BETWEEN EXALTATION AND INFAMY

Between Exaltation and Infamy

Female Mystics in the
Golden Age of Spain

STEPHEN HALICZER

UNIVERSITY PRESS

2002

OXFORD
UNIVERSITY PRESS

Oxford New York
Auckland   Bangkok   Buenos Aires   Cape Town   Chennai
Dar es Salaam   Delhi   Hong Kong   Istanbul   Karachi   Kolkata
Kuala Lumpur   Melbourne   Mexico City   Mumbai   Nairobi
São Paulo   Shanghai   Singapore   Taipei   Tokyo   Toronto

and an associated company in Berlin

Published by Oxford University Press, Inc.,
198 Madison Avenue, New York, New York 10016

www.oup.com

Oxford is a registered trademark of Oxford University Press

Library of Congress Cataloging-in-Publication Data
Haliczer, Stephen, 1942–
Between exaltation and infamy : female mystics in the golden age of Spain / Stephen Haliczer.
p. cm.
Includes bibliographical references and index.
ISBN 0-19-514851-7; ISBN 0-19-514863-0 (pbk.)
1. Mysticism—Spain—History—16th century.   2. Women mystics—Spain—History—16th
century.   3. Spain—Church history—16th century.   4. Mysticism—Spain—History—17th
century.   5. Women mystics—Spain—History—17th century.   6. Spain—Church
history—17th century.   I. Title.
BV5077.S7 H35 2002
248 .2'2'0820946—dc21   2001037314

9 8 7 6 5 4 3 2 1

Pnnted in the United States of Amenca
on acid-free paper

Contents

BETWEEN EXALTATION AND INFAMY

Introduction

One day in 1599, when she was just seven years old, María Ángela Astorch fell ill and died after gorging herself on unripened almonds. After some controversy, the family decided to move the body from the village of Saria, where she had been living in the home of her wet nurse, to a final resting place within the precincts of Barcelona's Convent of the Commanders of Santiago. But before the body could be taken for burial, María's sister Isabel insisted on seeing it one last time. Isabel arrived in Saria the following morning in the company of her mother superior, the ecstatic mystic and visionary María Ángela Serafina. As soon as she saw the serene and innocent face of the dead girl, María Ángela Serafina was overcome by a powerful impulse to offer her most fervent prayers to Christ and the Virgin Mary, begging them to return the soul to the body and restore the child to life. While Isabel prepared the corpse for removal and surrounded the little coffin with spring flowers, Serafina began to pray. Within a few moments she went into a deep trance and had a vision of the Virgin Mary holding the child's soul out to her, indicating that she should immediately restore it to the body. Emerging from the trance, María Ángela Serafina rushed to the coffin, where María Ángela Astorch was already showing signs of life. A moment later, the child had scrambled to the ground. In a few days, her health and strength were fully restored.[1]

All of this had been accomplished by prayer and its capacity to invoke the intervention of powerful supernatural forces. Blessed and restored to life by the Virgin Mary like some latter-day Lazarus, María Ángela Astorch would always be surrounded by the miraculous, and she herself would become known as a mystic and miracle worker capable of calling on supernatural forces for assistance to resolve the problems of her convent, city, and region.

During the Counter-Reformation, the church was confronted by an upsurge of feminine religious enthusiasm without parallel since medieval times. Inspired by new translations of the lives of the saints, devout women all over Catholic Europe sought to imitate these "athletes of Christ" through extremes of self-abnegation, physical mortification, and devotion. But, just as in the Middle Ages, women's piety expressed itself especially in mystical experiences frequently manifested in such phenomena as visions, revelations, voices, stigmata, and ecstasies. Phenomena of this kind, while susceptible to rational explanation, must also be understood within their cultural context. For these women, the paranormal was an accepted part of everyday lived experience, understood within socially constructed fields of meaning.[2]

The church's response to this revival of female piety was both wary and welcoming. On the one hand, a long-standing tradition held that women, as the weaker sex, were more emotionally unstable and therefore more susceptible to demonic manipulation. But visions, revelations, and other paranormal events that confirmed Catholic orthodoxy could represent genuine divine communication in defense of the true church. Feminine visionaries like Catherine of Siena, moreover, had been legitimized by canonization during the Middle Ages. The canonization of Teresa of Jesus (1622), Rose of Lima (1671), and Mary Magdelene de Pazzi (1669) demonstrated that the post-Tridentine church remained open to the creation of a new pantheon of female mystics.

Nevertheless, the spread of mystical piety, the imitation of the lives of the saints by so many women, and the potential for fraud and deception posed significant problems. How should the genuine mystical experience be distinguished from the demonically inspired? How could Catholic society separate the authentic saint from the counterfeit?

In Spain, this problem was particularly acute because of the Illuminist crisis during the early sixteenth century. Fortunately, Spanish society had a widely respected normative institution with a wealth of experience in dealing with issues of religious orthodoxy. By the middle of the sixteenth century, the Spanish Inquisition, originally founded to punish backsliders among Spain's numerous Jewish converts, had expanded its jurisdiction to include many kinds of heterodox religious expression. It was to this institution that Spaniards turned to separate the wheat from the chaff among the women mystics and would-be feminine saints of the period.

I have relied on two major sources for this study: thirty biographies and autobiographies of women mystics and fifteen Inquisition cases brought against women accused of "feigned sanctity." Such a charge meant that the women were perceived as only pretending to possess saintly virtues and powers and was usually accompanied by accusations of false or misleading revelations or mystical experiences, quite possibly of demonic origin. The use and juxtaposition of these two sources—on the one hand, a series of officially approved works, officially approved because they had to pass through official censorship, and on the other, inquisitorial cases of women convicted of pretended sanctity—will permit me to shed new light on many aspects of the relationship between women mystics and the wider society. These major sources have been complemented by numerous devotional works, theological treatises, and *Flos Sanctorum,* as well as material from other types of Inquisition cases that illustrate the problems that a woman might encounter in gaining and keeping a reputation for great spirituality.

Of course, sources are only as good and useful as the methodology applied to analyzing them. I have sought to use both quantitative and qualitative methods to interpret the social construction of female sanctity in early modern Spain. In general, however, quantification is used to extend and reinforce interpretations already suggested by qualitative research. Such an approach is inspired by the pioneering work of Ptirim A. Sorokin and Pierre Delooz, which was extended and improved by Donald Weinstein and Rudolph M. Bell in *Saints and Society: The Two Worlds of Western Christendom, 1000–1700.*[3]

In undertaking this project, I was very conscious of the differences between what I was attempting to do and what Sorokin, Delooz, Weinstein, and Bell had accomplished. My study contains a much smaller number of individuals and deals with "sainthood" only within the context of one European society at a specific period. Moreover, the most that the overwhelming majority of my women mystics could claim was popular sainthood. Only five of the thirty "approved" women mystics in this study ever received canonization, and most had cults that tended to die out after a generation or two. As for the fifteen women who were prosecuted by the Inquisition, their conviction as impostors put a definitive end to any claims to special status, and whatever cult had formed around them soon evaporated.

Still, the very fact that most of the women in my study were not necessarily exemplars of holiness so extraordinary as to merit canonization makes them that much more representative of the historical context in which they lived. By the mid-sixteenth century religious orders and the ecclesiastical hierarchy itself had become extremely conscious of the need to document the lives of those whom they wished to put forward for canonization. Careful documentation became even more vital after the decree issued by Pope Urban VIII in 1634, empowering ecclesiastical authorities and Inquisitors to act against any worship of saints not recognized as such by the Holy See. The high levels of documentation used in the biographies in this study, including autobiographical materials, detailed records kept by confessors, notarized accounts of miracles, and the spiritual writings of the women, meant that the facts about these women's lives were not lost in the mists of hagiographical convention, as were many of those studied by Sorokin, Weinstein, and Bell.[4] It is very hard to use saints' lives to illuminate broader social issues when very little about them can really be verified. The material upon which much of the work of Sorokin, Weinstein, and Bell is based tells us more about the mentality of the hagiographer than about the saint, and the hagiographer is always constrained to make the saint seem larger than life, a true athlete of Christ. Then again, after reviewing 113 autobiographies of Spanish women mystics written during the sixteenth and seventeenth centuries and comparing them with their respective biographies, Isabelle Poutrin concluded that while some authors occasionally removed items that might have offended the censors, most faithfully reflected the autobiographical material and even added valuable details about the lives or associations of the mystic that she had failed to mention.[5]

Arguably, as Poutrin has suggested, the biographies actually constitute texts superior to the autobiographies left by the mystics because the latter tend to be extremely fragmentary and contaminated by the influence of the confessors who ordered the women to write about their lives or the exaggerations of the women themselves. In the case of the seventeenth-century Italian mystic María Crocifissa, who has recently been studied by Sara Cabibbo and Marilena Modica, the mystic used her autobiographic works to bolster her family's efforts to generate a saintly reputation for her that would enhance family prestige and lead to eventual canonization.[6]

Of course, it would be hard to argue that even with the higher standards of proof that prevailed during the Counter-Reformation, the "approved" biographies did not contain a good measure of exaggeration, but I have been fortunate enough to have access to another type of documentation: Inquisition records. Inquisition case files constitute another kind of reality check for the "approved" biographies in that they provide a completely unvarnished view of a group of women who had gained or sought to gain a saintly reputation but lacked official support. The ability to compare and contrast two groups so similar in their aspirations and so different in their outcomes provides me with a level of insight into the realities of the social construction of sanctity in early modern Spain that goes far beyond what can be gleaned through traditional hagiographic sources.

Another problem connected with broadly based studies such as those of Sorokin or Weinstein and Bell is that the inclusion of so many saintly individuals drawn from different geographic areas, time periods, and national traditions seriously weakens the link between saints' lives and the historical context. Given their sample of 864 cases spread over 700 years in places as diverse as Hungary, Peru, Sweden, and Italy, Weinstein and Bell can speak only in generalities referring to broad (and quite possibly overstated) historical phenomena, such as the rise of lay culture in the fourteenth century or the increasing responsibility of individuals for their own spiritual choices in the sixteenth century, as key elements in determining the nature of sanctity. By painting with such a broad brush, Weinstein and Bell necessarily miss specific periods in national histories when sainthood and the imitation of sanctity took center stage to the point where they came to dominate the thinking of a large part of the ruling elite and played a key role in political decision making. Sixteenth-and seventeenth-century Spain, the background against which most of the women in my sample lived out their remarkable lives, was quite probably unique for the influence that saintly individuals—specifically, women credited with great spiritual powers—came to exercise and should not be conflated with other societies in the same or different periods.

Furthermore, however admirable the studies of Sorokin or Weinstein and Bell may be, the time for such general studies of sainthood may have passed. The increasing recognition among historians of the enduring strength of regionalism in medieval and early modern European society points the way to breaking down the study of sanctity into national and even regional traditions, or still further into urban and rural saint cults, which may well have coexisted and overlapped in the same society at the same time. Just as no two national *Flos Sanctorum* are the same in terms of the saints that they include, so the saints worshiped in cities and in the countryside are different and serve different purposes. William Christian's *Local Religion in Sixteenth Century Spain* marks a watershed in the study of saint cults and their social function in rural areas.[7]

At the same time, much more attention needs to be paid to the relationship between those who receive adulatory biographies and official approval and those whose writings were suppressed and who were subjected to penal sanctions. Isabelle Poutrin has begun this process by looking at inquisitorial censorship of the biographies of Spanish women mystics. Her conclusion that overall inquisitorial repression was relatively slight would be easier to accept if she provided us with a systematic analysis of the relationship of inquisitorial personnel to the censorship process or furnished us with a detailed comparison between "approved" mystics and those who were prosecuted.[8]

Even more interesting, perhaps, is the kind of unofficial sainthood that has the support of certain disaffected members of the elite but fails to receive complete official sanction because it poses a threat to political stability. These issues have barely been raised in the kind of literature on sainthood that attempts an overall synthesis but have been the subject of recent studies, especially Richard L. Kagan's *Lucrecia's Dreams: Politics and Prophecy in Sixteenth Century Spain*. This book offers us a fascinating account of the life of Lucrecia de León, who became the mouthpiece for a powerful opposition faction during the reign of King Philip II.[9] Of course, as I hope to demonstrate in this book, Lucrecia de León was not unique. After a woman attained a popular reputation for holiness by whatever means, she also gained the capacity to exert considerable influence on a local, regional, or even national level and even to exercise a form of political activity in an age when the political arena was the exclusive province of a tiny male elite. In Jodi Bilinkoff's recent study, late-sixteenth-century Avila is described as a city where several women with reputations for great spiritual power exerted considerable influence.[10]

Probably the most remarkable example of a woman mystic actually having some impact on national politics is contained in the correspondence exchanged between María de Jesús de Agreda, a cloistered Franciscan nun, and King Philip IV. Over a period of twenty-two years, from 1643 to 1665, the nun acted as a kind of informal advisor and confidante to the troubled ruler, who consulted her about everything from his health to foreign policy. The letters were first published in the last century by Francisco Silvela, and the relationship between nun and king was the subject of an article by Joaquín Pérez Villanueva, "Sor María de Agreda y Felipe IV: Un espistolerio en su tiempo."[11]

Another aspect of popular sanctity that the authors of more general studies have largely ignored is the issue of the confused and ambiguous attitudes of elites toward it. What were the standards by which an individual's claim to sanctity could be judged objectively? Official confusion in this key area is highlighted in Judith Brown's account of the seventeenth-century Theatine nun Benedetta Carlini. Benedetta was investigated by local Inquisitors after celebrating a very public mystical marriage with Christ and receiving the stigmata and a mysterious wedding ring. After carefully examining the stigmata and evaluating the nature of her visions, the Inquisitors concluded that she was directly inspired by God, thereby validating her claims to great spiritual authority.

Several years later, the Inquisition undertook a new inquiry after receiving several denunciations. Nuns testifying against her exposed her as a fraud who ate forbidden foods and punctured her skin to simulate stigmata. She was also denounced for sexual concupiscence for having a lesbian relationship with her companion Bartolomea.[12] Nevertheless, the fact that Benedetta was elected abbess after the first investigation and was permitted to carry on her activities unhindered for so many years in spite of her extravagant behavior speaks volumes about the real attitudes of Inquisitors toward the phenomenon of female mystics. The "pious credulity" that we will so often encounter in this book was not confined to devout friars or superstitious laymen; it also affected the judgment of the men serving the Inquisition, the one institution that almost everyone regarded as the highest authority in matters of the faith.

During the early modern period, as a direct consequence of the need to escape from the stress of religious conflict and endemic warfare into a world where the individual could bask in the certitude of divine communication, there was a revival of interest in mysticism. In France, beginning with the work of Lefèvre d'Étaples (c. 1455–1536), many editions of the works of both medieval and modern mystics were published in both French and Latin. In Italy, the Oratory of Divine Love, whose members played a major role in the development of the Counter-Reformation, relied on the works of such medieval mystics as Richard of St. Victor, Denis the Carthusian, and St. Catherine of Siena. Even among the persecuted English Recusants, Margaret Clitherow read the famous *Imitation of Christ*, that great monument to the mystical traditions of the Netherlands, as well as the *Spiritual Exercises* of William Peryystical, a Dominican who was inspired by medieval sources in addition to the *Spiritual Exercises* of Loyola.[13] But nowhere in Europe did mysticism come to play such a dominant role as in Spain, where it was not limited to a comparatively small number of devout individuals but took on the character of almost a mass movement, at least among the urban middle and upper classes. How did an entire society, or at least a significant part of it, come to see itself in terms of its capacity for self-abnegation and ecstatic worship? To answer this question, we must first understand the mental world of the Spanish middle and upper classes and apply that understanding to the particular circumstances and unique stresses of Spanish greatness and decline.

Spain and the Golden Age
of Mysticism

Notwithstanding the onset of the scientific revolution, the dominant intellectual concern in sixteenth- and seventeenth-century Europe was the search for the way in which humans could directly receive the influence of heavenly forces. Building on the work of the late-fifteenth-century philosopher Marsilio Ficino, who in turn was inspired by Stoic, Hermetic, and Neoplatonic sources, leading intellectuals like Pomponazzi, Francis Bacon, Paracelsus, and Campanella speculated that the flow of divine spirit to the individual depended fundamentally on the individual's receptivity. In other words, an individual's level of belief in the efficacy of the word itself, whether prayer or incantation, is the determining factor in calling down the occult. Furthermore, the "magical power of imagination" reinforced by belief operates to transform individuals making them more receptive to supernatural experience.[1]

By the 1620s and 1630s, however, a clear divide was beginning to open between southern and northern European intellectual life. In Holland, England, and France, science and technology were beginning to play an increasingly important role. The influence of the supernatural, even the very existence of the supernatural itself, was being called into question, and not only by scientists and philosophers like Pierre Bayle, Robert Boyle, or John Toland. The drunken trooper from Cromwell's New Model Army who asked, "Why should not that pewter pot on the table be God?" reflected the exciting period of free expression and skepticism that affected all classes during the English revolution and the interregnum, leading to the victory of experimental science in the universities.[2] The rise of such men as Robert Boyle and Robert Hooke

9

assured the place of serious science in English society and laid the ground-
work for the creation of the Royal Society of London in 1662.

In Spain, such a question might have been raised, but the questioner would
probably have been denounced to the Inquisition, which had been revived
under the energetic leadership of Diego de Arce y Reynoso, who served as
Inquisitor-General from 1643 to 1665. Arce y Reynoso, who greatly intensified persecution of converted Jews of Portugese origin (New Christians) causing thousands of them to flee the Iberian peninsula, also believed in the miraculous nature of the Plomos del Sacromonte, leaden tablets inscribed with
articles favoring the Immaculate Conception of the Virgin Mary and the
apostolate of Saint James. They were discovered in 1595 on a mountain near
Granada, accompanied by sets of bones said to be those of the earliest Christian martyrs. A shrine was erected on the spot, and numerous miracles were
recorded. Devotion to the site was further increased when the Jesuit Roman de
la Higuera wrote a chronicle of early Christianity in which the martyrs whose
remains were found along with the lead tablets figured prominently. Ignoring
the bull against the worship of uncanonized saints issued by Pope Urban VIII
in 1634, Arce y Reynoso ordered the saints and martyrs who figured in Higuera's
chronicle to be incorporated into litanies as legitimate objects of veneration.[3]
In spite of the fact that the tablets were condemned as forgeries by Pope Innocent XI in 1682, successive inquisitors-general continued to support the cult.
Official condemnation of belief in the tablets was included in the index issued
by Inquisitor-General Vidal Marin in 1707, but veneration of the relics of the
so-called martyrs was also specifically permitted. Certain late-eighteenth-
century inquisitors-general continued to support the cult that had taken shape
around the *plomos,* and critics, including the Valencian polymath Gregorio
Mayans y Síscar, found that opposition to the cult could damage their careers.[4]

Long before Inquisitor-General Arce y Reynoso came to the defense of
the "miraculous" Plomos del Sacromonte, Spanish scientific production had
begun a long and painful decline. While never precisely distinguished, the
contributions of Spaniards to mathematics, mechanics, and particularly navi-
gation and shipbuilding demonstrated that Spanish science and technology
had kept abreast of European developments throughout much of the sixteenth
century.[5] By the end of that century, however, the increasing weight of censorship, especially after the publication of the greatly expanded index issued
by Inquisitor-General Gaspar de Quiroga (1573–84), created a chilling effect
on Spanish intellectual life.[6] This repressive atmosphere was greatly reinforced
by inquisitorial activity against intellectual or academic discourse under the
heading of "heretical propositions," by which those participating in academic
debates or discussions could be denounced to the Holy Office for saying things
that another participant, or even a member of the audience, found less than
orthodox.

Given the intensity of repression, the natural tendency of intellectuals was
to take refuge in the well-worn paths of orthodoxy. Production of scientific
works fell from 14 percent of books published in Madrid between 1566 and
1600 to under 6 percent between 1601 and 1625. During the same period the

production of religious books rose from 32 to 42 percent of publications, while the production of literary works also increased dramatically.[7] While it is true that few of the key works of the scientific revolution were prohibited outright and that the prohibitions barely affected the reading habits of most of the literate population, all that tells us is that the plan to indoctrinate the Spanish reading public in the principles and values of the Counter-Reformation devised by conservative intellectuals like Arias Montano and Jerónimo de Zurita had succeeded brilliantly.[8] Becuase the Inquisition's role in censorship was strictly postpublication, it hardly needed to act against a type of book for which there was little or no demand. Official strictures against foreign authors, even if they were Catholic, and the blanket prohibition on the introduction of foreign works in Spanish translation had the effect of inoculating the reading public against anything new and dangerous. The effectiveness of this "pedagogy of fear" in largely eliminating the demand for works of science or political economy can be even be measured by its failures in that libraries that were discovered to contain prohibited books usually did not house anything really dangerous or revolutionary.[9] They certainly did not contain the key works of the scientific revolution, which had failed to make an impact on a society that had turned its back on rationalism in favor of the miraculous.[10]

The increased emphasis on the miraculous and the supernatural can be seen very clearly in the work of the Jesuit Juan Eusebio Nieremberg (1595–1658), one of the most influential figures in Spanish intellectual life during the middle years of the seventeenth century. Nieremberg, who was of southern German parentage, was born in Madrid. After a distinguished career, he was appointed professor at the Colegio Imperial, founded in 1623 to educate the sons of the nobility. Widely respected both in Spain and at the Habsburg court in Vienna, where Emperor Leopold I (1640–1705) read his *Historia Naturae* (Antwerp, 1635), Nieremberg was an anti-Copernican and, like many of his colleagues in the Habsburg monarchy, a supporter of the system that Tycho Brahe formulated in 1588.[11] Adopting the Tychonic system, which posited a stationary earth with the sun and moon revolving around it while the rest of the planets revolved around the sun, provided Nieremberg with a middle ground that was less dangerous theologically than wholehearted Copernicanism, but it made for a retrograde kind of science and boded ill for the kind of instruction this professor of natural philosophy would be imparting to his students.[12]

Nieremberg's theory of the relationship between man and the celestial spirit in his *Oculta filosophia de la sympatia y antipatia de las cosas,* published in 1636, looks backward to Ficino's spirit theory rather than forward to Boyle and Newton. According to Nieremberg, man is capable of receiving divine revelations, allowing him to predict future events, especially when his spirit is properly disposed either in sleep, as in the case of St. Joseph, or when listening to music.[13] Nieremberg's notion of the way in which music elevates the soul toward higher intelligence and "better disposes" it to receive the divine spirit is remarkably similar to Ficino's music spirit theory, by which planetary or celestial spirits may be attracted and absorbed by man, especially if his soul is made receptive by becoming as "celestial" as possible.[14] The whole idea of the disposition of the individual soul to receive the divine spirit was destined to have a long and prosperous life in early modern Spain but could hardly be considered the way forward in the area of science and technology. Instead, under the leadership of men like Nieremberg, Spain fell further and further behind and contributed virtually nothing original to the development of modern thought until the early twentieth century.

Within the territories of the northern Habsburg Empire, the reimposition of Roman Catholicism by force in large parts of Austria and Bohemia obscures the fact that the degree of intellectual repression imposed on the elite was considerably less than in Spain. In spite of a somewhat erratic episcopal censorship, the Habsburg Empire never published an index, never imposed a centrally controlled censorship apparatus like that operated by the Spanish Council of Castile, and, of course, never experienced the Inquisition. The Central European intellectual who was willing to accept a fundamentally traditional Aristotelian or Platonic framework would be allowed to freely engage in all kinds of "daring" occult speculations, including astrology, alchemy, and Cabalism. In the lands of the northern Habsburgs, therefore, there was considerable continuity between Renaissance notions of natural magic and seventeenth-century Baroque culture, and this made real scientific investigation possible.[15]

In the Spanish Monarchy, on the other hand, the indices of 1583 and 1612 substantially prohibited works of alchemy and sharply restricted the circulation of books in Hebrew and Arabic.[16] The Inquisition also acted against occult practices like efforts to find and liberate "enchanted" treasure through spells and incantations.[17] The repression of Erasmian and Illuminist thought with their strong Neoplatonic elements in the middle of the century meant that in the fusion of Renaissance and Counter-Reformation ideals that comprised later sixteenth-century culture, the Counter-Reformation element would be dominant.[18] The impulse that inspired the Renaissance magus to seek an influx of the celestial spirit through purely magical means continued, but it now had to flow into strictly orthodox and Christian channels, with God acting directly and even capriciously to deploy supernatural forces rather than as the creator and regulator of natural law, as understood by Newton and Boyle.[19] In his *Occulta filosofía,* Nieremberg specifically denies humans any "natural power" to receive revelations or foretell the future as believed by the ancients; the miracle of true prophecy can come only from God because only he knows the future and only he can reveal it.[20]

What became obvious as the scientific revolution went forward and Spain failed to participate in it is that there is an enormous difference between God considered as a regulating force and God considered as active agent. The former invites speculation and research, and the latter simply imposes awe and acceptance, backed up by all the coercive force that orthodoxy can command.[21] Instead of attempting to read the mind of God through the study of nature, therefore, Spanish intellectuals drew on their long mystical tradition and sought to apprehend God directly by opening themselves to his own acts of self-revelation.

Answering the criticisms of many Protestants who asserted that the age of miracles had ended when God succeeded in founding Christianity, Spanish theologians such as the Dominican Antonio de Lorea insisted that the God who had brought about the prodigies and miracles recounted in the Old Testament would be no less generous to his faithful in modern times.[22] The age of miracles and prodigies was not over, and to prove it Lorea presented his biography of the ecstatic nun Hipolita de Jesús y Rocaberti (1549–1624), in whose spiritual life God repeated the same favors he had awarded to St. Catherine of Siena two hundred years earlier. Moreover, according to the Augustinian Francisco de Acosta, preacher in ordinary to King Philip IV, divine liberality was so open-handed that God was not content to merely communicate the ability to work miracles to his elect but on occasion even gave that power to sinners.[23]

The power to work miracles could be found especially in the relics of the saints and martyrs of the church, and, fortunately for Spain, relics were abundant and housed conveniently in many convents, monasteries, and churches. The aristocratic Convent of Santa Clara of Zaragoza, for example, was reputed to contain the skulls of two of the eleven thousand virgins who were martyred with St. Ursula at Cologne, a piece of the true cross, one of the thorns from the crown of thorns, and pieces of the garments of the Virgin Mary, St. Francis of Assisi, St. Augustine, St. Peter of Alcantara, and St. Teresa of Jesus.[24]

Relics could be used for the relief of the faithful on numerous occasions. In 1647, when the seawall of the city of Barcelona was being battered by enormous waves and ships were in danger of being driven aground in the port, the body of St. María de Cervellon was brought out from the Convent of La Merced in solemn procession. When the procession arrived at the seawall, the sacristan of the convent touched the water with a piece of the saint's habit that the convent kept as a relic. The waves were said to have almost instantaneously calmed, and the storm abated, saving the ships from destruction.[25]

Ironically enough, in seventeenth-century Spain an uncritical belief in the miraculous was probably stronger among physicians than in any other educated group. This is all the more surprising because sixteenth-century Spanish medicine had been highly regarded all over Europe for its intellectual rigor. In the period 1475 to 1600 almost 47 percent of new scientific studies were in the medical field.[26] However, both academic and practical medicine were heavily dependent on converted Jews and Moriscos like the great Jerónimo Pachet, who once cured the future King Philip III. Growing hostility to Morisco physicians during the reign of King Philip II, many of whom were arrested and prosecuted by the Inquisition, had the effect of destroying the tradition of Islamic medical practice that had enriched Spanish medicine for so many centuries.[27] Converso physicians also found themselves under growing pressure with the upsurge in persecution of the New Christians in the 1630s and 1640s and the publication of anti-Semitic screeds like Discurso contra los judíos by the Portuguese Vicente da Costa Mattos, which was translated by Fray Diego Gavilán Vela in 1631. In this work, reprinted numerous times in the seventeenth and eighteenth centuries, the author accuses New Christian physicians of all the heinous crimes against their patients that Jewish physicians had been accused of in the Middle Ages.[28]

Loss of diversity and a growing insularity, leading to the rejection of medical advances from outside the peninsula, were perhaps best illustrated by Dr. Pedro Osorio's ad hominem attack on the brilliant Swiss German physician Paracelsus in *Vindica de la verdad* (1700).[29] The effect was to drive the Spanish medical schools back to a reliance on traditional Galenic medicine and make Spanish physicians all too willing to believe in supernatural causes for diseases and their cures. One of the depositions collected at the end of Antonio Arbiol's biography of Jacinta de Atondo is a touching and detailed account of the relationship of two generations of physicians with her that perfectly illustrates the credulous acceptance of marvels that characterized so many Spanish physicians. According to the deposition made by Dr. Antonio Borbón, who held a chair in medicine at the University of Zaragoza, his family's relationship with Atondo had started when his father, Dr. Felipe Borbón, served as consulting physician to the nuns of the Convent of Santa Catalina, where she once served as abbess.

The extremes of abuse and neglect that she had suffered as a child and the austerities that she practiced as an adult more or less guaranteed that Jacinta de Atondo would suffer a variety of ailments, including constant and severe stomach pain, headaches, and pains in her arms and legs. Toward the end of her life she also had great difficulty breathing, especially when she climbed stairs or scourged herself. She was also afflicted by numerous boils, which both doctors removed. While operating on one of these boils, Dr. Felipe Borbón told his son that in spite of its unusual size he experienced a remarkable ease and freedom from anxiety in removing it that he could attribute only to supernatural causes. On another occasion, he was so convinced that a miracle had intervened to allow him to successfully remove a boil on her knee that he took the boil home with him "like an object of great value that would turn into a relic." Dr. Borbón immediately gave the boil to his wife, admonishing her to "put it somewhere where you can find it because one day you will value it highly." In his deposition, Antonio Borbón confirmed that he had frequently seen the boil in his parents' home. He also asserted that in spite of the heat and humidity it had not changed or decayed in the twenty-three years that they had it in their possession. The lack of decay indicated the boil's saintly origin in that one of the sure indications of sanctity was an uncorrupted body. For his part, Antonio Borbón was also convinced that Atondo received divine favors; otherwise her frail body could not have withstood the abuse she inflicted upon it.[30]

Dr. Felipe Borbón was not the only physician to collect a relic from a patient whom he considered a recipient of divine assistance. When Dr. Juan de Guevara attended the Discalced Carmelite nun Gabriela de San Joseph on her deathbed, he unhooked her scourge from the nail on which it had been hanging and was overheard to remark that he had now "collected a relic" from the saint.[31]

Fundamentally, the concept that motivated physicians such as Felipe Borbón and Juan de Guevara to take "relics" from their seriously ill patients was the idea that illness itself was of supernatural origin and that the suffering experienced by the individual was itself a sign of God's favor.[32] Consequently, their inability to cure their patients was not a sign of their own inadequacy and ignorance but of God's inexorable will, and a patient's recovery, especially the recovery of an ecstatic mystic, was probably due to God's favor and not their ministrations. In his biography of Fray Tomás de la Virgen, Francisco de San Bernardo informs us that he was attended by several court physicians who were all convinced that his numerous illnesses were derived from supernatural causes. Royal physician Matamoros stated many times while treating Fray Tomás that "the saint's fevers were not of terrestrial origin."[33]

Perhaps because of his extreme suffering and the merit he had accumulated through his patience and uncomplaining endurance in imitation of the passion of Christ, Fray Tomás's possessions seemed to be able to effect cures. At any rate, a number of Spain's leading nobles seemed to think so since they routinely "prescribed" use of his pillow, towel, and scapulary to cure their own illnesses and those of their family members. After the Count of Medellín was instantaneously cured of tertian fever by applying one of Fray Tomás's towels to his forehead, his own physicians confirmed that this had been an "obvious and evident miracle."[34] After Fray Tomás died, the order immediately set about putting together a dossier for his beatification. Among the more than 140 witnesses was a cross section of Spain's political and social elite, including Inquisitor-General Diego de Arce y Reynoso.[35]

Belief in the supernatural causes of disease was hardly confined to the aristocracy. It was also extremely common among the urban middle class. During the early 1570s, when Francisca de Avila renamed herself Francisca de los Apostoles and founded a *beaterio* in Toledo, she told the other *beatas* that calling a physician when they became ill was useless because diseases were sent by the devil with God's permission.[36]

Such advice would hardly have been necessary for those whose faith in doctors was considerably less than their faith in those reputed to be able to intervene with God. For people like Juana Osorio, the wife of a prosperous hidalgo living in Madrid with her husband and children, calling a physician in a time of illness was almost inconceivable. When anyone in her family became ill, she asked Isabel de Briñas, a widow who lived nearby, to pray for them. She was apparently unfazed by the fact that one of her children and her husband had died in spite of Briñas's prayers and told the Holy Office that she still considered her a good person.[37]

The tendency to rely on divine intervention and eschew earthly solutions to practical problems was strongly reinforced by the penchant among Spanish intellectuals to regard Spain as having taken the place of the discredited Israelites as God's chosen people.[38] This belief, which seemed to be confirmed during the heyday of Spanish imperialism, was to suffer its most serious test during the crisis of the seventeenth century. Beginning in the mid-1570s, when the slow but steady demographic increase that had sustained the economy came to an end, Spain entered a long period of stagnation and decline. The plague of 1599–1600, one of the greatest epidemics to affect Europe in modern times, was responsible for approximately 600,000 deaths or about 7.5 percent of the population of around 8 million.[39] Waves of epidemic disease continued to lash the peninsula throughout the seventeenth century, especially in 1647–1652 and the great typhus epidemic of 1683–85.[40]

The constant ravages of disease were made even more serious because the population was already weakened by famine. The structural problems of Spanish agriculture—low levels of investment and innovation, lack of adequate rainfall, and poor soils—were greatly worsened by deteriorating weather conditions and natural disasters. In the diocese of Segovia, the records indicate a 30 percent decline in wheat production between 1580 and 1640, and there were similar declines registered in Seville and the Kingdom of Valencia.[41] In that unfortunate region, the problems of agriculture were substantially worsened by the ill-advised expulsion of the Moriscos, who made up fully 30 percent of the population. The expulsion of the Moriscos also had a major impact on Valencia's silk industry, which went into a serious decline mainly because of a lack of raw material from the Júcar valley and other producing areas, where Moriscos had traditionally provided much of the labor.[42]

In Castile, the industrial sector also experienced a serious crisis. Segovia, which had been the leader in the production of high-quality woolen cloth for much of the sixteenth century, experienced a sharp drop in production beginning around 1580. By the end of the seventeenth century, the approximately 600 looms working in the city in 1580 had been reduced to 159. At the same time, Segovia's industry changed its focus from high-quality cloth to cheaper varieties, leaving the high end of the market largely in the hands of foreigners.[43]

The crisis also had a negative effect on the city of Toledo, Spain's premier producer of high-quality silk. Drained by nearby Madrid and weakened by declining demand for silk from traditional markets, the city's population declined from about 61,500 in 1571 to around 20,500 in 1631, while the silk industry suffered a severe crisis in 1619–20 from which it never really recovered.[44] Similar declines in population and economic activity affected most of the cities of New and Old Castile, turning some of them into virtual economic wastelands colonized by innumerable religious institutions.

From 1640, Spain's economic problems, however serious they seemed, were almost eclipsed by a series of revolts and military disasters, both on land and at sea, that seemed to portend the breakup of the monarchy itself. The successful rebellions in Catalonia and Portugal in the spring and fall of 1640 had been followed by decisive military defeats in the Netherlands, especially at the battle of Rocroi on May 19, 1643. Even though Spain was able to recover control over Catalonia after a series of painful and expensive campaigns in 1650–52, the Treaty of Münster of October 24, 1648, marked the abandonment of the northern part of the old Duchy of Burgundy with the recognition of the United Netherlands as an independent state. Portugal was also lost after King Philip IV's ill-advised attempt to recover it was defeated at the battle of Villaviciosa in 1665.[45]

Spaniards at all levels from the king to the meanest commoner were aware of the crisis. Even heavily cloistered nuns were acutely conscious of the hard times and frequently expressed anxiety about the future of the monarchy. In a letter to her confessor from Zaragoza's Santa Catalina convent, Jacinta de Atondo declared that she would rather die than live to see Spain undergo greater hardships than it had already experienced.[46]

Responses to the crisis varied widely. It was precisely at this period of sharply increasing mortality rates that the number of new editions of works dealing with the "art of the good death" reached a peak.[47]

Some people tended to personalize the situation, feeling that their own bad behavior or lack of faith, or the sinful behavior of their neighbors, was the real cause of God's anger. Isabel de Jesús, a member of the Carmelite third order who lived in Toledo during the mid-seventeenth century, suffered from an extremely poor self-image, and in visions where she encountered Christ she accused herself of "ingratitude" and "disloyalty" and of not having "kept faith with you in anything." During one of her trances, she became convinced that she was in the presence of God and began begging him tearfully to have mercy on Spain, but the devil then appeared and informed her that her petitions would not be attended to because God had authorized him to destroy much of the country. It was presumptuous of her, moreover, to be asking for favors since she did not enjoy God's grace or friendship but instead was "abhorred by Him because you go against his will in everything." From this she understood immediately that "His Majesty has afflicted all of Spain solely on my account."[48]

In other instances, the focus of blame was turned outward, away from the individual's own sense of sin and toward the moral behavior of others. Catalina de San Lucas, a Dominican nun living in the Convent of the Encarnación in Almagro, was the recipient of numerous confidences from women in the area. During a winter of severe flooding in the 1630s, she was visited by a woman who, like Isabel de Jesús, was convinced that her sins had brought God's punishment upon the city. The woman left Catalina's cell in a much happier frame of mind after Catalina told her that it was not her sins but something far more serious that lay at the root of the problem. Nothing less than the abominable sin of incest being committed by a local man, which was known but quasi-tolerated, had incurred God's legitimate anger. Catalina took it upon herself to inform the local governor, who ordered the man's arrest and the girl's removal from the village.[49]

Still others saw in the crisis a failure of the entire society that would require a kind of mass atonement. In 1639, María Bautista, the wife of a commission merchant who had fallen on hard times, had a revelation in which a "spirit" informed her of the importance of public penance to appease God's anger and gave her to understand that the king as the head of the body politic should take the lead so that everyone else would follow his example.[50]

On a more hopeful note, the *arbitristas*, a group of reformers who were especially active between about 1580 and 1620, dedicated themselves to political economy and offered reform ideas ranging from banning imported goods to eliminating the entire fiscal system as presently constituted and introducing a "single tax" on some items in everyday use.[51] Most of the *arbitristas'* proposals made little sense and, rather than offering any realistic solutions, merely indicated the confusion that affected the thinking of Spain's policy-making elite.[52] Government under the Duke of Lerma and the Conde Duque de Olivares was fairly tolerant of this kind of political writing, especially since it only circulated among a small elite and sometimes provided support for ideas that the ministers themselves wanted to put forward. As Quevedo found to his cost, however, outright criticism directed against ministerial policy could result in swift punishment.[53]

Another approach to explaining the crisis, which was considerably more popular in official circles precisely because it absolved the king and his ministers from any direct blame, was to say that it was a manifestation of God's anger at a people who, like the ancient Israelites, had turned their backs on him, forgetting the sacrifice of his son and committing the sins of the flesh. Juan Eusebio Nieremberg advanced this idea in *Causa y remedio de los males públicos,* a work published in 1642 and dedicated to the Conde Duque de Olivares, whose mismanagement, political ineptitude, and wishful thinking had succeeded in making a bad situation substantially worse. From the outset, Nieremberg demonstrated that the crisis was of supernatural origin by the very suddenness of the decline itself: "Such a powerful empire could not fall to pieces so quickly. This itself argues that a force capable of disintegrating such a power could not have been natural." Because Spain's difficulties were caused by acts of God, official policies, no matter how effective, could have little impact on the situation, and the fact that so many things had been tried with so little effect was yet another demonstration of the supernatural origins of the crisis.[54]

In fact, according to Nieremberg, the rising chorus of complaints about the incompetence of the Conde Duque de Olivares and other royal ministers was quite beside the point because the people in general were at fault. It was their sins that God in his infinite wisdom had seen fit to punish, and those committed not only by the present generation of Spaniards but also by their fathers and grandfathers before them. Just as Spain's earlier conquests were due to the greater purity of "customs, justice, and equity" that it maintained at that time, its present defeats must be caused by a greater measure of sinfulness than that prevailing among the Dutch and other enemies of the monarchy. Victories are granted by God to those who deserve them so that "if we would but destroy our sins God would destroy our enemies."[55]

This kind of thinking lay behind much of the puritanical legislation of the period. It was King Philip IV, for example, who closed all of Spain's legal houses of prostitution in 1623. The hodgepodge Articles of Reformation that the Olivares regime issued on February 10, 1623, renewed and extended the stringent sumptuary regulations that had been promulgated and then suspended during the previous reign. The Madrid government also strongly supported the papal bull of August 30, 1622, which significantly broadened the Spanish Inquisition's jurisdiction over sexual solicitation by priests hearing confession. The result was a dramatic upsurge in solicitation cases, carrying the sexual repression of the clergy to a new and unprecedented level.[56]

Unfortunately, an interpretation like Nieremberg's raised many questions and merely served to heighten the uncertainty. If God were punishing present-day Spain for all the sins ever committed by previous generations, when would God's wrath be slaked and the punishment deemed sufficient? Would Spain be able to conserve its empire in spite of God's anger? What were the specific sins that had angered God the most, and how could these be corrected?

A partial answer to these agonizing questions was provided by Francisco Xarque, a curate and former judge of the ecclesiastical court in Potosí (Bolivia) who had recently returned to Spain. Like Nieremberg, Xarque dedicated his book to a high royal official, in this instance the Viceroy of Aragon D. Fernando de Borja, and saw the crisis as a product of God's anger directed not only at Spain but also at the entire House of Austria. After bemoaning the series of disasters that had affected the fortunes of the Habsburgs in recent years, however, Xarque went on to offer a curiously upbeat assessment. God was punishing the House of Austria but only as a father punishes his errant children. Out of this punishment would come cleansing and redemption such that this time of trial would enter the history books in letters of "gold and crimson" as the prelude to even greater triumphs. Spain's enemies are like "bees who sting once and then die" and can never do permanent damage so long as the House of Austria maintained its traditional devotion to the Eucharist. This devotion, which was so important to the greatness of Austria that Xarque even suggested that the name Osterreich be changed to Hostireich, would guarantee the ultimate success of the Habsburg cause. The host was "the bread of the valiant," which constituted a kind of secret weapon with the power of "battalions of fire" that they could use to subdue their enemies.[57]

Hope for future victories could not obscure the fact that in spite of its fervent eucharistic devotion, and extraordinary efforts to maintain the purity of the Catholic faith, Spain was still suffering from God's wrath, losing battles and in danger of collapse. The crucial question still remained, What could Spain do to more fully align itself with the will of God in order to appease him and avoid both present and future punishment? The need felt by Spain's governing elite to establish direct contact with God in order to know his will had never been greater than during this period of calamity, while those claiming to be able to provide divinely inspired advice and council had never been more numerous.

Spain, like other European societies, had a long-standing tradition of political prophecy—which tended to intensify and take on overt political overtones in times of crisis.[58] When Cardinal Cisneros served as archbishop of Toledo, his court played host to the French mystic and Erasmian Charles de Bovelles (1479–1553). Bovelles, who may have visited Spain to acquire manuscripts of the writings of Raymond Lull and Raymond de Sabunde, was the author of several extravagant prophecies, including the reconquest of Jerusalem by Christians and the complete reform of the church within a twelve-year period. The cardinal's immediate circle was also quite interested in the prophecies of one Fray Melchor, who was active in the Toledo area around 1512 and predicted the imminent destruction of the Holy Roman Empire and the papacy. The cardinal himself protected a circle of visionary *beatas,* including María de Santo Domingo, the famous Beata de Piedrahita, and Juana de la Cruz, who was predicted to be the mother of a future savior.[59]

The arrival of the young and inexperienced Charles of Ghent to take up the Spanish throne in September 1517 did little to calm the wave of dissatisfaction with royal government that had been increasing even before the death of Queen Isabella in 1504. Conditions were especially difficult in Valencia, where growing popular unrest fueled by plague, food shortages, economic contraction, and resentment against the nobility and their Mudejar vassals burst forth in the Revolt of the Germanías, which began in 1519. Beginning as a popular movement to convert the Mudejares, it soon turned violent. Hundreds of Mudejares were murdered by roving bands of militia, while thousands of others were given a quick and cursory baptism. After the death of Vicenç Peris, who had led the uprising in its early phase, it came under the influence of an individual who called himself el Rey Encubierto. Although little is known about his origins, el Encubierto can be placed squarely within the tradition of political prophecy best represented by Savonarola. Like his Florentine counterpart, el Encubierto had an apocalyptic vision and was constantly referring to the imminent arrival of the Antichrist and the end of the world. He claimed that he had seen Elijah and Enoch in a vision and that they had brought him to Valencia to extol the faith and render justice. He urged his hearers to destroy both "Moors and Jews who are my natural enemies."[60] After a brief but meteoric career, el Encubierto fell victim to hired assassins, and the Germanía collapsed shortly thereafter in the face of the resurgent power of the Valencian nobility.

Perhaps because of his own bad experiences with popular political prophecy both in Spain and later in Germany, King Charles V maintained a highly skeptical attitude toward all kinds of visionaries.[61] The fear of Protestantism led to official repression of the Illuminist movement in the 1520s and 1530s, even though some of those associated with that movement favored Charles's victory over the French and saw him as the possible savior of the church.

When King Philip II came to the throne in 1559, it was in the shadow of a growing Protestant threat both in Europe and within the Spanish monarchy. In Spanish Flanders, there was already a potentially dangerous Calvinist movement developing in the larger towns, and in Spain itself Lutheran or quasi-Lutheran cells had been discovered in Seville and Valladolid. The great series of autos de fé held between 1559 and 1562 succeeded in eliminating the native Spanish Protestant movement. Philip's plans to introduce a Spanish-style Inquisition into Flanders showed that he was preparing a similar fate for Netherlands Protestants, but he was also astute enough to realize that repression alone would not be sufficient.

Philip's new approach manifested itself in strong Spanish participation in the critical final session of the Council of Trent (1561–63), where sweeping reform of the episcopacy was decided upon. The decrees of the council were approved by the pope and incorporated into Spanish law by Philip on July

12, 1564.[62] King Philip II strongly supported the bishops in their attempts to gain more control over their dioceses by ordering regular provincial synods, and he promoted the establishment of seminaries as called for by the council to improve the educational level of the regular clergy.

At the same time, Philip was aware of the need to foster popular devotion so long as it could be channeled in acceptable ways. To that end he undertook an expensive campaign to bring the relics of several saints to Spain, including Justo and Pastor, Leocadia, Ildefonso, and Segundo. When the remains of Saint Leocadia arrived in Toledo, the king and queen, along with many of Spain's leading nobles, were there to receive them. The presence of the king legitimized the relics and provided a public demonstration of how such relics should be venerated. Before the relics were placed in the sanctuary, the king selected a good-sized bone for himself and several smaller ones for members of the royal family.[63]

Philip II also began to move away from his father's hostility or indifference toward mystics, especially if their orientation was purely religious. He offered strong support for the fledgling Jesuit order and for its founder, St. Ignatius of Loyola, and he threw official backing behind the Discalced Carmelite nun and visionary Teresa de Jesús in her efforts to found reform convents under strict claustration. In her *Book of the Foundations,* the saint gave ample credit to Philip for his support: "for our present King Don Philip, is very well disposed to religious who are known to keep their rule. When he had heard of our life in these houses of ours he gave us every kind of assistance."[64]

Support for the two mystics Loyola and Teresa de Jesús, however, did not mean that Philip II was in any way interested in any "divinely inspired" political, personal, or spiritual advice that they might have been able to offer. Philip's cautious attitude toward mysticism was reinforced by several politically dangerous cases evolving during the 1570s and 1580s.

Francisca de Avila—or Francisca de los Apostoles, as she later called herself—was the spinster daughter of a painter who lived with her sister and some thirteen or fourteen other women in a *beaterio* in Toledo. The women slept dormitory style, supported themselves by sewing, and tried to imitate the life of a convent as much as possible by conforming to the Jeronimite rule. Francisca was a visionary and mystic who had frequent trances and believed herself and her sister to be under the special protection of the Virgin Mary. She predicted that they were destined to play a major role in the much-needed reform of the church. The reform itself would be led by Archbishop Bartolomé de Carranza, who had been arrested by the Inquisition in 1559 on vague charges of supporting the Protestant heresy and transferred in 1567 to Rome, where he languished in the castle of Saint Angelo. Francisca, like many others in Toledo, had not forgotten the popular archbishop and told the women living in the *beaterio* that he would be released by divine intervention and go on to lead the church to renewal. Carranza would also issue the licenses for the establishment of a new religious order with two monasteries, one for men and one for women, who would set an example for the entire church through their piety and austerity.[65]

Francisca's open partisanship in favor of Archbishop Carranza, her demands for church reform, and her frequent denunciations of the clergy as sinful and materialistic made her dangerous to both church and state, so she was arrested in 1574. At her trial, which lasted from early 1575 to April 1578, she refused to present a defense, claimed to have been misled by the devil, and thanked the Holy Office for showing her the right path. On April 13, she was sentenced to abjure *de levi*, given a hundred lashes while riding through the streets of the city, and exiled from Toledo and its surrounding area for three years.[66]

A more serious case that confirmed Philip II's suspicion of political prophecy involved the so-called nun of Lisbon, Sor María de la Visitación. Sor María was thirty-three, and prioress of Lisbon's aristocratic Dominican Convent of the Annunciada when she first appeared marked with the stigmata on March 7, 1584. Given her impeccable social origins and exemplary religious life, there seemed little reason to doubt the validity of these divine favors, and within a very short time the "miracle" attracted the attention of the rich and powerful. Archduke Albert, the recently appointed Spanish viceroy, visited her and was so impressed that he immediately wrote to his uncle Phillip II and to Pope Gregory XIII, who accepted the events at Lisbon as a miracle. She also won the support of the saintly and influential Fray Luis de Granada, who interviewed her in her cell and was so impressed that he wrote her spiritual biography.[67]

Even though Sor María had to contend with a small but active opposition party within the convent, she might have continued to enjoy the reputation of a saint for some time had she not begun using her spiritual reputation on behalf of Dom Antonio, the exiled Portuguese pretender. Philip II, who had just seized control of Portugal in 1582, was outraged and ordered the inquisition to undertake an investigation into the validity of the divine favors that she claimed to have received. After first trying to brazen it out, Sor María broke down after the Inquisitors ordered her hands washed and watched as the soapy water carried away her stigmata. She confessed that she had painted on the stigmata, moistening them with her own blood whenever necessary to make them more convincing.[68] On December 6, 1588, Sor María was found guilty and sentenced to permanent reclusion in a convent outside Lisbon.

The fact that the "monja de Lisboa" had gained significant support among certain leading members of Spain's political and clerical elite, including the king's nephew, Archduke Albert, marked the beginning of a change in the status of mystics. In the years around the time of the defeat of the Armada, and especially in 1589, when Spain's navy had been largely destroyed and its coasts lay open to attack, widespread uncertainly about royal policies, military defeat, and growing signs of economic distress made political prophecy more acceptable. The meteoric rise of the street prophet Miguel de Piedrola and the even more dramatic career of Lucrecia de León seemed to indicate the greater acceptability of political prophecy and mysticism in general among certain members of Spain's social and political elite.

Nevertheless, the fact that both Piedrola and Lucrecia were ultimately arrested and tried by the Holy Office with support at the highest levels of government—Philip II himself and the royal confessor Fray Diego de Chaves—should raise a note of caution. The king himself never really took Lucrecia seriously and was galvanized into action only when the escape of his former secretary Antonio Pérez from a Madrid jail made any kind of opposition seem doubly dangerous. The principal supporters of both prophets, as far as can be discerned, were relatively minor figures with their own personal grudges against the government, while the inner circle of ministers remained immune.[69] It would take a larger, more serious, and more protracted crisis to open the way for political prophecy to penetrate Spain's ruling circles and gain the willing ear of the king himself.

The reign of Philip IV (1621–65) opened on an optimistic note with a new and energetic chief minister in the person of Gaspar de Guzmán, the Conde Duque de Olivares, who came into office with sweeping plans for reform. But Spain's growing economic problems and the failure to win decisive military victories against the Dutch soon triggered a wave of criticism and soul searching that brought the favorite high government officials and the king himself to seek the advice of mystics. For the count-duke himself, it was the death of his only daughter on July 30, 1626, and the bout of despair and pessimism that accompanied it that brought him to the doors of San Plácido, a reformed Benedictine convent in Madrid.

San Plácido had been founded in 1623–24 by Jerónimo de Villanueva, *protonotario* of the Crown of Aragon, and from 1630 secretary of state, the most powerful man in royal administration next to Olivares himself. Interestingly enough, Villanueva's decision to support the foundation was made in part because of a series of visions that foretold his involvement. These visions were experienced by Doña Ana María de Loyosa, the aunt of his betrothed, Teresa Valle de la Cerda, and by Isabel de Frías, who became one of the first nuns to enter the convent after it was actually founded.[70] Just before the marriage was to take place, however, Teresa encountered the noted preacher Fray Alonso de León, who convinced her to devote herself to God. She and Villanueva swore an oath of continence, and he eventually built a house right next to the convent so that he could be near his ex-betrothed. He and Teresa also gave a generous endowment to the convent.[71]

Informed of the death of Olivares's daughter, Teresa began corresponding with him on a regular basis. Although Olivares's own letters have been lost, we have eighty-nine letters to him from Teresa over a twenty-month period between November 12, 1626, and June 15, 1628, so that in some weeks they may have exchanged two or three letters. In most cases, the letters were carried directly to Olivares by the *protonotario*. Olivares also visited the convent on numerous occasions, and he and the countess exchanged gifts with Teresa.[72] Although most of the content of Teresa's letters was of a spiritual nature, she also encouraged the count-duke to believe that he had been selected by God especially to occupy his post and that he was a "great captain to whom the Lord hath entrusted his battles and with whom he wishes to destroy his enemies."[73]

The count-duke, who had turned to the works of Blosius, the sixteenth-century Flemish mystic, for consolation after the death of his daughter, evidently hoped that the prayers of the nuns would help his wife bear him a son.[74] For her part, Teresa prayed every day for the count-duke and even offered to sacrifice her own health to help him. Finally, her prayers were rewarded when she saw in a vision that St. Benedict had intervened in Olivares's favor and that he would have a son who would become a pillar of the church. This vision was later confirmed by the demons who were already speaking out of the mouths of several of the nuns, as well as Teresa herself. On one occasion, the demons confirmed the good news in the presence of the count-duke, who had come to the convent to visit Teresa. One of the other nuns, who was possessed by a demon called Fortaleza, was brought before Olivares, and her demon was induced to testify that he could expect a son. On another occasion, this same nun had been heard to cry out that "God is not God if the Countess is not with child."[75]

Eventually, with the countess's failure to produce a son and with the count-duke's failure to achieve the great victories promised by Teresa, the correspondence ceased. But, in spite of his bitter words about false prophecy contained in the *Nicandro* written just before he died, there certainly is no reason to believe that Olivares and his wife did not, at least for a time, completely accept the validity of the nuns' claims.[76] The count-duke may have been somewhat unusual for a well-educated man of his time in his disdain for astrology, but he was strictly conventional in his attitude toward visions and revelations. In a letter to the Duke of Medina de las Torres, the count-duke told him that while he should not feel compelled to believe in revelations that had not been approved by the church, he should not "presume to judge them either for or against."[77]

Apart from Olivares himself, other royal ministers eagerly sought out the revelations of mystics during the 1620s, 1630s, and 1640s. Jerónimo de Villanueva, as founder and patron of San Plácido, was of course in the best position to profit from the numerous revelations emanating from the nuns. Villanueva was intrigued when Josefa María, a lay nun, predicted that he would gain a habit and *encomienda* of the Order of Calatrava, and the fact that he did receive one made him even more receptive to whatever the nuns, or the demons speaking through them, had to say about his future. Another revelation concerned the office of *secretario del despacho*, the secretary who attended the king directly, then held by the aged Juan de Insausti. Sometime in May 1627, one of the "possessed" nuns predicted through her demon that he would soon be given a high office, placing him near the king. Villanueva then asked the nun for confirmation, and she told him that "yes, the old man would die and that he would have his office."

More generally—and consistent with the nuns' exalted vision of the foundation of San Plácido as the beginning of a great reform movement involving the entire church—Villanueva was told that he had been selected by God to perform great services for the faith.[78] Villanueva assiduously interrogated the demons and took down what they said in notebooks that he kept hidden in his home. He also commissioned a painting of his guardian angel as a pillar of the church, as described to him by the demon who spoke through the mouth of Josefa María.[79]

It would be a mistake to assume, however, that interest in mysticism among high government officials was confined only to Olivares and Villanueva. In fact, there is considerable evidence that Madrid during these crisis years was a hotbed of prophecy, as Dr. Atiria, a *calificador* of the Toledo tribunal, observed in March 1635.[80] One important official who was seeking out the advice of those whom Atiria qualified as "hare-brained *beatos*" was D. Diego de Cárdenas, a member of the Council of War and general in chief of royal forces in the Crown of Castile. On October 29, 1639, Cárdenas was the subject of a report to the Toledo tribunal regarding his relations with numerous individuals reputed to be able to "foretell the outcome of future battles" and receive revelations and other divine favors.[81] Since some of these persons had already been imprisoned by the Holy Office, Cárdenas was called before the tribunal to explain his contacts with them.[82]

Yet another indication at court of growing interest in prophecy and mysticism can be found in the career of Francisco Chiriboya. Chiriboya, who was a poor but pious hidalgo, came to court around 1625 and soon found himself appalled and alienated by the Olivares regime. One evening, while praying that the king would be given good advisors, he had a vision of the cross entering his breast and heard a voice, which he identified as the voice of God, telling him that he had the obligation to educate the king in the art of government.[83] In the months and years that followed, Chiriboya had numerous revelations that indicated that the king should remove Olivares and his confessor Francisco Aguado from court and that warned of the loss of Portugal three years before it occurred. It was also revealed to him that if the king heeded the voice of God he would be granted the money and soldiers he needed to fight off his enemies, but if he failed to do so he would be punished and his royal house irretrievably lost. Chiriboya communicated his visions to many well-known theologians and numerous members of the court and wrote to the king on several occasions. The attention and support that he attracted is evidenced by the remarkable memorial that was written in his defense by Pedro González Galindo, royal confessor, holder of the prima chair of theology at the Colegio Imperial and *calificador* of the Holy Office.

In his memorial, Galindo emphasized the long tradition of prophets at the service of good government. Chiriboya enjoyed the true gift of prophecy, which had been granted to him as a sign of "divine favor for this tormented monarchy." His revelations, therefore, should be considered a national resource, and Galindo drafted his memorial in the hopes that they would not be ignored because of fears that they may have come from the devil. Galindo told his readers that this was highly unlikely since Chiriboya was a model of saintly virtue, pious, charitable, and living a life of the utmost austerity. For Galindo, the remedy for all the ills of the monarchy was to be found in simply obeying what this divinely inspired voice had been saying for the last twenty-two years.[84]

As the culture of mysticism became a more and more decisive element in an urban middle-class society deprived of any legitimate means of political expression, prophecy was transformed into virtually the only way of indicting royal policies. Heavy expenditure on the construction and embellishment of the new Retiro palace, during a period when the ordinary citizen could barely make ends meet, provoked enormous public resentment, especially in Madrid, where two new sales taxes were imposed in 1633. While a court preacher like the Capuchin Father Ocaña could use his pulpit to denounce the construction of "useless buildings" in a time of crisis, a poor widow like María de San Joseph had no such forum.[85] Instead, María, who was well known in her Madrid neighborhood for her devoutly spiritual life, told visitors that it had been revealed to her that the world would end in 1640 and that the count-duke would find hell in the Buen Retiro.[86]

Whatever the vicissitudes of his reign, Philip IV had always been able to rely on the support of his chief minister. The fall of Olivares and his departure from court on the morning of January 23, 1643, meant that the king was alone and in complete charge of his government for the first time since his accession to the throne in 1621. But in spite of the euphoria that greeted the count-duke's departure, little had changed. Most of the high officials that Olivares had appointed remained in place, and his nephew Don Luis de Haro took over more and more responsibility for the affairs of government.[87] Above all, the war dragged on, with the French invading Aragon, laying siege to Lérida, and threatening Zaragoza. The Portuguese remained defiant and justified their rebellion by publishing a whole series of prophecies that appeared to presage the end of Spanish rule.[88] In the spring of 1643, the king decided, much against his will, to go personally to the Aragonese front to encourage his flagging armies and animate the resistance of the Aragonese.

But Philip IV had another important reason for hurrying to Zaragoza. For several months after the fall of Olivares, he had been seeking divine guidance for his government with the aid of several well-known visionaries. Now, with the strong encouragement of Queen Isabella of Bourbon and the support of the newly powerful Don Juan Chumacero, who had just been appointed president of the Council of Castile, the king had convened a veritable congress of mystics in Zaragoza. Mystics and visionaries had come from convents all over Spain and even from abroad to attend the conclave, although some, like Hernando de Santa María, who had just been released from his convent's prison in Germany, could boast few spiritual credentials.

According to the account of the congress written by Chumacero's confessor Fray Francisco Monteron, the king had promised to carry out the divine will as articulated by the attendees, many of whom he had already met with in Madrid. The message that these seers had to relate had come to each of them in separate visions and was remarkably consistent: the critical need for the king to rid himself of the protonotario, Don Luis de Haro, and the counts of Monterray and Castrillo. In short, these revelations pointed to the removal of the Olivares faction that still ran the monarchy, even after the count-duke's departure.

The stage appeared to be set for an unprecedented intrusion of mysticism into politics, but the seers reckoned without the wily Don Luis de Haro or the opposition that would come from the army. Fearing the loss of his position,

Haro spread the rumor that Philip had fallen under the influence of a cabal of mystics who "dominate him using fraud and deceit." Even more damaging to the cause of the mystics was the protest lodged before the king by the Marquis of Torrecuso, commander of the army besieging Lérida. Torrecuso told the king flatly that he wished to resign since he had learned that "his service to the monarchy was to be judged not on its merits but by revelations." The attitude of his army commander, combined with a growing chorus of protests from the judges of the Audiencia, *alcaldes,* and other officials, was enough to convince the king to disband the congress, and he ordered the mystics to return to their home convents. Francisco Monteron himself was bitterly disillusioned, and it appeared that all the mystics' efforts to prepare themselves to receive divine revelations through special prayers and extraordinary penance had been wasted; the king had refused to "rule and govern himself in harmony with their revelations."[89]

But even as the prophets dispersed, Philip IV could take comfort in the fact that he had already found a mystic to advise him and intercede with God on his behalf. On his way to Zaragoza, Philip had stopped off in the town of Agreda, on the border between Castile and Aragon, to see a most remarkable woman, María de Jesús de Agreda, prioress of the Franciscan convent that her mother had founded in their family home in 1618.[90] Already known for her writings, María de Agreda had gained the king's confidence at their very first meeting on June 10, 1643. From that year until the king died in 1665, they exchanged some 614 letters on a variety of matters, from the king's personal and family life to the need for peace to give the kingdom some relief from the strain of maintaining an overly ambitious foreign policy.[91] Throughout their relationship, one major theme stands out: the king's absolute confidence in Sor María's ability not only to intercede with God in favor of the monarchy but also to tell him what God wished him to do to regain his favor.[92]

Accepted at the highest levels of Spanish government, mysticism had come of age by the middle of the seventeenth century. Moreover, the fact that both the count-duke and the king had placed their trust in women mystics indicates that traditional ideas about women's emotional weakness and excessive vulnerability to demonic manipulation had given way to a new respect, even admiration, for the achievements of feminine spirituality. Probably the best indication of this new acceptability was the overwhelming support for the canonization of Teresa de Jesús. But acceptance of women prophets on the same level as their male counterparts would take time, and before it could occur a whole series of changes in Spanish culture and society would have to make it possible.

Women and the Saintly Ideal

In Spain, as in other Catholic states, the threat of Protestantism and the need to implement the Tridentine reforms called forth a powerful and many-faceted response both from church and lay authorities. Even though the nascent Protestant movement had been destroyed by the early 1560s, there was still the threat of foreign Protestants infiltrating the country, as well as the residual problem of the survival of elements of Islam and Judaism. The presence of large numbers of converted Jews and Moriscos meant that there was an ever-present threat that heterodox thought could filter into the consciousness of Old Christian Spaniards. Inquisition records from the sixteenth century gave ample support to these fears as well as attesting to a high degree of skepticism and confusion about fundamental Catholic concepts—the Trinity, the Immaculate Conception, penance, and indulgences to name a few. In fact, this skepticism expressed by Old Christian Spaniards may have itself reflected the influence of their converted Jewish or Morisco neighbors because these very beliefs were among those that they found most difficult to accept about their new religion. Even more troubling to the church hierarchy was the fact that, as inquisitors visited their sprawling districts, they found an abysmal ignorance of the basic tenets of Catholicism among the popular masses and even the parish clergy.[1]

To deal with this complex problem, the Spanish church and lay authorities adopted a two-pronged approach. The negative side involved the use of government agencies like the Council of Castile and the Inquisition in a broad campaign to prevent the penetration of heterodox ideas by placing controls on the publication, sale, and distribution of books. Religious imagery was also brought under control by setting standards for depicting religious scenes and scrutinizing and controlling the production of popular religious prints. The Inquisition and the ecclesiastical courts were also mobilized to enforce the new Tridentine norms on both clergy and laity through suppression of offen-

sive sexual behavior, disrespect for the sacraments, and anything that was seen
as "superstitious." Speech was also evaluated much more carefully, even if it
did not contain any serious heterodox tendency. Blasphemy and heretical
propositions formed the largest portion of the Inquisition's overall activity
(27.1 percent) between 1540 and 1700.[2]

But punishment by itself was not enough to produce conformity; the desire to conform had to be created through a process of education and indoctrination. For the clergy, both secular and regular, this process involved a
gradual but persistent effort to improve educational standards, which included
the establishment of seminaries and the dramatic expansion of educational
opportunities within the religious orders.

Acculturation of the laity, by contrast, required a multifaceted approach
that would generate real enthusiasm for Counter-Reformation devotions and
incorporate women more fully into the church. Above all, a new popular religious culture had to be created for the urban middle class that was based on
the publication of devotional works in the vernacular since few could read
Latin. If the urban middle and upper-middle classes could be won over to a
fervent religiosity, then the church would have little to fear from heterodoxy,
whether native or foreign.

Among those writers, playwrights, and theologians who crafted this vernacular religious culture in the years after the Council of Trent, it was generally agreed that one of its most essential elements had to be the dissemina-
tion of knowledge about the lives of the saints and martyrs who had contributed
so much to the progress of the Catholic faith. It was widely believed that reading the lives of the saints would inspire the individual to emulation. As the
prolific Jesuit writer Pedro de Ribadeneyra (1527–1611) said in the introduction to his *Flos Sanctorum* first published in 1599:

> What are the lives of the saints for us but a mirror and a model to have always
> before our eyes in order to understand and remedy our own depravities and
> vices, awaken us from our lethargy and inspire us to imitate them.[3]

Or as Alonso de Villegas, the author of a six-volume *Flos Sanctorum* that
was published between 1568 and 1603, remarked: "those who wish to raise
their voices to God in the interest of their immortal souls must follow in the
footsteps of the saints." But to find that path they must first "understand their
lives."[4]

The extraordinary popularity of the *Flos Sanctorum* is indicated by the fact
that they went through a large number of editions and appear in numerous
private libraries in spite of the fact that they were very expensive. Villegas's
massive work went through sixty editions between 1572 and 1794, including
six in Italian, one in English, and one in Aymara, the language of Indians living in Peru and Bolivia.[5] Ribadeneyra's three-volume opus appeared in 1599
and received eighteen editions up to 1761, including two in French. Unlike
Villegas, who composed all six volumes of his *Flos Sanctorum* during a lifetime of unremitting labor, Ribadeneyra's work gradually became transformed
into a collective effort representing the best available Jesuit scholarship as

other members of the order were invited to add to it in later editions. The 1643 edition has a considerable number of entries added by Eusebio Nieremberg, and the 1688 edition contains entries by Francisco García S.J. and by the Carmelite Fr. Andrés López Guererro. Needless to say, all of this added material was carried forward into later editions, such as the one issued in 1761.

As part of the church's campaign to bring popular religious expression under greater control, the Inquisition moved to suppress the vernacular Bibles and biblical excerpts that had proliferated during the early years of the sixteenth century.[6] Elimination of vernacular Bibles left a gap that the authors of the *Flos Sanctorum* hastened to fill by including a variety of biblical stories in their works, thus guaranteeing them a wider audience. Alonso de Villegas incorporated such biblical items as the life and passion of Christ, the life of the Virgin Mary, and the story of Adam and Eve and Cain and Abel. Villegas also included a grab bag of material calculated to appeal to the interest or prejudices of his readers, including homilies on chastity and in favor of marriage as a remedy against carnal temptation. At the same time, Villegas was quick to capitalize on popular anti-Semitism with a brief account of the so-called Holy Child of La Guardia, a blood libel that depicted Jews and converted Jews sacrificing a Christian child.[7]

For his part, the Jesuit Pedro de Ribadeneyra was much more in tune with the post-Tridentine religious program than the layman Villegas. Ribadeneyra incorporated some of the same basic elements—the life and passion of Jesus and the life of Mary—but was at pains to include a rather extensive description of the Trinity and an elaborate discussion and defense of the sacrament of the Eucharist, including various miracles that had occurred to demonstrate its veracity. Instead of repeating the Santo Niño story, Ribadeneyra's anti-Semitic anecdote is a miraculous proof of the real presence. In Poland, a Jew prevailed upon a Christian servant to get him a consecrated host. Once in possession of the host, he carried it to the synagogue, where he and several others proceeded to give it numerous kicks and blows. Much to the surprise of the Jews, however, the host began to bleed so profusely that they had to catch the blood in spoons and put it in a glass vessel. Once again the Christ killers had been at work, but the blood of the victim pointed to his assailants. News of what had happened reached the ears of the king, who had the Jews arrested and burned alive. Information about this new proof of the real presence was gathered by the papal nuncio, who sent a report to his holiness Pope Paul IV.[8] The addition of this sensational material to the *Flos Sanctorum* made them a more effective instrument of Counter-Reformation propaganda while further endearing them to the reading public, which saw them as a genuine substitute for the vernacular Bibles and biblical fragments that they had lost after the index of 1551.

The growing interest in the lives of the saints among the laity was also stoked by an extraordinary surge of publications of individual lives. In a recent study, the distinguished bibliographer José Simón Díaz has counted 443 individual hagiographies published in Spanish between 1480 and 1700.[9] Of that total, however, only 14 were published between 1480 and 1550. The dramatic increase in publication is a Counter-Reformation phenomenon, especially of the seventeenth century, with 357 works or 80.5 percent published after 1600.

Analysis of the authorship of these works and the relationship of authors to the wider Counter-Reformation agenda of the acculturation and indoctrination of the Catholic laity reveals the existence of a core of committed individuals who were involved broadly and continuously in the process and could operate comfortably in a variety of media. In the first place, twenty-six of the authors listed by Simón Díaz wrote at least two and in some cases as many as nine biographies. Such multiple authors included the Dominican Antonio de Lorea, who published four, including one of Pope Pius V, and the Trinitarian Francisco de Arcos, professor of theology and *calificador* of the Suprema, who wrote a biography of his fellow Trinitarian St. Simón de Rojas and another about the life of a young peasant woman named María Ruano, who took the name María de Jesús and became known as the "wise woman of Coria."[10] Pride of place for the most prolific author of individual hagiographies, however, must be awarded to lic. Luis Muñoz, who published nine, all of them on contemporary figures who exemplified some form of religious activity or religious expression that represented one of the ideals of the Counter-Reformation church.[11]

Perhaps the most extraordinary case of multiple authorship—and one that really demonstrates that educating the laity about the lives of the saints was a priority of the government as well as the church—is that of Miguel Batista de Lanuza. Unlike most of the authors, Batista de Lanuza was not a cleric but a high-ranking official of the crown. He succeeded Jerónimo de Villanueva as protonotario of Aragon and became regent of the Council of Aragon, as well as enjoying membership in the Order of Santiago, Spain's most prestigious military order. He was the author of no less than six spiritual biographies and, interestingly enough, they were all of women mystics, which he wrote to render service to the memory of St. Teresa.[12] The extraordinary efforts of someone as prominent as Batista de Lanuza could even inspire emulation by others. His biography of the Discalced Carmelite nun Isabel de Santo Domingo directly inspired Manuel de San Gerónimo's biography of Gabriela de San Joseph, who was a nun in the same order. Evidently, Manuel de San Gerónimo was an avid reader of these spiritual biographies because he mentions several others, including a life of St. Catherine of Siena by Fr. Raymundo de Capua and the Jesuit theologian Luis de Puente's biography of María de Escobar.[13]

Several individuals who contributed to later editions of Pedro de Ribadeneyra's *Flos Sanctorum* deepened their commitment to disseminating information about the lives of the saints by writing hagiographies. Ribadeneyra himself wrote a spiritual biography of St. Ignatius Loyola that was published in 1583. Francisco García, who contributed to the 1688 edition of Ribadeneyra's work, was also the author of spiritual biographies of three great Jesuit leaders, founder Ignatius Loyola, St. Francis Xavier, and St. Francisco de Borja, the eldest son of Juan Borja, third Duke of Gandía, who was accepted into the order in 1551 and became third general of the society in 1565.[14]

Reinforcing the concept of a "core" group, capable of moving easily between the various media of instruction and indoctrination, is the fact that several multiple authors of biographies were also responsible for works extolling post-Tridentine moral standards or devotions. Manuel Calisbeta, who was the author of biographies of St. Caietano di Tiene and St. Rosalia of Palermo, also wrote a devotional work in support of frequent or daily communion. In accordance with the Counter-Reformation stress on eucharistic devotion, Calasibeta praised the taking of the sacrament as "a magnificent and shining achievement" and a clear indication that the soul of the recipient was "unclouded by any serious sin." Calasibeta went on to criticize the lack of zeal shown by those who took communion only yearly; frequent or even daily communion was greatly to be preferred, as it demonstrated the individual's devotion to the sacrament and "is more beneficial to the soul than all of the indulgences that the Holy Father could bestow."[15]

Another versatile and prolific member of this core group, Alonso de Andrade, wrote biographies of his fellow Jesuits St. Stanislas Kostka and Pedro Claver; the founders of the Trinitarians, John of Matha, Felix de Valois; and St. Nicola di Mira. Andrade was also the author of a three-volume guide for laywomen who had taken simple vows; it dealt extensively with the issues raised by their growing number and provided them instruction in how they could live a more perfect spiritual life.[16]

The ubiquitous Juan Eusebio Nieremberg, whose theological-political meditations on the Spanish crisis have already been mentioned, was also an author of spiritual biographies. The subjects were the founder of his own Jesuit order, St. Ignatius Loyola, and St. Francisco de Borja.[17] Apart from his "scientific" writings and his theological-political works, Nieremberg also wrote numerous devotional works and *De la diferencia entre lo temporal y lo eternal*, an important and influential mystical treatise that emphasized the validity of mystical experiences. As noted previously, Nieremberg also made a major contribution to later editions of Ribadeneyra's *Flos Sanctorum*.

One of the most important and successful methods of indoctrination used all over Catholic Europe was religious theater. Pioneered by the Jesuits in France, Germany, Austria, and Bohemia, religious plays were an important reason for the success of the Catholic effort to solidify popular support for the church at a critical moment in its history.[18]

In Spain, where the church faced a less direct threat, *autos sacramentales*, which were essentially dramatizations of one of the mysteries of the faith, and *comedias de santos* were used for educational and propagandistic purposes. Because the overwhelming majority of Spain's seventeenth-century playwrights were in clerical orders, and many of them were also benefice holders or officials of the Inquisition, there could be little doubt that they had the church's program of indoctrination uppermost in their minds.[19]

The tremendous upsurge in the number of *comedias de santos* during the seventeenth century exactly parallels the dramatic increase in the number of individual hagiographies and was driven, at least in part, by a desire to solemnize the canonization of a particular saint or to foster the canonization process by creating a groundswell of popular support.[20] A number of Spain's greatest playwrights, including Quevedo, Mateo de Alemán, and Juan Pérez de Montalbán, wrote both *comedias de santos* and biographies. Pérez de Montalbán, who was a notary of the Holy Office, composed both *autos sacramentales* and *comedias de santos,* of which probably the most important was *La gitana de Menfis, Santa María Egipcíacia,* as well as a hagiography of St. Patrick.[21]

Spiritual biographies were also closely linked to pictorial art, yet another method of indoctrination widely used during the Counter-Reformation.[22] Almost all the biographies contained one or more engravings showing some especially dramatic moment from the spiritual life of the subject. For the biography of Gabriela de San Joseph, for example, the author, Fr. Manuel de San Gerónimo, commissioned Antonio Díaz to produce an engraving of an incident demonstrating the way in which a statue of Christ repaid her devotion. A wealthy widow had left the statue to the convent of Discalced Carmelites in Ubeda, where Gabriela was a nun, and almost as soon as it arrived Gabriela took charge of adorning it.

One day, when the convent was passing through a period of extreme necessity, a woman brought three beautiful carnations to the door. The doorkeeper gave the flowers to Gabriela, who handed them to the prioress, but the prioress, who was preoccupied with where the convent was going to get its next meal, returned them, remarking testily, "I need produce, not flowers; there is neither bread nor wheat in the convent." Then, raising her voice, she ordered Gabriela to present the flowers to the statue, ask it to send the convent some wheat, and bring its response back to her. Gabriela went to the statue, laid the flowers before it, and told it about the convent's needs. The statue immediately replied, "Tell the prioress that there will be wheat." In the ensuing months, Gabriela's simple faith paid abundant dividends as the convent received almost 450 bushels of grain from a variety of unexpected sources, which was more than it normally got even in years of abundant harvest. In the engraving itself, Gabriela is shown kneeling before the statue and presenting it with the flowers as an angel swoops down to place a crown on her head, while the statue's promise to provide grain for the convent is contained in a caption.[23]

Some authors of spiritual biographies were also artists. One of the finest and most prolific Mallorcan printmakers of the eighteenth century was the Trinitarian Fray Lorenzo Reynés (1709–86). Reynés, who held a chair in theology at the University of Mallorca, was also general representative of his order, author of a biography of Miguel de los Santos, and translator of an Italian version of the life of his fellow Trinitarian St. Simón de Rojas.[24]

There was also a considerable degree of cross-fertilization between printmakers and some of the greatest painters of the sixteenth century, especially those who specialized to some degree in portraying saints. One of the earliest examples of this kind of collaboration was between El Greco, who made many paintings of the saints, and the printmaker Diego de Astor, who wished to make engravings after some of El Greco's paintings.[25] Religious engravings also had a profound influence on many of the great painters of the period, perhaps because so many of them were clerics and therefore sympathetic to the church's program of indoctrination.[26] Because the Jesuits pioneered in the use of engravings to illustrate religious texts, it is not surprising that *Adnotationes et Meditationes in Evangelia* by the Mallorcan Jesuit Jerónimo Nadal (1599, 1606, 1607), exerted considerable influence over seventeenth-century Spanish painters.[27] This influence has been clearly demonstrated in the art of Francisco Zurbarán (1598–1664), especially in his *Exposición del cuerpo de San Buenaventura*, which he painted for the Jesuit college of San Buenaventura of Seville, and his paintings for the refectory and altarpiece of the Carthusian monastery in Jerez. The artistic ideas contained in these engravings, which were mainly from Italy and Spanish Flanders, were elevated into a standard of representation by the Sevillian Francisco Pacheco, who was an official censor for the Inquisition. Pacheco, who was himself strongly influenced by the Jesuits and had a Jesuit confessor, wrote *Arte de la Pintura,* which became the most influential work of art criticism in seventeenth-century Spain.[28]

There can be little doubt that the tremendous upsurge in the popularity of the cult of the saints had strong support at the highest levels of Spain's ruling elite, perhaps because the cult was fundamentally conservative and supportive of the existing distribution of power and property. If immersion in the fabulous stories of the saints and martyrs constituted a form of escapism, it certainly did not encourage attack on existing authorities, no matter what their level of responsibility for the bleak situation in which Spain found itself. Alonso de Villegas included a homily about how kings should be obeyed and respected by their subjects in book 2 of his *Flos Sanctorum,* while Pedro de Ribadeneyra taught that humility is "the most important of all the Christian virtues."[29] If the stories of the saints taught their readers anything, they taught them the futility of active involvement in the world. Like Ribadeneyra's aristocratic St. Fulgencio, who gave up his friends and the management of his estates for a life of contemplation and mortification "far away from the tumult and trafficking of the vulgar," the reader was invited to pursue spiritual perfection on an individual basis, leaving the affairs of the world to those who had been placed by God in a position to deal with them.

For their part, Spain's rulers sought to identify themselves with the saint cult for reasons of both internal politics and international prestige. In the international arena, the effort to canonize national spiritual figures was part of a wider struggle between Spain and France for influence in Rome. The stunning series of canonizations of the Spanish saints Tomás de Villanueva, Juan de Ribera, Teresa of Jesus, Ignatius Loyola, and Francis Borja exactly paralleled the rise of Spain to European and world domination during the last half of the sixteenth and early seventeenth centuries. Pride in the number of newly minted Spanish saints and the outstanding spiritual achievements of several remarkable contemporary Spanish women inspired Diego Díaz del Carrete to write a memorial in which he proclaimed the excellence of the names María and Ana, which taken together formed the name of Queen Mariana of Austria, and to claim that "there is not a hand's breadth of France that does not rightfully belong to his Majesty Philip IV." Díaz del Carrete, who was one of the typical political hacks of the period, claimed to have written thirty books, now thankfully lost, proving Spain's superiority over France.[30] Overall, Spain's herculean efforts appeared to have paid off. Of the fifty-five saints canonized between 1588 and 1767, seventeen were Spanish and only four were French.

Direct and highly visible royal support for the canonization of an individual who already had a significant popular following in one part of the monarchy was one way in which the king could identify himself with the people of that region and integrate its aspirations into a wider national agenda. This was especially true of Portugal, which was restive under Spanish rule and resented Spain's failure to protect Portuguese possessions from attack by the Dutch and English. Mindful of the need to win support in Portugal, both Philip III and Philip IV were quick to throw their influence behind the canonization of Isabella of Portugal, who had been married to King Diní s o Lavrador in 1282 and died a widow in 1336. During her lifetime she put up with the king's constant infidelities, accepted his seven illegitimate children, and never uttered a word of reproach. After the king died, this "perfect wife" devoted herself to good works and joined the Franciscan third order.

The move to canonize her began as a strictly Portuguese affair as she was beatified with the support of Joao III in 1525 and her cult was extended to all of Portugal under Sebastiao I during the middle years of the sixteenth century. In 1612 members of the Portuguese aristocracy, led by the bishop of Coimbra, visited her tomb and opened the casket. Incredibly, after 276 years they found the body to be uncorrupted and emitting a sweet odor, thereby convincing everyone present of the "rare, supernatural and miraculous" quality of everything that they had witnessed. After she effected a series of miraculous cures for those who invoked her assistance, the cult revived, and Philip III wrote Pope Paul V personally to request canonization. The pope proceeded to appoint the bishop of Coimbra and Francisco Vaz Pinto, royal chancellor for the Kingdom of Portugal, to accumulate the necessary evidence. Philip IV continued to pressure the Vatican on behalf of Isabella, and she was canonized on May 25, 1625. Given his own love for spectacle, Philip was not blind to the way in which the canonization could be used to win the hearts and minds of his Portuguese subjects, so he defrayed the expenses of a lavish celebration held in Lisbon.[31]

Of course not all regional saint cults received royal support, especially when local elites attempted to bypass the monarchy and deal directly with Rome. The cult that developed around Padre Francisco Simón, a Valencian parish priest with a reputation for supernatural powers, had the support of the kingdom's political elite, as well as an enormous popular following. Fearing violence and alarmed at the regionalist overtones of the cult, the government of Philip III charged the Inquisition with suppression of its more obvious manifestations, such as paintings representing Simón with the nimbus of sanctity or the illuminations in his honor.

In taking these measures, however, the government was merely trying to channel the cult and prevent it from degenerating into something that would seriously offend the Holy See. By 1622, however, the combined efforts of the Inquisition and the viceroy had succeeded in eliminating its worst aspects, and Philip IV felt comfortable about supporting Padre Simón's beatification in Rome. The monarchy's support for Simón continued during the reign of Charles II down to 1687, when the famous and controversial Spanish mystic Miguel de Molinos was arrested. Because Molinos had acted as solicitor for the case, it was immediately suspended and vanished into the darkest recesses of the Vatican archive.

Failure to resolve Simón's case to the satisfaction of the Valencians, however, led to frustration and attempts by members of the local elite to approach Rome directly. By 1710, the Valencia tribunal of the Inquisition had begun to be seriously alarmed when a biography of Simón, published by the auxiliary archbishop, described him as the "apostle of this city." The book reminded Valencians of the cult as it had existed during the early seventeenth century and attributed its popularity to "a superior and divine impulse." Fearing renewed trouble with Rome but also alarmed at the political implications of the cult in a city only recently recovered for the Bourbons, the Inquisition moved quickly to seize all copies of the biography.[32]

In the domestic political arena, royal favor for the canonization of worthy nuns and friars would gain the monarchy support from the powerful religious orders to whom those individuals belonged. In his 1663 biography of St. Diego de Alcalá, the Franciscan Antonio Rojo heaped praise on both Philip II and Philip IV, the former for his powerful support for the canonization process, the latter for building a sumptuous new chapel for the saint in the convent of Santa María de Jesús, which he had founded. In fact, Philip IV's devotion to the saint was so strong, and his eagerness to enlist him as an intercessor in the peace negotiations with France so intense, that he insisted on moving the sepulcher into the chapel before it was even finished so that he could venerate it in person.[33] Philip IV's support for the Franciscans did not end with his devotion to St. Diego de Alcalá, however; through his influence the cases of three other friars had been moved before the Congregation of Rites.

Championing the saint cults of a particular city was also an obvious way for the monarchy to maintain good relations with local elites who had an interest in strengthening the role of their cities as centers of religious devotion at a time when many of them were losing their commercial and manufacturing base. The impact of Spain's economic and demographic crisis was nowhere more apparent than in Toledo, which saw its population decline from a peak of 54,665 in 1591 to 25,000 in 1646, while its vital silk industry lost more than four-fifths of its capacity. Faced with this crisis, local elites fell back on Toledo's traditional role as an ecclesiastical center and home to sacred relics. By helping to bring the relics of Toledo-born saints back to the city, the monarchy was able to cement its relationship to Toledo's urban oligarchy, whose support in the Cortes of Castile was vital to maintaining the flow of new taxation. Following in the footsteps of his father, Philip III aided in the effort to bring the remains of the saintly princess Doña Sancha Alonso (1190–1270) to Toledo in 1608. The connection to the past glories of the city was obvious in that Doña Sancha had been the daughter of Alfonso IX of León and sister to Fernando III, who had made the city his capital after reuniting León and Castile in 1230.

After the arrival of the relics, the number of miracles and especially cures attributed to Sancha's intervention multiplied dramatically and were duly noted in the miracle book kept by the Convent of Santa Fe, where the body lay in the Bethlehem chapel, long the scene of intense popular devotion. In 1615, after the evidence of 430 witnesses to miraculous cures and other supernatural phenomena caused by invoking Doña Sancha had been recorded, Philip III himself visited the chapel, accompanied by many of Spain's leading nobles. Not surprisingly, it was after this royal visit that popular veneration of the relics intensified, involving "every sort of person" from the city and surrounding region. During the reign of Philip IV, the crown lent its support to a cult that could only redound to the benefit of the monarchy, and Queen Mariana of Austria wrote to the Holy See on behalf of canonization.[34]

Queen Mariana of Austria herself was extremely devoted to the cult of the saints and especially to those of the Counter-Reformation. The inventory of her possessions that was taken shortly after her death in 1696 reveals that she had images of St. Teresa of Jesus, St. Peter of Alcantara, and St. Anthony of Padua, as well as an altarpiece with numerous saints. The inventory also listed relics of John the Baptist and St. Charles Borromeo and a piece of the crown of thorns encased in a precious reliquary. The queen's strong interest in the canonization of Spanish religious figures also extended to contemporaries. She provided funds for the second edition of Luis de Mesa's biography of the Franciscan *beata* Mariana de Jesús, and the author dedicated the book to her in gratitude.[35]

Spain's cities and regions also competed for precedence. In this struggle, there were distinct political advantages to be gained by underscoring long-standing support for Roman Catholicism. This was especially true of the towns of Andalusia, whose conquest by the Moors and large Jewish presence made them vulnerable to charges of a lack of racial purity and consequently a less than fervent devotion to Catholicism.[36] As a result, during the early seventeenth century, when the entire country was debating the purity of blood issue, Córdoba and several other leading Andalusian cities commissioned Martín de Roa to write histories of their saints.[37] Interestingly enough, in light of the debate about purity of blood, these histories tended to emphasize ancient saints, martyrs to the faith either in Roman times or those who were killed when they resisted Islam at the time of the Moorish conquest.[38] By filling his Flos Sanctorums with such figures, Roa was indicating both the antiquity of Catholicism in southern Spain and the loyalty of Andalusians to the faith, for which they had gladly suffered martyrdom at the hands of the infidel.[39] All of this, of course, was in implicit contrast with the much vaunted racial "purity" claimed by the Basques, who had never been conquered by the Moors but who also had been mere savages when Spain was a Roman province and therefore played no role in the establishment of Christianity.

Given the sensitivity of local elites to issues of religious and racial purity, the monarchy's open patronage of ancient saints venerated in the Andalusian cities was a good way to guarantee their political support in a time of crisis. Both Philip II and Philip III made personal visits to the supposed tombs of Seville's patron saints Justa and Rufina, two aristocratic maidens who were tortured and killed after they refused to worship the goddess Venus.[40] The cult spread outside Andalusia, and chapels to the saints were established as far away as Daroca in Aragon and Lisbon and Coimbra in Portugal. A benefice holder in Seville's cathedral also founded a Colegio Mayor at Alcalá in honor of the two saints, and confraternities were founded all over Spain from Málaga to Barcelona.[41]

The fundamentally conservative nature of the cult of the saints also engendered support from among Spain's great landed magnates. Fray Pedro de la Corazón de Jesús dedicated his biography of the Discalced Mercedarian nun María Ana de Jesús to José Álvarez de Toledo and María del Pilar, dukes of Alba and Medina Sidonia, for their strong support of her cult and for having recently presented the convent where her body was kept with a beautiful and expensive urn to adorn her chapel. When she was beatified in 1783, the dukes helped defray the cost of the sumptuous banquet and other ceremonies held in her honor at the Mercedarian convent in Salamanca.[42]

Of course, some nobles had a direct pecuniary interest in fostering the cult to a particular saint. When D. Juan Cristóbal de Guardiola purchased the village of La Guardia from the archbishop of Toledo in 1581, he made every effort to foster the cult of the so-called Holy Child, which had already achieved a certain local and regional prominence. Shortly after acquiring the village, D. Juan founded a Trinitarian convent, which was dedicated to the service of this supposed victim of a Jewish conspiracy. Numerous pilgrimages of the famous and not so famous followed, confraternities were founded, and in 1649 Pope Innocent V conceded a plenary indulgence to all those entering the shrine. The yearly procession in honor of the "Holy Child" and the numerous pilgrims from as far away as Madrid must have significantly improved Cristóbal de Guardiola's return on what might otherwise have been a rather poor investment.[43]

Family pride also played a significant role in the aristocracy's sponsorship of a particular saint cult. Given the fact that the overwhelming majority of saints and noted spiritual figures came from the ranks of the nobility, it was not difficult for an aristocratic family to have an ancestor it could support for canonization. Juan Interain de Ayala's 1692 life of St. María de Cervellon (1230–90) was dedicated to the present Duke of Montalto and Bibona D. Fernando de Aragón Moncada Luna y Cardona, who was a descendant. The interlocking Moncada, Luna, and Cardona families started the canonization process for María de Cervellon in 1629.[44]

In rural areas, the cult of individual saints and advocations of divine figures remained traditional in the sense that they were mainly rooted in local

geography and related to protecting the harvest and guarding village boundaries.[45] The cult in the larger towns incorporated to a far greater degree national and international saintly figures and advocations as well as local ones.
It was nurtured by the printing industry, which profited from the publication
of hundreds of works designed to communicate with a literate and cultivated
audience that had other means of entertainment at its disposal. In the preface
to his *Flos Sanctorum*, Bartolomé Cayrasco de Figueroa referred to his readers as already acquainted with "profane and fantastic poetry" and "ingenious
plays both Tuscan and Spanish" and predicted that they would enjoy and profit
from the "famous and wonderful tales of the lives of the saints."[46]

The sophistication of those who purchased these works is evidenced by
the numerous references to figures from classical antiquity or the Bible that
fill its pages. Cayrasco de Figueroa mentions such figures from Greek and
Roman mythology as Galatea and Diana and uses numerous Latin quotations.
In the prologue to his biography of the Franciscan *beata* Mariana de Jesús,
Luis de Mesa refers to classical authors such as Horace and early Christian
writers such as Tertullian, as well as to more modern religious figures, including St. Anthony of Padua and St. Francis Xavier.[47] Manuel de San
Gerónimo, who was official chronicler of the Carmelite order when he wrote
his biography of Gabriella de San Joseph, went one step further by making
his graceful dedication to Doña Josepha Manuel de Hozes depend on an elaborate literary conceit comparing his portrait of Gabriella to Phidias's sculpture of the goddess Palas.[48]

We can catch a glimpse of some of the readers of these works through a
series of sonnets in praise of Cayrasco de Figueroa and his work that were
placed just before the dedication. These were written by the members of an
educated middle class of clergy and laymen, some of whom held offices of a
certain importance in the church or civil bureaucracy, including the general
representative of the Canary Islands resident in Madrid, a canon of the cathedral in Palma, and several simple licentiates.[49]

Among women, readers of the new hagiographies included educated nuns
like the author of an unpublished book of revelations written mainly in Latin
between 1663 and 1665. The revelations contained extensive references to the
Bible, the book of the Apocalypse, the works of St. Paul, the Gospel of St.
John, and Tertullian.[50]

Within the convents, diffusion of the lives of the saints was made easy by
high rates of literacy in Spanish. In some instances there is evidence that reading books written by or about saints was incorporated into convent routines.
In Zaragoza's aristocratic Convent of Santa Catalina, which had been founded
by an aunt of King James the Conqueror, it was customary to choose one of
the nuns to read a spiritual book or hagiography while the others sewed or
performed other labor. When Hipolita de Jesús y Rocaberti was mistress of
novices in Barcelona's Convent of Nuestra Señora de los Angeles, her own
extraordinary devotion to the saints led her to call together her novices on
the evening before a saint's day to teach them about the life and particular
virtues of that saint.[51]

Reading aloud from the lives of the saints was also a frequent pastime among aristocratic girls. When seventeen-year-old Brianda de Acuña Vela's father, Bernardino Gonzalez Delgadillo y Avellaneda, was appointed viceroy of Navarre, he decided to place her with his relatives, the counts of Miranda. During her time with the family, Brianda became very close to the two Miranda daughters, Aldonça and Tecla. After praying for several hours and performing spiritual exercises, all three girls would read the lives of the saints together.[52] Later on in life, when Brianda entered the Carmelite order, she not only took the name of the order's saintly foundress but also loved to read and listen to the lives of the saints. One evening, after listening to a particularly moving passage in the life of Peter the Hermit that was being read in the refectory, she was so overcome she had to leave the room.[53]

Given the relatively high rates of literacy that can be assumed for aristocratic and upper-middle-class women and the fact that they had a certain amount of discretionary income available to purchase books, it is not surprising that saint cults took firm root among them. In dealing with the possible diffusion of knowledge about saints of national or international reputation to the popular masses, we are necessarily on less firm ground. Literacy rates among the lower and middle classes in the towns was no more than 40 percent, and women in particular were at a disadvantage. Nevertheless, it can be assumed that lower-class urban women could and did learn about the lives of the saints, either by word of mouth or through their own reading. Gerónima de Noriega, whose father was a shoemaker and husband a tailor, was semiliterate, having learned basic reading skills from a parish priest in Madrid. When she was brought before the Holy Office in 1628, she had a number of books in her possession. Apart from a *contemptus mundi*, a catechism, and a work of spiritual exercises written by a Jesuit, she also had a recently published life of the German mystic Gertrude the Great. Gerónima was also aware of the reputation of the controversial abbess of the Convent of Santa Clara of Carrion de los Condes, Luisa de la Asensión, the so-called Monja de Carrion because she saw her in a vision.[54]

The case of Francisca Badia provides yet another good example of the diffusion of the saint cult to women of the urban lower middle class. Francisca came from a family of small shopkeepers who had a stall in Valencia's central market, where they all lived. Even though the family passed through hard times, Francisca was able to learn to read and write and was so devoted to the saints that she plastered her room with their images. On one occasion, after reading some of Teresa of Jesus' writings, she claimed that the saint appeared, praised her for spending her time reading devotional works, and explained some of the obscure points in her own writings to her.[55]

Diffusion of "outside" saint cults to the villages, where literacy rates were considerably lower, especially for women, is even more difficult to document. Because the saint cult as most rural people experienced it was designed around local "protectors" or the Virgin Mary, who was seen as an intercessor, worship of a saint that transcended the region would seem to call for a level of sophistication that was beyond the average peasant woman. Nevertheless, leaders did emerge who for one reason or another were able to forge a link between the village and the wider world of Counter-Reformation devotional practices. María Ruano was one such leader. Born to a family of poor peasants in the tiny village of Guijo in the diocese of Coria, on the border with Portugal, she was more or less abandoned to the care of a stern but pious widow from age six. In spite of the harsh regimen, she did learn how to read and write and acquired a fairly sophisticated understanding of Catholicism, which included the lives of certain saints. Perhaps unsurprisingly, given her social origins, the peasant Isidro Labrador was María's preferred saint. But her religious knowledge also extended to several other well-known saints, including St. Joseph, Francis of Assisi, and St. Dominic among the men and Teresa of Jesus, Mary Magdalen, and Martha, Mary Magdalen's sister, among the women.

Even villagers who were completely illiterate could pick up some knowledge of the lives of the saints simply from the conversations of others. Evidently that is exactly what happened to María Cotonilla, an illiterate pauper who lived in a rented room in the village of Colmenar de Oreja about fifty kilometers southeast of Madrid. When María was interrogated after her arrest on charges of "false sanctity," she was asked who had taught her to pretend to have the visions and revelations with which she had convinced others that she was a holy woman. She replied that no one had taught her anything but that she had simply listened to what the other villagers said about what had "happened to certain saints" to establish her persona.[56]

One of the most striking aspects of the saint cult in early modern Spain was the growing interest in female saints, especially in the seventeenth century. Among the medieval women saints, certain mystics stand out not only because of the number of individual hagiographies they received but also because their spiritual works and revelations were published in Spanish, making them accessible to a wider audience of educated women. Catherine of Siena's spiritual works were made available in a Spanish edition published in Alcalá in 1512.[57] In 1668, her dialogues were also published in a Spanish edition by the Dominican Luis de Loarte. There were also four Spanish biographies of the saint, one of which was written in octaves by a woman, Isabel de Liaño.[58]

While expressing modesty about the "homely" quality of her verse, Isabel de Liaño's achievement in publishing her biography was no mean achievement in an epoch when, as she declared in her prologue, "one of the things least accepted is the knowledge that is dispensed by feminine discernment." She herself had to contend with those who believed that she had not really composed the book, assuming that it had been written by a male author who put her name on it to increase its sales, since if people saw that the book was authored by a woman, they would buy it out of curiosity.

But early in the book, Isabel de Liaño made it clear that she cared little for men's opinion of her literary style in that she was writing mainly for women.[59] Whatever her spiritual accomplishments, the life of St. Catherine of Siena was mainly useful because it disproved the prevailing male idea that "women are incapable of accomplishing anything important."[60] Not only had Catherine revealed great religious truths in spite of having no theological training but also she had preached with great success before two popes,and was even chosen as a special emissary by one of them. She was equal or superior to even the greatest male saints and could provide contemporary women an example of God's power to raise a weak woman to spiritual greatness because in the eyes of the Creator both sexes were fundamentally equal:

> I am the one who created the human race
> And where I wish I spread my grace.[61]

But if the life of Catherine of Siena could point the way to a more prominent role for women in both religion and secular life, it was the revelations of the German mystic Gertrude the Great (d. 1302) that were the most influential in encouraging a climate favorable to the acceptance of the validity of divine communication bestowed on contemporary women. Gertrude the Great, Mechtild of Hackeborn, and Mechtild of Magdeburg were the most important members of a Benedictine community established in the mid-thirteenth century at Helfta near Eisleben in Saxony.[62] Her parents and place of birth are unknown, but from age five she lived in the convent at Helfta, where she received an excellent education. She became fluent in Latin and wrote spiritual works, treatises, and explanations of spiritual texts in both Latin and German. Her vernacular works are unfortunately lost, and what remains are two Latin works, the *Legatus divinae pietatis,* commonly translated as *Herald of God's Loving Kindness,* and *The Exercises.* The latter work is a series of exercises dealing with the best way to lead a Christian life, the responsibilities of persons leading a life consecrated to God, and the way in which a Christian should prepare for death. The *Legatus* is five books, of which only book 2 was actually written by Gertrude. Book 1 is a memorial to Gertrude written by her friends to demonstrate her sanctity. Book 2 is Gertrude's spiritual biography, and the remaining books deal with the soul and its relationship to God, the feasts of the church with special emphasis on the Eucharist, and the exemplary deaths of certain members of her community.[63]

The first printed edition of the *Legatus* was published in Latin by Lanspergius (Johann Gerecht) in 1536, and two other Latin editions followed in 1579 and 1599. The 1599 edition was published in Madrid by the first official chronicler of the Spanish Benedictines, Juan de Castañiza. But long before Castañiza's edition appeared, he and many other members of Spain's intellectual elite— Bartolomé de Carranza, Luis de Granada, and several of Teresa de Jesus' spiritual advisors including Domingo Báñez—had access to Gertrude's writings through the work of the Belgian friar Louis de Blois. Blois's *Conclave Animae Fidelis* (1558) contained his *Speculum Spiritualis,* an anthology of the works of the leading medieval women mystics, including St. Matilda, St. Catherine of Siena, Hildegard of Bingen, St. Bridget of Sweden, and Gertrude of Helfta. The *Conclave* also contained two of Blois's other devotional writings, which were suffused with Gertrude's ideas, expressions, and methods of prayer. The diffusion of this work in Spain prepared the way for the reception of editions of Gertrude's own writings, especially after Blois's complete works were translated into Spanish between 1597 and 1598.[64]

The fact that knowledge of Gertrude's spiritual life and revelations was filtering into Spanish religious and intellectual circles during the last half of the sixteenth century created some subtle and not so subtle relationships between the seer of Helfta and Teresa of Jesus. The evidence suggests that Teresa was certainly aware of at least some of Gertrude's visions either through oral transmission or through her confessors, who were very familiar with the work of Blois.[65] It is at least possible, therefore, that Teresa may have consciously patterned herself after the illustrious German nun. Certainly the famous vision of the transverberation of her heart, in which she saw an angel in bodily form pierce her heart with a fire-tipped spear, is remarkably similar to Gertrude's account of Christ piercing her heart with a triple-pointed arrow.[66]

Even more important, from the standpoint of Teresa's posthumous reputation, was Gertrude's impact on Teresa's supporters. Her first biographer, the Jesuit Francisco de Ribera, was at pains to compare Teresa's visions and revelations to those of the German mystic and other female saints since such a comparison would provide precedents for Teresa and make her appear less like a dangerous innovator.[67] Confusing Gertrude with her mentor Mechtild of Hackeborn, Ribera asserts that the lives of Teresa and Gertrude the Great were similar in that both were abbesses and reformers. He also specifically points to the vision of the transverberation as an example of both women enjoying similar divine favor and asserts that a vision of a multitude of persons dressed in white that was seen by one of the nuns attending Teresa while she was on her deathbed was the same as one seen by the nuns who attended Gertrude when she was dying. In both instances, Ribera assumes that the white-clad figures were a procession of holy virgins who had come to receive the soul of the dying woman and carry it to heaven, where "her glory would equal that of all the holy virgins who had shed their blood for Jesus Christ and been canonized."[68]

There can be little doubt that her supporters' success in identifying Teresa as a kind of Spanish reincarnation of Gertrude the Great helped deflect criticism of the somewhat controversial saint. By the same token, however, Teresa's increasing acceptability, and the successful publication of Ribera's biography with its copious references to Gertrude, helped swell the public's appetite to learn more about the German nun.[69] That need was filled with the publication of Alonso de Andrade's adulatory biography of Gertrude in 1663. In this work, Andrade underscores Gertrude's growing importance by referring to the enormous extension of her cult in the Hispanic world. He also quotes approvingly Ribera's linkage of Teresa and Gertrude. Both were perfect nuns who enjoyed the gift of prophecy, while Teresa's revelations were corroborated by those of Gertrude. Stretching historical truth more than a little, Andrade makes Teresa take Gertrude as her spiritual guide, "commending herself to her and seeking her intercession before the Almighty."[70]

Teresa's growing prominence, long before she was canonized in 1622, and the rapid growth of cultic veneration to Gertrude all over the Hispanic world after the publication of Leandro de Granada's Spanish translation of her *Legatus* in 1603 created a highly favorable climate for the revelations of other women mystics.[71] The fact that these revelations could be freely distributed, especially after 1600, stands in marked contrast to the reception they encountered for much of the sixteenth century, when the leading role played by certain women in the Illuminist movement made them the object of suspicion and hostility on the part of male theologians.[72] Even as late as June 1593, Fr. Juan de Lorenzana wrote the Suprema to demand that the recently translated works of Louis de Blois be withdrawn from circulation so that they could be expurgated.[73] But in the preface to the 1616 edition of his biography of St. Gertrude, Leandro de Granada presents us with a very different and far more optimistic picture. Noting that he had published the second edition at the request of nuns from Santiago's aristocratic Convent of San Payo because the 1603 edition was almost completely sold out, Leandro de Granada commented on the dramatic change that had taken place: "Until that time, works of visions and revelations written in romance did not circulate so freely."[74]

Teresa's role in bringing about this change of attitude on the part of male theologians was noted admiringly by her second biographer, Diego de Yepes. In general, such men tended to be highly skeptical of those, especially women, who claimed to receive extraordinary favors from God like trances, visions, and revelations. But in Teresa's case, "the greater and more learned they are the more they esteem her works and the more devoted to her they become."[75] Of course, the favor shown her by learned and influential theologians was no accident, as Teresa herself was acutely aware of the need to win them over. In judging the veracity of her revelations, moreover, they would have been cognizant of her endorsement by no less a personage than Juan de Horozco y Covarrubias, whose treatise on true and false prophecy was one of the most influential works of its kind. Horozco asserted that it was precisely because of the way Teresa had manifested "true" prophecy that the devil was trying so hard to discredit it by raising so many false prophets.[76]

With the dramatic growth of cults to both Gertrude and Teresa in Spain and Spanish America and tacit papal approval of the northern mystics around 1610, women mystics had at last gained the kind of respectability that would allow them to play an ever more prominent role in seventeenth-century society.[77] The availability of cheap "pocket" editions of the hagiographies of both medieval and contemporary or near-contemporary saints, moreover, ensured that their lives and religious practices would be imitated widely, especially by upper- and middle-class women.[78]

The effort that so many individuals were making to replicate aspects of the lives of saints or to imitate Christ through a lifestyle of austerity, mortification, and disdain for the material world was strongly reinforced by a tremendous outpouring of devotional literature that was specifically published in Spanish in order to reach readers of both sexes. In works like Francisco de Osuna's *Tercer abecedario espiritual*, Luis de Granada's *Guía de pecadores*, and Antonio Quintanadueñas's *Espejo grande*, writers emphasized humanity's infinite debt to God and urged their readers to meditate on Christ's passion as a way of driving home their constant ingratitude for God's favors. The individual's own worthlessness and guilt were manifest because the body was little more than a "dungheap of misery," while the soul was a "home for satan."[79] A program of systematic meditation on the parts of Christ's body and how each suffered for sinful humanity was prescribed in such works as *Theologia mystica sciencia y sabiduria de Dios*, first published in 1644 by the Augustinian Agustín de San Ildefonso. In this work, beautifully illustrated by the great Claudio Coello, San Ildefonso states that his main purpose was to provide his readers with access to that mysterious ladder, first discovered by Jacob, that permitted angels to pass from heaven to earth. By making use of this ladder, which consisted of a series of spiritual exercises, the reader could attain perfect union with God.[80]

The impact of devotional literature on the behavior and cultural expression of early modern Spanish women cannot be underestimated, especially since its message was being spread beyond the ranks of the literate by preachers who had themselves been nurtured on the same literature in seminaries and convent schools. Tomás de Montalvo's biography of the Franciscan ecstatic Beatriz María de Jesús details several instances of trancelike states induced by reading devotional works. On one occasion, she went into a trance so close to an open window that those observing her were afraid she would fall out.[81] In Granada's Convent of Santo Ángel Custodio, where she resided and later became abbess, it was customary to read from devotional works in the refectory. One day the reading was from the famous and controversial *Mystical City of God* by Sor María de Ágreda de Jesús. This work, which had been placed on the Roman index in 1681 and condemned by the Sorbonne in 1696 on the grounds that it contained false doctrine, remained extremely popular in Spain, especially among devout women, who found its descriptions of the life and tribulations of the Virgin Mary especially compelling. In spite of misgivings about the book in Rome and the condemnation by the Sorbonne and by the German theologian Eusebius Amort, the *Mystical City of God,* first published in 1670, went through eighty-nine complete editions and sixty-eight anthologies and summaries, making it one of the most popular Spanish-language devotional works ever written.[82] So powerful was the impact of hearing this work read aloud that when the lector arrived at the description of how the Virgin Mary suffered when her son went to fast in the desert, Beatriz María de Jesus could not contain her tears and was forced to leave the room. After finding somewhere more private, she gave full vent to her feelings. Sobbing piteously, she cried out for death so that her tie to the mortal flesh that imprisoned her would be broken and she could see God face to face. After an hour on her knees, she finally collapsed, confessing to those around her that she could no longer sustain such transports of love.[83]

For those women already embarked on a spiritual journey, certain devotional books struck a highly responsive chord. One of these key works was the *Noche Oscura* by St. John of the Cross. For St. John the image of the night is symbolic of the darkness in which the soul finds itself before experiencing the transcendent Deity. The Dominican María de San Andrés identified herself so closely with the spiritual journey described by St. John in the book that whenever she could not make her confessor understand her spiritual life, she would explain herself by pointing to passages and having him read them.[84]

For women who were completely or partially illiterate or could not afford devotional works, the sermon was probably the most important way of communicating the rudiments of the new religious culture of the Counter-Reformation. Because the Spanish Catholic Church had designated almost ninety holy days at which attendance at mass was obligatory in addition to Sundays, there was no shortage of opportunities for preachers to indoctrinate the faithful.[85] Sermons ranged from the simple Sunday homilies to the far more elaborate sermons by specially invited preachers on a holy day. Such sermons could draw large crowds from the city and surrounding countryside and fire the imaginations of their listeners.[86]

The impact that a particularly effective preacher could have on a woman's spiritual life is illustrated by a description of a missionary in the autobiography of Isabel de Jesús, a member of the third order of Carmelites. Before he began his sermon, Isabel saw "with the eyes of her soul" that he was accompanied by two beautiful angels and carried a crucified Christ next to his heart, which emanated a luminosity that lit up his entire body but especially his heart and made him very beautiful. After performing the stations of the cross with great devotion followed by large numbers of people, he preached a sermon with simple eloquence and great spiritual benefit to the public. From this moving experience, Isabel de Jesús professed that she had learned two great truths: the reverence that one should feel for preachers of the faith and the fact that "the worst time that satan spends is when he sees souls hearing sermons and understands the great profit they derive from them."[87]

Above all, whether it was disseminated by means of hagiographies, devotional works, *comedias de santos*, or sermons, the new religious culture that was being created in post-Tridentine Spain was a vernacular culture that included women to a far greater extent than the old Latin-based culture ever did. Even the aristocratic nuns of San Plácido read only Spanish and, as one of them testified, derived the stuff of their revelations from what was readily available: the lives of the saints and "from what they heard in sermons or picked up from reading books."[88] One of the keys to this religious culture was the imitation of sanctity by the ordinary individual illuminated by reading the lives of the saints and guided by the spiritual adviser.

Writing in 1678, when the tendency to imitate sanctity was already an entrenched part of the culture of Spanish women, the highly beneficial spiritual effects of such imitation were celebrated by Andrés de Maya Salaberria in the prologue to his biography of Martina de los Angeles y Arilla. The Dominican nun was just one example of the many "noble spirits" that the age had produced whose "prodigious lives" filled with "miracles, revelations and other singular divine favors" were the subject of so many spiritual biographies.[89]

But not all claims to sanctity or divine favor were valid. When Ana Rodríguez, the daughter of a muleteer, had a vision of herself holding the Christ child to her naked breast, which she conflated with another vision of her lover's soul merging with her own to conclude that it was her duty to nurture his soul so that he would become "another redemptor," she was merely using the language of mysticism to articulate her own obscene fantasies. Because those same terms and ideas had become deeply ingrained in popular culture, however, there was little point in complaining, like Toledo's inquisitors, that some "great disciple of the devil" must have taught her words and concepts beyond her station.[90]

The publication of growing numbers of spiritual biographies and autobiographies by and about highly spiritual nuns and *beatas* led other women whose spirituality was much less certain to try to publish their own material. In April 1639, at the trial of María Batista on charges of false sanctity, false revelations, simulated trances, and fraud, Pedro de Tapia, who held the prestigious Prima professorship of theology at Alcalá, testified that she had sent him her spiritual autobiography for him to evaluate for possible publication.[91]

As the mystical movement spread beyond its original centers in the convents and monasteries of urban Spain and the relatively well-educated women who had first embraced it to affect the lower classes of the towns and villages, it began to raise concern among the male theologians who dominated the universities and advised the Inquisition.[92] Confused and alarmed by the proliferation of female mystics but delighted by their spiritual progress and the signs of God's favor that they appeared to enjoy, male theologians sought desperately to find the appropriate criteria by which they could set aside the most doubtful claims while not disappointing the devout who found in the visions, locutions, raptures, and trances of women mystics renewed proof of the validity and vitality of the Catholic faith.

Women Mystics in a
Male-Dominated Culture

Inevitably, when confronting the issue of properly evaluating the claims of women to spiritual perfection and divine favor, theologians had to take a whole series of negative attitudes about women into account. Such views were not only hoary with tradition in the church but also shared by many of their contemporaries. Using Aristotelian dualities that made one element superior to the other, Thomas Aquinas and other medieval theologians saw men as perfect and complete and women as imperfect and deficient.[1] The inferiority of women was at once physical, psychological, and intellectual. According to the great sixteenth-century poet and theologian Luis de León, women were "weak, brittle and frail" to an extraordinary degree.[2] Psychologically, according to the late-fifteenth-century writer Martín de Córdoba, women were more attached to carnality than men, because emotion and not reason predominated in their psychological makeup. The weak-mindedness and generalized inconstancy and fickleness ingrained in the feminine psyche made them vulnerable to demonic suggestion. As a consequence, their spiritual lives were far more likely to be inspired by the devil than those of men, whose superior intellects allowed them to better resist demonic temptation.[3]

The ingrained idea that emotion predominated in women's psyches was also used to attempt to exclude women from being witnesses in civil and criminal cases.[4] Women's supposed intellectual inferiority made them unfit for any position in society (jurists, government officials) that required the use of learning, and it made education itself problematic.

That doubts about the effectiveness of educating women were not merely confined to an intellectual elite is demonstrated by the reaction of the Augustinian Fray Pedro Benimelis to his penitent Isabel de Riera when she informed him that she had numerous visions indicating that he should teach her Latin.

As Isabel was a mere beltmaker, Benimelis was astonished at her request and could simply not understand "what use it would be if she learned Latin." To his credit, Benimelis did not dismiss Isabel's request out of hand and consulted another priest, who told him that he could teach her a few times to see if she was learning anything. He gratefully accepted this advice and did give her a number of lessons, from which she picked up the rudiments of Latin.[5]

Curiously enough, however, firm belief in the inferiority of women did not make the men of old-regime Europe feel especially confident in dealing with them. It was precisely the sensual nature of women, the carnality that supposedly weakened their rational capabilities, that also made them dangerous in that men were so powerfully attracted to them because of it. Women, especially attractive women, were therefore automatically viewed with suspicion. Luis de León warned men against marrying a woman who was too beautiful because she would naturally wish to show off that beauty and in so doing attract the attention and desire of other men.

> So that whosoever seeks a very beautiful woman walks through a land infested with highwaymen carrying gold. Gold which he does not condescend to hide in his purse but instead flaunts before the very eyes of the thieves.[6]

To make matters worse, in Mediterranean societies like Spain, family honor was critically dependent on the unquestioned fidelity of wives and the equally undoubted chastity of daughters. It was for this reason that Luis de León declared that a spouse who attracted the attention and desire of other men ran the risk of compromising the family, even if she had done nothing wrong; even the possibility of her being able to commit adultery was enough cause gossip and "defame" her honor.[7]

The male need to assert control over women's sexuality is behind the multiple efforts to restrict their movements and remove them from contact with potentially dangerous men. The unmarried single girl was the object of special concern both because of her value as a pawn in the family's struggle to improve its status and because she could become the object of rape or forced removal from the home. Even relatively liberal writers like the humanist Luis de Vives agreed that *doncellas* should live secluded lives and not be allowed out of the house even to visit girlfriends except very occasionally. Other authors went even further. Juan de la Cerda advised anxious parents to "seal up every door and gate from where danger might be anticipated."[8]

Anxiety about maintaining the reputation of unmarried daughters affected all classes but was particularly acute among the urban middle and lower middle class because, unlike the nobility, their rank and status afforded them no automatic protection. Testifying in 1626 before the Canaries tribunal of the Inquisition about the family of his neighbor the swordmaker Diego González, Luis de Salazar provided a perhaps not atypical example of this concern. Apparently González was careful to keep the women of his household in some inner rooms where they could not be seen from the street or by the customers who entered his shop at the front of the house. Even though they had been neighbors for many years, González never allowed his daughter María Romero to visit the Salazars because they had boys as well as girls, and González believed that no man, "no matter how honorable," should be allowed to see María.[9]

The lives of married women were hardly less constrained. In Pedro Galindo's *Excelencias de la castidad y virginidad,* he wrote about how the husband began restricting the movements of his wife almost as soon as they were married. In a purely arbitrary manner and for no other reason than to exercise a despotic power over her, the husband prevents her from visiting her neighbors, cuts her off from her family, and does not even allow her to go to the window without his permission.[10] Even though this particular book was written to extol the celibate state, Galindo's long experience as spiritual director gives him a considerable amount of credibility, especially since his account is borne out by other evidence. In his well-known manual for confessors, Galindo obliges the confessor to ask male penitents if they had without just cause prevented their wives from seeing neighbors and their parents or stopped them from attending mass or other church functions.[11] This same concern about women being refused permission to attend church even to carry out such devotions as confession, which was obligatory under canon law, was expressed by authors as diverse as Manuel de Azpilcueta in the mid-sixteenth century and Fr. Alonso Cabrera, Juan de Soto, and the Jesuit Gaspar de Astete in the seventeenth.[12]

Such restrictions were also encountered by Isabel de Jesús when she went to Paterna to assist a young parish priest. While there, she had a nocturnal encounter with a married woman who told her that she had not been to confession or mass for fourteen years because her husband hardly let her out of the house during the day and that she was able to leave only at night, when everyone was asleep.[13]

Precisely because fear of sexual liberty fueled society's drive to restrict women, any woman who was not under the direct control of a husband or father was instantly suspect of actual or potential sexual excess. The fear of the masterless woman also lay behind the negativism about widows, who were excoriated if they married a second time and were expected to live lives of permanent mourning for their deceased husbands.

The fear of the unattached woman who was free of the control of male authority figures comes out quite clearly in testimony by two witnesses before the Canaries tribunal in the case of Luisa de Coriobada. Both Carlos Domingo y Montañez and Miguel de Abendaxe agreed that since she was an unmarried orphan living with a half sister and her brother was absent most of the time, "no one could stop her from taking any liberties she wished."[14] Suspicion of the unattached, unsupervised woman mounted if she also had a certain amount of economic freedom. In 1636, two unmarried sisters from Mallorca who owned an inn were widely rumored to be having an affair with their confessor, Diego Garoz. In this case, the rumors of sexual laxity led to even more serious accusations of unorthodox or even heretical religious behavior because Garoz was said to have given the sisters communion with unconsecrated hosts.

Adding to the background of male anxiety about women's sexual prowess was the fear that any form of education beyond the most rudimentary might induce them to challenge male control over religion and politics. Most of the leading playwrights of the seventeenth century satirized women who had received what to their minds was an excessive level of education. In *La doncella Teodor*, Lope de Vega warned men not to marry a highly educated woman:

> With her lofty intellect she will belittle you
> and hold you in contempt
> Wishing to seize the power
> That God has entrusted to men.[15]

In another play, *La boba para otros y descreta para sí*, Lope warned of married women whose "overweening pride in their cleverness" allows them to rule their husbands, while all they really need to know is "how to breed and rear their children."[16] But the misogyny of male theologians and playwrights was answered by feminists like the Dominican nun and prolific author Hipolita de Jesús y Rocaberti, who insisted that parents teach their daughters how to read and saw nothing wrong with girls learning Latin.[17]

With women like María de Zayas, Hipolita de Jesús y Rocaberti, and Isabel de Liaño knocking at the bastions of male privilege, it is no wonder that many men felt uneasy at women's desire for learning. Pedro Benimelis thought that Isabel Riera's desire to learn Latin might indicate a lack of "proper humility," but he really got upset when she used her new linguistic attainments to take an "excessive interest" in reading scripture. Her casual references to St. Augustine and other fathers of the church convinced him that she was showing an "inordinate thirst" for knowledge that "stemmed from vanity and conceit."[18]

But the real worry for male clerics was that women might use their knowledge of scripture and ritual to actually challenge male control over religion. Such fears increased alarmingly during the first decades of the sixteenth century when women like Isabel de la Cruz, María Cazalla, and Francisca Hernández took a prominent role in the Illuminist movement. In the advanced circles to which these women belonged, both men and women were openly questioning the basic precepts of the church. In testimony before the Holy Office about the activities of the lay preacher Pedro de Alcaraz, who was one of the leaders of the movement in the Guadalajara region, Francisco de Azeda remarked that he had communicated his ideas to many "unfit persons especially women and youths."[19] Both Alcaraz and Isabel de la Cruz taught that the external devotions mandated by the church were superfluous as far as salvation was concerned. Isabel de la Cruz also specifically denied the existence of hell, dismissing it as merely a fairy story that was "told to frighten children."[20]

The threat from Illuminism continued right to the end of the sixteenth century, punctuated by a series of autos de fe (1570–90) in Extremadura and Andalusia, during which several women were punished. This meant that church authorities were very nervous about any open involvement by women in giving religious instruction to the laity. This unease is probably why Spain never really developed groups of laywomen who became involved in teaching and catechizing the poor, like the Daughters of Charity in France. Even individual efforts were viewed with suspicion. In one curious case, the bishop of the Canaries issued permission to Felipa de Gracia and her sister Isabel de Cristo to use the parish church in Buena Vista to give women religious instruction that included reading out of the Roman catechism. A few months later, however, ordered them to suspend their activities on the grounds that "whenever something virtuous does more harm than good it should be abandoned."[21]

An even more direct threat to male control over the church was constituted by any attempt by women to take over male religious roles like preaching or giving benedictions. One incident occurred at the auto de fe of June 17, 1579, when María Sánchez, one of the leaders of the Extremadura Illuminists, formally blessed the Inquisitors after her sentence was read.[22] Ten years later, five women in el Pardo went even further in usurping male-controlled religious rituals. Having obtained several communion wafers, they organized an impromptu communion ceremony with one taking the role of the priest and raising the host high in the air, declaring, "Look, this is how priests raise it," while the others clamored to administer it to each other along with a sip of water they used as a substitute for wine. The general hilarity was brusquely interrupted, however, when twenty-one-year-old Ana García refused to kneel to receive the host that was being given out by one of the other women. She brought the women to their senses by telling them flatly that what they were doing was sinful. Stricken by remorse and fear of the Holy Office, the woman abandoned their activities, and three of them went to the Toledo tribunal to denounce themselves.[23]

The new, more intense religiosity of so many women during the late sixteenth and seventeenth centuries provoked an even more fundamental concern among male observers: it threatened to radically alter the political economy of the household. All male observers agreed that in the family the wife was clearly subordinate to her husband and obliged to obey him in all matters both large and small. That inferiority and subordination was centered on the domestic role of the wife. The home was not so much her province as her prison, where the husband could confine her and veto her desires to leave, even to pay visits to her friends.[24] Greater involvement with the church and its new or expanded Counter-Reformation devotions (rosary, sacred heart), as well as the spread of cults to saints to whom women were particularly devoted, like Gertrude the Great, meant that many women were spending more time warming the floors of churches than heating stoves to feed their families.[25] But if neglecting their families was bad, then neglecting and disobeying their husbands was even worse. "Among the many women who seek a life of virtue," wrote Fray Antonio Arbiol in a work he dedicated to Inquisitor-General Vidal Marin, "there are those who are no longer so respectful or obedient to their husbands and others, who out of a desire for greater purity, refuse to grant them their due in accordance with the laws of matrimony." Faced with such obduracy, Arbiol felt that the most drastic methods could be employed to restore the God-given order of the family and suggested that confessors deny communion to women guilty of such sinful disobedience.[26]

As if traditional misogyny and more contemporary concerns about women using their new spirituality to subvert the family were not enough, women mystics had yet another obstacle to overcome in their struggle for acceptance: a growing movement within the church to regulate and control all manifestations of popular religion. In the years after the Council of Trent, lay confraternities were brought under the supervision of parish priests, certain processions and popular festivals were suppressed, and priests were given a far more direct role in the administration of certain sacraments.

One aspect of popular religious culture that received considerable attention at the Council of Trent was the issue of canonizations and the saint cult in general. Stung by criticisms levied at the traditional and rather informal procedures that were used in the canonization process and concerned over the survival of numerous local and regional cults that flourished without Vatican approval, the papacy decided to bring the entire process of canonization under centralized control.

Well before the Council of Trent convened in 1542, the church had suspended canonizations, and when they resumed in 1588, with the elevation of Diego of Alcalá, a new Vatican department, the Congregation of Sacred Rites and Ceremonies, established at the beginning of 1587, was already in place to take overall responsibility for them.[27] In 1610, a papal rescript declared flatly that only the Roman pontiff had the authority to canonize.[28] The next logical step was to regulate the numerous accounts of miracles, revelations, and other divine favors received by holy people. Such accounts, as well as specially decorated altars or paintings in which the holy person was depicted with halos or other signs of sanctity, were key elements in developing precisely those informal saint cults that the papacy wished to control. The first of these briefs was published on March 13, 1625, by the Congregation of the Inquisition and confirmed in 1634. This initial brief was followed by another that was issued on June 5, 1631. Essentially, the purpose of these decrees was not to prevent the publication of the lives of holy people but to bring such publications and the claims made in them under the new system of centralized control. The 1625 brief stipulated prior authorization by the bishop in whose territory the life of a holy person was to appear before the book could actually be published. The 1631 document went even further. No longer could the author of a spiritual biography specifically refer to his subject as a saint, although the subject's deeds or lifestyle could be characterized as saintly. Moreover, all miracles, revelations, or prophecies were to be subject to approval by the Holy See and so could not be given any more credence than that they were the product of a sincere and honest account believed by reasonable and pious individuals.[29] At around the same time, it was decreed that canonization proceedings could not commence until fifty years after the death of the holy person. Finally, in 1734 Prospero Lambertini, a canon lawyer who later became Pope Benedict XIV, established a systematic method of evaluating an individual's claims to sanctity that included an elaborate way of defining and grading the favors that the person had enjoyed.[30]

The most immediate impact of the Holy See's more cautious attitude toward canonization was on the biographies of holy persons, which now had to be preceded by an elaborate disclaimer. These statements cited the two briefs and made it clear that the miracles that the author was about to relate were subject to approval by Rome and that until they were approved officially they merely had the authority of belief by credible and pious witnesses. Further-more, bureaucratization of procedures in Rome and the fifty-year rule itself led to an increasing officialization of the process at the periphery, with the need to fully document miracles, cures, and other supernatural events and assemble legalistic dossiers of evidence. The case then had to be brought before the congregation by experienced individuals, preferably with training in canon law. The increased expense and the demand for more complete docu-mentation and recordkeeping meant that for a canonization to be successful the holy person had to have the support of well-organized institutions with the resources to provide support on a long-term basis.

In Spain, the effect of the new situation was to create a somewhat more cautious attitude among theologians and the Holy Office toward visions, rev-elations, or any other outward manifestations of sanctity, especially by women. The arrest and conviction of Sor María de la Visitación, the "nun of Lisbon," could only serve to heighten concern about the pretensions of spiritual women.[31] In his famous *Sermón de las caídas públicas*, written just after Sor María's condemnation, Luis de Granada advised the devout to neither seek out nor pay attention to visions and revelations because "if the devil were to become aware of their desire to receive them, he himself would propagate them by transforming himself into an angel of light."[32]

Fear of demonic influence was also stressed by Antonio González de Rosende, one of Spain's leading seventeenth-century theologians, when he acted as censor of Antonio de Lorea's biography of Sor María de la Santissima Trinidad. After stressing the extreme difficulty of distinguishing between true and false revelations, González de Rosende warned against the devil, whose ability to disguise himself "like the actors in a play" should not be underestimated.[33]

For Francisco de Arcos, the biographer of St. Simón de Rojas, there was no more perplexing problem for theologians than deciding on the veracity of visions and revelations. Of course, there was the ever-present danger of de-monic influence, but even those whose spirits were so strong that the devil could not influence them were susceptible to false revelations. To demonstrate this, Arcos gave the example of St. Vincent Ferrer (1350–1419), who believed certain saintly monks when they told him that the end of the world was com-ing. He incorporated this prediction in his preaching, terrifying his hearers by informing them that the antichrist had already been born and warning them to repent. He also wrote to the Avignonese pope of the great schism, Benedict XIII, to inform him of this revelation, possibly to further his efforts to get him to resign in favor of the Roman Pope Urban IV. Since 253 years had elapsed, this prediction was proven false, but the fact that a divinely inspired spirit like that of St. Vincent Ferrer could be taken in at all should provide a salutary warning for "those of us who live in an age in which such matters are so commonly accepted." To drive his point home even more strongly, Arcos then gave several other examples of false mystics who had pretended revelations and other divine favors and then been exposed as frauds. These false mystics included Nicolasa, a Frenchwoman who had provoked a kind of "bonfire of the vanities" at the French court with her predictions of divine retribution for public immorality, and a young Flemish girl who had been informed that she was equal in merit to the Virgin Mary and then gave birth to a horrible monster. Normally, when theologians raised the difficult issue of demonic influence, they assured the timorous that they could avoid danger by relying on the advice of their spiritual directors. But Arcos was pessimistic, warning that the presence of a confessor, however useful in the spiritual life of the individual, was no guarantee against the demonic origins of any revelations that a person may have received.[34]

For some, the impact of the scandal caused by cases like that of Sor María de la Visitación and the warnings of well-known theologians like González Rosende and Francisco de Arcos were enough to thoroughly disillusion them about the value of a spiritual life dominated by extraordinary manifestations of God's favor. In the introduction to his biography of his mother, María de Pol, the Jesuit Marcos de Torres specifically compared her to the "nun of Lisbon." Unlike the latter, his mother had never sought or received extraordinary favors but had lived a life of exemplary piety and devotion to her children. She had been born at exactly the time that Sor María had begun to "show off her pretended sanctity," as a kind of antidote to her. She was the "other María," the one who was to demonstrate that spiritual perfection could be found in "a plain, ordinary life."[35]

For many others, especially the growing number of women mystics who were receiving what they believed to be divine communication through a variety of visions and revelations, the reservations expressed by theologians were enough to cause an enormous amount of anxiety and self-doubt. The Dominican nun Martina de los Angeles experienced such episodes with great frequency because she felt that she herself was sinful and therefore unworthy of any kind of divine favor. She told her prioress that she was afraid that all of her numerous visions were simply imaginary or that God had permitted the devil to deceive her. In spite of the abbess's attempts to comfort her, she was reassured only when St. Teresa appeared to her in a vision and told her that she was truly infused with divine grace. Then in a second vision, Teresa took her by the hand and led her to a seat in heaven alongside her own, thereby indicating that she occupied a place adjoining that of the saint in the eyes of God.[36] Although greatly comforted by the saint's intervention, Martina remained very apprehensive and needed periodic reassurance from her divine guardians for the rest of her life.

If, in spite of all of these misgivings about demonic manipulation, false or pretended sanctity and the dangers posed by women to the male religious monopoly, powerful male dominated institutions lined up solidly behind the canonization of certain spiritual women, part of the answer can be found in the complex relationship of the Counter-Reformation church to popular religious culture. In general, the major thrust of Catholic reform was to suppress those manifestations of popular religion that appeared to show disrespect for the sacred. As a consequence, dancing was forbidden in church, the laity were forbidden to dress as clergy during carnival, and the clergy were expected to observe a greater measure of decorum in dress and comportment. In Spain, the Inquisition was enlisted in the effort in to enforce these prohibitions so that by the seventeenth century it was spending the majority of its time and effort regulating the behavior of the perfectly orthodox majority rather than chasing the relatively small number of heretics.

Catholic clergy who went too far in suppressing traditional popular rituals ran the risk of seriously alienating their flock, however. In one instance, Scipione Ricci, the bishop of Pistoia and Prato, attempted sweeping reforms including transfer of some religious festivals to Sunday and clamping down on popular devotion to the sacred heart. These initiatives met with enormous opposition and provoked armed resistance, forcing Ricci to resign his post.[37]

Even more serious, perhaps, was the fact that popular culture in general frequently included a considerable amount of anticlericalism and skepticism about some of the basic tenets of the Catholic faith. In Galicia, the inquisitors recorded the case of the man in a tavern who declared to a priest, "Go on! God's in heaven and not in that host which you eat at mass!" These same inquisitors wrote to inform their superiors in Madrid that doubts about the real presence were widespread in the region but ascribed this unfortunate situation to "ignorance rather than malice," while skepticism about Mary's virginity was the result of "sheer thickheadedness rather than out of a wish to offend."[38]

Ignorance is the word repeated over and over again in the accounts of missionaries, inquisitors, and bishops, especially when they visited remote areas. In southwestern France, two late-seventeenth-century reforming bishops, Nicolas Pavillon, bishop of Alet, and François-Étienne Caulet, bishop of Pamiers, deplored the ignorance of the people living in upland regions of their sprawling diocese. In this region, it was not just geography that presented a barrier to the progress of basic Catholicism but language as well. To remedy this situation, Pavillon suggested a catechism in Occitan because his people did not understand French.[39] In Galicia, popular ignorance seems to have been the result of rural poverty rather than geography. At least that was the reasoning behind one inquisitor's request that a new inquisitorial tribunal be established in the region:

> If any part of these realms needs an Inquisition it is Galicia, which . . . has no priests or lettered persons or impressive churches or people who are used to going to mass and hearing sermons. . . . They are superstitious and the benefices so poor that there are not enough clergy.[40]

In the face of a population that was ignorant, blasphemous, anticlerical, and superstitious, the church did what it had always done: employ the doctrine of "accommodation." Overseas, this doctrine meant that Catholic missionaries adapted Catholic rituals to the culture of the Chinese, South Asians, or Japanese that they hoped to convert.[41] In Europe, this policy may be observed in the attitude of the hierarchy to popular saints. In spite of the tighter controls over the canonization process discussed previously, unofficial saints did not disappear, especially where the saint was extremely popular and filled an obvious social need. An excellent example is St. Roche, hermit and pilgrim, who was said to have caught and then recovered from the plague. He became the patron of plague sufferers, and given the extent of epidemic disease in early modern Europe, he remained extremely popular in spite of papal misgivings.[42] Venice, which prided itself on its independence from the papacy, made his cult official in 1576, and Tintoretto adorned one of its churches with a magnificent cycle of paintings depicting the life of the saint. Faced with the growing popularity of the cult, the papacy decided to align itself with it officially by approving his office for hermitages and churches dedicated to him.

But to deal effectively with the challenge of strengthening itself to confront the Protestant threat as well as the ignorance of the Catholic laity, the church needed to lead and form popular culture and not merely follow it, as in the case of St. Roche. Consequently, the church actively encouraged certain saint cults and helped to spread them far beyond the regions where they had originated. Some of these cults can clearly be ascribed to the need to focus attention on and engender public support for aspects of the Counter-Reformation program. A cult to the bishop of Milan, Carlo Borromeo, had begun in the city long before his actual canonization in 1610 but was fostered by the church because he exemplified the ideal of the Counter-Reformation bishop.[43] The rapid expansion of the cult of St. John Nepomuk, a Bohemian priest who was martyred because he refused to divulge the secrets of confession, and the stress placed on the veneration of St. Mary Magdalen were designed to promote the new and enhanced role of auricular confession and the priest as confessor in the post-Tridentine church.[44]

In back of all of this was the critical need to assert Catholic truth in the face of Protestant heresy. As a religion based in part on the use of holy magic and a firm belief in supernatural forces, Roman Catholicism had been thrown on the defensive by Erasmus, who condemned prayer in Latin as mere incantation, saint cults as pagan survivals, and indulgences as "paltry pardons." Lutheranism and Calvinism went even further in attacking church magic by sharply reducing the number of sacraments, denying transubstantiation, and eliminating the cult of the saints, all the while appropriating revelations and prophecy as a way of justifying their beliefs.[45]

Even in the Iberian peninsula, where the direct threat of Protestant subversion was relatively slight after the 1560s, there was a perception of the constant danger of implacable Jewish hostility toward the Catholic church. The existence of what was perceived by many as a large fifth column of converted Jews and New Christians in Iberia meant that the enemy was already inside the gates. Moreover, in the eyes of anti-Semites like the Portuguese Bizente Dacosta Mattos, Spain and Portugal could take little comfort in the lack of a powerful Protestant movement in their countries. The threat to the faith continued because Jews and Protestants were equal in their rejection of miracles, the cult of images, and other fundamental Catholic beliefs. To make matters worse, Dacosta Mattos informed his readers that all leading Protestants, including the "vile and detestable Luther," were either of Jewish origin or had Judaized before they became Protestants.[46]

Everywhere the Catholic leadership looked, therefore, the faith seemed to be threatened. As a result, it was impossible to compromise; to admit that certain traditional aspects of Catholicism were wrong or mistaken would be to give the enemy greater credibility. This conservative attitude was behind the decision at the Council of Trent to uphold the authority of the Vulgate, even though it was widely known to contain numerous errors. In the same way, the fact that the church had approved female saints, such as St. Catherine of Siena, in the relatively recent past made it impossible for Catholic theologians to reject the idea that certain extraordinary women could be genuine recipients of divine favors in the present in spite of their misgivings about women in general.

It was exactly this argument that Fray Luis de Granada used to justify his confidence in the miraculous events surrounding the life of the fraudulent Sor María de la Visitación. After detailing the miracles in the lives of such male saints as St. Dominic, St. Francis, and St. Vincent Ferrer, Fray Luis selected three outstanding women saints—St. Cecilia, St. Catherine of Alexandria, and St. Catherine of Siena—to demonstrate that women, too, could receive divine favors. Because God had not changed since biblical times and was as "rich and fruitful in loving kindness" as he had been when he bestowed divine favors on the holy women of the past, he could, and did, confer similar favors on Sor María and other women in the present. If anything, God's miracles were more likely than they had been when the church began since he now had to uphold his church, "which was to endure to the end of time," in the face of the "heresies that were defaming the faith." Miracles like those experienced by Sor María were themselves a magnificent reminder of God's power because they were bestowed upon a weak and insignificant woman who was unlikely to have received them through her own spiritual merits. At the same time, the kinds of miracles that she received (stigmata, wounds from the crown of thorns) were a salutary reminder of what Christ had to endure to save sinful mankind.[47]

It is perhaps not so surprising that we find Fray Luis de Granada writing in favor of holy women since he, after all, was the author of three other spiritual biographies apart from the *Historia de Sor María de la Visitación*.[48] But what really attests to the force of tradition operating in favor of spiritual women is the attitude of theologians who were normally antifeminine. Antonio González Rosende, who as censor of Miguel Batista de Lanuza's biography of Francisca del Santissimo Sacramento described women as weak-minded and irrational, not only approved publication of the book but also admitted that notwithstanding his pessimism there had been women whose willingness to suffer for the faith was equal to that of men. He affirmed, "No one could place limits on

God's ability to confide his secrets to women . . . through the favor of revelations."[49] In addition to González Rosende, the biography was approved by a number of other leading theologians, including Juan Eusebio Nieremberg. Of the total of thirteen censors who approved publication, five were professors of theology, five were *calificadores* of the Suprema, and one was the bishop of Segovia.

It is not too difficult to imagine that the church's "accommodation" to traditional religious culture and the hierarchy's reluctance to undermine popular support for the church should have played into the hands of certain women when their excesses provoked the anger or suspicion of the authorities. When Mariana de Jesús, a Franciscan *beata*, went to stay with the counts of la Puebla at their residence in Cuenca in 1610, she began having a series of very public trances in the cathedral and in several of the city's convents. In no time, she had attracted a large popular following, but the fact that she made no effort to conceal such divine gifts, as she should have done if she were truly humble, stirred the suspicion of a local friar who also served as a theological censor to Cuenca's inquisitorial tribunal. Obtaining permission from the bishop to conduct an inquiry, he proceeded to summon her to his cell, where he interrogated her at length and called her an "imposter and fraud, liar and hypocrite," and then tried to get her thrown out of the city. In light of her enormous popularity, however, the bishop intervened, sending his own provisor to conduct an investigation. This time the results were entirely different. After interviewing her, the provisor came away well satisfied and even asked her to commend his soul to God.[50] Regardless of how this account may have been embellished by the author, who was also her confessor, what emerges quite clearly is that her popularity in the city made it impossible for the bishop to follow the urging of the friar, even though his position with the Holy Office made him highly credible, whereas Mariana was in a position to ignore the friar's opposition.

An even more flagrant example of the failure of episcopal authority to curb the excesses of a woman mystic involved Joseph Argaiz, the powerful archbishop of Granada, and Beatriz María de Jesús, who, at that point in her life, was wearing the habit of a member of the Franciscan third order. With the support of her father, D. Lorenzo Enciso, who had written in his journal on the day that she was born, "Oh God, make her into a saint," Beatriz had been going about the city having public trances in the cathedral, parish churches, and public squares. While in the trancelike state, Beatriz was able to perform such feats as hold her body rigid in the shape of a cross, eat small amounts of food that she had previously agreed to consume, and give vent to exclamations of Christian piety that appeared to have been divinely inspired.

At one point, she even announced that she would experience the pain of being immersed in the lakes of fire that were used to torture souls in purgatory. After declaring that this particular trance would last just one hour, she thrashed about violently, cried out that the living should be told of the horrible torments being suffered by the souls in purgatory so that they would be more liberal in helping them with masses, and then asked if the hour was almost completed. Upon being informed that the sands of the hourglass that had been set had almost run out, she "awoke" from the trance as if nothing had happened, but those in attendance could see that her body was covered with a variety of brown and black marks indicating that she had indeed been present in the lake of fire.

This notoriety was the very opposite of the kind of decorum that Catholic reformers wished for in the post-Tridentine church, so Argaiz ordered his provisor, Dr. Gerónimo de Prado, a canon of the cathedral and noted theologian, to carry out an investigation. After examining her at her home on April 17, 1664, Prado ordered her father not to permit anyone outside the immediate family to be present at her trances on pain of excommunication. This warning fell on deaf ears, so the provisor was forced to make a number of further visits to her home, during which he treated her with great harshness and warned her against seeking the approval of the mob, which can "make or unmake whomsoever it wishes." For her part, Beatriz remained remarkably unfazed in the face of the threats and anger of the episcopal official, answering him with great calm and equanimity while her public trances, some lasting as long as five hours, continued as before.[51]

To the student of social history, what is truly impressive about the foregoing cases is not so much the relatively supine attitude of the church toward "excessive" public manifestations of spiritual power by women but rather the self-confidence of the women themselves. One of the elements that contributed most significantly to building that self confidence was the enormous amount of attention and approval that St. Teresa had received from influential male theologians. Between 1590 and 1677 there were no fewer than eleven biographies of Teresa published in Spain, the largest number for any individual saint between 1480 and 1700.[52] Teresa was also the subject of numerous public ceremonies all over Spain at the time of her beatification in 1614 and her canonization in 1622. At some of these ceremonies there were poetry competitions at which both men and women vied in writing poems in praise of her. The pride that educated, upper-class women took in Teresa's accomplishments and their feeling that other women could emulate her burst forth in a poem written for a competition held in Barcelona by Sor Teresa del Calvario, a Franciscan nun from Zaragoza. The poet celebrates Teresa's "rare wisdom" and the way in which she had overcome the limitations placed on her sex and "surpassed her condition." Then addressing herself to her female readers, the poet tells them that they should not be surprised:

> If you find inside yourself the valour
> A similar enterprise to endeavor.[53]

That women with high spiritual aspirations were inspired by Teresa's example is indicated by the fact that 35.5 percent of the women in my sample saw her in visions, making her the most frequently seen of all the women saints. One such vision in which a clear identification between Teresa and the aspiring spiritual woman was made manifest was experienced by the Dominican nun Martina de los Angeles one year before her death. In this vision, Martina saw a celestial procession with herself marching at Teresa's side. Feeling unworthy of this signal honor, she turned to Teresa and said, "I am vile, despicable, I am not even a Carmelite; I don't belong here." But after a long colloquy, Teresa convinced her that she had attained the spiritual perfection to take her place alongside her. Elsewhere in the vision, the equivalence between the two women was further revealed by the sight of Teresa lit up with a brilliant radiance and Martina glowing from within with the light of precious jewels, indicating her inner spiritual qualities, further reinforced by the presence within her of white lilies, the symbol of purity.[54]

Influential male clergy also had a great deal of respect for Teresa and her writings, which provided a model of mystic contemplation. In his biography of the Franciscan missionary Ignacio García (1641–1719), Antonio Arbiol tells us that when García headed a missionary college in Calamocha (Aragon) he regularly used St. Teresa's works, which he knew by heart, to instruct the novices.[55]

But what really indicated how far St. Teresa had come in winning the respect of a male-dominated society was the widespread support that greeted the proposal to make her the copatron of Spain (along with St. James the Great). The campaign began auspiciously when the Cortes of Castile voted in favor of a copatronage resolution in 1617. It enjoyed the strong support of the Carmelites and even received divine approval in the shape of a vision experienced by Francisca del Santissimo Sacramento, in which the Virgin Mary appeared to her along with Teresa and told her that "my son has decided that in heaven Teresa should be the firm support of Christianity and especially of Spain."[56]

In 1627 King Philip IV officially proclaimed Teresa as patroness of Spain. While the opposition of conservatives like Quevedo and assiduous lobbying by Fernando Andrade de Sotomayor, archbishop of Santiago, eventually convinced Pope Urban VIII to decree that Saint James should continue to be the sole patron of Spain, Teresa's popularity remained undiminished, and the controversy continued throughout the mid-seventeenth century.[57] According to Francisco Morovelli de Puebla, who published a book in 1648 defending the idea of copatronage and refuting Quevedo's objections, twenty-five major churches, including the cathedral chapter of Córdoba, had already gone on record as supporting copatronage. In addition to churches and cathedral chapters, copatronage also enjoyed the support of the Spain's three most important universities: Salamanca, Valladolid, and Alcalá.[58] Responding to the objections of opponents like Juan Pablo Martyr Rizo, who argued that St. James would be offended by having to share his role as patron, and that God himself had selected Santiago as Spain's only patron saint, Morovelli de Puebla replied that there were other places (Milan, Sicily) that had two patron saints and that Teresa was more popular than St. James who had been forgotten in large parts of Spain.[59] Moreover, Morovelli de Puebla argued that a patron saint did not have to be a warrior, leading Spain's soldiers in battle like St. James, but rather the patron must be able to effectively intercede with God to supply Spain's needs.[60]

Interestingly enough—and this is another indication that the debate about the role of women mystics was shifting away from a preoccupation with the inherent weakness of the female sex to more general issues like the validity and social utility of revelations—even a misogynist like Quevedo never questions Teresa's spiritual attainments and writes about her with great respect.[61] Juan Pablo Martyr Rizo also paid tribute to Teresa's status, even among those who opposed copatronage, by noting that "not one of the many who have written in defense of Santiago have ever spoken of the Saint with anything less than the esteem and reverence that is due to such a glorious Virgin."[62] But proponents of copatronage like Morovelli de Puebla went much further. For them, Teresa's sex was a positive benefit, pointing to the need for cooperation and equality between men and women, since "it took two sexes to effect the destruction of Paradise and it will take both sexes to repair and maintain the world."[63]

The growing self-confidence of women in the value of their spiritual lives and experiences is also evident from the number of devotional works by women that were being produced and published in the late sixteenth and throughout the seventeenth century. Once again, St. Teresa blazed the path for her sisters with the first edition of the *Maxims* and *Way of Perfection* appearing in Evora in 1583. The first Spanish edition of *Way of Perfection* was published at Salamanca in 1585, and that was followed three years later by the appearance of her complete works (with the principal exception of the *Foundations*) in a special edition prepared by Fray Luis de León. Further editions followed in 1592, 1597, 1604, 1615, 1613, 1623, 1635, and 1636.[64] The order eventually published a new and corrected edition in 1661, and that, too, received numerous reprintings. Without following in detail the long publication history of the saint's works, it is fairly obvious that the numerous editions of the spiritual works of a woman author must have encouraged other women to want to record and even publish accounts of their own spiritual lives.

One of the most interesting and suggestive of these devotional works was written by the Franciscan *beata* Mariana de Jesús in 1617. In this work, Mariana tells us that the secrets of Christ's passion were revealed to her in a series of visions that she had while praying or just after communion. At first she wanted to keep these visions to herself, but in one vision she was informed that she had been granted them specifically so that she could exercise a kind of spiritual apostolate by communicating what she had learned to others. As a result, with the encouragement of her confessor, Mariana sat herself down to write.

The resulting work consists of a sometimes harrowing description of the passion narrated by Christ, who invites Mariana and her readers to meditate upon it. So far Mariana's book is like a hundred other devotional works that evoke the passion to underscore the way Christ suffered to save sinful mankind. What really sets Mariana's book apart, however, is the way that Christ is made to speak constantly about the exemplary devotion shown by the women of Jerusalem at a time when his male disciples had deserted him. While the men "walked about sadly averting their eyes," the "women followed behind me and with tears and lamentations pitied me and shared my pain and torment." When his face became streaked with sweat and blood, it was the women who wiped it with a handkerchief and he rewarded them by impressing the image of his face upon it. These same devoted women, now including Mary Magdalen, the Virgin Mary, and "many other Marys sisters of my mother," followed him to the place of execution and witnessed the crucifixion.[65]

While the growing fame of St. Teresa and the repeated reprinting of her writings encouraged other women to believe that their own spiritual lives were valuable enough to communicate to others, another factor that created a favorable climate for holy women was the emergence and popularization of the concept of the *mujer varonil*, in the late sixteenth and seventeenth centuries. The *mujer varonil* was a woman whose behavior and personality differed significantly from the societal norm and who displayed a "manly" degree of moral and mental fortitude.[66]

In the theater, the term was used in reference to real political figures like the medieval Queen Urraca, whose valiant defense of Zamora against her brother King Sancho was the subject of a play by the sixteenth-century playwright Juan de la Cueva, or the Assyrian queen Semiramis, who was alleged to have founded Babylon and was famed for her beauty and sexual excesses. Playwrights also created entirely imaginary characters who flouted social conventions, such as Rosarda in Lope de Vega's *El alcalde mayor,* who had a long and successful career as chief magistrate of Salamanca and Toledo, or Ana in Moreto's *No puede ser*, whose literary attainments and intellectual leadership sharply contradicted the widely held view that women would not benefit from a liberal education.[67]

The popularity of the *mujer varonil* also gave rise to numerous works in praise of women. These works tended to follow a pattern, with the author choosing exemplary women to show how some were able to go beyond the limitations placed on their sex. Juan de Espinosa, a soldier who had served with distinction under both Charles V and Philip II, wrote one of the most famous of these books in this genre. His *Dialogo en laude de las mujeres* was published in Milan in 1580 and dedicated to Philip II's sister María of Austria. The author declares that his purpose in writing was to "enlighten those men who, in blind ignorance become furious with their own wives when they are delivered of girls."[68]

The book takes the form of a dialogue between Philodoxo and his friend Philalithes. Philodoxo is angry because his wife has just given birth to a girl. In his pique, he accuses women of causing wars, deceiving their husbands, and being inferior to men in both strength and wit. Philalithes refutes his friend by using exemplary women from ancient history to make his points. The war between the Greeks and Trojans was not caused by Helen but by Paris kidnapping her. The story of Ulysses's wife, Penelope, shows that women could resist the blandishments of men and remain faithful to their husbands over long periods. The lives of several contemporary queens (Isabella, wife of Charles V) and noblewomen (Ana de Córdoba, marquise of Ayamonte) demonstrate women's capacity for "prudence, piety and competence in government."[69]

In the introduction to his *Varia historia de santas y illustres mujeres*, Juan Pérez de Moya writes that women are superior to men in at least five respects of which the most important were greater devotion to the service of God; less involvement in serious crimes like homicide, blasphemy, and heresy; and a greater willingness to help other people in time of need. Women also "could not boast of anything more important than being the mother of God," which alone should be sufficient to "condemn those who speak ill of them to perpetual silence."[70]

In the rest of the book, Pérez de Moya draws upon an extensive knowledge of ancient and modern history, mythology, and the Old and New Testaments, both to refute traditional charges laid against women and to show that some women have been able to attain great heights of achievement. Women like María Coronel, who defended herself against the advances of King Peter the Cruel by burning her entire body with oil in order to make herself unattractive, have demonstrated extraordinary fidelity to their husbands. Women who excelled in war and government included Joan of Arc, Catherine of Aragon, and especially Isabella the Catholic, who greatly assisted King Ferdinand and gave such good advice that he continued to consult her, disregarding "the advice of those who told him to rule alone."[71]

Pérez de Moya was also particularly interested in refuting the traditional charge that "women are incapable of understanding any body of knowledge" by giving examples of women who had excelled in history, science, medicine, astrology, linguistics, philosophy, and rhetoric. Certain extraordinary women in the ancient world like St. Marcella, as well as contemporary women like Teresa of Jesus, also attained a profound knowledge of scripture, so much so that the latter was consulted frequently by some of Spain's leading male theologians.[72]

Interestingly enough, in spite of the fears expressed by Lope de Vega and others about the dangers of educated women expropriating male prerogatives, Pérez de Moya makes no negative comments after informing his readers that Spartan women were naturally "strong and manly" and "usurped power and dominion over their husbands." As *mujeres varoniles* they were presumably justified in ruling their husbands at home while "freely expressing their opinions about the most important affairs of state."[73]

For theologians, the concept of the *mujer varonil* was used to describe the numerous women who were devoting themselves to the church and seeking a more spiritual life, whether individually through penance, prayer and works of charity or collectively by joining a convent or one of the numerous groups of laywomen who would gather to pursue a life of prayer, meditation, and penance. It was this latter group of *beatas* to whom the Jesuit theologian Alonso de Andrade devoted an extraordinary three-volume work published in 1642–46. Andrade was a leading Jesuit theologian, *calificador* of the Suprema, and author of a biography of Estefania Manrique de Castilla, an aristocratic lady who had herself become a *beata*.

Although expressing certain reservations about the growing number of *beatas* and cautioning them to place themselves firmly under the control of male spiritual advisers, Andrade was generally positive toward them. They were truly worthy of the name of "religious" because although not cloistered they lived in disciplined communities just like those of the early church before the advent of formal monastic life. They offer their entire lives in the service of God and "spend every waking hour studying how they may gratify and serve their celestial spouse."[74] Throughout the book, Andrade is at pains to show how *beatas* exceed male religious in the degree of their devotion, mortification, abstinence, and service to God. These religious *mujeres varoniles* included such figures as Catalina de Herrera of Toledo, who went about catechizing children and the poor in the streets and plazas of the city, and Luisa de Carvajal y Mendoza, who attempted to convert the English to Catholicism while living in the home of the Spanish ambassador in London. The aristocratic Catalina de Mendoza, daughter of the fourth marquis of Mondéjar, also became a *beata* and "surpassed the most reclusive hermits" in her life of austerity, abstinence, and prayer.[75]

But if for most writers, even those favorably disposed toward women, the concept of the *mujer varonil* pertained only to certain exemplary women, some ecclesiastical authors appeared to be applying the concept to women as a whole, at least insofar as their devotion to the church was concerned. This was certainly the case with Bernardino de Villegas, Jesuit theologian, *calificador* of the Suprema, and author of *La esposa de Cristo instruida*. According to Villegas, men and women were equal before God and in the church, and women may even be superior in their spiritual lives. Referring to the "innumerable women who are genuinely seeking to make progress on the road to perfection," he questioned how many men were similarly outstanding in their "practice of mental prayer, observance of the sacraments, mortification or penance." The difference between the devotion shown by men and women had become so pronounced that the "God who finds himself abandoned will abandon the men who desert and forget him, and turn to the women who love him and serve him with more fervor, spirit and devotion."[76]

Not only were women demonstrating more intense devotion to God and the church but also their merit was so much the greater because they had to overcome the weakness of their sex. This at least is the approach taken by Batista de Lanuza to explain his eagerness to write a biography of Gerónima de San Esteban. Informing his readers that although it has always been important to record the lives of the saints to provide models of virtue for sinners, the lives of female saints are more edifying because "the more broken the vessel, the more remarkable the victory."[77]

Batista de Lanuza's views were echoed by the Franciscan theologian Pascal Ximénez, one of the censors assigned by the order to review Fray Tomás de Montalvo's biography of Beatriz María de Jesús. Great virtue was admirable in anyone, wrote Ximénez, but all the more so in women because of the inherent "fragility of their sex." Women were like delicate crystal that, "tempered by obedience, discipline and mortification, turns into a mirror and example for the strongest men."[78]

As far as the receipt of communication from God was concerned, more-over, many theologians had come to reject or at least question the traditional idea that women were less trustworthy recipients. They argued that the very lack of formal education, ability to read Latin, and access to scripture and sophisticated theological works made it highly likely that such communica-tion came directly from God. This was exactly the position taken by María Antonia Hortola's confessor Luis Poyo, when he praised her profound under-standing of Latin prayers in spite of her being able to read and write only in Spanish. Mentioning specifically the example of Inés de Benigánim, who was able to recite the divine office in the choir in spite of being completely illiter-ate, he commented that "we cannot presume to tie God's hands so that he will be unable to work his marvels in the souls of whomsoever he wishes, when-ever he wishes to do so."[79]

It was this belief that led many well-trained male priests to defer to the superior knowledge of certain women with great spiritual reputations. In Fray Francisco de Acosta's biography of María de Jesús, the abbess of Toledo's Convent of St. Joseph and St. Mary, he quoted another theologian to the effect that whenever we wished to really understand such mysteries as the Trinity, even from a theological standpoint, we should take lessons from her.[80] Of course, lack of theological training and an inability to read Latin or under-stand scripture were liabilities imposed by the male dominated society. This shortcoming was made into a positive spiritual virtue by male writers such as Luis de Mesa, whose biography of Mariana de Jesús was filled with visions she explained by using such a sophisticated terminology "that not even the greatest theologians could have devised, much less the mind of a woman who had never studied, unless it came directly from heaven."

Validating the visions of his subject by alleging her ignorance as proof of a vision's divine origin was designed to mollify those who had a visceral distrust of women. But it did a serious disservice to the middle- and upper-class women who were the subjects of so many biographies. Women like Mariana de Jesús, who was the daughter of a hidalgo, were literate in Span-ish and had considerable exposure to church services, sermons, images, de-votional works, and, above all, devout fathers and mothers who saw to it that they were given rigorous training in Roman Catholicism while they were growing up.

By the end of the seventeenth century, the feminization of the church in terms of greater church attendance by women, more frequent recourse to the sacraments of confession and communion, and greater involvement in devo-tions, processions, and holy days had done much to still the voices of their critics.[81] There were still those who harbored the old suspicions, and even supporters such as Juan de Espinosa had always shown that they remained tied to traditional attitudes by stressing the importance of chastity and warn-ing husbands to restrict their wives' freedom to leave the house because "the woman who is restless can easily bring about her own damnation."[82] But the general verdict was more favorable. Although *arbitristas* may have fulmi-nated against the proliferating number of religious, the pride many cities took in their communities of pious nuns can be glimpsed in Fray Tomás de Montalvo's dedication of his biography of Sor Beatriz María de Jesús to her native city of Granada; he averred it was not the city that created sanctity but the saintly persons living within it that created an atmosphere of holiness. In Granada, women were chiefly responsible for this, especially nuns, who provided the most precious "jewels in the diadem" of a city that had benefited from such "divine generosity in blessing it with so many strong and remarkable women."[83]

The pride that many women felt in their own spiritual achievements and the way that they had gained the confidence of leading members of a male-dominated church are reflected in a number of works written by women to celebrate the exemplary piety and austerity of nuns in particular convents. A typical example of this genre was a collective biography of the twenty-five founding nuns of Salamanca's Discalced Franciscan Convent of La Purissima Concepción, written by Sor Manuela de la Santissima Trinidad and published in 1696. These nuns included exemplary individuals such as Sor Catalina de las Llagas, the daughter of Pedro Solis de Frías, a knight of the prestigious military order of Santiago. Sor Catalina's specialty was the virtue of humility. As the daughter of a hidalgo, she evidently felt that she had to go to extraordinary lengths to humble her pride and therefore delighted in washing out the dirtiest pots and especially in cleaning chamber pots and latrines. On one occasion, when the duchess of Béjar came to visit her, she refused to stop cleaning a particularly dirty chamber pot and said that the vessel she was cleaning was more precious than "all the amber in the world" and that she "had more respect for what she was doing than for all the duchesses that ever existed."[84]

Just a few years earlier, in 1690, another remarkable work celebrated not just the nuns of one convent but all of the foundations made by Augustinian nuns of strict observance between 1589 and 1688. What is really noteworthy about this work is not its authorship, since it was written by Alonso de Villerino, an Augustinian friar, but rather the fact that the work was entirely funded by women, especially the prioresses of the majority of the thirty-three convents of the order who wished to offer their assistance when it became time to "publish to the world the virtues with which almighty God adorned his heroic consorts."[85]

Arguably, the real litmus test for the acceptability of holy women to the male-dominated institutional structure was the way in which their biographies or autobiographies were dealt with by the censorship apparatus. Because these were religious works and issues of orthodoxy would inevitably arise, the procedure was significantly more complicated than the one followed for a book dealing exclusively with secular matters. An ordinary book would simply be approved by the Council of Castile, which had enjoyed the right to control publication and issue licenses to print from 1554.[86]

Normally, each biography or autobiography of a spiritual woman had to be approved on three levels before publication: religious order, episcopal, and ministerial. After publication, the book was naturally subject to the jurisdiction of the Holy Office, which had been exercising postpublication censorship functions from the 1520s and published the indices of prohibited books.

Since the process and the people who carried it out have been largely ignored by historians, it might be instructive to briefly examine several examples. Fray Lope Paez published his biography of Francisca Inés de la Concepción in Toledo in 1653. Because his subject was a Franciscan nun, the manuscript was given initially to two Franciscan theologians by order of Fray Gaspar de la Fuente, provincial of the Franciscan province of Castile. Approval by the two Franciscans on May 13, 1644, led to issuance of a license to the author on September 12. The license specified that the author must first present the book in the Council of Castile and obtain permission from that body before it could be valid. The manuscript was then handed over to a Dominican, Tomás de Arellano, by order of the lieutenant vicar-general of the city of Madrid, who was acting for the archbishop of Toledo. The archbishop had had jurisdiction ever since the papal decree of March 16, 1635, which mandated that biographies of all those who died in the odor of sanctity must be submitted to the ordinary. Fray Tomás finished his review on September 15, and a license was issued by lieutenant vicar Aldama on the same day. Finally the Council of Castile issued its license after a third censor, the Mercedarian Juan Díaz Morquecho, finished his review on October 20, 1644.[87]

Those books published in the crown of Aragon would typically be submitted to high Aragonese authorities for evaluation, so that even in matters of censorship Castile and Aragon's unity was more apparent than real. In the case of Miguel Batista de Lanuza's biography of Gerónima de San Esteban, for example, D. Juan Chrisostomo de Exea, a member of the Council of Aragon, assigned the task of censorship to a secular, Diego Antonio Frances de Urrutigati, archpriest of Daroca and bishop-elect of Barbastro.[88] The average number of censors reviewing a book was five, although some could have considerably more, with Isabel de Jesús' *Tesoro del carmelo,* which was published in 1685, reaching a total of seventeen.[89]

As far as the Inquisition was concerned, while it did, for the most part, confine its formal censorship role to postpublication surveillance, it continued to exercise considerable informal prepublication control over these works. In my analysis of 98 individuals who carried out censorship responsibilities over the 30 books in my database, 26 were *calificadores* and 1 was an inquisitor, making 27.5 percent of the censors active officials of the Holy Office.

Furthermore, the authors themselves occasionally wrote the Inquisition requesting that it assign a censor to their book because they wanted more assurance as to its orthodoxy and, presumably, were trying to avoid potential problems after the book appeared. One of these authors was the prolific Miguel Batista de Lanuza, who as *protonotario* and member of the Council of Aragon was important enough to address himself directly to Inquisitor-General Diego de Arce y Reynoso about his biography of Francisca del Santissima Sacramento. In his petition, Batista de Lanuza gave as his principal reason for seeking approval from the Holy Office a certain amount of lingering discomfort with the number of "prodigious and extraordinary marvels" that were associated with her. Instead of assigning the book to a *calificador,* as he would have done for someone less prominent, Arce y Reynoso evaluated the book himself. On July 22, 1659, he lay Batista de Lanuza's fears to rest by warmly approving the biography and expressing the hope that it would serve to inspire others to greater devotion.[90] At the same time, Batista de Lanuza had also approached the renowned Jesuit theologian Juan Eusebio Nieremberg, asking him to evaluate the manuscript. Probably hoping for a favorable review because of Nieremberg's well-known views on supernatural phenomena, Batista de Lanuza was not disappointed. Nieremberg warmly endorsed the book, especially the second volume, which was full of Francisca's voyages to purgatory and the awful torments suffered by the souls, as this provided a warning to those who tended to dismiss the pains of purgatory as insignificant and consequently ignored their duty to the souls of the departed.[91] Illustrating a tendency among a few especially influential authors to choose at least some of the censors of their manuscripts, Batista de Lanuza was able to designate a total of eight out of the thirteen censors. However, picking the theologians who would review one's own manuscript was an option open to few authors, who in the main were relatively humble friars without significant political influence.

Sometimes it was not the author but the Council of Castile that requested censorship from the Inquisition in especially difficult or ambiguous cases. Antonio Daça's 1610 biography of Juana de la Cruz was evidently one of these, and the council decided to submit it to the Suprema after the other approvals had been received. When the manuscript arrived at the Suprema, it was assigned to a *calificador,* who approved its orthodoxy. Inquisitor-General Bernardo de Sandoval y Rojas then issued a license to print in his capacity as archbishop of Toledo to avoid any appearance of interfering in the jurisdiction of the Council of Castile, even though it was obvious that the council had decided not to approve publication without approval from the Holy Office.[92]

The key role played by the Holy Office and its officials in preapproving biographies explains why so few had postpublication difficulties or appeared on the index. As people who tried to clear their names after successfully defending themselves in an Inquisition proceeding discovered, the Inquisition was extremely unwilling to admit its mistakes. Instead of being dismissed for lack of evidence, the case would merely be suspended, leaving a cloud of suspicion over the individual, even one who was patently innocent. In the same way, the Inquisition was hardly likely to proceed against a work that had already received the stamp of approval from its own theologians. But the exception proves the rule. In the case of Antonio Daça, although the 1610 edition was published without emendation, the 1611 edition was prohibited, and the 1614 edition circulated in an expurgated version. The trouble was relatively minor, having to do with the use of the word *indulgences* to characterize the benefits to be derived from the magical beads that Juana de la Cruz distributed so liberally in her lifetime. In the expurgated version, the word was changed to *graces* to protect the papal monopoly over granting indulgences.[93] Needless to say, this minor change left room for plenty of miracles and supernatural events of all kinds in the book, while the change in terminology made little difference to those who venerated the beads.

Any discussion of the censorship applied to the biographies and autobiographies of mystics must begin with the fact that the censors themselves were as willing and eager as the rest of Spain's intellectual and social elite to accept the supernatural and the miraculous as part of everyday life. Indeed, as theologians and militant Catholics, they welcomed the miraculous as a way of confounding and refuting the international Protestant movement, especially if it expressed itself in a way consistent with Catholic dogma or confirmed God's continued support for the church.

When Fray Ignacio de Ibero was made responsible for reviewing the first edition of Antonio Daça's biography of Juana de la Cruz by Inquisitor-General Bernardo de Sandoval y Rojas, he was ordered to pay close attention to any miracles or revelations the book contained. But instead of producing anything critical, Ibero fully accepted the veracity of the principal source for the biography, which was an account written by a nun who had lived in the convent at the same time as Juana. He not only accepted the source as the product of a reliable eyewitness but also assumed that it was divinely inspired because of the tradition in the convent that the sister who wrote it was granted the ability to read and write by God specifically for that purpose. Having read the principal source for the life and learned of the miraculous way it came to be written, Ibero felt that he had fully discharged his responsibilities and therefore confirmed that "whatever is written in this account of the life, sanctity or miracles of this servant of God is true and certain," and it followed that all of her trances, visions, revelations and prophecies were of divine inspiration and that God really spoke through her. Ibero's credulity and lack of objectivity are all the more shocking because he formed part of the junta of theologians assigned to draw up the Index of 1612.[94]

A very similar approach—acceptance of sources, however biased or subjective, and automatic assumption of the divine origins of the miraculous events recounted in the biography—was taken by two of the censors of the life of Beatriz María de Jesús written by Tomás de Montalvo. The Franciscan Juan de Ascargorta, who carried out censorship on behalf of the archbishop of Granada fully accepted Beatriz's own writings as a valid account. He seemed at first to be a little troubled by the sheer number of trances, visions, and other miraculous events recounted in the biography, but he told his readers that they could place their faith in them since they conformed to the criteria for validity that he himself had outlined in a book entitled *Lecciones mysticas*.[95]

Fray Francisco de Silva, who was assigned to review the book for the Council of Castile, was perhaps even more credulous than his colleague. He confirmed that this "prodigious woman lived exempt from the laws of the flesh" and that the "hand of God was always at work within her." This was proven decisively by the stigmata that appeared and disappeared each year at the same time.[96] It seems that 151 years after the conviction of Sor María de la Visitación, the lessons of her false stigmata had been forgotten.

The eagerness displayed by so many censors to approve the biographies of holy women sometimes spilled over into overt attempts to assert the orthodoxy of the women's beliefs even when they differed from church teachings. Ignacio de Ibero was so biased in favor of approval that he went to considerable lengths to explain away Juana de la Cruz's assertions that not all the souls in purgatory expiate their sins there and that when St. Michael judged souls he wore imperial insignia and a king's crown. Ibero also saw nothing wrong with the idea that the rosary beads that Juana gave out carried indulgences. He justified his position by giving several recent examples of how God was intervening with miracles to demonstrate the importance of saying the rosary in the face of the doubt and incredulity of the Protestants.

In other cases, censors would explain away serious lapses from the saintly norm in order to justify approving publication of a biography. Francisco de Silva excused Beatriz María de Jesús of frequent and serious lapses in obedience to her superiors on the grounds that she was not free to obey them since her will had been taken over by God.

With censors abandoning all objectivity in their eagerness to approve biographies, the censorship process, at least as far as the biographies of women mystics were concerned, appears less a barrier than a filter designed to remove only the worst excesses. Furthermore, with certain influential authors, Miguel Batista de Lanuza among them, able to pick and choose the censors who would review their manuscripts, the process appears even less rigorous. Given the nature of the process, therefore, it is not surprising that dozens of biographies of women mystics were published and that very few ever figured on the index even after the mystic Miguel de Molinos was condemned in the late seventeenth century. It appears that so long as the biographies and autobiographies of women mystics supported the church and its dogmas and encouraged devotion, they could be published and circulate freely with little to fear from either ecclesiastical authorities or the Inquisition.

But the most important single factor in determining the reputation of a woman mystic was her relationship to her confessor. The reasons are fairly obvious: the confessor knew her spiritual life better than anyone else, and he was the woman's best connection to the male-dominated church hierarchy that alone could determine her status. A spiritual advisor who was favorably impressed by his penitent might easily become the author of her biography. Three of the biographies in my sample were written by clerics who had served as confessors to the women they wrote about. Even if he did not write a biography, the confessor would certainly be consulted by any biographer, he might be called upon to preach a sermon at the death of his penitent and any information that he could provide about her spirituality, miracles, visions, or other supernatural events would be recorded and placed in the woman's canonization dossier. As respected members of the clergy, moreover, their attitude toward her would weigh heavily with the censors when they came to evaluate the manuscript of a biography for publication.

The decisive importance of the spiritual advisor in making or breaking a woman's reputation for sanctity was the product of a profound change in the role of confession and confessors that took place after the Council of Trent (1545–63). Reaffirmation of the necessity of all seven sacraments for salvation, one of the high points of the council, began the transformation of the sacrament of penance from a marginal position in the life of most Catholics to a focal point for the inner spiritual life of the individual. At the same time, the role of the priest who heard confession was radically altered and greatly enhanced. Protestant and lay questioning of the efficacy of sacrament that depended on a fallible and frequently sinful priest to convey grace was silenced after the council confirmed that the sacraments bestowed the grace contained within them irrespective of the worth of the persons receiving or dispensing them.[97] The formula *ex opere operato* freed the penitent from worries about the effectiveness of the sacrament as administered by the clergy, while the hierarchy, through education, seminary training, and more effective discipline, prepared them to assume a broader role as spiritual advisors. The laity were being encouraged to go to confession more frequently, as the church saw the sacrament as its first line of defense against religious heterodoxy. In countries where inquisitorial tribunals were established, the confessors were tied directly to the system of repression by being told they could not grant absolution to a penitent who confessed something of a heretical nature but instead had to induce him or her to come to the Holy Office.[98]

The emergence of the confessor as spiritual advisor and "doctor of souls" was heralded in numerous devotional works of the period, which emphasized the need for penitents to follow the instructions of their confessors whether they agreed with them or not. According to Pedro Galindo, the author of an influential instructional manual designed to help penitents make acceptable confessions, the penitent should obey the confessor blindly, even if he was poorly informed or gave erroneous advice. The penitent should always bear in mind the fact that the confessor "should be obeyed as if he were God," because he exercised the power that God had delegated by saying to him, "he who hears you and obeys you, hears and obeys me."[99]

The growing insistence on the confessor as God's delegate on earth led some women to an almost slavish obedience to their confessors that, in many instances, was sealed by a special oath. At age thirty-six, Inés de Jesús y Franco made just such an oath, pledging in writing to her confessor Fray Guadioso Alexandre that she would "abandon herself totally" and stating that "her intellect would be entirely captive to the understanding of my spiritual father."[100] Evidently Inés's attitude must have pleased Alexandre because after her death he became one of the strongest supporters of her cult, speaking publicly about the miracles that she had performed and playing a key role in improving her tomb.

Some women even took literally the notion of the confessor as the stand-in for God. In Manuel de San Gerónimo's biography of Gabriela de San Joseph, he tells us that the Carmelite convent in Ubeda, where she was prioress, had a record of a incident that had occurred to one of the nuns most renowned for her sanctity. One day this nun was extremely eager to confess her sins before Christ himself. Imagining herself as a Magdalena throwing herself at Christ's feet and receiving absolution from him, she arrived at the confessional and found Christ himself there waiting to hear her confession. Then as she knelt before him, she looked up, only to see her ordinary confessor. Christ had disappeared, but the vision taught her that "the clergy sat in His place so that it was the same as if He Himself were hearing confession."[101]

At times such a degree of respect accorded to perfectly ordinary and extremely fallible male priests and friars led to abuse and bodily harm to the women who had entrusted them with their spiritual lives. From the moment that he assumed the responsibility of being her confessor, Fernando de San Antonio Capilla drastically increased the already severe austerities that María de Cristo had been subjecting herself to for many years, even though he admitted that she was already seriously debilitated. He insisted that she keep up these new austerities even after she became seriously ill and her doctors advised her to take a long period of bedrest. On his express orders, she disregarded her physicians and the tears of the other nuns and continued starving and scourging herself in a damp little room for twenty-six years until she became as "emaciated as a skeleton" and died in 1711 at age fifty-seven. According to her confessor, "mystical prudence" could not admit of any slackening off of her austerities as she sought not the health of the body but spiritual perfection.[102] Moreover, in spite of what may seem to a modern reader an almost sadistic disregard for María's suffering, Fernando de San Antonio Capilla greatly admired his penitent for the constancy with which she maintained her harsh regimen, which appeared to prove her sainthood. He became the author of her spiritual biography, where he generously lauded her virtues.

Spiritual advisors who were sincerely convinced of the sanctity of their charges would go out of their way to protect them. The Dominican Gabriel Ximénez, who acted as confessor to Martina de los Angeles y Arilla during the last three years of her life, was widely regarded as a person of saintly attributes both in the order and by the people of the village of Benaverre in upper Aragon, which Martina had helped to found. After a long and distinguished career during which he had served with distinction as a missionary in New Granada and provincial in Spain, Ximénez, by now quite ill from a lifetime of hardships, was sent to the Dominican house in Benaverre to recuperate.

It did not take very long acting as Martina's confessor for Fray Gabriel to become convinced that she was indeed receiving communication from God and that her trances and visions were genuine. She was, he once remarked in a letter, a "rare prodigy," and her life was of vital importance for "the consolation of sinners and even of the entire world." It is easy to imagine Ximénez's anger when two friars of the order who were visiting his convent suggested that he test Martina's humility by speaking harshly to her. Needless to say, Ximénez indignantly refused, commenting in a letter to one of his friends in the order that no one of even modest intelligence would dream of imposing such a examination on a person who had spent the last thirty years in the constant presence of "God, the Most Holy Virgin, angels and saints."[103]

Although some of the relationships between holy women and their spiritual advisors were manifestly unequal, there are many other examples of mutual interdependence. In a letter describing the details of his six years as spiritual advisor to Hipolita de Jesús y Rocaberti, the Jesuit Luis Vidal recorded the tremendous devotion with which she received absolution at his hands. She encouraged him in his career, and when he was sent on missions she prayed for him. For his part, Vidal had such faith in her that he was sure the spiritual benefits of his missions, in terms of greater numbers going to confession or mass, were more the result of her prayers than of anything he had done. After several years of hearing her confession, the emotional ties between confessor and penitent had become so strong that he claimed to have awakened out of a sound sleep in the very moment that her soul left her body.[104]

An unshakable belief in the supernatural powers of the penitents on whom they had lavished so much time and energy was common among spiritual advisors. Demonstrations of these supernatural powers in the lives of confessors would invariably be recorded and formed part of the spiritual biography. Martina de los Angeles y Arilla had a considerable reputation as a miracle worker in Zaragoza and upper Aragon while she was a nun in the Santa Fe convent and later in Benaverre. She was most famous for the rosary beads and crosses that she claimed to take up to heaven twice a day in order to have them blessed and then gave out all over the district. One of those crosses was in the possession of her last confessor, Jacinto Blasco. Blasco was something of a mystic himself and died in the odor of sanctity on the very day that Martina herself died. He would have met his demise much earlier had he not been carrying Martina's blessed cross with him while traveling from Zaragoza to Benaverre. While fording a river, Blasco's mule was carried downstream by the current, and he remembered the cross. No sooner had he taken it out of his habit and said the words, "Jesus, María!" than he found himself safely on the other bank and able to resume his journey. His experience with the wonderful crucifix so convinced Blasco of its value than he gave them out to other priests, some of whom had similar experiences. Duly grateful to Martina for the help that she had rendered him on this occasion, Blasco wrote an account of his experience with the magical cross that was placed in the file that the Aragonese Dominicans were building to support her canonization.[105]

Interestingly enough, the phenomenon of a spiritual advisor turning himself into the chief advocate for the reputation of a holy woman was not confined to those women who were the subjects of officially approved biographies. Priests who acted as spiritual advisors to women who were later exposed as frauds by the Holy Office could be just as partisan, sometimes even maintaining their support long after the women had been arrested.

Catalina Ballester, a poor widow who migrated from the village of Falaniche to Palma de Mallorca, would have never been able to gain a following in the city had it not been for the aid of several of her confessors who believed her fantastic stories and spread her reputation. Perhaps the most influential of all of her spiritual advisors was Dr. Juan Fuster, who was a canon of Palma's cathedral. Another of her confessors, Dr. Miguel Angelada, prior of the charity hospital, got her lodging at the home of the Morlana sisters, two respectable matrons well connected to the island's mercantile elite. Fuster gave the

Morlanas details about his penitent's spiritual life and protected her against criticism. When Ballester refused to do housework and spent most of her time lying in bed, Fuster informed the Morlanas that she was ill because of the pains of purgatory that she was suffering on their account. Fuster also told the sisters about Ballester's mystical marriage to Christ and sharply rebuked them whenever they expressed any doubts about her.[106]

Fuster and Angelada took it upon themselves to spread her reputation for sanctity among other members of the clergy. Fuster told Dr. Jaime Venrell, a parish priest who later became another one of Catalina's spiritual advisors, that she had suffered greatly from the severe penance she had inflicted on herself in her home village and that she undertook heroic fasting. In fact, testimony in her case revealed that no one had ever seen Catalina Ballester scourge herself in her home village, and Fuster himself had prohibited any scourging or fasting. Fuster also informed him that she had achieved "the highest form of contemplation." However improbable this was, Venrell and many other members of the clergy believed Angelada and Fuster in part because of their excellent reputation. During Ballester's trial, when Mallorca's Inquisitor Baltasar de Prado asked Venrell why he had gone about the city telling people that Ballester was "a great servant of God," and openly comparing her to St. Gertrude and St. Teresa, he had to admit that most of what he knew about her spiritual attainments had come from Fuster and Angelada.[107]

Another variant on the confessor-penitent relationship is provided by María Pizarro, a poor widow from the village of Siruela in Extremadura, and Francisco Camacho, the local parish priest. Pizarro had acquired a great reputation for her supernatural powers. Local doctors who examined her were so impressed by her abstinence that one of them swore that "she neither ate nor defecated."[108] She was also the subject of cult worship so intense that women from villages five leagues away would walk barefoot to Siruela to see her.[109]

Camacho, who had been her confessor for fourteen years when she was arrested by Inquisition, played a major role in creating and sustaining her reputation for spiritual power. Camacho firmly believed that she was a person of such saintly qualities that the devil was constantly torturing her to prevent her from praying and worshiping God. Pizarro nurtured his belief in her by telling him about instances when demons had choked her and carried her off on voyages to the mountains, where she saw strange animals. Fully aware of Camacho's credulity, Pizarro gave free rein to her imagination. Since she was very poor, Camacho had given her a room in his own home, making her his housekeeper. On one occasion, she climbed out the window and up to the roof and did not return until the following day, with her clothes torn and damp and her hair filthy and matted. When Camacho asked her where she had been she informed him that the demons had carried her off to the nearby mountains, pulled her hair, and torn her clothes. Another time, Camacho came home to find her tied to a bedpost by the neck. When he cut her loose, she pretended to be unconscious and told him that the demons had been choking her again.[110]

Such persecution by the evil one was familiar to Camacho from the hagiographies he had read and especially from the life of St. Antonio Abad, which he had told the illiterate Pizarro about on numerous occasions.[111] In the hagiographies, persecution by the devil was an almost infallible sign of sanctity, so that every time Pizarro was able to convince him that she was being singled out for persecution by demonic forces, his faith in her saintly nature increased.

Pizarro also pretended that she frequently appeared before God to plead for the souls of villagers who were seriously ill and in mortal sin. Using information that she gleaned from local gossip, it was easy for her to tell Camacho which sick people needed to make confession. He then would go to see these people and pressure them into making a confession with him in which he would sometimes hear about serious sins that had long been kept secret. Pizarro also claimed to have frequent visions of purgatory and to interview the souls of the dead, who begged her to tell their relatives that they needed more masses said for their immortal souls before they could escape to heaven. Pizarro would inform Camacho about the information that she had received, and he would then approach the relatives of the deceased and tell them the number of masses that they would have to provide.[112]

By controlling access to his penitent, confessing individuals with sins on their conscience, and deciding on the number of masses that families would have to provide for the dead souls of their relatives, Camacho appears to have benefited from his relationship with Pizarro. But any conclusion about a relationship of mutual benefit would have to be carefully nuanced. Since Camacho did not say any of the masses himself and instead assigned them all to the friars of a nearby Carmelite convent, it is hard to see any direct pecuniary benefit. His firm defense of her at her trial, where he lauded her spiritual life and testified that "she always spoke with great edification and devotion," reveals him as just another of those many confessors of holy women who sincerely believed in the powers they claimed. Of course, such belief would not in any way be inconsistent with the idea that association with someone who might become a second St. Teresa would bring them greater renown as spiritual advisors.[113]

A spiritual advisor who was overeager to believe any fantastic story told to him by his penitent was easy to deceive and could become a key supporter in creating and enhancing a woman's reputation for holiness. But that same uncritical eagerness could also have tragic consequences for the woman who was vulnerable to denunciation as a "false saint." Confessors who accepted uncritically whatever was told to them would tend to encourage their penitents to further embroider their stories of celestial favors, thereby increasing the risk of punishment by the Inquisition.

María Cotonilla was a young woman living in Colmenar de Oreja near Toledo. Since both her parents died when she was a child, leaving her with no money and no means of earning a livelihood, she was forced to beg from door to door to survive and to sleep anywhere she could. At about age twenty-six, she began to give evidence of having gone through a profound religious conversion. She became much more openly devout, arriving at the gates of the local Franciscan monastery before sunrise every morning to be admitted to mass. Public trances soon followed, and she began claiming that she had made spiritual voyages to heaven, hell, and purgatory.[114] On her visits to purgatory and hell, she said that she had been able to glean information about the fate of the souls of deceased villagers and then pass it on to their relatives. Realizing the importance of winning over a priest, she was quick to begin confessing with Fray Francisco Montero, an Augustinian who had been sent to Colmenar from his home convent in Chinchón to seek alms for his order.

According to his testimony at her trial in 1675, Montero was already predisposed in Cotonilla's favor by the reputation she had acquired in the village for visiting purgatory and returning with news of the deceased. Cotonilla was determined not to disappoint her new confessor's thirst for knowledge about the supernatural and regaled him with new anecdotes about her voyages to purgatory and other miraculous events every time he heard her in confession. Montero was so impressed by this that one day, while she was waxing on about having been carried to sea by her guardian angel, he exclaimed that the miraculous events of her life should be recorded and resolved to write the story of her spiritual life himself.[115] He was so proud of the manuscript that he remarked to one of the villagers that he would not take a thousand ducats for what he had written. Later, in conversation with Sebastian Navarro, a wealthy peasant, he boasted about the miraculous events that he had recorded in his spiritual biography of Cotonilla. But when Navarro looked through it, he began to laugh and warned the friar that he might get himself in trouble for writing down "phony miracles." In his reply, Montero revealed that it was precisely his attitude about the confessor-penitent relationship that had made it so easy for Cotonilla to manipulate him. Montero told Navarro that "when I am seated in the confessional booth I am obliged to believe whatever my penitent says, and by following that path no harm can come to me."[116]

A few months after her arrest on August 14, 1675, on charges of fraud, feigning sanctity for material gain, faking revelations, and heretical propositions, Cotonilla admitted that she had "fabricated everything." But she went on to blame Montero for letting the situation get out of hand. She said that a real confessor had the obligation "to know and inquire into the most minute details of his penitent's life." If only Montero had acted as a true spiritual advisor and admonished her, "she would have recognized her mistake and not gone astray," but instead he would "simply listen to her foolishness and not say a word."[117]

Just as the support of a woman's spiritual advisors was critically important to her reputation both during her lifetime and after her death, the opposition or hostility of a confessor could be disastrous. María Batista had a particularly difficult relationship with Fray Francisco de Soria, who was a *calificador* of the Toledo tribunal of the Inquisition. Although Soria testified that he thought Baptista was "essentially trying to be a good woman," he simply could not accept the idea that she received divine communication as she pretended. During the one and a half years when he acted as her spiritual advisor, they had a stormy relationship. On three or four occasions, he informed her that he no longer wished to hear her confession, but each time she begged him to allow her to return and he relented. She tried repeatedly to give him a kind of spiritual diary she kept to record visitations by Christ and the Virgin Mary and asked him to present it to theologians of his acquaintance on her behalf, but he always refused. To make matters worse, instead of returning the papers to her, he took them and tore them up in front of her, saying that he would do the same thing with any others that she gave him.[118] Batista's anger over his "incredulity" gave rise to a vision in which she saw a powerfully muscled arm raised above her head and heard God say, "Inform your confessor that I have manifested the strength of my arm in you."[119] Of course, Batista never dared to tell the formidable Soria about her vision, and soon afterward he dismissed her for the last time. Given Soria's firm conviction that Batista's revelations "contained not a germ of truth," it is hardly surprising that he registered a complaint about her to one of Toledo's inquisitors three days before he was called before the tribunal.

Nevertheless, it was perfectly possible for a woman who already had a considerable amount of social prestige and a well-established reputation as a recipient of divine favor to overcome the opposition of a spiritual advisor by invoking divine authority. When the Dominican Luis de Cozar assumed the role of spiritual advisor to Beatriz María de Jesús in 1678, she was a nun in Granada's convent of Santo Angel Custodio with a formidable reputation for receiving divine communication and the ability to carry out fasts of an extraordinary and miraculous length and rigor. Believing that his new penitent was proud and lacked the all-important virtue of obedience, Cozar decided to curb her excesses and reduce her to an ordinary nun who was content to live in the same way as all the rest. But he reckoned without the determination of this extraordinary woman. Using tactics similar to those that had worked so well against provisor Gerónimo de Prado when she was still a layperson, Beatriz refused to obey Cozar whenever he told her to do something she did not like on the grounds that she was entirely subject to the will of God and that God had instructed her to continue as before.

During Lent, Beatriz usually undertook an exceptionally long fast, in which she drank only a few sips of water, and then emerged from her cell smiling, happy, and full of energy, ready to take on all her obligations in the convent. Cozar objected strenuously to the ostentatious nature of this fast and wanted her to conform to the alimentary routine followed by the community as a whole, rather than try to excel and thereby call attention to herself. In 1693 Cozar finally ordered her to "abandon these novelties" and confine herself to eating exactly what the other nuns ate during the Lenten season. Beatriz could hardly have refused to obey and even told Cozar that his order could not have come at a better time because even though she had been unable to eat she had been feeling very hungry. Beatriz did caution him that she was afraid that in spite of his order God would not let her partake of food. In the next few days Beatriz came to the refectory and acted the part of someone who was trying to eat but without success. She would take a mouthful of food and "make violent efforts to swallow it," only to spit it up again. It became obvious to the entire community that a superior force was preventing her from eating, while Cozar's opposition began to look more and more like an attempt to thwart divine providence.

Away in his convent, Cozar probably assumed that his orders were being obeyed, so he was incensed to find Beatriz carrying on her usual Lenten fast when he returned for his regular visit. Brushing aside her claims that divine providence had prevented her from eating, he accused her of deliberately disobeying his orders, and pointed out that she could hardly claim to be seeking spiritual perfection and lack the supreme virtue of obedience. He was so angry that he even went so far as to say that he thought that her extraordinary fasting was "less a marvel of God than the work of the devil by whom you are possessed" and ended by threatening to resign as her spiritual advisor. Such a threat was not to be taken lightly. If Cozar had removed himself as Beatriz's spiritual advisor, it might have damaged her reputation and made it difficult to replace him with someone of equal stature.[120] But Cozar never carried through on his threat because he was in no position to do so. From 1679, when Beatriz had been widely credited for ending an outbreak of plague by undertaking special prayers and mortifications, she had enjoyed enormous support in the city. By the time Cozar attempted to curb her, she was corresponding with some of the leading nobles and churchmen in Spain. Instead of Beatriz giving up her extraordinary fasting, it was Cozar who backed down after Beatriz informed him of a vision in which Christ appeared and told her that she had nothing to fear from the devil because "I have chosen you as my instrument to make all men extol my glory."

The remarkable story of how Beatriz María de Jesús successfully defied both her confessor Luis de Cozar and the archbishop's provisor Gerónimo de Prado should give pause to those who automatically assume the powerlessness of women in early modern times. While the formal structure of power was denied to almost all women, some found ways of asserting themselves by taking advantage of opportunities opened to them by changing circumstances. All over Catholic Europe, the Counter-Reformation presented women with a variety of opportunities to employ their talents in the service of a church that had a critical shortage of well trained male priests. Women formed confraternities and devotional groups, engaged in catechizing and other educational projects, organized charitable giving, and founded new religious orders. But in an embattled church where divine communication was regarded increasingly as a critical demonstration of God's continued support, women mystics found special favor. By continuing and renovating the traditions of earlier female saints such as Gertrude the Great and Catherine of Siena, the women mystics of Catholic Europe were living proof that God continued to favor women as well as men. At the same time, their visions and revelations confirmed Catholic truth in the face of Protestant doubt and denial. But not all women were acceptable as potential recipients of God's favor. In a country with a social and economic organization increasingly favorable to the upper classes, a woman's social origins, family connections, and the influence of her supporters weighed heavily in the balance.

4

The Officially Approved
Woman Mystic and Her Supporters

A religion founded by poor fishermen and artisans might be expected to emphasize social equality and even to take a somewhat jaundiced view of the wealthy. Christian theology reflected the humble beginnings of the faith by stressing the equality of all believers. Christian eschatology foretold that at the day of judgment all were naked, the souls of rich and poor weighed according to their virtue regardless of their status in life. The Bible also contained passages that seemed to indicate that the poor automatically occupied a position of greater spiritual perfection. They were the beloved of God because their souls were not burdened by the numerous deadly sins required to get and keep wealth, while their poverty and humble status at least spared them the sins of gluttony and pride. The rich were said to find it very difficult to enter the kingdom of heaven, where Jesus promised that the last would come first.[1] In traditional Catholic thought, wealth had no intrinsic moral value, and since it could constitute a threat to the immortal soul, the rich were urged to use their wealth to help the poor or give it to the church. Theological censure of usury indicated just how strongly the medieval church felt about those who attempted to profit from the needs of their fellow man. Few bankers dared to question the church on this issue, and those who had an uneasy conscience attempted restitution in their testaments.[2]

Such a radical exegesis of scripture was increasingly embarrassing to a church that had benefited greatly from the behests of kings and great nobles and established itself as an integral part of the feudal system that was based on hierarchy and subordination. It could no longer afford to take a negative or pessimistic attitude toward the material world. Increasingly, the church accepted temporal lords as God's agents in rendering justice and the social hierarchy as divinely ordained. In the organic view of society, the head, identified with clergy and aristocracy, controlled the feet, identified as those who worked with their hands in order to live. Poverty may have been a holy state on a theoretical level, but the wealthy who embraced it voluntarily were seen as more virtuous than the poor who lived it because the rich had something to sacrifice. In a church that had fully accepted the importance of rank and family, the number of saints from noble or "good family" backgrounds exceeded any other social group by a ratio of roughly three to one throughout the medieval and early modern periods.[3]

In Spain, this tendency toward the aristocratization of those who gained a reputation for sanctity was accentuated by the revival and expansion of the aristocracy itself during the seventeenth century. Throughout the late sixteenth century, the "inflation of honors" by the massive creation of new titles of nobility, the sale of certificates of *hidalguía,* and knighthoods of the military orders all served to draw more and more men of wealth into the aristocracy.[4] With the bourgeois denuded of its wealthiest and most ambitious members, aristocratic values came to predominate, and working for a living became less important than living without working. It was symptomatic of this change that in the genealogical investigations that were mandatory for entry into honorable corporations like university colleges, military orders, or the Inquisition's corps of *familiares*, questions about office and occupation came to supersede those about race in weighing an applicant's acceptability.[5]

It was perfectly consistent with this trend that most observers agreed that aristocratic lineage predisposed the individual to scale the heights of spirituality, regardless of any loss of personal comfort or convenience. For Tomás de Montalvo, the author of the life of Beatriz María de Jesús, the noble was not only far more likely than the plebeian to be virtuous but also more likely to want to undertake "the tortuous path of spiritual perfection." While the former had the inherent moral advantages conferred upon them by their poverty, they lacked the valor to make the attempt, while the latter were like conquistadors "constantly inspired by the nobility of their blood to dedicate themselves to great undertakings."[6]

There were three compelling traditions that induced Doña Isabel de Rocaberti to seek spiritual perfection, according to her biographer Antonio de Lorea. One was the fact that she was descended from the bluest of blue-blooded aristocrats in the principality of Catalonia. Her father, D. Francisco Delmau, was viscount of Rocaberti, count of Modica, and marquis of Anglesola. Descent from such an aristocratic family meant that Isabel was "born with an obligation to seek sainthood."[7] An entirely different impulse in the same direction came from the traditions of sainthood as handed down in the Dominican order she joined. The order, in part because of its early emphasis on education, had always had a tradition of saints drawn from the nobility, and Lorea took the opportunity to list a number of these aristocratic Dominican forerunners in virtue to Isabel de Rocaberti.

A third ingredient that spurred Isabel to reach the highest levels of spiritual perfection was her own family's tradition of producing exemplary religious figures who died in the odor of sanctity. Her uncle Joseph de Rocaberti joined the Franciscan order instead of taking over the estate of Cabreñs to which he was entitled as eldest son. He became renowned all over Barcelona for his extraordinary humility and gifts as a preacher. When he died on December 12, 1584, a mute, one of the many residents who came to pay his respects, testified by gestures and facial expressions that he had seen the convent bathed in brilliant light with Joseph's soul in the middle of it, crowned with glory and rising to heaven accompanied by angels. With such a reputation, it is hardly surprising that his relics were reputed to have curative powers, and a Barcelona apothecary used some fragments of cloth that had come in contact with Joseph while he was on his deathbed to cure numerous individuals.

But the ability of this family to produce wonder-working mystics did not stop with one individual. D. Joseph's sister Estefania de Rocaberti refused to marry after her fiancé died and devoted herself to a life of abstinence and contemplation. She eventually provided the funds to found a Carmelite house in Barcelona, which she joined in 1589. While a nun, it was said that she could enter a trancelike state and remain on her knees immobile for several hours while shedding rivers of tears. After she died, her bones gave off a marvelously sweet odor and were reputed to have curative powers.

Finally, when Isabel de Rocaberti professed in 1565, she did so in the hands of her aunt Sor Gerónima de Rocaberti. Sor Gerónima had entered the Dominican Convent of Los Angeles at age seven and was elected abbess at nineteen. She served forty-four years in that capacity, presided over the convent's reform in accordance with the rules of strict enclosure as set forth by the Council of Trent, and died in the odor of sanctity in 1585.

The kind of pressure to excel in saintliness that elite families could place on their children is well illustrated by the dedicatory letter that Miguel Batista de Lanuza wrote to his daughter Teresa María de San Josef and had included in his biography of Gerónima de San Estevan. In his letter, Batista de Lanuza urged his daughter to "become very saintly" by emulating Gerónima, who had been placed in charge of her novitiate and mentored her during the first six years of her residence in Zaragoza's St. Joseph Convent. Doubtless assuming that Teresa María would read the biography, Fr. Gerónimo de San Josef, official historian of the Carmelite order and one of the ecclesiastical censors for the manuscript, addressed himself directly to her, pointing out that the entire biography had been written to provide her with a model and a measure. On the one hand, he explained, it was "designed to serve as incentive and example on the path to perfection," while on the other, it would always permit others "to indict or extol your actions in so far as they resemble or differ from those that we applaud in your mentor."[8]

But leaving aside family traditions, the harsh economic climate of early modern Spain made convent life an increasingly attractive option for the daughters of many aristocratic families. As the cost of providing dowries rose faster than the rate of inflation, more and more noble families were eager to have their daughters enter convents because the dowries they requested were so much smaller than what would have been required to launch the young women into matrimony. The aristocratization of convent life meant that the percentage of aristocratic women who gained a reputation for holiness also tended to increase. Given these factors, it is hardly surprising that the percentage of women mystics of aristocratic origin in my sample stands at 70 percent. Not only is this considerably higher than that among saints as a whole but also it excludes those whose parents could be classified as belonging to the urban elite. Including this group would raise the rate to 76 percent.

The only person of royal blood among the nobles was Margaret, the youngest daughter of the Holy Roman Emperor Maximillian II (1564–76) and the Empress María of Habsburg (1528–1603). She arrived in Spain with her mother in 1581 and joined the aristocratic Franciscan Convent of Descalzas Reales in 1584, where she professed as a nun and died in 1633 at sixty-six.[9]

Of those women with noble lineage, the largest number belong not to the upper group of grandees and *títulos* but to the simple hidalgos, many of whom experienced financial problems during the agrarian crisis of the seventeenth century. An interesting example of these decayed hidalgos is provided by the family of Beatriz María de Jesús. María was born in the city of Granada in 1632. Her father, D. Lorenzo de Enciso y Navarrete, came from a well-established hidalgo family from the province of Logroño that had seen better days. Lorenzo's great-grandfather, Pedro de Enciso y Navarette had been lord of the bedchamber to Ferdinand the Catholic and his ambassador to the papal court. But Pedro de Enciso y Navarette's descendants were unable to emulate his success, and by the time of Lorenzo's grandfather, the family had migrated to the city of Granada, where Sebastian became a city councillor and took an office with the Inquisition. Eventually, Lorenzo's father, Juan de Enciso, either lost or sold his office as *veinticuatro,* and Lorenzo himself was reduced to living on the income from some vineyards he owned in nearby Santa Fe. The story of the family of Barbara de Torres, Beatriz's mother, was much the same: distinguished ancestor followed by decline. Her great-grandfather had been city councillor of Málaga, but his descendants migrated to Granada, where they failed to enter the ranks of the urban patriciate.[10]

Throughout Beatriz's youth, the family lived in extreme poverty. Her father, who is described as "proud and haughty," ignored the sufferings of her mother, whose life was filled with "penury, illness and misfortune." But the family did have certain advantages. In spite of the fact that he had come down in the world, Lorenzo de Enciso was descended from a family that had once occupied a place at the royal court and, not so long ago, belonged to Granada's urban patriciate. Moreover, in a city whose political and social elite was uncomfortably aware of the descendants of the Moors living in its midst, Lorenzo de Enciso could boast of coming from a region of Spain that had always prided itself on being free of Jewish or Moorish influence. Such ancestry guaranteed Lorenzo de Enciso and his daughter access to the top drawer of Granada society in spite of their limited means.

A spectacular demonstration of the way in which her family was linked to Granada's elite was provided on June 1, 1665, when Beatriz was formally received into the Convent of Angel Custodio. Her sponsor was Granada's *alcalde de corte*, the official with overall responsibility for public order in the city. He was accompanied by all the judges of the Audiencia, Granada's high court of appeals, which had appellate jurisdiction for all of Castile south of the River Tajo. The ceremony was also attended by numerous members of the local nobility and a large concourse of common people who were confined behind a sturdy wrought iron fence.[11] The support of Granada's patriciate continued after Beatriz became a full-fledged nun, as her living expenses in the convent were defrayed by two of the Audiencia judges. Unlike some daughters of impoverished hidalgos, therefore, Beatriz did not have to endure a lifetime of frustration over her desire to become a nun. Her father's connections to Granada's patriciate of lawyers, Audiencia judges, and nobles allowed her to an enter an aristocratic convent whose abbess, María de las Llagas, was the daughter of the Marquis of Valençuela.

Of course, not all the parents in our sample suffered economically. Even among the lowest ranking strata of "good families," opportunities to better oneself were available, although it was probably easier in the mid-sixteenth century than it would become later. Francisca Inés de la Concepción was born in the village of Barcience, some 40 kilometers west of Toledo, which belonged to the Silva family, counts of Cifuentes. The fortunes of her father, Fernando de Molina, rested entirely on his attachment to the Silvas, whom he served in the administration of the estate. He was so highly regarded by the clan that when the third Count Fernando de Silva was appointed governor of Milan by Philip II, he insisted on taking Fernando de Molina with him as his secretary and chief steward. Fernando must have prospered because he was able to offer three hundred ducats toward his daughter's entry into a convent and purchase a seat on the noble's bench of the Toledo city council. But Francisca Inés also benefited from the paternalism of the Silva family. After Francisca Inés's mother died, Fernando de Silva's daughter-in-law, Ana de Ayala y Monroy, had her brought to the Silva palace in Toledo, where she treated her as if she were one of her own daughters. Later, after realizing that Francisca Inés had a strong religious vocation, the countess saw to it that she entered the Franciscan Convent of Belén in Cifuentes. On her own, Francisca Inés would probably have been unsuccessful in attempting to enter the convent since the nuns knew of her reputation for frequent and debilitating illness and even suspected her of having been bewitched. In spite of their obvious reluctance however, the nuns had to bow to the countess's wishes because the convent itself owed its foundation to the counts of Cifuentes.[12]

Francisca Badia came from the humblest of the two mercantile families in my sample. Her parents, Thomás Badia and Josepha Zapata, kept a stall in Valencia city's central market and lived a few paces away in a tiny one-room house under the porch of the parish church of San Juan de Mercado.[13] Born in 1711 just a few years after Valencia city had surrendered to the victorious armies of Philip V, Francisca's whole life (she died in 1754) was spent under the shadow of the food scarcities, high commodity prices, and increased taxation that depressed the economies of the eastern kingdoms during the reigns of the first two Bourbons.[14]

Poverty ruled out the possibility of marriage for Francisca, even had she been so inclined, but her attention turned to the church and religion at a very early age. Throughout her childhood and adolescence, it provided a way of reconciling herself to her poverty and a hope for a better life, if not in this world then in the next. As a sensitive child, Francisca was repelled by the noise and dirt of the market, but her parents forced her to stay at home all day while they tended their stall. Miserably unhappy, she longed for solitude, but a vision of Christ carrying a cross taught her that God had ordained that her place was right there at home. In 1734, she joined the third Mercedarian order. Not content to wear only the white scapulary that was normally worn by the members, she had made a special doublet with the symbol of the order embroidered on it. But simply belonging to the third order was not enough for Francisca. She really wanted to become a nun, but the family's penury made that impossible. All she could do was attend mass at the Mercedarian convent and watch enviously as the nuns intoned the divine office. Once again, consoling visions came to her rescue, teaching her to accept poverty and frustration in this life by promising fulfillment in the next. She had a series of visions of persons crowned with glory and dressed in the pure white of the Mercedarians; in one of these, God appeared, notifying her that "among these thou shalt also take thy place."[15] For Francisca Badia poverty served as a spur to the life of contemplation, while the consoling force of the celestial vision promised fulfillment in the next life and helped her to accept inequality, discomfort, and frustration in this world.

Paradoxically, in spite of the aristocratization of society outlined earlier, the second largest group of "approved" mystics were women of peasant origin. The fact that such women could become revered and receive official biographies no less flattering than those of their aristocratic sisters may indicate that the Spanish Catholic church was not as closed and immobile as some historians would have us believe. However, it is significant that only one of the five peasants ever became an abbess, while of the four that became nuns, two, Caterina Thomás and Josefa de Benigánim, were nuns of service charged with doing all of the convent's menial tasks. Of the fifteen nuns who did attain the position of abbess, fourteen were from aristocratic families.

Of the five peasant women, only Juana de la Cruz (1481–1534) came from a comfortably well-off family that had enough land to feed itself and provide a surplus to sell on the market. In fact, the family was so properous that numerous young men presented themselves as suitors when her father and uncles decided she should marry.[16] It is indicative of her superior status among the peasant nuns that Juana de la Cruz served as abbess for seventeen years. It is legitimate to wonder, however, whether she would have attained this status one hundred years later.

Although María de San Andres's parents are described as being "of limited wealth," she seems to have occupied a middle position, in that two of her aunts had become nuns in the Dominican Convent of the Incarnation in

Almagro, which she herself entered in 1599.[17] The fact that they entered the convent as choir nuns also indicates that the family was able to provide them with dowries. Although María never rose to become abbess, she did occupy several honorable offices during her period of residence in the convent.

At the bottom of the social hierarchy were the two servant nuns and the *beata* María Ruano, who later became known as the "Sabia de Coria." María Ruano's father is described as going out to plow with oxen, along with other peasants who performed the same task. This is a clear indication of working in common on land owned by the village, and he probably had little land of his own except for a garden plot.[18] Caterina Tomás was born in Valdemossa on the island of Mallorca in 1533, the last of seven children. Her father, Jayme, is described as a "poor *labrador*," and there is no indication the family owned any land. After both of her parents died when she was still a child, she was left destitute and had to be brought up by her uncles. According to her biographer, Bartólome Valperga she was able to enter the aristocratic Convent of Santa María Madalena only through God's direct intervention, after she had been rejected by every convent on the island because "her relatives were poor and she had no dowry."

Finally, Josefa de Benigánim came of a very poor family from the town of Benigánim, south of Valencia city near Játiva. Although a lay nun, her status in the convent was little better than maid, and she did all of the hardest work. She was also treated with the disdain with which the upper classes sometimes treated their servants. During her first few years in the convent, she was brutally teased and made the butt of numerous jokes and pranks because of her constant use of the Valencian dialect, then in the process of being abandoned by Valencia's upper and middle classes, to which the nuns belonged.[19]

In spite of the poverty and misfortune that affected the lives of certain of the humbler women in my sample, however, the fact that the two humblest— Josefa de Benigánim, beatified in 1886, and Caterina Thomás, canonized in 1930—received some of the highest honors the church could bestow is both a tribute to the women themselves and to the way sainthood had become identified with a series of attributes and powers that could be the province of any social group. The fact is that for poor uneducated women, entering a convent or becoming a *beata* provided an opportunity to rise socially, even if one was little better than a servant. Once in a religious order as a nun or a *tercera,* the woman "became visible," her "saintly" qualities had a chance of being noticed, and she might gain the support of powerful male figures who would trumpet her spiritual attainments and protect her reputation. After her death, the order might assume the burden of pushing her canonization, and by that time, a woman's social origins were less important than her achievements in the critical areas of spirituality, chastity, humility, mortification, and miracle working.

The relatively high social rank of most of the women mystics who received official biographies carried with it certain social and cultural consequences. One of the most important was that the literacy rate among these women was far higher than among the population as a whole. Of the thirty "official" mystics, only one, Josefa de Benigánim, can be said to have been truly illiterate, although significant differences did exist between the level of literacy attained by elite aristocratic women and the humbler members of the group.

Of course, literacy for most of these women meant that they could read and write Spanish but were ignorant of Latin. At times the biographies and autobiographies give us a very clear indication of how and when a woman learned to read and exactly how important reading was to her. In St. Teresa's autobiography we learn that her father, Alonso Sánchez de Cepeda, read to her from Spanish devotional works when she was six or seven years old. Teresa's mother, Beatriz Dávila y Ahumada, had less edifying tastes, and from her Teresa acquired the habit of reading tales of chivalry and became an avid reader: "unless I had an new book, I was never happy." Later in adolescence, she was given spiritual books, especially Francisco de Osuna's *Third Spiritual Alphabet,* by one of her uncles, and this work became very precious to her and helped to launch her on her career as a contemplative.[20] During her adult life, St. Teresa became a prolific author, writing several spiritual works, as well as her autobiography.

José Ximénez de Samaniego's brief biography of Sor María de Agreda also provides an interesting glimpse of the intellectual formation of a woman who was later to become the author of sixteen spiritual works, ranging from books like the famous *Mística Ciudad de Dios* to short tracts and spiritual exercises. As noted before, Sor María was also a prolific letter writer and, in addition to King Philip IV, her correspondents included several nuns and Pope Alexander VII. According to Samaniego, Sor María, like St. Teresa, was read to in her home. In Sor María's autobiography, she says that her mother "could read a little" and became particularly fond of devotional works, while Samaniego assures us that the mother taught the children how to read.[21] Howsoever it may have been, Sor María was very much a product of the vernacular scriptural literature that was available during the first half of the seventeenth century, and her knowledge of Latin was restricted to mouthing the words to prayers.

Of the six *latinas* in my sample, several were the daughters of *títulos*. Hipolita de Jesús y Rocaberti was an avid reader of Latin texts and was particularly devoted to the *Coelesti Hierarchia,* attributed to Dionysius the Areopagite, the influential fifth-century Christian Neoplatonist. She also borrowed or had access to numerous patristic and spiritual books, including the works of St. Augustine and the book of David.[22] Hipolita's literary achievements were impressive; she was the author of some twenty-six books in Latin, Spanish, and Catalan.

One of the most brilliant and remarkable of the *latinas* was the daughter of a bookseller from Barcelona. At age eleven, María Ángela Astorch entered Barcelona's Capuchin convent as a boarder, bringing a six-volume breviary with her when she arrived. She would make the breviary the basis of her religious devotion for her entire life, and when she was beatified in 1982 it was with the title of "the mystic of the breviary."

Showing an enormous aptitude for learning throughout her long career as nun and abbess, she excelled in reading Latin and gained such an extraordinary knowledge of scripture that her biographer, Luis Ignacio Zevallos, could attribute it only to divine intervention.[23] In fact, her Latin was so good that she once read a Latin work on hermit saints to her nuns and then immediately translated and explained the text. She also read widely in contemporary devotional literature in both Latin and Spanish, including works by St. Teresa and Nieremberg, as well as the *Revelations* of Gertrude the Great.

After she was sent to Zaragoza in 1614 to found another Capuchin house, her reputation for learning spread so quickly that it excited the suspicion and curiosity of the church hierarchy and Archbishop Juan Martínez de Peralta (1624–29) decided to convene a special commission to test her knowledge of Latin and holy scripture. The commissioners gave her a series of biblical citations to identify, which she did flawlessly, and then told her to make up a sermon based on three verses from the Bible. She met this last test with amazing erudition and left the commissioners so impressed that one of them commented, "What a shame that she is a woman and cannot be ordained . . . what a preacher she would have made."[24]

Literary attainments among the daughters of *títulos* and the better-off hidalgos and merchants should not surprise us because they had numerous educational opportunities. First of all, their parents were probably better educated than the majority of Spaniards so that they themselves could instruct their children. Comfortable economic circumstances also made it possible to hire tutors or send their daughters to convent schools. They typically had relatives who could offer instruction if their parents failed to do so. In the case of Martina de los Angeles y Arilla, simple neglect on the part of her father and not economic problems appeared to have denied her any formal opportunity to learn to read in her own home. She was fortunate, however, in living very close to her uncle, who was the priest in charge of a shrine to Our Lady of El Pueyo. She visited her uncle quite often, and one day when he was explaining certain biblical texts, she asked him how he knew so much about them. He explained that he had read these explanations in books. Amazed, the little girl asked, "Could I learn how to read?" Her uncle assured her that she could and offered to teach her, so with her father's permission she came to his house every day and was soon reading without difficulty. Martina was also fortunate in that her first confessor, a parish priest in Villamayor, where she was born, seeing her eagerness to possess devotional works, left her one hundred reales in his will so that she could purchase books.

But the story of Martina has an interesting twist and one shared by other women in my sample who, for one reason or another, found it difficult to obtain any kind of formal instruction but were still able to learn to read and write. On the way to her uncle's house, Martina always went into a hermitage to pray. While she was there, the Virgin appeared, took her by the hand, and gave her her first reading lessons. According to her confessor Fr. Jacinto

Blasco, these supernatural lessons better prepared Martina for working with her uncle so that she was able to progress much more rapidly.[25]

Altogether, eight of the women were said to have benefited from divine assistance in learning how to read or write. In most cases what this really meant was that the author was unaware of how his subject had managed to learn, given her lower-class origins or lack of means. At times the story of divine aid is also designed to demonstrate the extent of the subject's obedience to her confessor. A very dramatic demonstration of this occurred in the life of María Ruano, when her confessor ordered her to write down a vision that she had just experienced. Ignoring her protests that she had never written a word in her life, and not so much as taken a plume in her hand, he insisted that she write down the vision then and there. Blindly obeying her spiritual advisor, she was able to produce a brief but adequate account of the vision in clear letters, with the words separated from one another, so that it could be read without great difficulty. No miracles here, of course, because later in the text her handwriting is referred to as "rustic and unpolished," just exactly what could be expected from someone who came from a tiny village but who did live for a number of years with a widow who taught her the rudiments of religion and presumably her ABC's.[26]

The relatively high educational level of most of our "approved" mystics and their not inconsiderable familiarity with scholastic theology and holy scripture was another important plus when it came to achieving official approval. Having more than a nodding acquaintance with the cognitive structure underpinning Catholic dogma and ritual minimized the chance of going astray theologically, thereby forfeiting the all-important support of male religious.

Aware of the fact that women who claimed to receive divine communication continued to be suspect in many quarters, authors hastened to assure their readers—who might denounce their book to the Inquisition—of the strict orthodoxy of their subject. Addressing himself to both the revelations and the writings of Hipolita de Jesús Rocaberti, Antonio de Lorea lauded her for never having revelations different from "what is recorded in Holy Scripture." In her writings she was similarly discreet, "without meddling in novelties." She had never been the author of anything that the church itself had not "upheld, believed and observed."[27]

Since they themselves were highly conservative, those theologians involved in the censorship process tended to measure the acceptability of a biography by the degree to which the woman's spiritual life conformed to the teachings of the church. Eusebio Nieremberg's favorable verdict on Batista de Lanuza's biography of Francisca del Santissimo Sacramento was based in part on the fact that her beliefs were in complete agreement with "the dogmas of our faith". Francisca's many visions and revelations were also no cause for alarm because they, too, were firmly based on tradition and could be found in the writings of the saints and the masters of the mystical tradition.[28] For his part, Batista de Lanuza assured his readers that Francisca had told him that her visions of saints, celestial processions, and the like were always represented in exactly the same way as they were described in sacred works and accepted by church tradition.[29]

To doubt is human, however, and despite the efforts by authors to represent their subjects' religious views as strictly orthodox, even they sometimes lift the curtain just a little bit to reveal the inner travail experienced by at least some of the women. The dogma of the immaculate conception of the Virgin Mary was easily one of the most serious controversies to ever afflict the Roman Catholic church. In Spain, the dogma had powerful support from the state and the Franciscan and Jesuit orders, but it was bitterly opposed by the Dominicans and encountered a stratum of popular resistance as well. Inquisition trials for blasphemy, for example, frequently dealt with people who refused to accept the idea and sometimes expressed their rejection by using coarse and sexually explicit language. Disputants on both sides of the issue had to be careful because the papacy was reluctant to come down too strongly on either side and made the Inquisition responsible for punishing those publicly supporting or impugning the dogma.[30]

It is against this background of unresolved controversy and sporadic, if futile, efforts to silence the disputants that we must evaluate María de Christo's troubles with the devil. Even though she was a member of the third Franciscan order and therefore obligated to support the dogma, she had a vision in which the evil one appeared in the guise of an angel and insinuated that she should believe that "the mother of Christ had not been conceived without original sin." Of course, María saw through the devil's ruse and indignantly rejected his attempt to mislead her, crying out, "You lie, dog! From the first instant of her being this sovereign lady was purer than all the angels and seraphim combined." María recorded her pleasure at having "returned to the truth and purity" of the dogma, and in what could easily be interpreted as a form of overcompensation for the nagging doubts expressed in her "demonic" vision, she placed an image of the immaculate conception directly in front of her death bed so that it would be the last thing she saw before she died. Nevertheless, the fact that her biographer, Fernando de San Antonio, alluded to "other battles that served to make her faith firmer and more intense" indicates that her doubts not only persisted but also may have extended beyond the immaculate conception. Since San Antonio acted as María's confessor for the last twenty-six years of her life, he would have known about her religious doubts and had a motive for concealing any potentially embarrassing details about them.[31]

Interestingly enough, María de Christo's crisis of faith did not come from ignorance. In fact, in Badajoz, where she presided over a *beaterio* that followed the rule of St. Clare, she was very highly regarded by local theologians for her profound knowledge of devotional works and holy scripture. Although the details of María's "other battles" are hidden from us, it is safe to assume that too much knowledge of often conflicting and confusing religious texts may well have contributed to them.[32]

Devotion to the Eucharist was one of the main features of the new religious sensibility that characterized the Counter-Reformation, but there was always an undercurrent of popular skepticism. Like the man in a Galician tavern who exclaimed, "Go on! God's in heaven and not in that host which you eat at mass!" when a priest claimed that the communion bread changed into the body of Christ, common sense made it difficult for many to fully accept the idea of the real presence.[33] The popular debate about the presence of Christ in the host is reflected in another "satanic" vision, this time one that occurred to Martina de los Angeles. According to a nun who shared her cell, Martina was heard to cry out in her sleep, "Our Lord is in the host as he is in heaven," and later to threaten the evil one, exclaiming, "Do what you will, the Lord is on my side." In addition to her doubts about the real presence, Martina was tortured by other "temptations" in matters of faith.[34] It is at least possible that the author's reference to these religious doubts was one reason for certain delays in publication of the 1735 edition.

For all of the "approved" women mystics in my sample, doubts about Catholic orthodoxy were so dangerous and troubling that they had to be repressed or projected on an evil persona alien to themselves. Doubt was always the province of the "other"—the Jew, the Protestant heretics, the Moor, or the devil—but never the pious nun or *beata* who sought God in every thought and deed. Doubt appeared in dreams and manifested itself as a visit from the evil one but was never expressed openly, and what came from the devil could not come from inside oneself. Indeed, the devil could perform his mischief only with God's permission, so doubt and unbelief were transformed into yet another proof of God's omnipotent power and special love for his most loyal servants.

Faced with the combined influence of the monarchy, the church, and the Holy Office, the "holy woman" who wished to survive with her reputation intact would have to support not only the faith but also the entire structure of power as it then existed. A rather typical expression of this unequivocal support for the status quo is provided by an incident from the life of Isabel de Jesús, who was a member of the third order of Carmelites in Toledo. One day, right after she had taken communion, Christ appeared and told her that her prayers should be extended to the entire church, the Holy Father in Rome, bishops, kings and princes, and the entire ecclesiastical estate.[35] The willingness, even eagerness, of women mystics to align themselves ideologically and politically with the interests of Spain's power elite made it relatively easy for a broad cross section of that elite to offer them critical support.

Obviously, the most direct expression of royal favor for a holy woman would be the arrival of the king at her convent in order to honor her by his presence or simply to ask her advice. Although this was relatively unusual, it was not impossible given royal willingness to encounter the holy woman and the convenient location of the convent to the royal personage. It was convenience, as much as her exalted rank as the daughter of a *título* and former viceroy of Navarre, that brought Philip III and his wife, Margaret of Austria, to the ceremony at which Brianda de Acuña Vela took her novitiate at the Carmelite Convent of La Concepción in Valladolid on that day in mid-January

1602.[36] The previous year, much to the annoyance of his courtiers, Philip had transferred the court from Madrid to the city on the Pisuerga, where it was to remain until 1606.

Philip IV, by contrast, had to make a considerable detour to get to the Franciscan Convent of Agreda for his first interview with María de Jesús on June 10, 1643. Philip was travelling to Zaragoza to join the royal army at Segre. His desire to make contact with Sor María stemmed from the intense personal and political crisis that he was experiencing at that point in his life. To the French invasion of Catalonia had been added, on May 19, 1643, the crushing defeat at Rocroi. As if this were not enough, the resignation of the Conde Duque de Olivares, the king's chief minister for more than twenty years, left him feeling isolated. Since Philip IV was driven by an overwhelming sense of guilt for the calamitous events of the last few years, his meeting with Sor María formed a part of his attempt to rehabilitate himself in the eyes of God. It was from this meeting that the famous correspondence between the two began. Sor María's letters provided the king with much-needed emotional support through a difficult period, but the relationship was not all one-sided, as the king collected her writings and supported her when she was being investigated by the Inquisition. It would be disingenuous to suppose that inquisitor-General Arce y Reynoso's favorable verdict on her in 1650 had nothing to do with the fact that the king had been carrying on an intense correspondence with her for seven years. Moreover, the first edition of Sor María's famous and controversial work, *Mystical City of God,* was specifically approved for publication by inquisitor-General Balthasar de Mendoza y Sandoval in 1670. Although it is true that the Inquisition was forced to ban the book in 1672, it was allowed to circulate freely again in 1686, and it continued to circulate in spite of adverse censorship by the Sorbonne. Meanwhile, royal support for Sor María's beatification continued to be very strong under both Charles II and his Bourbon successors.[37]

Championing the goals and objectives of a holy woman by the king is quite evident in the relationship between Philip II and St. Teresa of Jesus. Philip intervened repeatedly to prevent the Calced Carmelite friars from stopping the reform movement in the order favored by Teresa. He also assisted with obtaining licenses for the new Carmelite convents that she wished to establish. In appreciation for the king's favor, Teresa asked her nuns to offer special prayers on his behalf, "for our present king . . . is very well disposed to religious who are known to keep their rule, and will always help them."[38]

Ana de Lobera, who joined the Discalced Carmelitesses under the name of Ana de Jesús, became one of St. Teresa's closest companions and was responsible for founding nine convents. She also enjoyed direct royal support from the Archduke Albert and his wife, the Infanta Isabella Clara Eugenia, when she went to Flanders in 1607. The princess not only helped with foundations but also it was she who commissioned Fr. Angel Manrique's biography, which was published in Brussels in 1632.[39]

Women mystics could also count on support from a broad cross section of the aristocracy. St. Teresa's *Book of the Foundations* is filled with anecdotes about members of the nobility who helped with new foundations, contributed houses and money, or even entered the convents themselves. Both Ruy Gómez de Silva, Prince of Eboli, and his wife, Doña Ana de Mendoza, whose father, Diego Hurtado de Mendoza, was first duke of Francavilla and president of the Council of Italy, asked Teresa to found a convent in Pastrana. The princess rebuilt and embellished the house that had originally been selected for the convent. After her husband died in 1573, she took the Carmelite habit and entered the convent, where she stayed for three turbulent years.[40]

Teresa was especially successful in attracting the support of wealthy widows whose husbands had combined aristocratic lineage with important positions in royal government. When the original house for her foundation at Valladolid was found unhealthy by the nuns who were first sent there, she was given a new house by María de Mendoza, widow of Francisco de los Cobos, the all-powerful secretary to Charles V.[41]

The widows of nobles or high-ranking members of the bureaucracy were frequently inclined toward the spiritual life, so that it was natural for them to spring to the assistance of foundering religious communities or to come out in support of a particularly impressive holy woman. Gabriela de San Joseph, three times prioress of the Carmelite convent in Ubeda, received regular assistance from Josepha Manuel de Hozes, the wealthy widow of Luis de la Cueva Carvajal, a member of the Order of Santiago. In fact, Gabriela was so accustomed to Josepha's regular contributions when she served as prioress that she came to anticipate them. One day, when the convent was experiencing a dearth of provisions because of poor harvests in the region, Gabriela remarked to the nun who was acting as doorkeeper, "Sister, do you know I have been wondering if my friend Doña Josepha Manuel is going to send us a side of mutton today?" The nun replied cautiously that that would be a good thing and thought no more about it, but not more than four hours later a servant of the lady in question arrived with the mutton. Both Doña Josepha and her husband had assisted the convent financially on numerous occasions, and Josepha counted herself as Gabriela's close personal friend.[42] The connection between the two women was so well known, and Josepha's support for the convent was so critical to its survival, that when Fr. Manuel de San Gerónimo wrote his biography of Gabriela, he dedicated it to Josepha Manuel de Hozes.

María de la Santissima Trinidad was another woman mystic who was able to elicit significant support from an aristocratic lady who became the widow of a noble with a record of service in royal administration. In this case, it was María Enriquez Porres y Gúzman Countess of Villaumbrosa. Her husband, Pedro Núñez de Gúzman, Count of Villaumbrosa and Marquis of Montealegre, was appointed president of the Council of Castile by Philip IV. Both the count and countess aided María repeatedly during her lifetime and venerated her after her death. The countess also subsidized the publication of Antonio de Lorea's biography of María, and he dedicated the book to her out of gratitude.[43]

But to maintain the support of the aristocracy, especially in the seventeenth century with its proliferation of status-conscious new *títulos*, a woman mystic had to be careful to demonstrate respect for the principle of hierarchy, especially if she herself came from the lower classes. María Ruano, the "wise woman of Coria," proved to be a slow learner when it came to the need to show deference to her social superiors. Deeply disturbed by the poverty and destitution that the Hispano-Portuguese conflict had brought to her native Extremadura, María had a vision in which it was revealed to her that peace could be achieved only if a Carmelite convent was founded in her village. With the conflict worsening, and her home village of el Guijo directly threatened with attack because of its strategic position near the border, her confessor Pedro de Estrada decided to take her to Madrid in 1644 to see if she could obtain a license to establish the convent.

Before braving the capital, however, Estrada was intelligent enough to realize that a project that originated from divine communication would need a considerable amount of support from theologians before it could be submitted to the political authorities. Estrada decided to take María to Salamanca, Spain's premier institution of higher learning, reasoning that if she could gain the approval of influential theologians there, her task in Madrid would be that much easier. In Salamanca, he was able to obtain support from eight leading theologians, including several senior professors, and each of them made a written deposition recording support both of the projected Carmelite house and of María herself as just the kind of person who would be likely to be favored with divine communication.[44]

As soon as they arrived in the capital, Estrada faded into the background, turning her spiritual direction over to Fr. Francisco Mançano, a high-ranking member of the Trinitarians who was very well connected at court and knew María from el Guijo because he came from a neighboring village. Mançano was able to get María introductions to some of Madrid's leading clerics, including Eusebio Nieremberg and, most important, St. Simón de Roxas, then acting as spiritual advisor to Queen Elizabeth of Bourbon. Armed with the support of so many prominent and influential members of the clergy, Mançano was also able to place María in certain key aristocratic households; indeed, as the fame of the "little peasant" from Guijo spread in the capital, the wives of *títulos* and government ministers vied to house her.

The high point of María's sojourn in Madrid was undoubtedly her reception at court, where everyone was impressed by her dignity and simplicity and Philip IV himself gave the project his blessing. A few days later, it was the turn of Queen Elizabeth of Bourbon to receive her. María spent most of one afternoon at the palace with the queen and Princess María Teresa, and both were sufficiently impressed by her to offer their support.

But beneath the surface of brilliant court receptions and interviews with famous theologians, trouble was brewing. María Ruano was not a nun and even though she had had a harsh upbringing, it had not broken her spirit. In the midst of a Spain in which the gap between rich and poor was widening and aristocratic privilege was the order of the day, the pride of the free Castilian peasant whose "pure" blood made her inherently superior to the "tainted" lineage of the upper classes still beat within her breast. María had also become a spiritual leader in her village. After the death of Juana Pérez, Guijo's first *beata*, who had taken her in after her father abandoned her, María took over the *beaterio* and made it into a center of religious devotion. Accustomed to the austerity of life in Extremadura and deeply concerned about the poverty in her own village, María was shocked at the atmosphere of splendor and gaiety with which holy week was celebrated in Madrid. Declaring that "instead of being filled with sadness for the loss of a Father they adorn themselves as if they were going to a wedding," she refused to attend any of the processions and took refuge in the Franciscan Convent of San Gil, where she could listen to the simple unadorned chanting of the nuns.

Even worse from the standpoint of the hoped-for new convent, María succeeded in alienating the aristocratic ladies who had once vied to take her into their homes. Throughout her stay in Madrid she had maintained the rigors of her regimen, which included scourging herself, wearing a penitential girdle, and, above all, consuming very little food. In a society where the most obvious distinction between rich and poor was the semistarvation of the latter and the sumptuous meals consumed by the former, to consciously reject a meal was to insult the person who offered it to you. This is exactly what María did at the home of the wife of one of the most important government ministers, whose good will was critical to the success of the project. María also had an unfortunate habit of speaking her mind a little too freely to her aristocratic hosts, and her critical comments stung them so much that she was forbidden entry into one home after another.

Finally, realizing that the entire project was in jeopardy, Mançano sent her to see the influential bishop of Badajoz, Gerónimo Valderas, who was then in the capital. Undoubtedly aware of her social transgressions, Valderas rebuked her without even allowing her to try to explain herself and then told her in no uncertain terms that she should forget about founding convents. Such an ambitious undertaking was unsuitable for an "insignificant little person" like her, and that if she wished he could place her in an aristocratic home as a servant. Since María had had enough of aristocrats, she demurred and was soon on her way back provincial obscurity. To no one's surprise, the proposed foundation was rejected by the bishop of Coria the following year in spite of approval by the Council of Castile and what appeared to have been strong support among the nobility of the region.[45]

Títulos and members of the royal family were vital to the success of holy women, but on a more mundane level they also depended on numerous other lay supporters. Some of these were drawn from the ranks of the lesser nobility, such as Doña Marina Ripoll, the wife of a gentleman (caballero) of Zaragoza, who had a very close relationship with Martina de los Angeles, visited her convent on numerous occasions, and left her one hundred reales annually in her will.[46]

The support of officials of local government was also important because they could make the difference between a relatively supportive environment in which the holy woman could develop her spiritual life and reputation and one of intolerance or outright hostility. Ownership of the village of Aracena, where María de la Santissima Trinidad lived as a member of the third order of Dominicans, had long been a source of friction between the leaders of two powerful Andalusian noble families. To avoid outright conflict in a sensitive region, the Council of Castile decided to send Gerónimo de Avendaño, who was already in Seville dealing with other matters, to the village to carry out an investigation into the conduct of local officials and serve as royal governor until the dispute between the two magnates should be settled. Hearing of María's spiritual reputation almost as soon as he arrived in the village, he went to see her to ask her to pray for the success of his assignment and came away very favorably impressed. Antonio de Lorea, María's biographer, describes him as her "great protector," and his devotion to her was such that he came to visit her while she was on her deathbed.[47]

Finally, on an even less exalted level, women mystics got a considerable amount of assistance from wealthy merchants and their families. St. Teresa, whose family had deep roots in the mercantile community of converted Jews, benefited at various times during her life from the generous financial assistance of merchants, especially during her efforts to establish new Carmelite houses. Given her family background, she was especially successful in obtaining aid from *conversos* for her foundations in Castile. When Teresa arrived in Medina del Campo in August 1567, she found that the building that had been set aside for the new convent could not be occupied without undergoing extensive repairs. With no place to stay and mounting opposition in the city to the foundation of a new convent, Teresa tried desperately but without success to find rented accommodations. Fortunately, after a week of searching, Blás de Medina, a wealthy merchant of probable *converso* origin, gave them the entire upstairs of his house to use until the repair work was completed.[48]

In Toledo, where Teresa went in 1569, she was rescued from possible disaster by Alonso de Avila, another *converso* merchant, after negotiations for a house for her foundation had broken down. Alonso, who was a bachelor of charitable disposition already known to Teresa, provided the surety the nuns needed to rent a house, which they were eventually able to purchase and make into a permanent home for the convent.[49]

The fact that María Ruano's failure to gain the support of either the bishop of Badajoz or the bishop of Coria ultimately doomed her project indicates the critical importance of the ecclesiastical hierarchy for the success of Spain's women mystics. The restoration of episcopal authority after the Council of Trent meant that bishops controlled what happened in their diocese to a far greater degree than they had since the early Middle Ages. Few new monastic houses could be established without the support of the local bishop. Moreover, as we have seen in the case of Beatriz María de Jesús, a bishop's overall responsibility for the moral and religious climate within his diocese meant that he could undertake an inquiry into the activities of any individual who showed signs of behaving in a way disrespectful to religion. It was hardly likely that any woman mystic would survive without being denounced to the Holy Office if she failed to win the support of her local bishop.

Specific examples of episcopal support can be encountered frequently in the biographies and autobiographies of women mystics. In both her autobiography and the *Book of the Foundations,* St. Teresa especially mentions the bishop of Avila, Álvaro de Mendoza, as a supporter of reform in the Carmelite order and in obtaining licenses for new convents.[50]

Francisca del Santissimo Sacramento was fortunate enough to enjoy the patronage of Bishop Christobal de Lobera when she was a nun in the Carmelite house of Pamplona. Knowing of her keen interest in the fate of the souls of purgatory, he purchased a large number of indulgences and then gave them to her to distribute. Needless to say, the authority to distribute indulgences to whomever she pleased greatly enhanced Francisca's prestige in the city. He also gave her convent some valuable ceremonial objects, including a silver lamp for the chapel.[51]

Finally, since it was almost indispensable for a holy woman to belong to a religious order to gain official approval, it was greatly to her advantage to remain on good terms with the male superiors of the order. These officials had more direct power over her life than the local bishop. They appointed the visitors who carried out periodic visitations to the houses of the order, and they also selected the male spiritual advisors and vicars who were the real force behind the administration of a convent and to whom the prioress was often compelled to defer.

Saint Teresa herself was very well aware of the power of the provincials of her order, who were all the more dangerous because they did not necessarily favor reform. Fate, however, intervened to send her a way of circumventing the authority of the provincials. In February 1566, Fra Giovanni Batista Rossi, the newly elected general of the Carmelite order, visited the Spanish Carmelite houses. Such visits were relatively rare, but this one had been encouraged by Philip II because he knew that Fra Giovanni favored the reform of the order. When Fra Giovanni arrived in Avila, Teresa made sure that he was treated with great respect by the bishop, who was one of her strongest supporters, and brought him to the convent that she had recently founded in the city. Fra Giovanni was duly impressed by the strictness with which the nuns were keeping the primitive rule and issued Teresa two patents, allowing her to found more houses in both Old and New Castile "so that no provincial would be able to stop me."[52]

After 1580, when the Calced and Discalced wings of the Carmelite order were divided, Discalced Carmelitesses with outstanding spiritual lives found their superiors extremely supportive because now the Discalced wanted to demonstrate that the products of their rule were superior to those of the unreformed. This new atmosphere certainly benefited Doña Brianda de Acuña Vela, who entered the Discalced Carmelitesses in 1602 and took the name

Teresa de Jesús Vela. Brianda's aristocratic origins, extraordinary religious fervor, and strong sense of obedience to her superiors made her the ideal reformed Carmelite nun. As a consequence, she had excellent relationships with a series of powerful generals and provincials, including Fr. Alonso de Jesús María, author, distinguished theologian and two times general of the order, and Fr. Pedro de los Angeles, who was her confessor for twenty-eight years and also served three terms as provincial.[53]

But the prevailing religious culture, with its emphasis on mortification, abstinence, and contemplation, meant that a holy woman would also benefit from gaining the support of friars who had demonstrated such virtues in the highest degree. The attitudes of such heroic servants of God were more important in validating the claims of a woman to high spiritual status than the favorable opinion of officials of the order. The most famous and successful relationship of this kind, of course, was between St. Teresa and St. John of the Cross, but lesser known women mystics were also able to benefit from such relationships.

The Dominican *tercera* María de la Santissima Trinidad, for example, gained the respect of a number of influential members of the order who were known for their own exemplary spiritual lives. One of her staunchest supporters was Fr. Antonio Ruiz de Cabrera, who, while admitting that he had always been skeptical of the claims of others to receive visions and revelations, found himself persuaded that she was genuine because "a woman to whom God had granted such beauty and modesty could not fail to be outstanding in virtue." Another friar called her a living portrait of St. Anne, mother of the Virgin Mary, while Juan de Salvatierra, a canon of Seville's cathedral who was greatly devoted to her, lauded not only her beauty and modesty but also her sweetness and lack of affectation.[54]

Finally, the element that perhaps most of all makes the phenomenon of the success of certain women mystics comprehensible is the support that they received from inquisitorial personnel. If inquisitors, officials, and commissioners could become the followers and even the acolytes of women mystics, then the tribunal itself could hardly be expected to take a firm stand against them.

One of the most extraordinary relationships between a woman mystic and an inquisitor involved Gabriela de San Joseph and Juan Miguelez de Amendaño, senior inquisitor of the Granada tribunal and later a member of the Suprema. Although she was a nun in the enclosed Discalced Carmelite Convent of Ubeda, Gabriela's fame as a mystic and miracle worker had spread throughout Andalusia. Soon after his arrival in Granada, Amendaño started a correspondence with her that was to last many years. He wrote her about all the intimate details of his life, sent her presents, and even went so far as to make a special trip to Ubeda to visit her before taking up his appointment in Madrid. He was so convinced of her holiness that he called her "a great woman and a great saint" and once remarked to the prioress of her convent that "they could beatify her with just what I have in her letters." By the time she died in 1701, he had become so emotionally dependent on her that he was devastated. In a letter that he wrote to the convent, he mourned her passing and lamented, "Now there can no longer be any consolation for me in this life."[55]

If Juan Miguelez de Amendaño needed no convincing to accept Gabriela de San Joseph's pretensions to sanctity, inquisitor Arganda of the Cuenca tribunal was led to Inés de la Concepción because he was assigned to carry on an investigation of two denunciations of "false sanctity" that had been received against her. Although skeptical at first, after interviewing numerous witnesses and actually interrogating her while she was in a trance, Arganda abandoned all pretense of objectivity and became a partisan. He was so convinced of her supernatural powers that he even told her to cure the countess of Cifuentes's children of an eye ailment. He was so impressed by the orthodox nature of her replies to his questions while she was in a trance that at one point he ordered the doors of the convent flung open and invited in the countess, local officials, and townsfolk to witness the phenomenon. As they fell to their knees before her, he addressed them, saying, "This is not a woman but an angel." After her return to Cuenca, he helped to spread her reputation throughout the district and carried on an extensive correspondence with her.[56]

But it was not just inquisitors who became devotees of particular women mystics. Support for mysticism also extended to other levels of officials. Lower level officials of the Granada tribunal who were devoted to Gabriela de San Joseph included Secretary Domingo del Corral, who carried on an extensive correspondence with her.

Commissioners, who were the eyes and ears of the Inquisition outside the seat of the tribunal, were also susceptible to becoming supporters and even devotees of holy women. The commissioner of the Cordóva tribunal in Ubeda, who was at first somewhat skeptical about Gabriela de San Joseph, ended up a believer and even asked for a relic after she died.[57] The commissioner of Castro in Aragon, Antonio de Ubierzo, was also a relic collector. After the death of Martina de los Angeles y Arilla, he procured one of her rosary beads, which he believed to have curative powers.[58] Nicolás Torrecila, one of the commissioners of the Murcia tribunal, dedicated a book to María Ángela Astorch, who was the founder of a convent in that city. Her confessor Alejo de Boxados eventually was appointed inquisitor of Murcia after a five-year struggle, during which she aided him with her prayers.[59]

The multiple layers of support from Spain's political, religious, and cultural elite that a woman mystic enjoyed during her lifetime made writing her biography an attractive project for authors looking for a theme that would probably receive the approbation of the authorities placed in charge of censorship. Then again, the academic distinction or high rank of the author served as a further guarantee of the orthodoxy of the subject.

Probably the most important motivation for authors to take up the task of writing a biography was the desire to broadcast the achievements of the exemplary members of their own religious order. Fully 71.4 percent of the biographers in my sample belonged to the same order as their subject. In certain instances, professional responsibility may have served to reinforce a personal interest in the holy women since several authors, such as the Dominican Antonio de Lorea and the Franciscan Antonio Daza, were official chroniclers of their order. Three of the biographers also served as spiritual advisors to their subjects so that they had a natural and understandable interest in writing a biography to showcase their own success with a penitent of such remarkable spiritual attainments.

While a number of authors were seemingly obscure priests or friars such as Luis de Mesa, a simple benefice holder in Toledo, 57.8 percent of them had attained significant rank or distinction within a religious order, in academic life, or as laymen in politics and law. Antonio Arbiol, the biographer of Sor Jacinta de Atondo, not only was the author of several other religious books but also had served as visitor and synodal examiner in the archdiocese of Zaragoza and as provincial of the Franciscan province of Aragon. Fernando de San Antonio, the author of the biography of María de Christo, also had a distinguished career in the Franciscans as both reader of theology and provincial of the Franciscan province of Andalusia, a position to which he was elected on two occasions.

Further underscoring the generally favorable position of the Spanish Inquisition toward the right kind of woman mystic is the fact that three authors were also officials of the Holy Office. Antonio Arbiol served as theological censor (*calificador*) for the Zaragoza tribunal, and Francisco de Arcos and Juan de Ellacuriaga carried out the same responsibilities for the Suprema. In addition, Fr. Lope Paez's biography of Francisca Inés de la Concepción was paid for by Miguel de Cardona, who, besides being Francisca's nephew, had the honor of being senior inquisitor on the Sardinia tribunal.

Some authors also achieved distinction in academic life, where their contacts and reputation would almost guarantee them favorable reviews from the censors. Of the four who held tenured chairs, the most distinguished was Fr. Ángel Manrique, who held the coveted Víspera professorship of theology at the University of Salamanca. Manrique, who wrote the biography of Ana de Jesús, later served as bishop of Badajoz (1645–49) and wrote memorials in favor of reforming the Spanish university system.[60] An excellent example of the way in which the closed circle of academic life could lead to a favorable outcome of the censorship process is the fact that the second censor to review Manrique's biography was his colleague Senior Professor Fr. Gaspar de los Reyes.

Another author and distinguished reformer was the Mercedarian Juan Interián de Ayala (1656–1730). Interián de Ayala, who was professor of Hebrew and philosophy at Salamanca, was a man of vast erudition who cofounded the Spanish Royal Academy and was one of the leaders of a movement that reformed and renewed Spanish preaching during the early eighteenth century.[61] These two academic luminaries far surpassed the other two authors with academic credentials, Fr. Andrés de Maya Salaberria, who was rector of the Dominican college in Zaragoza, and the Trinitarian Francisco de Arcos, professor at the shadowy University of Toledo.

Finally, another small but important group of authors were laymen who had attained distinction in law and royal service. The most obvious example here is the prolific Miguel Batista de Lanuza, regent of the Council of Aragon and *protonotario* of that kingdom. But eighteenth-century Aragon could also boast another distinguished lay author in the person of Diego Franco y Villalva, who published a biography of his relative Inés de Jesús y Franco while serving on the regional Audienca.

Judging from scattered references by censors, there can be little doubt that the distinction or reputation for orthodoxy of an author weighed heavily in the balance when they came to evaluate a work for publication. For some, an author's social status was sufficient to make them suspend their critical judgment altogether. Not surprisingly, the most blatant example of this occurred with the work of Miguel Batista de Lanuza, who had earned universal applause for his extraordinary dedication to recording the lives of women mystics while carrying out his governmental responsibilities. Commissioned to write a report on Batista de Lanuza's biography of Francisca del Santissimo Sacramento, Manuel de Salinas Lizana concluded that he must have been sent the book "simply for my pleasure, profit and delight," and without considering any of the rather serious doctrinal issues raised in the biography he approved it for publication.[62]

The increasing stress on the sacrament of penance in the post-Tridentine church, with its complicated arithmetic of sin, led to an increasing emphasis on the role of the confessor as infallible spiritual guide and "doctor of souls." Theologians and moralists writing about the struggles of individuals, especially women, to overcome religious doubt, fear or anxiety uniformly prescribed absolute and unquestioning submission to the guidance of the spiritual advisor as the way of "rising to heaven carried on the shoulders of another."[63] It was perfectly logical, therefore, for those involved in reviewing and judging the lives of women mystics to look to the quality of their spiritual advisors as the first and most important guarantee of their religious orthodoxy and the acceptability of any mystical experiences that they may have had. In fact, this approach was taken by no less a personage than Dr. Tomás Lop, senior professor of theology at the University of Valencia, who was given the task of reviewing Juan Bernal's biography of Francisca Badia by the Council of Castile. From the outset, Lop took the view that the fact that the author had also acted as her spiritual advisor for many years virtually guaranteed the orthodoxy and validity of the mystical experiences recounted in the book. Since Bernal was a seasoned spiritual advisor, he could be counted on to have directed his penitent along the "most secure path to spiritual perfection." Therefore, Lop's censorship of the book merely confirmed the conclusions of its author: that Francisca had been uniquely favored by God and called by him to the heights of spiritual glory.[64]

Since a woman's confessors played such a significant role in validating her mystical experiences in the face of a male-dominated society that was all too willing to either dismiss them or see them as demonically inspired, the quality of those spiritual advisors provided the woman's first line of defense against any potential critics. All the evidence suggests that the "true" mystics in my sample did enjoy the services of a distinguished group of spiritual advisors. While only 7 advisors were mere parish priests, fully 49 of the 117 that I have been able to identify had one or more of twelve key indicators of status in religious or academic life. Of the remaining 61 individuals, the lack of one of these indicators may simply indicate a lack of information in the biography or, more important, that that individual was very highly regarded by his contemporaries as priest and theologian without having ever exercised any kind of specific office. This would have been the case with Juan Bernal, who appears merely to have been an undistinguished member of the Mercederian order but is described in glowing terms by his fellow Valencian Tomás Lop as a "profound scholastic theologian" and expert in "mystical theology." The same would have been true of the Carmelite friar Diego de San Angelo, one of Teresa de Jesús Vela's confessors, who never held any office in the order but is described by Batista de Lanuza as "a monk of extraordinary perfection and in the opinion of those who knew him a man of saintly virtue." His reputation for holiness was so great that one of his penitents had visions of him with Christ, who was in the act of bestowing celestial favors upon him. Just after his death, this same penitent, described as being one of the holiest nuns in the Carmelite Convent of Valladolid, saw his soul, crowned with glory, rising to heaven.[65]

Spiritual advisors who attained distinction in their respective religious orders included twelve provincials and some who were elected to that office on several occasions. These men included two of Gabriela de San Joseph's confessors, Fr. Diego de San Alberto and Fr. Andrés de Santa Teresa, who was elected three times. Fr. Agustín de la Cruz, who served Gabriela as spiritual advisor for thirty years, served as a reader of theology in one of the Carmelite colleges but, more important, was so highly regarded for his spiritual attainments that Fr. Antonio de Santa María, another one of Gabriela's confessors, actually collected one of his fingers, which he used to affect cures. Sor María de Agreda also had a very distinguished member of the order in the Franciscan Andrés de la Torre. He served as her spiritual advisor for more than twenty years and was three times elected provincial.

Both St. Teresa of Jesus and her close disciple, Ana de Jesús, made their confessions to Fr. Domingo Bañes, one of Spain's most important neo-Thomist theologians. From occupying a comparatively lowly professorship of theology in the Dominican College of Saint Thomas in Ávila when Teresa first sent him a manuscript copy of her *Life* in 1566, he was elected to the coveted *Prima* chair of theology at Salamanca, where he promised to teach Thomist theology in its purest form.[66]

Officials and inquisitors also acted as spiritual advisors to women mystics, a fact that further reduces the already heavily compromised objectivity of the Holy Office with regard to the phenomenon itself. It would be hard to imagine a woman who had had a good relationship with a spiritual advisor linked with the Holy Office running afoul of the tribunal. Altogether nine spiritual advisors, including four inquisitors and two theological censors, heard the confessions of "official" mystics, including Dr. Juan Abrines, senior inquisitor on the Mallorca tribunal and canon of Palma's cathedral.

So devoted was Dr. Abrines to his penitent Catherina Thomás that he wrote her spiritual biography (unpublished) and the epigram that was placed on her tomb.[67]

Interestingly enough, a study of the confessors of someone like Catherina Thomás, who was the daughter of peasants and became a lay nun, underscores the role of class in understanding the phenomenon of women mystics in early modern Spain. With the exception of Dr. Abrines, who heard the confessions of all the nuns in her convent, her spiritual advisors were less distinguished than those who served women of the upper or middle strata. Her first confessor, Antonio Castañeda, was of hidalgo origin but had served as a soldier before he took ordination and never was accepted into a religious order.

The case for women of lower social origins getting a less eminent group of confessors is even clearer from the biography of Inés de Benigánim, whose two spiritual advisors were both simple curates. Nevertheless, it was perfectly possible for a woman to attract more eminent confessors as her reputation grew. María de Christo, who came from a poor hidalgo family, began making her confession to a simple Franciscan friar, but her last two spiritual advisors, Juan Rodríguez Pastrana and Fernando de San Antonio Capilla, cut much more imposing figures. Juan Rodríguez Pastrana was archpriest of the village of Parra but was also named to carry out a visitation to the entire episcopal see. Her last confessor was a reader of theology who was twice elected provincial for the Franciscan province of Andalusia and became the author of her biography.

Of course, a woman's spiritual advisor could do much more than provide her with a shield against criticism. While a small minority of confessors tried to prevent their penitents from reading devotional works or recording their mystical experiences, twenty-nine or 22.2 percent actively encouraged both their religious education and spiritual writings. In certain cases, encouragement by one confessor went directly contrary to the policy followed by another. In 1645, María de Agreda's regular confessor, Fr. Franciso Andrés de la Torre, left to attend a general conclave of the Franciscan order that was being held in Toledo, leaving her in the hands of Fr. Juan de Torrecilla. Torrecilla, who was an older, less "progressive" individual, strongly disapproved of women writing spiritual tracts and ordered María to burn the recently completed *Mystical City of God,* as well as all of her other writings. She complied instantly and without complaint, but when Andrés de la Torre returned, he made known his strong displeasure and ordered her to rewrite the book from memory.[68]

The multiple levels of support for women mystics revealed in the biographies and autobiographies go far to explain their successes in the Spain of the early modern period. Such support, as has been demonstrated here, even extended to the Spanish Inquisition, the chief normative institution functioning to guard society against all forms of religious belief or action that might threaten the faith. Direct support by individual inquisitors, as well as by secretaries and theological consultants to the several tribunals and the Suprema itself, made nonsense of any pretense of objectivity toward the phenomena of women mystics. But the Holy Office, like the rest of Spanish society, did have a crude conception of the kind of person likely to be favored with genuine divine communication. Analysis of a group of women accused of "false sanctity" before the bar of the Holy Office will shed considerable light on inquisitorial presuppositions and is a first step in understanding how the formal criteria handed down from the Middle Ages were supplemented and modified in light of the experience of the tribunal.

5

Sainthood Denied

The most fundamental difference between the group of women mystics whose lives were the subject of officially approved biographies or autobiographies and the women who were arrested by the Holy Office on charges of "false sanctity" concerns social status. While 70 percent of the approved women mystics came of aristocratic families, none of the "pretended" mystics could boast of social status greater than that of having a husband who was a struggling commission merchant. The highest percentage among the "pretended" mystics, 58.3 percent, came from the ranks of urban artisans, a group completely unrepresented among the "officially approved," while at the bottom of the social ladder, are 25 percent from peasant families, a figure considerably higher than the 16.7 percent found among the "official" group.

Even among the higher status merchants and artisans, however, there are signs of grinding poverty. With one brother practicing medicine in Madrid and another serving as a high police official attached to the Council of Castile, María Batista certainly could boast of better family connections than any of the other women in the group of "false mystics." But, according to testimony by witnesses brought before the Inquisition in her case, she lived a hand-to-mouth existence because her husband, a commission merchant, was crippled and frequently ill, and therefore they had no steady income. It was she, according to the testimony of her neighbor Isabel Hernandez, who had to find jobs for her husband, but even when he had a commission, he frequently brought nothing home.[1] Nevertheless, according to the inventory of her possessions that was taken on April 6, 1639, she was undoubtedly the wealthiest woman in the group of "false mystics" because it listed such luxury items as twelve oil paintings depicting the passion, pictures of St. Francis and several other saints, and a portrait of King Philip III. The family also possessed an adequate amount of furniture, including beds, writing tables, and chests of drawers, as well as clothing and kitchen implements. In addition, the tribunal's officers were able to lay their hands on 38½ reales in ready cash.[2]

In spite of her material possessions, the evidence suggests that María depended heavily on regular contributions of money and food from wealthy individuals at court who were convinced of her saintly life and spiritual powers. At her trial D. Diego de Cardenas, a member of the Council of War, and his wife, Ana Francisca de Portugal, testified that they gave her both money and food on a regular basis.[3] Another supporter, María de Butroni, the wife of a Genoese merchant, pledged to give María Batista a loaf of bread every two weeks after she had successfully predicted the end of an attack of gout that had incapacitated her husband.[4] The fact that the Holy Office accused 41.7 percent of "false" mystics of seeking to obtain material benefit from their saintly reputation indicates that for María Batista, like others in the group, mysticism may have been at least partially a survival strategy when more orthodox economic options were becoming increasingly limited. Nevertheless, those who receive charity may come to resent it, and María Batista risked losing one of her most important supporters when, after he had given her thirty reales, she remarked to D. de Cardenas that "those who betrayed Jesus Christ were given the same amount."[5]

The significance of social status in supporting or endangering the reputation of a woman mystic is very clearly illustrated in the case of Catalina Ballester. Catalina was a skilled shirtmaker from the village of Falaniche on Mallorca, where her husband was a weaver. When her husband died, Catalina experienced a kind of religious "conversion," and bringing both of her children before an image of the Virgin Mary, she begged her to take them under her protection. After doing this, she cut off her hair, took a vow of perpetual chastity, and joined the third order of Franciscans. She also began having visions, and in one of these, Christ taught her about mental prayer, and it seemed to her in that moment that the entire material world had disappeared and that there was nothing except God and herself. She also acquired a modest spiritual reputation in the village, and some people began saving items associated with her as relics.[6] All of this came to an end, however, after she quarreled with several of her neighbors and was accused of stealing. Fearing the impact on their reputation, the other members of the third order forced her to resign.

Although Catalina had been left an estate of two houses and a small piece of land valued at about two hundred *libras*, the income was not sufficient for her to support her family, so she decided to relocate to Palma, where she could ply her trade more profitably. Once in the city, she was fortunate enough to take as her spiritual advisor the widely respected prior of the charity hospital, Dr. Miguel Anglada. When Anglada died, leaving her fifty *libras* in his will, he was succeeded as her spiritual advisor by Dr. Juan Fuster, a canon of Palma's cathedral and a descendant of converted Jews. After witnessing several of her trances, Fuster became convinced of her spiritual powers, and it was he who convinced the pious Morlana sisters to take her into their home. Fuster also gave her money on numerous occasions, and, as her reputation as a mystic continued to increase, she also received money from the Morlana sisters and several wealthy and aristocratic women, including Doña Juana Juliana.[7]

Quite obviously, Catalina Ballester was using her spiritual reputation as a way of improving her lot both financially, through the contributions of supporters, and socially, by associating herself closely with persons of superior social status. But her very success acted to undermine her position. Carried away by her newfound prosperity and with no living expenses to be concerned about, she began spending money on finery, and this attracted unfavorable attention when she returned to the village to visit her family. In testimony that he gave before the tribunal, Juan Suñer, a local benefice holder, recorded his astonishment at her velvet hat festooned with flowers, elegant gloves, and veil. Such attire caused a sensation in the village, where she had always struggled just to make ends meet. Suñer himself was deeply shocked and testified that such dress was inappropriate because she was nothing more than an ordinary woman who supported herself by working with her hands, while "her dress was that of a great lady."[8] Even her own sister-in law Margarita Benimelis was outraged and told her that this finery was hardly appropriate for someone of her station who had "gained such a reputation for virtue."[9] Needless to say, both Juan Suñer and Margarita Benimelis turned up as witnesses for the prosecution when the Inquisition tried Catalina Ballester on charges of false sanctity.

Because the Inquisition itself was a deeply conservative institution that supported the principles of subordination and hierarchy, it would be surprising if its judges and officials did not share the feeling that Catalina Ballester was violating social norms by dressing in such finery. This social prejudice came out openly when the tribunal's prosecuting attorney asked Dr. Jaume Vanrell, one of her former spiritual advisors, if he did not "take it as scandalous that a woman of low condition and a seamstress should go about wearing a habit finer and more expensive than other *beatas* of gentler birth and greater wealth and quality."[10]

Dressing in a way inappropriate to her social status was a warning flag that something was not right about a woman pretending holiness. Not only did it seem to violate the norms of a divinely ordained social order but also it revealed a strong and unseemly interest in the material world that by itself would have been sufficient to invalidate a woman's claim to be leading a spiritual life.

As any social scientist or student of social movements can attest, poverty— or, perhaps more accurately, relative deprivation—can radicalize an individual. Francisca de Avila, who later took the name Francisca de los Apostoles, the daughter of a once-prosperous painter, was born in the village of Noblejas near Ocaña. Evidently her father had an excellent reputation in the region because she stayed for some time in the palace of Doña Francisca Sarmiento, who owned the village.

When she was sixteen, her family migrated to Toledo, where they failed to prosper. Francisca never married, probably because she lacked a sufficient dowry, and by age thirty-six, when she was denounced to the Holy Office, she was leading a small *beaterio* inhabited by fourteen or fifteen women who had pooled their resources while retaining certain private possessions. Within the *beaterio*, which followed the Jeronimite rule, the *beatas* had set up three altars, held processions, venerated an image of the child Jesus, and had numerous visions, which they recorded and placed on the altars. They slept dormitory style and gained a livelihood through dressmaking and needlework. They also had acquired a spiritual advisor in Miguel Ruiz, a benefice holder attached to Toledo's charity hospital. Ruiz not only heard the confessions of all of the *beatas* but also allowed them to come to the hospital chapel to hear mass and take communion. All seemed well within the *beaterio*, and when the vicar-general of the archdiocese made a visitation, he was favorably impressed by the altars and the intense religious life led by the *beatas*.

But beneath the placid surface of life in the *beaterio*, tensions were escalating that were to eventually lead to Francisca's arrest by the Holy Office. For one thing, its occupants were really frustrated nuns eager to enter one of Toledo's numerous convents but unable to do so for lack of money. The attempt to establish a monastic routine in the *beaterio* did not satisfy everyone, and Francisca petitioned the ecclesiastical authorities for the right to have mass said within the *beaterio* and permission to do charity work, help the sick, and teach poor children how to read. These requests to enhance the status of the *beaterio* were ignored, however, and an increasingly frustrated Francisca began having visions in which St. Peter appeared before Christ to demand punishment for the ecclesiastical estate because "while I followed you poor and naked they go overburdened with revenues and sin."[11] Basing herself on another vision, in which Christ urged the abandonment of material things, she demanded that her *beatas* give up all of the personal property that they had brought with them.[12] Since a lack of material wealth had frustrated the desires of all these women for marriage or monastic life, a radical rejection of the world seemed in order, but Francisca's demand unleashed a wave of protest from the other *beatas* and contributed to her arrest by the Toledo tribunal.

Deeply chagrined by being brought before the Inquisition, Francisca failed even to present a defense and was forced into a humiliating abjuration in which she had to admit that her visions had been of demonic origin.[13] Another woman had been silenced, but male-dominated society had been given a useful lesson in the effects of frustration about not being able to enter monastic life. Unfortunately, no one was listening, and the disappointment felt by women, endlessly propagandized about the virtues of religious life but denied entry into convents because of poverty, was all the more acute because they had so few other options.

In a society increasingly defined by aristocratic values and a hardening of the barriers to social advancement, the mere fact of belonging to the popular classes while claiming superiority in spiritual and religious life was enough to engender suspicion among one's own friends and neighbors. The possibility always existed that all the individual really wanted was to escape from a life of drudgery and live off others. Even for someone as astute as Catarina Ballester, who had many followers among Palma's elite families, there were always detractors who were all too willing to tell their story to the Holy Office.

But poverty or straitened circumstances had subtler, longer lasting, and more insidious effects that increased the danger to the woman mystic. For one thing, lack of means meant fewer opportunities for the woman to learn to read and write. Unlike the "official" women mystics, the overwhelming majority of whom were literate and some of whom became authors of spiritual biographies or works of devotion, 41.6 percent of the group tried by the Holy Office were either illiterate or semiliterate.

Illiteracy could be an enormous psychological burden, especially for a person like María Cotonilla who dreamed that somehow, magically, she would become able to read. María admitted to her friend and supporter Puiteria Sánchez that "all of her life she had wanted to learn how to read." She also told Sánchez that on one of her voyages to heaven she had been permitted to view certain glass tablets with letters written on them in gold, and in so doing she had learned her ABC's.[14]

The inability to read, combined with the poverty of most of these women, meant less exposure to the works of devotion and instruction (like catechisms) that could have formed their beliefs along the lines of Catholic orthodoxy. Only 33.3 percent of the "false" mystics had exposure to devotional works of any kind and, with one or two notable exceptions, that exposure meant a very few books. Even Francisca de los Apostoles, who had attended convent school as a boarder for eight years, had only a Roman catechism, one or two treatises on charity, and a prayer book when she was arrested by the Holy Office in October 1575.[15]

Confronted by sharp questioning on theological or biblical points at their trials, some were forced to admit their ignorance. At her trial in 1639, María Pizarra responded to the prosecuting attorney's accusations by admitting that she "knew nothing about Holy Scripture."[16] Even Francisca de la Santissima Trinidad, who was a nun, suffered from a lack of religious education. After interviewing her in her convent at the request of the Toledo tribunal, *calificador* Gerónimo de Ribera concluded that her knowledge of the most basic elements of Roman Catholicism was no greater than that of a child. Such ignorance, he remarked pointedly, was just the opposite of what could be expected of a person who was receiving divine communication.[17] In addition to her lack of basic knowledge, Gerónimo de Ribera and Gabriel de Morales, another *calificador* who was sent to interview her, commented on her ignorance or misunderstanding of the meaning and significance of baptism, the Trinity, and the incarnation.

Even the better educated "false mystics" subsided into confusion when confronted by an inquisitor in open court. In spite of the fact that María Antonia Hortola was literate, had read several hagiographies, and even knew a few words of Latin, her religious education was also seriously deficient. In response to questioning from Valencia's inquisitor Joseph de la Rassa Cassio, she was unable to explain the difference between meditation and contemplation and, in her confusion, was forced to say that she knew nothing more than that it was good to reflect upon the passion and sufferings of Christ as often as possible.[18]

With reduced access to the devotional works and catechisms by which the Counter-Reformation church wished to spread its message and educate the laity in Catholic orthodoxy, devout women from the lower classes were even more dependent on the support and guidance of their spiritual advisors than were their counterparts from the social elite. Unfortunately, this way of closing the educational and cultural gap between rich and poor was made extremely difficult by what can only be described as a maldistribution of confessional resources along class lines. If the "approved" woman mystic could count on having an average of four spiritual advisors during her lifetime who were fixed and heard her confession over long periods of time, many "false" mystics had a tenuous and difficult relationship with their confessors.

The experiences of Juana Batista, the illiterate daughter of a shoemaker, may be taken as typical of the experiences of many lowerclass women. Juana mentioned a total of seven confessors at her trial in 1636 but did not have more than occasional and rather superficial contact with any of them. In fact, her relationships with the men who were supposed to act as her spiritual advisors were so perfunctory that she failed even to remember the names of three of them. At her trial, she commented bitterly that she had changed confessors so often because "no one cares about the poor" and that they would usually mock her when she told them of her visions or tried to recount her spiritual life. She illustrated the offhand way that her confessors treated her with the example of one Fr. Vicente. One day when she entered the church of St. Peter Martyr, where Vicente had heard her confession on numerous occasions, she brought a bouquet of flowers that she intended to lay at the feet of a statue of the child Jesus. Fr. Vicente, who was present when she entered, told her to give the flowers to a woman friend of his who happened to be there. She obeyed, but then when she asked if he would hear her confession he refused. Furious, she told him that she would find someone to hear her confession, at the local Jesuit college and then stormed out of the church.[19]

But Juana Bauptista's relationships with other confessors were much the same. The Carmelite Gil Badillo who served as her confessor for several months had little respect for her and made light of her visions. On one occasion, when she told him that she had seen the image of the Virgin Mary suddenly fly out of a painting, he said that he was glad she had told him "so that people could throw stones at her and call her crazy." In all, five of her seven spiritual advisors openly rejected her visions, and several told her to be quiet about them as they might cause her to get a reputation as a madwoman. They were also extremely reluctant to hear her confession. Not only did she have to leave Fr. Vicente because of his attitude but also she had to beg her most distinguished spiritual advisor, Fr. Paulino de San Joseph, who was provincial of his order, to continue hearing her confession after telling her that he intended to quit.

The disdain and neglect that many of these women experienced at the hands of their spiritual advisors gave rise to feelings of anger and resentment that they could not possibly express openly. María Antonia Hortola, the impoverished daughter of a potter from Benisa in Valencia, was so infuriated at

Fr. Juan Ortiñana for abruptly refusing to hear her confession that she had a dream in which she saw him suffering the torments of hell.[20]

Perhaps the most striking and important difference between the two groups of spiritual advisors was the fact that 90.6 percent of those who heard the confessions of the "false" mystics belonged to a different religious order. As I have shown, support from the religious order was crucial to the reputation of a woman mystic both during her lifetime and after her death, when the order would frequently support canonization. Often, the woman's confessor determined the order's response to her. Through his contacts in the order, he made her reputation for holiness known. He also was instrumental in building up the dossier that the order needed for the canonization process. A strong association with her religious order, moreover, could provide a woman with some protection from the Inquisition, since most of the judges were members of an order and would therefore be loath to damage its reputation.

Sexual and emotional ties between confessor and penitent also served to complicate an already difficult situation. Such ties not only opened the priest to a charge of solicitation but also could cause jealousies among a woman mystic's other supporters that might leave her exposed to denunciation. This was doubly dangerous because, in so many cases, the links joining her entire network of supporters were that they frequently made their confessions to the same person. The stability of the network itself was called into question when the smooth priest-penitent relations upon which it depended was disrupted by jealousy or resentment.

Isabel de Morales, a wealthy widow who was one of Isabel de Briñas' most devoted supporters, was completely alienated after seeing Briñas sitting on her confessor's lap one day when she visited her at her home. She also testified that during most of her visits Confessor Domingo Daza would be present. As soon as he got there, Briñas would excuse herself and the two would go to another room, while Daza's companion, a friar from his own convent, and the rest of the guests would remain outside. Shocked at the way this attractive thirty-year-old would receive her spiritual advisor, Isabel de Morales turned from fervent supporter to prosecution witness for the Inquisition.

Manuela Ramos, a *beata* who was married to a comfortably off merchant somewhat older than herself, celebrated second nuptials with her confessor, Francisco Fernandez de Villegas, after experiencing a vision in which she was informed that they were destined to marry.[21] Even though Manuela denied the charges of illicit sexual relations with her confessor, another witness testified that they carried out their trysts at his house on numerous occasions. Her obvious interest in sex and her relationship with her confessor did not escape the notice of her neighbors, one of whom denounced her at her trial for her "filthy and suggestive conversation."[22] When Manuela was sentenced by the Toledo tribunal on September 27, 1711, she was told specifically to have no further contact with Villegas on pain of excommunication and other penalties.

Some "false mystics," whose illiteracy and poverty barred them from access to books that could have provided a religious education, were fortunate enough to have spiritual advisors who were willing to share their knowledge. María

Pizarra had a very close relationship with her confessor Francisco Camacho. In his testimony at her trial in 1638, Camacho recalled that he would regularly share with her the content of sermons that he had heard in the local churches. In this way, Pizarra, who was illiterate, was able to acquire a considerable degree of sophistication in the terminology and formulas of Catholicism, which she put to good use in articulating her visions and speaking to her followers during her numerous trances.[23]

However, a woman who had a tenuous relationship with spiritual advisors who either were unavailable, failed to take any real interest in her, or lacked the education and training to advise her properly was going to be left largely to her own devices as far as her religious life was concerned. Juana Batista told her inquisitors that although she took communion daily, it was frequently without confessing beforehand either because she did not have a regular confessor or because her confessor was not available. When asked by whose authority she received communion if she could not consult with a spiritual advisor, she replied that although she had had some anxiety, Christ had appeared to her and ordered her to take communion regularly, even without making confession.[24]

Of course, a woman whose spiritual advisor was inexperienced or poorly educated could not expect to acquire through him the religious training that she missed by being illiterate. In testimony before the Holy Office, María Cotonilla revealed that for some individuals the much vaunted mental prayer that was stressed during the Counter-Reformation could turn into little more than a mechanical exercise empty of spiritual content without the guidance of a competent spiritual advisor. María practiced two hours of mental prayer nightly, but when asked what she meditated on she replied that she thought about nothing but simply "stayed there and kept her place." Incredulous at her reply, the inquisitor then asked her what her confessor had told her about mental prayer. Astonishing the inquisitor still further, María replied that since her confessor had had no experience in leading such prayer, he could not help her and had not answered her questions about it.[25]

Because, in so many instances, the relationship between lower-class women and their confessors was so tenuous and unsatisfactory and the women's own poverty and lack of educational opportunities made it impossible for them to gain a complete and thorough understanding of church doctrine, they could easily fall into doctrinal error. It is not surprising to find that unlike the "approved" women mystics, who were renowned for their orthodoxy, one-third of the women accused of false sanctity were also cited for uttering heretical propositions, one-quarter were accused of superstition, and 16.7 percent were said to have been deceived by the devil.

Unorthodox visions and revelations played a significant role in Francisca de Avila's condemnation by the Toledo tribunal after a trial lasting almost three years. Predictably enough, the tribunal's theologians were unfavorably impressed by her visions, in which the clergy were condemned by Christ for their materialism and corruption. They also could hardly be expected to accept her prophecy that all sinners were to die at the beginning of the following year.[26] They also accused her of uttering a heretical proposition when she declared that physical mortification was "meant only for beggars."[27]

María Cotonilla's trouble with Catholic orthodoxy really stemmed from the fact that a considerable part of her standing in Colmenar de Oreja depended on telling the townsfolk the fate of the souls of deceased children or other relatives. To maintain her reputation, she had to make up wilder and more improbable stories that engendered doubts even among her otherwise credulous neighbors. When brought to the attention of the tribunal through the testimony of witnesses, these statements immediately raised concerns about her orthodoxy.

One of her most improbable and theologically incorrect statements was that the souls of all deceased infants had to pass through purgatory on their way to heaven in order to expiate the pain that they had caused their mothers during pregnancy.[28] She also told a suicide's mother that her son was currently in purgatory, a statement in clear violation of the church's position that suicides were condemned to hell. Claiming that she had the power to intercede successfully with God in favor of souls, she told her neighbors that she had even been able to remove a soul from hell and placed it in purgatory, a clear impossibility according to Catholic theology because hell was a permanent state of affairs and responded to God's inexorable choice.[29] Even more dangerous from the tribunal's point of view was the assertion that when she voyaged in spirit to heaven, hell, and purgatory her actual body was filled by the devil himself, who made confession and took communion in exactly the same way she did. It was this statement, with its implication of intimate collaboration with demonic forces, that caused a real scandal among her neighbors and cost her much of her support. Confronted by this testimony, the tribunal's *calificador* could conclude only that it was all "entirely contrary to what is professed by our Holy Mother church."[30]

In certain instances, the expression of an opinion that was later construed to be a heretical proposition by the Inquisition's theologians was not a product of ignorance but of delusions born of isolation, advancing age, or senility. Such expressions were harmless, but when they came to the attention of the Holy Office they sounded reminiscent of Illuminism, the native Spanish evangelical reform movement, which had been suppressed but not eliminated—or even worse, of the Protestant heresy itself.

When Fr. Sebastian de la Madre de Dios, prior of the Carmelite convent in Manzanares, was given orders to investigate ninety-two-year-old Catalina Ruiz by the Toledo tribunal, he first inquired about her lifestyle and reputation from some of the older friars. Much to his surprise, they informed him that not only had Catalina made her confession at the convent for many years but also she had lived a life of "mortification and seclusion" and was reputed to be extremely devout. Determined to carry out the tribunal's mandate, the prior decided to see for himself and went to her home to interview her. At first he was favorably impressed. Speaking of spiritual matters with her, he found her well informed and concluded, "The Holy Spirit dwelt in her soul." But when he began questioning her about how often she went to church to confess and receive communion, he was shocked when she asserted that God had dispensed her from both sacraments and that she was governed directly by God, who granted her greater favors than she could have gained from taking the sacraments.[31]

These statements probably reflected Catalina's state of physical decrepitude, which led to her being unwilling to attempt the long walk to the chapel to take communion, but they were couched in such a way as to raise an alarm in the minds of the tribunal's *calificadores* Gabriel González and Jerónimo Delgado. Instead of dismissing Catalina as an old lady who was attempting to justify her physical inability to go to church by claiming divine intervention, the overzealous theologians saw the germ of multiple heresies and demonic inspiration. They derived the likelihood of demonic intervention or illusion from her assertion that Christ had allowed her to dispense with taking the sacraments and saw Calvinism lurking behind the statement that God was bestowing great favors upon her outside the sacramental system, since the implication would be that the sacraments were unnecessary to attain grace. As to her complaints about feeling ill after attending church and preferring to stay at home, the *calificadores* considered her pain and discomfort a symptom of demonic intervention to prevent her from enjoying the benefits of being in church, while regarding her desire to remain at home as strongly reminiscent of the heresies of John Wycliffe, who attacked such practices as fasting and midnight prayer as damaging to health.[32]

Fortunately for Catalina Ruiz, Toledo's inquisitors chose to disregard the fulminations of their *calificadores*. Even though Catalina was accused of heretical propositions, suspicion of heresy, and feigning sanctity, the tribunal chose to reconcile her in its chambers instead of exposing her to the public humiliation of an *auto de fe*. After listening to a serious admonition, she was placed under the supervision of its local commissioner, who was allowed to dispense her from having to go to church when she was ill.[33]

Criticism of the Inquisition and its actions was also something that could get a woman mystic into deep trouble. Here again ignorance and lack of sophistication play a role. On the one hand, the officially approved women mystics were always careful to openly express support for the Inquisition. At the same time, women like Francisca Inés de la Concepción were sophisticated enough in their knowledge of theology and the language and practice of mysticism to turn the fact of being investigated by the Inquisition to their advantage. On the other hand, the attitudes of many of the "feigned" mystics to the Holy Office ranged from fear and apprehension to outright hostility.

Criticism of the procedures of the Holy Office was always dangerous, especially for a woman whose reputation for holiness depended on her orthodoxy and acceptance of the authority of the church. When Michaela Trivino, a widow who had a room in the same house where Juana Batista was living, told her that she had witnessed the public punishment of a woman accused of false sanctity or superstition, Juana became enraged and accused the Inquisition of "carrying out its investigations in any way it wished, and freeing those it saw fit." These were very serious charges indeed, and Michaela sprang to the tribunal's defense, maintaining that that its procedures were always "fair and just." She also warned Juana that if the inquisitors became aware of her attitude they would punish her. Instead of taking Michaela's warning to heart, Juana flew into a rage, and they had a violent argument that ended by Juana telling Michaela that she would never forgive her as long as she lived.[34] It is no coincidence that Michaela Trivino appeared before the Inquisition as a witness for the prosecution during the trial. But, even more important, Juana Batista was accused of having obstructed the work and jurisdiction of the Holy Office, a very serious charge that the Inquisition usually reserved for those accused of heresy.

By voicing open criticism of one of early modern Spain's most hallowed institutions—the one that exercised ultimate control over who could or could not be considered a valid recipient of divine favor—the one-third of "sham" women mystics who were accused of obstructing the jurisdiction of the Holy Office had made an error that would prove fatal to their chances. In this instance, a fundamental ignorance about how the Spanish Inquistition functioned undermined these women, rather than any lack of knowledge of theology or basic dogma. But that very ignorance stemmed from the lower social origins of the "false" mystic. Aristocratic women such as Ana de Jesús and even upper-middle-class women such as Francisca Inés de la Concepción knew instinctively that they had to remain in the good graces of the Inquisition because they and their families were much more familiar with the operations of Spain's leading institutions.

But disparities in social status, with all of their accompanying handicaps in education, religious culture, and political savvy, were not the only differences between the "officially approved" women mystics and their "false" counterparts. Equally important is the contrast between the supporters and followers of the two groups. As noted previously, the reputation of the officially approved woman mystic benefited from a multilayered support system. Beginning with her own religious order and members of her own family, the system continued through her confessors and spiritual advisors and those who believed in her virtue and spiritual powers and ended with the authors of adulatory biographies and the censors who were charged with reviewing both biographies and autobiographies for publication.

Any effort to describe the support system enjoyed by the "feigned" mystic has to begin with the fact that it had failed to protect her against the obloquy and humiliation of a trial by the Inquisition. Yet even the "false" woman mystic had a support system that succeeded in sustaining her for long periods of time. Describing the character and extent of that support is in many ways more difficult than describing the support system that sustained the officially approved, but careful analysis of testimony from the Inquisition cases themselves enables the historian to unravel it.

Looking first at the results of analyzing the social status of some 111 supporters, both lay and clerical, that can be identified from the trial records provides a mixed and perhaps even surprising result, especially given the foregoing discussion of the relatively low social status of most "false" mystics tried by the Inquisition. In general, the "false" mystics, like the "official" group had a certain number of supporters (9 percent) among Spain's social elite. Nobles such as Antonio Mexia y Paz, eldest son of the count of Molina and a member of the prestigious military order of Calatrava, were favorably impressed by the exemplary spiritual lives of these women. They fully accepted their claims to be able to communicate with the spirit world and relied on them for guidance in such difficult and problematic areas as predicting the course of an illness or forecasting the fate of the souls of deceased relatives. Mexia y Paz himself was a devotee of the *beata* Isabel de Briñas. He admired her especially for her ability to induce a trancelike state. He believed in her supernatural powers and repeatedly pressed her to tell him if his father would survive a serious illness.[35]

The families of simple hidalgos and caballeros supplied 7.2 percent of supporters. Here again, as in the case of the nobility, admiration for the exemplary lifestyle practiced by the individual led to acceptance of her claim to supernatural power. Isabel de Velasco, a forty-year-old spinster from a reputable hidalgo family, joined a group that said the rosary with Isabel de Briñas after she had sought spiritual advice from her and Isabel had told her to say the rosary with special fervor. She was so impressed with Isabel's inner spiritual life and visions that she asked her for a written record of all of God's special favors to her. Isabel complied with her request, only to take back the account when she heard that she would be arrested by the Holy Office.[36]

She also relied on Isabel's intervention when she became ill. Once, when she had a high fever her physician could not reduce, she asked Isabel to come to her bedside. Isabel complied, and her very presence caused the fever to disappear, much to the amazement of her doctor.

High social status and prominent positions in local communities also made hidalgos excellent defense witnesses. Several local hidalgos testified to the honesty and good reputation of Catalina Ruiz, who had lived in Manzanares all her life. Francisco Oroposa Morales, a hidalgo and long-time resident, knew her well and testified that she lived a life of "singular virtue" and that "everyone took her for a saint."[37] Diego de Saludo, a hidalgo and perpetual city councillor of the town, knew her quite well, and his daughter visited her frequently at home. Don Diego testified that in his opinion she was an "exemplary woman of exceptional virtue," while Blas de Quesada, another local hidalgo, agreed and added that she came from one of the oldest and best local families.[38]

Professional and bureaucratic families at 7.2 percent were also well represented among the supporters and followers of "sham" women mystics. Isabel de Briñas's residence in Madrid, her relatively higher social status and wealth, and the fact that her brother was an attorney meant that she had more contact with individuals with a professional and bureaucratic background and that such persons figured conspicuously among her supporters.

Like many of her more socially prominent followers, Juliana de Castro, the seventy-year-old widow of an official of the *audiencia* of Valladolid, one of Spain's most important appellate tribunals, was introduced to Isabel de

Briñas by her spiritual advisor, the Dominican Fr. Domingo Deza, who also presented Isabel to Juliana's son, Fr. Diego Teran de la Peña. Fr. Diego and his mother were both greatly devoted to Isabel. Diego and his sister visited her on numerous occasions, and his mother gave her both money and food on a regular basis. Juliana accepted without question Isabel's claim to know the fate of souls, and Juliana used Isabel's powers to find out about the soul of one of the family's devoted servants. Informed by Isabel that her former servant's soul was indeed suffering in purgatory, Juliana promptly paid the ubiquitous Deza to say several masses for her.[39]

The families of merchants, financiers, and artisans together comprised 10.8 percent of the supporters of the "false" women mystics. Such individuals ranged from the prosperous banker Pedro María Bibaldo, who was grateful to Isabel de Briñas for her intercession with God in favor of his scheme to cheat the government, to Juana Jiménez, the widow of a merchant who resided with her twelve-year-old niece in the *beaterio* directed by Francisca de los Apostoles. At the bottom end of this group were the wives of humble artisans such as María del Castillo, whose husband was a tailor. María went out of her way to praise Isabel de Briñas when she testified at her trial on March 26, 1639, and felt that she had every reason to be grateful to her because she had used her supernatural powers to cure her family of the plague on numerous occasions.[40]

So far, this analysis of the support enjoyed by "sham" women mystics has shown that they had a relatively large number of followers among the upper and middle classes of lay society. It is when clerical supporters and spiritual advisors are thrown into the balance, however, that we can really see the qualitative differences between the two support networks.

A little more than one-quarter (25.2 percent), of the supporters and followers of the feigned mystics can be identified as members of the clergy, but few had attained any distinction either in their religious orders or as secular clergy. In short—and the significance of this for a woman's political position and social standing cannot be overstated—they were mainly simple friars, nuns, parish priests or benefice holders.

Of course, it is true that there were a handful of abbesses (3.6 percent), among the clerical supporters, but the abbess was normally not an influential figure outside her own convent, and since she was elected by the other nuns for a limited term, she could easily be replaced if she displeased the majority. But this is not to say that an abbess was of negligible importance or that she could safely be ignored. Frequently, the nuns would choose one of their most aristocratic members to be abbess. An aristocratic abbess had political influence outside the convent through her extended family. She could legitimately call upon her family for political protection for the convent and for financial assistance when times were hard. An aristocratic lineage also gave her more influence over the male vicars and officials of the religious order who really made the final decisions about the convent.

The importance of cultivating a politically powerful and socially superior nun who would probably be elected prioress was certainly not lost on Clara

de San Francisco. Because she was the daughter of a shoemaker and therefore despised by some of the nuns in Palma's Bernardine Convent of San
Ildefonso, Clara went out of her way to cultivate several nuns who became
prioresses. During one of her trances, she was heard to cry out, "The mother
abbess is a saint." In this instance, she was referring to Ana María de la
Encarnación, who later told the Inquisition that she firmly believed that Clara
was a recipient of God's favor and averred that "it cannot be assumed that
she is faking sanctity."[41]

Of even greater significance in securing her future was the support of the
aristocratic Magdalena del Sacramento because of her influence both inside and
outside the convent. Clara gained her favor by telling Magdalena that she had
seen her in a vision placed next to the twelve apostles in heaven.[42] Completely
won over by this blatant flattery, Magdalena not only told the Inquisition that
Clara was "an excellent nun" but also became her staunchest supporter in the
convent, going so far as to imprison a nun who spoke against her.

Of course, as indicated previously, the overwhelming majority of clerical
supporters of "false" women mystics were male priests and friars of no particular distinction. One of the secrets of María Pizarra's success as a mystic
seer in the village of Siruela was the extraordinary support she received from
the clergy in the village and surrounding district. This was partly due to the
influence of Francisco Camacho, the local curate and María's spiritual advisor. It was Camacho who welcomed Diego González de Viera, a benefice
holder in nearby Talarubia, into his home, where he could watch María's
extraordinary trances for more than six months. Diego González became a
true believer, participated in saying the rosary with María and Camacho, and
carried back with him the story of María's marvelous spiritual exploits.[43] But
Camacho's influence was also critical in gaining her the support of *alcalde*
Joseph Olivar, the highest royal official in the village. Olivar just happened
to be making his confessions with Camacho, who used every opportunity to
praise María and talk up her supposed supernatural powers. The recently
widowed Olivar inquired about the state of his wife's soul and was only too
happy to pay Camacho to say whatever masses María told him were necessary for her welfare.[44]

There were also a number of simple friars who could be counted as supporters of "feigned" mystics. The *beata* Manuela Ramos, for example, could
count on three friars from Toledo's Carmelite convent, one of whom was her
confessor Fr. Francisco de Villegas.[45]

María Antonia Hortola enjoyed the unstinting support of two Dominicans,
Thomas Guell and Luis Poyo, both of whom served as her confessors. The
two friars, who were both described as credulous and sincere by the master
of novices of their convent, were more convinced of María's spiritual powers than she was herself. Early in their relationship, Guell assured her that
God had conferred the grace of prophecy upon her, even though she told him
that she was unaware that she had any such gift. For his part, Fr. Luis Poyo
told Valencia's inquisitors that she was a "saintly woman." He also gave it as
his opinion that it would be good if she died in the city of Valencia because

then her "holy body" would remain to benefit the city, while her hair could be distributed as relics to surrounding villages.[46]

But the fact is that none of these friars could provide the women with any protection against prosecution because they lacked any significant support among inquisitors and officials. Of 111 supporters (excluding confessors), only three had any connection to the Holy Office. All three were supporters of Francisca de la Santissima Trinidad, and none were inquisitors or secretaries. The three included her confessor, the Franciscan Fr. Antonio de Rivera, who was a *calificador* of the Suprema, a commissioner in a village outside Toledo, and another *calificador*, Baltasar Fernandez, who described Francisca as "a saint" during his appearance before the tribunal on April 20, 1638.[47] None of these men were able to intervene effectively on behalf of their idol, and the one serious attempt to do so, when Antonio de Rivera went personally to plead with Fr. Luis Apacicio, a *calificador* who had been assigned to review the evidence against Francisca on behalf of the Toledo tribunal, was a complete fiasco.[48] The contrast between "approved" and "feigned" women mystics in this critical area could not be more dramatic.

The relatively low status of the "false" mystic's ecclesiastical supporters might have been compensated for if their spiritual advisors had been distinguished by intellectual and academic accomplishments or the offices they held in religious orders and the ecclesiastical bureaucracy. Such was not the case, however, so that once again their support system proved itself to be considerably weaker than those that sustained the officially approved.

Of course, this is not to say that none of the fifty-three spiritual advisors had attained important positions. In fact, six individuals (11.3 percent) were wardens of convents, including Fr. Domingo Daza, Isabel de Briñas's confessor and confidant. Daza also joined eight others (16.9 percent) as a *calificador* of the Holy Office. Daza, who was the only one of this group of confessors to have any connection with the royal court, may have had even greater ambitions for himself. At least he did nothing to discourage Isabel de Briñas from publicizing her vision of him in the robes of archbishop of Toledo or of commissioning a portrait of him in a devout pose.[49] Two of Catalina Ballester's nineteen spiritual advisors, fathers Maso and Mezquida, had also served as wardens of their respective convents. According to Catalina Morlana, one of the most important witnesses at her trial, Fr. Pedro Maso, was so in awe of Catalina Ballester's spiritual powers that he would regularly prostrate himself in front of her and kiss her feet. He even had a Te Deum sung in his chapel when she did something he regarded as especially noteworthy and was grateful to her because he thought that she had miraculously rescued him from a storm at sea.[50]

The position of warden, while not unimportant, had little influence outside a specific convent, and it was the highest that most of the friars among this group of confessors were able to attain. Among the fifty-three spiritual advisors, only one was elected provincial of his order. Furthermore, none of the group achieved the rank of bishop, which stands in marked contrast to the 3.4 percent who were selected to fill those coveted positions among those who heard the confessions of the officially approved women mystics.

The same lack of high position characterizes the secular clergy among the confessors. It is true that two were canons of cathedrals. Don Miguel Esqueba, one of Manuela Ramos's spiritual advisors, was canon in the cathedral chapter of Toledo, one of Spain's most prestigious religious institutions. Catalina Ballester was fortunate in having Dr. Joan Fuster, canon in the cathedral of Palma, as her spiritual advisor. But canon was the highest rank attained by any of the secular clergy. Many were simple parish priests (9.4 percent) such as María Pizarro's confessor Francisco Camacho, or benefice holders (7.5 percent) such as Juan de Mengohechea, who acted as rector of the charity hospital in Toledo.

As if this were not enough, in a country that had an almost exaggerated respect for scholarship, the group who heard the confessions of the "sham" mystics could boast few intellectual attainments. Only two were readers in convent schools, there were no university professors of any rank in the group and none managed to publish any theological works or works of devotion. While nine were *calificadores,* which does indicate an adequate training in theology, their relative lack of distinction in academic life meant that their opinions could be easily discounted by other *calificadores* when their penitents were brought to trial.

If the relationship between spiritual advisors and "false" women mystics suffered from a high degree of tension and instability, the same must be said of the entire network of support, which had a tendency to break apart into squabbling fragments or even turn wholly against the woman that it had once sustained. The inherent instability of the support system made it relatively easy for the Inquisition to find ample evidence it could use to neutralize the supposed "threat" posed by the "counterfeit" woman mystic to religion and society.

Of course, some supporters demonstrated an almost fanatical loyalty, even to the extent of lying to the Inquisition and thereby running the risk of being accused of perjury, a very serious charge with its overtones of protecting heretics. Francisco Cornado, one of Isabel de Briñas's neighbors and staunchest supporters, made a desperate effort to defend her, not only by lying to the Holy Office about her but also even urging another supporter to perjure herself. According to Isabel Morales in testimony she gave on October 25, 1639, Cornado had approached her just before the Toledo tribunal sent its commissioner to take her testimony and begged her not to aver that Briñas was a woman of extraordinary virtue if she were called. But she replied that she could not possibly do that since Fr. Domingo Daza, who was also her spiritual advisor, had affirmed not only that Briñas was virtuous but also that God had chosen her as someone to whom he would "reveal his secrets." Cornado became alarmed at this, saying, "No! No! For the love of God, she will be ruined. . . . You must tell them that you know her as simply a good Christian and not a woman of rare virtue; that you know nothing about her either good or bad."[51]

Denied the political and moral support of a religious order and unable to count on their own spiritual advisors, "feigned" mystics were forced into demonstrating their supernatural powers in very concrete ways that would benefit supporters and their families. It goes without saying that any failure to deliver would redound to the detriment of the woman mystic's reputation. For this and other reasons, the support systems that protected and sustained the "false" mystics were inherently unstable. With more than 26 percent of supporters registering disillusionment with the women they once idolized, it is easy to see that the Inquisition could count on a significant number of witnesses with intimate knowledge of the affairs of the mystic and her inner circle if it ever chose to undertake a prosecution.

Isabel de Briñas had the largest number of followers of all the women (31) and went to the most extraordinary lengths to maintain them. Since many of her followers were widows, she hatched a scheme to found a new convent for them in cooperation with her confessor Fr. Domingo Daza. Because illness and disease were so common among her followers and their families, she and her confessor publicized her powers to cure the sick. The public's tremendous fear of purgatory, with its indeterminate period of suffering before the soul could be released to heaven, created anxiety among the families of the deceased, anxieties that Isabel was all too eager to assuage by reassuring her followers about the souls of their relatives.

But if these undertakings and assertions were essential to maintaining and extending her reputation, her failures in these same key areas created a germ of doubt in the minds of her supporters that eventually made them willing to testify for the prosecution at her trial. Whether or not she and her confessor actually meant to establish a new convent, such foundations faced formidable opposition in seventeenth-century Spain and could not succeed without backing at the highest level. Isabel de Briñas had no such support, so the project came to nothing. Furthermore, Briñas admitted at her trial that in any case she had spent the money that her supporters had entrusted to her for the project. Her failure to make any serious effort to establish the new monastic institution that many of her supporters had contributed to out of their own meager capital created intense dissatisfaction and turned such would-be nuns as Ursula Vazquez and Angela del Portillo into willing prosecution witnesses.[52]

Extravagant and unrealizable promises to found a convent also played a major role in undermining the trust that several of Francisca de los Apostoles's key supporters had placed in her. In this instance, her failure was compounded by the way she built up their hopes by flattering them and making them feel that they were ideally suited to be a part of the new and purer form of religious life that she hoped to establish. This approach worked wonders with her more naive or less well educated followers. When Francisca told María de San Agustin that she "had the face of a saint or a great servant of God," she was extremely pleased and began accompanying her to hear mass at local convents.[53] Ana, a servant in the *beaterio* to whom she had promised entry into the new convent because of her exemplary spiritual life, even had a dream in which she saw Christ seated on a magnificent throne with two empty chairs on either side of him. Christ informed her that the seats "were reserved for my servants Francisca and Isabel," referring to Francisca de los Apostoles and her sister Isabel Bautista.[54]

But not everyone was taken in. When she informed María de Jesús that she would become a nun in the new convent, where she would enjoy a cell hung with silk and brocades, María was a little skeptical, but this daughter of an accountant in the service of the marquis of Getefe was really startled when Francisca told her that she was "more saintly than John the Baptist." Too well educated not to realize that such a remark bordered on the sacrilegious and too well disciplined to commit the sin of pride, she remarked tartly, "Watch what you are saying! I don't believe you because I know I am nothing but a great sinner."[55] Francisca's attempt to gain the support of María and her sister Isabel, whom she compared to Catherine of Siena, had backfired, and María went voluntarily to denounce Francisca to the Inquisition.

The high-risk strategy of building up the self-confidence of supporters and making them believe that they were persons of extraordinary merit who deserved to form part of a splendid new religious community carried with it an additional danger: the possibility that a supporter would lose respect for or even feel that she could replace the leader. This was precisely what happened to Luisa de los Angeles, one of Francisca's strongest supporters. Encouraged by Francisca, who lavished praise on her for her great spiritual gifts, she began having visions in which the success of the new foundation appeared certain. She also assured the other *beatas* that they were all under divine protection so that if they were ever to be arrested by the Holy Office, "the strong hand of God would remove them from there."

Armed with a swelling sense of her own spiritual powers, Luisa soon turned against Francisca and her sister. According to testimony from some of the other *beatas*, she declared that their visions were false and decried the fact that they had so much control over Miguel Ruiz, who acted as spiritual director for the *beaterio*. More ominously still, she began to think of herself as leader. In one particularly grandiose vision, she was informed that she, and she alone, would be the founder of the new convent and that Francisca and her sister would be "disgraced and defamed."[56] Given Luisa de los Angeles's rejection of her leadership, it was only a matter of time before she appeared voluntarily before the Inquisition to denounce Francisca, thereby helping to bring about the very disgrace that she had predicted.

A more traditional way of gaining and holding supporters was to promise to cure their diseases. Isabel de Briñas accomplished this with a certain amount of success by employing special prayers or by "prescribing" concoctions for them to take. When she was called before the Inquisition during Isabel's trial, María de Saavedra, the wife of a small farmer, testified that she had indeed been helped by a powder that Briñas gave her when she was seriously ill. But in something as unpredictable and poorly understood as disease, such interventions could easily fail, thereby doing serious damage to the reputation of the seer. When Francisca de Silva's husband, Francisco de Villagomez Viviano, became seriously ill, she turned to Isabel de Briñas for assistance. Egged on by her confessor, Briñas prayed repeatedly for his recovery but to no avail since he died shortly thereafter, leaving his wife bitterly disappointed. Briñas's failure converted an erstwhile supporter into an eager prosecution witness at her trial.[57]

Isabel de Briñas's reputation with another supporter, María Pinelo, suffered because she guessed wrong about the outcome of a disease. María had heard that the family of someone who was seriously ill had approached Briñas's as a last desperate measure. But when Pinelo asked her if the man would recover, she informed her that in spite of her prayers on his behalf, she had seen him dead in a vision. In this instance, Briñas's reputation as a visionary suffered, along with her reputation as a *curandera,* because, as María Pinelo commented wryly during her testimony before the Inquisition, "It was all a lie and a deception since he is alive and healthy to this day."[58]

Finally, the thing that really served to disillusion many fervent supporters was the woman mystic's failure to live up to the saintly ideal. Fed by the increasing availability of hagiographies, supporters and followers were demanding that the women mystics they idolized demonstrate the degree of control over bodily impulses that they had read about in the lives of the saints. As such fantastic feats as complete abstinence from food and water for very long periods and extremes of physical mortification were obviously impossible, the woman mystic was forced to engage in a variety of tricks to simulate them. Exposure meant that supporters became rapidly disillusioned and disposed to cooperate with the Inquisition.

Clara de San Francisco's reputation among the nuns in her convent depended largely on her claim that she had abstained from eating or drinking for an entire year. It was this feat that convinced most of the nuns and the abbess Magdalena del Sacramento that she was a "saint." Of course, Clara's miraculous fast was actually being sustained by an inner group of supporters who were providing her with food, which she would eat surreptitiously in her cell, after making a great show of vomiting up whatever she was given in the refectory.[59]

In the meantime, Clara's reputation had reached the ears of the bishop, who decided to test her supernatural powers by keeping her confined in a hermitage without food or water. This was a major test for her supporters, and the fact that she was able to endure what became a twenty-two-day ordeal and emerge thin but healthy is a tribute to their persistence and imagination in finding ways to introduce a minimal amount of food into a locked and supposedly secure building. Unfortunately for Clara's future, however, the comings and goings between convent and hermitage could not be entirely concealed. Certain nuns who counted themselves among her supporters but did not belong to the inner circle began to have serious doubts about her. One of these nuns was Catalina de la Presentación, whose father, Francisco Gallegos, had been opposed to her entering the convent. After learning from his daughter that "they brought her eggs and oil" while she was supposedly fasting, Francisco Gallegos decided to denounce Clara to the Holy Office.[60]

The story of Clara de San Francisco's failure to maintain her reputation for holiness and her eventual trial by the Holy Office contains within it all the elements of vulnerability that undermined the "false" women mystics. Clara's modest social origins made her pretensions to spiritual excellence automatically suspect while depriving her of the family support that was enjoyed by such "official" mystics as Teresa de Jesús Vela or Hipolita de Jesús Rocaberti. It is difficult to imagine a bishop ordering an investigation into the extraordinary abstinence from food or the incredible physical mortification claimed for these women because their social status would have protected them from any such indignity, even though their claims were as obviously false or exaggerated. As Clara's position in the convent weakened, she made a last desperate effort to restore it by inducing a young girl who boarded in the convent to claim that she had seen the Virgin Mary in her cell and heard her urge Clara to "have patience in this time of trouble."[61] After the girl retracted her story, Clara lost the support of her abbess, and her prosecution on charges of *fingida santidad* was only a matter of time.

In early modern Spain, reputation was more important than accomplishment, more important than life itself. But reputation depended on complicity, the willingness of others to make one's faults disappear or be forgotten. On a fundamental level, the failure of some women mystics to gain official support and the success of others—the difference between the "sham" and "genuine" saintliness—was similar to the difference between a successful and unsuccessful "purity of blood" investigation for a subject of dubious ancestry. In any genealogical investigation, the procedure used to establish an individual's freedom from Jewish or Moorish antecedents relied heavily on what people could remember about the family. Such memories were highly subjective and vulnerable to influence. The power of money or the political importance of the individual or his family could and frequently did make doubts disappear, but the lack of such advantages could result in a drastic failure of the process of obfuscation, revealing the individual's claims to "pure" Old Christian origin to be false. In the same way, the claims of the mystic, her reputation for sanctity, divine communication, and the like rested on what others said about them. This, too, was highly subjective and vulnerable to manipulation on the part of families, patrons, religious orders, municipalities, and even the crown. It was a woman's failure to mobilize such support and thereby gain a reputation for supernatural power that all too frequently led her before the bar of the Inquisition.

It remains to ask, however, how did the Inquisition deal with accusations against women whose chief crime could be construed as being little more than an excess of enthusiasm? After all, the behavior of the "false" saint was modeled on that of the real saint at a time when the saint cult itself was becoming more popular. At the same time, the Inquisition had to tread warily. The case of the "nun of Lisbon" had demonstrated just how subversive a popular saint cult could become. By its very nature, the "reality" of divine favor bestowed on a particular individual was impossible to prove, but the Inquisition had always worked with probabilities and could draw upon a long tradition of theological writing going back to the early Middle Ages to help it make its decisions.

6

An Uncertain Sword

*The Spanish Inquisition and
the Repression of Feigned Sanctity*

As the fervor for mysticism spread from an elite group of adepts to the popular masses, the church hierarchy and especially the Inquisition became more and more concerned about the problem of fraud. Of course, it was generally agreed that the divine communication a genuine mystic had received could not and should not be ignored. The Franciscan Gerónimo Planes, a reader in theology at the Convent of Jesus Nazarine in Malloca, emphasized this in a work dedicated to differentiating between true and false trances and revelations, which he published in 1634. After indicating several ways in which those who make false claims to receiving divine communication may be discovered, he cautioned spiritual advisors not to automatically adopt a negative attitude toward those of their penitents who told them about their visions and revelations. Instead, the confessor should respond like an impartial judge, neither showing excessive skepticism nor a willingness to believe that might border on credulity. The excessively credulous were "more demonic than the devil" in showing an absurd and inappropriate degree of respect for their penitents that would make it impossible for them to provide spiritual guidance. But confessors who treated their penitents with asperity may have committed an even worse offense by breaking the spirit of a penitent who may have actually been receiving divine communication. The good Christian was obligated to believe in the visions and revelations of saints but could not automatically discard those experienced by ordinary private individuals. In the last analysis, Planes believed that the existence of so many impostors who claimed to enter trances and receive revelations said nothing about the validity of such phenomena. Instead, such widespread fraud probably constituted a plot designed by the devil to discredit belief in mystical experiences precisely because that was the way that "God has chosen to confirm His truth."[1]

Then again, all observers agreed that the church had always been plagued with false mystics whose goal was to secure "applause and approbation out of pride and conceit."[2] The effect of the actions of such false mystics, warned the *calificadores* in the case of María de Legarda, a woman tried on charges of "pretended revelations" in 1648, was to "discredit real virtue and genuine revelations in a manner highly prejudicial to the true faith."[3] Moreover, according to Planes, false mystics are far more common among women than among men. Women experienced the sin of pride much more intensely than men. Because their sex barred them from gaining the esteem of the public through offices and honors, they were tempted to gain it by publishing their own sanctity through visions and revelations that they had "read about in some book or simply made up themselves." Women, he warned, were "the most effective instrument the devil had to deceive men." They would use the power that these false revelations gave them to "rule their husbands and give orders to their spiritual advisors." It goes without saying that such a drastic inversion of sexual roles was to be avoided at all costs. Planes admonished those with responsibility for the spiritual lives of women to be aware of their "natural propensity toward evil" and to "move with prudence and circumspection" when evaluating their visions and revelations.[4]

Papal recognition of the very real dangers posed by feigned sanctity led Pope Urban VIII to issue the bulls of March 15, 1625, July 5, 1631, and July 5, 1634, which were designed to prohibit any worship of saints or martyrs not approved by the Holy See. The 1634 bull vested enforcement power in inquisitors and bishops, but in Spain and its dependencies those confronting difficult cases tended to turn automatically to the Holy Office to resolve the issue.[5]

For its part, the Inquisition showed little inclination to share its jurisdiction over mysticism with the bishops, no matter what papal bulls might say. Ever since the fourteenth century, the medieval and then the modern Inquisition had dealt with a variety of mystical beliefs that seemed to challenge both church authority and public morality. Even Meister Eckhart, the greatest of the medieval mystics, was prosecuted for certain of his ideas, especially his belief that in the eyes of God sin and virtue are equal. In Spain, the *dejados*, who maintained that there could be no sin in anything that came from God, were frequently investigated and punished by the Holy Office.[6]

All across Christian Europe, the late-fifteenth- and early-sixteenth-century challenge to the church that culminated in the Reformation took part of its inspiration from medieval mystics such as Johann Tauler, a favorite of Martin Luther, and the Netherlandish *devotio moderna*.[7] Both the German and Netherlandish schools greatly influenced the development of Spanish mysticism, especially that peculiarly Spanish movement the Alumbrados or Illuminists, who became extremely popular in certain regions of Castile during the early sixteenth century. As manifested in the beliefs of such extremists as the lay preacher Pedro Ruiz de Alcaraz, who was arrested by the Toledo tribunal in 1524, the Alumbrados denied the need for oral prayer as unnecessary to those adept at mental prayer and denounced as worthless such works as charity, sacraments including confession, and suffrages such as the purchase of indulgences. Alcaraz also denied transubstantiation and the existence of hell.[8] After a long trial, Alcaraz was severely punished for holding these beliefs on July 22, 1529.

Alarmed by what appeared to be a threat to the purity of the faith, the Inquisition took a series of measures to repress Illuminism, including an edict issued by inquisitor-General Manrique on September 23, 1525, which spelled out forty-eight heretical propositions commonly held by them. Leaders of the Illuminist movement and the related but more sophisticated Erasmians were either arrested or driven into exile. But the Alumbrados were never entirely suppressed, and the Spanish Inquisition was to confront scattered outbreaks of the movement in Extremadura in 1576–79 and Seville in 1622–24. After the trials in Seville, the Inquisition's heightened concern with mysticism in general, and not just its aberrant manifestations, was demonstrated by the Edict of Grace, listing seventy-six errors attributed to the Alumbrados, including a number that were common beliefs of all mystics, even the most orthodox.

On this occasion, the tribunal's complete disdain for episcopal jurisdiction, which it had demonstrated by not even notifying the archbishop about the edict, gave rise to an interesting memorial. The author, Juan Dionisio Portocarrero, examined the condemned propositions one by one and concluded that many of them were outside the jurisdiction of the Inquisition and were simply matters of discipline and therefore squarely within the province of the ordinary. Needless to say, the memorial had no effect, as the archbishop died shortly after he received it. The tribunal then proceeded to try the cases without even calling a representative of the archbishop to sit on the *consulta de fe,* which determined sentencing. Interestingly enough, the cogency of Portocarrero's arguments brought his abilities to the attention of the Inquisition, which in 1624 appointed him inquisitor of Mallorca, where he made use of his considerable talents as a polemicist to write a book defending the Inquisition against royal jurisdiction.[9]

Certainly the theologians employed by the Inquisition as *calificadores* had no doubt that it should be responsible for evaluating questions related to mysticism, pretended sanctity, or false or doubtful revelations. Francisco de Parejas, the noted Jesuit theologian who was consulted by the Toledo tribunal in the case of María de San Bartolomé, explained it very simply: these cases involved controversial matters of faith that cast doubt on the orthodoxy of the accused. It was therefore up to the Inquisition to set guidelines and make determinations because it had always been responsible for maintaining the purity of the faith.[10]

It was the Inquisition, and only the Inquisition among Spain's normative institutions, that had the accumulated knowledge and experience in dealing with issues of heresy and heterodoxy that would enable it to separate the sheep from the goats among those who pretended sanctity. An excellent example of this ability to make distinctions on the basis of a considerable erudition in hagiography and scripture can be found in prosecuting attorney Dr. Baltazar de Oyanguren's evaluation of Mateo Rodriguez's claims to special favor from God. One of Rodriguez's most important assertions was that he had received the stigmata "in a sweet and pleasing manner" while on a mystical voyage to Jerusalem. Oyanguren exposed this assertion as false on the basis of his own reading of the lives of the saints, none of whom had received the stigmata without experiencing "intense pain."[11]

But proving or disproving claims to specific divine favors like the stigmata by comparing them to the hagiographical literature is relatively easy. Unlike stigmata, which were claimed by relatively few mystics, visions and revelations were extremely common, so common as to constitute perhaps the most important manifestation of the divine favor shown to a particular individual. Here, making distinctions was far more difficult. Among the possible sources of confusion was the issue of what kind of person was likely to receive valid divine communication. Gerónimo Planes thought that he could rule out both the very rich and the very poor. The former, he averred, would pretend to have revelations out of "greed, ambition, or pride"; the latter would pretend to have visions, especially of souls in purgatory, to obtain alms. But it was far less easy to rule out other groups. Even though children who claimed to have visions and revelations could not be trusted because their brains were "excessively humid and full of vapour," the biblical story of Daniel shows that God could infuse children with the wisdom they needed to understand the visions and dreams that he sent them. As far as women were concerned, they were less than ideal recipients of divine communication because of their emotional weakness and greater vulnerability to demonic suggestion, but even Planes had to admit that some especially virtuous and devout women had received the gift of prophecy. In short, with regard to the recipients of valid divine communication, "there was no general rule that did not admit of an exception."[12]

Even more dangerous and confusing, especially from the standpoint of the Holy Office, which was responsible for establishing a set of guidelines by which claims to sanctity could be judged, was the constant activity of the devil in deceiving the faithful. By using the imaginative faculty common to all men and especially lively in women, the devil routinely inspired visions that appeared to be of divine origin but really were designed to serve his own sinister purposes. Such demonic visions were impossible to tell from those directly inspired by God and, according to Gabriel de Morales, a *calificador* in the trial of Francisca de la Santissima Trinidad, the devil had routinely deceived even the greatest of mystics.[13] Juan de Horozco y Covarrubias, whose *Tratado de la verdadera y falsa profecía,* published in 1588, was one of the most influential works in the field, asserted that false, demonically inspired prophets had always existed because the devil has sought to discredit true prophecy. Such contemporary false prophets as Martin Luther, Thomas Müntzer, and Miguel Serveto existed only to "spread heresy and divert mankind from the true faith."[14]

Probably the most serious manifestation of the devil's insidiousness was the way in which he undermined the Inquisition's attempts to exercise its normative function. Theologians were in general agreement that a divine revelation could be distinguished from a demonic one by the profoundly spiritual effects it had on the behavior of the recipient. A demonically inspired vision or revelation would have a negative effect, whereby the recipient would become more materialistic and tend to covet sex, money, or fame. The adept who was fortunate enough to receive a divine communication, however, would become more spiritual, less in love with the body, and more eager to carry out the will of God through good works and acts of personal abasement. Unfortunately, the devil who had proven himself so adept at counterfeiting divinely inspired visions was also perfectly capable of inspiring genuinely good deeds in a fundamentally evil person precisely to lend credence to her false claims to sanctity.

In his discussion of the case of Francisca de la Santissima Trinidad, the *calificador* Gabriel de Morales commented on the one incontestably perfect thing that she claimed to have done: convince two young men to leave secular life and join religious orders. Without denying the value of this accomplishment, Morales cited Martín del Río's example of how the devil had inspired a young woman to become a nun just so that she could disrupt the tranquility of a convent he wanted to subvert. Luckily, the young woman, through her own humility and prudence, realized just in time that she had become part of a demonic plot and refused to enter the convent. In the same way, Francisca's excellent advice to the two young men could have stemmed from demonic inspiration because good deeds might have been a stratagem designed to conceal Francisca's real character and support her undeserved reputation for sanctity. Morales pointed out that the devil's ploy appeared to have worked because, after Francisca joined the Convent of San Miguel de los Angeles, a once happy community had dissolved into "incivility, hatreds and anger; ill will and vile language."[15]

In spite of this uncertainty, the Inquisition had little choice but to rely on standards of evaluation of "genuine" and "counterfeit" mystics that had evolved from the Middle Ages. The long argument that led to the widespread if somewhat tentative acceptance of these standards evolved out of a controversy over the revelations of St. Bridget of Sweden at her canonization hearings during the Council of Constance (1414–17). The two protagonists in this struggle were Cardinal Juan de Torquemada, who took a lenient attitude toward the revelations, and the French theologian Jean Gerson, who tended to be far more critical. Among the Inquisition's *calificadores*, Gerson's two key works *De distinctione verarum visionum a falsis* and *De probatione spirituum* were constantly being cited. Additional sources that the Inquisition relied upon included Martín del Río's famous *Disquisitionum Magicarum Libri* and the works of several Spanish experts, especially Juan de Horozco y Covarrubias. By the early seventeenth century, the Inquisition had even drawn up a set of instructions for its judges, providing them with guidelines for detecting false visions and revelations.

Drawing on these sources, as well as the case law of the Inquisition itself, *calificadores* derived a rough set of standards by which they could evaluate the claims of any person receiving divine communication. The first and perhaps most important criterion was the lifestyle of the individual. The absolute requirement for a life marked by a notable degree of "virtue, chastity, modesty, devotion, abstinence and obedience to confessors" was emphasized in a treatise written in 1620 by Juan de Roa, an Inquisition defense attorney. Roa, who cites a number of the works mentioned previously, declared that if revelations came to such a person and were approved by his spiritual advisors, "they could not be condemned and must be taken as true and not of demonic origin,"[16] but a lifestyle that failed to meet these criteria would disqualify the individual from receiving certain kinds of visions. Although the Dominican Fr. Jacinto Juan, who acted as *calificador* in the case of María Cotonilla, admitted that it was very difficult to make a distinction between true and false visions, he was certain that María was not sufficiently virtuous to have merited the visions that she claimed to have received and therefore must have lied about them.[17]

A second key concept, which went all the way back to Cardinal Torquemada's position at the Council of Constance, was that revelations of divine origin could not possibly contradict the basic tenets of the Catholic faith or even the customs and decretals established by successive popes. Such a revelation, according to Juan de Horozco y Covarrubias, could not possibly be of divine origin because it denied "God's truth as declared by His church."[18] Juan de Roa also observed that to be valid such revelations should also concern something of general utility to Christian society and not simply to the individual who received them.[19]

Finally, since the goal of the false prophet was always to elicit public approbation for prophecies, the very opposite should be true of the person who received a genuine divine communication. According to Planes, publicizing the vision or revelation oneself without clearing it with a spiritual advisor automatically condemned it as false. The surest sign of a valid recipient is a notable reluctance to advertise divine gifts and an appropriate willingness to subordinate their individual's will to that of the confessor. Although Planes leaves no doubt that the divine communication must be made public for the greater good of humanity, it was up to the spiritual advisor and not the mystic to make decisions about where and when this was to occur.[20]

An excellent example of the way in which these standards were applied is provided by *calificador* Fr. Gerónimo de Ribera's evaluation of the evidence in the case of Francisca de la Santissima Trinidad. Relying mainly on Gerson, Ribera began by arguing that the first and most important consideration in judging the divine origin of any supernatural communication was the life of the recipient, which must be both pure and chaste. Francisca spectacularly failed to meet this test because of a very well documented lesbian relationship with her cellmate Ana de Brazandi.

Francisca's life also failed to meet another standard: intense religious devotion, abstinence, and mortification beyond what would be expected from a simple nun. Depositions by many of the nuns, even those who counted themselves among her supporters, revealed that she did nothing more than what was expected of any nun in the convent and even ate meat on Fridays, even though she was not ill. She also failed to demonstrate any pattern of exemplary religious observance. Unlike the overwhelming majority of mystics, Francisca did not engage in any special program of mental prayer, nor did she undertake any exceptional penance or fasting, or lose sleep with nightly vigils in the chapel. The unexceptional nature of her life and her failure to imitate Christ undermined the credibility of her visions. In one of these, which she had announced to many members of the community, she was tied to a cross, and numerous saints came from heaven to cut her bonds and sooth her, but as far as Ribera was concerned the idea that she could legitimately see herself as suffering in imitation of Christ was absurd, given her comfortable life in the convent.

Finally, instead of seeking to avoid publicizing the favors that God was bestowing upon her and subordinating herself to the judgment of her spiritual advisors, Francisca had gone into her trances in front of numerous other nuns and even persons from outside the convent. As if this were not bad enough, Francisca had spoken to those in attendance during her trances, asking them if she should reveal the visions that she was experiencing. Receiving a reply in the affirmative, she would then relate exactly what she was seeing in her visions, much to the delight of her admirers. It was clear, Ribera concluded, that Francisca wanted to publicize her visions and revelations for no other purpose than to promote her reputation for sanctity.[21]

Unfortunately for the Holy Office and the theologians attached to it, the case of Francisca de la Santissima Trinidad was considerably more straightforward than others, where the accused appeared to be imitating successfully the abstinence and physical austerities that were so often mentioned in the hagiographies. In 1635, the entire country was astonished when the Inquisition removed the famous ascetic Sor Luisa de la Ascensión from her convent in Carrión de los Condes and placed her in reclusion in the Convent of the Augustinians in Valladolid, where she was to die nineteen months later. The major accusations against her were false sanctity, erroneous propositions, and a hypocritical faking of extraordinary fasts. The case itself dragged on long after her death, finally concluding on May 23, 1648, when the Suprema decreed that her reputation and memory should be absolved of all charges but that the crosses and other items that she had distributed to her followers, as well as her writings and any paintings or prints depicting her as a saint, should be taken out of circulation.[22]

Such a lenient verdict, despite the testimony of numerous hostile witnesses, was partly the result of a spirited defense of her mounted by the Franciscan order which entered the lists after her death to prevent any damage to its reputation. Faced with the open opposition of a powerful religious order that had furnished it with numerous inquisitors, the Suprema reacted weakly, allowing the appointment of twenty-five *calificadores* from several religious orders, including her own Franciscans, to evaluate the evidence and render a verdict. It also permitted the Franciscans to appoint a defense attorney for Luisa's reputation, an opportunity that they took full advantage of by selecting Fr. Pedro de Balbas, longtime *calificador* of the Suprema and a reader in theology.

Balbas's 1645 memorial, which he dedicated to the committee of *calificadores*, takes many of the traditionally accepted standards for judging the validity of a person's claim to be receiving divine illumination and uses them to refute the prosecuting attorney's accusations. In replying to the charge that her trances and revelations were demonically inspired, Balbas asserted that their genuineness was proven by Luisa's exceptionally virtuous lifestyle in the convent, especially the alacrity with which she attended sick nuns and prepared them for a good death. The positive effects that real divine communication were said to have on the spirit of those receiving them were shown in Luisa's case by her extreme humility. This was demonstrated by the eagerness with which she sought out the humblest and most demeaning occupations that the convent had to offer, even if they were not her responsibility. In fact, Balbas noted, Luisa's disdain for herself was so great that she even lay down in the path of the other nuns and encouraged them to step on her as they passed, even though she had twice been abbess of the convent. Finally, far from becoming enamored of her own body or wallowing in sensuality, as would be expected of someone seduced by demonically inspired visions, Luisa macerated her own flesh and regularly wore iron chains and a crown of thorns during holy week. Beneficial effects such as these left little doubt as to the divine origins of her trances, visions, and revelations. Balbas dealt with other parts of the arraignment, such as the fact that she had advertised the favor she was receiving by distributing crosses and beads that she claimed to have taken to heaven, by claiming, rather disingenuously, that there could be nothing wrong with this practice as it had been approved by her spiritual advisors.[23]

The effectiveness of Pedro de Balbas's defense of the "Monja de Carrión" notwithstanding, the fact that her reputation was reestablished after such a long and arduous proceeding may have more to do with doubts in the minds of the Inquisition's theological assessors about the nature and seriousness of the offense itself than with the difficulties of applying a set of poorly defined criteria. In certain cases, especially where the *calificador* had concluded that the visions and revelations of the accused were demonically inspired, the question of whether the individual could be held accountable for her actions was very much a matter of debate. At the conclusion of a long and highly critical evaluation of Francisca de la Santissima Trinidad, Fr. Gabriel de Morales found that he could not pronounce on her guilt or innocence. His confusion stemmed from his conviction that her fraudulent visions and revelations were the product of demonic influence and therefore he confessed that he had "serious doubts about whether this deception was her fault or not." In the end, he simply called for a rigorous examination of the witnesses in the case and left the final decision up to his superiors on the tribunal.[24]

But the question of culpability would concern only those who were regarded as the victims of demonic intervention, and only a few more than half of the "sham" holy women in my sample were accused of colluding with the devil. The real controversy that affected directly or indirectly all of the accused in these cases was just how seriously the offense should be taken. In addressing the evidence against María de San Bartolomé, the Jesuit Francisco de Parejas was specifically asked to consider whether those who were convicted of false revelations or feigned sanctity should be considered "lightly suspect of heresy." Parejas concluded that it was most probable, given the weight of opinion among the authorities that he had consulted, that María was guilty only of superstition and not heresy. It was superstitious to attempt to demonstrate religious truth by concocting false miracles or revelations, but it was not heresy. False sanctity, if anything, required that the individual intensify her devotions precisely in order to gain a reputation for holiness, and that certainly did not constitute suspicion of heresy. To bolster his position, Parejas cited the fact that in general the Holy Office itself had concluded that such offenders could not be considered as suspect in the faith, although he had to admit that at least some inquisitors felt differently and that some accused were sentenced to abjure *de levi*.[25] The split on the tribunal between hardline inquisitors, who felt that feigned sanctity and its related offenses did constitute some suspicion of heresy, and their more liberal colleagues is confirmed by looking at the sentences of the women in my sample, in which one-third were designated as "lightly suspect" of heresy.

Other *calificadores* in the same case went even further in absolving the accused of guilt. The famous Jesuit theologian Alonso de Andrade spoke for a whole group of Jesuit *calificadores* who resided in the Colegio Imperial in Madrid and had been assigned to review the case. In their opinion, María was guilty of seeking to gain a false reputation as a holy woman to win the good will and esteem of others, but feigning sanctity does not constitute heresy, and she had done nothing to undermine or deny any of the fundamental principles of the Catholic faith. In this respect, Andrade claimed that María was less culpable than those convicted of solicitation or bigamy because they had deliberately distorted the meaning of the sacraments of penance and holy matrimony and were therefore at least lightly suspect of heresy.[26]

But what really lay behind the Inquisition's doubts, hesitations, sporadic enforcement, and weak sentencing in cases of *fingida santidad* is probably best summed up by Fr. Luis de Granada in his famous *Sermón contra los escandalos en las caídas públicas*. Although the entire sermon was dedicated to giving examples of persons with an immense reputation for holiness who fell into disgrace and to discussing the way the public should react to such distressing events, Fr. Luis had no intention of discarding his belief that persons of holy and sanctified life did exist and that the vast majority were loyal servants of God. "It would be wrong," he wrote "to condemn everyone who follows the path of virtue because of the false or feigned sanctity of a few."[27]

Fr. Luis's fervent desire to believe that God could and did choose persons with whom to communicate, thereby constantly confirming and reconfirming the fundamental principles of Catholicism, seems almost pathetic, given the fact that the sermon was written after his own bitter experience with the fraudulent Sor María de la Visitación, the "Nun of Lisbon." But that very desire to believe was shared by many inquisitors, officials and *calificadores,* as evidenced by the numbers who gave favorable censorship reports on the biographies of women mystics or who acted to protect them during their lifetimes. Pious fraud was nevertheless piety and therefore not to be discouraged excessively, even if it manifested itself in ways that were not entirely desirable. The result of this attitude on the cases themselves was to create a bias in favor of the accused among many *calificadores* and judges and to seriously blunt enforcement efforts by the tribunal in the area of false sanctity.

The first three *calificadores* assigned to review the materials in the case of Francisca de la Santissima Trinidad had only her confessor's letter to review, and that letter, which placed blame on the devil for her blasphemies and lewd behavior, could hardly be considered a document from an unbiased source. Notwithstanding this obvious fact, the three *calificadores* took a favorable view of her and simply explained away a number of the troubling issues raised by the confessor's letter. Francisca's filthy language and lewd gestures, which her confessor excused because he claimed that she was possessed, became transformed by the *calificadores* into a positive sign of her election by God since such things were "permitted by God and have been experienced by many saints." They also accepted, without any corroborating evidence, her confessor's assertion that she was extremely humble and did her most to conceal the spiritual favors that God showered upon her, and they concluded by stating their conviction that Francisca was a "great servant of God" and that "God lives within her."[28] Faced with this favorable opinion by all three of its theological advisors, the tribunal had little choice but to suspend the case. At the beginning of 1634, however, enough new evidence had accumulated for the Suprema to appoint Gerónimo de Ribera to interrogate Francisca. His report led to her arrest and reclusion in the nearby Convent of Jesús María. On September 11, 1638, more than two and a half years after her arrest, she was merely sentenced to be admonished in a private session in the convent and assigned Gerónimo de Ribera as her spiritual advisor for the next two years. At the same time, in a clause curiously reminiscent of the case of the "Monja de Carrión," inquisitorial personnel were assigned the task of finding and confiscating the rosaries, crosses, and beads that she had "blessed" and given out to her admirers.[29]

This case and many others illustrate the difficulties experienced by the Holy Office in enforcing the strictures against false snactity in all of its forms. To a certain extent, of course, the Inquisition's problems can be ascribed to a set of somewhat vague and necessarily subjective criteria. What constitutes a lifestyle sufficiently rich in spiritual values as to warrant divine communication was open to debate. The evidence for a given individual's conformity to that ideal depended on the testimony of witnesses, who might take a favorable or unfavorable attitude, based on matters extraneous to the charge. In short, like so many other kinds of criminal offenses in old-regime Europe, with its paucity of objective and scientific methods of proof, *fingida santidad* depended on an individual's reputation and especially on her or his position within the community, whether village, town, *beaterio,* or convent. Any decline in that position, any weakening of the individual in relationship to critical members of that community, and denunciation to a judicial tribunal became a possible way of resolving the conflict. In a very real sense, therefore, the trial of a woman on charges of false sanctity appears to be, at least in part, the outcome of a process of winnowing out individuals who, for one reason or another, failed to make a successful adjustment to their community.

An excellent example of the way in which changing circumstances could drastically undermine an individual's situation is provided by the case of Clara de San Francisco. Despite having numerous enemies and detractors, Clara's position in her convent remained strong because she had the support of two abbesses, Ana María de la Encarnación and Magdalena del Sacramento. Ana María firmly believed that Clara was the recipient of divine favor, and Magdalena was convinced that Clara had the power of prophecy, especially after she successfully predicted the safe arrival in the Canaries of the convent's spiritual advisor Joseph Vaniverde. Magdalena even went so far as to imprison Sister María de San Bartolomé for openly criticizing Clara's claims to sanctity, releasing her only after she made a public apology to Clara in front of all the other nuns.[30]

Clara's luck began to change, however, when Susana de San Esteban, a nun from another convent, was brought in to replace Magdalena del Sacramento as abbess. Obviously fearful of this change of regime, Clara sought to head off the arrival of the new abbess by magical means, using her power as mistress of novices to force them to pray that Susana would suddenly become severely crippled and therefore be unable to take up her new position.[31] Notwithstanding the fervent prayers for her destruction, Susana de San Esteban arrived healthy and energetic at the convent and, after hearing from certain of Clara's detractors, decided that everything she claimed was "a fake and a fraud." Susana then ordered the removal of the bandages that Clara used to hide the "stigmata" that she claimed had been bestowed upon her by Christ. Instead of wounds, however, there was only a little of the dried blood that Clara had used to daub herself.[32] Given the new regime in the convent, which now encouraged Clara's critics to speak out, it was not long before a flood of accusations reached the Holy Office, even from nuns who had been extremely unwilling to testify earlier.

Unattractive personality traits were another thing that could generate enough resentment among others to lead to greater scrutiny of a mystic's lifestyle and beliefs and to eventual denunciation to the Holy Office. The atmosphere of hostility that many of those accused of feigned sanctity managed to create around themselves is shown by the fact that 50 percent could actually name their enemies, something that was extremely rare in Inquisition cases, where many accused had no idea of who had brought charges against them. Even more significant perhaps was that 66.7 percent had had fights or argued with their neighbors seriously enough to alienate them and turn them into potential prosecution witnesses. Ana de Medina, a witness in the case of María Batista, was extremely hostile toward her and went about their Madrid neighborhood calling her a fraud and accusing her (falsely) of having had two illegitimate children by a man she had been living with. But Ana de Medina was hardly an unbiased observer since she admitted to having had a violent falling out with María not long before presenting herself to an official of the Holy Office.[33]

At times the case files are sufficiently rich to indicate a link between a woman's difficult behavior toward her neighbors and symptoms of emotional instability. Periods of mental illness are specifically mentioned in witnesses' testimony in 16.7 percent of the cases in which women were also accused of fighting and arguing with their neighbors. Three of the witnesses in the case of Juana Batista testified that she had had episodes of mental breakdown in which she wandered raving through the streets and even interrupted sermons in the parish church by screaming at the priest. Pedro de Galves, a local artisan who knew her quite well, even linked her periods of mental instability to a change in her character, testifying that even after her recovery she "did not converse as before."[34] Certainly Juana's interpersonal relations were characterized by an extreme unwillingness to forgive anyone who had slighted her even unintentionally, and she named a long list of enemies when she testified before the tribunal.

The indifference or skepticism of confessors and the opposition or downright hostility of neighbors or family members who openly expressed doubts about their supernatural powers caused some of these women to overcompensate by asserting that they were the beneficiaries of extraordinary and even unheard-of divine favors. Such exaggerated claims were dangerous from a theological standpoint and increased the risk that *calificadores* would take a dim view of her case. Evidence presented during María Batista's trial indicated that she had claimed not only that she would become a doctor of the church but also that God would grant her more favors than he had given to St. Teresa. Noting that nothing in her lifestyle would seem to indicate that she had the characteristics of a person chosen by God to reveal great truths to the faithful, all three *calificadores* who reviewed her case for the Toledo tribunal condemned both of these propositions as "imprudent, unfounded and presumptuous."[35]

Such delusions of grandeur, which occurred in no less than 76.9 percent of the cases of "false" mystics, manifested themselves in excessive demands for deference from followers and supporters and left the women open to charges of false pride that a true saint would never display. It was exactly this conclusion that Juan Pardo de Castro, a hidalgo attached to the court of the count of Castro, drew when he heard that Isabel de Briñas had refused to attend the count when he was ill because he had not shown her proper deference. She insisted that he treat her as "Señora," "if not for being a woman then for being the spouse of Christ." Pardo de Castro told the count that she must be a fraud because "true virtue is free of any ambition and pride." Pardo de Castro's anger at Briñas's treatment of his master eventually led to his appearance before the Holy Office as a witness for the prosecution.[36]

Even though Inquisition procedure was highly professionalized and controlled by university-trained jurists, it still depended on the willingness of certain individuals to come forward to make initial denunciations and then upon a much larger number of witnesses who could be called to corroborate and expand on that initial denunciation. Only after receiving the testimony of an average of twenty-one individuals did the Inquisition have its *calificadores* evaluate the evidence in a case of feigned sanctity to see if an arrest was warranted. Receipt of such a large number of depositions before taking action was itself unusual for the Inquisition and is a further indication of its reluctance to intervene in such cases.

Systematic analysis of the testimony of 252 witnesses who provided evidence used to prosecute women for false sanctity reveals some interesting differences between witnesses and accused. The first and perhaps most important of these is the marked disparity in social origins and relative wealth. On the whole, witnesses called by the prosecuting attorney were of significantly higher social rank than the accused, with 7 percent either nobles or hidalgos and 11.1 percent professionals. The women accused of false sanctity however, overwhelmingly the daughters of artisans (61.5 percent) and peasants (23 percent) and were frequently poorer than their parents had been.

The fact that women accused of being false saints came from significantly lower social strata than the witnesses testifying at their trials may not necessarily indicate that the impetus for prosecution came from a higher-class milieu that felt cheated and disillusioned by the behavior and pretensions of these women. While it is certainly true that some prosecution witnesses had a deep sense of grievance against a woman mystic for swindling them and their families and others came from the ranks of disillusioned supporters, the fact that only 22.2 percent came forward without being specifically called before the tribunal or its agents may indicate a certain reluctance to testify against a woman that so many had believed in. The significance of the disparity in social status, therefore, may simply be a function of the fact that Spain's upper and middle classes had a high degree of receptivity to all kinds of mysticism, thereby forming as natural a "market" for the services of the "false mystic" as they did for the biographies of those who were officially approved.

Regardless of the position taken by the *calificadores*, the tribunal was required to send a summary of the evidence to the Suprema in order to receive permission to make an arrest when the accused was a cleric or religious. Such deference to the Suprema had become the rule during the seventeenth century, when the once largely autonomous regional tribunals were brought under an increasing degree of central control.[37] In cases involving most laypersons, however, the tribunals still retained the right to proceed on their own, except where there was only one witness against the accused or when flight was expected. The minuteness of the Suprema's oversight in matters of arrest and incarceration, as well as the dilatory nature of its activity, is demonstrated by its actions in the case of Clara de San Francisco. After sending a summary of the evidence and its recommendation that she be placed in the secret prison to the Suprema on December 12, 1642, the Canaries tribunal had to wait until

May 22, 1644, for a reply. Far from agreeing with the tribunal's opinion, moreover, the Suprema ordered that she be placed in a secluded cell in her own convent and interrogated in the porter's lodge.[38]

After a decision was made to put the individual on trial, the tribunal made use of its agents to carry out an arrest. If the accused lived outside the seat of the tribunal, it employed the agents it had throughout the district to make the arrest. If she lived in the chief city where the tribunal was headquartered, it made use of its own *alcalde mayor*.

Incarceration during the trial could take several forms. In general, a lay-woman was consigned to the secret prison, while nuns were placed in reclusion in either their own convent or another convent in the same city. For Francisca de la Santissima Trinidad, the Toledo tribunal took the unusual step of not just placing her in a different convent but even one of a different religious order, where she was to be interrogated by *calificador* Gerónimo de Ribera, who was appointed as special commissioner.[39] In making its decision, the tribunal was responding to the fact that Francisca's agitation for reform of her own convent had so divided the community that life in her convent had been seriously disrupted.

The Inquisition also made exceptions to its general policy because of the illness or frailty of the accused, in which case she would be placed in a local hospital. After arresting Catalina Ruiz, notary Francisco Martín Barragan wrote the Toledo tribunal that the age and physical condition of the accused made it impossible to send her to Toledo by way of the houses of *familiares* living along the route, as he had been ordered. He took advantage of the local commissioner's offer to accompany her to send her by special coach, and after she arrived, the tribunal ordered her placed in a local hospital.[40]

After a layperson was arrested, an inventory of her possessions was drawn up, and an *audiencia de hacienda* was held, at which the prisoner had to specify any other property she held. Her possessions were placed in the hands of a *depositario,* who held it until the end of the trial, at which time, if confiscation was part of her sentence, he handed it over to the receiver; if not, what was left of it was returned to the accused.[41]

A short time after an arrest was carried out, the prisoner was given her first regular audience. A gold mine for historians, this audience was where the inquisitors established the basic facts about the accused's family, social origins, literacy, and degree of familiarity with the fundamentals of Roman Catholicism. Also at this audience the tribunal invited her to discourse about her life, and from this narrative the historian can learn precious details about the childhood and adolescence of the accused. At the end of the first audience, the accused was warned that the Holy Office did not arrest people without sufficient evidence that they had done or said something injurious to the Catholic faith and was urged to confess the truth.

Before recalling the accused for a second and third official audience, the Inquisition let the "solitude and silence" of the secret prison and her own fears and insecurity work on her conscience for a certain period of time. Several weeks or even months were normally allowed to go by until the prisoner was called back, although she could ask for an audience at any time. At the conclusion of these *audiencias,* the accused was once again admonished to tell the truth, and the third monition ended with the warning that the prosecuting attorney was prepared to present an accusation. The prisoner was informed that it would be better if she would tell the truth before it was actually presented so that she could be given the merciful treatment that the Holy Office was wont to dispense to those who confessed early in their trials.

Throughout these hearings, the inquisitors carried out interrogations of the accused, asking her to clarify her statements or writings. Frequently this questioning was carried on in a spirit of doubt or skepticism and an unwillingness to accept at face value claims of divine revelations or demonic persecution. María Pizarra's tales of physical torture and persecution by the devil were closely questioned by inquisitor Dr. Baltasar de Aranguren, who asked her if anyone was present during these episodes and if they had left any mark on her body. Of course, María could provide only the vaguest of answers, simply replying that anyone who had been present could have perceived the pain that she was enduring only through the expression on her face and that the torture had left no marks upon her body beyond a disease of the liver as a result of them.

Aranguren also questioned her about her claim to have lived for several years without food. The inquisitor was frankly incredulous and told her bluntly that she was a "fraud" and that "the human body cannot live without eating." The inquisitor urged her to tell the truth about her fasting, but Pizarra insisted that she had, indeed, fasted for long periods, although she could not remember if it was for three or five years.[42]

In his interrogation of Francisca de los Apostoles, inquisitor Juan de Llano de Valdes asked her about certain aspects of her visions, especially one in which she said that she had seen Christ holding a folded paper in his hand containing the "divine justice" that would be apportioned to mankind. The skeptical inquisitor demanded to know how she could be so sure of what the document contained if it was folded over as she said. But Francisca was completely unfazed by Llano de Valdes's questioning and declared that she did not have to read the document to know what it contained because God had already declared its contents to her soul.

Llano de Valdes also asked her about the content of certain visions in which she claimed to have seen a procession of celestial beings accompanying God. Warning her that her word alone was not enough without sufficient details, he questioned her as to which saints accompanied God, what they wore, and how they could be recognized. Sensing that the inquisitor was testing her knowledge of the saints and their characteristic dress and insignia and that she might be caught making an error, she deftly parried by claiming that she could not be more specific because during the trance her soul had become so absorbed by an "incomprehensible light" that she did not notice exactly which saints were present in the heavenly host.[43]

Another striking example of inquisitorial skepticism regarding the claims of mysticism comes from the prosecuting attorney in the case of Isabel de

Santa Teresa, who had claimed to have had a series of revelations regarding the future of certain people living in her village. He charged her with faking these revelations since some had proven false but, even more important, because of the likelihood that she could have known in advance about the things that came true because of her large number of local contacts.[44]

For his part, Fr. Gabriel de Morales, who interrogated Francisca de la Santissima Santidad for the Toledo tribunal and then acted as one of the *calificadores* in her case, censured her for feigning trances simply because she spoke to the persons gathered around her and invited them to touch her. Such ostentatious behavior was "inconsistent with the humility and perfection that could be expected if she had really enjoyed God's favor, and could not be observed in the behavior of true saints who were ruled and governed by the Holy Spirit."[45]

Anyone familiar with the biographies of officially approved women mystics will agree that they are full of the most fantastic stories of extreme deprivation of food and liquids, visions with celestial hosts of an unspecified nature, public trances, and mysterious revelations of divine justice. Because their conduct was so remarkably similar, the historian can only speculate as to what would have happened to the reputations of certain of the women mystics who received official biographies if they had been subjected to the kinds of interrogation that those accused of false sanctity had to undergo. Just to give one example, St. Caterina Tomás would frequently go into extended trances during which she would interact with the other nuns in her convent. On one notable occasion, in the presence of the prioress and several of the nuns, she was handed a needle and thread and began to put stitches into a piece of linen with her eyes closed. The prioress, who was astonished at the perfection of her sewing, something that she was unable to achieve while awake, asked her how she was able to accomplish it. Sor Caterina, still in her trance, responded that St. Catherine Martyr and St. Clare were helping her and indicated with her needle the stitches that each had placed in the cloth.[46]

Of course, the officially approved mystics did not have to undergo any such indignity. Protected by their families and firmly supported by their religious orders and spiritual advisors, most were unconcerned about being hauled before the Inquisition. For all of the theatrics during her numerous trances, Caterina Thomás was beatified in 1792 and canonized in 1930, while Francisca de la Santissima Santidad was accused of simulating trances and revelations, dragged through a humiliating trial, and punished by the Inquisition.

Throughout all of this questioning, most of the women not only were extremely reluctant to admit that they had faked the rudiments of sanctity but also continued to insist that they had the powers that their followers attributed to them in the face of an increasingly skeptical tribunal. Even when they were forced to admit the truth, many tried to salvage something of their reputation for sanctity, which was such an important part of the inflated self-image that they had built for themselves. This reluctance to relinquish the idea of specialness and abandon completely the image of sanctity that she had worked so hard to create can be observed at work in the attitude of Clara de San Francisco during her hearings. After admitting that she had fabricated all of her visions of saints, she continued to insist that she had actually seen Christ and the Virgin Mary. She also insisted, in the face of sharp questioning by the tribunal, that Christ had appeared to her and impressed the stigmata on her body. These stigmata could no longer be seen, however, because she had prayed that they be removed. In response to increasing pressure from the judges, however, Clara was forced to admit that her visions were all imaginary and that the stigmata were nothing but a "fiction." Later in the trial, after admitting that all of her heroic fasting was a fraud because she had been able to secrete food that she consumed unobserved, she threw herself on the mercy of the court, declaring that she was a "weak and miserable woman" and that she "regretted with all her heart that she had been an impostor."[47]

For María Batista, the potential collapse of her fantasy world in the face of the skepticism of the one institution universally respected as the arbitrator in matters of faith, impelled her to try one last desperate gamble to convince the inquisitors that she genuinely had the qualities of a saint and mystic. On July 13, 1639, as she was describing a vision of the devil to inquisitor Juan Santos de San Pedro in open court, her body went rigid, her face took on an abstracted expression, and she began to cry and tremble. A few moments later, when she came out of her "trance," the prosecuting attorney asked her what had happened. María informed the court that she had been in the presence of God, who had told her to notify the inquisitors that "our Lord speaks to you from his divinity." Far from being impressed by this message from above, however, inquisitor Juan Santos de San Pedro was furious at María, accusing her of faking the trance, which represented nothing more than a "frantic effort to confirm the humbug that is contained in your writings and that is nothing more than lies."[48]

Immediately after the prisoner's reply to the third monition, the prosecuting attorney presented the accusation, in which the offenses committed by the accused were arranged in a series of articles and presented in such a way as to flesh out the principal charge of feigned sanctity. In the first set of articles, the women were accused of heretical propositions (33 percent), faking revelations (84.6 percent), false prophecy (46.1 percent), and outright fraud (83.3 percent).

A second group of articles were more general and tried to give the impression that the accused's offenses were comparable to those of the heretics and apostates that the Inquisition had combated so effectively in the past. In pursuit of this goal, prosecuting attorneys accused the women of being suspect of heresy (53.8 percent) and protecting heretics (16.7 percent), undermining the free exercise of the Inquisition's jurisdiction, and, perhaps most damaging of all, collaborating with the devil through an explicit or implicit pact (53.8 percent). The fact that more than half of the women were accused of Illuminism or Molinism reflects the Inquisition's underlying concern that mysticism itself had a potentially subversive effect because it tended to support the individual's own efforts to forge a relationship with God and call into question the value of the formal channels of grace mediated by the institutional church.[49]

After the accusation was read out, it was repeated, and the accused had to reply to it article by article without the help of a defense attorney, who was chosen only after this session was concluded. The intense anxiety that many of these women must have felt when confronted with these accusations is reflected in an exchange that took place between Toledo's senior inquisitor Juan de Llano de Vargas and Francisca de los Apostoles when she was required to answer the charges against her. Complaining that Llano de Vargas was so "harsh in his questioning" while she was a "weak and irresolute woman" who feared him "as if he were Jesus Christ come to judge her," she begged him to give her the assistance of a defense attorney because she was afraid that she would be unable to express herself as she wished. In his reply, Llano de Vargas offered the poor frightened woman little comfort, merely remarking that she had to answer the charges "before anything else" and that her replies were meant to help ferret out the truth.[50]

In providing defense attorneys for the accused, the Spanish Inquisition was far ahead of the times, but sadly the quality of the defense and the zeal of defense attorneys frequently left a great deal to be desired. Quite apart from the numerous strictures against overzealous defense attorneys contained in inquisitors' manuals, they were themselves officials of the court and would be unlikely to risk the disapproval of the inquisitors. Some accused persons failed even to offer a defense. The shock of being arrested by the Holy Office, so closely associated in the public mind with rooting out heresy, was so great that some of the accused simply confessed their guilt at earlier hearings and threw themselves on the mercy of the court.[51]

Those women who continued to deny the charges against them even after the accusation had been read out had to accept the defense counsel presented to them by the tribunal. After briefly interviewing his client in the presence of the secretary and inquisitors, a defense counsel then drew up a defense brief. This document could be extremely flowery and filled with recondite marginalia, such as the statement that was prepared for the defense of Francisca de la Santissima Trinidad by Juan Diaz Suelto, a canon in Toledo's cathedral, or simple and straightforward, such as the statement presented on behalf of María Antonia Hortola. Regardless of the form it took or the erudition of the defense attorney, the statement had to deal effectively with the major charges against the accused and not simply make references to her character as a way of demonstrating that she was above reproach and therefore could not possibly have committed the crimes with which she had been charged.

What were some of the ways in which defense attorneys attempted to exonerate their clients? One approach, which was used in the defense of Francisca de la Santissima Trinidad, was to identify her enemies and accuse them of trumping up the charges. Another way of dealing with the charges was to project the blame onto the evil one. This tactic was adopted by Juan Diaz Suelto to defend Francisca de la Santissima Trinidad against charges of using foul language, which was unworthy of a person in religious orders and damaging to her reputation for holiness. According to Diaz Suelto, Francisca could not be held responsible for these foul utterances because they were a result of the demonic torment that God had permitted in order to test her.[52]

Equally important for the defense, the statement had to be backed up by a significant number of credible defense witnesses who supported the general line of argument that it set forth. Unfortunately for Isabel de Briñas, her witnesses failed to confirm the points raised in her defense. The defense statement claimed that she lived a life of exemplary virtue and raised the issue of the prejudice and bias of the witnesses against her.[53] But the defense witnesses proved almost useless in substantiating these key arguments. While several of the witnesses did testify that she was "humble, observant and a good Christian," the majority admitted that they knew her only slightly and could therefore say little as to her character. Even more ominous for the defense, sixteen of nineteen defense witnesses failed to corroborate her allegations of bias on the part of certain of her enemies as the source of her misfortunes.

In contrast, witnesses called by Francisca de la Santissima Trinidad were able to substantiate the defense's most important point, which was to blame the charges against her on a plot by her enemies in the convent. Nuns like María and Lucia de Vargas corroborated her list of enemies and confirmed her charge that they had conspired to remove her from the convent.[54] Moreover, her confessor Fr. Antonio de Ribera, who was made even more credible because he was a *calificador*, testified about her exemplary life of physical mortification, fasting, and helping the poor and sick.[55] One of the nuns even proved that her plans to reform the convent's dress code were actually in accord with tradition and testified that her enemies burned the rule book when they found out that it supported her position.[56]

How much difference did any of this make? The answer seems to be very little indeed. In most trials, the guilt of the accused was decided by the judges and the Suprema long before the defense statement was ever presented. This impression of the irrelevance of the defense is confirmed by the sentences handed down in the cases of Francisca de la Santissima Trinidad and Isabel de Briñas. Tried by the same tribunal, roughly at the same time (1636–38) and (1639–41), and accused of virtually the same offenses, they were given almost the same sentence even though, by any measure, the defense offered for Francisca was far superior to the one offered for Isabel.

However surprising this may be to the modern reader accustomed to the American courtroom, with its contest between two equally matched sides, neither prosecution nor defense played the same role in the courtroom of the Inquisition as they now play in the criminal courts of the United States. Both attorneys had purely formal functions, the one to draw up and present a well-ordered set of charges and the other to provide a semblance of fairness and representation, but the Inquisition trial remained firmly under the control of the judges, who carried out interrogations of both prosecution and defense witnesses and decided on the admissibility of evidence. The guilt of an individual brought before the Holy Office had already been determined because, as the inquisitors never ceased to declare in hearing after hearing, no one was arrested without cause. None of the cases in my sample was suspended, and woman was absolved for lack of evidence. The real issue was the degree of guilt, and that was for trained jurists to consider. But in evaluating the guilt of the accused and especially in assessing punishment, the provincial inquisitors had to defer to the judgment of their superiors in Madrid, since the Suprema had to confirm all sentences and did not hesitate to change those handed down by the tribunals if doing so suited its purpose.

Once the defense concluded its phase of the proceedings, which could be done either after the presentation of a defense statement, as in the case of María Antonia Hortola, or after a list of defense witnesses had been interviewed, the case entered its concluding phase and was ready for judgement. Instead of deliberating alone, however, the inquisitors called in a representative of the bishop of the offender's diocese and sometimes certain law or theology graduates called *consultores*. Called the *consulta de fe*, this committee arrived at a sentencing recommendation that was forwarded to the Suprema for review.

It is perhaps an indication of the serious concern that the Roman Catholic church felt about the excesses of mysticism during the early modern period that 41.6 percent of the "feigned" mystics were termed "suspect" or "lightly suspect of heresy" in the final sentence. In most cases, it is difficult to see why this designation, which was normally reserved for the hated Judaizer or Protestant heretic, was ascribed to a woman whose chief faults may have consisted of little more than vanity or excessive zeal. But the female mystic, however orthodox her beliefs, could pose a threat to a male-dominated church unless she kept her ambitions very much within bounds and accepted the status quo. One of the keys to the widespread support that St. Teresa received from the male-dominated political and religious establishment was certainly the fact that the order she founded followed a regimen of strict claustration from the very beginning. To avoid even the possibility of criticism, she even went so far as to refuse to undertake the education of girls within the walls of her convents, unlike certain other newly established orders of women.[57]

But when Francisca de Avila took the name Francisca de los Apostoles and began talking about visions in which God spoke angrily against male clergy or named the other women in the *beaterio* after the apostles and told them that they were destined to lead the reform of a corrupt church, it was too much for the tribunal. As one of the *calificadores* in her case wrote:

> giving the names of the apostles to these women and leading them to believe that they would be carrying out the office of St. Peter and the rest of the apostles is heretical . . . because it involves imparting the function of St. Peter and the other apostles to women.[58]

On the whole, though, actual punishment of offenders in cases of *fingida santidad* was fairly light, especially considering the way the Inquisition dealt with Judaizers, Moriscos, or Protestants. Even the women who were designated as suspect of heresy were not punished with any exceptional harshness although, unlike the others, they were sentenced to be scourged through the streets, which was both painful and humiliating. Those whose offenses seemed less serious were merely admonished (58.3 percent) in a private ceremony and, like the elderly and infirm Catalina Ruiz, sent back home to undergo a regimen of spiritual instruction. Sometimes if the *consulta de fe* or the Suprema felt that the woman's vanity had been stoked by being allowed to take communion with excessive frequency by her spiritual advisors, the sentence was very specific about how many times she could receive it. In the case of María Pizarra, whose confessor Francisco Camacho had allowed her to take communion on a daily basis for the last three and a half years, the Suprema ordered her not to receive it more than three times a year. Furthermore, to humble her even more, it was ordered that the sentence be read out in her home village of Siruela.[59]

In general, the way the Inquisition dealt with women accused of false sanctity was right in line with its treatment of the other minor offenses not involving heresy with which it became increasingly concerned after the Council of Trent. By the 1620s and 1630s, instead of dealing almost exclusively with religious and ethnic minorities like converted Jews and Moriscos, the Inquisition dealt mainly with the offenses of the Old Christian majority. In this new role, the Inquisition's task was not the physical elimination or forced assimilation of obdurate ethnic or religious minorities but rather the removal from popular culture of anything superstitious, immoral, or unorthodox. From the standpoint of the Counter-Reformation church, the mystical transports of women were to be encouraged as long as those women trod the path of orthodoxy. The mainly lower-class women who ran afoul of the Inquisition were operating in a gray area that made them vulnerable to an increasingly repressive hierarchy. Unfortunately for them, they also lacked the support of powerful religious orders and influential spiritual advisors. The very fact that criteria for judging the veracity of any claim to exceptional spiritual favors was necessarily vague and subjective made it imperative for the Inquisition to establish a body of case law that would serve to set limits to the phenomenon of female mysticism. An example had to be made, and these women were not only available but vulnerable. The fact that actual punishment was not especially harsh merely demonstrates that the main thrust of the Inquisition's activity in this area was to instruct, educate, and set limits and not to repress and destroy.

A Counter-Reformation Childhood

It would be difficult to overemphasize the extent to which the child-rearing practices and intense religiosity of the post-tridentine Spanish home created the psychological conditions that could turn a child toward a life of mystic contemplation. The peculiarly Spanish combination of parental piety, monastic austerity, harsh discipline, and economic distress and dislocation created what the anthropologist Philip Greven has called a "psychic warehouse" of behavioral norms, religious images, and disassociative fantasies that propelled the individual toward the life of a holy woman.[1]

The great majority of the biographies and autobiographies in my sample of "official" women mystics (76.7 percent) stress the extreme piety of both the fathers and mothers of these women. Even more significant, perhaps, given the fact that the inquisitors who interrogated the "false" mystics did not ask specifically about religious practices during childhood, is that in 23 percent of the cases there are strong indications of an atmosphere of fervent religious devotion in these homes as well. The pious behavior of parents set the tone for the entire household; it was imitated by their children and, in many cases, continued to influence the development of their religious practices throughout their lives.

Juan Correa de Tapia and Isabel de Acosta, the parents of Gabriela de San Joseph, were extremely pious. Both parents insisted that Gabriela and her four siblings join them for two hours of mental prayer every day. The family prayed in the small chapel that Correa de Tapia had built into one of the rooms of their home.[2] Isabel de Acosta's piety became even more intense after the death of her husband. According to Gabriela's biographer, Fr. Manuel de San

Gerónimo, she came to resemble "another Judith in her fasting, devotion and retirement from active life." Given this upbringing, it is hardly surprising that all of the five surviving children of this couple chose religious vocations, with Gabriela's only brother becoming a parish priest and all four girls entering convents.

The fate of little Teresa Henriquez provides a sobering example of the negative impact that a perfervid religious environment could have on an impressionable child. By the time she was three years old, Teresa became her mother's favorite of all her eleven children. As a result of her husband's long absences as pilot of vessels crossing the Atlantic, Teresa's mother fell into a serious depression and is described as weeping uncontrollably for long periods.[3] Religion became her only solace, and she would bring Teresa with her on her pilgrimages to pray before the image of Our Lady of the Rule, which was in an Augustinian convent in the nearby village of Chipiona. Teresa also became extremely fond of the image and defended her devotion to it when she was asked why she venerated such a dark-skinned image when there were so many lighter-skinned ones that she could have chosen. Her mother also encouraged her to identify herself with the nuns of the nearby Mercedarian convent. At age two and a half, she was made to dress in a Mercedarian habit, and she began to organize her day around the routines of the convent as signaled by its bells. Whenever she heard the bells sounding the hour for mental prayer, she would call out, "Come brothers and sisters, it is time to pray and praise the Lord."[4]

Drawn into an intense and morbid religiosity entirely inappropriate to her age and state of health, Teresa failed to thrive. Encouraged by her mother's confessor, she began to isolate herself from the rest of the family and insisted on withdrawing from her mother's bed and sleeping alone on a cot, where she refused to cover herself properly in winter. She also began to engage in a series of physical austerities that further undermined her already fragile constitution. Every Friday she would scourge herself until blood flowed, and, spurred on by a misguided sense of charity, she would give most of her food to the poor.[5] After developing a severe case of erysipelas she became feverish and bedridden and died at just five years of age.

Examples of parental piety and its influence on the lives of siblings can also be found among the women who were later charged with feigned sanctity In her testimony before the Toledo tribunal, Francisca de la Santissima Trinidad declared that she became a Franciscan nun in part because her mother and grandmother had dedicated her to St. Francis even before she was born.[6] Her mother also took her to San Miguel de los Angeles, the convent where she eventually became a novice, for mass and jubilees.

In her testimony about her childhood, María Cotonilla testified that her mother had taught her the necessity of prayer by saying that through prayer one could "see God." In spite of the fact that she was a beggar who lived wherever she was offered lodgings, she incorporated regular mental prayer in her daily routine of religious observance, which also included saying the rosary and going to mass.[7]

Just as in the case of the "false" mystic María Cotonilla, several of the "official" holy women could trace aspects of their later religious life to parental influences. Francisca Inés de la Concepción's mother, María de Olmedo, was greatly devoted to San Diego de Alcalá, who she believed had brought her daughter back from the dead after she invoked his assistance. Shortly after Francisca recovered, her mother brought her to Alcalá, and when they arrived before a portrait of the saint that had been set up in a special chapel, she announced that "that is he; the one who was with me and revived me when I was dead." Later in life, Francisca continued her devotion to San Diego, and when she became the abbess of the Franciscan convent in Cifuentes, she set up an altar to the saint with a relic in the breast of his statue.[8]

The habit of exercising charity toward the poor was also inculcated into many of these women from a very early age. Whenever Gabriela de San Joseph's parents wanted to give out alms, they would entrust them to a servant who would carry Gabriela to the door of the house and give the money to her to distribute.[9] After she became abbess of the Convent of the Discalced Carmelitesses in Ubeda, Gabriela encouraged the nuns to give alms and engage in other charitable exercises as a way of teaching humility.

Another woman whose childhood training in aiding the poor carried over into later life was the aristocratic Brianda de Acuña Vela, daughter of the count of Castrillo. As a small child, she acquired the habit of waiting at the top of the staircase leading to the entrance of the palace in Aranda de Duero until the door opened and someone presented himself asking for alms. She would then signal to a servant, who would bring her down and give her a few coins, which she would present to the beggar on her knees.[10] This early training in charity and humility stayed with her for the rest of her life.

In as many as 30 percent of the homes of the "official" mystics, parental piety reached such an extreme that the household became organized as if it were a convent. Gabriela de San Joseph recorded that from the time that she was eight years old until she joined the Discalced Carmelitesses at age twenty-one, "We led our lives as if we were nuns." Since her father was a wealthy attorney who practiced before the *audiencia* of Valladolid, he could afford to establish a chapel and have mass said in his own home. In fact, the family was largely self-sufficient from a religious standpoint, even enjoying the luxury of its own spiritual advisors, men well known for their spiritual and intellectual accomplishments, who came to their home to hear their confessions.[11]

The adoption of a monastic lifestyle in so many homes proved an excellent preparation for the religious careers that so many of the children would later follow, while at the same time creating the basis for intense frustration for so many who, for one reason or another, were unable to enter religious life. María de Agreda's mother, Catalina de Arana, found an original if drastic solution to the problem of establishing her children in a profession by creating a convent in her own home. Prepared in advance by her own extreme piety and the quasi-monastic routine she imposed on the family and spurred by the fact that both her daughters were approaching an age when critical decisions had to made about their future, she had a vision that indicated that she had to sacrifice her entire family for Christ. In 1618, when María was sixteen, the decision was taken. Forcing her husband, Francisco Coronel, a man of sixty with serious health problems, to join the Franciscan order as a lay friar (servant) and her two sons to become Franciscan friars, she established the convent for herself, her two daughters, and three nuns from a convent in Burgos in January 1619.[12]

The intense religiosity that marked the homes of women mystics also had a profound impact on children's play activity. Little Teresa Henriquez, who took the name of Teresa de Jesús, devised an elaborate game in which she organized the neighborhood children into a religious community like that of a convent and named herself *madre comendadora*. The children would stage religious processions, carrying an image of the Virgin Mary, and Teresa would take on the role of spiritual advisor, even preaching sermons to them and exhorting them to greater devotion.[13]

Processions also figured in the play activity of the children in the home of Juan Díaz y Ortiz and Ana de Cardenas, parents of the child who was to eventually join the Dominican third order as María de la Santissima Trinidad. Both parents were ardent believers. Ana de Cardenas was a Dominican *tercera,* and Juan Díaz was a devotee of the Virgin of the Rosary. When María was four, her house was full of children, including her brother and two other boys, the children of relatives that her parents were bringing up. Entranced by the docility and comeliness of the little girl, the boys began calling her "saint." Once, when her mother was absent, they made a holy week float out of chests and a writing table and, with María perched precariously on top, marched around the house waving homemade pennants and singing "Santa Mariquita ora pro nobis" at the top of their lungs.[14]

Not surprisingly, a little girl's play activity could easily become centered around the image of the child Jesus, which had become such an important part of Counter-Reformation art.[15] In her autobiography, Isabel de Jesús recalled that, when she was four or five, her brothers made a nativity scene. At first, they let her hold the doll representing the infant but then took it away. She was very hurt by this but continued sitting alongside the nativity scene and reading her catechism aloud to the doll. As she read out the various parts of the catechism describing the majesty of God, she had a fantasy of the doll responding to her, thereby affirming his identity. This was the first of many fantasies about the child Jesus, to whom she remained devoted throughout her life.[16]

The child Jesus also became important in the fantasy life of Inés de Jesús y Franco when she was a girl. Somewhat older than María, the seven-year-old imagined herself as becoming engaged to the holy child in a ceremony in which she promised to be his "grateful and devoted wife."[17] She even boasted that on that occasion the child had presented her with a ring whose existence was attested to in a memorial drawn up after her death by her last spiritual advisor, Fr. Gaudioso Alexandre.

Behavior that was little more than childish fantasy or the imaginary trying on of adult roles frequently took on greater significance in the eyes of adults who wanted to interpret it as indicating a unique spiritual calling. One day when Jacinta de Atondo was four, she hid herself in the stables, and when the adults found her she was on her knees, praying with her arms stretched out as if she were being crucified. This incident and others of a similar nature became widely known in the village, and people began asking themselves if "by any chance God had created in this little girl a saint of the Catholic Church."[18]

Martina de los Angeles y Arilla's favorite pastime when she was a child was making altars, adorning them with holy images, and praying before them. These and other devout practices attracted the attention of her confessor, who declared that she was "a soul without a body" and told her father that he was very fortunate to have a daughter who "gave evidence of becoming a second St. Catherine of Siena."[19] One person who took the confessor's words quite seriously was one of Martina's uncles, a priest who began telling her about St. Catherine's childhood and then gave her a biography of the saint to read. Martina, who could read from age six, loved the book, and St. Catherine became one of her favorite saints, appearing to her in visions many times during her life.

The adult tendency to read into childish behavior a precocious spirituality and a deeper understanding of the mysteries of the faith than was cognitively possible could lead to tragedy, as in the case of the death of five-year-old Teresa de Jesús. But it could also lead to greater self-confidence for the child and a special place in the family that could provide her with certain privileges. Behaving in ways that appeared "saintly" to adults was one way of pleasing them, but it was also a way of marking oneself as a special person especially favored by God and therefore somewhat immune from parental authority. Whatever the reality in individual cases, the way adults interpreted childish behavior had a profound impact on the child herself and on her future as a mystic and holy woman.

The growing numbers of devotional works and saint's lives being published in Spanish meant that many children had access to some of these works in their parents' homes. In the biographies and autobiographies of the "true" women mystics in my sample, 40 percent specifically mention access to devotional works as an important part of the child's intellectual development.

Even though María de Christo came of a modest hidalgo family living in a village near Badajoz, she did have considerable access to devotional works because her extremely pious parents had decided to dedicate a considerable portion of their limited income to acquiring them. María recorded that she read the works of San Pedro de Alcántara and St. Teresa of Jesus at an early age and completed her early religious education by listening to sermons at the local parish church. In later life, when she founded and directed *beaterios*, she stressed the education of the other women and personally taught them to read Latin and Spanish.[20]

María de Agreda was another avid reader of spiritual and devotional works when she was a child. María greatly impressed her mother, who was only marginally literate, by learning to read at a very early age. Her favorite recreation during periods of rest from doing chores around the house was to find a quiet spot to read works of a "devout and spiritual" nature.[21] In later life, María de Agreda's interest in scholarship continued. Her letters to King Philip IV are studded with references to the New and Old Testaments, saints' lives and the Psalms of David, and she became the author of a number of devotional works.

But a child could be exposed to devotional works in places other than her own home. After Martina de los Angeles was taught to read by her uncle, she spent all her time hunting for more books that she could borrow. Impressed by her commitment, Dr. Abenia, the parish priest who had first alerted her parents to Martina's spiritual potential, left her one hundred reales in his will so that she could purchase the devotional works she wanted.[22]

Since the only direct questions about the reading habits of those tried by the Inquisition were confined to prohibited books, it is very difficult to know the extent to which the "false mystics" had access to devotional works as children. Catalina Ruiz was the only one whose testimony indicated clearly that she did have access to such works as a child. Evidently she must have continued reading them as an adult, and her familiarity with the ideas contained within them may well have contributed to her sense that she no longer needed to be governed by male priests, as God spoke to her directly.[23]

Reading spiritual works, especially those with mystical overtones, could reinforce the child's precocious religiosity and help set her on the path toward the contemplative life. At the same time, such works, especially hagiographies in which all too often pious authors exaggerated the self-denying exploits of these "athletes of Christ," could lead a child to excesses far beyond her physical capacities. In the case of eight-year-old María de Christo, it was her attempt to imitate the real ascetic San Pedro de Alcántara by refusing food and scourging herself nightly that broke her health and left her "pale, sick and exhausted."[24]

Of course, the most fascinating question about the childhood of these women is how their experiences led to the kinds of behavior that marked them as mystic contemplatives who communicated with God through visions and trances. From the foregoing discussion, it is easy to see that their imaginations were filled with the images conjured up by reading vernacular devotional works and hagiographies, reinforced by sermons, paintings, and religious theater. But thousands of women in early modern Spain had exposure to such stimuli and never had the dissociative experiences that would mark them out as mystics. To explain the appearance of the more dramatic manifestations of mystical behavior, especially trances and visions, we must turn to a description of the interaction between historical, personal, and intrapsychic factors, especially as they affected the families of the future mystics and induced the kinds of reactions in the child that set her firmly on the path of mystical experience.

A family tradition of mysticism was certainly an important element in creating a receptive atmosphere for the child's own mystical transports while also providing an admired, if somewhat eccentric, family member to emulate. Lorenzo Enciso, Beatriz María de Jesús' father was himself something of a mystic who had frequent visions and was given to trances. Even though he himself had no special virtues, his reputation as a mystic was so great in his native Granada that when he died such a large number of people came to venerate the body that several *alcaldes* had to be posted at the doors of the house. Even though Enciso opposed María's desire to become a nun for purely selfish reasons, there can be little doubt that he wanted her to live a spiritual life, even writing in her diary on the day she was born, "God, make her a saint."[25]

An even more impressive tradition of mystic contemplation and rejection of the world in favor of a life of religious austerity can be found in the aristocratic Rocaberti family. Both of Hipolita de Jesús y Rocaberti's aunts, Estefania de Rocaberti and Gerónima de Rocaberti, were renowned for their virtue, and both became nuns and prioresses of their respective convents. In fact, Doña Gerónima was prioress when Hipolita entered the Dominican Convent of Nuestra Señora de los Angeles at the age of sixteen. Estefania was reputed to have received many divine revelations when she lived shut up in a little apartment with three like-minded women. After entering the Discalced Carmelitesses, she was known to have a supernatural degree of insight into the thoughts of each of the other nuns. On one occasion, when Hipolita herself was suffering serious doubts about her vocation, Estefania visited her, announcing that she had been sent by the Divine Spirit and that she knew exactly what ailed her.[26]

In Antonio Arbiol's biography of the great seventeenth-century missionary Ignacio García, he stresses the importance of the spiritual advisor in the life of the child. According to Arbiol, choosing a confessor during the years when the child first becomes able to reason is critical because the confessor can help to shield the child from the wiles of the devil, who first begins to reveal himself in this same period.[27]

Whether influenced by the writings of moralists like Antonio Arbiol or out of fear for their child's immortal soul, mothers began bringing their children to a spiritual advisor, usually their own, at younger and younger ages, when the child could be most easily influenced. At age four, Francisca Inés de la Concepción was placed under the spiritual direction of the Franciscan mystic and preacher Francisco de Torres. By age five, she was already beginning to have the visions that would stay with her for the rest of her life. It was also because of Torres, who was extremely concerned about issues of sexuality and celibacy, that she took a perpetual vow of chastity on the same afternoon as her first communion at age ten.[28]

An especially painful and difficult relationship with her parents was the most important factor that could accentuate the child's natural desire to withdraw into a world of fantasy. Early modern parents were sternly advised to avoid excessive affection toward their children by such theologians as the Franciscan Antonio Arbiol, *calificador* of the Holy Office and synodal examiner for the archbishop of Zaragoza. In an influential work first published in 1715, Arbiol portrayed pregnancy, birth, and childhood itself as the scene of a titanic struggle between the devil and the child's guardian angels over the child's soul.[29] In this struggle the behavior of the parents toward the child played a critical role. Parents who neglected their responsibility to give children a good religious education risked their immortal souls, but just as serious and as dangerous to children was showing them excessive affection. Such parents made the cardinal error of "loving the creature more than the Creator." To avoid violating divine law in this respect, Arbiol advised parents to avoid intimacy with their children: "You must not laugh with them, play with them or cry over their misadventures." Instead, he counseled parents to show a "prudent severity" and solemnly warned them that they risked their children's eternal damnation if they loved them to excess.[30]

Parents had to be especially careful in their handling of girls because of the extreme danger to the family's reputation that was posed by any sexual misconduct. To avoid future problems, Arbiol advised parents of little girls to observe their behavior very closely and to instantly correct even the most minor of faults. On the whole, he averred, a "stern" attitude should be maintained toward them, and they should be taught to "cry rather than to laugh" in order to induce a proper level of modesty and attentiveness to the needs of adults.[31]

In many middle-class and aristocratic families, the ideals set forward by moralists like Antonio Arbiol were achieved but at the cost of repressing the child's need for affection. Clara de Jesús María's memory of accompanying her mother to church, and listening while she read from a devotional book reminds us that a child's relationship to her mother could be warm and loving. But not all mothers were as solicitous of their children's welfare. The custom among many middle-class mothers of putting their infants out to a wet nurse and then neglecting them for long periods placed the child at risk of dying.

It took Isabel de Acosta six months after she turned her infant daughter Gabriela over to a wet nurse in a village near Granada to decide to pay her a visit. Arriving at the village, Isabel was shocked to find her daughter dressed in rags, playing in the dirt, and eating a plate of stale bread fried in pork fat. Instead of receiving adequate milk from the wet nurse, she was seriously ill from being given goat's milk after the wet nurse's breasts dried up.[32] Gabriela's mother was forced to take the child back home, but she never fully recovered from the abuse to which she had been subjected and continued to have serious health problems for the rest of her life.

Caterina Tomás's mother had little to learn from Arbiol's child-rearing manual, as she treated both her daughters harshly without any prompting. Both children were sent to hear mass when they were between three and four years old and told that they could not return for lunch until it was over. One day, when the priest was late in arriving at church, Caterina's older sister was heard to complain that she was hungry, and was whipped when her mother found out. Forced to watch while her sister was beaten, Caterina burst into tears but was consoled by a vision of a resplendent angel who told her not to be sad because her sister deserved her punishment.[33] This was the first of the consoling visions that Caterina would have at moments of extreme stress when she was neglected by caregivers. Throughout her childhood, these visions served not only to dissociate her from a painful and frequently incomprehensible reality but also to reconcile her to situations that she could do nothing about. They also served to provide her with a warm and loving mother figure very different from the cold and unfeeling mother that she had in reality.

An excellent example of this imaginary substitution of the saintly mother for the real one is related to a time when she became upset when she was unable to join the other children in singing Christmas songs because she did not know the words. Her feelings of embarrassment were assuaged with the appearance of her favorite saint, Catherine of Alexandria, who told her not to feel bad about missing the singing because "you are destined to become his special servant and praise him with greater perfection." Then, in a gesture of affection that the little girl must have often wished her own mother would have shown her, the saint took her by the hand and led her to a seat in the church apart from the others.[34]

But as Antonio Arbiol indicated when he wrote about the key role that fathers played in disciplining children over the objections of their wives, the tone in families was frequently set by fathers who tended to be harsh and hypercritical. During her first audience before the Valencia tribunal, María Antonia Hortola described her father as "tyrannical" and mentioned frequent beatings and denial of food. In later life she had virtually no relationship with her parents, and the tribunal's prosecuting attorney spoke disapprovingly of a "lack of charity" in the way she referred to them.[35]

Marina de Escobar's father was the brilliant Dr. Diego de Escobar, a practicing attorney before the Audiencia of Valladolid and holder of the prestigious Sexto chair of canon law at the university. In spite of his comfortable circumstances, Escobar led a life of great personal austerity and fervent religious devotion. He scourged himself once a week, habitually wore a girdle of netted wire with bristles, and fasted much more frequently than the rule of the church required.

Marina was Escobar's fourth daughter, which was probably where her problems with her father began, since he made no secret of the fact that after having three girls he wanted a boy. At one and a half years old, Marina was removed from the parental home and sent to live with her grandmother, a pious lady from whom she learned to read, pray, and say the rosary. Marina returned to her home at age nine as a virtual stranger with almost no experience of living with her father. Given the circumstances, conflict with him was almost inevitable, especially since it was about this time that she began taking better care of her appearance and abandoned some of her religious exercises. Her father was furious at her for giving in to "temptation" and treated her with cold contempt.[36] He chose another confessor for her who roundly criticized her faults and set her firmly on the path of religious aus-

terity, but no matter how hard she tried to please her father by prayer, studying devotional books, abstinence, or wearing a penitential girdle, he never
forgave her earlier transgressions.

Reading Luis de la Puente's biography of Marina de Escobar, which was
mainly based on her own writings, it is difficult to escape from the conclusion that her entire childhood and adolescence was marred by her father's
rejection of her. From age fourteen, she suffered what modern psychiatrists
would probably diagnose as schizophrenia, had numerous visions, and became dissociated from the world around her, "living as much with God as
with the people of her household."[37] During this period, which lasted until
age twenty-seven, she experienced waves of guilt and self-loathing and
thought of God as the harsh and demanding father who insisted on an exact
account of what she had done with all the gifts he had bestowed upon her.
She felt unclean and was afraid to appear before this demanding and disap-
proving God, afraid that she would disgust him and "make him vomit at the
sight of her."[38]

Later in life, Marina continued to experience trances and had visions of
God the Father as a figure inspiring awe and fear, much as her real father had
done. In certain of these visions, Christ would appear to reproach her for her
faults. In one vision, she was dressed in torn and filthy clothing, and Christ
ordered her guardian angel to give her three blows across her shoulders. In
other visions, however, it appeared as though God was willing to forgive her
for her faults in a way that her real father never did, assuaging her fears of
rejection by assuring her that he would never desert her.[39]

But a difficult and painful relationship with her parents was not the only
experience that might have induced a girl to take refuge in a comforting world
of religious fantasy. The Spain of the late sixteenth and seventeenth centuries, when mysticism reached its peak as a social phenomenon, was also a
society in crisis, wracked by wave after wave of epidemic disease and an
economic depression that placed families under stress as never before. As
pressure on the family mounted from the outside, its ability to offer an emotionally nurturing and economically supportive environment diminished, and
the child was exposed to a series of shocks that threatened her sense of security. As the family's capacity to nurture and sustain the child dwindled, the
child was more likely to tend to withdraw into a world of visions peopled
with helpful saints or an emotionally nurturing Virgin Mary.

The illness and death of a parent or parents was probably the most serious
emotional shock experienced by any of these children. Whether caused by
the rigors of childbirth or the ravages of diseases that the medical practice
of the day was unable to treat effectively, the death of a parent was traumatic
for the young child and could by itself be the cause of greater psychic investment in fantasy. More than 43 percent of the "true" mystics experienced the
death of one or both of their parents during childhood, sometimes after a long
and painful illness. In the case of Isabel de Jesús, the five-year illness and
death of her mother proved highly traumatic and triggered a severe depres-

sion that was intensified by her own feelings of guilt over being a "poor sinner" unable to measure up to the piety and absolute resignation to the will of God manifested by her "saintly mother."[40]

The death of María Ángela Astorch's mother, Catalina, when she was five proved equally traumatic and was clearly associated with her first mystical experience.[41] The shock of her mother's death was made all the more serious for the little girl because as the youngest child she was clearly her mother's favorite, so much so that María was the only one of her four children that she wanted at her bedside during her final illness.[42]

Death of a parent or parents, especially the mother, constituted a serious blow to the child's sense of security and frequently led to her being placed in the care of someone outside the immediate family. Even though such brusque changes of caregiver and home could be difficult and even traumatic for the child, some such changes may have worked to the child's advantage. After María Ángela Astorch was left an orphan at age six when her father died, she was placed in the care of a wet nurse from a nearby village. Evidently the child flourished under the care of the wet nurse Apolonia, who loved her and took good care of her.

But not everyone was lucky with a substitute caregiver. The death of Brianda de Acuña's mother, Doña María Vela de Acuña, when Brianda was only four years old and the fact that her father was usually absent from the home because of his important position as viceroy of Navarre meant that Brianda and her siblings were placed in the unsupervised care of a young relative, who treated the children with considerable brutality.[43]

The childhood experiences of Caterina Tomás after she lost her father at age two and her mother at age four are instructive of the kind of neglect and abuse that a child could be subjected to at the hands of relatives and the general insecurity of life that affected the entire population. After her mother's death, Caterina was sent to live with her grandmother, but her stay ended abruptly and horribly when her grandmother was murdered during one of the all-too-frequent raids that North African corsairs mounted against Spanish coastal towns.[44]

At age six, therefore, little Caterina had to move again, this time to the home of her uncle. Not surprisingly, considering the tragic events that had filled her young life and the lack of any understanding or sympathetic person in whom to confide, Caterina became more and more dissociated from her immediate environment and had increasing numbers of "visits" from saintly figures who appeared whenever she needed help or consolation. Her uncle and aunt seemed to feel no special affection for a child they took in as a matter of charity, and they not only burdened her with numerous household responsibilities but also assigned her tasks well beyond the capacity of a seven- or eight-year-old child. As an orphan, entirely dependent on her uncle and aunt for survival, Caterina was frightened of offending them and could not refuse anything they asked her to do, no matter how dangerous or difficult. On one occasion, her uncle sent her to a dangerously high place in the hills to gather herbs, and she was "rescued" only when St. Catherine of Alexandria appeared and helped her descend, telling her not to come back to such dangerous heights, "even if they order you to do so."[45] While it is perfectly possible that Caterina really saw her favorite saint in a vision, since her cult was quite widespread all over Europe, there seems little doubt that what was really operating here was her own instinct for self-preservation allowing her to defy her aunt and uncle, which she was normally afraid to do, through the intercession of a "superior" force.

Visions containing "helping" saints also appeared whenever she was nervous or frightened. Once when she went out very late at night to fetch water from a well outside the village and became frightened, St. Antonio Abad, another of her favorite "parental" saints, took her by the hand and brought her back home, admonishing her not to go out so late in the future.[46] Another incident occurred when she was seven years old. Passing through a dark wood with a message for her uncle, who was making charcoal, she saw some men carrying a corpse to the cemetery. Frightened by the presence of the corpse, she lost her way and sat down under a tree in tears, begging her divine helpers to show her the right path. Her prayers were answered as they had been on numerous other occasions, and Catherine of Alexandria appeared to take her to her uncle.[47]

In the psychoanalytic literature, dissociative disorder is highly correlated with physical abuse and neglect, especially sexual abuse, which must have been at least as high in early modern Spain as in modern Western societies, where studies report an incidence of 40 percent and above for women.[48] While sexual abuse is never spoken of directly in the biographies, it may be strongly inferred for at least two of the children because of their behavior around men. From about age four, little Teresa de Jesús had dethroned her father and mother from their positions of authority and informed her mother that she would henceforth consider them as her brothers, giving the name of father only to God and of mother to the Virgin Mary. That the real cause of the underlying anger and resentment toward her parents that manifested itself in this way was sexual is indicated by the extreme rejection of men that she exhibited around the same time, by not allowing any male to come anywhere near her, even if he happened to be an uncle or a cousin her own age.[49]

Sexual abuse is even clearer in the case of Martina de los Angeles y Arilla because of an extreme fear of men and desire to avoid their company that began in childhood. One of the first incidents occurred when one of her childhood friends asked her to accompany her to visit the home of a sick person, and Martina replied by asking if any men were to be present, because "if any are there I don't want to go." In fact, so strong was her aversion to male company that she was called "the enemy of men" by the people of her village.[50] Another indication of probable sexual abuse was her desire as a child to mutilate or efface her breasts by taking metal scrapers used in sheep shearing and tying them so that they would cut into her flesh.

Later in life, when she became a Dominican lay nun, she exhibited an extreme reluctance to talk with men in the locutory parlor of the convent. On one occasion, when one of the convent's wealthiest supporters became aware of her saintly reputation and insisted on consulting with her on spiritual matters, the abbess had to order her to see him. The fact that she was to be alone with a man, even though they would be separated by an iron screen, was enough to trigger a hysterical response and a resort to her divine protectors, St. Dominic and St. Catherine of Siena. Her biographer records that she was fearful of even the male saints who would appear in visions, which, on one occasion, earned her a sharp rebuke from St. Dominic himself.[51] Because she was pathologically afraid of real men, Martina resorted to the world of fantasy and had a vision of Christ as a "beautiful youth, affable and kind."[52]

High mortality rates among women in the early modern period meant high numbers of remarriages. Remarriage meant bringing a stepmother into the home who had little reason to care for the children of her husband's previous marriage and could very easily see them as competing with her own for his affection. In certain cases, the arrival of a stepmother could signal a sharp deterioration in the level of care that the child received. During her first audience before the Toledo tribunal, María Cotonilla recalled that after her mother died when she was five, she was placed in the hands of her stepmother, Isabel de Ballestros, who put her out to beg.[53]

Martina de los Angeles y Arilla's biography provides a more extreme example of the negative impact that a stepmother could have on a child's life. A few years after her mother died in childbirth, Martina's father remarried but the new wife was so jealous of any attention that her husband gave Martina and treated her so harshly that Martina begged her father to be allowed to retire to the desert in imitation of the hermits of the early church. Although he dismissed this as a childish fantasy, her stepmother's hostility and ill treatment increased to such a point that he was forced to remove Martina from her home and place her with a widow who lived nearby. While living with the widow, Martina was neglected and hardly ever saw her father.[54] It was during this turbulent and lonely period in her life, when she felt completely unloved, that she took refuge in a fantasy world peopled with saints who would comfort her.

But the arrival of a stepmother was not the only reason that so many children experienced removal from their homes. The economic crisis that began in the 1580s had a negative impact on families, making it difficult for them to support their children. Consequently, some 36.7 percent of the "true" mystics were placed with relatives for extended periods. These alternative arrangements, however expedient or necessary for the family, were frequently disastrous for the child.

Jacinta de Atondo, who was born in the village of Valtierra (Navarre) on September 11, 1645, was the second of three daughters of a hidalgo family that was struggling to maintain its status in the face of growing financial problems. There were six children in the family, but most of the available resources were earmarked for the boys, one of whom eventually entered the prestigious Order of Santiago. The girls fared considerably worse, with only enough money to provide one dowry for the eldest. Jacinta's younger sister eventually entered a convent, while Jacinta herself was sent to live with an elderly aunt in the nearby village of Mallen.[55]

From the very beginning of her stay, her aunt treated her with brutal harshness. In later life Jacinta recalled that she screamed at her constantly about even the slightest fault. Since the woman was living on a shoestring herself, she could not afford to buy the girl any clothing, and Jacinta was forced to wear hand-me-downs from her more fortunate older sister.[56] She was given a tiny dark room without furniture in the worst part of the house. Her confessor, Fr. Pedro Garces, decided to cut off her hair and forced her to dress in a coarse nun's habit. To complement this garment, she wore rope sandals without stockings even in harsh winter weather. It was Garces who made her limit her food consumption and fast regularly on bread and water. Although this was supposed to be a way of teaching her humility, it is hard not to believe that the real reason was to spare her aunt further expense. During this period, Jacinta describes herself as "suffering terrible hunger" and becoming so thin that the cartilage in her nostrils became translucent.[57] To help her further along the path of spiritual perfection, Garces decided that she should beg for her food at the door of the local Franciscan convent and eat with the poor. Whatever the "spiritual benefits" that traditional Catholic theology might have found in this treatment, it is easy to imagine that the psychological impact of being forced to beg for food in public, perform menial tasks, and associate herself openly with the dregs of society must have been devastating to the daughter of a hidalgo. Sadly, and in spite of biographer Antonio Arbiol's attempt to hold up her childhood as a model of Christian virtue, Jacinta de Atondo seems to have been just another example of a vulnerable child abused by an unfeeling relative who was aided and abetted by her spiritual advisor.

Jacinta's reaction to this treatment was to withdraw emotionally and psychologically. In Jacinta's case, the trauma of sustained and systematic physical abuse and neglect was compounded by the fact that this treatment came from a member of her own family.[58] She describes herself as feeling as though she were "bewitched" and as "paying attention to nothing" and "heeding nothing that they said to her."[59] During this period that she began seeing visions and having trances in public. For Jacinta de Atondo, therefore, the brutal physical and emotional abuse that she received caused her to dissociate from a reality that threatened her very existence, while her religious training and the sermons she heard in the convent chapel gave her the language of piety and devotion that filled her visions.

During the early modern period, there was a complex relationship between childhood experiences and the development of the dissociative behavior that translated into trances, visions, and prophecy and gained the individual the reputation of being a mystic. Devotional works and sermons, combined with exposure to visual media like *estampas* and religious painting and sculpture, stimulated the imagination of children and provided the imagery that filled their visions. Confessors and spiritual advisors whose own commitment to a life of mystical contemplation was strong could also have a profound influence on the child. In addition, Spanish parents at that time can generally be described as detached, hostile, and restrictive toward their children. A home environment was created in which warm and loving parent-child interactions were rare and the child's spontaneous behavior and striving for autonomy were blocked by a despotic patriarchy. When social stressors like war, economic dislocation, and plague are added to the outright abuse that many of them experienced, it is only natural that such imaginative and sensitive children should seek to separate themselves from a painful reality and take refuge in a world of helping, loving divine figures. In this way, the child passed from lesser to greater states of dissociation and evolved into an adult for whom the world of religious imagery was more real and meaningful than the social and material world itself.

Adolescence and the Struggle for Self-Assertion

Adolescence for the women of early modern Spain, like their counterparts in modern society, was a period of increasing maturation and self-assertion that could bring on conflict with adults and caregivers. Confronted with an ideology that called for heightened vigilance of the adolescent girl or *doncella* and greater control over her activities, and given the fact that choices for the future were extremely limited, most girls were destined to lose the struggle and end up caving in to their parents' desires for them or compromising their own goals in the interests of the family. At the same time, however, adverse social and economic conditions continued to place intolerable burdens on the family, further exposing adolescent girls to dislocation, instability, and abuse.

But not all of the adolescents in this study were crushed by the pressure. Exceptional individuals could rise above their situation or even turn it to their advantage. Parents could be forced or persuaded to allow their children more freedom in choosing their future situation, and some adolescents were already discovering that gaining a reputation for saintliness was a way of invoking powerful external support against formerly all-powerful parental figures.

According to the late-sixteenth-century Franciscan moralist Juan de la Cerda, in a work specifically dedicated to describing all of the stages in a woman's life, the period of adolescence ran from ten to twenty because at that age the girl was ready for marriage.[1] Of course, the majority of the women in this study who took a husband married before age twenty, so that Juan de la Cerda's definition of the *doncella* cannot be taken as anything but a rule of thumb.

The concern expressed by so many observers about limiting the freedom of the *doncella* was based squarely on the fear of a sexual liaison that would compromise the honor of the family. To avoid unnecessary and potentially dangerous situations that might ruin a *doncella*'s reputation, the Jesuit Alonso de Andrade was of the opinion that she should not be allowed to leave the house except when absolutely necessary and that mothers should make themselves responsible for preventing any contact between their daughters and "young men or those of a licentious disposition."

But as the seventeenth-century Dominican Andrés Ferrer de Valcedebro observed, a man would need "all of Argos' one hundred eyes" to monitor her movements.[2] The only way to be absolutely certain of controlling the *doncella,* therefore, was to condition her in such a way as to make her cooperate willingly with the restrictions imposed upon her. To this end, Juan Luis Vives described the ideal *doncella* as "chaste, sober, frugal and devout," whereas Pedro de Lujan and Vicente Mexia stressed the importance of inculcating a strong dose of shame or modesty, which would protect her better than anything else from the snares of the world.[3]

In a society in which the incidence of rape was relatively high and special legal procedures had to be developed to force young men to fulfill the promises that they had made to marry or compensate the young women with whom they had had intercourse, such restrictions could be considered a crude form of protection for the *doncella.* But the socially sanctioned restrictions on the *doncella*'s freedom were open to serious abuse.

In the case of Jacinta de Atondo, the enormous power that law, custom, and the prevailing ideology gave to the girl's family was sufficient to thwart her desperate efforts to attract attention to her plight. Because Jacinta could not go home without her parents' permission, and could not openly revolt against her ill treatment, she sought to get help by falling down as noisily as possible both at home and in public. By calling attention to herself in such a dramatic manner, she must have felt either that her parents would take her back or that the scandal that she would cause would put pressure on her aunt to improve her living conditions. She took the opportunity of the visit of one of her brothers to fall down right at the entrance to his room, probably hoping that he would be alarmed enough to get her parents to take her back. She also fell down the stairs of her aunt's house, thereby forcing her to call a local physician to inspect the swellings and sores on her face. Carrying her efforts a critical step further, she began falling just before entering the confessional, which constituted a thinly disguised way of embarrassing her brutal confessor. To call public attention to her plight, she also fell at the entrance to the church, where many people were gathered. After a few weeks of this, when she had fallen so often that her face was a swollen mass of bruises, the village was in a uproar, with the majority blaming her confessor, Pedro Garces, and others denouncing her family and especially her aunt. Some villagers even went so far as to threaten to give Garces a thrashing or denounce him to the Inquisition.[4]

Jacinta's attempt to call attention to her situation seemed to be working, but instead of improving her living conditions, her family became infuriated and closed ranks with Garces to isolate her from the outside world and either destroy her health or kill her through a brutal regimen of torture, isolation, starvation, and overwork. Because every moralist from Vives to Andrade recommended that the *doncella* be kept from public view and restricted in her movements, their conduct was irreproachable. If she were to die, the family could claim that she did so as a result of heroic religious austerities. The first step was to change the time of her normal confession to force her to come before dawn to the chapel where Garces was waiting so that no one was present to see her fall. But Jacinta continued her resistance, falling down at home so often and making so much noise that her aunt and brother could not fail to notice. Since her aunt also employed servants who would tell other villagers about Jacinta's distress and Jacinta continued falling in church, her confessor decided to isolate her completely and subject her to a regimen designed to break her spirit or even kill her.

Jacinta's new Calvary began with her removal to another room in the darkest and most secluded part of the house. The room was extremely small and had only a bench for furniture. She was to spend most of the next three and a half years in that room, never leaving it except at night, when she was forced to do most of the housework and clean out the stables. To avoid further public scandal, Garces also decided prevent her from going to church to take communion. This upset her profoundly, but in the best tradition of the *doncella* who is silent, meek, and obedient to authority, she accepted this arbitrary and spiteful ruling by her confessor because "it was better not to inquire into the ways of God." Deprivation of the right to take communion in public had the effect of reinforcing Jacinta's already significant dissociative tendencies by forcing her to look directly to God for solace through spiritual communion.[5]

Lest she remain idle during her imprisonment, spiritual advisor Garces and her aunt devised a series of spiritual exercises that filled almost every moment of her day and much of the night. During this entire period, she was half starved and remembered being fed only bread and water many times. Her normal diet was a bowl of thin vegetable soup and a little bit of fruit, for which she had to beg on her knees. She was also required to wear two *cilicios* next to her flesh and scourge herself each day.

As a final refinement on this regimen, a woman was engaged to beat and humiliate her for an hour every weekday. On Monday, for example, the "virtuous" woman was permitted to place a collar around Jacinta's neck and drag her around the room while kicking her in memory of the mistreatment that Christ had received. On Wednesday, her hands were tied behind her back, and she was forced into a corner where the woman beat her unmercifully.[6]

Sadly, throughout this entire period, Jacinta felt herself to blame for what was happening to her and at times even begged for more punishment. She had an extremely poor self-image, describing herself as a "piece of dung." In general she coped with her brutal treatment by becoming more abstracted, and she had many more visions than previously. The beating and semistarvation that she experienced at the hands of her aunt and confessor finally succeeded in breaking her will to resist, and she stopped the falling behavior that had brought her family so much unwelcome public notice.[7] In later life, after she was able to enter the Convent of Santa Catalina thanks to one of her brothers who had become wealthy in America, she became known for her extended trances and the numerous visions that she received, so that it could be said that her early "training" as a child and adolescent played an integral part in making her into a mystic. By the time of her death in 1716 at age 71, she had become so famous that the provincial of the Franciscan order in Aragon undertook an investigation aimed at gathering evidence for her canonization.

The case of Jacinta de Atondo perfectly illustrates the way that patterns of abuse and neglect established in childhood persisted into adolescence. Another example of this continuity is to be found in the life of Caterina Tomás. From age ten until she entered a convent, Caterina remained in her uncle's home. During her adolescence, her problems were compounded by her aunt and uncle's reaction to her desire to became a nun. Both adults mocked and abused her, as did other members of the family who visited the house. As if this were not enough, the servants and farmhands took their cue from the masters and abused and persecuted her. One day she fell off a hill and nearly died trying to escape from one of the farmhands, who had amused himself by frightening her with lizards and throwing them on her body.[8]

Caterina reacted to this treatment by continuing her religious exercises and resisted any attempt by her aunt to adorn her in ways she felt were inappropriate to the religious lifestyle. On one occasion when her aunt dressed her in the elaborate silk coif that village girls wore on special church holidays, she tore it off and went to church in her ordinary garments, much to the distress of her aunt, who upbraided her, calling her "crazy" and "malicious," and accused her of trying to bring the family into disrepute. Caterina was seriously depressed over the reaction her desire to be a nun had caused, and she took refuge in supernatural communication as she had done so often as a child. Divine voices assured her of God's continued support, and the apostle St. Peter appeared to her in a vision to tell her that she would get her wish and become a nun in spite of her family's opposition.[9]

If adolescence brought no relief from abuse to some of the least fortunate young women in my study, for others it brought a worsening in their life situation. The same stressors on the continuity and stability of the family that had caused so much instability during the childhood of certain women mystics remained a serious threat as the women grew into adolescence and disrupted the lives of some whose families had remained intact during their childhoods. Altogether, an additional 11 percent of the women in my sample suffered the death of a parent, and one the death of a stepmother. Taking into account the five who lost one or more parents when they were children, twelve or 26.6 percent of the women mystics had lost one or both of their parents by the time they were eighteen.

The death of a mother could have an especially profound effect on an adolescent girl's attitudes and life choices. Since their mothers were their most important role model, what happened to them provided an object lesson that would be difficult to ignore. The sudden death of Francisca de la Concepción's mother, María de Olmedo, during childbirth, for example, powerfully reinforced her childhood decision to make a vow of perpetual chastity and resist any attempt by her father to find her a suitor. Her decision was made all the more inevitable by the fact that her mother died so quickly that she was unable even to make her last confession and receive absolution, something that was extremely shocking to the devoutly religious young girl.[10]

For some individuals, however, the death of a mother could provide an emotional and psychological relief from burdensome obligations that the parent had laid upon them from childhood. Francisca Gomez's mother and grandmother had dedicated her to Saint Francis of Assisi even before she was born and naturally assumed that she would enter a convent. As a child living in a strongly religious home, Francisca became withdrawn and reclusive, but when she was sixteen her mother died and everything changed. "Giving up all manner of virtue," she began socializing with other girls her own age and expressed a strong desire to marry.[11] Francisca's wishes ran squarely into opposition from her father and stepmother, who were unable or unwilling to provide her with the dowry that she would need. As a result, Francisca Gomez became the novice Francisca de la Santissima Trinidad in the Convent of San Miguel de los Angeles of Toledo. Francisca had become one of those numerous women in early modern Europe forced into religious life against their will, but, like so many other reluctant members of religious orders, her emotional instability and disrespect for authority figures made her into a negative and disruptive influence on any religious community she entered.

Unlike a mother's death, which would have probably eliminated any modicum of affection that the child was receiving, the demise of an often-absent father would have its major impact on the family's financial security. María Pizarra's father was a moderately prosperous *labrador* in Extremadura, but after his death when she was thirteen the family began experiencing serious financial problems. As a result of this decline in the family fortunes, she was unable to marry as well as she might have. Her husband was considerably poorer than her father had been, and by the time of her arrest by the Holy Office in 1638 she was almost destitute.[12]

The high percentage of adolescents who had lost one or both of their parents by their eighteenth birthday allows us to see adolescence as another stage in the breakdown of family life that goes to the heart of so many of the social problems that plagued early modern Spain. By the time many of the women mystics reached adulthood, they not only had little or no contact with their families but also were remarkably ignorant about even the most important details of the lives of their siblings or nearest relatives. Thomasa Dolz, the Carmelite nun whose first audience with the Valencia tribunal took place when she was forty-seven, had lost her father and could provide very few details about the lives of her siblings, all of whom lived in the Kingdom of Valencia relatively near Valencia city. She had one brother and three sisters but was unable to name her brother's wife or children and could not give the names of any of her middle sister's nine children. Sadly, her testimony also records a tragically failed marriage in the family, the relationship between Vicente Ibañez and his wife, Magdalena. After a short period of living together, Vicente took an oath of chastity, left his wife and infant daughter, and went to live in solitude. Such a decision, which left his wife destitute and led to the death of his daughter, was not atypical in a society that had such a pessimistic attitude toward marriage that marital sex was denounced from the pulpit as sinful by no less a luminary than Dr. Francisco Bezerria, a canon of the collegiate church of Antequera.[13]

But adolescence could also be a period during which the soon-to-be woman mystic began the process of achieving the understanding of religion, self-mastery, and control over others that were to be the hallmark of her later career as nun, *beata,* or spiritual mother. Interestingly enough, in spite of his stern warnings about the need to inculcate obedience and break the potentially rebellious spirit of the *doncella,* even Juan de la Cerda saw adolescence as a time of growing maturity. In the all-important area of religious instruction, he told mothers that adolescence was the time to teach their girls about such arcane mysteries of the faith as the Trinity, something they could not have undertaken when they were children.[14]

In spite of many painful and difficult moments, the adolescence of Brianda de Acuña Vela provides an excellent example of how a girl could be given significant opportunities for growth and maturity during this critical period of her life. Throughout her adolescence, Brianda's father, Bernardino González Delgadillo y Avellaneda, continued his firm opposition to her becoming a nun. When she was seventeen, however, he removed her from the convent, where she had been a boarder since age twelve, and placed her in charge of his estates, and she distinguished herself by establishing a pharmacy and giving the tenants regular religious instruction. Management of the Castrillo estate from 1593 to 1602, when she was finally allowed to enter the Carmelite Convent of La Concepción in Valladolid, provided excellent training for her later career in the convent, where she was put in charge of novices and then elected prioress.[15]

The life of María de Agreda furnishes us with an excellent example of how adolescence could provide opportunities for spiritual and psychological growth that prepared her to take a leadership role as an adult. During her childhood, María recalled that her parents, especially her domineering and controlling mother, treated her harshly and reprimanded her for the slightest misdeed. María also experienced a series of childhood illnesses that incapacitated her for long periods and made her unable to help with household chores. Eventually her relationship with her parents had deteriorated to such a degree that they began referring to her openly as useless for marriage or for the cloister.[16]

María, who had been taught to revere her parents, was extremely upset by their lack of affection and tried desperately to please them, but it was not until she became an adolescent that she found the keys to her mother's heart. She began the process of winning over her mother by imitating her charitable activities. Since Catalina de Arana was deeply committed to helping the poor and would visit their homes regularly to distribute alms, María began giving away her own clothing. It was not very long before her mother began taking her on her rounds and, as she gained more confidence in María, actually sending her out alone when she was unable to go herself. By throwing herself wholeheartedly into charitable activity, María was performing one of the few tasks outside the home that moralists like Juan de la Cerda approved for the ideal *doncella*.[17]

But this was not enough to fully establish her position in the family. As a child, María had already impressed her parents by her ability to read, memorize prayers, and perform devotions, but she now sought a more systematic approach to leading a spiritual life. Realizing that she needed help from outside the family, she enlisted the aid of her confessor, who taught her not only the principles of mental prayer but also how to comport herself in the manner of a spiritual person by maintaining "a modest expression on her face, a sober attitude about idle conversation and a tempering of the natural ardor of youth." He also taught her to become more abstracted and stoic when she experienced pain and illness.[18] Gradually, as she began to excel in imitating the manner of the mystic, she attracted more and more favorable attention, first from the servants in her own household, then from her confessor, who began telling others about her extraordinary behavior, and finally from a distinguished cleric who was also a good friend of her parents. The latter was so favorably impressed by María's new "spiritual" lifestyle that he told them that he had venerated María from the time of her birth because he had always known that she would become a saint.[19] Invocation of powerful outsiders to assist her in her struggle to overcome opposition within her own family had worked, and it was an approach that she would use again and again throughout her adolescence and adult life when she was faced by obstacles.

Finally, she told her parents that she wished to become a nun. This was something she knew would please them since they had always strongly discouraged their children from marrying. Gratified by her daughter's decision, her mother immediately began to canvas the possibility of having her enter the Carmelite order and later turned the family home into a convent of Poor Clares.[20]

Having received training from her confessor and followed a quasi-monastic routine in her own home for a number of years, María was extremely well prepared for convent life. As a novice and during her first year as a nun, she excelled in performing the ordinary routines of the convent and in following her own program of austerity and mystic contemplation. But it was about this time that she ran into the opposition of the three nuns who had been brought to Aranda from the Convent of San Luis of Burgos to act as founders of the new convent. Whether out of concern for María's poor health, as her biographer Samaniego suggests, or out of spite, they criticized her for spending so much time on her own devotions, claiming that she had adopted such an extraordinary regimen solely to show off and put the other nuns in a bad light.

Once again, María found herself confronted with opposition from within, but this time the eighteen-year-old was well prepared to overcome it. Not only did she continue her extraordinary devotions in secret but also she began to have trances in front of the other nuns. This behavior split the convent, with some supporting her and others openly expressing doubts about whether her trances were genuine. The factions lost no time in appealing to higher authority and succeeded in attracting the attention of Antonio de Villalacre, the father provincial of the Franciscan province. Villalacre made several personal visits to the convent to examine María de Agreda. After she managed to convince him that her trances were genuine, he decided that she was to be given a new spiritual advisor capable of guiding the religious life of such an un-usual individual and put a stop to any further opposition to her in the con-vent.[21] For a second time, María had won over internal opposition, this time not from her family but from within the religious community. Using outside support to circumvent opposition from parents, relatives, or other nuns proved to be successful, and in the future she would seek the aid of the powerful to counterbalance any threat, even from the Inquisition itself.

But for some adolescent girls, spiritual and emotional maturity involved not so much their own efforts as the influence of adults. In her autobiogra-phy, Hipolita de Jesús y Rocaberti records that she entered Barcelona's aris-tocratic Dominican Convent of Nuestra Señora de los Angeles at eleven and professed at age sixteen, all to please her parents and without any religious vocation whatsoever.

Three months after her profession, however, her life changed radically when she and four other young nuns were placed under the direction of a spiritual advisor especially chosen by the abbess to give them a course of intense religious instruction. For two months, the five nuns were forbidden to have contact with anyone, even within the convent, and were trained in meditation and mental prayer. After the training period was over, Hipolita returned to the routines of convent life, but the two months of reclusion had made a profound impression on this sensitive adolescent, who had already decided that the world and its works had little value for her. Breaking radi-cally with the friends she had before, she sought out the humblest nuns and made them her role models, while spending as little time as possible outside her cell. The two months of solitude had had their desired effect. Hipolita's ties with her friends in the convent had been broken, and she now had the opportunity to radically reorganize her life on the basis of a new set of crite-ria. The indifferent convent boarder, the nun who entered religion to please her family, was transformed into the mystic, the visionary, and the future author of so many spiritual works.[22]

In one sense, adolescence has not changed; it is still a period of anxiety during which the young person has to at least begin to make some critical decisions about the future. In his influential manual on widows and *doncellas*, the Jesuit theologian Gaspar de Astete warned parents of their responsibility for helping their adolescent children choose their future "estate" in a timely manner.[23] For the middle-class or upper middle class woman living in early modern Europe, however, the choices were extremely limited, essentially three: remaining in the parental home as a spinster, marrying, or entering a convent.

Remaining single was unattractive not least because it condemned the young woman to a life of celibacy under the careful eye of her family. The option of becoming a concubine, which was not only tolerated but honorable during the Middle Ages, was increasingly difficult to manage for respectable women after the Fifth Lateran Council (1514), which interdicted the practice among the laity.[24]

Marriage also presented significant hurdles, given the fact that by the mid-eighteenth century approximately 180,000 men had chosen ecclesiastical life, while tens of thousands of others had emigrated to the colonies or perished in Spain's wars.[25] The reaction of a woman who had an obvious but unfulfilled desire for marriage when confronted by an attractive man who was off limits because of his clerical status emerged in a conversation that the Augustinian Juan de Alcocer had with an attractive middle-aged lady he met while attending to a sick person. After complimenting her on her appearance, Alcocer declared his astonishment that no one had ever asked for her hand in marriage and jokingly asked her if she would like to marry him. Much to Alcocer's surprise, she responded by telling him that if he put aside his habit she would marry him immediately.[26] This rather pathetic conversation between two individuals who by choice or necessity found themselves unable to marry is illustrative of the enormous frustration that the myriad difficulties besetting the establishment of a household could cause.

Despite the obvious desire of many women to marry, only four of the thirty "officially approved" mystics and four of the fifteen "false" mystics ever succeeded in doing so. Undoubtedly, the low percentage of married persons among the "feigned" mystics (26.6 percent) is a reflection of their family's inability to provide acceptable dowries. Affording dowries was almost certainly impossible for a number of the families of the "approved" mystics as well, many of whom were struggling to maintain themselves in the face of highly adverse economic circumstances. For poor families with more than one daughter, it was frequently impossible to find the money for more than one dowry. After María Ruano's elder sister married, she was told by her father that she "could marry Christ and bring her virtues as her dowry."[27] Nevertheless, lack of money for dowries certainly does not explain the aversion to marriage that was so strongly expressed by 56.7 percent of the official mystics, many of whom came from families with sufficient means to provide them with a generous dowry.

Certainly money did not even arise as an issue when King Philip II sought to marry his fifteen-year-old niece Margaret shortly after she arrived in Spain from the Austrian court. Even though her intention had always been to enter Spain's famous Convent of the Descalzas Reales, the young girl came under enormous pressure to marry the king not only from her mother, the Empress Maria, who saw it as a service to the Habsburg family, but also from her own servants, who stood to benefit if their mistress became queen. Juan de Borja, the empress's majordomo, even sought to appeal to her religious and charitable impulses by telling her to accept Philip because of all the good works that she could perform as queen.[28] Nevertheless, in spite of all this pressure and feeling as though she had been deserted by everyone, including her mother, Margaret stuck to her resolution. On her seventeenth birthday, January 25, 1584, in the presence of the king and his chief courtiers, Margaret entered Descalzas Reales as a novice, taking the name of Margaret of the Cross and saying good-bye forever to marriage, children, and the brilliant court life that might have been hers.

It seems plausible that at least some of the blame for the low rate of marriage among the "true" mystics can be placed on the theologians and moralists whose writings and sermons depicted it in such a bad light. It was a sermon by an itinerant Franciscan, for example, that was responsible for Mariana de Jesus's sudden decision to abandon the idea of marriage, cut her hair, and take an oath of chastity.[29] Although the effect of this pessimistic view of marriage might have been greatest among the literate and better-off officially approved mystics, the fact that the church's negative attitudes about marriage reached down into the lower classes is illustrated by evidence taken in the case of the "fraudulent" mystic Isabel de Riera, a ropemaker from Mallorca. In testimony before the Inquisition in 1622, her chief clerical supporter declared that Isabel had once voiced support for a young woman who was pretending to be possessed in order to avoid marrying a man she disliked because if "she failed to marry she could serve God better."[30]

One of the most representative and influential of the theologians who wrote against marriage writers was Pedro Galindo, author of *Excelencias de la castidad y virginidad* (1681). Galindo was a priest who had acted as spiritual advisor to hundreds of women.[31] His hair-raising descriptions of fearful wives and brutal and unfeeling husbands were based on the experiences of his penitents and not entirely on traditional Catholic attitudes that favored the celibate life.

Galindo felt that marriage greatly disadvantaged the woman, placing a "heavy yoke on her frail shoulders," saddling her with a husband who was unlikely to support her or her children, and exposing her to beatings or worse. He warned eager young women that the handsome *novio* who had treated her with such consideration, love, and generosity when they were courting would later show her unpleasant aspects of his personality that she had never even suspected. As soon as the last piece of bread from the wedding feast had disappeared, that affable young man she had married would turn into a domestic tyrant, restricting her movements, preventing her from visiting her parents or girlfriends, limiting her attendance at mass, insulting her, and even hitting her.[32] Galindo was so concerned about the frequency with which husbands presumed to dictate their wives" religious lives and church attendance that he specifically mentioned such restrictions as a mortal sin and in his manual for confessors advised spiritual advisors to ask men about the practice during confession.[33]

Yet because of her complete economic dependence on this same man, the wife would tremble every time he left the house on a trip for fear that he would be drowned or killed by brigands, leaving her destitute and with children to support.[34] Galindo even went so far as to compare marriage to the way in which the ancient tyrants martyred certain saints, tying them firmly to a rotting corpse and waiting "day and night until the horror, evil odor and corruption of the dead body brought about their martyrdom." In the same way, a marriage between a man and a woman who were incompatible was a perpetual martyrdom because in the absence of divorce they were condemned to stay together until death. Instead of loving each, other they "nursed a deadly hatred; instead of consoling each other by supplying each other's needs and soothing their afflictions they helped each other to fall further and increased their afflictions every instant."[35]

Testimony in Inquisition trials involving accusations of false sanctity, solicitation, and bigamy allows us to demonstrate that the gloomy descriptions of marriage in Galindo's book were all too real. Spain's growing economic problems, which were turning into a full-fledged depression by the first decades of the seventeenth century, reduced employment and drove men to desert their families. Pedro Foil, a Trinitarian accused of solicitation before the Mallorca tribunal, testified about one such woman who asked him to hear her in confession. In replying to one of the obligatory questions that the spiritual advisors had to ask concerning her feelings of hatred toward others, she replied that there was someone she hated and wished dead. It was her husband, a sailor who had deserted her, leaving her completely impoverished and having to provide for several small children.[36]

Even when a young woman did marry, however, the sudden death of a spouse could trigger such a negative reaction and such strong feelings of guilt that remarriage was highly unlikely, even if the marriage had not been consummated. Catalina de San Lucas was forced by parental pressure to marry at age fifteen, but immediately after the wedding ceremony her new husband caught malaria, and six months later he was dead. Although the sixteen-year-old was still a virgin and came from a moderately prosperous family, she determined not to marry again and entered the Dominican Convent of the Encarnación as a novice when she was eighteen.[37]

At age eleven, Mariana de Tapia had been sent to serve at the court of the marquis of Villena, one of Spain's richest and most powerful nobles. Four years later, when Mariana was fifteen, her father arranged for her to be married to Andrés de Cuellar, a singer at the court, but he died just a few weeks later. Since Mariana was an attractive girl and her marriage had never been consummated, she was able to marry for a second time at the age of eighteen. Unfortunately for Mariana, her second marriage was also to end quickly, with the death of her husband only three weeks later. These tragic events administered a serious shock to the psyche of this sensitive adolescent. She began seeing visions of skeletons and blamed herself for what had happened.[38] Feeling that it was her own sexual desires and sexual appeal that were ultimately responsible for the deaths of two young men, she swore an oath of chastity and began punishing her body, especially her breasts, which she beat bloody with stones on numerous occasions.[39] She became a Franciscan *beata* and took in a sadistic companion who administered regular beatings over a nine-year period. For the rest of her life, Mariana suffered serious body aches and chest pain and died at age forty-two, emaciated from fasting four days a week and wracked by fever.

Taking into account the pessimism about marriage and marital sex shared by so many leading moralists and theologians and disseminated in moral treatises and confessor's manuals, as well as from the pulpit, the negative reaction of many adolescents toward the prospect of marriage could be anticipated. What is astonishing, however, is the hostility that some middle- and upper-class parents expressed to their adolescent child's expression of desire for a celibate life, especially since they themselves had allowed or encouraged them to set up a conventlike lifestyle in the home.

The anomaly between a homelife that imitated the convent and a parent who was opposed to a daughter actually becoming a nun can perhaps be best seen in the conflict between Juan Correa de Tapia and his daughter Gabriela. When Gabriela was a child, life in the home was modeled so closely on that of a monastic institution, with regular fasting, scourging, and mental prayer, that her older brother and two sisters mocked her because she was too weak to maintain the regimen. Juan Correa de Tapia set the tone for the house because he was extremely devout and spent most of his spare time saying the rosary or absorbed in contemplation and mental prayer. Since little Gabriela had known nothing but a monastic routine conducive to a celibate lifestyle since earliest childhood, it should have come as no surprise when, at age twelve, she asked in a letter to her father to be allowed to enter the nearby Carmelite convent as a boarder. Seeing this as a direct challenge to his parental authority to decide on the *estado* that his children would take up, he indignantly denied the request and ordered her never to mention her desire to enter religious life in his presence.[40] Gabriela's reaction, and that of her sister Clara, was to intensify and formalize their conventual routine, while Gabriela refused all suitors and swore that "she would take no station other than that of a nun."[41] Nevertheless, and in spite of the fact that her father respected her desire for a celibate life to the extent that he never tried to pressure her into marriage, it was not until his death in 1648, when she was twenty, that she was finally able to enter the Carmelite order.

Even though Gabriela described herself in later life as "harsh and inflexible," she did not directly oppose her father on the matter of entering religious life, perhaps because he himself was a cold and distant person who would have been unresponsive to her complaints, but there were other adolescents who were quite prepared to challenge their parents directly when they attempted to marry off their daughters. Juana Vazquez, who later took the name Juana de la Cruz, had wanted to become a nun ever since she was seven years old, after a favorite aunt had entered a Dominican convent in Toledo. Her father had different plans for her, however, and when she was fourteen he began encouraging her to marry. After several young men had presented themselves as suitors, she became seriously alarmed. Behaving just like heroine of a play by Lope de Vega or Calderon, Juana escaped dressed like a man and walked six miles to the Franciscan Convent of Santa María de la Cruz, where she begged the nuns to admit her as a novice. The nuns agreed even though she lacked a dowry, while her father, having failed to convince her to return home, ended by reconciling himself to her vocation.[42] She had a long and successful monastic career, including a seventeen-year stint as abbess of the convent.

In Marcos de San Antonio's biography of Sor Clara de Jesús María, he relates an incident from her adolescence that provides us not only with an example of how a teenager could defy her parents over the issue of marriage but also the way that she dramatized her obedience to a higher calling. Clara had been brought up by her extremely devout mother in an atmosphere of frequent attendance at mass and reading aloud from the lives of the saints and the life of Jesus. Her mother was extremely devoted to the child Jesus and was able to communicate this devotion to her daughter, who conceived a strong love for him and dreamed that someday he would come to possess her. This early religious training and the idea that somehow she belonged to Jesus continued through early adolescence, when her parents allowed her to withdraw to a deserted part of the house, where she slept on the floor on a straw mattress filled with thistles and stones.[43] During this entire period, while she and her sister carried out a variety of religious exercises and fasted four days a week, they sensed that the child Jesus accompanied them and approved of what they were doing.

It is easy to imagine how shocked Clara must have been when, after this education in religious austerity and chastity that included even encouraging her to imitate the lives of the anchorites of the desert, her father allowed a young man to come to the house and present himself as her suitor. Learning from the servants that he had arrived and was talking to her father and other members of the family, she draped an old blanket around her shoulders, fashioned a halter from some ropes, and had one of the servant girls lead her into the room where they were conversing. At first, the guests reacted with amusement, and her suitor asked her if she were performing some kind of farce. Clara confirmed this and told the servant to take off her halter. Then, addressing the company, she said, "Halt ass! Your masters want to sell you." She then had the servant lead her around the room until she stopped in front of the visitors and cried, "My lords, the ass is here ready for sale." Going along with what appeared to be a joke, the young man said immediately that he would buy her but she responded, "That cannot be . . . ever since earliest childhood I have given my word and promised my hand to a shepherd of sublime beauty."[44] Needless to say, after this dramatic confrontation the young man withdrew his suit, and Clara was free to enter a monastic community.

It was by no means the case, however, that all families, even relatively prosperous ones who could afford dowries, were opposed to the young women's desire to enter monastic life. In certain families the wish to become a nun was fully accepted as the logical outgrowth of the kind of religious training that girls had received as children and adolescents. For María de Cristo, the option of marriage was never seriously considered by her or her parents. Growing up in an extremely devout hidalgo family where she got attention by expressing piety and memorizing devotional works, she took a vow of chastity at fourteen years of age, formally renounced the world at eighteen, and entered the *beaterio* of La Parra as a founding member four years later.[45]

Family financial interests seemed to have played a more important role in María Rivas' decision to join the Carmelite order. María, who is described as a quiet, shy girl, lost her father when she was four and was removed from her home and forced to live with her grandparents and then with her uncle. Nevertheless, as her father's only child, she was the heiress to a substantial estate that was protected under the laws of entail so that it could not be legally transferred without her permission. The size of the estate evidently excited the cupidity of her uncle and a number of her other relatives, so her uncle used every opportunity to encourage her already strong ambivalence about married life and overcame her doubts about being able to withstand the rigors of monastic life because of recurrent illnesses. At age fifteen, she decided to take an oath of chastity and give all her property except for five thousand ducats to her uncle for him to distribute among her poor relatives. At age seventeen, María was received by St. Teresa herself when she entered the Carmelite Convent of San Joseph y Santa Teresa of Toledo, using the five thousand ducats as her dowry.[46]

For lower-class families, however, excesses of religious devotion on the part of an adolescent that might lead her to attempt to enter a convent were actively discouraged. María Antonia Hortola, who grew up in the village of Senicha (Valencia), was the daughter of an artisan family that clearly expected her to marry. But María was extremely devout and from age seven had begun a series of special prayers and devotions that included fasting, saying prayers at nightfall, and disciplining herself several times a week. Although she tried to conceal her devotions, they became known to her parents when she was thirteen since people in the village had started calling her "the *beata*." Fearing that her reputation might destroy the possibility of matrimony, her parents and relatives began ridiculing her, claimed that she was possessed, abused her by denying her meals, and even had her exorcised on several occasions. Finally, when she was sixteen, she took advantage of the disruption caused by the English attack on Játiva to flee to the home of an uncle in nearby Xalón.[47]

At times, it was the girl herself who was reluctant or unwilling to enter monastic life, while the family did its best to convince her. The life of Gerónima de San Esteban presents one of the most surprising cases of this attitude because as a child and adolescent she had devoted herself to the practice of such austerities as nightly vigils, regular scourging, and wearing of a penitential girdle. At the same time, for whatever reason, the girl had a pronounced aversion to the Carmelites, and when her uncle offered to bring her to the Franciscan Convent of Santa Catalina in Zaragoza, she told him flatly that she had no interest in life as a nun. It was not until age twenty-four that the once reluctant Gerónima was finally persuaded to enter religious life as a member of that same Carmelite order that she had once disliked so intensely.[48]

The most tragic case of remorse over feeling reluctant about entering religious life concerns Hipolita de Jesús y Rocaberti, who admitted in one of her writings that she had experienced strong sexual desires as a teenager and therefore had little desire to join a religious community.[49] Pressured by her father and other relatives, who pointed to a long tradition of exemplary religious leaders coming from the family, Hipolita joined the Dominican Convent of Nuestra Señora de los Angeles in Barcelona at age sixteen and went on to have a distinguished career that spanned almost sixty years. During her life as a nun, she became well known for her mystical experiences and wrote twenty-six spiritual works in Latin, Catalan, and Castillian. Even though her ambivalence about entering religious life ceased shortly after she professed, she was so overwhelmed by guilt at having felt any doubts about becoming a bride of Christ that she concluded that she was an "evil sinner," "unworthy of being a member of the order," and a "Judas among the apostles."[50] Haunted by these strong feelings of guilt and by such low self-esteem that she did not even want to sign her name to one of the letters she wrote to her confessor, she embarked on a program of self-punishment so intense that in four years she managed to completely ruin her health. In fact, if it had not been for the intervention of Raymundo Sanson, her first spiritual advisor, who ordered her to sharply reduce her fasting, scourging, and other austerities, she would probably have died in her early twenties. Even so, her piteous letters to her spiritual advisors, begging them to allow her to resume at least some of these practices, indicated that she was never able to feel fully vindicated in the sight of God and that her feelings of guilt remained with her throughout her life.[51]

Interestingly enough, when an adolescent girl chose to enter religious life, she was not necessarily alone. Sometimes members of her family were already in the convent, and occasionally they even occupied positions of authority. But what frequently made the transition from home to convent or *beaterio* easier was the existence of a group of young women who provided support for the decision or entered religious life at the same time. Just a few days before Margaret of Habsburg entered Descalzas Reales, several young women attached to her court and strongly influenced by her did the same thing. These girls included Luisa de Pernestan, the daughter of the grand chancellor of Bohemia, whom she had brought with her from the imperial court, and several young Spanish noblewomen who became attached to her after her arrival. Luisa de Pernestan went on to become abbess of Descalzas Reales, a position that Margaret herself refused.[52]

On a much less exalted level, the adolescence of María Christo, the daughter of a modest family of hidalgos from the village of La Parra in Andalusia, illustrates the same phenomenon of a group of girls who gave each other moral support and mutual encouragement to give up the world and enter religious life. In María's case, entry was not to an aristocratic convent but the foundation of a humble *beaterio* in her home village of La Parra. Joining her in making the foundation were her older sister Ana, who had accompanied her in her regimen of penance and devotion during the time they lived in the parental home, and two sisters from another leading local family. This nucleus was soon joined by five other girls of good family and a young widow who gave her home to the group so that they could establish the *beaterio*.[53]

In spite of occasionally enjoying the company or protection of a family member, the young women entering a religious order in early modern Spain found that, in most convents, living conditions were spartan at best. As the Spanish economy deteriorated and the number of convents increased, things got so bad that some convents, such as Seville's Santa María la Real, could provide food for the nuns only three days out of the week.[54] Such deprivation was not unusual, especially for convents established in the seventeenth century, even if they had aristocratic sponsorship. Granada's Convent of the Santo Angel Custodio, which was founded in 1626 by the marquis of Camarasa's youngest daughter, who acted as its first prioress, seems to have been little more than a convenient place where aristocratic or middle-class families could stash their unwanted daughters at little or no expense. The convent followed the rule of Poor Clares, so that the nuns were sworn to live in absolute poverty, while at the same time prohibited from begging. The nuns slept dormitory style and were not even allowed to have a chest or trunk for personal use.[55] To make matters worse, the marquis himself, who might have been expected to favor a convent that he had founded, was feuding with his daughter and visited the convent only once. Even though the community did receive some financial aid from the relatives of a nun who had transferred from another convent, it remained extremely poor, as a much-hoped-for behest from the Camarasa estate failed to materialize.[56]

Of course, the living conditions were not as bad in every convent. At Zaragoza's aristocratic old Convent of Santa Catalina, which was founded by an aunt of King James the Conqueror, the nuns all had roomy, well-furnished cells.[57] When Margaret of Habsburg joined what was arguably Spain's most prestigious convent, Madrid's Descalzas Reales, in 1584, however, she found that although the nuns had their own cells they all slept on straw pallets, had a limited and monotonous diet of vegetables and eggs, and did all the kitchen work themselves.[58]

If conditions were bad in convents with aristocratic founders, they could be far worse in Spain's numerous *beaterios,* which generally drew their members from the daughters of the impoverished middle class or poor widows. Before she entered the *beaterio* of La Parra as a founding member, María de Christo renounced her inheritance and gave away all her property. In the *beaterio* itself, the women followed a harsh regimen with one meal a day eaten out of a common vegetable stew that was prepared once a week so that, in the words of her biographer Fernando de San Antonio Capilla, "there was no time wasted serving the pleasures of the flesh." The house was almost bereft of furniture, even beds, so that the *beatas* slept on the floor, using their serge cloaks as a pillow. In any case, beds would have been superfluous because they spent so little time sleeping, occupying their nights with prayer and penance.[59]

Conditions in convents, moreover, were made far more restrictive by a provision of the Council of Trent calling for strict enclosure or cloistering and by harsh rules that made it very difficult for nuns to maintain contact with the outside world. At the Ángel Convent in Granada, for example, the nuns were strongly discouraged from receiving visitors, especially family members in the porter's lodge. If a nun wished to write a letter, it first had to receive authorization from the abbess. All letters arriving at the convent were read before they were passed to their recipient.[60] Both the Franciscan rule of the Poor Clares and St. Teresa's 1567 Constitutions for the Discalced Carmelite nuns stipulated that another nun be present whenever a layperson came to visit. Saint Teresa even insisted that all trivial conversations be brought to a rapid conclusion under pain of imprisonment if the nun involved failed to heed the warnings of her chaperon.[61] Saint Teresa also went to extraordinary lengths to eliminate anything that might delight the senses from her convents, declaring in her constitutions, "Neither in the habits of the nuns nor on the beds must there be any color not even in so small a thing as a girdle."[62]

It was this harsh environment that so many middle- and upper-class adolescent girls entered, frequently of their own volition but just as often under strong pressure from their parents and relatives eager to save on dowries. But it would be a mistake to portray all of these young women as delicate creatures brought up in the lap of luxury and therefore entirely unprepared for the harsh life of the convent or *beaterio*. This is precisely the way the novices who entered the Convent of Santo Angel Custodio were depicted by Beatriz María de Jesús' biographer Tomás de Montalvo, but the fact that in so many middle- and upper-class homes an austere environment akin to that of a convent was the rule indicates that Montalvo's description reflects the baroque love of contrasts and dramatic change more than social reality.[63] Nevertheless, the evidence suggests that many young women—and not only those without any special vocation for the life of the cloister—had great difficulties in making the adjustment. Novices had a particularly hard time, in part because so many were emotionally immature adolescents and in part because the novitiate was a testing time designed to weed out girls who were unable to meet the physical and psychological demands of convent life. These aspects of the novitiate were laid out by St. Teresa of Jesus in her constitutions, where she states that no postulant was to be received as a nun unless she had a clear vocation and was apt to be a useful addition to the community. Pressure on the novice to prove herself was increased by the fact that profession was subject to the consent of the majority of the community.[64]

As if this were not enough, in certain convents novices were treated with special harshness to break them of any bad habits that they might have acquired in secular life. Perhaps because the nuns were aware of just how difficult life in their convent would be, the novices at Santo Ángel Custodio were not only expected to endure an especially harsh regimen of silence and penance but also trained in humility by the novice mistress by being "punished without having committed any offense, admonished without transgression and humiliated for no special reason." Moreover, the saintly virtue of obedience was instilled by not allowing them to protest their innocence, no matter how arbitrary the punishment.[65] Even Margaret of Habsburg was not spared this treatment. During her novitiate, Sor Juana de la Cruz, Descalzas Reales's austere abbess, went out of her way to upbraid her for the slightest fault, humiliate her by telling her that she was not strong enough for convent life, and made sure that she performed the humblest tasks in the kitchen and laundry.[66]

In most convents, successful adjustment for novices depended critically on the attitude of the nun placed in charge of their training. The novice mistress was all powerful, and her charges not only were under her direction but also had to report to her on a regular basis as to the progress of their spiritual lives. In convents where the novice mistress was truly compassionate and had real insight into the emotional and psychological needs of her charges, the transition from layperson to nun was made much easier. In the Carmelite Convent of Saint Joseph and Santa Teresa of Toledo, the novices who entered during the 1580s were fortunate in having María de Jesús as novice mistress. Perhaps because of doubts about her health and fitness for convent life when she professed at age seventeen, she had unique insight into the problems of the novices placed under her direction and would make it her business to be available to them at any hour of the day or night. She was aware, from her own experience, of the doubts that tormented young girls faced with making a lifetime commitment to convent life and was ready and able to provide them with the kind of counseling that would help them to overcome these "snares of the Devil." One of the nuns, Isabel del Sacramento, recalled that as a sixteen-year-old novice she had a series of horrible nightmares filled with demons, but as soon as she cried out María de Jesús would come to her cell and the evil ones would hide their faces and disappear.[67] She also coped with the high levels of anxiety and insecurity that her young charges felt, especially at night, by sprinkling holy water over them just after they went to bed.[68] This gesture was especially comforting because of the widely accepted idea that holy water had protective and curative properties.

Nevertheless, it was not unusual for novices to have a harsh and austere novice mistress who would use the most brutal means to remold their personalities. During the time that Ana de Jesús served as novice mistress at the Carmelite Convent of Beas, which had been founded in 1575 by Teresa of Jesus, she specialized in inventing ways to break their will. One of her favorite methods of instilling blind obedience in the novices was to make them move a pile of stones from one end of the courtyard to the other and back. Questioned by one of the novices as to why they were being forced to perform such a seemingly useless task, she told her be aware that "you do not search for reasons to obey but keep your mouth shut and do as you are told." Once she ordered a pot of stew to be placed on the stairs and left it there for several days until it began to stink. Finally, one of the novices complained about the smell, only to be rebuked for the lack of humility and forced to wear the stew pot around her neck for several days until Ana allowed her to take it off.[69]

In Saint Teresa's constitutions, she makes a point of emphasizing that no novice who fails to demonstrate commitment and aptitude for convent life should be accepted into the community: "Anyone who does not feel herself to be called by the Lord to this state, must on no account be received."[70] But just how easy was it to leave a religious institution? Some novices who were dissatisfied with convent life simply had no place to go. That was certainly the case of Catarina Tomás, who, as a lay nun of eighteen, found herself working like a slave, cleaning the nuns' cells, doing all the kitchen labor and a variety of other chores, and not even being allowed to attend mass with the other members of the community.[71] Her fantasy about going home was expressed in several "demonic" visions. In one, a dignified man presented himself to her and told her that he was on his way to Rome on behalf of a large number of novices and nuns who wanted the holy father to allow them to break their vows. He asked her to inform everyone in the community that he was prepared to represent them as well. Temptation also presented itself in the form of a gray-bearded hermit who expressed sympathy for her suffering and offered to remove her from the convent if she wished.[72] Of course, according to her biographer, she indignantly rejected both offers, but from what has already been said about her childhood it would seem that she really had no viable choice. Leaving the convent would simply have meant thrusting herself back into an abusive home with her relatives.

The tendency of novice mistresses and others with responsibility over young postulants to dismiss their dissatisfaction with convent life as the work of the devil is perfectly natural, considering the fact that to admit the validity of such complaints might reflect badly on the convent itself. The convent would lose whatever financial support it might have hoped to gain from the novice's family and might get a bad reputation among other local families as a place that could not retain the young women placed there. Even the well-meaning provisions of the Council of Trent, which condemned the practice of forcing children into religious vocations, may have worked to the detriment of novices who wished to leave the convent since it could be assumed that after that legislation the young women who entered the convent must have had at least some vocation. Faced with a novice who felt that convent life was too difficult for her and that she could better pursue her spiritual goals in another venue, Teresa de Jesús Vela reacted by dismissing these complaints as the work of the evil one and offered her help in struggling against these perfidious suggestions. Later, when the girl's parents and relatives came to visit her, she insisted on being present during the interview and warned her ahead of time not to say anything to them.[73] After the girl's parents left the convent, unaware of their daughter's plight, her best chance of leaving monastic life was gone as well, and she was "saved" for the life of the convent in spite of her lack of real vocation.

Unwilling or reluctant novices "saved" by novice mistresses like Teresa de Jesús Vela turned into unhappy and maladjusted nuns, of which there were not a few in the Spain of the early modern period. Complaints about convent life that nuns commonly made, as recorded by Antonio de Lorea in his biography of Hipolita de Jesús Rocaberti, included likening the convent to a prison and a place of constant melancholy. Dissatisfied nuns would also complain that they had been forced into religious life.[74] Overhearing some of the members of her own religious community complain about the boredom of seeing the same faces and the tedium of the choir while she was in a trance, Francisca Inés de la Concepción preached a kind of impromptu sermon, telling the nuns that in exchange for the gloom and austerity of religious life God had reserved for each of them a city resplendent with gold and precious stones, surrounded by a wall with twelve gates inscribed with the names of the twelve apostles.[75]

Such fantasies, however, could do little to mitigate the harshness of convent life and still less to change the personalities of those who simply could not adjust to it. Francisca de Binvessa, who joined the Carmelite Convent of San Joseph in Pamplona in 1583 under the name of Francisca del Santissimo Sacramento, was described by Joseph de Santa María, the chronicler of the order, as of a "harsh and angry disposition."[76] She herself admitted to having little aptitude for devotions and to finding spiritual exercises "repugnant." During her novitiate and early years as a nun, she experienced long periods of spiritual desolation and was disturbed by so many nightmares that she sometimes obtained permission to sleep in the prioress's cell, where she felt more secure because "demons would respect the leaders of religious orders."[77] Francisca was also one of those persistent troublemakers who did so much to perturb the life of religious communities in the post-Tridentine church. She was always intolerant of the faults of the other members of the community and took every opportunity to criticize them. She managed to cause so much dissension that she was punished by order of the provincial, who also transferred her favorite spiritual advisor to another convent because of his support for her.[78]

In extreme cases, the problem nun, the nun who was bored and dissatisfied with community life, could come to believe herself to be possessed by demonic forces. Such feelings of possession may be traced to feelings of having lost control and being powerless over her own life, but they could also have been derived from the fact that novice mistresses and other superiors routinely blamed all manifestations of dissatisfaction, however solidly based, on the nefarious activity of the evil one. Moreover, as the Augustinian Pedro Benimelis found when he had to deal with a case of demonic possession in the Convent of La Concepción in Palma de Mallorca, the feeling of being possessed tended to spread from one nun to the rest of the community.

The epidemic began with Catalina Maura, an eighteen-year-old lay novice who was making a very difficult adjustment to convent life by being late for choir and prayers and refusing to learn to read. About six months after she entered the convent, she began showing signs of possession, going into trances and speaking in the voice of a demonic spirit. Obviously, part of the motivation here was a desire to break the taboos of convent life, since she would routinely curse and blaspheme while under the influence of the demon. Having experienced these kinds of situations previously and alarmed by reports that other nuns were coming to her cell to listen to her and converse with the "spirit," Benimelis intervened to exorcise her in front of the abbess and most of the nuns. He also took the precaution of having a thirteen-year-old boarder removed from the convent because she, too, was showing signs of possession.[79] Quick action by Benimelis and the local bishop sufficed to prevent the outbreak from getting out of hand, but as similar outbreaks on the island demonstrated, the frustrations and tedium of convent life could not always be sublimated into a denial of the flesh and a focus on divine favor.

In early modern Europe, as in the modern world, adolescence was a testing time and a time of struggle for self-actualization. By their early or midtwenties, however, most of the women in this study had come to terms with their situation and, as they became adults, began to gain increasing mastery over their social environment. In that struggle, the experiences and hardships of childhood and adolescence would play a key role in promoting a strong amount of self-reliance on the one hand and a high degree of dissociation and abstraction on the other. This was a potent combination, especially within the context of a society that placed a high degree of reliance on the ability to communicate with the divine and led many of these women to leadership positions in their convents, religious orders, and the wider society of the region and even the monarchy as a whole.

9

Adulthood

For most of the women in this study, adulthood, which began after age twenty according to Juan de la Cerda's somewhat arbitrary schema, was a period of growing self-confidence when they proved their mettle as leaders in whatever milieu they happened to find themselves, whether convent, *beaterio,* or secular society. But what made these women into leaders, what distinguished them from the other women around them who frequently had the same or greater advantages? Put another way, what strategies or combination of strategies did they adopt that allowed them to succeed, given the constraints that Spanish society placed on women during the early modern period?

The first approach, successfully adopted by Gabriela de San Joseph a few years after she entered the Discalced Carmelite convent in Ubeda, was to slowly but surely establish a moral ascendancy over the other nuns by criticizing their faults and deficiencies. After the members of her own religious community had been sufficiently cowed, this strategy was extended successfully to the order itself. While this approach was not designed to win the love of the community, it was well calculated to elicit respect and even fear and to discredit any opposition.

Interestingly enough, Gabriela may have actually adopted this strategy out of resentment after overhearing a conversation highly critical of her shortly after she entered the convent as a novice at the age of twenty-one. Be that as it may, by age twenty-six she had begun her lifelong habit of making it her business to call aside any nun that she found transgressing the rule or committing any minor fault and "with a terrible sweetness, correct and cajole them." It was as if she could peer into the souls of every member of the community with a crystal-clear mirror to "discover faults and imperfections even better than the one who had experienced them."[1] The nuns soon learned that Gabriela had a sharp tongue and could be extremely harsh if they failed to obey her slightest whim. Once, when Juana de la Purificación saved up what little money she had to spend on celebrating a religious holiday with slightly more than the usual display, Gabriela somehow found out that she had hidden the money in the bottom of an old stocking and began asking the nun for money to buy eggs for the convent. Sor Juana, who was trying to keep her money for the fiesta, replied innocently that as a cloistered nun she had no access to money, but this reply merely served to infuriate Gabriela, who replied tartly, "Traitress! Go to the stocking, bring the money you have there to me immediately and stop offending God."[2] The poor nun, who was completely nonplussed by Gabriela's seemingly miraculous knowledge of her little trick, had little choice but to fetch the money, which was restored to the common pool. Gabriela had her way again, and who could question her? The Carmelite rule enjoined absolute poverty and an absence of personal possessions, even though the offending nun had every intention of spending her pittance on enhancing a religious ceremony that would be taking place in the convent itself.

It did not take too long for Gabriela to extend to the order as a whole a strategy that already had the nuns of her own convent tremble whenever she looked in their direction. She began her campaign with her longtime spiritual advisor, Andrés de Santa Teresa, who not only was extremely devoted to her but also had sufficient influence to have been elected provincial on three separate occasions. To gain moral ascendancy over her spiritual advisor, Gabriela made use of a vision involving the foundress of her order, St. Teresa of Jesus.

Writing to her confessor in 1679, on the occasion of the conclave of the order at which he had been elected as provincial for the second time, she described her own dream visit to the meeting in the company of St. Teresa. Her vision occurred at the beginning of the conclave, when Teresa appeared to summon her to be present. As the friars settled down to take their vote, Teresa beckoned Gabriela to follow her to the door of the kitchen and then disappeared. Inside, Gabriela noticed tables laden with sumptuous food and turned away in disgust. Significantly enough, Teresa had avoided entering the kitchen, and when Gabriela encountered her again, she said that "less pampering would be more than sufficient for a few poor friars, this is not what I struggled to achieve." Informing her spiritual advisor that she herself had attended such conclaves in spirit and had seen both virtuous friars who worked for the benefit of the order and many others who were driven by personal ambition, she warned him that God was displeased and had told her to "weep and pray" for them. Even though Teresa confirmed during the vision that his own election had been in accordance with the will of God, that was not enough to protect him from Gabriela's disapproval as someone who "having just finished a term as provincial found a way to be elected to another term." She informed him that God was deeply pained by such arrangements, which implied a lack of charity and equal treatment for other members of the order, and offered one thousand lives if she had them to remove this "scab" from the moral conduct of the order.[3]

These were harsh words indeed for someone as powerful as Andrés de Santa Teresa, who had authority over her both as her confessor and as chief executive of the order in Andalusia. Not only did she escape punishment for her temerity, however, but also in ensuing years she was able to considerably expand her control over the order by developing a network of correspondents in all of the religious houses, both male and female, in the Carmelite province. Using this unrivaled intelligence network, she became privy to all of the scandals and abuses in each convent long before they came to the attention of the male superiors of the order. Then, in keeping with her strategy of establishing her own moral ascendancy, she wrote to the provincial, informing them of what she had learned. These notes, in turn, frequently formed the basis for the investigations carried on by the superiors when they made their periodic visitations to the religious houses.[4]

Gabriela's amazing ascendancy over the Andalusian province continued throughout much of her adult life. She was elected prioress of her own convent in 1675, 1683, and 1689 and was frequently consulted by the male provincials about the politics of the order. A letter from her to the general of the order, Juan de la Aunciación, demanding that he take action to expedite the canonization of Juan de la Cruz, was enough to get him to undertake a major effort to obtain vital information about his miracles and to order prayers for the success of the process.[5] The nuns of her own convent were so awed by her that eight days after her death, two of them swore that they saw her enter the chapter meeting and take her accustomed seat. As it happened, the prioress had allowed two of the nuns to be absent from the meeting to attend to some important community business. But Gabriela, who had dominated convent life for so long, had always been so insistent on the presence of all the nuns at community events that there must have been considerable uneasiness about the prioress's decision so soon after her death. Consequently, one of the nuns saw Gabriela's ghost turn toward her and demand that the prioress order the two nuns to return and attend the meeting, since they could perform their business after it was over. Ever obedient to Gabriela's wishes, even after her death, the nun went privately to the prioress and informed her of what had transpired, and the prioress responded by recalling the two nuns.

If Gabriela de San Joseph had relied only occasionally on visions and revelations as part of a wider strategy of controlling the nuns of her convent, there were other women, both "genuine" and "fake" mystics, who relied almost exclusively on such divine communication to facilitate their rise to power. The ability to convince others that their words were inspired by the Holy Spirit, or that the Holy Spirit was actually speaking through them, gave them the courage and the authority to put forth their own ideas about running their religious communities and gain a degree of authority that might have been denied them otherwise.

Juana de la Cruz (1498–1534), the earliest "genuine" mystic in my sample, rose to become prioress of the convent of Santa María de la Cruz in spite of the fact that her parents were simple peasants from the village of Hazaña in New Castile. One of the most powerful weapons in her arsenal was a vision in which the Virgin Mary appeared to announce that those nuns who had offended her would have to suffer the wrath of God. She then ordered all of the nuns to appear before her and asked Juana to tell her what grievances she had against them. Juana responded by declaring that she had no complaints against them. The Virgin Mary then called them before her individually and asked Juana again what complaints she had, and Juana responded as she had before. The Virgin Mary complimented her for "leaving it to God to render justice and exact vengeance for the offenses which you have suffered" and disappeared after assuring her that she would intervene with Christ on her behalf, since she held "the key to my house."[6]

What was Juana de la Cruz attempting to achieve by announcing this vision to the other nuns? On the one hand, by invoking the powerful intercession of the Virgin Mary, who had absorbed many of the powers and responsibilities of the ancient goddesses, she frightened them by demonstrating that she had such powerful support.[7] On the other hand, by not informing the Virgin about any of the complaints she had against them, she emerged as their protector, at the same time holding over their heads the certainly of divine punishment if they offended her further.

Gratitude and fear proved themselves powerful allies. After she was elected prioress, she achieved such absolute ascendancy over the community that the nuns "counted themselves fortunate" if they were permitted to kiss her hand or touch the hem of her garment. They were in such awe of her that whenever she called any of them, they would arrive trembling, and she had to calm them down before proceeding to discuss the matter in question. Powerfully reinforcing her authority as prioress were the visions that she had before every general meeting of the community. In these visions, all the faults and sins of each nun were revealed to her, and her guardian angel told her exactly what to say to deal with each situation. At the meeting itself, she would reveal her vision to the assembled community and punish each individual in accordance with what had been ordained by the Holy Spirit. In this way, of course, she herself avoided being blamed for any harsh measure that she had to take, since she was merely the instrument and not the author of the punishment, while at the same time she maintained her role as intercessor with supernatural forces. This strategy worked to perfection, and the nuns were so loyal to her that they supported her against the hostility of the provincial, who had briefly removed her from office.[8]

Visions and claims of divine communication were also frequently used by "false" mystics in their struggles for power inside convents or in secular society. Such claims, however, tended to be viewed with a considerable degree of skepticism by at least a significant minority of the people in their immediate circle. These doubters not only helped to undermine the women's reputations but also frequently turned up as witnesses against them at their trials.

As a novice in the Convent of San Miguel de los Angeles of Toledo, Francisca de la Santissima Trinidad could not have expected to have much influence, especially considering her humble social origins as the daughter of an artisan and the minuscule dowry that she had been able to bring with her. Nevertheless, within a few months of her arrival in May 1633, she had the convent in an uproar over the attire worn by the nuns, which she claimed violated the ancient rule. The only evidence for her assertion that the nuns had strayed in matters of dress came out of her frequent trances, during which she either spoke directly to God or addressed the nuns who came to see her. During one of these trances, she was heard to ask, "And what do the elders have to say?" Receiving the answer, which was evidently favorable to her ideas about changing the coif, she immediately went to consult with the convent's spiritual advisor, who forced the community to adopt the linen coif that she was demanding.[9]

Fresh from her triumph over the matter of the coifs, Francisca then began to focus on her next demand for reform: substituting sandals for the clogs that the nuns were permitted to wear. Her opportunity to interpose divine authority to assist her campaign came when the novice mistress asked her to find out if it was God's will that the nuns should remove their clogs. Francisca agreed to do so and entered a cell, shutting the door behind her. In a few moments, the nuns who were gathered outside the door heard her asking God about the clogs in a loud voice. Francisca then emerged from the cell and, predictably enough, informed the community that indeed God had confirmed that they should wear sandals instead.[10]

Not surprisingly, however, given Francisca's social disabilities and her status as a novice without enough time in the convent to build up a solid network of support, the community became deeply divided over her claims to divine inspiration and her program of reform. On the one hand, as Antonia de Briones, one of her worst detractors, claimed, her supporters "accepted her as the oracle of the Holy Spirit," while other nuns rejected her completely, insisting that they would not permit "a novice to dictate new precepts to them even if she were Saint Catherine of Siena."[11] Faced by the obduracy of a number of the nuns, including some of the oldest and most aristocratic, Francisca once again resorted to her supernatural powers, claiming that she had seen the souls of her opponents in hell and that they were all possessed by the devil. Dismissed as empty threats by her opponents, these revelations merely exacerbated the situation and led them to denounce her to the Holy Office.

Laywomen, even the illiterate pauper María Cotonilla, were also able to improve their position by pretending to have visions and mystical transports. Impoverished and in rags when she began to have trances and travel to hell and purgatory in spirit, María rapidly improved her situation as several local families began giving her their used clothing and providing her with fixed amounts of money on a regular basis. Even her landlady, who doubted her spiritual vocation from the very beginning, admitted at her trial that she believed that evil spirits did try to prevent María from taking communion, which would certainly have been a sign of virtue.[12] Other local people were less skeptical and believed her stories about visions of hell and visits to purgatory, where she claimed to have seen and talked to the souls of dead family members.[13]

Taking the path of the mystic visionary had benefited María Cotonilla, transforming an illiterate and virtually friendless pauper into something of a local personage received by the best *labrador*, merchant, and artisan families. But her good fortune had already caused eyebrows to be raised among those who regarded the slight improvement in her circumstances as entirely inappropriate to her station and a sign that she was merely pretending "sanctity." Desperate to shore up her support among the good families of the village, María overplayed her hand by staging a series of spasms, followed by a two-hour trance in the upstairs bedroom in the home of Manuel Pantoja, one of her staunchest supporters. The attempt to impress Pantoja backfired, however, as he found her trances completely unconvincing and ordered his servants to bar her from the house.[14] Exclusion from the home of a man who had once invited her to his daughter's wedding and had frequently had her stay overnight carried a great deal of weight, especially as he and his wife told the story to other persons of influence. One of the people they talked to, Fr. Juan Carrascosa, a Trinitarian in a nearby convent, concluded that María had simply tried to gain a reputation as a "saint" in order to feed herself. The failure of the trances also led to her dismissal by her confessor and chief supporter, the Carmelite Juan Maroto, who bitterly denounced her as a "fraud" and ceased his efforts to supply her with alms from devotees in the village.[15]

Catalina Ballester was another laywoman who succeeded in rising economically and socially primarily by convincing others that she could communicate directly with God through trances and visions. But in this case it was not the visions themselves but the elaborate performances connected with them that really gave her the ability to gain a large following. Catalina began building her spiritual reputation in Falaniche, her home village, when a local woman recovered from a life-threatening illness after she brought her some medlar fruit. This cure was considered so remarkable in the village that the remaining fruit was distributed among other women, who cherished it "as if it were a relic or something miraculous."[16]

After she left Falaniche for the greener pastures of Palma de Mallorca, however, and especially after she became established in the home of the devout Morlana sisters, she abandoned curative magic, with its aura of folk remedies and rural culture, for long ecstatic trances during which she became "as rigid as a piece of wood."[17] During these trances she would act out Christ's passion and raise her arms to receive the Christ child. In other trances, she would also sustain prolonged dialogues with God and was believed by Juana Terrasa, the Morlana's niece, to be receiving spiritual communion at the hands of an angel. In fact, these trances and the performances connected with them so impressed Terrasa that she admitted to being afraid of Catalina during her testimony before the Inquisition.[18]

One of her most influential male followers, the Carmelite Nicolas Masso, firmly believed that Catalina traveled in spirit during her trances and that she had been able to rescue him from a storm at sea.[19] Catalina acted out this "spiritual sea voyage" one day when the Morlana sisters found her lying in bed soaking wet. She also managed the convince Masso that every time she returned from taking communion she sat down to a supernatural feast at a sumptuous table set with a snow-white cloth.[20] The shirts that she made were also highly prized in Palma because she claimed that St. Catherine of Siena helped her to complete them.[21] Like Catherine of Siena, moreover,

Catalina had a mystical ring that Christ gave her during one of her trances to signify their spiritual marriage. Of course, Catalina's "miracle" differed from Catherine's in that the ring was visible and, in fact, had probably been stolen from the Morlana sisters, who had been showing her their jewelry only the day before.[22]

The third and perhaps most remarkable way in which women mystics established their reputations and enhanced their power was through performance. To make manifest their recipt of divine favor, these women acted out trances, spoke with the voice of God, preached elaborate sermons, and pantomimed the sufferings of Christ. Following the tradition of the religiously based theater that emerged in sixteenth- and seventeenth-century Spain, with actors taking the part of saints, the Virgin Mary, or the Holy Spirit, these performances deeply impressed their audiences, helping to convince them that the woman mystic was the recipient of divine communication.

Juana de la Cruz deployed an impressive range of acting skills to gain a national reputation as a mystic and prophetess, in spite of serious efforts by her superiors to repress her. Eventually, this daughter of a local peasant family became prioress of her convent, a position that she held for an unprecedented term of seventeen years.

Juana's period of notoriety began when she was twenty-two, with a vision in which Christ appeared to her and ordered her to remain mute. Her silence had the effect of focusing a good deal of attention on her in a convent that did not follow the rules of strict enclosure and in which visitors were allowed in to speak with the nuns on a regular basis. Several months after this first vision, Juana experienced another one in which Christ ordered her to resume speaking, but with his voice. For the next thirteen years, Juana assumed the voice and authority of the Holy Spirit during a series of impressive public trances.[23]

The performance would always begin with Juana entering a trancelike state and "seeing" the approach of Christ accompanied by numerous angels, apostles, and saints. She would make the presence of these celestial figures known to the audience—which came to include not only the nuns of the convent but also numerous outsiders and even prominent political figures—by speaking to the heavenly company, mentioning their names, motioning them to come closer, and bowing deeply to them as they did so. These preliminaries took about an hour, and then Christ himself would approach. She would speak loudly and clearly, assuming his voice and announcing his presence in the room. She then began beseeching his divine mercy for the souls of purgatory and for all humankind of whatever state and condition, from emperors to the humblest peasant. As she did this, she would clasp her hands and pray in a very low voice while bowing her head numerous times and then prostrate herself on the ground. At this point the other nuns would play their part by lifting her up and carrying her to her cell, where she would be placed on her cot.

Act two of this little drama would commence when Juana would begin preaching in the voice of the Holy Spirit about such matters as the interpretation of scripture, the immaculate conception, or the saints' days according to the ecclesiastical calendar. During these sermons, which could last six to seven hours, Juana remained absolutely still in a trancelike state so profound that when a woman spectator jabbed a pin into her head to test her, she failed to react, although she did complain about pain from the wound after she emerged from the trance. At the end of the sermon, the Holy Spirit would give his blessing to the assembled audience, who would go on their knees before Juana's cot and then be ushered out of the convent. So that such miraculous events would not to be lost to posterity, three of the nuns acted as scribes and took copious notes in a book that remained in the convent and provided information that served in her process of beatification.[24]

Since these events took place in the early years of the sixteenth century, when the authorities and the Inquisition were showing increasing concern about the Illuminist movement and the "spiritual mothers" who frequently provided the focus for groups of acolytes, it was not long before Juana's performances attracted the attention of the Holy Office and her superiors in the order. As it turned out, the Inquisition presented no great threat. Hearing of her reputation and following, an inquisitor from the Toledo tribunal did come to attend one of her sermons, but he was so impressed by her that he fell on his knees and declared himself convinced that she was indeed speaking the word of God.[25]

But worse opposition was to come from her superiors in the convent and the order. Concerned about the notoriety that she was attracting and afraid of a possible scandal, the superiors of the order told the abbess that whenever she began preaching she should be shut away in a cell in the remotest part of the convent. Juana first tried to thwart this effort to silence her by simulating the famous miracle of the preaching to the birds by the founder of her order, St. Francis of Assisi. One day Juana was shut in her cell and took such a long time to wake from her trance that the prioress sent a nun to investigate. Opening the door, the nun was astonished to find a large number of birds of many colors grouped around Juana's cot, with their heads raised as if listening to her sermon.[26]

However much this "miracle" appeared to indicate divine intervention, her superiors were not convinced and continued to insist that she be isolated every time she went into one of her trances. Realizing that she needed to do something much more dramatic to force them to accept her, Juana decided to take advantage of her superior's orders and fabricate a "miracle" that would so impress them that they would stop interfering with her. Knowing full well that she would be immediately taken to her cell if she showed any signs of having a trance, she suddenly went rigid with her arms held out in the shape of a cross one Holy Friday just before the community had to go to the choir for divine office. Obeying the instructions they had been given in such cases, the nuns picked Juana up and took her to her cell and then left for the choir as she expected. A short time later, as they were finishing their singing, Juana entered the choir weeping copiously, holding on to the walls, and walking on heel and toe as if she were afraid to put her feet fully on the floor. Filled with curiosity and concerned because of the pain she seemed to be experiencing, the nuns examined her feet and hands and found round marks the same size as a silver real. The marks were reddish, very fresh, and moist, although containing no blood. Overcome with emotion at this latest miracle, the nuns carried her back to her cell and asked her how she had acquired these marks. Juana replied that she had been carried to the crucified Christ by her guardian angel, and that as she approached the cross he impressed them upon her. The stigmata manifested themselves each Friday, Saturday, and Sunday until Ascension day, when they completely disappeared.[27]

The presence of stigmata on Juana's person, which simulated a miracle that had happened to St. Francis, was finally enough to convince the leaders of her order that she was uniquely favored by God. From then on, she was left in peace, and her incredible career as a preacher and counselor to the great and humble was allowed to continue unhindered. She was elected prioress with the unanimous support of the nuns and informed the provincial that he had to confirm her by speaking to him in his native Basque during a trance in which she once again assumed the role of the Holy Spirit. During her time in office, she transformed a poor convent with a few miserable acres of land and a tiny endowment into an important and wealthy ecclesiastical institution with the help of donors like Cardinal Francisco Jiménez de Cisneros and the "Great Captain," Gonzalo Fernández de Córdoba.

Another performance-based tactic that sought to demonstrate that the individual was uniquely favored by God was to pretend to be experiencing the physical and emotional torture of demonic persecution. Since the evil one could act only with God's permission, demonic persecution was regarded as a kind of rite of passage that had the effect of testing the saint's courage and perseverance in the path of virtue. Such acting was a favorite tactic of the "false" saint Vicenta Orval from Torrente in the kingdom of Valencia.

According to the parish priest Juan Pérez, one of Vicenta Orval's most ardent followers, she "suffered exceedingly from persecution by evil spirits." He testified that on three separate occasions he had seen her so exhausted from this torture that she collapsed into a state of semiconsciousness, interrupted by deep sighs and brief dialogues with the devil, in which she appeared to be resisting his demands and blandishments.[28]

A performance-based strategy designed to convince others that one had been singled out by God for demonic persecution proved to be highly effective in altering Caterina Tomás's position in her convent from downtrodden servant to highly respected, even feared member of the community. At around age seventeen, Caterina's luck began to change when her virtue and religious devotion came to the attention of a local hermit who happened to have some valuable connections in Palma. He brought her to the city and placed her as a servant in the home of Mateo Forteza, a wealthy knight who was preparing one of his daughters for life as a nun. The girl taught Caterina how to read and write, and the entire family was impressed by her hard work and humility.[29]

But, as we have seen, Caterina's first year in the convent was miserable, and she nearly died of overwork and mistreatment. Like Antonio Abad, one of her favorite saints, she also experienced the blandishments of the devil, who argued that she should leave religious life. The strategy of representation and dramatization of demonic persecution was born out of her struggle to survive in the convent and her knowledge of the story of Antonio Abad, whose struggles with the devil went on throughout his life.[30]

Even though her biographer Bartolome Valperga was at some pains to insist that Caterina really wanted to suffer in silence and obscurity, he had to admit that when the devil tormented her, it was usually in a highly public place where all the nuns could witness it. During one of these episodes, Caterina made believe that she was being carried off by the devil, began crawling around the floor of the convent, and pretended that she was being dragged by demonic forces. Her screams alerted the other nuns, who rushed to her assistance and tried desperately to hold her while Caterina encouraged them by shouting, "Have no fear my sisters. Christ is with us!"[31]

Caterina made sure that the nuns were aware that she was about to suffer demonic torments by such devices as ringing the convent bell just before an incident. In one of her most spectacular and successful performances, she even went so far as to warn the prioress in advance that the devil had threatened to either push her down the stairs from the cloister or throw her into the cistern or into the well. Having created an atmosphere of anxious expectation, she carefully picked a time when she knew that one of the nuns was nearby and jumped into the cistern, which was full of water. Her shouts of "Jesus! Jesus! Jesus!"—greatly magnified and made all the more frightening by the echo from the sides of the cistern—quickly brought the prioress and the other nuns, who managed to reach Caterina with ladders. After hoisting her up, they noticed that throughout the ordeal she had held a relic of St. Catherine Martyr in one hand and part of a rosary in the other. Possession of these two holy objects at the time of her fall indicates the care and planning that went into this little scene, since she would have to have prepared both relic and rosary well in advance. Later on, this incident became so famous in Palma that the rosary beads that she used were treasured as a relic in their own right.[32]

Caterina was also well aware of the credulity and timidity of the prioress and the rest of the community and sought to frighten and impress them with loud and unexpected noises. One day Caterina threw stones around her cell, and when the prioress came running, crying, "What is all this noise and banging?" Caterina told her that the devil had been throwing stones at her and showed her the wounds and scratches that they had caused.[33]

Later in life, Caterina deployed a wider range of strategies to strengthen her control over the community. Accustomed to long spells of dissociation from earliest youth, she impressed the community and her superiors with deep trances that sometimes lasted two or three days. Interestingly enough, however, these trances were not so very profound as to stop her from performing normal activities, even when she supposedly had her eyes closed. She found it especially easy to manipulate Sor Elizabeth Calvona, a prioress who had always been one of her most fervent supporters. One evening she fell into a trance after having been bled to cure the most recent wounds that the devil had inflicted on her. The prioress, who was a little worried about her because she had lost so much blood, hoped to bring her out of the trance by ordering her to pick up her sewing. Always obedient to her superiors even while in a trancelike state, Caterina did as she was told, but instead of coming out of the trance, she began doing needlework that was far more beautiful than she had ever done while conscious. Astonished, the prioress asked her how she was able to do such work, and she answered that she was being helped by St. Catherine of Alexandria and St. Clare and pointed out the stitches that each one had put in. Of course, news of the miracle soon reached every corner of the convent, and the nuns came running to see the marvelous piece of linen. Unfortunately for the faithful nuns, however, the linen with its saintly stitching later disappeared, presumably carried off to heaven by one of the heavenly seamstresses.[34]

Performance could also be used to establish a reputation for exemplary devotion that went so far beyond the ordinary that it indicated the individual's special relationship to God. The biblical injunction from Christ to "take up the cross and follow me" had numerous mystics acting out the pain, torment, and humiliation of the passion as Christ himself must have felt it.

María Ángela Astorch was extremely devoted to the passion, which she would act out on a regular basis in the refectory, but she was particularly adept at inventing new ways of self-abasement related to the passion, thereby giving full rein to the strong masochistic urges that she had felt since adolescence. In 1642 she described with obvious relish how she had herself whipped by two of the nuns in the dead of night and made them treat her like a jailed criminal "with leg irons, handcuffs and a chain around my neck."[35] To dramatize the humiliation that Christ must have felt when being accused before the authorities and the people, she invented something called, significantly, "the exercise of the holy theater." The "holy theater" in this case consisted of an Inquisition-style examination, with the other nuns as accusers, and it ended with María being found guilty and forced to admit her sinfulness before the entire community.[36]

Devotion to the Eucharist could also become the subject of dramatization by mystics. The "false" mystic Sor Luisa de la Ascensión, who became known popularly as the "monja de Carrion," would regularly stage an impressive trance every time she took communion. Blessed with great strength and an iron constitution, she would go down on one knee and keep the other leg in the air. She was also capable of descending the stairs on one foot, while in a trance like state a feat she once performed in the presence of King Philip III.[37]

Luisa was also very devoted to helping other nuns die a "good death" and would frequently enter a trancelike state when a nun was seriously ill and about to die. These trances involved profuse crying, and the paintings that were made of her and the prints that circulated with her portrait normally showed her with tears streaming from her eyes. After she emerged from these trances, she would force herself under the dying nun's cot, lifting it up several times and then hitting the floor loudly. Since Luisa was extremely strong, nuns who attempted to pull her from under the cot would sometimes be injured, and

she insisted that they sprinkle holy water and make crosses over her to release her, since she blamed the devil for her behavior.[38]

But it was also possible to involve others in these theatrics not just as mere
spectators but as active participants. One of the most impressive examples of
this can be found in the elaborate ceremony that María Angela Astorch staged
to celebrate her betrothal to Christ. This ceremony, which was held after she
had been elected prioress, involved all of the nuns and even her confessor,
Dr. Arbués, who took the role of Christ. After more than nineteen months of
preparation, the performance began with an all-night vigil, during which María
knelt before an image of the crucified Christ. Early in the morning on October 21, 1626, María woke up the other nuns by banging on the doors of their
cells and calling out in Latin, "Awake, daughters of Zion, and behold King
Solomon." Responding eagerly to this rather flamboyant salutation, the nuns
streamed out of their cells and followed María down to the choir, where they
heard mass. After mass, Dr. Arbués delivered a sermon, and then María re-
cited fervent declarations of love, which were responded to by Arbués, taking the part of Christ. Then, with each nun holding a burning candle, María
solemnly pronounced her covenant of betrothal promising faithfully:

> That out of a vehement desire to contract
> spiritual marriage with my lord Jesus Christ
> I will never again sin against God either
> venially or mortally.[39]

The elaborate religious theater staged by women mystics, whether "feigned"
or "officially approved," illustrates not only the similarities in the behavior
of the two groups but also the fact that this behavior was shaped by the social,
cultural, and religious context. Audiences, whether predominantly made up
of religious or of a mixture of religious and laypeople, had certain expecta-
tions and models for the performance provided by hagiographies, *comedias
de santos*, and word of mouth. Dissociation, which began in the lives of so
many mystics as a reaction to a distressed childhood, now became part of a
conscious or semiconscious strategy to attract attention and gain power and
authority within the religious community itself and in the wider society.
Trancelike states inspired a mixture of fear and awe, offered a safe means of
criticizing others, and allowed the mystic to express her genuine theological
and devotional convictions.

The fact that no fewer than sixteen (53 percent) of the "official" mystics
were elected prioress or subprioress of their convents should be enough to
indicate the success of the group in attaining leadership positions. But what
kind of leadership did these women provide, how did they get others to follow them, and what was the overall impact of their leadership on the religious
community?

The harsh circumstances of life in many an early modern convent meant
that effective leadership was leadership by example, especially if the goal was
to induce the members of the community to make their lives even more difficult by undertaking greater austerities. This was certainly the leadership style

practiced by Ana de Jesús, both as novice mistress and as prioress. A description of her leadership style that comes down to us from the time that she was novice mistress at Veas indicates that she herself participated in several exercises designed to teach humility and toughen the young women physically and emotionally so that they could bear the hardships of life as a Carmelite.

One of these exercises, shocking in its brutality, involved forcing each of the novices to take her turn at being a martyr, with the other novices playing the role of torturers and executioners. Ana would then browbeat the other novices into beating and whipping the unfortunate victim until she collapsed bleeding and exhausted. But she herself gave the example, playing the role of the "martyr" more often than any of the novices and urging them to scourge and beat her without mercy so that she could gain the "crown of martyrdom that she had so ardently desired."[40]

Setting an example of religious austerity and driving the members of her community to greater heights of self-abdication also formed a key element in the leadership style of María de Christo when she founded the *beaterio* of La Parra. Even though she herself and most of the other women were weak, sick, and undernourished, she refused to call in a physician, insisted on greater austerities, and took on the humblest and dirtiest tasks in the kitchen herself. She also imposed a special regimen of penance in which two of the women would retire to a small room at the back of the house and practice a series of particularly harsh physical mortifications on each other. Having little to give them of a material nature, María would encourage the other women by speaking to them with great fervor about the passion and sufferings of Christ and exhort them to embrace holy poverty without fear in the confidence that God would provide for their needs.[41]

Unlike the nuns of the Carmelite order, the *beatas* of La Parra were not in a regimen of strict enclosure so that as their reputation for austerity and devotion spread, people could come and see for themselves. A number of locally important clergy availed themselves of the opportunity, including an archpriest and a prebendary from Alcalá, all of whom were favorably impressed by the *beaterio* and by María herself, who appeared to have a real flare for interpreting scripture. The fame of the *beaterio* spread, and after María managed to obtain the privilege of having the host reserved in the chapel, money began to flow in from numerous supporters, including a wealthy caballero, Francisco de Silva y Vargas, who gave enough money for an elaborate gilt altar piece in which she placed statues of St. Francis and St. Clare.[42]

Apparently, María chose to spend the money she was receiving on additional cult objects rather than on improving living conditions in the *beaterio*. One thing that we do know for certain is that she indignantly rejected suggestions that she use some of the money to aid her starving relatives by declaring, "I have no relatives other than Jesus Christ." This attitude was praised by her biographer Fernando de San Antonio Capilla as simply following the words of Christ recorded by St. Matthew: "Whosoever loves his father or his mother more than he loves me is not worthy of me," but it may be surmised that María, who had been forced to renounce her inheritance before she founded the *beaterio*, felt some resentment toward relatives who were now demanding assistance from her.[43]

Another way in which women mystics provided leadership was by establishing new devotions that would serve to distinguish the nuns of her convent from other nuns. Such new devotional practices would not only raise morale within the religious community itself but also open the possibility of establishing a stronger link with the laity, who might then emerge as supporters and contributors. One "true" mystic who did this very effectively was Gabriela de San Joseph during her long reign as prioress of the Carmelite convent in Ubeda. Gabriela instituted four important new devotions, one of which, commemorating Jesus Nazarene, attracted financial support from the marquis of Santa Cruz. It was symptomatic of the powerful impression that Gabriela's personality made on the nuns and how strongly they associated her with the devotions that she had founded that for one entire year after her death, two or three of them saw her attending the ceremonies with an expression of singular happiness and satisfaction.[44]

A woman mystic could also provide leadership by making herself into a kind of cultural intermediary, bringing the devotional forms fashionable among the elites of major cities to her less sophisticated followers. This is exactly the role that María Ruano played when she returned to her native El Guijo after her stay in Madrid. Reuniting her supporters among the women of the village, she organized them into a kind of *tableau vivante* in exactly the same way as certain "pious souls" were doing in Madrid. The *tableau vivante*, which was to be presented every day in the parish church, called for two of the women to prostrate themselves and kiss the ground, another group to stand with their arms spread in the form of a cross, and the remainder to kneel and make various gestures of humility and gratitude for the favors that God had bestowed.[45] All of this was dedicated to support María's ill-fated proposal to establish a Carmelite convent in the village, which she hoped would help to ward off Portuguese attack.

Finally, what the biographies reveal beyond a shadow of a doubt is the enormous benefit that a convent or *beaterio* could derive from choosing as its leader someone with a reputation for great spiritual power. Generally poorer and less well endowed than their male counterparts, female religious committees were also greatly restricted in the things that they could do to raise money by the imposition of strict enclosure. Barred from begging for alms like the mendicant friars, preaching, hearing confessions, and even teaching children like the French Congregation of Notre Dame, Spanish nuns and *beatas* became even more dependent on the reputation of their leading members to ensure the flow of lay support.

The positive impact that a woman mystic could have on the fortunes of a convent is evident in the biography of Beatriz María de Jesús, especially after 1680, when she experienced a vision that informed her that she was to "help humanity to know and love God."[46] Already in the previous year, when the city was wracked by plague, Beatriz had received permission from her confessor to undertake special penance to expiate the sins that she believed had angered God and caused the pestilence. Since the weakening of the plague later that year was widely attributed to Beatriz's prayers, her reputation in the city grew tremendously.

Beginning in 1680, she began giving spiritual advice to a group of influential upper-class women, and she was soon in touch with leading members of the aristocracy, both male and female, who were eager make contact with this "exceptional woman." For their part, the clergy, including the archbishop of Granada, Alfonso Bernardo de los Ríos, became extremely devoted to her, frequently coming to the convent to consult with her and treating her like an "oracle."[47]

Needless to say, wealthy clergy and laity were exactly the kind of people that the convent needed to lift it out of the poverty to which its founder's neglect had condemned it. Grateful for her prayers, advice, and protection, they were prepared to give generously to the convent. Contributions poured in, not only from the city of Granada but also from numerous other places and from the court in Madrid, and people "counted themselves fortunate if Beatriz would accept them." Generous contributions meant that the community could now not only provide for its basic needs but also embellish its chapel with beautiful and expensive cult objects.[48]

The success that so many of the women mystics achieved as leaders of convents, *beaterios,* or lay society also led to significant changes in their relationships to their own families. Bernardino González Delgadillo y Avellaneda's strong opposition to his daughter Brianda de Acuña Vela's desire to join the Discalced Carmelitesses gave way to admiration and devotion as the extent of her commitment to the spiritual life became clear to him. Regarding her as a person of great holiness, he came to her convent to thank her for interceding with God for his immortal soul, something she had been doing because she feared that his soul would be condemned for his brutal treatment of her mother and his political misdeeds.[49]

An even more remarkable change came over the family of Caterina Tomás. Caterina's growing reputation as a miracle-working mystic and her success in the convent significantly changed her uncle and aunt's opinion of her. Even though they treated her little better than a servant and were openly disdainful of her religious vocation while she lived with them, they came to regard her as a powerful ally both in this world and in the realm of the supernatural. In fact, her uncle had such a high opinion of her ability to effect supernatural cures that he sent his own son Miguel to see her on three separate occasions when he was ill.[50] In gratitude for her efforts on his behalf, Miguel Tomás, who later became a prosperous benefice holder on the island, paid for the publication of Bartolomé Valperga's 1627 biography.

For some women mystics, adulthood also meant having the leisure and support to write. Spiritual autobiographies, in which the woman would give an account of her doubts, struggles, visions, and divine favors, were insisted upon by 22.2 percent of the confessors of the "approved mystics" and 7.5 percent of those who served the women who feigned sanctity. Such writings, whether or not collected in book form, provided the spiritual advisor with valuable insights into the thoughts and feelings of his charge as they gave the woman an unprecedented opportunity for self-expression. Even Jacinta de Atondo's brutal confessor, Pedro Garcés, insisted that she produce a written account of her inner thoughts and feelings, although he paid scant attention to them. Like many other women, Jacinta was wracked by feelings of insecurity and begged Garcés repeatedly to let her stop writing, but he refused and she had little choice but to obey her confessor, whom she identified with the power and authority of Christ.[51]

Some of the women also wrote devotional works, many of which remain unpublished, and created poetry and songs. Some of the devotional works that they produced can be counted among the most influential of the early modern period, the two most obvious examples being St. Teresa of Jesus' *Way of Perfection* and *Interior Castile*. Less well known to modern readers but almost as influential among contemporaries was María de Agreda's *Mystical City of God,* first published in Madrid in 1670. This book went through eighty-nine complete editions and sixty-eight summaries and anthologies. In the end, however, María de Agreda was much less fortunate than Teresa of Jesus because many of her other works remained unpublished until the early years of the twentieth century, while others have yet to appear.[52]

Spanish women mystics, like those in other countries, also produced a very respectable body of verse, but with very few exceptions this verse, where it still exists, remains in manuscript. Every so often one of the biographers would be struck by the quality of the poetry written by his subject and reproduce it in his text. It is because of Antonio de Lorea's interest in the poetry of María de la Santissima Trinidad that we have a few precious lines of her verse, which has otherwise been lost. These poems, which were mainly inspired by visions, deal with such themes as the soul's yearning for God, the passion, and Christ the divine pastor and savior of sinful mankind. Even though Lorea reproduced only three of her poems, he recorded with admiration that she was proficient at every kind of verse form that was in vogue during the first half of the seventeenth century.[53]

It is to biographer Andrés de Maya Salaberria that we owe the preservation of some of the simple but charming songs composed by the Dominican Martina de los Angeles y Arilla. Like the poems of María de la Santissima Trinidad, Martina's songs were directly inspired by visions, and they celebrated Christ's love for humankind and his sacrifice, as well as the longing that she felt as "a captive in this world" to free her soul from the constraints of material existence.[54]

Interestingly enough, in spite of a generalized mistrust of the feminine intellect, it was frequently the woman's confessor who played a key role in encouraging her to write devotional works. At the same time, certain confessors were steadfastly opposed to allowing women to write about spiritual matters, especially those of a particularly sensitive nature. A confessor of this kind was perfectly capable of ordering the woman to destroy her work, no matter how high its quality and no matter what amount of effort or sacrifice had gone into composing it.

Saint Teresa of Jesus and María de Agreda experienced both kinds of spiritual advisors. Most of St. Teresa's confessors, including such distinguished theologians as the Dominican Domingo Báñes and the Jesuits Baltasar Álvarez and Jerónimo Ripalda, encouraged her writing while she, in turn, was careful to submit her work to them before releasing it to the nuns of her order. These same men conserved her manuscripts, providing future scholars with an invaluable resource. But when Teresa composed a gloss on the Song of Songs in the early 1570s, her confessor at that time, Diego de Yanguas, ordered it burned on the grounds that, as St. Paul said, "Women should keep silence in the Church of God."[55]

María de Jesús de Agreda had gone through ten years of soul searching and self-doubt before she sat down to write the first draft of *The Mystical City of God* in 1637. During the entire gestation period of this famous work, she had benefited from the firm support and guidance of her confessor Francisco Andrés. But when Andrés, who was provincial of the order, was called away to preside over a chapter meeting that was being held in Toledo, an older friar was called in to substitute for him as her confessor. This father was much more conservative than Andrés, and when he found out that María had written a biography of the Virgin Mary he told her flatly that "writing was not women's work" and ordered her to destroy her only copy, as well as anything else that she had written. Faced with such a demand from a man whose role of spiritual advisor gave him absolute authority over her, María had little choice but to obey and may even have felt a certain relief in destroying the manuscript of a work that she herself felt anxious about having written.

After Francisco Andrés returned from the chapter meeting, however, he was furious to find that the only copy of *The Mystical City of God* had been destroyed. He ordered María to compose it again and, faced with yet another demand from a male spiritual advisor, she reluctantly agreed but was prevented from doing so by her own poor health. The death of Andrés in March 1647 seemed to put an end to the project, but when Andrés de Fuenmayor took over as her confessor in 1650, he insisted that she rewrite *The Mystical City of God* as his predecessor had demanded. During his fifteen-year term as María de Agreda's principal confessor, Andrés de Fuenmayor also saw to it that she gave him periodic written accounts of her spiritual life and made her begin an autobiography.[56] Although the autobiography remained incomplete at María's death in 1665, it provided her biographer, José Ximénez de Samaniego, with invaluable reference material.

In spite of their successes as the leaders of religious communities, writers, and poets, the majority of the "approved" mystics openly expressed strong feelings of sinfulness and felt themselves unworthy of the favors that God was bestowing upon them. In some women, such feelings could manifest themselves in extreme self-loathing. During a conversation with her spiritual advisor, Jacinta de Atondo once referred to herself as little more than "a piece of excrement."[57]

Such feelings could also transform themselves into intense anxiety about being "found out" by others and, even more important, by God himself as hiding a deeply flawed and sinful inner being beneath the façade of spirituality. For Isabel de Jesús, the feeling that she was living a lie and projecting a completely false image manifested itself in the idea that she was like a "dungheap covered with snow." The snow, in all its whiteness, signified purity and innocence, but the observer who dug a little below that "perfect whiteness" would discover things that were so "filthy and loathsome" that he would turn away from her in disgust.[58]

The post-Tridentine emphasis on the crucial importance of communion created a great deal of anxiety among many Catholics concerning their moral and spiritual readiness to receive it. Not surprisingly, many of these women focused their sense of worthlessness on communion, and some became reluctant to take the sacrament. Isabel de Jesús invented the image of the "dungheap covered with snow" to describe herself late one night when she was preparing to take communion. She feared that God would be deeply offended by the state of her soul, immersed in the "maloderous filth" of her own sinfulness. Teresa de Jesús Vela was convinced that she was so "impure" that her own confessor would refuse to give her communion after he had heard her confession. Since Teresa was an ideal nun and the prioress of her convent, her confessor had no reason to deny her communion, but receiving it at his hands did little to quiet her apprehension, and there were times that she refused to take it because she felt so unworthy.[59]

The source of at least some of these feelings of worthlessness can be found in the theology of the period, with its emphasis on the incalculable debt owed to God because he sacrificed his only son to redeem sinful humankind. Theologians insisted that instead of repaying God for his sacrifice, people had continued to sin, thereby increasing their indebtedness. In a passage strikingly similar to Isabel de Jesús' description of her own soul, the prolific Jesuit theologian Antonio de Quintanadueña called upon each individual to consider that his soul was a "dungheap of misery . . . more worthy of being despised and trod under foot than the very mud and filth of the plaza."[60]

But there was another reason for the self-loathing experienced by many women mystics that emerges clearly in the biographical material and Inquisition cases: they experienced numerous and troubling fantasies springing in one way or another from sexual frustration or desire. The erotic desires and the emotional and psychological need for marriage and children that such fantasies reveal were a fertile source of guilt and self-loathing among women religious who had been taught to value chastity above all other virtues from girlhood. In fact, the entire Christian tradition, from early patristic fathers like Origen and Tertullian through the early modern period, had condemned sexual desire as "the most foul and unclean of human wickedness, the most pervasive manifestation of man's disobedience to God's designs."[61]

But in spite of the fact that Augustine taught that those who sought to live a genuinely spiritual life and gain salvation must overcome sexual desires, specific sexual dreams and fantasies are mentioned in the biographies of more than one-third of the officially approved mystics and in 41.7 percent of cases involving "false" mystics. It would seem, therefore, that post-Tridentine theologians such as Juan de Avila y Chicona were correct in regarding nuns and female religious in general as especially vulnerable to lascivious thoughts and fantasies that could invade their minds at any time.[62]

The inability of women who had dedicated themselves to God to purify themselves of sensual desires must have caused strong feelings of guilt that were compounded by the fact that, as Avila y Chicona assured his readers, God permitted the devil to torment religious women because of their "disrespect" and "failure to serve Him properly."[63]

The woman, therefore, was made to feel guilty not only for having impure thoughts but also for the sin that caused her to be punished with them. In his *Cartas del esposo Christo a las religiosas sus esposas*, the Franciscan theologian and mystic Francisco de Posadas assumes the voice of Christ to express disappointment with the nuns who betray him: "Oh wife where is your chastity and purity of heart? How many impure words. How many filthy thoughts?"[64] A woman's only recourse was to adopt an attitude of constant vigilance and choose a spiritual advisor capable of helping her through her time of trial, but even here the snares of concupiscence awaited her, since, if he was young and attractive, "nothing is easier than for spiritual affection to become carnal attraction."[65]

Typically, the complex feelings of guilt and frustration that engendered these sexual fantasies began well before puberty, when the child took an oath of perpetual chastity, probably hoping to please her parents, other relatives, or confessor. What these vows actually meant to the child and the adults is certainly open to question. Judging by the later attempts made by many parents and relatives to bring prospective suitors into the home and convince the adolescent to consent to marriage, adults sometimes thought of the vow as little more than an indication of the girl's spirituality and rejection of "the world," something that was considered by the moralists as just as valuable for married life as it was for a life of celibacy. As for the child, she could have had little or no idea of what a vow of celibacy really meant. While many adolescent girls stubbornly upheld their girlish vows in the face of adults' attempts to convince them to marry, their determination was probably grounded more in rebellion than in fidelity to the vow of celibacy.

Generational misunderstanding about the meaning of the vow of chastity can be seen clearly in the life of Ana de Jesús, who took an oath of chastity at age ten with the support and approval of her parents, other relatives, and spiritual advisor, only to be confronted by the very same people when she was fourteen, who then insisted that since she had taken the vow so young it could be broken without sin.[66] Ana was genuinely horrified at this advice and informed them that she renewed the vow every day, but when an attractive young man who also happened to be a distant relative began paying attention to her, she was greatly tempted. Like St. Teresa of Jesus at a similar stage of life, she began taking care of her appearance, and like St. Teresa felt guilty about it.[67] Moreover, Ana had taken a vow of chastity, and the fear of violating that vow, even in spirit, so preyed upon her mind that she was ripe for "conversion." A sudden shock, the untimely death of a girlfriend, tipped her over the edge.

Formally renewing her vows of chastity, she rejected the attentions of her suitor, put aside her secular garments as "instruments of the devil for trapping men's souls," and appeared before her family in a nun's habit.[68]

But forcing ourselves to reject something we need and desire has a high price in mental anguish and frustration. Ana de Jesús was satisfied with what she did, but in other cases the decision to turn away from the attentions of a young and attractive suitor was not wholehearted and left the young girl with unfulfilled longings and recurring sexual fantasies centered on the young man who might have become her husband. Like Ana de Jesús, Francisca Inés de la Concepción had taken an oath of chastity at age ten with the approval of her parents, but when she was fifteen her father procured a dispensation that would allow her to set aside the oath and contract marriage.[69] Her father had even picked out the prospective groom. He was a good-looking young caballero named Juan de Ribadeneyra, and Francisca was very attracted to him, but in the end her fears of marriage and guilt about violating the oath of chastity caused her to reject him and enter the Franciscan Convent of Nuestra Señora de Belen of Cifuentes in 1570, when she was nineteen. In spite of this decision, Francisca could not forget Juan de Ribadeneyra and had recurring sexual fantasies about him for many years. In these dreams, the young man would appear attractively dressed or even lying on a cot in a lascivious posture and caress and kiss her with great tenderness. Francisca would defend herself with fervent prayer, and the image would leave her, only to return in another guise the next night.[70]

Sexual and emotional frustration resulting from an inability to marry or even establish a long-term relationship also gave rise to sexual fantasies among "false" mystics. María Cotonilla, whose poverty made marriage impossible and whose reputation for sanctity would have been seriously undermined if she had a lover, experienced recurrent fantasies involving men. In one of these, she fantasized about a young man who accosted her as she left the parish church, spoke to her affectionately, and then asked her to marry him, promising to take her to Madrid and offer her other advantages. Before she could reply, however, he had disappeared. On another occasion, she dreamed that a man entered her room and had intercourse with her. After this incident, she experienced a hysterical pregnancy during which her stomach swelled so much that her friends commented that she looked exactly like a person about to give birth.[71]

Serious doubts about entering religious life and thereby abandoning any hope of sexual pleasure or marriage could also give rise to sexual fantasies when a girl was facing the critical decision of whether to profess in a convent after her period as a novice. For Isabel de Jesús, the entire year before she was to profess was a period of terrible anxiety, during which she imagined demons threatening her with bodily harm and strange voices screaming blasphemies from holes in the earth. But her most vivid fantasy during this period involved two demons in the guise of handsome men who took her arms and asked her, "Why have you run away from us; don't you think that men know how to comfort you?" "We love you more than you can imagine." The two men then urged her not to become a nun, warning her that she would be making an irrevocable decision that she would later come to regret.[72]

As Francisca Inés de la Concepción's level of sexual frustration became more intense, her fantasies about Juan de Ribadeneyra became darker, incorporating visions of rape and resulting in genital manipulation. In one vision, the devil assumed the form and dress of her putative fiancé and arrived with a group of his retainers armed with various instruments, which they attempted to thrust inside her. Francisca recalled that she tried to fight them off with her hands, but nothing could prevent the devil himself from penetrating her vagina with a burning brand. The fact that masturbation probably occurred on this occasion is indicated not only by the penetration itself and the vigorous use of her hands during the struggle with the devil but also by the fact that she concealed the incident from her confessor and the other nuns, even though she had hurt herself and was in pain for several days. As one of the few women mystics who could read Latin, Francisca Inés de la Concepción was undoubtedly aware of the strictures against voluntary "pollution" in the morality texts of the period and, as her biographer observed, did not wish to "offend against modesty" by admitting to something so roundly condemned, even though the incident had taken place in her sleep.[73]

Several incidents of masturbation are also clearly indicated in the testimony of witnesses at the trial of María Cotonilla in 1675. One night her landlady, Ana Ruiz, entered her bedroom to find María on the floor, wedged between the bed and the wall, with her feet in the air and a wooden candlestick thrust into her private parts. Even though she blamed the devil for her situation, it is obvious that María had been using the candlestick as a dildo while masturbating. On another evening, when Ana entered the stable to check on the stock, she found María propped up against the wall with her private parts exposed, this time making use of three small stones to help her masturbate. Astonished, Ana asked her what had happened, and María replied that they— the demons—had simply left her that way.[74]

Fantasies involving animals, especially dogs, were common among both "genuine" (33.3 percent), and "fake" (41.7 percent) mystics. As a young widow, Catalina Ballester had taken an oath of chastity after the death of her husband in order to enlist the help of the Virgin Mary in furthering her son's career. Since her son was successful in acquiring a rudimentary education and entering the Mercedarian order, she felt herself under a great obligation to the Virgin and continued to abstain from sex, even after she moved to Palma from her home village. But avoiding sexual intercourse simply added fuel to Catalina's fantasy life, and she told her hosts, the Morlana sisters, about numerous sexual fantasies, including being surrounded by a group of young men who yelled obscenities at her while several priests looked on.[75] Most of her sexual fantasies revolved around visions of animals. In testimony before the Mallorca tribunal on December 6, 1669, she admitted that she had frequent visions of toads, tortoises, and dogs and that she also saw men and women copulating and beckoning her to join them.[76]

Catalina Ballester was not the only "feigned" mystic to experience erotic visions involving animals. During her trial before the Toledo tribunal, Francisca de la Santissima Trinidad told the court that she masturbated frequently and copiously, especially after she scourged herself. These incidents were normally accompanied by visions of large dogs with enormous deformed penises, which they laid in her lap, provoking in her "a more powerful urge to have intercourse with them than with any man."[77]

Similar fantasies involving animals were also experienced by "genuine" mystics. Inés de Jesús y Franco had numerous highly charged erotic visions, both before and after she became prioress of the Franciscan convent in Miedes. In her visions, she saw what she described to her confessor as "filthy lascivious acts" involving lions and other animals and a "dark man carrying a torch." She admitted that she was so attracted by these visions that she was strongly tempted to give up the convent, where she had been a resident since age fourteen, and "return to the pleasures of the world." She tried everything to dampen the fires of sensuality, including dragging her tongue over the floor of the chapel three times a week, but nothing helped, and she became so frustrated that she wanted to take a knife and cut out pieces of her flesh.[78]

An irresistible impulse to hurt one's own body, especially to wound or mutilate the breasts, was not uncommon among "genuine" mystics frustrated by their inability of rid themselves of sensual urges. Teresa de Jesús Vela, who was so ashamed of her erotic visions that she was unable to tell her confessor about them, decided to take drastic action after spending several days struggling with a particularly strong wave of sexual desire shortly after she joined the Carmelites. Going into the fields around the convent, she cut two branches from a rosebush with particularly sharp thorns, took them back to her cell, and placed them on the floor in the form of a cross. Stripping to the waist, she threw herself on the branches and rolled around on them, scratching her breasts and seriously wounding herself with one of the thorns.[79]

Less overtly sexual perhaps but evidencing unfulfilled desires for male companionship, marriage, and children were fantasies taking shape around Christ himself in the role of either husband or infant. Such visions were extremely common among both officially approved and "feigned" mystics, with 30 percent of the former and 33.3 percent of the latter experiencing some form of mystical marriage. Even more remarkable, 73.3 percent and 40 percent, respectively, had visions involving the Christ child.

Most mystical marriages were visions that were either recorded by the women when they wrote about their spiritual lives or told to their confessors. For María de Christo, the "marriage ceremony" was a simple affair with strongly religious and spiritual overtones that took place on two occasions after she had taken communion. After falling into a deep trance that lasted several hours, María recalled that she had a sensation of a precious ring being slipped on her finger. Shortly thereafter, Christ the bridegroom appeared and manifested to her the same qualities that he had revealed to his apostles: "meekness, humility, works and deeds of infinite sanctity and love."[80]

For Martina de los Angeles, however, the ceremony itself was not only brilliant and full of sensual delight but also succeeded by a long-term fantasy relationship in which she imagined Christ as the ideal husband that she could never have. The marriage took place in heaven, in the presence of the entire celestial court, with the Virgin Mary acting as godmother and bringing Martina into the presence of her son, who formally received her and placed a ring on her finger. She was then dressed in resplendent white garments and took her place in the "choir of virgins." In later years, the vision of this magnificent ceremony was to repeat itself many times.[81]

But unlike most women mystics who experienced some form of mystical marriage, Martina's marriage ceremony was the prelude to a long "relationship" with Christ as husband and the Virgin as mother-in-law. In Martina's fantasy world, Christ was the perfect husband who not only showered her with expensive gifts like rings and a necklace but also behaved with great affection, calling her his "angelic beauty," his "rose," "emerald," and "lily," among other adoring names. Like a good husband, moreover, Christ was solicitous of her welfare. Once when she had difficulty mounting the stairs because of a recent illness, Christ took her arm and helped her up, saying, "You are tired, my wife, give me your hand and let me help you."[82]

It is difficult not to see in the elaborate ceremonial of marriage Martina imagined, which even her otherwise uncritical biographer, Fr. Andrés de Maya Salaberria, thought highly unusual, and the fantasy of Christ the adoring and attentive husband a way of compensating for her terrible fear of men. Christ the imaginary husband represented an ideal inconceivable to Martina, who was so anxious about men that when St. Dominic appeared to her in a dream, she woke up and nearly ran out of her cell.[83]

The cult of the child Jesus was one of the most important new devotions to emerge in the post-Tridentine church. Beginning in the sixteenth century, devotion to the holy child inspired the work of dozens of artists, including such masters as Le Brun, Van Dyck, Murillo, and Gentileschi. It was in the early seventeenth century that theologians began to seriously evaluate the enormity of Christ's sacrifice in condescending to participate in the lowest state of humanity. In assuming this state, which they equated with that of a brute beast without possible knowledge of God, Christ demonstrated the greatness of his love for sinful humankind and his determination not to avoid tasting any of its miseries in his effort to save us.[84]

But for the women living in convents under strict enclosure, such arcane theology was irrelevant. Instead, the cult was driven by a frustrated desire for the sensual and emotional satisfactions of pregnancy and motherhood. This connection could not be made clearer than in the case of Margaret of the Cross, who rejected marriage with King Philip II in favor of becoming a nun in Madrid's Franciscan Convent of the Descalzas Reales and spent most of the rest of her life taking care of her mother, the Empress Maria.

According to her biographer, Juan de Palma, Margaret was extremely unhappy in Descalzas Reales because illness, physical disability, and the demands of her position as a Habsburg princess made it impossible for her to be treated like an ordinary nun. Her only solace appears to have been an extreme form of devotion, verging on obsession with the child Jesus. She kept a statuette of the child with her at all times, calling it the "firstborn." She would frequently take it out and, laying her head at its feet, break off a conversation to ask the other nuns, "Look at him carefully, tell me what you think . . . isn't my child handsome?" She also kept numerous images of the child Jesus in her cell and delighted in dressing and adorning them. She made up names for all of them, calling one "the lost child," another "the German" and "the serious one," and even had one of the doll-like images brought to the refectory, where she dined at a table separate from the other nuns. While dining, she would kiss and caress the image and then take it to the reliquary, where she would remain alone with it for hours.[85]

At the Christmas season, Margaret's devotion to the child Jesus really engulfed her. Her preparations would begin as early as All Saints Day (November 1) and continue right up to Christmas week, with an intense series of special devotions and exercises designed to "form a spiritual manger in her heart so that the child of God could be born within it." As Christmas got closer, the entire community began to notice her becoming extremely agitated. In the words of her biographer, she had become "intoxicated" with devotion and desire, and one of the nuns even remarked, not without a certain irony, "How wonderful that Your Highness has drunk so deeply from the wine cellar of love." On Christmas Eve, she ordered them to bring her favorite statue of the child Jesus, which she would worship on her knees with adoring words and copious sobs, and she would sometimes be so overcome with emotion that she would fall into a trancelike state in which she imagined that she met with the Virgin Mary, who gave her the child to hold.[86]

The Christmas season, with its obvious associations with the birth of Christ, was also when the "false" mystic Vicenta Orvall tended to have the largest number of visions of the Christ child and feel his presence most strongly in her room. In fact, according to testimony before the Valencia tribunal by Juan Pérez, a local curate, Vicenta had become well known in the entire rural area around Valencia city for her devotion to the child Jesus and for maintaining a small statue of the child that was reputed to work cures and other miracles. So widespread had the fame of this image become that when Pérez visited her he found the image surrounded by ex-votos donated by those who had been cured through its intercession.[87]

María Antonia Hortola was another "false" mystic with a strong attachment to the child Jesus. On one occasion, while in a trancelike state before several spectators, she manifested such powerful expressions of love for the child that the audience was moved to tears. This performance was so moving that one spectator, Fr. Luis Ruiz, had to leave the room and go to the porter's lodge, where he could be heard sobbing and sighing so loudly that the others were afraid he was going to have a heart attack.[88]

That Margaret of the Cross's frenzied devotion to the child Jesus did not obey purely religious motives and was connected to genuine frustration over never being able to conceive a child is amply demonstrated by her behavior around real children. She would have poor children brought to her in the convent, caress them tenderly, and buy them clothing. Whenever any of the other nuns would make the children cry to see how she would react, she would burst into tears herself.[89]

The connection of the worship of the child Jesus to conception was even more direct in the case of María de Jesús. Every Christmas during her long and at times despotic rule as prioress of the Convent of St. Joseph and St. Teresa of Toledo, she would personally decorate the crèche and prepare the cradle, even going so far as to force the nuns to warm the pieces of cloth upon which the figure of the Christ child was to be placed. Her biographer records that she became so upset when one of the nuns brought her a cloth that was not warm enough that she apologized to the image with tears in her eyes for the neglect shown by her sisters.[90]

For Mariana de Jesús, who had been married twice and had a daughter by her first husband, devotion to the child Jesus afforded the opportunity to reprise the pleasure of giving birth. On Epiphany in the year 1611, she had a vision in which the Virgin Mary shared with her the five principal joys that she experienced in giving birth to Christ: the moment of his birth, sharing the pleasure that St. Joseph took in presenting the new baby, embracing him, swaddling him for the first time, and giving him the breast.[91]

But the cult of the child Jesus, however beautiful the artistic expressions that it inspired, could hardly be expected to compensate cloistered nuns for the sexual and emotional frustrations of convent life. Instead, like so many others living in the Europe of the Counter-Reformation, they were the victims of a new sexual policy of unprecedented austerity that affected both clergy and laity.

If sexual and emotional deprivation was the almost inevitable consequence of the more restrictive sexual politics introduced by the post-Tridentine church, physical suffering from a variety of illnesses accompanied most of these women throughout their lives. Although these sufferings were, in many cases, needlessly exacerbated by the primitive and inadequate medical practice of the day, they themselves interpreted suffering as a form of divine communication that helped them experience the joys of suffering for Christ.

Diseases common among officially approved mystics included various forms of malaria, especially tertian (23.3 percent) and quartan (6.7 percent). As bad as these percentages are in terms of human suffering, the actual incidence was probably much higher in that 66.7 percent were reported as experiencing unspecified recurring fevers, many of which were probably malarial.

The records the Inquisition maintained were far less likely to indicate the illnesses "false" mystics suffered than were the biographies of "true" mystics, whose authors were eager to demonstrate the sanctity of their subjects by the suffering they experienced, but the testimony of Inquisition witnesses sometimes reveals that the accused went through bouts of sickness. The Dominican *tercera* María Antonia Hortola, for example, used the severe recurrent fevers she suffered as a defense at her trial by claiming that many of the unorthodox statements that she was accused of making were said while she was sick and "deranged"with fever and therefore not responsible for her actions.[92]

Heart disease was probably the leading cause of death among "true" mystics, who complained of severe chest pains (36.7 percent), difficulty in breathing (13.3 percent), or heart flutter. Even though the women in convents and *beaterios* consumed a low-fat diet, thereby avoiding the cholesterol-related causes of heart disease so prevalent in Western societies today, their diets were also not very balanced and lacked nutrients, such as calcium and vitamins C and B, that are essential for a healthy heart. The famous transverberations of the heart that were described as an angelic lance thrust of joy and pain by several mystics, including Teresa of Jesus, may have been connected with heart disease. Certainly in the case of Martina de los Angeles y Arilla, the connection is made crystal clear by the fact that she experienced her trans-verberation two years before her death and that from that time on she had intermittent but severe chest pains and had to spend most of her time in bed. Tortured almost as much by the supposed cures of her doctors as by the chest pains, Martina consulted with her confessor about dismissing them, since she had no doubt that the pains came from the supernatural and were therefore not susceptible to treatment.[93]

Stress, which is almost universally agreed to play a major role in high blood pressure and other precursors of heart disease, was also present in the lives of women mystics. Disappointing the hopes of their founders, many convents and *beaterios* were the very opposite of the secure and tranquil places of prayer and contemplation that they had intended. As both Inquisition records and biographies reveal, these institutions were frequently divided into rival factions who engaged in acrimonious squabbles over offices and preferment. Books for and about such cloistered and semicloistered women, moreover, reveal that they felt intense anxiety about such critical matters as a full and complete confession, the Eucharist, and the individual's state of grace. Such feelings of anxiety were exacerbated by guilt about lingering sexual desires and the fear that the devil might invade and take over the psyche.

Dysentery and other forms of stomach ailments were as common among our women mystics (33.3 percent) as they must have been in the society as a whole. To the problems of bad food and contaminated water that affected everyone in a country where sanitation was primitive should be added the austerities and physical mortifications that the women imposed on themselves. The constant and severe stomach pain that plagued the Carmelite María de Jesús, for example, was probably related to her drinking out of the cups into which sick nuns spat during the time that she ran the convent infirmary.[94] Other nuns, such as Gabriela de San Joseph, deliberately ate bad or rotten food in order to mortify the sense of taste. In Gabriela's case, such austerities caused constant vomiting and such terrible and continuous stomach pain that she thought she was going to die.[95]

Finally, perhaps the most tragic form of physical disability experienced by women mystics (10 percent) was total or partial blindness. In the case of Margaret of the Cross, deterioration of her eyesight was exacerbated by her doctors, who prescribed corrosive drops to "cure" her and also botched a cataract operation, leaving her totally blind.[96]

In examining the biographies of women mystics, the modern reader is struck by the stoicism with which so many of them faced the excruciating pains of illness and the no less terrible suffering brought on by the treatments attempted by their physicians. Although the people of early modern Europe were accustomed to a level of hardship and discomfort unacceptable in modern society, many saw pain and suffering as conferring a positive spiritual benefit.

In a remarkable work by the Jesuit theologian Luis de la Puente, first published in 1688, illness is regarded positively as a gift sent by God to save the souls of the excessively healthy and vigorous from sin, especially the sins of the flesh to which the robust body is all too prone.[97] Illness, moreover, tends to promote certain Christian virtues, especially obedience in that the individual is forced to accept the will of God, compassion since the sick person learns to sympathize with others, and patience in that someone who is ill learns to endure "the torment of the body with gladness of spirit."[98] In other places, de la Puente bids those who experience illness to thank God for the opportunity to suffer as he did during the passion. To be ill is to imitate Christ and to make a cross for oneself with the "pain, tedium, fear and agony" experienced during an illness. Illness may also be a means by which God seeks to test his chosen ones by giving them an opportunity to prove their mettle in the face of adversity.[99] In this interpretation, illness is caused by God's supernatural power and controlled by him.[100] The physician is as powerless as the patient to affect the course of the disease, and the sickbed is transformed into a place where the elect may glorify God with their joyous acceptance of pain and suffering, while transforming themselves into the living image of the crucified Christ.

Even allowing for the hyperbole of official biographers who did everything possible to make the lives of their subjects conform to the model set forth by hagiographers and theologians, a number of the women did internalize many of these ideas about the virtues of illness. Certainly in her memoirs María Ángela Astorch made a point of telling her confessor that the terrible angina pains that she experienced had no physical cause but were sent to her by God to "purify me with this great heat and pain."[101] By the middle of the seventeenth century, physical suffering had become so strongly identified with holiness that the "false" mystic Clara de San Francisco, who was in robust health, sought to make herself look pallid by scourging herself until her blood ran.[102]

The reaction of Margaret of the Cross to her blindness was even more in line with the model of sanctity. She was fifty-four when she began noticing her sharply increased sensitivity to light, but instead of complaining she welcomed failing eyesight as a way of mortifying the sense of sight, since she believed that she had taken too much pleasure in admiring church ornaments. Later, after botched medical treatments condemned her to blindness, she told the other nuns not to feel sorry for her; she claimed to have reached a higher state of spiritual perfection as a blind person. For Margaret, the spiritual results of illness and disability far outweighed any physical loss that may have resulted; forced deprivation of the "light coming from the body" had made her more acutely aware of the light from her soul, and after she went completely blind, she felt the sensation of being surrounded by "a clear and soft presence far superior to earthly light."[103]

Sadly, the mental illness that afflicted 20 percent of the "true" mystics and fully one-third of their wayward sisters was never regarded as affording its victims any kind of spiritual benefit. If anything, mental illness, which was routinely attributed to diabolical influence or possession, had to be cast out by supernatural means, particularly through the intervention of an exorcist. Moreover, the symptoms of depression were generally viewed with suspicion as a sign of sin or divine displeasure, and theologians taught that the only solution was to completely subordinate oneself to a spiritual advisor.

The experiences of the "feigned" mystic Thomasa Dolz, a Carmelite nun in Valencia's Santa Ana Convent, with her superiors and the Inquisition provides an excellent example of the way in which both male clerics and the female victims themselves accepted the idea of the demonic origins of mental illness. Sor Thomasa's delusional system involved the belief that she was "confirmed in grace" and that Christ's love for her was greater than his love for the saints and second only to his love for the Virgin Mary. Because her spiritual progress was so vitally important to the true church, she declared that Christ communicated directly with her and dispensed her from the need to carry out the normal duties of a nun, including attending mass and taking communion. She also did not need to take communion from the prior of the convent; Christ, dressed in a habit of a Carmelite friar, appeared to administer it to her directly.[104]

Reaction within the convent to Thomasa's assertions was mixed, with some of the nuns admiring her as a "saint" and listening raptly to her pronouncements, while others, including the prioress, were increasingly resentful of her disobedience and refusal to abide by the rule.[105] Finally, Felix Dura, the prior of the convent, became so concerned about the threat to the community posed by Thomasa that he decided to imprison her in one of the cells and attempt exorcism as a way of ridding her of the demons that were causing her to challenge the authority of her superiors. On balance, though, exorcism proved disappointing. On the one hand, Thomasa's failure to react negatively to the sight of the crucifix or to speak with the preternatural voices of demons seemed to indicate that she was not suffering from possession. It was also difficult for Dura to conclude that she was "obsessed" because sometimes she would appear to accept the learned explanation of her conduct as a result of demonic trickery and deception.

After several months of observation and faced with Thomasa's wild mood swings and refusal to eat for three and four days at a time, Dura became so frustrated that he stopped her from having any visitors and began verbally abusing her. At length, he decided to denounce her to the Inquisition for unorthodox statements and disobedience to authority, although he was also careful to raise his concerns about her mental health.[106]

The decision was logical within the context of seventeenth-century Spanish society, where it was the Holy Office that acted to adjudicate matters of

belief and expression. Furthermore, although inquisitors had no special procedures for dealing with mental illness, they could all bring to bear a certain
amount of experience with prisoners who went mad or committed suicide
during their trials, since occurrences of that kind were not uncommon.

Surprisingly enough, given its reputation as a harsh and uncompromising
tribunal, the Inquisition took a moderate attitude toward Thomasa Dolz. In
the final vote on the case taken on February 20, 1673, the *consulta de fe*, consisting of the inquisitors Dr. Joan Casteldases and Hermenigildo Ximenez
Navarro; Dr. Christobal Marco, canon of Valencia's cathedral, representing the archbishop; and Dr. Marcos Roig from the *audiencia*, decided that
Thomasa was *illusa passive, non sane mentis*, meaning essentially that she
was delusional. This decision was confirmed on May 18, 1673, after the
tribunal's physician had examined her and decided that she was suffering
from melancholy brought on by an excess of black bile.[107]

Things had changed drastically since the 1630s, when the Toledo tribunal
had completely ignored the overwhelming evidence of mental disorder
brought out by defense witnesses in the case of Juana Bautista and sentenced
her to be flogged through the streets and *abjure de levi* for offenses considerably less serious than those committed by Thomasa Dolz.[108] In 1673, the
Valencia tribunal recognized the claims of mental illness, at least insofar as
mentioning it in the sentence, and refrained from assigning any harsh physical punishment or public humiliation.

But apart from giving her a new spiritual advisor who was to be a *calificador*
attached to the tribunal, the Inquisition was unable or unwilling to do anything
more for Thomasa, even though as an *illusa passive* she was presumably not
responsible for her actions. Instead, the elaborate clauses of the sentence indicate that the tribunal was far more concerned with restoring discipline in the
convent than it was with dealing with her mental illness. Obviously disturbed
by the fact that Thomasa had a following in the convent, the tribunal went to
great pains to discredit her and her beliefs in the eyes of the religious community. The sentence was first read out in the tribunal's audience chamber in
the presence of six nuns and then for a second time in the convent with the
entire community in attendance, so that "all of the nuns can learn the truth
about the things she has professed in this convent."[109] After this sentence was
carried out, Thomasa Dolz drops from the historical record, but it is probably
safe to say that her future in the convent, where she had already suffered from
abuse and mistreatment, must have been bleak. As far as the Inquisition was
concerned, however, the fact that she was mentally ill and in need of assistance was far less important than reestablishing the principles of obedience
and hierarchy that her aberrant behavior seemed to threaten.

But illness, regardless of any merit that the individual might gain from
patiently enduring suffering, was simply part of the torment that the Christian had to endure in the temporal world, and only the death of the body could
provide access to eternal life. It was for this reason that María de Jesús de
Agreda's final words, as recorded by the nuns who attended her, were, "Come!
Come to me!" and why she told her confessor that her soul would be "mournful

until death arrives to claim me."[110] This attitude is also responsible for the strong death wish so often expressed by Margaret of the Cross, who constantly prayed that God would remove her soul from the "prison" of her body and had the crowned skulls of her royal ancestors painted in the breviary that she used every day.[111]

Beginning in the late Middle Ages, however, a new conception of death and dying transformed the days and hours before death into a final testing time, an ordeal in which the dying person had to engage in a titanic struggle with the forces of darkness that were trying to lay claim to the soul at the moment of greatest vulnerability. In this struggle, God stands to one side, no longer judging but observing the contest in which the dying person, with the aid of a guardian angel and divine and human intercessors, must triumph and find salvation or yield to the blandishments of the demons and be lost.[112]

To instruct the dying in how best to comport themselves in this struggle so that a "good death"—that is to say, a death that led to salvation—would result, a whole literature was developed. In the *Ars Moriendi*, which were designed for both clergy and laity, the dying person was provided with a road map of the kind of behavior required for a "good death," while spectators were told how to judge whether the individual was winning or losing the struggle. Above all, the *Ars Moriendi* stressed that the dying person had to become resigned to death as the will of God, renounce worldly things, and demonstrate a sincere contrition for all sins.[113]

A sure sign of victory in the struggle against the demonic forces filling the bedroom was the calm or beatific expression that would pass over the face of the elect just before death. Ideally, the death agony should take place in the presence of clergy and especially the spiritual advisor, who should hear the dying person's confession and administer the all-important sacrament of extreme unction, which confers special assistance against the fear of death and damnation.

Even though the *Ars Moriendi* literature originated in the fifteenth century, it became really popular after the Council of Trent and especially during the seventeenth century. A recent survey of ninety-nine Spanish *Ars Moriendi* indicates that 35.3 percent were first published in the sixteenth century and 56.5 percent during the seventeenth. Analysis of new editions reveals an even greater preponderance in the seventeenth century. Of the 125 reedited works surveyed, more than 68 percent were issued in the seventeenth century, while only 31.2 percent belonged to the sixteenth. Authors were drawn mainly from the religious orders, especially the Franciscans and Jesuits, and the *Ars Moriendi* appear to have been widely distributed among the literate classes, especially in the libraries of convents and monasteries and among members of the governing elite.[114] The ideals of the good death were also diffused to a wider and illiterate or semiliterate public through the funerary sermons that were becoming increasingly popular during the seventeenth century.

The cultural diffusion of the ideal of the good death can be seen clearly in a number of the biographies whose authors were undoubtedly as familiar with the literature as many of their subjects. In 20 percent of the biographies, the woman either expresses frustration because she cannot aid others in achieving the good death or actually does so, as in the case of the Franciscan *tercera* María de Christo. Following the model as set forth in the *Ars Moriendi*, the woman's victory over the forces of evil at the moment of her demise was evidenced by a beatific expression, which is described in 56.6 percent of the cases.

Some of the biographies go into much greater detail about the whole spiritual struggle involved in death and dying and are at pains to demonstrate just how closely the death of their subject conformed to the ideal of the good death. One of the best descriptions comes from the pen of José Ximénez de Samaniego, the biographer of María de Jesús de Agreda. Samaniego describes her as a person obsessed with death who had adopted the ideas of Jesuit theologians such as Francisco Arana, who advised his readers that they must prepare for death long before they had to confront it during a final illness through a systematic program of spiritual retreats and nightly examination of conscience.[115] Following the Jesuit model, María's program included a series of meditations on the last judgment and a constant and rigorous examination of conscience. She also sought to obtain a divine promise of assistance in providing some of the elements most closely associated with the good death, especially the presence of numerous members of the clergy at her bedside and the assistance of a guardian angel to help her resist the demonic host. This was followed by a series of long spiritual retreats, sometimes lasting a month or more, during which she meditated on death and the futility of material existence and is said to have received many favors from God.[116]

Even before María fell ill with malarial fever on the eve of Ascension Day in 1665, she was aware that it would be her final illness. The last ordeal had begun carrying with it the tremendous possibility of winning or losing everything during the struggle. During this period, which lasted from Ascension Day to her death on May 24, 1665, María was to provide a model for the good death by demonstrating the Christian virtues of resignation, contrition for her sins, humility, and obedience to the authority of her superiors. She even sought to increase her suffering in imitation of Christ's passion by eagerly embracing the painful "remedies" prescribed by her doctors, even though she knew full well that her illness depended on supernatural forces and was not curable by any human means.[117]

Finally, after her doctors warned her that the end was near, she received extreme unction. It was then that the many spectators who crowded the infirmary saw a beatific expression spread over her face. The titanic struggle with demonic forces had been concluded successfully, and she informed her confessor that she was now prepared to die "inspired and comforted."[118]

In Samaniego's description of María de Agreda's final hours, the presence of demonic forces is only implied, and the favorable outcome of the struggle seems almost assured from the beginning. The same cannot be said for the death agonies of the Carmelite *tercera* Isabel de Jesús. Throughout her life, Isabel had suffered from periodic bouts of depression and had even contemplated suicide when she was an adolescent. She also had an extraordinarily low self-image. Addressing God toward the end of her life, she pointed to herself, saying, "Here is the ungrateful one; the one who has entirely failed to discharge her obligations to you; the one who has betrayed your love."[119]

Given this background of emotional stress, added to the fact that the tertian malaria that she eventually died of induced periods of delirium, it is perhaps hardly surprising that the bedside struggle with demonic forces should take on an especially dramatic character. According to her confessor Francisco Clarissa, who completed her autobiography after she died, she saw horrible demonic visions in the days before her death, consisting of balls with numerous eyes that emitted a terrible smell while shooting out jets of fire. Six days before she died, these visions were replaced by an even more horrible one: a head with one gigantic eye that emitted the same fire and surrounded itself with the same evil stench.

Clarissa remained by her bedside throughout her last agony and recorded that she amply demonstrated all of the elements that made up the good death. Even as her pain and fever increased, she eagerly embraced the sickness that God had sent to test her and praised the spiritual benefits of illness to her confessor. While making her last confession, she demonstrated sincere contrition and displayed an utter disdain for the material world by ridding herself of what little property remained to her. Finally, just before the end, when Clarissa asked her if she still felt as plagued by demons, she answered that she felt "belabored but not afflicted." Victory was at hand and demonstrated for all to see by the changes on her face as this woman accepted eternal life with joy. Gone were the wrinkles of age; the anguished expression of deep suffering was replaced by the mild and pleasing appearance of a twenty-year-old experiencing a soft and restful sleep.[120]

In the case of the "authentic" mystic, success in conquering the forces of evil during the deathbed struggle can be seen as the ultimate goal of her adult life. While this trial may have carried the same risk for her as it did for any ordinary Christian, the mystic's own virtue, honed during her earlier struggles with sensuality and tempered by her patience and resignation in the face of illness, guaranteed victory. Even more important, however, was the fact that the "true" mystic had lived out much of her adult life as a "life in death," channeling most of her psychic energy into a succession of devotions and mystical "states" that had served to separate her more and more from involvement with the material world.

10

Religious Life and Devotions

The Tridentine decrees asserting the necessity for salvation of all seven sacraments and condemning Lutheran ideas of justification began the process whereby a new Catholic religious sensibility was created. Trent had revived the notion of freedom of will and rejected the idea of human passivity under the influence of grace. The renewed emphasis on good works, whether material, as in an act of charity, or spiritual, as in the taking of communion, led pious individuals, especially contemplatives, to seek spiritual merit through devotions that both reaffirmed the validity of key Catholic beliefs in the face of Protestant rejection and asserted a strong Christocentrism, as in the prominence given to the passion and the sacred heart. Belief in the efficacy of these devotions was reinforced by visions that were accepted as intimations from the divine that they were valid expressions of the true faith and therefore pleasing to him.

Ever since the thirteenth century, when eucharistic visions and miracles seemed almost a female genre, the central importance of the Eucharist to women and their key role in the transmission of eucharistic devotion can be demonstrated with little difficulty.[1] That this pattern of female devotion to the Eucharist continued into the early modern period is amply demonstrated by the fact that eucharistic concerns played a central role in the religious lives of 86.7 percent of "genuine" and 40 percent of the "feigned" mystics in this study.

Even more significant, however, is that the desire for frequent or even daily communion, which had largely been confined to a few exceptional women like Ida of Nivelles or Saint Hedwig of Silesia (c. 1174–1243) during the medieval period, became transformed into an integral part of middle-class religious culture in much of Catholic Europe by the mid-seventeenth century. As early as 1648, the ecclesiastical censor Bernabe Gallego de Vera commented favorably on the proliferation of works advocating the practice in his review of Juan Daza y Berrio's *Tesoro de confesores y perla de la conciencia,* while the author himself praised daily confession as "salutary, laudable and becoming."[2] For his part, Diego Pérez de Valdivia argued that it was far more appropriate for women to take frequent communion than men because they led lives of greater piety.[3] Moreover, the fact that more women than men were heeding the call for frequent or daily communion was noted by the late-sixteenth-century theologian Fr. Luis de Granada in his famous *Sermón de las caidas públicas.*

The popularity of communion among the spiritual women in this study is attested to by the fact that 40 percent of the "genuine" mystics and 41.7 percent of the "fake" mystics in this study took it on a daily basis. Eucharistic concerns are also manifested by the way that these women would fantasize about receiving spiritual communion whenever it was impossible for them to take communion as frequently as they wished. Like 17.7 percent of the women mystics in this study, the "sham" mystic María Antonia Hortola had a recurring fantasy of Christ personally administering the sacrament to her every day. In her dream, she was given communion at the end of a magnificent pontifical mass attended by St. Dominic, who acted as deacon, assisted by St. Thomas Aquinas. María Antonia Hortola, like some of the other poor women in this study, had difficulty in maintaining a stable relationship with a spiritual advisor or even finding one who would take her spiritual needs seriously. It was her frustration over the offhand way that she was being treated by some of her confessors and the difficulties that she had in persuading them to provide her with frequent or daily communion that was probably responsible for triggering the fantasy, since communion administered directly by Christ would be a way to circumvent the restrictions placed upon her by male priests.[4]

Other women, such as the Capuchin nun María Ángela Astorch or the "false" mystic María Pizarra, were allowed by their spiritual advisors to take daily communion for only certain periods but arranged to take it very frequently at other times. María Ángela Astorch even founded a convent in Murcia that was dedicated to "the exaltation of the Holy Sacrament." In this convent, the members of the community were permitted to take communion Sundays and holidays, as well as every Monday, Wednesday, and Friday.[5]

Ever since the host began to be stamped with the image of Christ, the believer could more easily persuade herself that taking communion was tantamount to a mystical feeding on his body. To eat Christ was to become Christ; the act of taking in the host was sufficient by itself to achieve union with God.[6] It is easy to understand from this how some very devout women could be tremendously anxious to receive the host and why they experienced ecstatic states afterward. The "false" mystic María Cotonilla was said by those who knew her to have risen every morning before dawn and waited in front of the door of the local Franciscan convent to attend the first mass and receive communion.[7] María Ángela Astorch wrote that she frequently felt an unbearable desire to beat her breast against the case where the consecrated hosts were kept "in order to break the little door and encounter Him there."[8]

Spectacular trances after communion were also an important part of the religious "show" managed by Francisco Camacho, the parish priest of the

Extremaduran village of Siruela, and starring his favorite penitent, María Pizarra. After her screams and cries during mass in the parish church gave rise to complaints from some members of the congregation, Camacho decided to say mass in a nearby hermitage for the benefit of María and some of her numerous local supporters. At the conclusion of the mass, after she had taken communion, Camacho would usher the congregation out of the hermitage, leaving María in a profound trance that would sometimes last six or seven hours. At other times, she would follow Camacho to his home, still in a deep trancelike state. Entering the principal room, Camacho would divest her of her shawl, and she would fall to her knees, thanking God for granting her the favor of receiving him in the host in front of numerous admirers who had gathered to see her.[9]

Such trancelike states and the extreme anxiety focused on the communion bread were symptomatic of a general societal preoccupation with the Eucharist emanating from the monarchy itself and including most of Spain's educated classes. As late as the 1770s, crowds of *madrileños* watched as the "enlightened" King Charles III descended from his carriage and walked beside it, as his place was taken by a priest who was carrying the viaticum to a dying person.[10]

One hundred years earlier, an even more spectacular example of devotion to the viaticum was given by D. Manuel Alfonso Pérez de Guzman el Bueno, the wealthy and powerful duke of Medina-Sidona. In San Lúcar de Barrameda, where he maintained his court, the duke gave his subjects proof of his devotion to the holy sacrament by personally accompanying the viaticum each time that it was carried through the streets to the bedside of a sick person. Since they could hardly avoid following the duke's example, the members of his court, including no less than ten commanders of the military orders, as well as the court musicians, joined the procession, so that the simple carrying of the viaticum through the streets of San Lúcar was celebrated with more pomp than Corpus Christi in many surrounding villages.[11]

The Christological dimension in the spirituality of these women is represented most strongly by fervent devotion to the passion. Such devotion is hardly surprising, given the number of theologians and moralists who urged people to meditate on Christ's sufferings. The Jesuit Pedro de Ribadeneyra, whose *Flos Sanctorum* received numerous editions in the seventeenth and eighteenth centuries, called the life and passion of Christ "our treasury" and urged his readers to imitate the many saints who had taken the passion as inspiration for their prayer and meditation.[12] Antonio de Quintanadueñas, another Jesuit, wrote *Espejo grande de los trabajos de Jesús crucificado* as a vernacular account of the passion specifically to encourage the literate middle classes who did not know Latin to meditate upon it. He hoped that writing in the vernacular would allow the wonderful story to become an object of contemplation for both sexes so that "there would not be a single woman, no matter how withdrawn from the world, who would not be exposed to the "splendor and clarity of Christ's great sacrifice." Following in the tradition of Loyola and other Jesuit writers who stressed a systematic approach to spirituality, Quintanadueñas advised his readers to meditate on each part of Christ's tortured body and contemplate the fact that "while our legs and arms are free, those of Christ, who died to save us, were torn and imprisoned by huge nails."[13]

The importance of the passion in the spiritual lives of these women is indicated by the fact that some 80 percent of the "officially approved" mystics and 53.3 percent of the "sham" mystics in this study were intensely devoted to it. At her trial in 1675, for example, María Cotonilla told the court that for the last twenty-five years she had meditated on the passion every day.[14]

For the Dominican nun Martina de los Ángeles y Arilla, meditation on the passion meant that she would enter a trance during which she would actually accompany Christ on all the stations of the cross. Tears streaming from her eyes, she would see the blood on Christ's body and witness his torturers tying him to the column. In one vision, she even threw herself across his shoulders to spare him the beating and emerged miraculously spattered with his blood. On other occasions, she would find herself accompanying the Virgin Mary and other women at the foot of the cross. In these visions, the Virgin Mary always appeared wearing widow's clothing stained with drops of the blood that were falling from his wounds. These meditative states became much more frequent and intense during Corpus Christi and would sometimes evolve into trances that went on for several hours.[15]

Some women even wrote books about a spirituality that took its departure from constant meditation on the passion. In an unpublished work written in 1617, the Poor Clare Mariana de Jesús recounted a number of the secrets that had been revealed to her while she was praying or after she had received communion. She began by recounting that her need to put these "mysteries" on paper stemmed from the fact that she had been given to understand that she had been chosen to carry on a spiritual apostolate that would affect many people. Mariana was informed that she had to live her life in imitation of Christ and that the best way to prepare herself for this was to meditate on the stations of the cross. Only by doing this could she be made to feel not only the physical torture but also the psychological torment of being brought through the streets of Jerusalem past jeering mobs crying, "Traitor, you have deceived us all." Finally, Christ himself confirmed the importance of the passion in her devotional life by inviting her to "feel in your heart the terrible pain that I felt when they nailed me to the cross."[16]

It was precisely this desire on the part of so many spiritual women to imagine and even to actually feel the torments of the passion that led to the manifestation of the stigmata, surely one of the most fascinating and remarkable "outward" signs of sanctity in the annals of mysticism. In fact, the experience of the stigmata carried with it a double identification. On the one hand, the woman identifies herself with the suffering Christ and on the other with the great stigmatic saints.[17] It is hardly surprising, therefore, that all of the women mystics in this study who experienced the phenomenon of the stigmata also saw visions of St. Francis of Assisi.

The emotional and psychological link between devotion to the passion and the appearance of the stigmata can be appreciated in the fascination that some mystics had with the wounds of Christ. María Antonia Hortola, whose fervent devotion to the passion began when she was seven years old, told her confessor that she "was moved to pity by Christ's sufferings in the house of Pilate." She was most affected by his wounds and would say three credos each day in honor of them, especially the lance thrust that Christ received in his side. Eventually, she became so obsessed by the wound in Christ's side that she began feeling pain in the same place. While María's stigmata never appeared on her body, she joined the numerous women mystics who felt pain or swelling in places where Christ received his wounds.[18]

Unlike María Antonia Hortola, Beatriz María de Jesús claimed to have really suffered the stigmata on the outside of her body. But this outward manifestation began with an "interior" invisible phenomenon on September 16, 1663, the day before the church celebrates the Impression of the Stigmata of Francis of Assisi. Already prefigured by pains that she had experienced in her extremities during the previous year, Christ now appeared to inform her that he had chosen to impress the stigmata on her at the same time every year, although in such a way as to prevent them from being apparent to anyone else. Two years after she had experienced her first pains, Christ once again appeared to inform her that he had decided to actually impress the stigmata on her body as a way of claiming her for himself, in the same way a prince would place his shield over the entrance to his castle.

Of course, given Beatriz's penchant for self-dramatization, she could hardly be expected to keep such a marvelous event a secret. On the afternoon of September 16, 1664, in front of her entire family, her confessor, and other spectators, she struck the same pose that St. Francis is shown assuming in countless paintings: kneeling with her arms outstretched and the palms of her hands open and facing heaven to receive the stigmata. Interestingly enough, when the stigmata did appear, they bore no resemblance to the wounds that Christ suffered but instead resembled the buds of tiny red roses.[19] The following year, when she claimed to have had a vision during which her heart was purified by being burned with a torch carried by her guardian angel, the stigmata appeared as smudges of black ash. The fact that Beatriz's stigmata were so dissimilar to those depicted in religious painting and were different each time she showed them probably indicates that she faked them with whatever material came to hand; if some kind of red dye was not available, she could always fall back on using the ashes from one of the cooking fires that were always kept burning in the house.

Of course, Beatriz's family, her confessor Jerónimo de Allyón, and provisor Jerónimo de Prado were convinced that her stigmata were entirely genuine. Prado's decision to place her in the Franciscan convent of Santo Ángel Custodio the following year was probably motivated by a desire to retain someone of such obvious and impressive spiritual powers within the walls of a convent belonging to the fabled Franciscan order.[20]

Clara de San Francisco, the Bernardine nun in the Canaries, was much less fortunate in her attempt to enhance her reputation by "outward signs" of sanctity. As a devotee of both St. Francis of Assisi and Catherine of Siena, she was well aware of the potent symbolism of stigmata and used various methods to simulate them, including pricking herself in the side until she began to bleed and scratching her forehead in order to claim that she had the crown of thorns impressed upon her. She also allowed hot wax to drip on her hands and feet and then claimed to have had the stigmata burned on her flesh by supernatural forces.[21]

But her most successful attempt to convince the other nuns of her sanctity by showing exterior signs was when she borrowed a little piece of red paper from her cellmate and, using a bit of lemon, rubbed the paper until the dye started to come off. Clara then took the moistened paper and daubed it on her hands, feet, and side to make it appear as though she were bleeding from stigmata.[22] Although this trick should have been transparently obvious, Clara's claim of divine favor was accepted as genuine by Abbess Ana María de la Encarnación, who was one of her strongest supporters in the convent. Her luck changed, however, when Susana de San Esteban y Santa Ursulina was elected abbess. The new superior distrusted Clara and even threw her in the convent jail after she claimed, improbably, that she could provide the nuns with relics of the Japanese Christian martyrs and that one of John the Evangelist's fingers was buried near the convent. Needless to say, the chilling effect of the atmosphere of skepticism created by the new abbess soon put an end to all of Clara's "wounds and miracles," including the stigmata, which somehow disappeared.[23]

Sadly, Clara's emotional and psychological commitment to demonstrating her spiritual perfection through external signs was so great that she continued to insist that her stigmata were genuine when she was called before the Inquisition. She persisted in asserting this even though she had previously admitted to the archbishop of the Canaries that she had faked them with wax, blood, and dye.[24] Of course, the tribunal was well aware of Clara's previous admission of guilt and, after calling twenty-nine prosecution witnesses, finally wore her down to the point where she admitted that the stigmata were no more than an *invención suya*, and begged the tribunal for merciful treatment.[25]

Catalina Ballester was another "fake" mystic who tried to enhance her reputation for sanctity by various "exterior signs," including falsifying at least one of the stigmata, the wound in Christ's side, by cutting herself with a knife. To make the deception even more realistic, she even went to the trouble of calling in a local *curandera* (healer) to treat the wound. The wise woman, who just happened to be the sister of Catalina's strongest supporter, Dr. Fuster, sewed up the wound and when she returned the following day told everyone in the neighborhood that she had found it completely and miraculously healed.[26] Catalina was so convinced of the value of these "exterior signs" in enhancing her spiritual reputation that she openly boasted to the Morlana sisters that someday she would be venerated as a saint and that the people would made up *gozos* (couplets in praise of the saints) in her honor.[27]

Even though the Inquisition and the hierarchy continued to support and protect those mystics who evidenced "external signs" as long as their behavior approximated the saintly ideal, the very fact that the Holy Office kept on arresting and punishing women mystics may have deterred some who might otherwise have exhibited stigmata. Certainly, the condemnation of Sor María de la Visitación, the "nun of Lisbon," probably the best known of the "false mystics" tried by the Holy Office, was uppermost in the mind of María Ángela Astorch when she contemplated showing stigmata in the 1640s. María had just received a wound to the heart administered, so she believed, by Christ himself, and the stigmata would seem to be the logical next step in receiving divine favor. But one day as she was helping the other nuns do the convent's washing, she recalled that part of María de la Visitación's sentence provided that she was to walk about her convent with her arms and feet bare, since that is where she had painted her stigmata. The thought that she might have to expose her arms if she were to be tried and convicted before the Inquisition was so intolerable that she dismissed the idea of having stigmata from her mind.[28]

Ever since the concept of purgatory was set forth at the Councils of Lyons (1274) and Florence (1439) as a place where souls could pay the penalty for sins that they had failed to fully expiate while they were living, there was a growing interest in "pious works" that could reduce their time in purgatory. The Protestant belief that salvation was God's free gift to whomsoever he chose during their earthly life negated the idea of purgatory and denied the value of any "pious works."[29] But the Council of Trent's ringing reaffirmation of the existence of purgatory and the importance and efficacy of "pious works," especially the mass, served to reinforce the determination of devout Catholics to aid the souls and shorten their time in purgatory by whatever means they could.

By the end of the seventeenth century, devotion to the souls in purgatory had become an integral part of the religious life of large sections of the Spanish population. The devotion was spurred by the publication of numerous works in the vernacular that detailed the sufferings of the souls and the ways in which they could be assisted by the living. In one of these books, written by Dr. Joseph Boneta, theologian and benefice holder in Zaragoza cathedral, the author warned that few souls could avoid condemnation to purgatory because the penalties incurred by the ordinary Christian for sins committed in this life were so great that hardly anyone would be successful in expiating them during a lifetime. Consequently, he averred that no living person could avoid an obligations toward the souls, because it was almost certain that one's own parents, relatives, and friends were among them.[30]

Furthermore, echoing earlier writers like St. Thomas Aquinas, St. Bernard, and St. Gregory, Boneta warned that the sufferings of just one soul in purgatory were equal to those of all the martyrs that had ever existed, which Boneta, with pardonable exaggeration, estimated at more than eleven million. But even this level of suffering, however unimaginable, was insufficient since to this had to be added the pains that all the women who ever lived had experienced in pregnancy and all of the torture that criminals had been made to suffer during their trials.[31]

As if this were not enough, Boneta went on to point out that each soul's time in purgatory was likely to be lengthy because one year was required to fully expiate each venial sin, and considerably more time was needed for each mortal sin.[32] To justify his pessimism, Boneta cited Batista de Lanuza's recently published biography of Francisca del Santissimo Sacramento. In this remarkable work, which includes a richly detailed description of the visit of numerous souls to her cell, Francisca is described as being depressed because so many of them had already endured ten, twenty, or even sixty years of torment. Even more upsetting was the fact that a large number of the souls who asked for her intercession were from her own Carmelite order. The needy souls included two popes, several bishops, the former prioress of the convent in Pamplona, a close associate of St. Teresa who was responsible for founding two Carmelite houses, and several deceased members of her own community who had enjoyed excellent reputations while they were still alive.[33]

Taking into account their sufferings and the indeterminate duration of their time in purgatory, it was hardly surprising that the souls should "cry out" to the living. As Boneta described it, the souls blamed the living for their indifference in allowing them "to suffer and burn while you laugh, eat and play." Out of the depths of their anguish and torment, they cried:

> Pity! Have pity for my grief, mortals.
> Pity friends! Pity my affliction.[34]

When we consider the fact that the millions of souls trapped in purgatory were not only calling out for help but also even visiting certain living persons to recount their sufferings, it is hardly surprising to find that devotion to the souls ranked as third most important among the "true" mystics (80 percent) or that it shared first place with the passion (53.3 percent) among their "wayward" sisters. By the seventeenth century, devotion to the souls affected all social classes. It started at the top with the king himself. As Miguel Batista de Lanuza noted in a memorial to Philip IV dated June 21, 1659, the king had gone out of his way to procure indulgences in Rome for the souls. Taking this expression of the royal interest into account, Batista de Lanuza, who was a member of the Council of Aragon, presented a copy of his biography of Francisca de la Santissima Santidad to the king for his library. Philip IV replied by graciously accepting the book "on account of the particular devotion that I have to the souls."[35]

Devotion to the souls of purgatory was also widespread among the nobility, especially noblewomen like Doña Elvira de Mendoza y Córdova, to whom the Jesuit Martín de Roa dedicated his early-seventeenth-century work *Estado de las Almas de Purgatorio*. According to Roa, Doña Elvira was not only extremely devout but also had dedicated herself especially to helping the souls through works of charity, prayer, and, above all, paying for numerous masses.[36]

The fervent atmosphere of devotion to the souls even reached down to the level of María Pizarra, the poor widow of a peasant. Testifying before the Toledo tribunal in 1638, María stated that she was inspired to become devoted to the souls by a sermon that she had heard from some missionaries. Shortly after hearing the sermon, she had a vision in which she visited purgatory and saw many souls "suffering in flames both dark and bright." Some of the souls were familiar to her since they were people from her own village who had recently died. She understood without talking to them that they wanted her to ask their relatives to carry out the provisions in their wills providing for masses to be said for their souls, which was the most effective way of reducing their time in purgatory.[37]

But how could ordinary Christians help the souls? Fortunately, there were a number of acts called suffrages that contained sufficient grace to redeem all or part of the debt owed by souls and thereby reduce their time of suffering, or even release them immediately.[38] Apart from paying for masses, the devout could dedicate their own sufferings from illness and fasting to the relief of the souls. Prayer could also be effective. In his discussion of the suffrages, Martín de Roa underscored the way in which the repetition of even the most common prayers, such as "Our Father," entered into the moral accounting by reducing each soul's term of purgatory by a certain number of days, thereby gaining merit for the living and relief for the dead.[39]

During the sixteenth and seventeenth centuries, the growth of lay confraternities was connected to their role in offering intercessory prayers, which were thought to be effective in reducing the suffering that the souls were obliged to undergo in purgatory. In 1640, María Ángela Astorch took the confraternity idea a critical step further by founding one whose sole purpose was to provide prayers and suffrages for the souls of its members and their families. The members of the confraternity included both living and dead, clergy and laity, and a member who passed away would automatically receive a seven-day credit toward the time of the member's soul in purgatory. The members agreed to pool their own merits in the common interest, and the entire confraternity was placed under the protection of the Sacred Heart and the Virgin Mary.[40]

Since most women and especially those who had entered religious life could not join confraternities and did not have the means to buy masses for the dead, devotional authors went out of their way to stress how they could help by accepting or even seeking out suffering on earth to the relief of the souls. To illustrate this, Joseph Boneta gave the example of St. Catherine of Siena, probably the best known and most revered woman saint among religious women in the early modern period, who had accepted a lifelong pain in her liver to free her father from purgatory.[41] Such descriptions appealed greatly to women who wished to gain spiritual merit from self-sacrifice, since by dedicating her sufferings in life to the relief of a soul in purgatory, she was giving up the benefit of that suffering for her own soul. A sacrifice of this kind was likely to extend the time that her own soul had to remain in purgatory, because theologians were agreed that suffering in this life carried with it a higher redemptive value than the penalties paid in the afterlife.[42]

In spite of the pain and suffering that their souls might have to endure in the afterlife, however, many women mystics were eager to sacrifice themselves to relieve the torments of souls in purgatory. Whenever any of her sister nuns in the Franciscan Convent of Nuestra Señora de Belen died, Francisca

Inés de la Concepción committed herself to a full year of self-inflicted pain and deprivation on their behalf. She even invented a new practice that seemed to offer the souls effective relief. During that same first year, she would frequently lie across the tomb of the deceased. Even though she modestly told the other nuns that this practice was just a way of anticipating the circumstances of her own death, she had a vision in which one of her friends, who had just died, appeared and told her of the tremendous benefits that the souls were deriving from this practice.[43]

It was fortunate indeed that the souls had the ability to actually visit their benefactors or to appear in visions to inform them of the effectiveness of the pious works and suffrages they performed on their behalf. On the very same evening of the day when Gabriela de San Joseph formally renounced in favor of the souls the exculpatory grace contained in all of the pious works that she would perform until the end of her life, a procession of souls visited her cell to thank her for her sacrifice. A number of the souls in the procession, especially the souls of friars and nuns, indicated that she had succeeded in freeing them from purgatory and that they would soon be on their way to heaven.[44]

Anxiety over the afterlife ran so deep in early modern Spanish society that the ability to intercede to alleviate the torment of souls in purgatory became a key element in creating and sustaining a reputation for sanctity. Women mystics were well aware of this, and "genuine" and "fake" alike went out of their way to advertise their success. Since it was commonly assumed that the souls would ask for the intercession of only persons who were already enjoying a state of grace, familiarity with the souls and the ability to help them could redound only to the credit of that person's spiritual reputation. The "false" mystics were also cognizant of this. Several of them made their relationship with the souls in purgatory the linchpin of their attempts to gain a reputation for enjoying extraordinary spiritual gifts and being favored by God. Francisca del Santissimo Sacramento's almost nightly visits from the souls of the dead and her extraordinarily successful efforts on their behalf became very widely known in Pamplona, to the point that they alone constituted the primary reason that people thought of her as a saint.[45] In the case of Isabel de Briñas, claims of an extraordinary relationship with the souls not only constituted the chief means whereby she was able to stake a claim to having great spiritual powers but also allowed her to acquire a substantial piece of property.

Apparently, Briñas gained her reputation by replying with a great show of assurance whenever people asked about the souls of one of their relatives. One day, while having a conversation with Catalina de Guidiel, the wealthy widow of a notary, Briñas casually informed her that she frequently received visits from souls in purgatory who asked her to intercede on their behalf.[46] She told other people in her Madrid neighborhood that she had frequently visited purgatory in the company of the Virgin Mary and that together they had liberated numerous souls. She even went so far as to assert that God could deny her nothing and that she had just seen the soul of the recently deceased count of Molina leave purgatory as a result of her intercession.[47]

Briñas's self-created reputation spread quickly, and soon a number of people from the district were asking her about the souls of their dead relatives. Those who consulted her included Juliana de Castro, the seventy-year-old widow of a government official, and Andrea María Barahona y Gudiel, a wealthy spinster who wanted to know the fate of the souls of her father and her uncle, who had been bishop of Oviedo. Briñas informed each of these women of the number of masses that the soul was requesting and was even able to tell Andrea María Barahona y Gudiel that she had seen her uncle's soul rising heavenward after they had been said. This must have been extremely gratifying to Barahona y Gudiel because, as she told the Inquisition, she had originally consulted with Briñas because she had heard that she "could take souls out of purgatory."[48] Briñas's reputation also got a boost from the active and vocal support of her confessor Domingo Daza, a Dominican friar and royal preacher who praised her to his other penitents and frequently decided who was to perform the masses she recommended.

But the pinnacle of Briñas's success in using the fear of the hereafter for her own benefit was to convince lic. Quadros, a local benefice holder, to leave her his house and property. Briñas and her confessor, Domingo Daza, were able to accomplish this by telling Quadros that they both had a revelation that told them that God had destined his house to be transformed into a Dominican convent.[49] Quadros, who had a strong fear of divine punishment for a variety of misdeeds, agreed that Briñas should receive his house and told his son-in-law Simon Ximenez that he was doing this for "the sake of his soul."[50] After his death, it was learned that he had made Briñas his universal heir, trusting her to found the convent. Like other madridleños who left their entire estates to be consumed in masses for their immortal soul, Quadros evidently believed that such a "pious bequest" would shorten his soul's time in purgatory, but his trust in Isabel de Briñas proved to be sadly misplaced. She never even considered starting a convent and simply moved into the house herself after his death.

Queen of heaven, exemplar of the ideal for women, intercessor with her all-powerful son, mother, inheritor of the attributes of the pagan fertility goddesses, and symbol of the church itself, the Virgin Mary was as compelling an object of devotion for both approved and "fake" mystics as she was for Spanish society as a whole. Among the "fake" mystics, devotion to her was indicated in 46.6 percent of the cases, right behind the passion and the souls of purgatory in their devotional systems. The Virgin Mary also ranked high among the "genuine" mystics, taking fourth place at 50 percent, just after devotion to the souls of purgatory.

The post-Tridentine stress on the family as a model for divine-human relations and on the role of Mary as wife and mother virtually guaranteed that, for at least some women mystics, devotion to Mary was a way of coping with the emotional deprivation that they experienced as children through neglect or the loss of a parent. María de Jesús' first vision of the Virgin Mary, for example, occurred at age five, a year after her father died, when her mother's new husband objected to her presence in the home and forced her to live with her grandparents. In a clear reference to the child's feelings of loneliness and rejection, the Virgin Mary appeared in resplendent garments, smiled warmly, and announced, "I want you as my daughter."[51]

For Jacinta de Atondo, abandoned by her parents at age three and given into the care of her abusive aunt, the Virgin Mary was the only solace throughout her childhood and adolescence, and, as she wrote in one of her letters, she frequently saw visions of Mary with her heart opened to all mortals. At such moments, Jacinta felt that her own heart was inside the heart of the Virgin Mary and she admitted that she "would have felt like an orphan" without that divine presence. She also likened the intense love that she felt for the Virgin Mary to the love of a daughter for an admired mother and claimed to have really felt that she was "the true daughter of the Most Holy Mother."[52]

If the maternal qualities ascribed to the Virgin Mary inspired the devotion of children and adolescents neglected by their parents and relatives, her role as intercessor was most compelling for others. In a particularly intense passage from her *Mystical City of God*, María de Jesús de Agreda describes Christ on the cross as entrusting Mary with power over the entire universe and explicitly promising that "whatever she asks on behalf of mortals, now afterwards and forever, we shall concede."[53]

Other women looked to the Virgin Mary not so much for intercession as for validation of their own particular goals. In the midst of her struggle to gain acceptance for the founding of a new convent, Francisca de los Apostles saw a vision of a procession of saints led by the Virgin Mary and concluded that the proposed foundation would be successful and that it would attain "great perfection."[54]

Perhaps the clearest indication of the growing belief in the powers of the Virgin Mary was the massive use of the rosary to invoke her intercession. According to tradition, the devotion originated with the Virgin Mary herself, who appeared to St. Dominic while he was leading the Inquisition against the Albigensians during the early thirteenth century. After handing him the rosary, the Virgin Mary told him that men and women should invoke her assistance by prayer on the beads. Even though the legend is apocryphal and seems to have been invented by a fifteenth- century Dominican, the explicit intercession of the Virgin Mary associated the rosary with her very strongly and gave it a substantial claim to divine institution and validity.[55]

All classes in Spanish society, from King Philip IV's second wife, Mariana of Austria, who had eleven rosaries in her possession when she died in 1696, to the pauper María Antonia Hortola, who told the Valencia tribunal that she had been saying the rosary since childhood, became devoted to the rosary.[56] In fact, the Franciscan theologian and provincial Antonio Arbiol went so far as to assert that the family that did not say the rosary together every day could not be really considered a Christian family.[57]

Reflecting the attitudes of society as a whole, fully one-third of both groups of mystics were also extremely devoted to the rosary, sometimes to an extraordinary degree. According to her spiritual advisor Jaime de Albert, Josefa Inés de Benigánim not only said the rosary every day but also urged others to do the same on the grounds that God would reward those who offered such devotion to his mother.[58]

As devotion to the Virgin Mary became more widespread, numerous confraternities formed that were dedicated to reciting the rosary. Apart from these formal associations, it was not uncommon for groups of friends, especially women, to come together to recite it on a regular basis. At her trial in 1639, Isabel de Briñas recalled how she had led a group of women from her neighborhood in Madrid in saying the rosary with the encouragement of her spiritual advisor the Dominican Juan de la Puente.[59] Francisco Camacho, the parish priest in the village of Siruela, was another priest who encouraged reciting the rosary. At María Pizarra's trial in 1640, Diego Gonzalez de Viera, a benefice holder in a neighboring village, testified that he, Camacho, and Pizarra had joined together to say the rosary in unison nearly every day during the two and a half years he lived with them.[60]

Because saying the rosary had become widely accepted as the key to obtaining the Virgin Mary's mercy and protection, it is not surprising to find that a number of women who sought to establish reputations for great spirituality would give out rosaries or individual beads that were said to contain thaumaturgic powers. María de Agreda was well known for this, and hundreds of people from the surrounding region would come to her convent to receive the rosaries and beads that they believed would protect them against illness or misfortune. She herself encouraged this belief by telling her confessors that she had obtained a special concession from God in favor of those who accepted these items and invoked him in their hour of need.[61]

The "false" mystics were not far behind their more acceptable sisters in exploiting the potential of the rosary for increasing their reputations. Like her contemporary María de Agreda, Luisa de Carrión was well known for distributing rosary beads and medals, as well as portraits and other items, to increase the importance of the cult that was forming around her person. Like the feigned mystic Francisca del Santissimo Sacramento, Luisa even asked her followers for their own rosaries, which she claimed to take to heaven to have blessed before she returned them.[62] Interestingly enough, such extravagant claims left María de Agreda completely unfazed, and she went out of her way to inform herself about the Inquisition's case against Luisa and intervened with Philip IV to nullify the proceedings.[63]

Altogether, some 26.6 percent of the "false" mystics claimed either to be able to carry rosaries to heaven for blessings or, as in the case of Vicenta Orval, to have received rosaries from the Virgin Mary herself.[64] One of the most interesting cases involved the Bernardine nun Clara de San Francisco, who presented the novices in her convent with beads that she claimed had been blessed by angels and then invited them to give her their rosaries, which she promised she would take to heaven for similar blessings.[65] These extravagant promises formed part of a pattern of behavior by which Clara felt compelled to make ever more incredible assertions and undertake arduous penance in order to maintain a reputation for sanctity among the novices.

Notwithstanding such abuses, official approval for this popular devotion came in 1717, when the feast of the rosary, which began in 1573 after the battle of Lepanto, was extended to the entire church as an expression of thanks to God for another great victory over the Turks at Petrovaradin.[66] But the growing importance of the rosary in obtaining the intercession of the Virgin Mary produced the same kind of anxiety in some individuals that taking the Eucharist had produced in others. Testifying before the Inquisition's Toledo tribunal in 1634, Francisca de la Santissima Trinidad blamed demonic intervention for the foul taste that she had in her mouth every time she took the Eucharist. But saying the rosary was even worse because she reported experiencing so much anxiety when she started that she was hardly ever able to finish it.[67]

Devotion to the Virgin Mary reached its peak in the seventeenth century and was fostered by the Habsburgs as part of a deliberate policy of creating the myth of Austrian piety as a way of imposing religious unity and distracting the popular masses from the burdens of famine, war, and massive fiscal mismanagement. Both northern and southern Habsburgs focused especially on the dogma of the immaculate conception of the Virgin Mary as a way of demonstrating the extent of their devotion to her cult. In Vienna, Ferdinand III (ruled 1637–57) raised a Marian statue in the Am Hof square and imposed an oath to the immaculate conception on all privy councilors, university teachers, and graduates. This oath was extended and made even more absolute under his successor Leopold I.[68]

In Spain, where devotion to the Virgin Mary was already at a fever pitch, the monarchy threw its support behind the immaculate conception and conducted protracted and expensive lobbying efforts to get the papacy to give it public approval. The Spanish rulers were strongly supported by Margaret of the Cross, who, as a true daughter of the Habsburgs, wrote the pope and cardinals on numerous occasions in support of the efforts of Spanish ambassadors.[69] These efforts were rewarded in 1661, when Pope Alexander VII issued a brief specifically describing the opposing view as heresy and forbidding anyone from teaching or writing in favor of it.[70]

But acclamation for the immaculate conception by official bodies like the Inquisition and the hierarchy masked the savage conflict between the Jesuit order, which was among its earliest and strongest proponents, and the Dominicans, who had long opposed it. Prominent Dominicans preached sermons and wrote books against the dogma, and the controversy became so acerbic that the Inquisition had to warn its officials that they must exercise extreme circumspection in enforcing the provisions of the 1661 brief.[71] Earlier in the century, the mystic Mariana de Escobar, who had written to congratulate King Philip III after he had dedicated all of Spain to the dogma in 1616, dreamed of a reconciliation between Jesuits and Dominicans and had a vision in which Christ ordered the two orders to unite.[72] Mariana de Escobar's wishes notwithstanding, the controversy was to drag on for almost another two hundred years until 1854, when Pope Pius IX proclaimed the immaculate conception as an official dogma of the Catholic faith.

Strongly oriented toward dissociative states from earliest childhood and living in a cultural and religious environment in which the mystical works of such figures as Luis de Granada and St. Teresa of Jesus had attained great currency, an overwhelming majority of both the officially approved (86.7 percent) and "false" (93.3 percent) mystics experienced trances and saw visions. These visions were of two main types: those confirming the holiness of the devotions supported by the church, and visions of saints, which not only demonstrate the ongoing importance of the saint cult in Spanish popular religion but also indicate the particular saints venerated by the women mystics. Although there is ample evidence for the materialist causes for these visions, it is nevertheless the case that for the individual, they were genuine "meaning giving experiences," as understood by Husserl.[73]

Apart from the childhood experiences already discussed, several other influences tended to extend and even increase mystics' propensity to experience dissociative states. For one thing, as we have already observed, both groups of mystics were prone to serious illnesses, especially malaria and influenza, that produced high fevers, which are frequently associated with periods of intense visions. At about age twenty-seven, Hipolita de Jesús y Rocaberti recorded that she had been stricken with a case of quartan malaria so serious that she suffered from constant bouts of fever for the next twenty-seven years. Needless to say, a number of her visions were directly associated with periods of high fever.[74]

In her diary, Francisca del Santissima Sacramento records several occasions when visions were closely associated with or occurred during periods of fever. On one occasion when she had been sick with a high fever for two days, innumerable souls from purgatory filled her cell to overflowing.[75] Her entry for April 17, 1620, records that she had been suffering from influenza and had experienced "high fever" for several days when she saw a terrible vision of Christ tied up and bleeding and surrounded by his torturers. Christ addressed her angrily, denouncing her for lying about while he was tied up and beaten, and she immediately leaped out of bed and fell on her knees with tears streaming from her eyes.[76] This vision reflected not only the strong Christological orientation of her devotions but also her own sense of guilt, frequently expressed in her writings, about not having entered wholeheartedly into the life of the convent.

Mental illness, although not very glamorous, exalted, or mysterious, was another obvious source of vision states. Juana Baptista, who told the Toledo tribunal in 1636 that "God had favored her" with more than thirty trances over the last fourteen years, experienced several well-documented incidents of mental breakdown. In fact, Bartolome Osorio, one of the defense witnesses, told the tribunal that he had taken her into his home on more than one occasion when he found her wandering the streets. He also believed that her bout with mental illness had left her permanently impaired so that she was likely to commit any kind of "folly" without being aware of what she was doing. Juana had numerous visions of the crucified Christ during her trances, as well as of the Virgin Mary and of Satan in the form of a cat.[77]

The Carmelite Tomasa Dolz was described by witnesses, including the tribunal's own officials, as having wild mood swings, and she would probably be diagnosed today as manic depressive. Needless to say, Tomasa had frequent trances and saw visions involving the Eucharist, the child Jesus, and demons. One of the most bizarre of her visions was when she saw the green cross of the Inquisition emerge from a consecrated host.[78]

But illness, even given the frequency with which many of these women suffered from recurring bouts of different strains of fever-producing malaria, was probably less important than sleep deprivation as a principal cause of hallucinatory states in our women mystics. Whatever the circumstances of their lives, whether they lived at home, in *beaterios* or in convents, their social environment strongly encouraged or mandated that they exert a high degree of control over the amount and duration of their sleep. Such demands were, of course, part of a systematic effort to control and subordinate bodily needs to the higher goals of the inner spiritual life. According to Jacinta de Atondo's biographer Antonio Arbiol, sleep, while necessary for work, should be kept to the absolute minimum in order to provide more time for contemplation and spiritual exercises.[79] Jacinta herself took the injunction against excessive sleep to the extreme and did everything possible to keep herself awake. Spurred by her longtime confessor, Pedro Garcés, who insisted that she sleep on her knees with her head resting on a small table, Jacinta regarded sleep as her "enemy" and did everything possible, including scourging herself until she bled, to stay awake.[80]

In all, 63.3 percent of "approved" and 40 percent of "feigned" mystics limited their sleep to between two and six hours per night on a regular basis, while 43.3 percent of "true" mystics maintained vigils that would periodically keep them awake for entire nights. Women who lived in highly regulated environments like convents or *beaterios* had to follow the rule of the order, and these rules not only restricted the duration of sleep but also usually mandated interruptions in sleep for obligatory prayers. The Franciscan rule followed by Margaret of the Cross at Madrid's Descalzas Reales Convent stipulated a total of no more than four hours of sleep. The nuns would go to their special chapels at 8 P.M. to ask God for permission to sleep and only then retire to their cells. Shortly before midnight, they would be summoned to matins, the first of the canonical hours in the breviary, followed by one hour of prayer. The nuns would then typically remain in the chapel until 5 A.M., when they would recite the first canonical hour and hear mass.[81]

While St. Teresa did prescribe a more liberal rule for her Carmelites, which allowed them to say matins at 9 P.M. and then sleep continuously until 5 A.M. in summer and 6 A.M. in winter, many of the nuns were zealots who restricted their sleep as part of a general program of harsh austerities.[82] Gabriela de San Joseph limited her sleep to four hours by remaining in the chapel for prayer for several hours after matins and rising at 4 A.M.[83] Gabriela also had a series of illnesses, including painful stomach aches, severe chest pains, and vomiting, that woke her up and served to fragment her sleep.

Many of these women also came from devout homes where limitations on sleep were prescribed for children. Isabel de Jesús, who was later to become a member of the third order of Carmelites, never slept for more than five hours before she left home. After praying between midnight and 2 A.M. she would sleep until 6:00 in the morning and then take a nap, which usually lasted for one hour, sometime in the early afternoon.[84] After leaving home and setting up housekeeping with an older woman, Isabel decreased her hours of continuous sleep by usually praying until 3 A.M. and going to mass one hour earlier. By following this regimen, Isabel rarely got more than three hours of sleep during her entire adult life.[85]

Psychologists who have studied sleep patterns, especially the effects of sleep deprivation and interrupted sleep, have concluded that progressive sleep deprivation and fragmented sleep tend to produce perceptual distortions and hallucinations in experimental subjects.[86] Hallucinosis is particularly common among people with Parkinson's disease (which may well have affected some of the women mystics) and those who experience a high degree of sleep disruption, but hallucinations have also been shown for normal individuals awakened about an hour after rapid eye movement (REM) sleep begins.[87] In one instance, a normal twenty-year-old student had several hallucinations strangely reminiscent of the "sense of presence" experienced by our women mystics during their visions when returning to sleep after interruption. These hallucinations included hearing someone come into the bedroom and walk around the bed although, in actual fact, no one came into the room.[88] The literature also presents numerous examples of both auditory and visual hallucinations during transitional states of drowsiness between waking and sleeping. Such hallucinations can occur during the day or at night before sleep and are believed to be caused by a disruption in the REM dream state. Jacinta de Atondo, who was described by her confessor as drowsy and "lethargic," would have frequent visions as she drifted in and out of consciousness, and her auditory hallucinations were similar to those described in the results of modern dream laboratory experiments.[89]

Of course, it would be a gross overstatement to attempt to establish a rigid causal connection between lack of sleep and the number of visions an individual experienced. Nevertheless, it is probably no accident that María de Agreda experienced her famous vision of the soul of the deceased Queen Isabel de Borbón at matins, during a period when she was sleeping about two hours per night. It is also probably significant that Francisca del Santissima Sacramento, who limited her sleep to no more than three to four hours, had the largest number of visions (41) and apparitions of individual saints (100) of any of the women in this study. But it was left to the brilliant María Ángela Astorch to make a systematic record of her dreams for the edification of the nuns of her convent. Like many other women mystics, Astorch spent much of the night awake and wandering the darkest recesses of the convent, and she would frequently interrupt what little sleep she did get for special prayers. Not unexpectedly, she was also prone to dreaming and could sometimes not even tell the difference between dreaming and being awake.[90]

Whether induced by child or adolescent trauma, illness, fever, sleep deprivation, or ardent belief, the mystical states of consciousness experienced by so many of these women were filled with religious visions. Apart from those that were specific to the struggles and trials of each individual, the visions fell into three major groups, which were largely consistent with their devotional concerns.

The first group is Christological in nature and directly relates to the intense devotion that so many of these women felt toward the image of the crucified and suffering Christ and toward the Christ of the passion. Overall, 66.7 percent of "true" mystics and 53.3 percent of those who came before the Inquisition experienced visions in which Christ appeared. Christological visions varied in both content and meaning. Many of them related directly to the passion itself, with 46.7 percent of the "true" mystics and 26.6 percent of the "false" experiencing visions containing the image of Christ on the cross or carrying the cross.

In one vision, experienced by the "false" mystic Manuela Ramos, Christ appeared carrying the cross. Manuela approached Christ and asked if she could share his burden. Even though a voice told her that it would be a great weight, she replied bravely that "even if it weighed much more," she still wanted to carry it. Christ then placed the cross on her right shoulder and, as she told the inquisitors in Toledo, carrying the cross had caused her fifteen days of agony in that same shoulder.[91]

In other instances, Christ appeared as a consoling presence, either to reassure the woman of his favor in times of trial or to relieve her physical suffering by making her appreciate how much more he had suffered during the passion. Ana de Jesús experienced both kinds of visions. Visions of Christ as a consoling and encouraging force were particularly common during Ana's frequent struggles with the male superiors of her order. On one occasion, Christ appeared just after she had been denied permission to create a barred window in a parish church that adjoined a convent that she had founded so that the nuns could hear mass and sermons. Christ informed her that no one could prevail against her because "you and your nuns are the light of my eye." Later in life, however, when she fell seriously ill and suffered great pain, Christ appeared and made her understand fully what he had gone through during the passion, while informing her that she would have the honor of suffering as he did and looking very much like him just before she died. Predictably enough, her biographer relates that she spent the last few months of her life in intense pain and suffered from severe bedsores that left scars, making her body an imitation of Christ.[92]

A second group of visions took shape around the Eucharist, which, as noted before, both appealed powerfully to these women's imagination and caused them intense anxiety. This ambivalence was so pronounced in the case of Isabel de Jesús that it led to visions in which the devil appeared and mocked the Eucharist, telling her it was a lie because "God does not need you to take him in your mouth." Isabel felt so guilty about this vision that she fell on the ground. With tears in her eyes, she begged to be forgiven for her "rebellion" and made a deep and profound profession of faith in the Eucharist and all of the other teachings of the church.[93]

More common among the 40 percent of "genuine" and 20 percent of "counterfeit" mystics who experienced visions involving the Eucharist was the kind of reverence expressed by María Cotonilla when she told her friend Quiteria Sánchez about a particularly beautiful vision that she had while waiting to take communion in the Santa Ana parish church. Standing a few feet from the priest as he gave communion to members of the congregation, María saw a statue of the crucified Christ pull a rose from its side and present it to each person who received the host.[94]

The third major group of visions were, broadly speaking, related to the cult of the Virgin Mary and everything most closely associated with it. In all, some 73.3 percent of "genuine" mystics and 40 percent of the "fake" mystics saw visions of the Virgin Mary. Such visions, as suggested previously, frequently had a consoling aspect, like her many appearances to Caterina Tomás when she was a child. In addition, of course, the strong support that the Jesuit order, the hierarchy, and the state gave to the immaculate conception of Mary was reflected in visions. Francisca del Santissimo Sacramento, who was especially devoted to the dogma, had two spectacular visions that confirmed its validity beyond any doubt. In the first vision, she saw the Virgin Mary as a recently born infant nestled in the arms of her mother, St. Anne, and surrounded by a celestial court of angels and saints whose very presence seemed to indicate the miraculous and unique nature of the event. In the second vision, which took place just two months later, Christ and the Virgin Mary appeared, surrounded by a celestial host, and gave her to understand that "the Queen of Heaven was conceived without original sin."[95]

The powerful upsurge of Marian devotion that characterized the early modern period, epitomized in the struggle to establish the immaculate conception, should not be allowed to obscure the fact that the cult of the saints continued to flourish in Spain. Analysis of the saints who appeared in visions to both groups of women mystics provides fascinating insights into a key aspect of popular piety and sheds light on the relationship between the lives of the saints contained in the hagiographies and *Flos Sanctorum* of the period and the emotional, psychological, and spiritual needs of the individual. It also allows us to weigh with some precision the relative importance of new Counter-Reformation saints such as Teresa of Jesus, Francis Xavier, or Ignatius Loyola, as opposed to older, more traditional figures such as the apostles, the martyrs of the early church, and the great teachers of the Christian faith such as St. Augustine and St. Thomas Aquinas.

The continued importance of the saint cult among both "genuine" and "fake" mystics, however, should not be allowed to obscure the fact that there were considerable differences in the intensity and sophistication of saint worship both within each group and between them. For one thing, the overall number of saints seen in visions differs, with the "true" mystics experiencing 4.3 per biography while the women tried by the Holy Office mention an average of only 2.0 per case file. While the case files cannot be equated with the biographies and autobiographies as a source for the devotional lives of women mystics, nevertheless the significant differences in literacy rates between "approved" mystics (90 percent) and "fake" mystics (66.6 percent) and the greater access that "approved" mystics had to saint images and hagiographies would seem to account for at least part of the numerical differences.[96]

Detailed analysis of the occurrence of saint visions among "approved" mystics further confirms the importance of literacy in determining the number of saints that appeared in visions. Illiterate or semiliterate "true" mystics such as the lay nun Josefa Inés de Benigánim saw many fewer saints in their visions (9) than highly educated women such as Hipolita de Jesús y Rocaberti (25), who lived in an aristocratic convent and was able to obtain a variety of devotional works.

Qualitative differences among and between the two groups are also traceable to such cultural factors as literacy, exposure to hagiographical literature, and social status. The 129 saints who appeared to the "approved" mystics included such exotic figures as Stephen Protomartyr, the first-century Hellenistic Jew allegedly appointed almoner by the apostles, and Ignatius of Antioch (d. c. 107), who was thrown to the lions in the Colosseum. Needless to say, such exotica were unknown to the "feigned" mystics who lacked access to the collected of lives of the saints where they were mentioned. Instead, their devotions were organized around a fairly small number of saints, with the top eight accounting for 46.4 percent of those mentioned in the case files, while the top eight referred to by the "true" mystics were responsible for only 28.3 percent of the appearances cited in the books.

Given the fact that this study deals exclusively with women, it is perhaps surprising that only 22.4 percent (29 of 129) of the saints that they venerated were female. Nevertheless, that percentage is significantly higher than the 17.5 percent of female saints in Weinstein and Bell's sample, and it runs counter to the pattern of declining numbers of female saints during the sixteenth and seventeenth centuries.[97]

Among the female saints, two stand out: the fourteenth-century penitent, visionary, and reformer Catherine of Siena (1347–80), who was the most popular among the "false mystics," mentioned in 46.1 percent of the case records, and Teresa of Jesus (1515–82), who was tied with St. Joseph for third place in the number of biographies mentioning her (13 of 30 or 43.3 percent) as appearing in visions. The cult of Catherine of Siena, who was popularly credited with bringing the papacy back to Rome from Avignon, was boosted by the appearance of a biography by Raymond of Capua. It was almost certainly a Spanish translation of this biography that was referred to by the *beata* Francisca de los Apostles in her testimony before the Toledo tribunal of the Inquisition.

In the woman mystic's quest for spiritual perfection, Catherine of Siena provided a much-needed role model of a woman who won the respect of popes and cardinals for her teaching and who remained chaste and engaged in penance that would have daunted the strongest man. Her success demonstrated that, in spite of physical weakness and social disability, women could still aspire to spiritual greatness because in the eyes of God both sexes were equal.[98]

The popularity of St. Teresa among the "approved" mystics may be attributed, at least in part, to the fact that so many of them were Carmelites. For the woman or man belonging to a religious order, the founder was an imposing, inescapable figure. The frequency with which Francis of Assisi, founder of the Franciscans, appeared in the biographies of "true" mystics (17 of 30 or 56.6 percent) and the popularity of St. Dominic (33.3 percent) and St. Peter Nolasco (6.6 percent) are also partly due to the fact that they were the founders of great religious orders.

All of the Carmelite nuns had visions in which St. Teresa encouraged them, admonished them, or, in the case of Francisca del Santissimo Sacramento, promised to punish their enemies within the community. Teresa de Jesús Vela, who was so convinced of her inadequacy as a Carmelite nun that she did not even dare look at Teresa's portrait, enjoyed one of the most powerful of these "encouragement" visions when she was a novice. One night while she slept, the saint, appeared seated and deep in conversation with another Carmelite nun. Much to her delight, Teresa saw herself in the vision seated right alongside the saint who gave every indication of welcoming her into her company and showed no reluctance to include her in the conversation, which involved grave matters concerning the order. From this intimacy with the saint, Teresa understood that she was fully accepted as a Carmelite and, from then on, whenever she saw a portrait of the saint, she smiled and felt happy and secure in her protection.[99]

But Teresa of Jesus had something working for her that none of the other Counter-Reformation saints could match: the printing press, by which her spiritual and autobiographical writings became known to a wider public. In 1583, not even a year after her death, an edition of the maxims and *The Way of Perfection* was published in Evora, and by 1588, a volume of more than a thousand octavo pages incorporating her autobiography and five of her spiritual works had appeared in Salamanca. Thirteen more editions of her complete works were published between 1588 and 1636. During the same period, numerous editions of individual works were published in Spanish, including the *Spiritual Maxims* and *The Way of Perfection*, and Teresa's life was the subject of biographies written by such leading figures in Spanish ecclesiastical life as Jerónimo Gracián (1608, 1611), Diego de Ypes (1615), and Francisco de Ribera.[100] With all of these editions, including some that were relatively inexpensive, Teresa's writings spread her reputation far and wide, reaching not only the palaces of the great but also even the hovels of the poor. Even Francisca Badia, who lived behind her parents' stall in Valencia's main market, read several of Teresa's books in the 1720s, including an edition of the *Mansions*. During one vision Teresa appeared and informed her that she was very pleased to see her reading her spiritual works.[101]

Even though María Bautista did not name any of Teresa's books in her testimony, she did tell the Toledo tribunal that she had read them, as well as several other spiritual works. Evidently, María must have felt highly ambivalent about Teresa. If, on the one hand, the powerful imagery in one of Teresa's visions inspired her to have one of a similar kind, on the other she was jealous of the saint and confidently assured her supporters that she would receive more divine favors than Teresa and that she, too, would become a "doctor of the church."[102] Unfortunately for María, both of these statements were classed as heretical propositions by the tribunal's theological advisors and figured in the charges brought against her by the prosecuting attorney at her trial.

Interestingly enough, in spite of the stress that the Counter-Reformation church laid on the cult of the new saints, who were helping it to reclaim lost territory in Europe and spreading the faith through foreign missions, most of the saints that appeared to the women mystics were the apostles, martyrs, and teachers of the ancient and medieval church. Of the 129 saints who appeared to the "authentic" mystics, 55 percent died before 400 A.D., and 27 percent came from the medieval period. The percentages are remarkably similar among the "counterfeit" mystics. Of the 31 saints appearing in their visions, 54.8 percent came from the ancient world and 15.4 percent from the medieval period. The popularity of the saints of the Counter-Reformation was limited among both the "true" (10.8 percent) and "false" mystics (9.6 percent), in spite of considerable efforts by both the religious orders and the monarchy to promote their veneration. In fact, it appears that some women mystics had a distinct preference for the traditional saints as opposed to those of the Counter-Reformation. In 1618, María Ángela Astorch, whose overactive imagination was always leading her to create new devotions, devised what she called a "consistory of saint-confessors" to monitor her compliance with the particular virtue that she assigned to each one. All of the fourteen saints in this pantheon were from the ancient or medieval periods, including such relatively obscure saints as the seventh-century Ildifonsus of Toledo and Basil the Great (c. 330–379), bishop of Caesarea, along with better known saints such as Francis of Assisi. She was assisted before the tribunal by St. Thomas Aquinas, and the prosecuting attorney was none other than St. Clement (d. 100), who was one of the early popes.[103]

In excluding all Counter-Reformation saints from her pantheon, Astorch was simply reflecting the continuing interest in the saints of the early and medieval church that was characteristic of Spanish society as a whole. Perhaps Hipolita de Jesús y Rocaberti put it best in her autobiography when she explained her own strong preference for the saints of the ancient world by the fact that "those of the primitive Church lived at a time when Christians had greater fervour because they were closer to the blood of Christ."[104] Or perhaps it was simply that the new saints, whose major contributions were to provide leadership as bishops (Carlo Borromeo) or founders of new religious orders (Ignatius Loyola or Gaetano Thiene, founder of the Theatines) were a bit dull compared with the martyrs, ascetics, and miracle workers of earlier periods. As a consequence, Ignatius Loyola appeared to only three of the thirty "true" mystics and is not mentioned at all in the case files of the women who ended up before the bar of the Holy Office.

On a deeper level, however, it appears that the heroic character of the lives of the saints of the late Roman period, especially their role as martyrs and teachers of the faith, reflected the aspirations that the women mystics had for themselves. Among the "approved" mystics, for example, fully 40 percent aspired to martyrdom and 36.7 percent wanted to preach. While none of the testimony in the case files indicates any desire for martyrdom among the "feigned" mystics, one-third contained evidence of the accused's desire to preach the faith.

Such aspirations, expressed by so many of the women, led to the popularity among them of such relatively obscure martyrs as Pope Clement, reputedly killed by being thrown into the sea with an anchor around his neck, or the late-third-century Marcellus the Centurion, who sealed his fate by resigning from the army and claiming publicly to be a soldier of Christ.[105] But the greatest saints of early Christianity were known for their ability to teach and communicate the word of God. Included among the most popular of the saints who appeared to the women mystics, therefore, were the apostles Matthew and Mark (10 percent) and John the Evangelist (50 percent). Other great teachers of the faith in the ancient world who appeared in these women's visions included Augustine (10 percent), as well as more obscure figures like Ambrose (339–397) bishop of Milan and Denys the Areopagite, whose myth conflates several figures responsible for the conversion of France.[106]

Since extreme forms of self-mortification and denial of the senses were still widely accepted as a path to greater spirituality, many of the women also saw visions of some of the great ascetics of ancient Christianity. Like Hilarion (c. 291–c. 371), who gave away his property and lived as a hermit, most of these ascetics embraced a life of solitude and voluntary poverty.[107] These saints were frequently pioneers of the monastic movement, which shifted a part of the energy of late Roman Christianity away from urban areas.[108] The decision to leave the world and devote oneself to a life of contemplation further strengthened the appeal of these ascetics to the women, most of whom had more or less willingly made the same choice, and many consciously tried to cut themselves off as much as possible even from the other members of the community.

Among the medieval saints venerated by these women were a number of martyrs, but, reflecting the Counter-Reformation concern with religious orthodoxy and protecting the rights of the church, these saints lost their lives defending the faith against heretics or the excessive demands of lay authority, rather than against pagans. Such concerns explain the presence of the Dominican Inquisitor Peter the Martyr, who fell victim to a Cathar assassin, among the saints seen in visions by the "officially approved" mystics.[109] Resistance to monarchs who wished to injure the prerogatives of the clergy is exemplified among the medieval saints by the appearance of Thomas à Beckett (1118–70), who was murdered for resisting King Henry II's refusal to allow clerics the right to appeal to Rome against the verdicts of English ecclesiastical courts.[110]

National and regional pride, which is evident in the hagiographic traditions of different parts of Europe, determined that saints of Spanish origin accounted for just over 20 percent of those appearing in the visions of the "true" mystics and just over 16 percent of those seen by the "false." Not surprisingly for those familiar with the contents of the *Flos Sanctorum* across Europe, some of the Spanish saints, especially the medieval ones, were fairly obscure and would not have figured in the traditional saint lore of other regions. Examples of obscure saints virtually unknown in the *Flos Sanctorum* of other parts of Europe included Diego de Alcalá, who was cited in five biographies and one case file, and Ildephonsus of Toledo (607–677), who may have remained popular in Spain because of his fervent devotion to the immaculate conception of Mary.

Within Spain itself, regional traditions of saint worship that originated in the Middle Ages were kept alive well into the early modern period. An excellent example of an exclusively regional saint cult among our women mystics is the appearance of St. Eulalia of Barcelona to three of the women, all from Catalonia. Saint Eulalia of Barcelona's story was almost certainly lifted from that of Eulalia of Merida, a fourth-century martyr to the persecutions of Diocletian. Interestingly enough, the entire hagiographic literature on Eulalia of Barcelona, beginning with an eleventh-century Latin martyrology, consisted of four items, all in Latin or Catalan. One of these items actually was a Catalan edition of James of Voragine's *Golden Legend*, with the life of Eulalia of Barcelona added. By inserting Eulalia of Barcelona into what was undoubtedly the most widely known *Flos Sanctorum* of medieval times, the Catalan editor undoubtedly hoped to lend her enough credibility to eclipse her rival from Merida.[111]

Certain regional saint cults were encouraged by the monarchy, which sought to gain political advantage by demonstrating its support for a cult that was part of popular religious culture. The supposed remains of the obscure martyr Leocadia of Toledo (d. 303), which had lain for many centuries in the Flemish abbey of Saint-Ghislain, were brought back to Toledo by order of King Philip II in 1587 as partial compensation to that city for making Madrid the capital in 1561.[112] Leocadia appeared to four of the approved mystics, all born in Toledo.

In one particularly beautiful vision, the Carmelite *beata* Isabel de Jesús saw Leocadia, dressed in the habit of a Carmelite, descending a heavenly staircase and holding a cross. She wore a resplendent white cape, and white butterflies resembling snowflakes issued from her mouth and flew upward toward heaven. Leocadia informed the *beata* that she had been chosen by God to be Toledo's link to heaven because God loved the city very much. The butterflies that came from her mouth were, in fact, a sign of this communication since they represented the supplications for assistance made to her from its citizens. These petitions took the form of butterflies and rose to heaven, where God would deal with them directly. Leocadia vanished, but not before assuring Isabel of her continued protection for the city.[113]

Apart from some fairly obvious distinctions, such as the regional basis of a cult or the fact that a particular saint was the founder of the religious order to which the individual belonged, it is far from easy to understand why certain saints appeared to some women and not to others. Adopting a series of broad categories to classify saints and then attempting to apply those categories to understand individual preferences might obscure more than it reveals. The published Life of a saint frequently contained many different features, which made it easy for individuals to pick characteristics that interested them regardless of the major thrust of the saint's real contribution. It seems quite clear, for example, that the great Thomas Aquinas, the author of the *Summa Theologica*, should be placed in Weinstein and Bell's category of evangelical activity for his teaching and writing, but for the lay nun Inés de Benigánim, the most important thing about St. Thomas was that he had defended his chastity against a woman that his brothers had sent to seduce him.[114] The illiterate lay nun had probably never heard of the *Summa Theologica* but did spend a great deal of time talking up the virtues of chastity, so that what appealed to her about St. Thomas was what seemed to tie his life most closely to her personal preferences and opinions.[115]

Nevertheless, in spite of the difficulties inherent in any classification of saint cults, I believe that the preferences of the women in this study for certain specific saints can be roughly broken down into three broad areas: saints whose lives compensate for some emotional, psychological, or material deprivation; saints who validate and support the individual's life struggles and ambitions; and those who stimulate her fantasy life by providing models of exceptionally heroic activity, which early modern society normally denied to women.

Jacinta de Atondo's visions of Margaret of Cortona (c. 1247–97) provide an excellent example of the first category because of the abuse and emotional deprivation suffered by both women. Like Jacinta herself, Margaret was rejected by her family and engaged in dramatic public penance somewhat reminiscent of Jacinta's own. Margaret really had committed the sin of concupiscence and had an illegitimate child, whereas Jacinta herself had never offended against the moral standards of the day, but both shared a terrible sense of guilt.[116]

Caterina Tomás's visions incorporating saints Praxedes, Cosmas, and Damian, all known for charity and a lack of interest in financial gain, helped to sustain her emotionally in the face of the grasping, miserly relatives who exploited her unmercifully.[117] Saint Catherine of Alexandria's frequent appearances were even more suggestive of a form of emotional compensation for her family's lack of understanding and support. In addition to being the patron of young girls, Catherine of Alexandria's legend makes her an adolescent who was persecuted for her Christianity and who argued successfully in its defense before fifty renowned philosophers.[118] As we have already seen, Caterina must have felt like an early Christian faced with the indifference and hostility of pagans in the home of her uncle and aunt, where she was mocked and abused for her religious devotion and forced into silence about her desire to become a nun.[119]

Saints who appeared to support the woman's ambitions for herself or her chosen form of devotion or observance were extremely popular. One of the most frequent saint visions was the appearance of the founder of a religious order who came to encourage her to believe that she could become a nun in spite of parental opposition or lack of means. Beatriz María de Jesús' most frequent saintly visitor, for example, was Francis of Assisi, founder of the Franciscans, since she quarreled with her father over her desire to join the order. Her diary records the constant presence of St. Francis and St. Clare, the founder of the Minoresses or Poor Clares, the companion order for women. Both of these saints would accompany her to and from church and appear to her at moments of extreme tension with her father in order to reassure her about her inevitable entry into the religious life.

Saints whose lives indicated that they had rejected marriage and eagerly embraced a life of celibacy also appeared in visions to strengthen the resolve of young women who were choosing the same path for themselves. Of these saints, Catherine of Siena was the most popular because her Life not only appeared in *Flos Sanctorum* but also was available in individual hagiographies. Martina de los Angeles y Arilla, who eventually joined Catherine's own Dominican order, read a biography of Catherine while she was still a child and swore an oath of chastity when she was ten.[120] Catherine appeared to Martina in numerous visions; Martina, who frequently meditated on Christ as the ideal husband, experienced a mystical marriage similar to the one described in St. Catherine's life.

The "sham" mystic Vicenta Orval also experienced numerous visions in which St. Catherine of Siena appeared to her dressed in the rags of a beggar and asking her for alms. According to Dr. Joseph Guillem, the vicar of her parish in Torrente, the forty-year-old spinster was extremely devoted to Christ and considered herself married to him in the same way as St. Catherine was.[121]

Given the opposition of a male-dominated intellectual establishment to women writers, it is hardly surprising that a woman with intellectual ambitions should choose to model herself on saints who were outstanding as writers and teachers. The remarkable Hipolita de Jesús y Rocaberti, who wrote so many books in spite of experiencing episodes of severe depression, regularly received visions of saints who had themselves contributed valuable works to the corpus of Catholic theology. The "helper" saints who appeared with greatest frequency and specifically encouraged her to press on with her writing included Augustine, Thomas Aquinas, Paul, and Gregory the Great (c. 540–604), the author of *Homilies on the Gospel* and numerous other works.[122]

Saints whose Lives indicated that they had contended with established institutions or challenged tradition to bring about innovations or reforms were popular with women who saw their lives as a struggle with recalcitrant religious communities or an unfeeling male-dominated religious establishment. Francisca de los Apostoles, another "false" mystic, was very critical of the ecclesiastical establishment and even dreamed of approaching the pope about establishing a new reformed religious order. She saw visions of Catherine of Siena, who had written letters critical of both Gregory XI and Urban VI and helped to end the Great Schism.[123] In conversation with Luisa de los Angeles, one of her supporters who later turned up as a witness at her trial before the Inquisition, Francisca boldly compared herself to St. Catherine in the sense that she, too, had offered to suffer "persecution and dishonor" to save sinful Christianity.[124]

Women who chose an unusually harsh penitential regimen tended to venerate saints who embraced similar forms of extreme asceticism. Teresa de Jesús Vela, who employed harsh penance to expiate her strong feelings of guilt, greatly admired the German Dominican Henry of Suso for his almost superhuman penitential practices, which included carving the name Jesus on his breast with a knife. Her devotion to Henry was so great that she thought of emulating him but was dissuaded from doing so by the thought that she was so vile and unworthy that God might not accept such a gesture from her.[125]

Attitudes toward saints among our women mystics were also affected by the way in which the lives of some of them seemed to point in new directions and at least offer the possibility of doing things that were generally denied to women in early modern society. The wave of enthusiasm that generated so much proselytizing and missionary activity during the Counter-Reformation could not fail to affect devout Catholic women who wished to contribute to the process of rolling back the Protestant tide and converting new souls for Christ. Unfortunately for Spanish women, the conservatism of Spanish society and the emphasis on total claustration after the Council of Trent prevented the development of groups like France's Congregation of Notre Dame, who took simple vows and dedicated themselves to helping the poor and furnishing basic religious education to young girls.

The failure to provide real-world opportunities for women to participate actively in the Counter-Reformation meant that such desires emerged as fantasy. One of the most recurring fantasies experienced by all "official" mystics in this study was to participate in missionary activity (26.7 percent), even if doing so meant suffering martyrdom. It is not surprising, therefore, that some women should choose to venerate saints who had dedicated themselves to missionary activity. Isabel de Jesús fantasized about journeying to North Africa and ministering to the spiritual needs of the Christian captives in the infamous baños (prisons) of Algiers.[126] Not surprisingly, one of the saints who inspired her with special veneration was the Portuguese Franciscan Anthony of Padua (c. 1193–1231), who had joined other Franciscan friars in a mission to Morocco in 1220. Even though Anthony was forced to return because of ill health, he continued his active preaching (another one of Isabel's fantasies) and proselytizing activities among the Cathars of southwestern France.[127]

Spanish Catholicism from the time of the Council of Trent through the end of the seventeenth century and beyond tended to preserve a structure of belief and observance that stressed the supernatural elements in religion. From sacraments to the cult of the saints, from the vast numbers of relics collected by such monarchs as Philip II to the outpouring of officially approved literature on the mystical and the miraculous, both the ecclesiastical hierarchy and Catholic secular authorities emphasized the importance of the approved channels of grace and intercession that linked man to God and offered the possibility not only of redemption in the afterlife but also concrete assistance with human difficulties here on earth.[128]

But within the framework of a Spanish church militant that tended to see heresy behind every novel idea or question about established observances, the role of women remained highly ambivalent. Frustrated by the refusal of the hierarchy to allow them to participate directly in the process of Catholic renewal through the organization of lay congregations, they could only resign themselves to a life of prayer and contemplation or seek to expiate the sins of humankind by torturing their own bodies, secure in the knowledge that this sacrifice was pleasing in the sight of God. But by excelling in the forms of holiness that the hierarchy itself so strongly supported, many of these women gained a reputation for spiritual power that brought persons from all walks of life to seek their advice and rely on their intercessory capabilities. The public role denied them by strict enclosure and social prejudice, therefore, they recovered to some extent by excelling in the private realm of the spirit.

Between Power and Impotence

Social Role and Social Fantasies

Extraordinary piety, harsh asceticism, chastity, and, perhaps most important, a reputation as someone who was favored with divine communication elevated the status of the woman mystic and gave her a certain social and even political importance that her sex normally could not claim. But that influence, such as it was, came at a heavy price. Acceptance of strict claustration, the power that male vicars and spiritual advisors had over convent life, and the ever-watchful eye of the Holy Office meant that many of their aspirations remained on the level of fantasy.

The influence that at least some women mystics could attain was indicated by the fact that they were much sought after as advisors and intercessors by all classes, from royalty to the meanest *labrador*. The royal family began consulting with spiritual women during the reign of Philip III, who sought out the advice of Beatriz Ramírez de Mendoza, countess of Castellar, a pious and mystical *beata* from an important noble family. During one long interview with the monarch, the countess was permitted to freely criticize the policies of the duke of Lerma, the king's first minister and favorite.[1]

Philip III also went out of his way to meet Francisca Inés de la Concepción, whose reputation for chastity, piety, and prophecy was spreading throughout New Castile. As it turned out, the meeting was fortunate for both of them because shortly after her death in October 1611, Queen Margaret of Austria had appeared to Francisca and gave her important information for the king about the governance of the monarchy. Francisca promised to write to the king and let him know what she had been told, but the queen stopped her and ordered her to speak to him in person at a time and place to be arranged by

God. In his infinite wisdom and with the interests of the Spanish monarchy uppermost in his mind, God caused Francisca to become one of the founding nuns and first abbess of the new convent that her order was founding in Oropesa. The foundation was complete and the nuns fully installed when, in 1618, Philip was returning from Portugal and stopped in Oropesa to meet her. During the hour and a half they spent together, the king sat on a small bench in the choir while Francisca told him all about her vision and relayed the queen's message, which he heard with great interest. Just before he left, Philip thanked Francisca, urged her to continue to pray for him, and promised to carry out the suggestions that had been given to him insofar as possible.[2]

But it was Margaret of the Cross, of all the pious and mystical women of his kingdom, who was able to exert the greatest influence over Philip III. As a member of the Habsburg family and daughter of the emperor, Margaret would naturally have had a claim on the king's attention, but she also had a well-deserved reputation for extraordinary piety and a visceral hatred for all forms of heresy. The potent combination of piety and rank gave her the opportunity to play a political role, which she felt would be in the best interests of the Austrian Habsburgs and the revival of the Catholic church in the embattled lands of Central Europe. As a nun renowned for her piety, Margaret of the Cross found it easy to invoke the need to ensure the survival of the Catholic faith whenever she petitioned Philip III for assistance to Emperor Rudolf II (1576–1611) or her brothers in Central Europe. This strategy was eventually successful with the pious king, who reversed his earlier policy of concentration on peninsular issues and intervened to help the Austrian Habsburgs suppress the revolt in Bohemia.[3]

An perhaps even more telling example of the intervention of women mystics at the highest levels of the Habsburg royal family during the reign of Philip III, was the relationship between the archdukes governors-general of the Spanish Netherlands and St. Teresa's great collaborator, Ana de Jesús. Both Archduke Albert of Austria and his wife, the Spanish *infanta* Isabella Clara-Eugenia, were extremely pious, with the archduke having been named Archbishop of Toledo in 1577 and later elevated to the rank of cardinal. After being reduced to lay status to marry, he and his wife made every effort to promote the Counter-Reformation within the Spanish Netherlands.[4]

Ana de Jesús' reputation for piety had preceded her when she arrived in Flanders, and that the archdukes should invite her to come to Brussels was only natural. Ana's good judgment and experience in founding and running Carmelite houses, as well as her role in dispute settlement in Palencia before she entered the order, qualified her to become an advisor to the archdukes, who consulted her about "the gravest matters of state." But Ana was not just an ordinary advisor. She was also credited with supernatural powers, including the power of prophecy. This proved to be especially beneficial to the archdukes, who were concerned over a possible attack by the French King Henry IV. Ana was able to put their fears at rest by telling them that she had a divine revelation that God would stop Henry before he could put his plans into effect. Henry IV's assassination at the hands of François Ravaillac appeared to

confirm Ana's prophecy.[5] After this, the archdukes became even more devoted to Ana, and, after she died, the *infanta* not only visited her tomb but
also hired Angel Manrique to write her biography.

The best documented relationship between a woman mystic and a Spanish monarch, the lengthy correspondence between Philip IV and Sor María
de Ágreda de Jesús, has already been mentioned. Historians have long known,
of course, that the king was originally drawn to Sor María because of her piety
and reputation as a wonder-working mystic, but little serious consideration
has been given to the overall effect that the relationship had on his morale.
Even though Philip wrote María detailed letters regarding such critical military and political issues as the siege of the fortress of Rosas in 1645 and the
excruciating negotiations that eventually resulted in the Treaty of Münster,
she had little to offer in reply, merely platitudes about the need for peace or
urging him to do things that he had already thought of on his own.[6] Her complete inability to intercede with God in favor of the monarchy should have
been painfully obvious to anyone but the most uncritical observer after the
failure of her efforts to save Rosas. In a long and rambling letter to Philip dated
May 22, 1645, she informed him that in response to the French siege she had
added a special devotion to her nuns' already heavy burden: the entire community would lie prostrate with their bodies in the form of a cross and be-
seech God for mercy. This intervention failed, of course, and Rosas fell on
May 28, 1645.[7]

Undaunted by this disappointment, Philip remained a true believer. In the
same letter in which he informed Sor María about the loss of the fortress, he
implored her to intercede with God to prevent any further losses. In her reply,
the nun stressed that these losses were a consequence not of human activity
but of God's displeasure with Philip himself and with Spain for the excessive
"vanity and depraved customs" that had been allowed to creep into public
life. According to Sor María, God was punishing the king to bring him to a
state of penance in which he would act to reform public morality. Then and
only then would his just anger be appeased and the blows that he was aiming
at the monarchy and at the king himself be deflected. Philip IV, who already
felt terribly insecure after having been forced to dismiss the Conde Duque de
Olivares, his longtime chief minister in 1643, needed little urging to blame
his own moral failings for Spain's tragic reverses and adopt an attitude of
resignation that could not fail to sap his will to struggle on. Moreover, by
constantly urging the king to focus on reforming public morality, especially
in matters of dress, as a way of regaining God's favor, Sor María was setting
him up to fail, because the enforcement of sumptuary laws could have no effect
on Spain's military or strategic position.[8] As that situation worsened, in the
1650s and early 1660s, Philip's sense of guilt and self-doubt tended to increase,
especially since Sor María continued to harp on the very same need for the
reformation of morals as she had in the 1640s. As a result, Philip always felt
that he had not done enough and engaged in even more painful bouts of self-
examination.[9] Even though it is impossible to pinpoint any specific policy
moves that were affected by Sor María, this was probably because the king

had surrendered active control to Olivares's nephew Luis de Haro. By convincing the king that Spanish defeats and the tragedies that afflicted his family were the result of his own failings, Sor María added to an already formidable weight of guilt that made the king's final years even more depressing than they might otherwise have been.

Interestingly enough, down the social scale from the exalted ranks of royalty were several "sham" mystics who maintained regular contacts with members of the aristocracy, providing them with moral and religious advice and even intervening to help them when they were seriously ill. Of course, there were significant differences between "approved" and "sham" mystics, in terms of both the intensity of their involvement with the aristocracy and the social status and political importance of their aristocratic clients.

Male aristocrats, who were generally more prominent and politically important than their wives, tended to seek counsel mainly from "approved" mystics (53.3 percent) in contrast to only 13.3 percent who consulted "feigned" mystics. Prominent among the members of the high aristocracy who regularly sought advice from María Ángela Astorch, for example, were Lope de Francia, viceroy of Mallorca, and the Milanese noble Teodoro Trivulzio, who was named viceroy and captain-general of Aragon in 1642.[10]

The high social rank and educational and cultural level attained by such "true" mystics as Ana de Jesús and María Ángela Astorch would seem to make them the natural advisors of powerful members of the male governing elite but, interestingly enough, Inés de Benigánim had a similar range of contacts. Her confessor recorded that she was regularly consulted by leading figures in the Kingdom of Valencia, including the viceroy, the count of Paredes, and the dukes of Gandía.[11] The fact that this illiterate servant nun was so popular in Valencia's ruling circles indicates that the real attraction was not political savvy or administrative experience but rather the woman's reputation as a miracle worker and recipient of divine communication.

But the "approved" mystics did not have a complete monopoly on contacts with the male aristocratic elite. The same spiritual attributes that attracted leading members of the Valencian nobility to Inés de Benigánim also worked to open the aristocratic home of Diego de Cárdenas to the "false" mystic María Bautista. During the mid-1630s, both Diego de Cárdenas, who had recently been appointed to the Council of War, and his wife, Ana Francisca de Portugal, frequently witnessed María Bautista's amazing trances in their own home. They both consulted with María about family problems, Diego de Cárdenas gave her money and food, and his wife defended her publicly against her critics, including her own chaplain.[12]

Interestingly enough, female nobles seemed to have somewhat less access to approved mystics (40 percent) and somewhat more interaction with "false" mystics (20 percent) than their male counterparts. Domestic conflict over women leaving their homes too frequently, even to go to visit religious institutions, may have been partially responsible for this disparity. The "unofficial" mystic, who was generally a layperson or *tercera*, was usually freer to visit the homes of her clients than the cloistered nuns who made up the bulk of the approved mystics in this study. One good example of this freedom of movement is the fact that all four of the aristocratic women who became Catalina Ballester's clients met her when she came to their homes to fit them for dresses.

Female nobles also had sex-specific reasons for seeking the services and advice of a woman mystic. While both sexes were interested in the health of family members, for example, successful pregnancies were usually more a concern of the women. Doña Fabiana de la Cueva, who came from a prominent knightly family in Ubeda, had been unable to have children, even after many years of marriage. She complained of her lack of progeny numerous times during her visits to Gabriela de San Joseph, but Gabriela avoided committing herself to assisting her and usually changed the subject. Finally, Fabiana brought the matter up again, angrily accusing Gabriela of doing less for her than she did for many others. But Gabriela responded by asking her why she would want a child who "would cause her nothing but constant sadness and pain." Thoroughly aroused, Fabiana interposed the authority of the abbess, who happened to be a close relative, and the abbess ordered Gabriela to intercede in Fabiana's favor. In due course, Fabiana gave birth to a boy, but disregarding Gabriela's veiled warnings proved disastrous, since he was born partially paralyzed and developed a serious speech defect.[13]

Not surprisingly, it was St. Teresa of Jesus who knew best how to exploit a network of women from the highest ranks of the aristocracy to help found her convents. In many instances. these women had spiritual and emotional needs that could be satisfied only by direct contact with Teresa. In some extreme cases, like the princess of Eboli, Ana Mendoza de la Cerda, or Beatriz de Beamont y Navarra, a descendant of the royal house of Navarre, these needs were fulfilled only by entering the Carmelite order. The princess herself entered the Discalced convent at Pastrana, which she had helped to finance, and Beatriz de Beamont gave her own house for the Soria foundation and then entered the Pamplona house herself, taking the name of Beatriz de Cristo. While Eboli lasted only three years as a Discalced, Beatriz de Beamont earned an enviable reputation for piety at Pamplona and died there in 1660.[14]

The contrast between the social status of the female nobles who consulted with the "feigned" mystics and those who sought out officially approved mystics clearly favors the latter. While María de Jesús, the Carmelite prioress of Toledo's Convent of San Joseph and Santa Teresa, received frequent visits from such luminaries as the countess of Arcos and the marchioness of Pomar, all four noblewomen who consulted Catalina Ballester were from the humbler strata of hidalgos or caballeros.

Overall, a relatively high percentage of both groups had significant involvement with members of the clergy, with 66.7 percent of the "true" and 26.6 percent of "false" mystics providing some form of advice, counsel, or guidance. What really separates the two groups, however, is the fact that fully 30 percent of the approved mystics served members of the ecclesiastical hierarchy, bishops and archbishops, while their less favored sisters mainly confined their attention to the humbler strata of simple parish priests, benefice holders, and friars.

Inés de Benigánim's success in attracting the highest religious figures in the kingdom of Valencia is just another example of the way a reputation for unimpeachable orthodoxy counted with the elite in early modern Spain. When he first became archbishop, Luis Alfonso de los Cameros was rather suspicious of Inés and thought that his predecessor was mistaken to place so much trust in a woman whose reputation might have been more a product of popular credulity than genuine spiritual attainments. He decided to see for himself, but after interviewing Inés at some length he concluded that her beliefs were well within acceptable limits and that God had genuinely favored her with miraculous powers. After this visit, he had no hesitation in consulting her about the most important matters in the archdiocese.[15] The Augustinian lay nun also received numerous visits from other Valencian archbishops, including Juan Tomás de Rocaberti, who served as inquisitor general from 1695 to his death in June 1699.[16]

Another group of high-ranking clerics almost entirely off-limits to the "false" mystics were the superiors of religious orders. In contrast to a traditional historiography that continues to stress the power that male clerics had over the lives of cloistered nuns, the evidence from Spain would seem to indicate that certain women with great spiritual reputations could gain an astonishing amount of influence in their orders. In 1604, when the reformed Franciscans were at odds over a proposed change in the way they elected the vicar general, one of the leading Franciscan theologians wrote to Francisca Inés de la Concepcíon to ask for her opinion. In her reply, Francisca Inés informed him not only that she strongly disapproved of the proposal but also that it would fail to be adopted at the upcoming conclave. In this instance, as in so many others, Francisca Inés was to prove correct when the leaders of the Franciscan reformed province rejected the proposal at their meeting in Valladolid. While Francisca herself could not have attended the meeting, it is difficult to imagine that her views were not made known to the delegates by the theologian who had written to solicit them. Once her views were known, they probably carried considerable weight since she was already famed for her prophecies.[17]

Catalina Ballester's trial record provides us with our only instance of a "false" mystic who provided counsel to the male superior of a religious order. Dr. Pedro Fuenbuena was the warden of the Mercedarian convent in Palma de Mallorca when he became Catalina's spiritual advisor. As their relationship deepened, Fuenbuena came to admire Catalina, praising her "virtue and saintliness" in a conversation with Gabriel Sitjar, one of the friars in the convent. Fuenbuena was so convinced of Catalina's spiritual perfection that he even went so far as to write her spiritual biography.[18]

Several "true" mystics with significant reputations for sanctity were also able to intervene with the prioresses of other convents to resolve problems or demand reforms. Gabriela de San Joseph's moral stature and spiritual reputation, as well as the fact that she had been elected prioress of her convent on three occasions, gave her a tremendous amount of authority in the entire Carmelite province. Whenever she felt that the rule was being less than fully observed in any of the Discalced houses, she made it her business to intervene, especially when property was the issue. In one instance, Gabriela heard about what appear to have been some relatively minor lapses in the Carmelite rule that Discalced nuns should have no personal possessions. She quickly wrote to the prioress of the offending convent, pointing out the faults of the nuns with such force and precision that, after her letter was made known to them, they rushed to remove even the smallest items from their cells and donate them to the common store. In fact, the nuns were so impressed by Gabriela's letter that when Manuel de San Gerónimo, the official historian of the order, visited that convent while gathering information for his biography of Gabriela, they told him that they periodically took out the letter and read it aloud, believing that it had been inspired by a divine revelation.[19]

Whereas exercise of the advisory function among the ecclesiastical hierarchy or the superiors of religious orders was almost entirely confined to the approved mystics, at the level of the friar, simple parish priest, benefice holder, or *beata,* the two groups are on a more equal footing. In fact, in certain cases involving "feigned" mystics, most notably among the three secular priests who fell under the influence of Francisca de los Apostoles, the degree of dependence was very reminiscent of the followers of the "spiritual mothers" of the Illuminist movement during the early sixteenth century. All three were strong supporters of Francisca's proposed new religious community and relied on her advice in spiritual matters as well as in relation to their careers in the church. She was especially close to Pedro Chacon, who consulted her on several occasions about how to overcome the stigma of being the illegitimate son of a priest and obtain a benefice.[20]

One of the most curious examples of a priest consulting a "female" mystic involved Dr. Joseph Guillem, vicar of Torrente, his house guest Juan Pérez, a benefice holder from Rusafa, and Guillem's maid, Vicenta Orval. One day at the end of July 1703, while Pérez was staying with Guillem to resolve a financial matter connected with his benefice, he asked him if he could recommend someone to whom he could unburden his conscience. Instead of hearing Pérez's confession himself, Guillem offered to take him to Orval, whom he described as a "woman of marvelous sanctity and virtue." Suitably impressed, Pérez accepted his friend's offer and went with him to see Orval, who lived in a tiny house filled with religious images. After introducing them, Guillem left the house, and Pérez unburdened himself of the thing that was "oppressing" his soul. Incredible as it may seem, Guillem valued Orval's spiritual advice so highly that he routinely sent all his own penitents to her as well.

Frequently, when nuns or friars sought the advice of a woman with a great reputation for spirituality, they sought help in dealing with problems of adjustment to convent life. Predictably enough, given the fact that their influence depended ultimately on their reputation for unimpeachable orthodoxy and support of the religious and political status quo, the women mystics always gave them the same advice: stay with the religious life and set aside all doubts and questions as the work of the devil.

Knowing of Beatriz María de Jesús's reputation for receiving divine illumination through her public trances, the nuns and friars of Granada did not
hesitate to write to her whenever they felt a serious urge to leave monastic
life. One story involves a professed nun who had repented of her decision to
join the convent and was considering filing a lawsuit to nullify her vows.
Before taking this drastic step, however, she wrote Beatriz to ask her advice.
Without even taking into account the reasons for the nun's dissatisfaction,
Beatriz told her that instead of nullifying her vows she should formally reit-
erate them in front of the entire community. Inspired by this letter from someone she greatly admired, the nun followed Beatriz's advice and renewed her
vows, thereby closing off her last possibility of returning to secular life.

In her zeal to prevent anyone from backsliding from the religious life that
she herself had struggled so long and hard to enter, Beatriz did not even wait
to be asked to give her advice. With an excellent network of contacts in
Granada's monastic institutions, she was frequently made aware of the plans
of poorly adjusted religious to renounce their vows or leave the community.
Hearing of a friar who was planning to absent himself from his convent and
renounce his vows after a dispute with his abbot, she immediately wrote to
warn that he was about to fall into a snare set for him by the devil. Her letter
proved to be just the medicine that the friar needed; instead of fleeing his
convent, he decided to remain in the community and make peace with his
superiors.[21]

What probably demonstrates the "popular" nature of the phenomenon of
the woman mystic in early modern Spain better than anything else is the fact
that these women were consulted by members of the humbler classes as well
as by the social elite. Artisans, peasants, and even beggars found a warm
welcome at the doors of many convents and could hope to speak personally
with a famous world-denying ascetic whose supernatural power gave her
extraordinary insight into the complexities of the human condition. Laywomen
mystics were even more accessible because they lived, for the most part, within
the community and could be approached for advice without the cumbersome
restrictions imposed by enclosure.

Perhaps because so many of them came from artisan families themselves,
the percentage of "feigned" mystics who provided advice and counsel to artisans (53.3 percent) was significantly higher than that of their officially approved counterparts (23.3 percent). Francisca de los Apostoles, whose father
was a painter, had a considerable number of clients among Toledo's artisans
and merchants. On her first visit to Francisca, Inés de la Concepción, the wife
of a silk weaver, was probably rather shocked when she prophesied that Inés
would become a widow and join a religious order. Seemingly undaunted by
this rather dreary prognosis, Inés consulted Francisca a second time just after
having given birth. This time the forecast was considerably more encouraging, as Francica informed her that the baby would grow up to serve God with
great aptitude.[22]

Nevertheless, it appears that "genuine" mystics may have had more contact with peasants and beggars (23.3 percent) than the "fake" mystics. Since

apart from one or two cases, like the servant nun Inés de Benigánim, they came from a higher social rank, the explanation must lie in the fact that Spain's poor were accustomed to going to convents for handouts.

The same desire to provide solace and spiritual comfort that made María de Agreda maintain her correspondence with King Philip IV in spite of injury and illness also impelled her to assist the poor who flocked to the gates of her convent. According to her biographer Samaniego, whenever she was informed that a peasant or beggar had arrived, she literally "flew" down to the porter's lodge to see to the visitor's needs. In addition to receiving food and alms, they would beg her intercession with God to help them in their afflictions, while she would seize the opportunity to instruct them in the faith and try to help them lead more spiritual lives.[23]

What kind of advice and counsel did the women mystics provide those who came to consult them? Broadly speaking, there were two areas where women mystics seemed to feel most comfortable: advising about an individual's lifestyle and moral conduct and offering religious or spiritual advice.

One of the most difficult choices that young people have to make in any society is the selection of a career. In early modern Europe, where there were relatively few career options and life in the world was routinely denigrated for its strong temptation to sin, this choice frequently presented itself in a particularly dramatic manner as ascetism versus materialism: work, marriage, and family or the life of the cloister. Predictably enough, the women mystics always advised against secular life and felt that they were gaining a victory for Christ whenever a young man or woman chose to enter a religious order. One story involved a vision in which Beatriz María de Jesús was informed that it was her mission to help humanity better understand and worship God. The vision inspired Beatriz to persuade a young caballero who stood to inherit a substantial estate to join a religious order instead.[24]

Among the "feigned" mystics, Francisca de la Santissima Trinidad was particularly effective in such matters. According to her spiritual advisor Juan de Mengohechea, she was able to persuade two young men, one of them a Toledo city councillor, to join the Franciscans in spite of the fact that neither had ever seriously considered the religious life. In a conversation that he had with Mengohechea after joining the order, one of these men paid tribute to Francisca's powers of persuasion by remarking that "even if she presented me with the most difficult thing in the world to do I would find it impossible to refuse her."

Improving the moral conduct of those she came in contact with was also one of Francisca's most important goals. Before she entered the convent, Francisca would frequently walk from her home to the chapel of Toledo's charity hospital to hear mass and take communion. As rector of the hospital, Juan de Mengohechea had ample opportunity to observe Francisca's behavior. He told the tribunal that she always gave a good example of humility and devotion and sought to convince those who came to speak with her to adopt a life of penance and mortification, as that was the road taken by Christ. Her moral counsel was particularly effective with Diego de Mesa, the chaplain, who was much addicted to pleasure and neglectful of his responsibilities. After conversing with Francisca on several occasions, Mesa became much more serious about his vocation, took major orders so that he could say mass, and lived a "virtuous and exemplary life." Francisca's conversation even had an edifying effect on Mengohechea's niece Paula, who reformed her own lifestyle and eventually joined the Convent of Santo Domingo del Antiguo.[25]

In matters of sexual morality, women mystics did not feel the need to wait to be consulted. The severe moral and legal strictures against sodomy, the enforcement of the celibacy laws, and the closing of municipal houses of prostitution were all signs of a new and stricter sexual morality and a growing fear that God would punish a society that tolerated sexual transgressions.[26] Some female mystics made themselves responsible for taking on the role of enforcing this new post-Tridentine sexual morality and had little compunction about bringing pressure to bear on transgressors, whatever their social position.

At the end of December 1687, a priest who was well acquainted with Beatriz María de Jesús came to her convent to beg her to pray for the soul of a prominent local caballero who had been living publicly with his mistress. Since Beatriz considered herself responsible for the city's welfare and was generally accepted as an intercessor before God in times of plague or famine, she felt that she could not content herself with prayer and was determined to confront the caballero directly. But the strict enclosure of nuns that was imposed after the Council of Trent made it impossible for Beatriz to arrange an interview. The impact of strict enclosure, however, was not as great as some recent studies have suggested, especially for a woman as resourceful and influential as Beatriz María de Jesús. Making use of a lay friar (servant) in Granada's Franciscan convent who was free to wander the city because of his responsibilities, Beatriz was able to get a stern message to the caballero, warning him that God would punish him severely if he did not cease his illicit affair. Already under pressure from friends and associates to break off the relationship, an admonition from someone so universally admired could not fail to have a profound effect. The caballero entered the Franciscan house as a way of distancing himself from his mistress and prepared to make a general confession, which he did some days later with every sign of profound contrition. The affair was over, and Beatriz could congratulate herself on having restored the moral and sexual balance in the city. As for the lay friar, Beatriz had used him before on similar missions and would use him again many times to evade the cumbersome restrictions imposed by strict enclosure.[27]

It is hardly surprising that advice about individual lifestyles and moral comportment far outweighed the purely religious or spiritual counsel provided by "true" (73.3 percent versus 33.3 percent), and "false" (33.3 percent versus 20 percent) women mystics. With the increasing importance of the confessor and spiritual advisor during the post-Tridentine period and significant improvements in the training of both secular and regular clergy, this was a task that male clerics were able to undertake with confidence.[28] That is not to say, however, that in some special instances, women mystics did not furnish religious guidance and spiritual counsel even to male clerics. Ana de Jesús, who was extraordinary in so many ways, became spiritual advisor to the renowned court preacher Antonio de la Madre de Díos. He would frequently come to visit her cell when she was prioress of Veas and confide in her about his ardent desire to seek martyrdom and convert the infidel.[29] María de Jesús, another Discalced Carmelite, assumed a similar role with María de Mendoza, countess of Arcos, who consulted with her about spiritual matters, especially after she became seriously ill.[30] A third example comes from the life of Mariana de Escobar, who, when she began making her confession at the local Dominican convent, instructed her confessor in the finer points of mental prayer.[31]

But, given the preponderant role of the spiritual advisor and parish priest in the area of religious instruction and guidance, women mystics mainly acted to urge compliance with the sacrament of penance that perpetuated the male-dominated church's control over conscience. So, for example, when Joseph Guillem brought his friend Juan Pérez to see Vicenta Orval, and he confided in her about the thing that was afflicting his conscience, she burst forth with a veritable sermon and urged him to make a general confession. Not surprisingly, he chose to confess with Guillem, who probably expected this to happen as a result of Orval's counseling.[32]

The work of a "false" mystic in channeling guilt-ridden individuals to her own confessor is even clearer in the relationship between María Pizarra and Francisco Camacho. Camacho consciously used Pizarra to build up his clientele by supporting her reputation for sanctity. He was so successful that women from surrounding villages would make a pilgrimage to seek her spiritual advice, walking barefoot all the way. When they were admitted into her presence, she would ask them how they could expect to gain God's help if they failed to reform their own lives and urged them to remove the impediments to divine mercy by making a full confession of their sins. Needless to say, Francisco Camacho, who rigidly controlled access to Pizarra and decided who would be allowed to see her, garnered the great majority of these penitents.[33]

Advising, shaming, or even forcing those with something on their consciences to confess their sins in order to receive absolution was an important but indirect way of aiding clerics in carrying out their responsibilities for the spiritual health of the faithful. But many obstacles—parental opposition, social prejudice, and strict claustration, to name just a few—stood in the way of a woman's direct involvement in rendering assistance to a priest in carrying out his parish responsibilities. Among our forty-five women mystics, therefore, just one, the Carmelite *tercera* Isabel de Jesús, was able to play such a role successfully. Liberated from an unhappy family situation by the death of her last surviving sibling and both her parents, Isabel joined a young priest on the trip from Toledo to the village of Pastrana. Finding the village church sadly neglected and the village itself impoverished, Isabel dedicated herself to taking care of the poor and infirm, while the priest saw to the spiritual needs of his parish. This division of labor was not absolute, however, because Isabel was also able to facilitate his spiritual and sacramental functions by getting local women to confide in her and then urging them to make a formal confession with the priest. Isabel was also able to clear up the irregular and incomplete baptism of three women who had been baptized by a layperson during a time that the parish priest was not in attendance.[34]

Isabel's arduous labors on behalf of the poor and sick of the village seemed to be fully recompensed when she had a highly emotional encounter with Christ one evening while she was walking in the countryside. As she walked, absorbed in her own thoughts, a man fell in beside her. For a long time, he said nothing until he asked her what troubles could have brought her to that lonely spot, risking her reputation by walking alone in the darkness, and guessed that it was "because your family has so little regard for you?" Isabel was moved to tears when she realized that he had put his finger exactly on what had been bothering her the most. Keeping silent but overcome with emotion, Isabel walked on until the man stopped her and told her that she was to continue to pray for the souls of those living in the village and that silence, humility, and charity would do a great deal of good with the poor. Feeling more strongly than ever before that she was in the presence of the Redeemer, Isabel could contain herself no longer and cried out that she was unworthy of his favor and that her tears were "no more than two little drops of water from a mean, despicable, little well." It was then that she noticed that the man was barefoot and humbly offered to give him her sandals, saying that she had another pair and that it was not seemly that he should walk barefoot. But the man said, "I have never worn anything on my feet" and told her to give them to the next poor person who needed them. He then blessed her and disappeared.[35]

Apart from their efforts to assist the poor and infirm, either at the parish level or at the doors of their convents, women mystics could have a direct and positive impact on their communities by intervening to resolve disputes between individuals and families. Such conflicts, which could convulse entire towns in years of violent rivalry, were best solved by mediation, but when the usual channels failed, local political leaders might turn to a woman mystic of recognized holiness to conciliate the rivals. In one example, the Franciscan *beata* Mariana de Jesús received a delegation of local leaders from Escalona who begged her to settle a dispute between two politically powerful nobles, since they had tried and failed to bring about a reconciliation. In spite of her initial show of modesty and hesitation, Mariana had already established herself as an advisor to most of the town's leading families. Encouraged by an appearance of her guardian angel, who informed her that God had ordered her to resolve the conflict, Mariana went directly to the most obdurate of the two men and was able to convince him to embrace his enemy.[36] Although it is difficult to assess the long-term effectiveness of Mariana's intervention, her well-established reputation for extreme penitential asceticism, as well as her stigmata and other signs of sanctity, ensured the respectful attention of even the most tumultuous caballero.

On a more exalted plane, the presence of a female mystic was believed to be of particular value because she could be expected to use her intercessory powers to mitigate the effects of catastrophic events, both natural and man-made. During the first half of the seventeenth century, when Catalina de San Lucas and María de San Andres were nuns in Almagro's Convent of the Incarnation, the entire region was hit by a series of harvest failures and natural disasters. Fortunately for the townsfolk, both women were numbered among God's just and therefore had extraordinary powers of intercession. During one of these crises, when a serious and prolonged drought threatened the harvest and left livestock with nothing to drink, the prioress of the convent ordered María de San Andrés to go to the choir to pray for rain and not to emerge until "Our Lord sees fit to provide comfort to His people." María obeyed and descended to the chapel, where she begged God to show mercy. In less than fifteen minutes, the wind increased, clouds rolled in, and rain began falling heavily. For the rest of that year the peasants enjoyed abundant harvests.[37]

Catalina de San Lucas's most famous intervention on the part of her beloved town came in a form that seemed to confirm in an open and public manner that human sin was the root cause of natural disasters. Depressed and anxious over flooding that had washed away houses and damaged crops over a wide area, Catalina became convinced that she herself was the cause of these maladies. One day, however, while she was begging God not to punish others for her faults, she was informed that the real problem should be ascribed to the sin of a man who was committing incest with his daughter. Appalled at learning about this terrible sin (which she had probably heard about from one of the numerous women who visited her cell), she made haste to inform the governor, who had the man arrested and forced his wife into exile. Predictably enough, once the underlying sin had been punished, God's anger was appeased, the waters receded, and the wide currency given to this affair served to greatly increase Catalina's reputation in the entire region.[38]

Intercession with God to prevent or mitigate some expression of divine wrath through disasters like flood or famine was only one way in which the woman mystic could use her powers to protect her people. War was a man-made calamity that could be far worse, and of longer duration, than any natural disaster, and unfortunately parts of Spain were to experience it directly for the first time in 150 years or more during the mid-seventeenth century.

The village of Guijo was close enough to Portugal to be caught up in the interminable cross-border skirmishing that characterized Philip IV's ill-fated attempts to regain the Portuguese throne in the late 1650s and mid-1660s. Even though Spain's military forces suffered serious defeats at Elvas (1659) and Villaviciosa (1665), and much of the region between the two countries was devastated by the passage of armies, the village remained unharmed, protected by the powers of its resident mystic, María de Jesús. As one of the enemy generals later explained it, Portuguese forces had wanted to seize the village on several occasions but had been prevented from doing so by a series of mysterious events, such as a sudden heavy downpour just when they were preparing to attack.[39]

The terrible uncertainties that affected people in early modern times and their inability to even understand, much less control, the physical environment created a society that depended on magical remedies to deal with the risks and hazards of ordinary life. It was only natural, therefore, that people who credited women mystics with the power to protect their communities against flood, famine, drought, and war would also look to them for a cure when they were sick or injured.

The practice of healing was widespread among the "genuine" mystics (66.7 percent) but considerably less so among the group of "false" mystics (26.6 percent). One important reason for this disparity might be because a woman whose reputation for sanctity was supported by powerful ecclesiastical institutions could employ "curative" powers more freely since she was in a better position to avoid charges of superstition or demonic assistance. It is perhaps significant in this regard that 46.6 percent of the "false" mystics who came before the Holy Office were accused of collaborating with the devil.

Medical practitioners among both groups of mystics, like the "wise" or "cunning" women in other parts of Europe, used a combination of natural and magical remedies to effect cures. But this did not exclude the possibility that at least some of these women might have had genuine insights into illness. In one concrete instance, the Dominican lay nun Martina de los Angeles y Arilla, who acted as chief of the infirmary in her convent, was asked by a local notary to pray for his little son, who was suffering from high fever. Instead of invoking divine intercession, however, Martina merely smiled and told the worried father that the child's permanent teeth were probably coming out and that condition was frequently accompanied by fever. She predicted that he would soon recover, and when the notary returned home he found his son feeling much better.[40]

Herbal or other "natural" remedies were frequently used by women mystics, sometimes alone and sometimes in combination with incantations, prayers, consecrated objects, or other forms of "ecclesiastical medicine." Isabel de Briñas, who had a significant reputation as a healer in Madrid, once prescribed an herbal powder to cure María de Saavedra, even though she was convinced that she would die anyway. Notwithstanding this gloomy prognosis, when María recovered unexpectedly, Briñas was not unwilling to take the credit and use the "cure" to enhance her reputation.[41]

Frequently the powders, potions, or unguents prescribed or applied by women mystics as treatment for wounds or illness were little more than a nod in the direction of natural medicine, while the cure itself lay in the realm of the supernatural. María de San Andres would fry up some eggplant and mix it with wax, thereby creating an unguent that she would apply to all her patients. But for her biographer Antonio de Lorea, this "natural" treatment was little more than a "cover" or "cloak" of humility designed to disguise the fact that God had given her the ability to effect cures. Lorea's opinion was seemingly confirmed when one of her patients took a sample of the unguent to two local doctors, who declared that its contents could not have any effect on the illnesses and that the cures she effected must have been caused by a miracle.[42] Of course, given the pious credulity that dictated a suspension of the critical faculties in evaluating the claims of a "true" mystic, no one even thought of ascribing the cures to natural causes.

María de la Santissima Trinidad, another of Lorea's subjects, was famous for her cures and attracted patients from the entire region around her home village. Even though she habitually made use of herbal concoctions to effect cures, she usually combined them with consecrated objects, like articles of clothing from particular saints, or devotional images of the Virgin Mary. If all else failed, she would "take on" the symptoms of an illness that someone else was suffering. As a consequence, while her patients recovered, María herself hardly had a day's rest and was continually tormented by the symptoms of malaria, liver ailments, worms, fevers, and other common illnesses of the period.[43]

Detailed analysis of the "cures" effected by María de la Santissima Trinidad and other women mystics reveals the presence of certain modes of thinking that, even in today's skeptical world, provide the basis for superstitious beliefs. The hypothetical but false relationship between two separate events leading to a positive outcome is what cognitive psychologists call illusory correlations.[44] Such thinking, reinforced by socially conditioned prior belief, was clearly operative in the case of María Rodero, who asked María to cure some sores that had emerged on her skin. María responded by bringing her the tunic from a locally venerated image of Our Lady of the Rosary and applying it to the inflammation. The sores disappeared, and María naturally attributed her cure to the intervention of the Virgin Mary through the medium of a consecrated cult object. As psychologists studying cognition have discovered, however, our perceptions of correlations between events that have no necessary connection are frequently flawed by wishful thinking, bias, and a willingness or desire to believe, based on social conditioning.[45] María Rodero, who had been cured by Trinidad twice before, had a propensity to believe in her, especially since local doctors had frequently failed to take her maladies seriously.[46] This bias, combined with the intensity of such social influences as the widespread belief in the supernatural power of consecrated objects, probably led to the correlation that she made between the disappearance of her sores and her contact with the Virgin Mary's chemise.

The inherent variability of the course of numerous diseases also served to strengthen belief in the curative powers of women mystics. Even in the case of terminal diseases, while the overall trend is negative, the path is anything but linear and is punctuated by periods of relative health. Since people typically call for medical intervention when we are at a low point in the progress of the disease, an ineffective medical strategy may receive the credit for a temporary improvement that would have happened anyway.[47] The malarial fevers common during the early modern period, especially tertian and quartan malaria, in which paroxysms occur every third and fourth day, respectively, provided an excellent opportunity for the intervention of an amateur practitioner employing magical treatments. The variability factor in these diseases meant that the patient would inevitably move from a low point of pain and distress to a high point of relative freedom from symptoms on a regular schedule. It was precisely this ignorance of the variability factor that allowed María de la Santissima Trinidad to take the credit for a dramatic improvement in the condition of Nicolás de la Peña, who was suffering from tertian malaria. María was called in while Nicolás was having an attack, presumably at the low point of the cycle; she visited with him and comforted him, and shortly after her departure he began to show significant improvement. Not surprisingly, given her reputation for miraculous cures, María was given full credit for Peña's "recovery."[48]

The Counter-Reformation campaign of reforming popular religion involved education, catechetical instruction, and the selective repression of practices and beliefs that the church defined as superstitious. In Spain, this campaign intensified after 1560, and between that year and 1700, 2,520 persons were brought before the Inquisition and charged with superstitious practices, principally love magic and magical healing.[49] Evidence from the case files indicates that this campaign was successful not only in identifying and punishing numerous offenders but also in creating a climate of fear that inhibited folk healers from taking on patients that they normally would have been only too happy to treat.

One of the most interesting stories of a reluctant wise woman comes from testimony given to the Valencia tribunal by María Antonia Hortola at her trial in 1725. María's problem was that she had succeeded only too well in convincing everyone of her spiritual powers. Her confessor Luis Poyo was so impressed by this "saintly woman" that he kept pushing her into new situations where she could exercise her powers. As she herself observed in her testimony, he was remarkably "ingenuous and easy to deceive" in such matters.[50] He was also eager to have more miraculous incidents so that he could spice up the spiritual biography that he was writing about her. Hearing of the illness of one of her supporters in Masamagrell, Poyo insisted that she pray for her recovery and visit her at home. Fearing possible arrest on charges of curative magic, María initially refused but later, on a visit to the village, she did enter the home, where the family beseeched her to help the sick woman. Finally, taking pity on the woman and her six small children, María broke down and said some prayers on her behalf. Of course, the woman recovered, as María's intervention probably took place at some low point in the cycle of the disease, and the entire family, as well as her confessor, began broadcasting the news of María's success to the world. While such a success might have pleased María at an earlier time, the "pedagogy of fear," taught by inquisitorial persecution of practitioners of magical healing, made her uncertain. She concluded her testimony by informing the inquisitors that she herself did not believe that her prayers had had any real impact on the disease and that "it was all just a fable made up by the family and Father Poyo."[51]

In the increasingly repressive atmosphere caused by inquisitorial persecution of both white and black magic, only the best protected and well-established practitioners could hope to survive without fear. It is at least possible, therefore, that by the seventeenth century traditional magicians and sorceresses had become marginalized and were being replaced by "approved" mystics who could operate with relative impunity.

A very suggestive example of the direct substitution of the services of an approved mystic for those of a traditional wise woman comes from the biography of the Dominican *tercera* María de la Santissima Trinidad. Already famous in Seville and its surroundings for her miracle cures and power over demonic forces, María had an enormous clientele who consulted her about all manner of concerns relating to the power of supernatural forces in their lives. In 1658 a woman from the nearby village of Alcalá del Rio came to Seville and took up lodging in a hostel belonging to Sebastiana Guerra Garzon, one of María's strongest supporters. Obviously upset, the woman confided to her host that she had come to engage the services of an "evil woman" in order to find out what had happened to her husband, who had disappeared some eight months earlier after telling her he was going to visit some relatives in Jaén. Rather than encourage her in such a "foolish" enterprise, Sebastiana presented her to María, who listened to the case and assured her that her husband would soon come home. Greatly reassured, the woman went back to her village and, a few days later, was reunited with her husband, just as María had predicted.[52]

While a great deal of research would be necessary to establish the connection between the rise of the officially approved mystic and the activities of traditional sorceresses, it is at least possible that the relative lack of intensity of Spain's witch craze stemmed in part from the fact that the post-Tridentine reform did not imply the complete removal of magical remedies. Instead of eliminating the magical weapons that those who believed themselves the victims of sorcery could employ and leaving them only with the option of legal retaliation, Spanish reformers persecuted semiprofessional practitioners and repressed "superstition" while supporting a network of approved mystics who practiced an orthodox ecclesiastical magic.

The Protestant challenge to the authority of the Catholic church elicited a powerful reaction from women all over Catholic Europe. Carried away by their enthusiasm for the faith, some women even were tempted to "try out" roles traditionally reserved for male clerics, such as preaching, hearing confessions, or missionary work, even if these efforts were sometimes more imaginary than real.

Commended by important theologians like the Jesuit Alonso de Andrade for the power of their sermons, Spanish preachers became wildly popular during the late sixteenth and seventeenth centuries.[53] But preaching, like missionary work or hearing confessions, was confined to men, even though there was absolutely no intrinsic reason that women would not be equally successful. Given the strength of their religious convictions, many women mystics, especially the better educated ones, felt extremely frustrated at their exclusion from the work of proclaiming the word of God.

At times, women did get the opportunity to "rehearse" the preaching role in a safe and protected setting where they did not need to be concerned about male resentment. During the three carnival days before Ash Wednesday, the nuns of the Convent of Our Lady of Bethlehem of Cifuentes would put costumes on over their habits and engage in a variety of games. As a popular mistress of novices in the convent, Francisca Inés de la Concepción was encouraged to join in the fun by her young charges. Going to a chapel, she put on a friar's cowl and entered the room where the nuns were playing. Getting their attention by assuming the air of a preacher, she mounted a chest in the middle of the room and launched into a two-and a-half-hour sermon that was so compelling that the nuns ignored the visitors who were calling at the gate because they did not wish to lose a moment of such eloquence.[54]

But given the intense suspicion of any attempt by women to encroach on male prerogatives, it was probably safer to attempt preaching under the pretense of a trance, during which the women was presumed to be infused with knowledge and inspiration by God. Based on the well-established idea that the purpose of a trance was to "allow God to communicate with souls," this notion adroitly skirted the issue of a deliberate and conscious female challenge to the male monopoly over preaching.[55]

After Beatriz María de Jesús entered the Franciscan Convent of Santo Ángel Custodio in 1665, she made a practice of favoring the nuns with extended sermons delivered during her frequent trances. Inspired by some revelation of the fundamental meaning of a particular dogma like the Trinity or the immaculate conception, she would hold forth with a long and edifying disquisition to justify and explain it. She particularly loved using these trances to show off her extensive biblical and patristic knowledge. On August 27, 1677, the night before the Feast of Saint Augustine, she went into an extended trance during which she gained a clear awareness of the depth of Augustine's love of God and saw him as a seraph with his three pairs of enormous wings extended over the members of many religious orders. Suddenly infused with a deeper appreciation of his teachings, Beatriz began what even her biographer Tomás de Montalvo called a "sermon," in which she expounded the finer points of his doctrine in a "thin, light voice of great solemnity."[56]

Altogether, some 36.7 percent of the approved mystics and 33.3 percent of the "feigned" mystics tried some form of preaching, but not every woman mystic felt completely confident about preaching. After hearing a particularly impressive sermon in Toledo's cathedral, Isabel de Jesús was inspired to preach a sermon to her own soul. Even though her spiritual advisor approved what was, after all, little more than a harmless illusion, the very idea of preaching made her feel so guilty that she began to see visions of horrible monsters who admonished her for daring even to contemplate preaching. They informed her that she was clearly incapable of assuming such a heavy responsibility and that if she persisted they would make sure her "heresy" was made known to the Inquisition. Isabel de Jesús' feelings of inadequacy and fears of committing heresy were probably not uncommon among women who contemplated preaching, but by projecting them onto demonic, alien forces outside herself she was able to overcome them. She felt a sudden, powerful force supporting her and addressed her soul with a sermon full of faith in a God who loved even the meanest of his creatures.[57]

The growing popularity of confession during the post-Tridentine period and especially the increasing respect, sometimes amounting to adulation, accorded to male spiritual advisors made the role of the confessor extremely attractive to several of the women mystics. Of course, as described previously, a large number of these women were already being consulted about spiritual matters by their devotees. In several cases, however, several of the women, especially Martina de los Angeles y Arilla and Francisca de los Angeles, appeared to be taking that critical step further and assuming the role of actual confessors by hearing sins, assigning penance, and authorizing some form of absolution or perhaps even giving it.

Martina de los Angeles y Arilla, who had carefully fostered her own reputation as a miracle worker throughout upper Aragon, was frequently consulted by people from all walks of life about matters of conscience that would normally have been under the jurisdiction of male clerics. On one occasion, her own confessor, the Dominican Jacinto Blasco, overheard her speaking earnestly to a "penitent" about the need to take the road of virtue and about the flames of hell with which God punishes the unrepentant sinner. Seemingly chagrined by Martina's insight, the man confessed that all he really had on his conscience was some minor blasphemies, but she told him that she was well aware that he was thinking about committing a much greater sin. Far from being outraged by this obvious usurpation of the role of the male confessor, Jacinto Blasco's reaction was merely to tell the other friar who had accompanied him to the convent that they should leave because "we do not want to create any obstacles to the benefits that this soul may be receiving."[58]

None of the "official" mystics, even Martina de los Angeles y Arrilla, went as far as Francisca de los Apostoles in imitating and usurping the role of the male confessor. According to the testimony of María de Jesús y Jiménez, one of the women living in the *beaterio*, Francisca forced the other *beatas* to kneel before her and confess their sins while she sat in a chair and prescribed the appropriate penance. When some of the women protested against this practice, she lied and told them that she had already informed the vicar general of the archdiocese about what she was doing and that he had left it up to her by taking no position for or against the practice.[59]

If one thing can be identified as a unique and extraordinary aspect of the Counter-Reformation, it would probably be the tremendous vitality of Catholic missionary work. All over Catholic Europe, devout young men were entering religious orders, particularly the Jesuits, to inform and instruct the faithful. At the same time, oblivious to the risks that led many of them to martyrdom, they sought to convert heretic and heathen alike. Notwithstanding the serious restrictions that the male-dominated society placed on their freedom of movement, women mystics dreamted of becoming Christian warriors, missionaries, and, if necessary, martyrs. It is precisely in this area, where faith and the impulse to self-sacrifice intersect with a longing for exotic adventure, that some women mystics took their greatest leaps into fantasy. Projecting themselves into far-off places, directed by God, assisted by angels, and free of the shackles placed upon them by men, they, too, could become soldiers of Christ.

In a society that had already defined religious orthodoxy as its fundamental organizing principle, it is hardly surprising to find that women mystics had a visceral hatred for all forms of heresy. Martina de los Angeles y Arilla became so carried away by her hatred for heresy that she imagined herself as a warrior who won a decisive victory over the Protestants. In one fantastic vision that she later described to the prioress of her convent, she and another nun were magically transported to Germany just before the start of the battle of Lützen on November 16, 1632. Once on the field, an angel handed Martina a lance and told her to stab the leader of the Protestant forces. She obeyed and thrust the lance deep into his body, thereby killing the great Swedish King Gustavus Adolphus and seriously weakening the Protestant cause.[60] Her account was believed without question by the ever credulous prioress and by her equally gullible confessor, Jacinto Blasco, but her description of killing Gustavus Adolphus before the battle started betrays the vision as just another tall tale because the Swedish king died during the battle at the head of his cavalry.

Faced with persecution by Roman emperors such as Nero and Diocletian, early Christians had the choice of worshiping the pagan gods or giving their lives for the true faith. Those who made the supreme sacrifice were called witnesses or martyrs and became the earliest Christian saints. Particularly intense during the early church, the veneration of martyrs gave way to that of intercessors and miracle healers during the Middle Ages, only to be revived in the sixteenth and seventeenth centuries. With missionaries going forth in unprecedented numbers to win souls for the faith among the heathen of South America, Asia, and Africa and the heretics of Central Europe, the reform decrees of Urban VIII (1623–44) specifically authorized preservation of martyrdom as a form of heroic virtue sufficient for canonization, without the requirement of miracles or other proofs of sanctity.[61]

The revived interest in martyrdom was not lost on women mystics, with 40 percent of the "approved" mystics indicating their desire to suffer some form of martyrdom at the hands of the enemies of the faith. Not only did they have the news of the heroism of numerous recent martyrs to spur their imaginations but also, in at least one instance, a woman mystic had an example in her own family. Catalina de San Lucas had lost her first cousin, the Augustinian Fernando de Ayala y San Josef, to the fierce persecutions of Christians unleashed by the Japanese ruler Hideyoshi.[62]

Of course, given the restrictions imposed by strict enclosure and the social prejudice that limited their freedom of movement, the pursuit of martyrdom remained a mere fantasy for most women. The only woman to escape from these restrictions was the remarkable Luisa de Carvajal y Mendoza, who pursued martyrdom by undertaking open missionary work in England, where she died in 1614 after two periods of imprisonment.[63]

Nevertheless, the desire to emulate the heroic martyrs of the early church could give a woman exemplary courage when danger appeared to threaten.

Just after King Philip III issued his decree expelling the Moriscos on April 9, 1609, there was fear of a revolt in Barcelona. Even though such fears were greatly exaggerated, in that Catalonia itself had relatively few Moriscos, the nuns of the Dominican Convent of Nuestra Señora de los Angeles shut the gates and trembled for their safety. But among all these nervous nuns, Hipolita de Jesús y Rocaberti stood out for her glacial calm in the face of what seemed to be impending disaster. Asked how she could remain so tranquil, Hipolita smiled and asked why she should be unhappy when her dearest wish was to see herself in the "hands of the enemies of Jesus Christ."[64]

While it was relatively easy to imagine martyrdom in Counter-Reformation Spain, it was considerably more difficult to actually experience it, so that after the fear of a Morisco riot in Barcelona died down, Hipolita, too, had to resort to the realm of fantasy to assure herself that she was worthy of sacrificing herself for the faith. On the feast day of her favorite saint, Vincent of Zaragoza (d. 304), a victim of the persecution of Diocletian and Maximian, she went into a trance during which she saw the saint asking the other martyrs to accept her as their equal. The martyrs agreed, but after she emerged from the trance, she began to wonder if she was really worthy of such an honor. Turning to Christ, she humbly asked if she had merely imagined the saint favoring her. Christ responded by assuring her that St. Vincent and the other martyrs loved and accepted her as one of their company "because of your desire to die in my name."[65]

For the rest of her life, Hipolita's thoughts turned constantly to those who were risking martyrdom by undertaking missions to convert Jews and Muslims, heathens and heretics. As a cloistered nun, she could not join them, as much as she wished to do so, but as a member of a wealthy aristocratic family, she was able to pay the cost of educating a young man who could act as a substitute.[66] But for the other women mystics who wanted to risk martyrdom by participating in the great age of Catholic missions, the dream journey had to suffice.

Perhaps the most famous of all these dream missions was the series of five hundred imaginary voyages to Mexico by María de Agreda. Undertaken after she had offered to suffer martyrdom in exchange for the opportunity to convert the heathen, these fantasies involved both preaching to and catechizing the Indians and then ordering them to seek baptism at a Franciscan mission. After she convinced her confessor that these voyages were genuine, he made haste to publicize them within the order, and soon it was common knowledge that María, or an angel taking her form, had proselytized among the Indians of New Spain.[67]

Interestingly enough, however, in spite of the enormous missionary effort that Spain was putting forth in its American colonies, the Philippines, and Japan, it was North Africa that attracted the attention of the one "fake" mystic and the overwhelming majority of the 26.7 percent of "true" mystics who dreamed of undertaking missions. This can be accounted for by the increase in the frequency of attacks on Spanish shipping and coastal regions and the expansion of corsair activity to the Atlantic coast after 1610.[68] These raids meant that a steady stream of prisoners were being taken to North Africa, where they were held for ransom while being forced to work as slave labor. It was also widely, if erroneously, believed that the Moors would try to force their Christian captives to convert so that both their bodies and their immortal souls were in extreme danger.[69] Wide publicity was given to the plight of these Christian captives by the Mercedarian and Trinitarian orders, which undertook missions to redeem the prisoners.

The decided increase in the size of the problem after 1610 and the propaganda carried on by the redemptionist orders captured the imagination and sympathy of "true" and "false" mystics alike. María Pizarra, the only "false" mystic whose trial record reveals any notion of participating in missionary activity, told the curate of her village that she had experienced a vision in which she was informed of the possible apostasy of several Franciscans and two laymen who were being treated with great brutality in a North African prison. While praying to God on their behalf, she was told to provide them with the emotional support they needed to face their ordeal. No sooner was this order issued than she was magically transported to North Africa, where she encouraged the men so effectively that they all died as martyrs.[70]

Rescue of a soul in danger, rather than encouraging martyrdom, was the goal of Martina de los Angeles y Arilla when she took a dream journey to Algiers in the company of the Virgin Mary. Typical of the aggressive approach toward the enemies of the Catholic faith taken by one who had played such a "heroic" role in the defeat of the Swedes, Martina invaded the home of a Moor who was attempting to force a mother and her son to convert. The captives were freed without the need to pay ransom to the despicable Moor, and Martina's "exploit," carefully advertised by her confessor, Gabriel Jiménez, became so famous that blind street singers made it a subject for their ballads.[71]

A direct relationship between a woman's frustrated desire for martyrdom and persistent fantasies about missions to North African prisons can also be established for Isabel de Jesús. In her autobiography, she wrote that she frequently had ardent desires for martyrdom. She begged God to give these desires to someone who was more likely to act on them, as she was tied down by her oath of obedience to her confessor and could do nothing without his permission. She was particularly tormented by her inability to help the prisoners in North Africa. In a vision that must have been inspired by the lurid accounts of the redemptionist friars, she imagined the prisoners in an enormous dark dungeon weighted down with heavy chains, their faces wearing expressions of fatigue and desperation.

Obsessed with this terrible image, Isabel was unable to put it out of her mind and was again overwhelmed with a desire to take the place of one of the prisoners and suffer martyrdom in "the land of the Moors." At the same time, she was aware that she would never be permitted to go to North Africa. It was in this state of hope and despair that she felt someone take her hand and heard a voice saying, "Come sister Isabel, let us go to assist our captive brothers because that is what our Lord desires us to do." Looking around, she saw her two favorite saints, Leocadia of Toledo and Anthony of Padua, along with her guardian angel, who told her that all four of them would journey to that prison together. Better company could not have been found because they both would fully understand the misery and torment that the prisoners were experiencing. Leocadia herself had been martyred in the early fourth century by the prefect Dacianus, and Anthony of Padua was a spellbinding preacher who had once tried to take up a mission to North Africa.

Arriving at the same prison that she had seen in the previous dream, the party began consoling the prisoners. Isabel and Leocadia were also given bread and apples to give out to the prisoners. After all had eaten, Anthony of Padua stood on top of a bench and delivered a magnificent sermon in which he spoke of God's love, his passion, and the need to have patience in the face of adversity. Even though Isabel was informed that the time to free the prisoners had not actually arrived, the four voyagers left them greatly consoled and much more willing to bear the trials that they had still to undergo in a spirit of Christian resignation.[72]

For some women, missionary work was no substitute for a genuine reform of the church. Like Mary Ward, whose Jesuit-inspired teaching and missionary order was suppressed, these women dreamed of a reformed church led by the members of a new, female religious order.[73]

Without a doubt, the best known of all these fantastic projects took shape during the demonic possession of the nuns of Madrid's aristocratic San Plácido Convent. With twenty-two out of the thirty nuns possessed, including the abbess, Teresa Valle de la Cerda, the exorcists were kept extremely busy recording the pronouncements of the demons inhabiting their bodies. Since it was believed that a powerful exorcist could compel demons to reveal hidden truths, it is easy to imagine their astonishment when they were told that San Plácido would be the mother house of a sweeping reformation of the entire church.[74]

Some fifty years earlier, however, a similar but even more daring project, with overtly anticlerical overtones, was concocted by Francisca de los Apostoles, the Jeronimite *tercera* from Toledo. Even though Francisca was probably having a sexual relationship with Miguel Ruiz, the priest who acted as confessor and spiritual advisor to her *beaterio*, she was deeply resentful of a clergy that had strayed from the path of righteousness. She even told Toledo's inquisitors about a terrible vision in which St. Peter came before the celestial throne to ask God to punish the clergy, who "go about loaded up with revenue and vices while I stripped myself to follow He who was naked."[75] Concluding that the church itself needed to be completely "rebuilt," she had received permission from God to found a special convent that would be the first house of a new religious order dedicated exclusively to "establishing virtue and putting evil to flight."[76] But, even before the new religious order was established, the pope himself was to be placed under the tutelage of a committee of five devout women headed by her sister Isabel Baptista. In a complete inversion of the structure of the male-dominated church, the pope was to consult with them on all aspects of church governance, while they would pray to God and receive their guidance directly from him. Francisca herself would become abbess of the new convent, which would be founded by exactly twelve nuns without dowry, each taking the name of one of the apostles.[77]

Francisca's inversion of the sexual roles in the church was not absolute because she also believed that Bartolomé de Carranza, the archbishop of Toledo, who had been arrested on suspicion of heresy in August 1559, would be magically released, help to finance her new order, and play a key role in the reform program. Nevertheless, it was sufficiently daring to incur the wrath of the Inquisition's theologians, who denounced her as a heretic for "wanting to found a new religion and confer upon women the office of Saint Peter and the other apostles."[78] In the end, of course, Francisca's scheme, like the demonically inspired fantasies of the nuns of San Plácido, came to nothing. Denounced to the Inquisition, she was arrested and had to go through a difficult and painful trial that lasted from October 1575 to April 1578. Meanwhile, Archbishop Carranza, on whom she had pinned such extravagant hopes, was a broken man who died shortly after his release from a Roman prison in April 1576.[79]

Of course, in the real world, women were not allowed to undertake dangerous missionary work, just as they were not permitted to give absolution or preach in public. In the end, after the exciting fantasies of exotic voyages, battlefield heroics, and revolutionary new female-controlled religious orders had passed, most of the women came to accept the limitations that society had imposed upon their sex. As the *tercera* María de Christo realized after she experienced a vision of St. Francis of Assisi begging God to be merciful to sinful humanity, her true role was to "eschew all forms of ostentation." Instead of the noisy and clamorous role of the preacher that she had once so ardently wished to assume, she knew that God wanted her to remain in her cell and work with prayer and penance for the redemption of all humankind.

The Perception of Sanctity

Reputation, Cult Formation, and Canonization

The relationship between the life of a woman mystic and the development of a cultic veneration for her that might lead eventually to beatification or even canonization is highly complex, with many elements. In the first place, there were the efforts made by the woman herself to create or enhance her reputation for sanctity, especially by demonstrating that she enjoyed a special closeness to God. But advancing up the ladder of sanctity from popular saint to official canonization required more than the extraordinary penitential practices and parapsychological manifestations that most women mystics of any reputation could deploy. The elaborate and expensive procedures for canonization that were gradually introduced after 1588 meant that key long-term support would have to be forthcoming from religious orders, municipalities, regional authorities, and the monarchy itself.

Because the production of spectacular outward signs of grace was the traditional way in which such support could be elicited, these women acted out trances, spoke with the voice of God, preached elaborate sermons, and pantomimed the sufferings of Christ. Their audiences, which could include not only the members of their own religious community but also spiritual advisors, other members of the order, secular clergy, judges and officials of the Inquisition, and laypeople, were well prepared for the performances they were about to witness by the elaborate theater of the day, with its emphasis on the lives of the saints and other religious themes.

Francisca Inés de la Concepción, the prioress of the Franciscan Convent of Belén in Cifuentes, was not only a woman of considerable beauty but also a performer of no mean ability. On one occasion, when the chapel of the convent was full of people, she knelt in front of the screen in the upper choir where the nuns were observing mass. Having attracted the attention and admiration of the congregants with the extraordinary beauty of her pose and the expression on her face, she addressed the angels in heaven, urging them to sing and dance in honor of God. Seemingly carried away by religious fervor, she then turned her eyes to heaven and asked if she could be admitted to that sacred company. Indicating the success of this supplication, she arose from the kneeling position and commenced a slow and graceful dance around the upper choir in full view of the spectators and the other nuns. With "exquisite dexterity," she returned to her original position, all the while keeping up a soliloquy devoted to the holy sacrament that was so moving that the entire congregation was overcome with tears.[1]

An even more direct and convincing sign of divine favor was to be infused with the Holy Spirit so that one actually spoke with the voice of God. One of the most impressive examples of this phenomenon was the cycle of divine sermons that the Holy Spirit is said to have preached through the mouth of the Franciscan Juana de la Cruz. At age twenty-two, after a long period of remaining mute, she was informed directly by God that henceforth he would speak through her. During the next thirteen years, Juana would enter a trancelike state and "preach" before large numbers of people who had been invited into the convent for the occasion.

Many of her sermons were recorded by three nuns who were miraculously granted the ability to write for the occasion. Bound into a book, the sermons were kept in the convent and venerated as a relic. It is no wonder, therefore, that Juana de la Cruz was already the subject of a cult long before she died in 1534 and that her funeral was the scene of a massive outpouring of popular devotion.[2]

The "feigned" mystic Clara de San Francisco was highly cognizant of her need to build her saintly reputation among the other nuns in her convent by convincing them that she enjoyed divine favor. She accomplished this by staging a series of trances in highly public places, such as the choir, when she would either speak directly with Christ or relate what Christ had been saying to her. In the first type of vision, the object was to impress upon the other nuns the extreme favor that Christ, as her spouse, was showing her. Maintaining a trancelike state, she spoke in the third person of how "dressed in purest white, Clara savored dallying with her spouse who had presented her with a crown of rubies." After convincing her hearers that she indeed enjoyed extraordinary favor, she addressed them directly, assuring them, "Our Lord loves all of them exceedingly, and that they all enjoyed a state of grace."[3]

Aware that modesty and humility were considered to be an indispensable attribute of sanctity, Clara carried on a second "dialogue" with Christ, during which she appeared to reject his favors because she was not worthy to receive them. Making sure that she chose a night when another nun was sharing her cell so that her vision would be widely reported, she called upon Christ to take back his gifts. She exclaimed that she was unworthy to have that beautiful wedding ring or that cross of gold and precious stones that he had presented to her. She would content herself instead with a "cross of pain and suffering," like the one that he had been crowned with during the passion.[4]

Even though Clara's reputation for sanctity had not spread far beyond the walls of her convent when she was arrested by the Canaries tribunal in August 1644, she was successful in convincing most of the other nuns of her saintly qualities. Several of her most ardent supporters had visions that appeared to validate her pretensions. In one instance, Magdalena del Sacramento, the former abbess, testified that she had seen Clara seated next to the apostles in heaven.[5] María de Santa Clara, another supporter, described Clara as a woman of "saintly life" and had a vision of her surrounded by an aura of splendid light.[6] Given time and the support of her spiritual advisors and superiors in the order, Clara might have been able to build a formidable "saintly" reputation outside the convent, but the pressure to constantly perform new "miracles" and provide the nuns with encouraging prophecies proved her undoing. Forced to risk her "saintly" reputation by undertaking superhuman feats of abstinence, she ended by quarreling with one of her spiritual advisors, who just happened to be a notary of the Inquisition. Once he had decided that she was a fraud, Clara's arrest on charges of "false sanctity" and fake revelations was a foregone conclusion. Instead of enjoying the adulation of a cult following, therefore, Clara was to undergo a humiliating trial and suffer permanent exile from the convent for which she had tried to do so much.

But perhaps the most important way in which individuals could demonstrate that God's favor had been bestowed upon them was to be permitted to experience the pain and suffering that Christ had undergone during the passion. Described in luxuriant detail in such popular works as Pedro de Ribadeneyra's *Flos Sanctorum*, the passion became such an accepted sign of divine favor that fully 60 percent of the "true" mystics and 26.6 percent of the "false" mystics attempted to simulate the experience.

Beatriz María de Jesús made a specialty of acting out the passion during her time as a nun. Every year on the anniversary of the impression of the stigmata on Francis of Assisi, she would be informed in vision that it was her time to suffer. One story from her biography relates how on September 16, 1687, having first asked and received permission from the abbess, she commenced her sufferings by extending her arms and placing her legs one on top of the other, just as Christ had been forced to do on the cross. This was accompanied by a vision in which she saw St. Francis and her own guardian angel attaching her to a cross. For the next three hours, for so she had been ordered in the vision, she manifested every outward sign of intense suffering to an admiring audience of nuns, while her body remained as rigid as marble. Arriving at a climax of suffering, she concluded the performance by seeming to expire, although as soon as the prescribed three-hour interlude was over, she was as healthy as ever before.

But Beatriz did not confine herself to performing the passion on the anniversary of St. Francis's stigmata. Lent, as the traditional season for penitential discipline, served her purpose equally well. During one Lenten season, when she still lived at home, Beatriz assumed the form of the crucified Christ on several occasions, and once she could be heard to cry out, "Oh my God! Oh my God" and to breathe heavily and audibly, much to the amazement of her family and the numerous spectators who were invited to see her during such performances. As the three-hour interval drew to a close, her breathing was heard to diminish in strength, until she remained pale and seemingly near death.[7]

Equally impressive, in terms of both the performance and the impression it made on spectators, were the passion "sufferings" of the "false" mystic Catalina Ballester. Catalina, who boasted that she was destined to be canonized, frequently acted out the pains of the passion in front of the Morlana sisters, with whom she was living, and other spectators. On one occasion, with seven people watching, including her confessor Dr. Anglada, she began imitating the passion while lying in bed. Assuming the position of Christ on the cross with her body so rigid that no one could move it, she screwed up her face, grimaced, experienced great suffering. After several minutes of this, she seemed to be dead and was able to use her power to control her own body so effectively that one of the spectators who attempted to feel her pulse found nothing. Although everyone in the room wanted to understand what had happened, they were so impressed that they asked no questions and concluded that all of these things were "divine and celestial."[8]

Adopting a tactic designed to enhance the prestige of Dr. Anglada, her confessor and one of her principal supporters, Ballester made it a point to "suffer" the pains of the passion almost every time he heard her in confession. Taking to her bed, she would remain rigid, with her arms outstretched and one leg over the other, crying, "Oh my legs! Oh my arms! Oh my ears! Oh my side!" as if she were really experiencing pain in the places where Christ had suffered. Because Anglada was writing her spiritual biography and openly spoke of her as a "saint," it was very much in Ballester's interest to associate the divine favor of suffering the pain of the passion with his spiritual ministrations.[9]

Isabel de Briñas, another "pretended" mystic who demonstrated an ability to attract a following, sought to strengthen their devotion by imitating the passion in their presence. Ana del Christo, one of the witnesses at her trial, recalled that once, when Briñas was said to be ill, she went to her home to see if she could help her. Once she entered the room where Briñas was confined, however, she was surprised to find that many people were present, including a Dominican friar and her confessor Domingo Daza. Briñas was lying in bed in a trancelike state; taking various poses connected with the passion, including the position that Christ assumed on the cross; and crossing her hands over her chest like a cadaver. Murmuring their approval of this trance, the spectators were ushered out while Briñas remained alone with her confessor. Briñas's success in increasing her cult following by using this tactic was demonstrated a few days later, when Ana visited her again and found seven or eight people in the room, including one man kneeling in front of her bed devotedly saying the rosary.[10]

Another tactic designed to create and maintain a wide popular following was to distribute cult objects reputed to have magical or preservative powers. The existence of such objects would not only spread their cult during their lifetime but also help create the basis for compiling dossiers of sanctity after death, as followers ascribed miraculous events to them.

One of the easiest and most direct ways to create a large number of cult objects in the shortest possible time was to use rosary beads. Apparently the early-sixteenth-century mystic Juana de la Cruz enjoyed considerable success with rosaries that she claimed her guardian angel would elevate to heaven. After her death in 1534, her followers (or certain individuals who hoped to profit from owning the "blessed" rosaries) circulated a false indulgence purportedly issued by Gregory XIII (1572–85), attributing all kinds of powers and virtues to them up to and including those of the Agnus Dei.[11]

Judging by a crudely printed indulgence that was turned over to the Valladolid tribunal in 1635, Juana may have set a standard for counterfeit indulgences that inspired other would-be saints. This paper, which was circulated widely all over Castile, listed a series of indulgences enjoyed by those in possession of the rosary beads and crosses distributed by Sor Luisa de la Ascensión, the famous "nun of Carrión." Perhaps influenced by a tradition in the Franciscan order stemming from the time of Juana de la Cruz, the indulgences listed included the "virtues of the Agnus Dei" and those attributed to the "beads of Santa Juana."[12]

But the "nun of Carrión" seemed to have gone considerably further than her predecessor and made a real industry out of creating a saintly reputation by distributing cult objects. An inventory of cult items in the possession of her brother Francisco Colmenares included hundreds of rosaries, metal hearts inscribed with her name, *estampas*, crosses, and items of personal use. Domingo de Aspe, one of her spiritual advisors, even wrote the Franciscan commissioner general on March 26, 1633, to bemoan the fact that in Valladolid there were entire stalls devoted to selling her rosaries and cult objects, something he believed detracted from her reputation.[13]

The "sham" mystic Isabel de Briñas, who was active at about the same time as Luisa de la Ascensión, not only claimed a spiritual relationship with the "nun of Carrión" but also shared a supporter with her.[14] She also appears to have taken a leaf out of Luisa's book by distributing "blessed" rosary beads to the sick as a way of increasing her own cult.[15]

To spread her reputation as a miracle worker, especially in her Madrid neighborhood, Isabel also commissioned a local painter to make pictures showing her magical cures, which she then had hung up in the parish church. Unfortunately for Isabel, however, this strategy backfired, resulting in the alienation of a powerful official at the court of Philip IV who later testified against her at her trial. Called to the home of royal *aposentador* Santiago Vigil after his wife had suffered from a bleeding administered by an inept barber surgeon, Isabel claimed to have cured the woman after she applied a poultice to the wound. In accordance with her usual practice, Isabel then commissioned her painter to make a miracle painting of the cure and hung it in the chapel of the nearby Dominican convent in the name of Santiago Vigil's wife.[16] As he later testified before the Toledo tribunal, Vigil was incensed at Briñas's presumption in taking credit for a cure that he considered due entirely to natural causes and then publishing his wife's name without permission. Even though he was too afraid of Domingo Daza, the powerful warden of the convent and one of Isabel de Briñas's strongest supporters, to have the painting removed, he approached the painter and tried to force him to cover over his wife's name so that she would not be associated with such a fraud. Much to his chagrin, however, the painter refused on the grounds that covering the name would indicate a lack of devotion to Isabel de Briñas. Confronted by this refusal, Vigil could do little more than beg the tribunal to order that his wife's name be removed from the painting.

But, lest she be seen as immodest or accused of seeking the kind of publicity for herself that would automatically arouse suspicion and possibly attract the unwelcome attention of the authorities, a woman could go just so far in creating her own "saintly" reputation. To spread her reputation to its fullest extent during her lifetime, she needed the help of her supporters, spiritual advisors, and even her servants.

To spread her cult, Martina de los Angeles y Arilla, the Dominican lay nun from Zaragoza, was able to make extensive use of the services of Mosen Juan Paladilla, the parish priest from Villamayor. Paladilla, who was credulous enough to believe Martina when she told him that she had actually appeared to one of the women of the village when she was on her deathbed, was eager to spread her reputation as a miracle worker because he depended on it to supplement his meager benefice. Located in the foothills of the Sierra de Alcubrerre, Villamayor was an ideal location to practice weather magic by conjuring the damaging hailstorms that were so common in the region. Traveling throughout the district, Paladilla used crosses she had blessed and invoked her name in order to control the forces of nature and collect fees from the rural people for his trouble. As a sideline to his weather-conjuring business, Paladilla made use of Martina's rosary beads to effect magical cures all over the district. His success in fostering her cult is attested to by the fact that in her home village it became customary to invoke her whenever someone was seriously ill.[17]

Since Paladilla intended to continue invoking Martina and using items associated with her in his business as a weather conjurer after her death, it was very much in his interest to promote the idea that she had died in the odor of sanctity. To accomplish this, he carefully publicized two visions. In the first one, which took place shortly before her death, he claimed to have seen Saints Dominic, Luis Beltrán, and Peter the Martyr at the door of her cell. Then, just after her death, when her coffin had already been put in the ground, he claimed to have had a vision of her surrounded by flowers and wearing a diadem that emitted a splendid, unearthly light.[18] Both visions, of course, clearly indicated that she enjoyed extraordinary divine favor and that the probability of her actually being a saint was extremely high. Helped by these visions and her growing reputation, Mosen Juan Paladilla was able to continue invoking her name and using cult objects connected with her in his conjuring business for many more years.

After the woman mystic's death, the maintenance of her reputation for sanctity mainly depended on the loyalty of a core group of supporter families. In Martina de los Angeles y Arilla's case, it was Juan Luis Seyra, a prebendary of Zaragoza cathedral and his two sisters, Jacinta and Inés, who kept the flame alive. The three siblings were the children of Antonio Seyra and Josefa Vinós, two of Martina's most dedicated supporters in the village of Benavarre. The children evidently internalized the tradition and were generous in using pieces of Martina's habit and other cult items left to them by their parents to cure local people of a variety of maladies.[19]

Servants could also be counted on to spread a woman's fame. Not only were they dependent on their masters for their livelihood and therefore likely to do as they were told but also they could hope to benefit personally from any alms or contributions made by the pious. This is exactly what happened after Isabel de Briñas inherited her house from Quadros. Along with the house came two servants, Pedro Rodríguez and Juana de Guevara, and both proved more than willing to advertise Isabel's reputation for sanctity. Rodríguez, who was eventually brought to trial by the Holy Office for assisting Isabel in her deceptive practices, was accused of benefiting personally from at least part of the contributions made to her in return for telling others about such marvels as her stigmata, trances, and the way Christ had presented her with the crown of thorns that he had worn during the passion.[20] Both servants told stories about how St. Inés appeared to Isabel looking "exactly" the same as she was shown in a painting that they had in the house, and both spoke reverently, if inaccurately, about how instead of going to bed at night Isabel remained tied to a cross. Of course, at Isabel's trial, her servants strenuously denied that they had said or done anything to inflate her reputation, but their stories failed to convince the inquisitors and *calificadores* and were directly contradicted by prosecution witnesses.[21]

Last but not least, a woman's spiritual advisor could play a key role in spreading a woman's reputation for sanctity and encouraging cultic veneration for her. Luis de Mesa, who acted as confessor to the Franciscan *tercera* Mariana de Jesús and also wrote her biography, made a point of inviting large numbers of people to view her when she was in a trance and made public any predictions or revelations that he felt would enhance her reputation. On one occasion when she told him that she would recover from a serious illness within eight days, he spread the news all over Toledo. Sure enough, on the day that she predicted she would recover, numerous persons were present, including two physicians. In Luis de Mesa's case, one reason he insisted on manifesting publicly the remarkable spiritual powers of his charge was the prestige that would accrue to him from being her confessor. A no less important motive, however, was the belief, which he shared with many other committed Counter-Reformation Catholics, that the miraculous recovery was just another wonderful example of God's work in the world, a favor he bestowed on those who had remained faithful to him in a time of religious conflict.[22]

No less direct, in terms of seeking to enhance his penitent's following, was Isabel de Briñas's powerful confessor-protector, Domingo Daza. According to Isabel de Morales, a wealthy woman who was one of the witnesses at her trial, it was Daza who had first told her about Briñas, describing her as a woman of "rare virtue" and the "most perfect creature in the world." He encouraged Morales to visit Briñas frequently and consult with her about her spiritual life.[23]

Interestingly enough, on one occasion Daza even gave Briñas information that allowed her to plausibly advance a claim to supernatural power, thereby solidifying her reputation with one of her key followers. One feast day after preaching a sermon, Daza was invited to dine at the home of one of Briñas's friends and supporters, and while he was there her son fell down the stairs. Even though the boy landed unharmed, his mother was extremely upset by the incident. That same evening, Daza hastened to see Briñas and tell her about what had happened, including the exact time that the child fell. The following day, Briñas went to see the woman and, naming the exact time of the incident, indicated that the child was saved from serious harm only by her intervention. She urged the woman to use her name while invoking divine assistance in any such future accident. But, as the tribunal's prosecuting attorney pointed out in his accusation, even though Briñas had pretended that she was magically present at the time of the child's mishap, in fact she knew about the event only from her confessor.[24]

In many cases, self-promotion, plus the efforts of supporters and spiritual advisors, resulted in significant cultic veneration being paid to the woman during her lifetime, thereby laying the basis for efforts to initiate canonization proceedings after her death. Interestingly enough, even though the post-Tridentine papacy was extremely suspicious of unsanctioned saint cults, popular veneration was still very much accepted as a key validating element for any individual's reputation for sanctity. After reviewing Tomás de Montalvo's biography of Beatriz María de Jesús for his brother, the archbishop of Granada, the distinguished theologian Juan de Ascargorta concluded that her immense popularity in the city simply confirmed the good opinion that her spiritual advisors and the nuns of the Ángel Custodio Convent had of her. While the "importunate clamor" of the popular classes could not be accepted as proof that her soul belonged to God, it at least tended to confirm the other proofs and make it more likely. Greatly reassured by his brother's opinion, Archbishop Martín de Ascargorta issued a license to print the book on October 17, 1713.[25]

Cultic veneration for Beatriz María de Jesús had begun long before she entered the convent. Spurred by her successful public trances and the support of her family and spiritual advisors, public adulation had reached such a frenzy by the time she was in her late twenties that people would crowd into the alley next to her house or simply walk past it, hoping for a glimpse of her or thinking that being physically close to her would benefit them in some way. To avoid being mobbed when she went to church, Beatriz had to leave her house heavily disguised and tried to avoid going to the same church too often. But these precautions, by increasing her scarcity value, made some people even more desperate to see her perform her devotions. One of the most bizarre attempts was made by a woman from one of the city's distinguished families. Discovering a hole in the wall of Beatriz's house that offered a view of a gallery where she sometimes said her prayers, the woman knelt there for hours in hopes of catching a glimpse of the saintly creature. In fact, Beatriz was so successful in building a cult following that she invited imitation. In 1664, another woman began pretending to have trances, feigning paralysis, and manifesting the same kind of suffering that formed part of Beatriz's religious persona. Exposed as a fake, probably because she lacked the kind of political and family support that Beatriz had always counted on, the woman was punished. Needless to say, the fact that someone had imitated Beatriz so exactly that she had attracted a significant popular following and then been exposed as a fraud did nothing to discourage her supporters, who had already decided that she enjoyed God's special favor.[26]

The more popular the mystic was in life, the more her death would be the occasion of universal lamentation, and the more people would demand to see the body. After Beatriz died in the Ángel Custodio Convent on February 15, 1702, the community was forced to bring the cadaver to the main choir to accommodate the numerous people who wanted to view it and touch it with their rosaries and other devotional objects. The numbers became so large that the crowd threatened to burst through the iron screen that protected the choir, and a sturdy wooden barrier had to be built to provide additional protection.[27]

Something very similar happened when Martina de los Angeles y Arilla and six other nuns from the Dominican Convent of Santa Fe in Zaragoza travelled to the village of Benavarre to found the convent of San Pedro Martyr. On Martina's last day in Zaragoza, when she and the other nuns left the convent to worship at the statue of the Virgin of Pilar, she was literally mobbed by hundreds of people who wanted to catch a glimpse of someone about whom they had heard "so many wonders and prodigies." Similar scenes were repeated throughout the journey, especially in Martina's home village of Villamayor, where she had built a strong following by effecting numerous miracle cures. On their arrival at Benavarre, the nuns were met by the entire city council and other local notables and then brought in procession to the collegiate church, accompanied by the friars from the local Dominican and Augustinian convents.[28]

During her three years in Benavarre, Martina de las Angeles y Arilla was so successful in creating an intense cultic veneration around her person that, after her death, the nuns of San Pedro Martyr were forced to leave her body on view in the choir for three whole days to satisfy the hundreds of people who came to touch their rosaries to it. She had come to be regarded as the protector of the village with a unique power to intercede for its denizens and propitiate the supernatural forces that threatened to overwhelm it with hailstorms, flood, drought, or disease. This belief, so firmly ingrained in the popular mind by Martina herself and her spiritual advisor Jacinto Blasco, the warden of the nearby Convent of Our Lady of Linares, nearly led to an ugly incident when it came time to remove her body for burial. Fearing that during the procession to the cemetery some people in the mob would throw themselves on the body and cut pieces off it for relics, Blasco decided to have it brought there in a closed coffin. But this plan immediately stirred the suspicion of local officials, who were afraid that it was really a scheme to remove the body to Zaragoza, where Martina had spent most of her life as a nun. As the rumor of this supposed conspiracy spread through the village, hundreds of people arrived at the gates of the convent to prevent the removal of the body, which they believed to have thaumaturgical powers. Violence was averted only when Blasco agreed to open the top of the coffin before allowing it to be lowered into the ground, thereby showing the people that Martina was really being buried in the village cemetery.[29]

Hoping that intense cultic veneration would turn one of their own into another Teresa of Jesus or Rose of Lima, the nuns of the religious community and the superiors of the order vied to engrave the events of the days immediately after the death of a renowned mystic deeply into the popular memory. When Gabriela de San Joseph died in 1701, the nuns of the Carmelite convent in Ubeda rang the bells of the chapel to summon the largest possible number of people to the convent. Soon the streets were filled with people, and even little children shouted, "Let's go to see the saint who has just died in the discalced convent." Hundreds of people soon appeared at the door, and the two nuns on duty could barely keep up with all the requests to touch rosaries and religious medals to the corpse.

To further intensify public adulation, the nuns brought the corpse down to the choir and allowed people to enter the chapel to venerate it. Since the corpse had remained tractable, they sat it up, placed a palm frond in its hand, and later, acceding to requests by the people crowded against the choir's ornate iron screen, raised her arm as if to bless the multitude.[30] The nuns also let a number of artists approach near enough to make portraits of the corpse. These sketches formed the basis for *estampas* and were distributed all over southern Spain. To satisfy the demand for relics and spread the cult still further, the nuns cut up all her habits, shirts, blankets, and other items and gave them out to the people waiting at the screen. Her longtime confessor, Andrés de Santa Teresa, also sent her veil as a relic to enrich the new Carmelite convent that was founded in Velez-Málaga. After Gabriela was buried, the nuns sent numerous letters to religious institutions and influential members of the hierarchy, like the bishop of Merida, detailing the "life and virtues of the saintly Gabriela de San Joseph."[31] The funeral itself was celebrated with the greatest pomp that the order could muster. The friars from all of the city's convents came to venerate the body and hear mass in the chapel. So many people crowded into the courtyard of the church and the streets immediately surrounding it that the pulpit had to be erected at the door so that the sermon could be heard.[32]

Funeral processions could also be effectively exploited by the religious community to dramatize the importance and holiness of a deceased nun or *tercera*. After the Franciscan *tercera* Mariana de Jesús died on July 9, 1620, the order went to court to overturn her expressed desire to be buried in a pauper's grave and insisted on interring her in the cloister of the aristocratic

Convent of San Juan de los Reyes. Completely ignoring Mariana's extreme modesty in life, the Franciscans paraded her body, with its head uncovered, through the widest streets of Toledo so that it could be exposed to a great many people, who were allowed to touch the body with their crosses and rosaries. When the procession finally arrived at San Juan de los Reyes, it was buried with the greatest ceremony in the presence of such an enormous crowd that even nobles were afraid of being trampled.[33]

Shortly after the burial of a noted female mystic, her order would arrange for a mass to be said in her honor and a sermon to be preached, extolling her virtues. Even though she was only a *tercera*, Mariana de Jesús' reputation for sanctity was so great by the time of her death in 1620 that the Franciscans decided to go all out in paying her honor. Eight days after her death, the local Franciscan convent where she had worshiped arranged to have a mass for her said by the warden and a sermon preached by Fr. Juan de Guzman, who later became bishop of the Canaries. The order also made sure that copies of the sermon were printed and distributed as widely as possible, even going so far as to send a copy to the pious Archduke Albert of Austria, governor of the Netherlands.[34]

Largely disregarding the papacy's deep suspicion of anything that smacked of popular veneration for someone who had not been properly investigated by the Congregation of Rites, high officials of certain religious orders went out of their way to demonstrate support for a popular mystic in order to legitimize and deepen popular devotion. After the Dominican *tercera* María de la Santissima Trinidad died in 1660, amid scenes of popular devotion so intense that her funeral cortege was mobbed and her body stripped of its habit by relic seekers, Alonso de Santo Tomás, who was acting as visitor to the province, made a highly public pilgrimage to her home village of Arazena. While in the village, he went to the parish church and prayed before an image of Our Lady of the Rosary in the same chapel and in the same place that María herself had occupied so often during her lifetime. He also developed a scheme to establish a Dominican convent in the village. Ever since María was age twenty-four, when she saw a vision indicating that she was to found a Dominican house with fifteen nuns, such a convent had been her greatest wish, but it was only at her death that the order threw its support behind the project. Alonso de Santo Tomás traced out a convent that would incorporate the house in which she had lived and the land immediately around it. After completing his inspection of the site, Santo Tomás wrote to the owner of the village, the duke of Medina de las Torres, to inform him that the Cortes, Castile's chief legislative body, had approved the foundation and to ask for his support.

Yet another story of dramatic intervention by a high official of the mendicant orders to legitimize popular devotion comes from the events surrounding the death of the Franciscan nun Francisca Inés de la Concepción in 1620. Shortly after her death, none other than the order's general commissioner for Spain arrived in Oropesa, where Francisca had lived during the past two years. Commissioner Juan Venido remained in the town for the three days that the body remained exposed to the adulation of the public and then attended the funeral and her burial in an elaborate tomb paid for by Count Fernando Alvarez de Toledo, one of her strongest supporters.

Given the political and economic power of the religious orders in early modern Spain and the unwillingness of the authorities to do anything that might diminish piety, even the most flagrant promotion of cultic veneration toward an especially ascetic friar or nun was deemed acceptable. When a woman mystic was suspected of being a fraud, thereby undermining respect and reverence for the church, however, overt manifestations of support by the religious order were precisely what the authorities wished to avoid. When the famous "nun of Carrión" died on October 28, 1636, she was a prisoner of the Holy Office and being tried for fraud, false sanctity, and a host of other charges. In this instance, any public ceremony or procession including members of the Franciscan order would have undermined the Inquisition's attempts to curb the growth of her cult. Appraised of the dangers by the Valladolid judges, the Suprema hastily prohibited the officials of the Franciscan order from "making any show of support for the said Luisa in sermons or honors paid to her without explicit permission from this council."[35]

Since burial took place within the precincts of a convent, usually somewhere in the chapel, the order had control over the body itself and could enhance its location or upgrade the tomb as part of a general strategy for maintaining or increasing cultic veneration. Three years after the death of Caterina Tomás, funds were donated to improve her tomb by Juana Paz, one of her most dedicated supporters, while the order completed the construction of an underground chapel just below the one dedicated to Catherine of Siena, Caterina's favorite saint. On the day when Caterina's body was scheduled to be moved, her coffin was opened and the body was dressed in new and more splendid garments and covered with a white silk veil trimmed in gold. After hearing an inspiring sermon by Caterina's longtime spiritual advisor, Canon Juan Abrines, the entire community marched in solemn procession from the church to the convent, where they circled the choir very slowly as if reluctant to part with their Caterina for a second time. Finally, singing hymns of praise, their eyes filled with tears, the nuns marched back to the church, which was crowded with hundreds of worshipers, and down to the subterranean chapel where Caterina was laid to rest.[36]

Throughout the seventeenth and eighteenth centuries, the order kept supporting Caterina's canonization process in Rome, while in Mallorca itself a number of *estampas* printed by the famed Guasp publishing house kept her memory alive among the popular masses.[37] The order's persistence was finally rewarded when Caterina was beatified in 1792 and canonized in 1930, amid scenes of popular rejoicing by pilgrims from Mallorca who had traveled to Rome on pilgrimages organized by the religious orders.

When Canon Juan Abrines opened Caterina Tomás's coffin just before she was to be moved, he and the nuns who were present wept openly when they saw that her body had remained uncorrupted in spite of the dampness that had stained the sides of the coffin. Even the elements seemed to respect Caterina's body, doubtless because God himself had intervened.[38] Incorruptibility itself had always been accepted as a positive indication of sanctity, and this belief accounts for the frequency with which the authorities of religious orders authorized opening the coffins of those who had died in the odor of sanctity. The state of the body would indicate the strength of God's protection against the universal forces of decay and destruction; an uncorrupted body would encourage supporters to persevere and confound the doubters. It was to demonstrate and prove incorruptibility that Franciscan authorities allowed the coffin of the Poor Clare María Ángela Astorch to be opened no less than eight times, beginning one year after her death in 1666 and ending in 1867. The results were always favorable enough for the order to tenaciously pursue canonization, although, ironically enough, beatification was achieved only in 1982, after her tomb had been vandalized and her bones scattered during the Spanish Civil War.[39]

Of course, opening a coffin could prove quite disappointing or even dangerous to the integrity of the body within. When María Ángela Astorch's coffin was opened in 1725, even the devout nuns of her convent had to admit that the body was somewhat deteriorated. In 1643, twenty-three years after her death, the Franciscan order had the tomb of Francisca Inés de la Concepción opened for the first time. Much to the disappointment of the observers, the face was significantly deteriorated. While this evident decay did not prevent the nuns from taking the body out of the coffin, washing it, and dressing it in a silken garment, or stop the author of her biography from kissing her hands and feet, the coffin was never opened again, and Francisca never rose even as far as the rank of venerable.[40]

Sadly, pious relic hunters frequently did more damage than the elements to the bodies of holy women. In marked contrast to the magnificent Bernini sculpture in Rome's S. Maria della Vittoria, which shows her whole and enthralled by the love of God, Teresa of Jesus' cadaver was seriously mutilated as early as nine months after she was first buried, when her left hand was cut off by the Carmelite provincial.[41] By 1606, when Diego de Yepes published his biography, a truly amazing number of bits and pieces of Teresa's body had found their way into private hands and were being used to cure everything from malaria to blindness.[42]

The same fate was in store for the corpse of the *tercera* María de la Santissima Trinidad, who died in 1660 and was buried under the altar in the Dominican convent in Arazena. In early November 1662, the countess of Villaumbrosa and Castronuevo and her sister, Antonia Niño Enríquez de Guzman, were preparing for a difficult and perhaps dangerous trip to Madrid. Because both aristocratic ladies had been greatly devoted to María during her lifetime, they decided to say good-bye to her cadaver before embarking. Using their influence with the prior of the convent, they had the coffin opened and were gratified to discover that the body was in an extremely good state of preservation. Giving way to a sudden and powerful impulse, the countess insisted that the prior allow her to cut off one of María's fingers to take as a relic. He agreed, but the countess's example proved contagious, as both her sister and a friend who had accompanied them demanded and obtained fingers, which were cut off by their personal chaplain. In addition to the fingers, which the women wrapped carefully because they were described as very "sappy," they cut pieces off her habit and distributed them to friends and devotees of María's growing cult.[43]

Because the ultimate goal of the religious order in staging elaborate funeral processions, exposing the cadaver to the curious eyes of the public, and encouraging cultic veneration of a particular woman mystic was to achieve canonization, it was vitally important to maintain good records of the woman's spiritual life in order to form a dossier that could be submitted to Rome. Some orders did this on a routine basis. At the conclusion of each chapter meeting of the Dominicans of the Province of Andalusia, for example, it was customary to record the spiritual lives of any particularly outstanding friar or nun who had died since the last such meeting.[44]

But if the order was really committed to seeking canonization, especially after procedures were formalized after 1588, it had to create an elaborate dossier that its representatives could use to win over key members of the college of cardinals and the Congregation of Rites. Above all, evidence needed to be gathered within living memory of the nun's death to prevent the oral tradition about her life from being forgotten or hopelessly garbled.

Immediately after the death of Jacinta de Atondo, for example, the provincial of the Franciscan province of Aragon, having decided that sufficient signs from heaven had been received to warrant an all-out effort at canonization, conducted an extensive inquest among the nuns of her convent concerning her spiritual life. At the same time, he appointed two commissioners, one to conduct investigations among those who had known her in the village of Mallen, where she spent the first thirty-four years of her unhappy life, and another to interview Catalina la Fita, the woman with whom she had lived just before she became a nun.[45]

Finally, if the order was really serious about pursuing canonization, it would have to appoint a special representative to undertake a lobbying effort in Rome. In the eternal city, the canonization process, however, could stretch over the lifetimes of several such candidates. In the case of María Ángela Astorch, the dossier gathered by the ecclesiastical tribunal at the diocese was completed in 1670, only four years after her death, but was not actually submitted to Rome until 1760, when the first of the postulators was appointed to act in the name of the abbess and nuns of the Capuchin Convent of Murcia. In spite of the fact that postulator Tomás de Azpuru doubled as Charles III's ambassador to the Holy See, all he was able to accomplish was to get the future Clemente XIV, Cardinal Ganganelli, to plead María's case before the Congregation of Rites.

After Azpuru's death in 1772, Archbishop Francisco Javier Zelada succeeded him. Zelada was one of those prelates who was considerably fonder of life in Rome than he was of life in his archdiocese. But, in spite of the fact that he was made a cardinal in 1773 and was appointed secretary of state to Pius VI, he was able to do little for María's cause. Zelada was succeeded by five more postulants, including two papal private secretaries, who had similar ill luck down to the year 1845, when the case was taken over by the general representative of the Capuchins. Five years later, María reached the first rung on the ladder that might lead to sainthood when she was granted the title of venerable on September 29, 1850. Finally, on May 23, 1982, 316 years after her death, María received beatification, even though only one of her miracle cures was approved by the Vatican's medical commission. In this instance, the Congregation of Rites agreed to waive the normal requirement for two miracles because of the spiritual benefit that those who invoked her intercession were continuing to receive.[46]

From the standpoint of the church, the position of a woman's spiritual advisor regarding her saintly virtues was perhaps even more important than that of her religious order. Even though slightly more than 70 percent of the confessors of "genuine" mystics were members of the same religious order, what was really important about them was their in-depth knowledge of the spiritual life of the individual gained through years of hearing her confessions.

Apart from writing spiritual biographies, there were several other important ways that a spiritual advisor could assist in the canonization process. For one thing, he could cooperate in the collection of material for the dossier by making notarized statements regarding the woman's spiritual life, the divine favor shown to her, or any miracles that she might have performed. Even more important perhaps, especially to enhancing her reputation for sanctity on a local and regional level, was to express a willingness to preach a sermon either at the time of her funeral or later, during honors paid to her by her religious order. Two years after the demise of the Carmelite *tercera* Isabel de Jesús, honors were paid to her at the elite Carmelite house in Toledo. On this occasion, a sermon filled with references from both the Old and New Testaments was preached by Francisco Clarisse, one of her longtime confessors, and published by Manuel de Paredes, who had taken over her spiritual direction after Clarisse assumed other duties.[47]

The episcopal authorities, the bishop or archbishop or his officials, could also provide key support for the canonization process either indirectly, by encouraging cultic veneration through example, or directly, by assisting in the accumulation of evidence and providing financial assistance. Given the fact that Hipolita de Jesús y Rocaberti was related to many of Catalonia's leading families, it is hardly surprising that Alonso de Sotomayor, the archbishop of Barcelona, took a very active role in seeking her canonization. The eagerness with which this scion of an aristocratic Castilian family embraced the cause of a Catalan mystic of similar social standing must also be related to the difficult relationship between Catalonia and Madrid in the 1670s and 1680s. Castile had fully recovered the principality only in October 1652, and it remained restive and dissatisfied, even though Philip IV had conceded a general pardon and promised to maintain its laws and customs as they had been when he came to the throne.[48] Obviously, official support from the archbishop for the canonization of someone from an old-line, well-established family of Catalan aristocrats might go a long way in reconciling local elites to renewed Castilian control.

The archbishop's campaign began around 1670, with a major effort to identify and review all of Hipolita's copious writings in order to determine their orthodoxy. This was a critical first step because the slightest doctrinal slip would have doomed the possibility of canonization and might have entailed problems with the Holy Office. After careful review by a committee of local theologians selected by the archbishop, Hipolita's works were declared entirely orthodox, thereby earning the approval of episcopal officials. Emboldened by this declaration, the archbishop ordered his officials to put together a formal dossier and submitted it to the Congregation of Rites in 1671. But with his sense of urgency greatly increased by the rumblings of renewed unrest in various parts of the principality, the archbishop was too impatient to let events take their course and bombarded the pope with letters asking for Hipolita's canonization in April and May of 1674. The archbishop's efforts on behalf of Hipolita were seconded by the viceroy, who also wrote a series of letters to the holy father in April 1674.[49] In the end, all the trouble taken by the leading political and ecclesiastical authorities of Catalonia proved fruitless. Hipolita's writings were placed on the index in 1687, and she never achieved even the rank of venerable.[50] An initiative that might have proven effective in rebuilding the popularity of the Castilian administration among the Catalan elite had failed, and unrest in the province increased until another series of popular uprisings broke out in 1688–89.

Barring the political considerations that drove the campaign in favor of the canonization process for Hipolita de Jesús y Rocaberti, the involvement of bishops appears to have been limited to supporting local figures with a strong popular following and employing episcopal officials to supplement the order's efforts. The enormous outpouring of popular adulation that greeted the death of Gabriela de San Joseph in 1701 convinced the bishop of Jaen, Antonio de Brizuela y Salamanca, to send episcopal officials out to take oral depositions from witnesses who could attest to her miracles. The material that they were able to gather not only contributed to the official biography written by Manuel de San Gerónimo, the historian of the Carmelite province of Andalusia, but also was included in the canonization dossier that was sent to Rome.[51]

Local and regional authorities were a third major force that could provide both political and financial support for cultic veneration and canonization. Pride in the heroic religious history of a city frequently manifested itself in a spate of works dedicated to providing information about little-known martyrs, frequently women, who had given their lives in the struggle to preserve Christianity against both Roman and Islamic persecution. In a typical example, the Jesuit Martín de Roa's *Flos Sanctorum, fiestas y santos naturales de la ciudad de Cordova*, ancient martyrs such as Santa Pomposa and Saints Adolfo and Juan are held up as evidence for the city's long commitment to the Catholic faith. The example of these martyrs is then carried forward to modern times—that is, the fifteenth and sixteenth centuries—with the stories of aristocratic women from the city, such as Sancha Carillo and Ana Ponce de Leon, who had sacrificed their material well-being for Christ by devoting themselves to a life of prayer and abstinence.[52] Such works by Roa,

Antonio de Quintanadueñas, and others were one way of competing with other cities and regions for royal attention, deflecting charges that local elites were infected with *converso* blood, or simply compensating for economic decline by recalling a glorious past.

But recalling past glories or even finding instances of fervent devotion among contemporaries or near contemporaries was not the same as actually attaining the beatification or canonization of a native son. Canonization would provide impressive evidence of the continued loyalty of a city or region to the faith and would renew and reinforce regional pride at a time when the power and authority of the central institutions of the monarchy were breaking down. An excellent example of municipal sponsorship is provided by the leading role that the Granada city council took in promoting the collection of materials for Beatriz María de Jesús. Impressed by the enormous outpouring of public adulation at her funeral on February 16, 1702, and the impressive series of events, sermons, masses, and obsequies that lasted until May 4, the city council held several meetings and decided to appoint commissioners to assist with the canonization dossier.[53]

In dedicating his 1627 biography of Caterina Tomás to the bishop and city council of Palma de Mallorca, Bartolomé Valperga urged them to support her canonization because of the debt that the city and region already owed to her and the fact that so many other cities had succeeded in making saints out of local religious figures. Comparing her to another Jeremiah in her unceasing prayer for the good of her people and constant intercession on their behalf, he assured the *jurats* that she could be expected to continue her support from heaven as long as she was not forgotten. He also reminded them of the fact that many other cities had met with considerable success in supporting the canonization of local religious figures. By supporting Catherine of Siena, that city had not only won honor and glory by petitioning the pope to make her a saint but also gained an important intercessor who could act along with its guardian angel to protect it from divine retribution. Closer to home, Valperga gave the example of Valencia with its recent (1618) success in achieving the beatification of its Archbishop Thomas of Villanova. Moreover, the city was not content to rest on its laurels and had recently embraced the cause of Padre Francisco Simón, a local parish priest and mystic. In addition to Valencia, Valperga also mentioned Madrid's successful campaign on behalf of its patron Isidro Labrador, canonized in 1622, and Zaragoza's efforts on behalf of its first inquisitor, Pedro Arbués, who was assigned a feast day in Spain but not actually canonized until 1867.[54]

Evidence confirming the increasingly important role that cities were playing in the struggle to canonize more Spaniards comes from the Mercedarian Francisco Guzman Ponce de Leon, who was appointed censor of Luis de Mesa's biography of Mariana de Jesús in 1673. In discussing the support that Mariana had received, Ponce de Leon gave pride of place to the city of Toledo, which both "acclaimed and implored" her canonization. While Toledo's efforts were ultimately unsuccessful, at least a formal investigation was authorized by the Congregation of Rites, which appointed apostolic judges to carry it out.[55]

The final major player in the canonization struggle was the monarchy it-self. While the crown could not commit its prestige to every canonization effort, it was obvious that, at least to some extent, the number of saints that a great Catholic monarchy could boast was a strong indication of its political importance. The fact that a region that had lagged well behind the Holy Roman Empire and France throughout the Middle Ages surpassed both in the six-teenth and seventeenth centuries, with a total of thirty-eight canonizations, is a strong indication of Spain's leading role during the Counter-Reformation.[56] Even though the monarchy's role was not always decisive, the evidence sug-gests a great deal of activity on the part of Spanish ambassadors, as well as direct intervention by Habsburg rulers and their families.

Certainly the hand of the Spanish government was evident in three of the four Spanish saints canonized at St. Peter's on March 12, 1622, just after Spain entered the Thirty Years War. Philip II himself initiated canonization pro-ceedings for Teresa of Jesus by writing directly to Nuncio Camillo Gaetano in 1595. The nuncio in turn sent commissioners to interview all those who could attest to her saintly virtues, and those interviews were dispatched to the pope, along with supporting letters from Philip himself in 1597.[57] The monarchy also intervened to support Isidro Labrador, who became patron saint of the new Spanish capital. When the general congregation of the Society of Jesus requested the opening of canonization proceedings for Ignatius Loyola in 1594, their request was supported by letters from Philip II, and Maria of Austria and a personal appearance by the Spanish ambassador to argue the case in front of the Congregation of Rites.[58]

Apart from such "national" saints as Isidro Labrador or Ignatius Loyola, the monarchy was also prepared to intervene in favor of the canonization of saints with a more regional focus in order to demonstrate its support for the region's aspirations. Such support extended to two pious medieval women, María de Cervellon (1230–90) and Isabel of Portugal (1271–1336). Apart from their impeccable spiritual credentials, both women represented the cream of Iberian society. María de Cervellon was the daughter of D. Guillen de Cervellon, one of Catalonia's leading nobles, and Isabel had been queen of Portugal. Both Portugal and the Principality of Catalonia had proven difficult to reconcile to Spanish rule, and direct royal intervention in the canonization process was clearly a way of favoring regional aspirations while not undermining the authority of Madrid. In the end, however, the failure to achieve the canoniza-tion of María de Cervellon was to matter as little as the success scored by the monarchy in the case of Isabel of Portugal, who was canonized by Urban VIII in 1626, because both provinces rejected Spanish control in 1640.

Changes in the theological virtues and clerical roles that the saints of the Counter-Reformation were expected to model notwithstanding, sanctity re-mained first and foremost the ability to work wonders and perform miracles for both the papacy and the popular masses.[59] When Clement VIII denied the Jesuits' first request to open canonization proceedings for Ignatius of Loyola in spite of the fact that he was the hero who had founded the Counter-Reformation's most important religious order, it was because he was not known as a miracle worker. It was only after 1601, when Pedro de Ribadeneyra, the author of one of Spain's most popular *Flos Sanctorum*, published a new biography of Ignatius, illustrated with woodcuts showing him performing miracles, that support for his canonization really solidified. In 1605, Paul V opened the canonization process. In the same year, the Bavarian Jesuits published *Life of Ignatius,* which presented their founder as both hero and miracle worker and compared him with Francis of Assisi. Jesuit efforts to paint Ignatius as a wonder-worker intensified after he was declared blessed in 1609. These efforts culminated in a painting by Rubens showing Ignatius standing at the head of a row of Jesuits, casting demons out of tormented Christianity and illuminated by a divine light. The painting was completed in time for Ignatius to join four others in the glorious canonization ceremony of March 12, 1622.[60]

The transformation of Teresa of Jesus from ecstatic contemplative and founder of a new religious order to miracle worker began just after the coffin containing her body was opened in 1586, in the presence of the bishop of Avila and several physicians. Finding the body intact, the order began to advertise the "miracle" all over the city. After the body was returned to its resting place in the Carmelite convent at Alba de Tormes, the order continued focusing public attention on its miraculous character by distributing the pieces of cloth that had been used to wrap it as relics. Each of these pieces of cloth had an aroma of rotting flesh, described as smelling like jasmine by her first biographer, Francisco de Ribera. Finally, Ribera himself completed the process of transformation by including thirty-two pages of posthumous miracles, from apparitions to miracle cures, in his 1590 biography.[61]

In an age when various epidemic diseases were widespread and medicine was almost entirely ineffective, healing was the most frequently cited miracle in favor of canonization. In the vitae of the "true" mystics, the mythography of wonder-working is perfectly consistent with this bias toward healing, which was attributed to 66.6 percent of the women, much greater than any other form of miracle.

Miraculous healing could take on several forms. Perhaps the most impressive kind involved willingly assuming an illness being suffered by someone else. Based on the magical principle of contagion, by which powers or influences contained in one body can be made to flow into another through "the magical power of imagination," such effects demonstrated a woman's heroic willingness to sacrifice herself for others, itself a fundamental attribute of sanctity.[62]

One especially compelling story of taking on the suffering of another involved Mariana de Jesús, whose sympathy for a local notable as a friend and supporter was increased by the fact that his charitable benefactions supported many poor people. After being informed that he was so seriously ill that the doctors had warned him to make his final confession, Mariana had a vision in which Saint Diego de Alcalá appeared and told her that to save him she would have to assume his illness. Having agreed to this bargain, Mariana began suffering the very next day, while the sick man commenced a rapid and complete recovery. Convinced that Mariana had really sacrificed herself for him,

Mariana's faithful supporter made sure that the miracle became widely known all over Toledo, further enhancing a reputation that already included freeing numerous souls from purgatory, aiding pregnant women, and other forms of miracle cures.[63]

The role of St. Diego de Alcalá in this miracle cure points to yet another way in which such cures could be effected: through a woman's intercession with a favorite saint. Testimony at the trial of Isabel de Briñas indicates that she also sought to heal by invoking the intercession of St. Domingo Soriano. On July 15, 1639, Beatriz Ponce de Leon testified that a woman who frequented Isabel's home told her that once, when her arm had become infected to the point that the physicians told her that it would have to be amputated, Isabel arrived and offered prayers to St. Domingo for her relief. Just after Beatriz returned from the prayer room, the woman's arm was seen to have recovered totally.

Isabel de Briñas's fame as a healer evidently spread well beyond her Madrid neighborhood. At this same hearing before the Toledo tribunal, Beatriz Ponce de Leon testified that she had been present when someone from Madrid's poorer barrios arrived, carrying a seriously ill child. This time, instead of imploring St. Domingo Soriano's intercession, Isabel resorted to using a remedy whose power was derived from association with the saint. Mixing with water a little of the dirt in the bottom of the baptismal font that the saint had used, she administered it to the child, who was said to have recovered almost immediately.[64]

Stories of cures being effected by touch are among the most common of all the miracles, in part because they had become so widely accepted by the general public. Thaumaturgic powers were commonly attributed to royal persons whose touch was believed to be especially effective in curing scrofula.[65] Ana de Jesús, whose prophecies of the death of prominent political figures such as the French King Henry IV were widely known well before her death, frequently used touch to effect magical healing of wounds. One incident while she was prioress of a Carmelite convent involved a nun whose hand was crushed by a marble pillar. Alerted by several of the other nuns, Ana rushed to the scene and took the wounded hand in hers. No sooner had she done so than the wound healed and the nun's hand was restored to its former condition. Something very similar occurred in that same convent when another nun got a splinter in her finger. Receiving information about what had happened in a divine revelation while she was praying in the choir, Ana removed the splinter, and this wound, too, healed up immediately, leaving almost no trace. Suitably impressed by a long series of cures that he found in the dossier that was made available to him by the order, Ana's biographer, Angel Manrique, concluded that "the ability to effect miracles implies great powers."[66]

An interesting variation on the use of touch to carry out wonder cures is provided in the biography of María de la Santissima Trinidad. In one instance involving an aristocratic nun, Ana Josefa de Cordova y Figueroa, who was suffering from a partially paralyzed hand, María told her to have faith and say a prayer to the Virgin Mary. As the woman spoke the words, María placed her own hand upon her, and just as Ana finished the Salve she began moving her hand as if nothing had ever happened. Of course, this miracle cure, which was effected through a combination of touch and prayer, was duly recorded and notarized in the canonization file that was being put together with the support of Ambrosio Spinoza, archbishop of Seville.[67]

The use of material objects associated directly with a woman mystic was also very common in magical healing. When Ana de Jesús was superior of the Carmelite convent in Madrid, she was able to heal the sacristan of a broken bone by merely placing her handkerchief over the wound. She was also successful in curing the wife of an influential judge by using her scapular.[68]

The employment of personal items to effect cures by a respected woman mystic sent a powerful message about the value of such items. Consequently, anything physically associated with a woman mystic was deemed to have thaumaturgic power and could be used to cure oneself and others. But in making cult objects of such items and treating them as holy relics, the followers and supporters of women mystics were merely following the lead of the woman herself.

Tantalizingly close to the remedial practices of women who were convicted of performing "superstitious medications" by the Holy Office were those officially approved women mystics who "signed illnesses" with the sign of the cross. Of course, those charged with superstition by the tribunal were guilty of mixing magical and clerical remedies, while the approved mystics were consistent in employing only orthodox remedies that were fully within the accepted limits of "ecclesiastical medicines."[69]

Beatriz María de Jesús employed the sign of the cross quite frequently, along with an arsenal of magical remedies that included touching and invocation. Believing, as she once remarked to her sister Francisca, that "God grants us many favors through the Holy Cross," she used signing especially with her own family. Making use of the sign of the cross, she was able to cure Francisca of a severe pain in her leg. In that same year of 1664, she employed the signing method to cure her brother of a serious fracture that he had received in a scuffle.[70]

The miracle cure effected by María de la Santissima Trinidad on the paralyzed arm of the head of one of Arazena's most important families was somewhat more ambiguous insofar as the fine line between curative magic and "ecclesiastical medicines" was concerned. In this case, the cure was to be the result of what could easily have been an incantation, since María touched the paralyzed arm while mumbling something that the family could not overhear.[71]

Neither María de la Santissima Trinidad nor Beatriz María de Jesús ever had any problems with the Holy Office over superstitious practices. But, consistent with its relative moderation in dealing with evidence of magical healing, the Toledo tribunal also resisted the temptation to accuse Isabel de Briñas of superstition, preferring to concentrate instead on what appeared to be the far more dangerous issues of false sanctity and Illuminism. Making use of curative magic, even if such orthodox religious practices as the sign of the cross were used inappropriately, indicated piety, but faking sanctity and Illuminism threatened to undermine respect for the church.

The intimate relationship between cultic devotion to a woman mystic and her ability to bring about miracle cures is demonstrated by the way people began invoking her in time of need even during her lifetime. After María de la Santissima Trinidad cured Ana Josefa de Cordova y Figuero's paralyzed hand, it was natural for Ana to invoke her during all of her subsequent illnesses. Her belief in the supernatural powers of María and of anything even remotely connected with her was so great that she applied a letter that she had received from her to the bodies of the sick and injured nuns in the convent.

Perhaps the most curious example of invocation involved Pascual Lopez, a devotee of Martina de los Angeles y Arilla. One evening, instead of going home, Pascual got involved in a game of dice with some strangers and, before he knew it, lost his house and property. Desperate at the thought that he could lose everything his family had struggled to accumulate over several generations in a few hands of cards, he invoked Martina's intercession in the name of his wife and children, who were about to become homeless. Instantly, the dice began to turn in his favor, and he ended the game with a small gain. Several days later, Pascual went to Martina's convent to visit her, telling her nothing about what had happened. She received him coldly and warned him not to ask for her help again during dice games because "God is becoming tired of your foolishness." Astonished at her knowledge of what had happened, Pascual thanked her for her assistance and promised that he would give up gambling forever.

Miracle cures were the most important but not the only way that a woman could demonstrate her supernatural power. Prophecy, the ability to foresee events in the future, had long been accepted by hagiographers as a sign of God's special favor and a strong indication of sanctity.[72] Accurate prediction of their own demise or the death of others was the most common form of prophecy attributed to "true" mystics in the "official" biographies. Such prophecies not only permitted the biographer to demonstrate the woman's acceptance of her own mortality in the spirit of the theological virtues of faith and hope but also allowed the subject to be seen in the role of urging others to do the same. But the ability to predict death itself was also an awesome demonstration of a woman's understanding of the course of disease. Demonstration of such insight powerfully reinforced her claim to work miracle cures since it gave evidence of a degree of knowledge that could have come only from God.

Seeming foreknowledge of the exact day of their own death was attributed to 46.7 percent of the approved mystics. The story of Martina de los Angeles y Arrilla demonstrates how some women mystics deliberately used such awareness to increase their reputation for supernatural powers. As early as three years before her death, Martina was already taking every opportunity to inform her closest supporters that she would die on November 11, the feast day of her patron saint, Martin of Tours. It is interesting to speculate, given her familiarity with devotional works and conscious imitation of the lives of the saints, that she may have known that Martin himself had a premonition of his coming death, which was shared by certain of his followers.[73]

Finally, a few weeks before she died on November 11, 1635, she began intimating that her death was near to the prioress of her convent and the other nuns. Even though she never responded directly when asked if she knew the exact day that she would die, by inquiring over and over again how many days it was until the feast of St. Martin, she indicated that it would be her next saint's day.[74]

María de Jesús, the Carmelite nun and three times abbess of the Convent of St. Joseph and Santa Teresa in Toledo, signaled that she had a presentiment of her own demise six months before it actually happened. She petitioned the order for the right to bury "a nun" within the cloister of her convent. Later, María gave an even more pronounced indication of miraculous prescience by declaring that this space was not to be used to bury the first nun to die but, rather, the second—that is, María herself. Then, just twenty-two hours before her death, she had a last interview with a Carmelite friar, whom she had treated almost like a son for a number of years. To the friar's extreme distress, she announced her imminent demise and asked for his benediction in terms so moving that Francisco de Acosta, the author of an adulatory biography published in 1648, felt that he could not adequately render them in print.[75]

Curiously enough, 60 percent of the approved mystics could predict the death of others, which is significantly higher than those who forecast their own. The popularity of such a formidable claim is probably due to the enormous amount of power that could accrue to someone who could convince others of the validity of such a prophecy. Certainly, María de Jesús' unsettling habit of calling certain nuns into her cell, lecturing them about the contemptible nature of life in this world, and then telling them that their time on earth was approaching its end proved to be one of the keys to her authority as abbess of her convent.[76]

One may presume that the predictions made by María de Jesús were based on the intimate knowledge that an abbess must have had concerning the state of health of her charges. But it is less easy to account for the many prophecies made by Ana de Jesús regarding the demise of such prominent figures as the French King Henry IV, the Marquis del Valle, or Lucas Gracián, the celebrated author of the *Galateo Español*.[77] The element of the miraculous in such prophecies begins to fade, however, when we take into account the fact that Ana had always played a prominent role in the affairs of the order and was very well informed; so there was a high probability of prior knowledge of the physical condition of the individuals concerned. Even her biographer Angel Manrique admitted that the Marquis del Valle was seriously ill when Ana prophesied his demise. Ana could also have received information about the death of the French king from her contacts among the Carmelites of Paris, where she had founded a convent.

Even more important in evaluating the miraculous element in such prophecies are the discoveries of modern psychology regarding perception. The impact of temporal contiguity on the way we organize knowledge and the irrational thinking that it can produce probably accounts for most of the credibility so easily granted to prophecies of death. Temporal contiguity means that a prediction occurred around the time of an individual's death, not that the prophecy itself was in any way accurate.[78] Such a conclusion could be drawn as a consequence of the respect and admiration that people ascribed to the person making the prophecy, which would lead to an automatic tendency to "confirm" her predictions. Such a tendency was certainly operating in the case of Ana's prediction of the death of the Marquis del Valle. The prophecy took place in the Carmelite convent that Ana founded in Brussels, where she stopped a prayer and then informed the other nuns that the marquis had died in that moment and that his soul needed their prayers to escape from purgatory. It was only later that the mail from Madrid confirmed that he had, in fact, died at that moment. Such a confirmation, however, should be greeted with considerable skepticism. The two events took place far apart, and those reporting the connection had a strong interest in building Ana's reputation for possessing supernatural powers.

Clairvoyance, the ability to read people's innermost thoughts, was another form of supernatural power that could be seen as a sign of sanctity. Shared by 30 percent of the approved mystics, the uncanny ability to intuit the sins, foibles, or deepest desires of others was just another addition to an impressive arsenal of powers that further enhanced cultic veneration toward a particular individual.

According to her biographer, Martina de los Angeles y Arilla was clairvoyant to a "heroic degree." No matter how hard they tried, people could hide nothing from her; she could understand both the intentions of those she spoke with and whether they were inspired by God or the devil. A member of Zaragoza's urban noble class had occasion to encounter Martina's insight, as well as her sharp tongue, one day when he came to her convent to ask her to intercede for him with a judge she happened to know. Before he even began his plea, Martina interrupted him to demand "how anyone who has fallen out with God could come here demanding favors." Astonished by Martina's seeming insight into the deepest recesses of his soul, the man confessed the sin that he had been concealing and withdrew, admitting later that he "did not dare to remain in her presence."[79]

But not everyone's uncanny ability to read the thoughts of others was a product of clairvoyance. Testifying in response to an inquisitor's question about whether Caterina Ballester had the power to penetrate the meaning of things kept secret, Isabel Miro responded that Caterina was an "extremely inquisitive woman." She would deliberately stir up trouble between her hosts, the Morlana sisters, and their niece in order to discover family secrets and then used what she had found to "reveal" their innermost thoughts to the Morlanas. The credulous Morlana sisters were always profoundly impressed by Caterina's seemingly uncanny ability to read their minds. Even Miro admitted that she was unwilling to confront Caterina because of her reputation as a "saint" and out of fear that whatever she said would be repeated to the Morlanas, who would invariably "attribute it to a miracle."[80]

The stronger a woman mystic's reputation for supernatural powers during her lifetime, the more certain it was that she would continue to be invoked after her death. Such invocation was directly encouraged by the religious order, her former spiritual advisors, supporters, and even biographers, who used articles of her clothing or other personal effects as if they were relics to "cure" a variety of illnesses.

The home convents of Beatriz María de Jesús and Caterina Tomás both retained articles of their clothing that they used to assist people who came to seek help. The Ángel Custodio Convent in Granada actually conserved Beatriz María's entire habit, which they allowed people in distress to use. One story of a miraculous cure involved using the sleeves of the habit to cure a woman of a serious throat infection. After the sleeves were applied, the infection cleared up so quickly that when her physician arrived to minister to her he could find nothing wrong. Another story involved a judge of Granada's powerful Audiencia who was suffering from pain in his kidneys. Even though the doctors despaired of treating him, the mere touch of a piece of the shirt that Beatriz wore during her final illness was enough to relieve his pain. For years after Beatriz's death, the convent exploited the marvelous powers of her habit to cure a variety of illnesses and, no doubt, benefit from the alms of a grateful public.[81]

Probably the most unusual "curative" relic that was retained by any woman mystic's home convent was held by the Augustinian house where Caterina Tomás had been resident for the last twenty-three years of her life. Because Caterina was immensely popular in her lifetime for public trances and credited with numerous miracle cures, the convent hoped to perpetuate her reputation by using her hat to aid those suffering from serious illnesses. Two of the instances recorded by her biographer, involved application of the sombrero to the bodies of young girls suffering from high fever. Both girls were cured almost immediately, and the girls' families, as well as their physicians, gave thanks to God for the "miracle cure." All of these cures, both before and after Caterina's death, were carefully recorded by the Mallorcan inquisitor Juan Abrines, her longtime spiritual advisor, and two Carthusian monks, Vicente Mas and Pedro Caldes. Both monks were inveterate and uncritical admirers of Caterina Tomás, and both received brief biographies from Abrines, who also wrote an unpublished spiritual biography of Caterina herself.[82]

Some spiritual advisors unabashedly made use of items closely associated with a deceased woman mystic to effect miracle cures. After Inés de Jesús y Franco's death, her confessor Guadioso Alexandre took possession of an umbilical cord that she had used to relieve her own headaches and cure a variety of illnesses. Since she had informed him that the umbilical cord had been given to her by the Virgin Mary herself, there seemed no reason to believe that it would not continue to perform miracles. Happily for numerous persons in and around the town of Miedes, this assumption proved correct, and Alexandre used the umbilical cord to carry out a series of miraculous cures.[83]

Alexandre also gave a small cross mounted on a pedestal to the new abbess of the convent. Reputedly bestowed upon Inés by the Virgin Mary, this "holy relic," as her relative and biographer, Diego Franco y Villalva, described it, not only cured the abbess of a serious illness but also became quite popular in the entire region. The nuns repeatedly acceded to requests for it by individuals and even local physicians but noticed that when it was returned it had pieces cut out of it. Eventually, the people who used the cross chipped off so much of it that it lost its shape and could hardly stand on its pedestal. One woman, whose doctor used the cross to treat her when she was possessed, became so attached to it that she had to be taken to court to force her to return it.[84]

Wide disbursal of items with an intimate connection to the body or person of a woman mystic virtually guaranteed that those who had been among her main supporters while she lived would be able to obtain something after her death. Since anything that had been in contact with such a woman was reputed to be a relic with thaumaturgic powers, supporters in possession of such objects found it almost impossible to resist the demands of those who believed that contact with the object would cure their maladies. By using items from the wardrobe of a deceased woman mystic to cure or lending such items to others, the supporter became an important disseminator of her cult.

Unable to resist the importunities of friends, neighbors, and even perfect strangers, Teresa Montes, one of Jacinta de Atondo's strongest supporters, lent the rope belt from her habit to numerous women who were having difficult pregnancies. Application of the belt to the swollen belly of the woman would guarantee the success of the pregnancy. Evidently Jacinta's personal effects were widely disbursed in and around Zaragoza because of the twelve miracle cures recorded after her death, eleven were produced by using personal items, and the twelfth involved a difficult pregnancy that was resolved when the woman prayed before an *estampa* representing Jacinta in a devotional pose.[85]

An instance of how the spirit of a "woman of power" could take revenge on those who scorned her relics comes to us from the biography of Gabriela de San Joseph. Andrés de Lara, one of Gabriela's supporters, was visiting the home of María and Teresa de Viedma one day when María was quite ill. Lara, who happened to have a piece of Gabriela's tunic in his possession, offered it to both women, but María insisted on taking it first. Her sister, offended at having to wait before touching the cloth, became angry and told Lara that she really did not want it because "I don't have much respect for uncanonized saints." At that moment, her sister applied the cloth to her forehead and instantly felt better, while the doubting sister felt the pain of the illness.[86] But the story of the two sisters provides us with more than a dramatic demonstration of the power of relics. It also stands as an ironic commentary on the effectiveness of Pope Urban VIII's 1634 edict against the veneration of uncanonized saints. Nearly sixty-nine years after that edict, the author Manuel de San Gerónimo, official historian of the Carmelites of Andalusia, could tell a story directly supporting unofficial "popular" canonization, which was still considered by many to be more important than the cumbersome and expensive process carried on before the Congregation of Rites.

An accurate description of the manner by which a woman mystic attained one of the three stages in the process of canonization—"venerable servant of God," beatification or "blessed," and saint—must begin by admitting that many were called but few chosen. Of the thirty officially approved mystics in this study, only eight had attained any of the stages by the time this book was written. Of course, as any student of the byzantine workings of the Vatican knows, the wheels of policy grind very slowly and, when enough influence is brought to bear, even cases seemingly closed forever can be reopened. The effects of persistence are demonstrated in the case of Juana de la Cruz, the controversial abbess and reformer of the Franciscan Convent of Santa María de la Cruz near Cubas in New Castile. In spite of strong royal support and a fervent local cult, her cause stagnated for centuries at the Congregation of Rites because of doubts about the value of her revelations, only to be revived in 1981 with the appointment of a new postulator.[87]

For a woman mystic to be pronounced worthy of any of the degrees of sanctity, it would appear that apart from demonstrating the required number of miracles, four significant elements would have to be present: strong and persistent cultic veneration, support from the religious order, endorsement by regional and national elites, and a lack of concern about the orthodoxy of her statements, writings, or actions. Of these four elements, the last was by far the most important.

The failure of Ana de Jesús to gain a foothold on any of the rungs of the ladder that led to sainthood, in spite of her brilliant collaboration with Teresa of Jesus during the formative years of the Discalced Carmelites, may be attributed to her support for Teresa's constitution during the conflict that convulsed the order in 1590–94. Ana would seem to have all of the requisite qualifications. She had been instrumental in the development of one of the most important new Counter-Reformation religious orders, her writings were of impeccable orthodoxy, and her miracles were numerous and well attested. Even more important perhaps, she had the support of the powerful Infanta Isabella Clara Eugenia, who ruled the Spanish Netherlands after the death of her husband, Archduke Albert, until her own death in 1633. The infanta had not only gone out of her way to make a formal declaration before the officials charged with assembling the official canonization dossier but also visited Ana's tomb with members of her court. Nevertheless, in spite of Ana's support among the Spanish monarchy's governing elite, beatification proceedings were not even introduced until May 1878 and then failed to prosper, even though her writings were approved as orthodox in 1885.

Ana's failure to achieve beatification stands in marked contrast to the success of Ana de San Bartolomé, who was beatified on May 6, 1917, by order of Pope Benedict XV. Arguably, the difference may be attributed to the fact that Ana de San Bartolomé was closer to Teresa herself. Ana served as Teresa's personal secretary from 1577, and the saint died in her arms in 1585. But there can be little doubt that Ana de Jesús was more important to the expansion of the order, founding nine convents to Ana de San Bartolomé's three. The real difference between the two women lies elsewhere, in their attitudes toward the conflict over preserving that part of Teresa's constitution that permitted the prioresses of Carmelite convents to select extraordinary confessors from other orders.[88] Confronted by demands from the Carmelite friars to eliminate that right, Ana de Jesús led a group of five prioresses in successfully petitioning Pope Sixtus V for confirmation of Teresa's original constitution, thereby alienating the male superiors of the order. Ana de San Bartolomé chose the opposite side, believing that obedience to superiors constituted the first duty of a nun.[89] Since the issue of female subordination and obedience to male superiors in a male-dominated church was, and remains, highly controversial, it is easy to see how Ana de Jesús's courageous stand might have cost her beatification.

Conclusion

Spiritual advisor, social worker, prophet, royal confidant, and privileged recipient of divine communication—the multiple roles played by the woman mystic during Spain's golden age defy the conventional wisdom about female weakness and subordination. But it would be a serious error to conclude that this new perspective does anything more than add nuance to a generally depressing picture. Whatever their achievements in the real world, their dreams were far grander and provide us with a measure of the frustration that must have been felt by many women refused entry into trades, professions, and offices solely because of their sex. Missionary, preacher, teacher of the word of God, warrior, and martyr for the faith were the fantasies that social reality made impossible.

Then again, if this general observation is true, it is likewise true that the Counter-Reformation provided women with new opportunities to demonstrate their loyalty to the church and prove their utility in areas where men could not or would not serve. In France, where Catholicism faced the powerful Huguenot movement, women organized in such orders as the Sisters of Charity tended to the sick and educated the poor. All over Catholic Europe, the Ursuline Order, founded by Angela Merici in 1535, spread rapidly during the post-Tridentine period to become the most important teaching order of women.

In Spain, where there was no serious competition from an organized Protestant movement, the Spanish church was less constrained to use women to supplement the services of male clerics. Saint Teresa's Discalced Carmelitesses, the most important new order for women founded in early modern Spain, were from the first an enclosed order dedicated to prayer and contemplation. At the same time, Teresa herself and her brilliant associates, Ana de Jesús and Ana de San Bartolomé, were writing a new chapter in the history of women by showing uncommon ability as founders and leaders of conventual institutions.

Mysticism provided Spanish women with a way to transcend but not disrupt the control of the male-dominated church. Encouraged by certain influential male theologians who praised women for their piety and spiritual attainments, many sought to imitate the great female contemplatives of the past. The late-thirteenth-century mystic Gertrude the Great, whose writings were known through a Spanish translation of the works of Louis de Blois, inspired Teresa herself, while her own spiritual biography and mystical writings served as an inspiration for such figures as Rose of Lima.

The remarkable influence gained by such figures as Gabriela de San Joseph and María de Jesús de Agreda, however, should not be allowed to obscure the fact that the reception of female mystical experiences depended absolutely on the approval of the male-dominated church and monarchy. Sor María de la Visitación, who offended the government of King Philip II by openly calling for Spain to relinquish control over Portugal, immediately lost the support of the Holy Office in spite of her high rank, position as prioress, mystical fervor, levitations, and stigmata. As for the so-called feigned mystics, whose story has been chronicled in this book, their lower social status, uneven educational attainments, and weak understanding of theology left them open to persecution by a tribunal already deeply concerned by the persistence of Illuminism. The powerful influence that "spiritual mothers" such as Isabel de la Cruz had exercised over their male followers during the early sixteenth century was a warning that the Inquisition could not ignore.

Paradoxically, alongside this cautious, even hostile approach to female mysticism, the Holy Office and the male-dominated hierarchy were eager to believe and accept the validity of such supernatural phenomena as visions, revelations, and stigmata. In an age of religious competition, mystical transports were a sign that God still favored the devout Catholic with divine communication. If these favors were bestowed upon women in spite of their generally accepted emotional weakness, intellectual inferiority, and vulnerability to demonic manipulation, so much the better as a manifestation of God's wonderful generosity to his faithful. Pious credulity, as shown by the eagerness with which certain of the censors charged with reviewing the biographies of women mystics overlooked or explained away the faults of their subjects, has always been and still is a part of the institutional culture of the Roman Catholic Church. But to enjoy this degree of indulgence, the women had to have the correct pedigree, belong to a powerful religious order, and enjoy the support of prominent religious advisors and wealthy laypeople. Above all, the content of her visions and revelations had to confirm orthodox catholic belief and practice as defined by male theologians. Even with all of these advantages, as both Teresa of Jesus and María de Jesús de Agreda were to discover, the woman mystic was not immune to the scrutiny of the Holy Office.

During the post-Tridentine period, the spiritual transports and worldly achievements of Spain's women mystics succeeded only in reinforcing the power and control of the male-dominated church. But in the long run, the remarkable record left behind by some of these women, especially Teresa of Jesus, inspired other women all over the Catholic world and gained the grudging admiration of men. The long and arduous road to the emancipation of women, probably the most important social phenomenon of our times, once passed through the narrow, tortured path blazed by Spanish women mystics whose lives were held up for imitation by a growing chorus of admiring male hagiographers.

Epilogue

As the editors of the new theological journal *Iglesia Viva* indicated in their first issue in 1966, the Spanish church was woefully unprepared to appreciate, understand, and implement either the new ecclesiology or the new liberalism of the Second Vatican Council.[90] Several years later, Archbishop Vicente Enrique y Tarancón described the singularly uncomfortable position in which the church found itself when he commented, "The Council surprised everyone. But for historical reasons and because of the social context in Spain, the surprise was much greater for us Spaniards."[91]

The historical and social context that Archbishop Tarancón was referring to, of course, was the continuing strength of the values, theology, liturgy, and ecclesiology of the Counter-Reformation, which had endured in Spain so much longer than in other Catholic countries. It was that same Counter-Reformation ethos, with its emphasis on the ways in which the deity demonstrated continued support for his church through miracles and revelations, that created and sustained the great age of Spanish women mystics in the sixteenth and seventeenth centuries.[92] During that period, the miraculous achievements of spiritual women (and men), published in officially approved biographies, could be used to confound Protestants, Jews, and heretics and perhaps win converts for the true faith. At the same time, those who advanced false claims to sanctity could be punished by the Inquisition, thereby making it clear to the faithful that only the most ascetic, penitent, and spiritual of women would be honored by divine communication.

After King Ferdinand VII's failure to reestablish the Inquisition when he reassumed full power in 1823, the church found that it had lost the one institution that could make valid and acceptable normative decisions in matters relating to the receipt of supernatural favors. At the same time, the church needed the miraculous and the supernatural more than ever. This time, however, the enemy was not heresy or Protestantism but irreligion, skepticism, and anticlericalism. In spite of the lack of a normative institution, therefore, the church continued to sponsor and support women mystics who claimed divine revelation, curative powers, and the stigmata. Sor María Florencia Trinidad, the Mercedarian nun who had remarkable visions of the passion and carried the stigmata on her body, and the Dominican Bárbara de Santo Domingo, who died in 1872 after a brief but glorious career of penance and mystical transports, were just two in a long line of women mystics during the nineteenth and early twentieth centuries.[93] In the relationship between Queen Isabel II and the stigmatic María Micaela del Sacramento, the nineteenth century even saw a repeat of the emotional and spiritual dependence of a guilt-ridden monarch on a woman mystic that was reminiscent of the relationship between King Philip IV and María de Agreda.[94]

But the church could no longer command the unswerving and almost uncritical loyalty of Spain's cultural, political, and intellectual elite. The sharp divisions between the liberal Catholics of the nineteenth and twentieth centuries, who were willing to accept constitutional monarchy, toleration, and republicanism, and conservatives who rejected the institutions of modern society created tremendous conflict.[95] However much the faithful demonstrated their support for traditional values and beliefs, there were many others who expressed open skepticism.

The Madrid journalist José Nakens, whose satirical pieces entertained a whole generation of anticlericals at the turn of the century, mocked the credulity and ignorance of Spain's conservative Catholics. Among his favorite targets were women who pretended sanctity through visions, miraculous cures, and visits from the souls of purgatory. One story, included in a collection of Nakens's work published in 1913, involved Bernarda, a celebrated miracle worker from Fontiveros, a rural hamlet about midway between Salamanca and Segovia. To increase her reputation, Bernarda concocted a scheme with a local innkeeper to have one of his friends pretend to be crippled so that she could "cure" him in a particularly spectacular way. On the appointed day, in front of a multitude of Bernarda's followers, the false lame man appeared on crutches, ready to be cured. But unbeknownst to Bernarda, who had never met the innkeeper's friend, man who was really disabled had slipped in among the throng, and it was he that Bernarda interviewed.

After going through a series of routine questions, the miracle worker announced in a loud voice that with God's inspiration and the "assistance of my relative Saint John of the Cross, I declare you cured as of this moment." She then ordered the man to cast away his crutches. Without hesitating more than a few seconds, he abandoned his crutches and promptly fell to the ground, almost breaking his one good leg. Astonished by the failure of the miracle cure, the crowd began laughing, and the entire scene threatened to turn ugly. But Bernarda proved able to cope with the situation and reconciled her followers by blaming the crippled man. The failure of her efforts to cure him, she said, was a direct result of his own lack of faith.[96]

José Nakans filled this book—and another one he published in 1912—with these anecdotes of clerical cupidity and superstition, but a more serious indictment of the penitential life in general and mysticism in particular is contained in a novel by S. Pey Ordeix published in Barcelona in 1931. In *Sor Sicalipsis*, Pey Ordeix tells the story of a young girl from a comfortable middle-class family who fell under the influence of her confessor and decided to join his religious order.[97] So far, the story could have been taken out of the pages of one of the adulatory biographies that have provided the raw material for so much of this book, but in the ensuing chapters, we realize that instead of finding God through her decision she loses her true self.

Depressed by the loss of her pretty clothes and reflecting bitterly on the fact that she was now a "mother without children," Ipsis made an extremely difficult adjustment to convent life, further complicated by her fear that she was pregnant by her confessor.[98] After the pregnancy proved a false alarm, Ipsis resolved to dedicate herself to a life of mystical contemplation in order to "rise to that level of perfection that is attained only by those who reach union with God."

At first, the life of prayer, abstinence, physical penance, and austerity that Ipsis had chosen for herself gave her great satisfaction. The painful *cilicio* became her friend, and even scourging, which she had at first detested, became agreeable. Like the women mystics of the Counter-Reformation, she rejected the corruption and materialism of the world and "seemed more like the burning flame of divine love than a creature of mere flesh and blood."[99]

But Ipsis was soon disabused of the notion that these mystical transports would make her happy. Already warned by her second confessor, a hard-bitten old monk who had seen many spiritually ambitious postulants fall by the wayside, Ipsis became disillusioned by the meaningless rounds of monastic routine and the rules that began to seem more and more senseless. She rapidly abandoned the mysticism that had once seemed so satisfying and began to spend sleepless nights and lose weight. She realized that the needs of the body could not so easily be denied, and that flesh and spirit were part of the same organism and could not be separated. Bitterly reproaching Father Sical, her lover and first confessor, for deceiving her into taking up a life that she now detested, she asked him whether he had brought her into the order "in the name of God or the devil."[100] Stricken by remorse for having destroyed the woman he loved, Sical could no longer function as a preacher and spiritual advisor. Since both were now an embarrassment to the order, the father superior decided to send Sor Ipsis and Father Sical as missionaries to an area from which few had emerged alive. When asked by the captain of the ship what they expected to find in such a savage land, they answered, "Death, the only true nuptials of the godly, whose embrace is the first signal of eternal love."[101]

In an increasingly secular world, where the mysteries of disease were slowly but surely falling victim to science's growing knowledge and the insecurities of life were yielding to improved social organization, the age of the mystic was passing. Today, the Congregation for the Causes of Saints considers few mystics for canonization and approves none on the basis of their mystical experiences alone.[102] Moreover, reform of the Roman calendar in 1969 and the changes introduced by Pope John Paul II in 1983 had the effect of significantly reducing the mythical and supernatural as fundamental components of sanctity. The Roman calendar no longer includes many saints whose cult had no solid foundation in historical scholarship. In 1983 the number of miracles required for the beatification of nonmartyrs and for canonization itself was reduced by half. These reforms led to a substantial increase in the pace of canonization in recent years, but dethroning the miracle as the basis for sanctity does not necessarily resonate well with the Catholics who still define themselves as practicing. For many of these people, the supernatural and the miraculous remain the touchstone of their faith. The continued relevance of the cultural ideals of the Counter-Reformation in today's world is evidenced by the amazing popularity of the Medjugorje site in Bosnia. Braving primitive roads and the threat of violence, ten to twenty million pilgrims have visited the site since 1981, when local children reported that Mary appeared to them, calling herself the Queen of Peace.[103]

Confronted with the need to modernize and "rationalize" its canonization procedures on the one hand and the evidence of popular devotion to the miraculous on the other, the church's response has been divided and hesitant.

Taking into account the fact that medical advances have left little room for the miraculous cures that comprised the overwhelming majority of miracles, the congregation has begun taking up the causes of holy individuals with nonmedical physical miracles.[104] The church hierarchy has also investigated but so far failed to endorse popular devotion to the Dutch visionary Ida Peerdeman and the Worcester, Massachusetts, cult surrounding Audrey Santos.[105] But whatever the criteria for canonization, the church still needs saints whose superabundance of faith and outstanding spiritual gifts will continue to provide inspiration for the faithful.

Notes

Introduction

1. Luis Ignacio Zevallos, S.J., *Vida y virtudes, favores del cielo, milagros y prodigos de la V. Madre Sor María Ángela Astorch, religiosa capuchina fundadora en la ciudad de Murcia de su illustre convento de capuchinas de la exaltación del santissimo sacramento* (Madrid: Gerónimo Roxo, 1733), 7–9.

2. Jean Clandinin and Michael Connelly, "Personal Experience Methods," in *Collecting and Interpreting Qualitative Materials*, ed. Norman K. Denzin and Yvonna S. Lincoln (Thousand Oaks, Calif.: Sage, 1998), 156, 159.

3. Other pioneering works on the sociology of sainthood include the numerous works of Hippolyte Delehaye, especially *Les légendes hagiographiques* (Brussels, 1955), and John Mecklin, *The Passing of the Saint: A Study of a Culture Type* (Chicago: University of Chicago Press, 1941). I have also found inspiration in the fascinating work of the sociologist Ptirim A. Sorokin, especially *Altruistic Love: A Study of American "Good Neighbors" and Christian Saints* (Boston, 1950; New York: Kraus Reprint, 1969). For another interesting approach to the social history of sainthood, see Pierre Delooz, "Pour une étude sociologique de la sainteté canoniseé dans l'église catholique," *Archives de Sociologie des Religions* 13 (1962): 17–43.

4. Evidence of the quantity of material available to the authors of spiritual biographies abound in the text and commentary by the official censors. The religious orders were particularly willing to furnish these materials to anyone who wished to write a biography of one of their number because that would reflect favorably on the order and help in the canonization process. In the introduction to his biography of Francisca del Santissimo Sacramento, Miguel Batista de Lanuza mentions that he made use of accounts of her spiritual life written by two nuns who lived in the same convent, as well as other records that had been furnished to him by several generals of the Carmelite order. Batista de Lanuza's access to the well-stocked archive was confirmed by Fray Joseph de Santa Teresa, the order's official chronicler, who acted as one of the censors of the biography. For its part, the order was extremely happy to provide Batista de Lanuza with material because he was a member of the Council of Aragon and had already written

five other spiritual biographies of Carmelite nuns. Miguel Batista de Lanuza, *Vida de la sierva de Dios Francisca del Santissimo Sacramento* (Pamplona: Joseph Martínez, 1727), 36, 37, 232. For an example of a notarized account of a miracle that was later used by a biographer, see Andres de Moya Salaberria, *Vida prodigiosa de admirable exercicio de virtudes de la V. M. Sor Martina de los Angeles y Arilla religiosa del convento de Santa Fe de Zaragoza* (Madrid: Antonio Marín, 1735), 103–104.

5. Isabelle Poutrin, *Le voile et la plume: autobiographie et sainteté féminine dans l'Espagne moderne* (Madrid: Casa de Velázquez, 1995), 268, 276–277. For an example of how a biographer was able to produce a text superior to the autobiography itself, see the life of María Vela written by her last confessor, Miguel González Vaquero. Evidently, Vaquero was able to interview certain close associates of his subject and thereby correct the false impression of extreme solitude that she sought to give in her autobiography, no doubt because it more closely matched the ideal of sainthood.

6. Sara Cabibbo and Marilena Modica, *La Santa dei Tomasi. Storia di suor Maria Crocifissa* (Turin: Editorial Enuadi, 1989).

7. William Christian, *Local Religion in Sixteenth Century Spain* (Princeton, N.J.: Princeton University Press, 1981). Rural saint cults and their relationship to popular pilgrimages or *romerias* are discussed in Pierre Sanchis, "The Portuguese 'Romarias,'" in *Saints and Their Cults: Studies in Religious Sociology, Folklore and History*, ed. Stephen Wilson (Cambridge: Cambridge University Press, 1983), 261–289.

8. Poutrin, *Le voile et la plume*, 250.

9. Richard L. Kagan, *Lucrecia's Dreams: Politics and Prophecy in Sixteenth Century Spain* (Berkeley: University of California Press, 1990).

10. Jodi Bilinkoff, *The Avila of Saint Teresa: Religious Reform in a Sixteenth Century City* (Ithaca, N.Y.: Cornell University Press, 1989).

11. Francisco Silvela, *Cartas de la Venerable Madre sor María de Agreda y el rey Felipe IV* (Madrid: Establecimientos Sucesores de Rivadeneyra, 1885); Joaquín Pérez Villanueva, "Sor María de Agreda y Felipe IV: Un epistolerio en su tiempo," in *Historia de la Iglesia en España*, ed. Ricardo García Villoslada. 5 vols. (Madrid: La Editorial Católica, 1979) 4, pt. 1:359–417.

12. Judith C. Brown, *Immodest Acts: The Life of a Lesbian Nun in Renaissance Italy* (Oxford: Oxford University Press, 1986).

13. A. G. Dickens, *The Counter-Reformation* (New York: Norton, 1979), 22–26.

Chapter 1

1. D. P. Walker, *Spiritual and Demonic Magic from Ficino to Campanella* (London: Warburg Institute, 1958), 108.

2. Christopher Hill, *The Century of Revolution, 1603–14* (New York: Norton, 1966), 179–180.

3. Henry Charles Lea, *A History of the Inquisition of Spain*, 4 vols. (New York: Macmillan, 1906–7), 4:357–358.

4. Antonio Mestre, *Ilustración y reforma de la iglesia; pensamiento político-religioso de Don Gregorio Mayáns y Siscar* (Valencia: Ayuntamiento de Oliva, 1968), 161–162. Inquisitor-General Manual Quintano Bonifaz (1755–74) was a strong supporter of the cult (202).

5. José María López Piñero, *Ciencia y técnica en la sociedad española de los siglos XVI y XVII* (Barcelona: Labor, 1979), 146–147.

6. Ibid., 142–43.

7. Henry Kamen, *Spain 1469–1714: A Society of Conflict* (London: Longman, 1991), 253.

8. Henry Kamen, *Inquisition and Society in Spain in the Sixteenth and Seventeenth Centuries* (Bloomington: Indiana University Press, 1985), 84.

9. Marcelin Defourneaux, *L'Inquisition espagnole et les livres français au XVIII siècle* (Paris: PUF, 1963), 146–147.

10. Traditional Aristotelianism and an intense interest in the occult dominated intellectual life in the Habsburg monarchy as well. There were also strong, but as yet not well understood, cultural relations between Spain and leading intellectuals active in Austria and Bohemia. R. J. W. Evans, *The Making of the Habsburg Monarchy 1550–1700* (Oxford: Clarendon Press, 1979), 318–323, 348–380. In England, even after the Restoration removed many leading scientists from the universities, the Dissenting academies maintained the tradition. It is difficult to imagine such institutions developing in the repressive atmosphere of Counter-Reformation Spain. Hill, *The Century of Revolution*, 293.

11. Juan Eusebio Nieremberg, *Oculta filosofía de la sympatia y antipatia de las cosas, artificio de la naturaleza y noticia natural del mundo* (Madrid: Imprenta del Reino, 1636), 33.

12. It is doubtful that open advocacy of the Copernican system would have been possible in Spain after Galileo's condemnation, given the extremely repressive atmosphere described here. The difficulties that Galileo and other Copernican advocates faced stands in sharp contrast to the freedom with which Copernican ideas could be espoused in Holland and England. John Hedley Brooke, *Science and Religion: Some Historical Perspectives* (Cambridge: Cambridge University Press, 1991), 100–109.

13. Nieremberg, *Oculta filosofía*, 21v–22.

14. Walker, *Spiritual and Demonic Magic*, 13–14.

15. Evans, *The Making of the Habsburg Monarchy*, 346–380. Valuable scientific work was conducted in optics, hydraulics, and atmospheric pressure.

16. Virgilio Pinto Crespo, *Inquisición y control ideológico en La España del siglio XVI* (Madrid: Taurus, 1983), 287–292.

17. AHN, Inquisition, March 18, 1680, leg. 804, exp. 2; October 7, 1732, leg. 514, f. 60.

18. J. H. Elliott, *Imperial Spain 1469–1716* (New York: New American Library, 1966), 242.

19. Gale E. Christianson, *In the Presence of the Creator: Isaac Newton and His Times* (New York: Free Press, 1984), 353.

20. Nieremberg, *Oculta filosofía*, 86v-87.

21. In his *Sueños del infierno,* Francisco Quevedo condemned natural scientists for transgressing the prerogatives of the Creator and located astrologers and alchemists in hell immediately behind the leaders of the Protestant movement. They had been condemned for their "diabolical activities." Alessandreo Martinengo, "De la intolerancia intelectual: algo más sobre los herejes del Sueño del Infierno," in *Les problèmes de l'exclusion en Espagne*, ed. Augustin Redondo (Paris: Publications de la Sorbonne, 1983), 219–226.

22. Fr. Antonio de Lorea, *La venerable madre Sor María de la Santissima Trinidad religiosa de la tercera orden de Santo Domingo* (Madrid: Francisco Sánchez, 1671), 81–82.

23. Fr. Francisco de Acosta, *Vida prodigiosa y heroicas virtudes de la V. M. María de Jesús Carmelita descalza de Toledo* (Madrid: Domingo García y Morrás, 1648), 434.

24. Fr. Antonio Arbiol, *Ejemplar de religiosas en la penitente, virtuosa y maravillosa vida de la venerable Sor Jacinta de Atondo* (Zaragoza: Manuel Roman, 1716), 167–169, 172–174.

25. Fr. Juan Interian de Ayala, *Epitome de la admirable vida, virtudes y milagros de Santa María de Cervellón* (Salamanca: Eugenio García, 1695), 157–168.

26. Kamen, *Spain 1469–1714*, 192.

27. Antonio Domínguez Ortiz and Bernard Vincent, *Historia de los moriscos, vida y tragedia de una minoría* (Madrid: Revista de Occidente, 1978), 122–124.

28. Vicente da Costa Mattos, *Discurso contra los judíos*, trans. Fr. Diego Gavilan Vega (Madrid: Viuda de Melchor Alegre, 1680), 126–131.

29. López Piñero, *Ciencia y técnica de*, 395. (see note 5)

30. Arbiol, *Ejemplar de religiosas*, 567–570.

31. Fr. Manuel de San Gerónimo, *Edades y virtudes, empleos, y prodigios de l a V. M. Gabriela de San Joseph, religiosa carmelita descalza en su convento de la concepción de Ubeda* (Jaen: Tómas Copado, 1703), 103.

32. Luis de la Puente, S.J., *Tesoro escondido en las enfermedades y trabajos* (Madrid: Manuel Fernandez, 1750), 2–6, 11–21.

33. Fray Francisco de San Bernardo, *Vida del prodigioso Job destos siglos, el Venerable Padre Fray Tomás de la Virgen* (Madrid: Roque Rico de Miranda, 1678), 37.

34. Ibid., 460.

35. Ibid., 505.

36. AHN, Inquisition, January 25, 1576, leg. 113, exp. 5.

37. AHN, Inquisition, June 3, 1639, leg. 102, exp. 5.

38. Louis Cardaillac, "Vision simplifcatrice des groupes marginaux par le groupe dominant dans l'Espagne des XVI et XVII siècles," in Redondo, *Les problèmes*, 17. Jack Weiner, "La *Numancia* de Cervantes y la alianza entre Dios y Israel," *Neophilologus* 81 (1997): 63–64.

39. Bartolomé Bennassar, *Recherches sur les grandes épidémies dans le Nord de l'Espagne à la fin du XVI siècle* (Paris: S.E.V.P.E.N., 1969), 11.

40. Vicente Pérez Moreda, *Las crisis de mortalidad en la España interior* (Madrid: Siglo Veintiuno, 1980), 280, 304–305.

41. Angel García Sanz, *Desarrollo y crisis del Antiguo Régimen en Castilla la Vieja: economía y sociedad en tierras de Segovia, 1500–1814* (Madrid: Akal, 1977), 94–95; Kamen, *Spain 1469–1714*, 226; James Casey, *The Kingdom of Valencia in the Seventeenth Century* (Cambridge: Cambridge University Press, 1979), 65–66.

42. Casey, *The Kingdom of Valencia*, 69, 86–89.

43. García Sanz, *Desarrollo y crisis*, 216–219.

44. Michael Weisser, "The Decline of Castile Revisited: The Case of Toledo," *Journal of European Economic History*, 2 (1973):625–627, 631.

45. Elliott, *Imperial Spain*, 337–353.

46. Arbiol, *Ejemplar de religiosas*, 254.

47. Fernando Martínez Gil, *Muerte y sociedad en la España de las Austrias* (Madrid: Siglo Veintiuno, 1993), 39.

48. Isabel de Jesús, *Tesoro del carmelo escondido en el campo de la iglesia, hallado y descubierto en la muerte y vida que de si dexó escrita por orden de su confesor la venerable madre Isabel de Jesús* (Madrid: Julian de Paredes, 1685), 522.

49. Fr. Antonio de Lorea, *Las siervas de Dios Sor Catalina de San Lucas y Sor María de San Andrés religiosas de la esclaracida orden de Santo Domingo en el monesterio de la Encarnación de la villa de Almagro* (Valencia: Vicente Cabrera, 1671), 102–104.

50. AHN, Inquisition, July 17, 1639, leg. 102, exp. 2.

51. Kamen, *Spain, 1469–1714*, 234.

52. Jean Vilar, *Literatura y economía: la figura satírica del arbitrista en el siglo de oro* (Madrid: Revista de Occidente, 1973), 247–272.

53. J. H. Elliott, *The Count-Duke of Olivares: The Statesman in an Age of Decline* (New Haven: Yale University Press, 1988), 553–558.

54. Juan Eusebio Nieremberg, *Causa y remedio de los males públicos* (Madrid: María de Quiñones, 1642), 3, 17.

55. Ibid., 27.

56. Stephen Haliczer, *Sexuality in the Confessional; A Sacrament Profaned* (New York: Oxford University Press, 1996), 56–57.

57. Francisco Xarque, *Sacra consolatoria del tiempo en las guerras y otras calamidades púbicas de la Casa de Austria y Católica monarquia* (Valencia: Garriz, 1642), 35, 120, 241.

58. Ronald Cueto Ruiz, "La tradición profética en la monarquía católica en los siglos 15, 16, y 17," *Arquivos do Centro Cultural Portugues* 17 (1982):412–413.

59. Marcel Bataillon, *Erasmo y España* (Mexico, D.F.: Fondo de Cultura Ecónomica, 1950), 54–55, 63–65, 69–71, 177–178.

60. Ricardo García Cárcel, *Orígenes de la Inquisición Española: el tribunal de Valencia* (Barcelona: Península, 1976), 101–107.

61. Richard Kagan, *Lucrecia's Dreams, Politics and Prophecy in sixteenth Century Spain* (Berkeley: University of California Press, 1990), 129.

62. Ibid., 181.

63. Palma Martínez-Burgos García, *Ídolos e imágenes: La controversia del arte religioso en el siglo XVI español* (Valladolid: Universidad de Valladolid, 1990), 128, 137.

64. *The Complete Works of Saint Teresa of Jesus*, trans. E. Allison Peers, vol. 3, *Book of the Foundations* (London: Sheed and Ward, 1946), 142.

65. AHN, Inquisition, January 25, 1576, leg. 113, exp. 5.

66. AHN, Inquisition, April 13, 1578, leg. 113, exp. 5.

67. Fray Luis de Granada, *Historia de Sor María de la Visitación,* ed. Álvaro Huerga (Barcelona: Juan Flors, 1962), 31, 188–189.

68. Ibid., 54–55, 58–59.

69. Kagan, *Lucrecia's Dreams*, 95–99, 101–113.

70. AHN, Inquisition, June 12 and 15, 1628, leg. 3691.

71. Carlos Puyol Buil, *Inquisición y política en el reinado de Felipe IV* (Madrid: CSIC, 1993), 59.

72. Ibid., 71–73.

73. Ibid., 84.

74. Elliott, *The Count-Duke of Olivares*, 278–279.

75. Puyol Buil, *Inquisición y política*, 78–79.

76. Ibid., 81.

77. Ibid., 80.

78. Ibid., 156–159, 251.

79. Ibid., 234.

80. AHN, Inquisition, March 14, 1635, leg. 106, exp. 2. For the public trances that were being held in Madrid at that time, see the testimony of Fr. Pedro Yañez, AHN, Inquisition, November 7, 1639, leg. 102, exp. 5, and the report about the situation in Madrid made to the Toledo tribunal by Francisco Ortiz, AHN, Inquisition, May 19, 1639, leg. 102, exp. 5.

81. AHN, Inquisition, October 29, 1639, leg. 102, exp. 2.

82. AHN, Inquisition, November 11, 1639, leg. 102, exp. 2.

83. AHN, Inquisition, April 23, 1645, leg. 103, exp. 9.

84. BNM, MSS 4015–P51, Pedro González Galindo, "Memorial al rey dando por divinas las revelaciones y visiones de D. Francisco de Chiriboga."

85. Jonathan Brown and J. H. Elliott, *A Palace for a King: The Buen Retiro and the Court of Philip IV* (New Haven: Yale University Press, 1980), 100–104.

86. AHN, Inquisition, July 13, 1639, leg. 102, exp. 2.

87. Elliott, *The Count-Duke of Olivares*, 654–655.

88. AHN, Inquisition, May 22, 1645, leg. 4463, exp. 2.

89. BNM, MSS 2080, Fray Francisco Monteron, "Historia apologetica donde se cuenta el beneficio singular que ha hecho Dios en estos tiempos del año 1643 al rey D. Felipe IV en haverse enbiado a muchos siervos suyos con el espiritu profetico desde diversas partes de la christianidad."

90. José Ximénez de Samaniego, "Prólogo Galeato," *Vida de Sor María de Ágreda* in *Biblioteca de Autores Españoles*, vol. 109, ed. Carlos Seco Serrano (Madrid: Atlas, 1958), 276–277.

91. Joaquín Pérez Villanueva, "Sor María de Ágreda y Felipe IV en epistolario en su tiempo" in Ricardo Garcia Villosiada ed. *Historia de la Iglesia en España*, 5 vols. (Madrid: La Editorial Católica, 1979), 362–363.

92. Samaniego, "Prologa Galeato," 109:22.

Chapter 2

1. The ignorance of the parish priests in the Basque region shocked Inquisitor Alonso de Salazar Frias when he visited the region. AHN, Inquisition, January 28, 1617, leg. 1679, exp. 2.

2. Jaime Contreras and Gustav Henningsen, "Forty-Four Thousand Cases of the Spanish Inquisition (1540–1700): Analysis of a Historical Data Bank," in *The Inquisition in Early Modern Europe: Studies on Sources and Methods*, ed. Gustav Henningsen, John Tedeschi, and Charles Amiel (DeKalb: Northern Illinois University Press, 1986), 118.

3. Pedro de Ribadeneyra, *Flos Sanctorum, de las vidas de los santas* (Madrid: Joachin Ibarra, 1761) "prologo al lector," np.

4. Villegas, *Flos Sanctorum*, f. 6v.

5. Fernando Martínez Gil, *Muerte y sociedad, en la España de las Austrias* (Madrid: Siglo Veintiuno, 1993), 74.

6. Virgilio Pinto Crespo, *Inquisición y control ideológico, en la España del siglo XVI* (Madrid: Taurus, 1983), 276.

7. Villegas, *Flos Sanctorum*, ffs. 88–96. 163–164, 23v–24.

8. Ribadeneyra, *Flos Sanctorum*, 1–65, 66–76.

9. José Simón Díaz, "Hagiografías individuales publicadas en español de 1480 á 1700," *Hispania Sacra*, 30 (1977):6–60.

10. Ibid., 50, 52, 58.

11. Muñoz's biographies included one on St. Charles Borromeo, who represented the ideal of the resident bishop personally involved in fostering the spiritual welfare of his flock; the aristocratic Luisa de Carvajal y Mendoza, who went to England in order to convert the English to Catholicism; and the mystic Fr. Luis de Granada.

12. Batista de Lanuza wrote biographies of Francisca del Santissimo Sacramento, Isabel de Santo Domingo, Feliciana de San Joseph, Gerónima de San Estevan, Teresa de Jesús Vela, and Catalina de Cristo.

13. FR. Manuel de San Gerónimo, *Edades y virtudes, empleos, y prodigios de la V.M. Gabriela de San Joseph, religiosa carmelita descalza en su convento de la concepción de Ubeda* (Jaen: Tómas Copado, 1703), ffs. 92, 138, 142v, 169v.

14. Simón Díaz, "Hagiografías individuales," 22–23, 27, 29.

15. Manuel Calisbeta, *Enseñanzas espirituales para el mayor provecho de las almas, doce doctrinas a favor de la comunión cotidiana* (Madrid: Pablo de Val, 1663), 37–38, 41; Simón Díaz, "Hagiografías Individuales," 14, 53.

16. Simón Díaz, "Hagiografías individuales," 17, 19, 43, 47; Alonso de Andrade, *Libro de la Guía de la virtud y de la imitación de Nuestra Señora* (Madrid: Francisco Moroto, 1644).

17. Simón Díaz, "Hagiografías individuales," 22, 28.

18. Jean-Marie Valentin, *Le théâtre des Jésuites dans les pays de langue allemande (1554–1680)*, 3 vols. (Bern: Peter Lang, 1978), 1:386–500; for the northern Habsburgs, especially the influence of Calderon, see 2:839–847. Jean-Marie Valentin, "Gegenreformation und Literatur: das Jesuitendrama im Dienste der religiösen und moralischen Erziehung," *Historisches Jahrbuch*, 100 (1980):240–56.

19. Rafael María de Hornedo, "Teatro e iglesia en los siglos XVII y XVII," in *Historia de la Iglesia en España*, ed. Ricardo García-Villoslada, 5 vols. (Madrid: La Editorial Católica, 1979), 4:312–313.

20. Ibid., 354–355. For the popular appeal of Jesuit theater in Spain, see Jesús Menéndez Paláez, *Los Jesuitas y el teatro en el siglo de oro* (Oviedo: Universidad de Oviedo, 1995), 40–43.

21. Simón Díaz, "Hagiografías individuales," 45.

22. Alberto Vecchi, *Il culto delle immagini nelle stampe popolari* (Firenze: Leo S. Olschki Editore, 1968), 62–65, 72–86.

23. San Gerónimo, *Edades y virtudes*, 97–98.

24. Jerónimo Juan Tous, *Grabadores Mallorquines* (Palma de Mallorca: Diputación Provincial de Baleares, 1977), 57.

25. Fernando Checa Cremades, "La imagen impresa en el Renacimiento y el Manerismo," in *El grabado en España: siglos XV al XVIII* in *Summa Artes: Historia General del Arte,* ed. Juan Carrete Parrondo, Fernando Checa Cremades, and Valeriano Bozal, 32 vols. (Madrid: Espasa Calpe, 1987), 31:165.

26. Émile Mâle, *L'Art religieux de la fin du moyen âge en France* (Paris: Armand Colin, 1932), 14–15.

27. Mario Praz, *Studies in Seventeenth Century Imagery* (Rome: Edizioni di Storia e Letteratura, 1964), 170–171.

28. Inocencio V. Pérez Guillen, "Nuevas fuentes de la pintura de Zurbarán. La estampa didactica Jesuitica," *Goya* 213 (1989), 152–154.

29. Villegas, *Flos Sanctorum*, 2:313–14, Ribadeneyra, *Flos Sanctorum*, 13.

30. Juan Alonso Calderón. *Memorial historico-juridicio-politico que dio a la Magestad Católica del Rey D. Philipe Quarto* (Madrid: Díaz del Carrete, 1651), ffs. 13–14, 20v.

31. Fr. Juan de Torres, *Vida y milagros de Santa Isabel Regna de Portugal* (Madrid: Imprenta Real, 1625), ffs. 9–11, 14–17v, 21v, 42–43.

32. AHN, Inquisition, June 23, 1710, leg. 503/3, exp. 7, ffs. 142v–144. The city of Valencia fell to Bourbon forces on May 8, 1707, but other parts of the kingdom re-

sisted much longer. Henry Kamen, *The War of Succession in Spain 1700–1715* (London: Weidenfeld and Nicolson, 1969), 296.

33. Fr. Antonio Rojo, *Historia de San Diego de Alcalá* (Madrid: Imprenta Real, 1663), 300–301, 309, 311. Philip IV also had the body of the saint brought to the palace in the vain hope that its presence would cure his only son, Prince Felipe Prospero.

34. Antonio de Quintanadueñas, *Serenissima infanta, gloriosa virgen, Doña Sancha Alonso, su vida, sus virtudes, sus milagros* (Madrid: Imprenta Real, 1651), 90–92, 111, 133–135.

35. BNM, MS 9196, March 24, 1696.

36. According to Fr. Gerónimo de Santa Cruz, the author of *Defensa de los estatutos y noblezas españoles,* which appeared in Zaragoza in 1637, only converted Jews stayed behind in the cities of Andalusia when the Moors invaded. The Christians who returned with the victorious armies of the reconquest made no effort to conceal their disdain for these turncoats. Albert Sicroff, *Les controverses des statutes de pureté de sang en Espagne du XV au XVII siècle* (Paris: Marcel Didier, 1960), 240.

37. For the rediscovery and use of the ninth-century account of the Christian martyrs of Córdoba by the sixteenth-century bishop and Inquisitor-General Pedro Ponce de León, who was of Córdoban origin, see Kenneth Wold, *Christian Martyrs in Muslim Spain* (Cambridge: Cambridge University Press, 1988), 36–38.

38. In the introduction to his work on the saints of Córdoba, Martín de Roa announces that his purpose was to celebrate the lives of those who had suffered persecution for their loyalty to the faith by "the Romans because of the conflict over the cross and by the Moors because of their hatred for Christians." He emphasized, however, that although the Romans had been guilty of persecuting Christians, they had been made to suffer to a far greater extent under Moorish domination. Martín de Roa, *Flos Sanctorum, fiestas y santos naturales de la ciudad de Córdoba* (Seville: Alonso Rodriguez Gomarra, 1615).

39. Martín de Roa, S.J., *Ecija, sus santos, su antigüedad ecclesiastica y segular* (Seville: Manuel de Sanda, 1629), 109–109v, 110.

40. Antonio de Quintanadueñas, S.J., *Santos de la cuidad de Sevilla* (Seville: Francisco de Leyra, 1637), 73–75.

41. BNM, MS 6732, "papeles varios de D. Francisco Bejar."

42. Fr. Pedro del Corazón de Jesús, *Glorias de la beata María Ana de Jesús mercedaria descalza publicados en los solemnes fiestas de su beatificación* (Salamanca: Domingo Cosero, 1783), f. 9v.

43. Fr. Antonio de Guzmán, *Historia del inocente trinitario el Santo Niño de la Guardia* (Madrid: Diego Martínez Abad, 1720), 223, 246, 253.

44. Fr. Juan Interain de Ayala, *Epitome de la admirable vida,* virtudes y milagros de Santa María de Cervellon (Salamanca: Eugenio Antonio Garcia, 1695), 162.

45. William A. Christian, *Person and God in a Spanish Valley* (New York: Seminar Press, 1972), 50–76.

46. Bartolomé Cayrasco de Figueroa, *Templo Militante, Flos Santorum y triumphos de sus virtudes* (Lisbon: Pedro Crasbeeck, 1613), "al lector," np.

47. Luis de Mesa, *Vida, favores y mercedes que Christo N.S. hizo a la venerable hermana Mariana de Jesús* (Madrid: Imprenta Real, 1678), "prologo al christiano lector," np.

48. San Gerónimo. *Edades y virtudes,* "dedicatoria a Doña Josepha Manuel de Hozes," np.

49. Cayrasco de Figueroa, *Templo Militante,* ff. 4–4v.

50. BNM, MS 7083.

51. Fr. Antonio de Lorea, *La venerable madre Hipolita de Jesús y Rocaberti, religiosa de la orden de Santo Domingo en el monestario de Nuestra Señora de los Angeles de la ciudad de Barcelona* (Valencia: Vicente Carrera, 1679), 121.

52. Miguel Batista de Lanuza, *Virtudes de la V. M. Teresa de Jesús Vela Carmelita descalza* (Zaragoza: Jusepe Lanaja y Lamarca, 1656), 13.

53. Ibid., 19.

54. AHN, Inquisition, June 8, 1628, leg. 115, exp. 1.

55. Fr. Juan Bernal, *Compendiosa noticia de la ejemplar vida y singulares virtudes de la venerable hermana Francisca Badia* (Valencia: Joseph García, 1755), 191.

56. AHN, Inquisition, December 9, 1675, leg. 114, exp. 6.

57. Poutrin, *Le Voile et la plume*, 72.

58. Simón Díaz, *Hagiografías individuales*, 13–14.

59. Isabel de Llaño, *Historia de la vida, muerte, y milagros de santa Catalina de Sena compuesta en octava rima* (Valladolid: Luis Sánchez, 1604), 2.

60. Ibid., prologue, np.

61. Ibid., 135.

62. Mary Jeremy Finnegan, *The Women of Helfta: Scholars and Mystics* (Athens: University of Georgia Press, 1991), 1.

63. Ibid., 71.

64. José Adriano Moreira de Freitas Carvalho, *Gertrudes de Helfta e Espanha* (Porto: Instituto Nacional de Investigação Científica, 1981), 153, 182.

65. Ibid., 226–227.

66. Finnegan, *The Women of Helfta*, 68–69.

67. Francisco de Ribera, S.J., *La vida de la Madre Teresa de Jesús, fundadora de las descalças y descalços Carmelitas* (Salamanca: Pedro Lasso, 1590), 31–33.

68. Ibid., 89–92, 301–302.

69. Teresa was extremely fortunate in having a biography published only eight years after her death. The biographer, Francisco de Ribera, was a distinguished theologian who would go on to publish a commentary on the Apocalypse of Saint John in 1591 and another on St. Peter's Epistle to the Hebrews in 1598, along with several other biographies of holy persons. Ribera's productivity could only add to his reputation and enhance the value of his endorsement of Teresa.

70. Alonso de Andrade, S.J., *Vida de la gloriosa virgen y abadesa S. Gertrudis de Eyslevio Manspheldense de la orden del glorioso patiarca San Benito* (Madrid: Joseph Fernández de Buendía, 1663), 243–244, 247. In 1647, Andrade had published a two-volume edition of Teresa's *Spiritual Advice* in which he took pains to draw parallels between Teresa's spiritual experiences and those of Gertrudis. Alonso de Andrade, *Avisos espirituales de la gloriosa Madre Santa Teresa de Jesús*, segunda parte. (Madrid: Carlos Sánchez Bravo, 1647), 864, 869–873.

71. In Madrid, miracle-working images of Gertrude were worshiped in two parish churches: San Ildefonso and San Miguel. Both churches commissioned *estampas* of these images to advertise the devotion. BNM, INV. 14328, Juan de la Peña, *Verdadero retrato de la milagrosa imagen de Santa Gertrudis la Magna que se venera en la iglesia de San Ildefonso de Madrid*. BNM, INV. 14329, Bernardo Alviztur, *Gloriosa Virgen Santa Gertrudis La Magna que se venera en la parroquia de San Miguel*.

72. Henry Charles Lea, *A History of the Inquisition of Spain*, 4 vols. (New York: Macmillan, 1906–7) 4:7–12.

73. Moreira de Freitas Carvalho, *Gertrudis de Helfta*, 181. Worries were still being expressed about the publication in Spanish of the revelations of early mystics as late

as 1648. See AHN, Inquisition, April 22, 1648, leg. 4480, exp. 6 for the negative comments of censor Thomas de Herrera concerning publication in the vernacular of the works of Pseudo-Denys the Areopagite.

74. Fr. Leandro de Granada, *Vida y revelaciones de Santa Gertrudis la Magna* (Madrid: Melchor Alcarez, 1689), prologue, np.

75. Diego de Yepes, *Vida, virtudes y milagros de la bienaventurada virgen Teresa de Jesús madre y fundadora de la nueva reformación de la orden de los descalços y descalças de Nuestra Señora del Carmen* (Zaragoza: Angelo Tavanno, 1606), prologo, np.

76. Juan de Horozco y Covarrubias, *Tratado de la verdadera y falsa prophecia* (Segovia: Juan de la Cuesta, 1588), ffs. 24–24v.

77. Moreira de Freitas Carvalho, *Gertrudis de Helfta*, 285, 287.

78. Fr. Pedro de San Cecilio, *Díos prodigioso en Teresa de Jesús niña que murió a los cinco años un mes y diez y siete días* (Madrid: Dionosio Idalgo, 1669), "Al lector," np.

79. Antonio de Quintanadueñas, S.J., *Espejo grande de los trabajos de Jesús crucificado* (Valladolid: Bartolomé Portoles, 1656), 54.

80. Fr. Agustín de San Ildefonso, *Theología mystica, sciencia y sabiduria de Dios misteriosa, oscura, y levantada para muchos* (Madrid, 1683), 102.

81. Fr. Tomás de Montalvo, *Vida prodigiosa de la extatica virgen V. M. Sor Beatriz María de Jesús abadesa que fue del convento del Ángel Custodio de la ciudad de Granada* (Granada: Francisco Domínguez, 1719), 44.

82. Thomas D. Kendrick, *Mary of Agreda: The Life and Legend of a Spanish Nun* (London: Routledge and Kegan Paul, 1967), 163–164.

83. Montalvo, *Vida prodigiosa*, 313.

84. Fr. Antonio de Lorea, *Las siervas de Díos sor Catalina de San Lucas y sor María de San Andrés* (Valencia: Vicente Cabrera, 1671), 184.

85. Antonio Mestre, "Religion y cultura en el siglo XVIII español," in *Historia de la Iglesia en España*, ed. Ricardo García Villoslada, 5 vols. (Madrid: Biblioteca de Autores Cristianos, 1979–80), 4:590.

86. Hilary Dansey Smith, *Preaching in the Spanish Golden Age* (Oxford: Oxford University Press, 1978), 6.

87. Isabel de Jesús, *Tesoro de carmelo escondido en el campo de la iglesia, hallado y descubierto en la muerte y vida que de si dexó escrita por orden de su confesor la venerable madre Isabel de Jesús* (Madrid: Julian de Paredes 1685), 391–392.

88. AHN, Inquisition, June 17, 1628, testimony of Sor Catalina Manuel, leg. 103, exp. 7.

89. Andrés de Moya Salaberria, *Vida prodigiosa, y exercicio admirable de virtudes de la V.M. sor Martina de los Angeles y Arilla.* (Zaragoza: Herederos de Pedro Lanaja y Lamarca, 1678), prologue, np.

90. AHN, Inquisition, September 17, 1730, "meritos de la causa de Ana Rodríguez," leg. 106, exp. 1.

91. AHN, Inquisition, April 8, 1639, leg. 102, exp. 2.

92. AHN, Inquisition, May 22, 1639, leg. 102, exp. 5; April 3, 1634, leg. 107, exp. 4.

Chapter 3

1. Ian Maclean, *The Renaissance Notion of Women* (Cambridge: Cambridge University Press, 1980), 8.

2. Fr. Luis de León, *La perfecta casada* (Barcelona: Hymsa, 1953), 58.

3. Fr. Antonio Arbiol, *Desengaños misticos a las almas detenidas o engañadas en el camino de la perfección* (Zaragoza: Manuel Roman, 1706), 8.

4. AHN, Inquisition, November 6, 1689, leg. 227, exp. 7.

5. AHN, Inquisition, November 12, 1688, leg. 1705, exp. 5.

6. Luis de León, *La perfecta casada*, 275.

7. Ibid.

8. Juan de la Cerda, *Libro intitulado vida política de todos los estados de mujeres* (Alcalá de Henares: Juan Gracián, 1599), 8–9.

9. AHN, Inquisition, April 22, 1626, leg. 1821, exp. 12.

10. Pedro Galindo, *Excelencias de la castidad y virginidad* (Madrid: Mateo de Espinosa y Arteaga, 1681), ffs. 5v-6.

11. Pedro Galindo, *Parte segundo del directorio de penitentes y práctica de una buena y prudente confesión* (Madrid: Antonio de Zafra, 1680), 160.

12. Mariló Vigil, *La vida de las mujeres en los siglos XVI y XVII* (Madrid: Siglo XXI 1986), 37–38.

13. Isabel de Jesús, *Tesoro del carmelo*, 100.

14. AHN, Inquisition, December 1, 1690, leg. 1825, exp. 14.

15. Ricardo del Arco Garay, *La sociedad española en las obras dramáticas de Lope de Vega* (Madrid: Escélicer, 1942), 321; quoted in Vigil, *La vida de las mujeres*, 59.

16. Meelvena Mckindrick, *Women and Society in the Spanish Drama of the Golden Age: A Study of the Mujer Varonil* (Cambridge: Cambridge University Press, 1974), 224; quoted in Vigil, *La vida de las mujeres*, 59.

17. Hipolita de Jesús y Rocaberti, *Libro primero de su admirable vida y doctrina, que escribió de su mano por mandado de sus prelados y confesores* (Valencia: Francisco Mestre, 1679), 326–327. For Hipolita's struggle to learn Latin and her love of Latin books, see Hipolita de Jesús y Rocaberti, *Discurso de mi vida,* ed. Lazaro Iriarte (Madrid: Hermanos Menores Capuchinos de la Provincia de Navarra-Cantabria-Aragón, 1985), 59–61.

18. AHN, Inquisition, November 16, 1688, leg. 1705, exp. 5.

19. AHN, Inquisition, December 28, 1525, leg. 106, exp. 5.

20. AHN, Inquisition, April 26, 1520, leg. 106, exp. 5.

21. AHN, Inquisition, September 9, 1686, leg. 1827, exp. 20.

22. Alvaro Huerga, *Historia de los Alumbrados*, vol. 1, *Los alumbrados de Extremadura (1570–1582)* (Madrid: Fundación Universitaria Española, 1978), 271.

23. AHN, Inquisition, June 13, 1589, leg. 231, exp. 7.

24. Alonso de Andrade, S.J., *Libro de la guía de la virtud, y de la imitación de nuestra señora. Primera parte: para todos los estados* (Madrid: Francisco Maroto, 1642), 94.

25. Alonso de Andrade S.J., *Vida de la gloriosa virgen y abadesa, S. Gertrudis de Eyslevio Mansheldense* (Madrid: Joseph Fernández de Buendía, 1663),"prologo al lector," "toman infinitas mujeres por su santa."

26. Arbiol, *Desengaños misticos*, 65.

27. Pierre Delooz, *Sociologie et canonisations* (The Hague: Martinus Nijhoff, 1969), 37.

28. Peter Burke, "How to Be a Counter-Reformation Saint," in *Religion and Society in Early Modern Europe*, ed. Kaspar von Gregerz (London: George Allen and Unwin, 1984), 46.

29. Fr. Antonio de Lorea, *La venerable madre*, "protestación del autor," np.

30. Peter Burke, "How to Be a Counter-Reformation Saint," 47.

31. BNM, MS 6035 "Sentencia de la priora María de la Visitación priora que fue del monasterio de la anunciada de la ciudad de Lisboa," ffs. 180–198v.

32. Fr. Luis de Granada, "Sermón contra los escándalos en las caídas públicas" in *Monjas y beatas embaucadoras,* ed. Jesús Imirizaldu (Madrid: Editorial Nacional, 1977), 260.

33. Miguel Batista de Lanuza, *Vida de la sierva de Dios Francisca del Santissimo Sacramento* (Pamplona: Joseph Martínez, 1727), 60–61.

34. Francisco de Arcos, *La sabia de Coria, Vida de la venerable María de Jesús* (Madrid: Francisco Nieto, 1671), 164–173.

35. Marcos de Torres, S.J., *Vida y virtudes de la V. S. Doña María de Pol* (Madrid: Pablo de Val, 1661), prologo, np.

36. Andrés de Moya Salaberria, *Vida prodigiosa de la VM Sor Martina de los Angeles* (Zaragoza: Herederos de Pedro Lanaja y Lamdrca, 1678), 240, 254.

37. Peter Burke, *Popular Culture in Early Modern Europe* (New York: Harper and Row, 1978), 237.

38. Henry Kamen, *Inquisition and Society in Spain in the Sixteenth and Seventeenth Centuries* (Bloomington: Indiana University Press, 1985), 202.

39. Burke, *Popular Culture,* 236.

40. Kamen, *Inquisition and Society,* 199.

41. Burke, *Popular Culture,* 229.

42. Burke, "How to Be a Counter-Reformation Saint," 47.

43. Ibid.

44. Stephen Haliczer, *Sexuality in the Confessional: A Sacrament Profaned* (New York: Oxford University Press, 1996), 30.

45. Keith Thomas stressed the way in which the Catholic church blurred the distinction between spells and prayer and "appeared as a vast reservoir of magical power." I follow Thomas in referring to this as "church magic" or "ecclesiastical magic." Keith Thomas, *Religion and the Decline of Magic* (London: Weidenfeld and Nicolson, 1971), 41, 45, 50, 277.

46. Bizente Dacosta Mattos, *Discurso contra los Judíos,* trans. Fr. Diego Gavilan Vega (Madrid: Viuda de Melchor Alegre, 1680), 113, 163, 316–317.

47. Fr. Luis de Granada, *Historia de la admirable vida de Sor María de la Visitación,* ed. Alvaro Hverga (Barcelona: Juan Flors, 1962), 174–179, 296–297, 312–313.

48. Ibid., 147.

49. Batista de Lanuza, *Vida de la sierva de Dios,* 61.

50. Mesa, *Vida, favores y mercedes,* 257–259.

51. Tomás Montalvo, *Vida prodigiosa de la extatica virgen, y venerable Madre sor Beatriz María de Jesus* (Granada: Francisco Dominquez, 1719) 34, 41–45.

52. Carlos Eire, *From Madrid to Purgatory* (Cambridge: Cambridge University Press, 1995), 508.

53. Jusepe Delmau, *Relaciones de los regozijos y fiestas con que celebró esta ciudad de Barcelona la felice beatificación de la Madre Santa Teresa de Jesús* (Barcelona: Sebastián Mathevat, 1614), 628–629.

54. Moya Salaberria, *Vida prodigiosa,* 253.

55. Fr. Antonio Arbiol, *Epitome de la virtuosa y evangelica vida de Fray Ignacio García fundador y guardian del colegio seminario de misioneros apostólicos de la regular observancia de S. Francisco de la villa de Calamocha* (Zaragoza: Pedro Carreras, 1720), 66.

56. Batista de Lanuza, *Vida de la Sierva de Díos*, 237.

57. BNM MS 20711–8. Those who expressed doubts about Teresa's miracles, like the Bishop of Guadix, had to face the hostility of her supporters, especially among the Jesuits. BNM, MS. 20711–9. Eire, *From Madrid to Purgatory*, 379–380.

58. Francisco Morovelli de Puebla, *Defiende el patronato de Santa Teresa de Jesús, patrona illustrissima de España, y responde a Francisco de Quevedo* (Malaga: Juan Renè, 1628), ffs. 6, 14, 17.

59. Francisco de Quevedo, "Memorial por el patronato de Santiago," in *Obras Completas*, ed. Felicidad Buendia, 2 vols. (Madrid: Aguilar, 1981).

60. Morovelli de Puebla, *Defiende el patronato*, 15.

61. Quevedo, *Memorial*, 232, 234.

62. Juan Pablo Martyr Rizo, *Defensa de la verdad que escrivió D. Francisco de Quevedo Villegas en favor del patronato del apostol único patron de España* (Malaga: Juan Renè, 1628), nf.

63. Ibid., f. 23v.

64. Teresa de Jesús, *The Complete Works of Saint Teresa of Jesus*, trans. and ed., E. Allison Peers 11th ed., 3 vols. (London: Sheed and Ward, 1982), 1, xliv.

65. BNM, MS 872. Mariana de Jesús, "Espejo purissimo de la vida, passion, muerte y resurrección de Cristo bien nuestro manifestado por el mismo a una sierva suya religiosa descalza de la orden del seraficio padre S. Francisco en San Antonio de la ciudad de Trujillo" (1617), ffs. 202–204.

66. Mckindrick, *Women and Society*, 80.

67. Ibid., 52–58, 68–69, 227, 232.

68. Juan de Espinosa, *Dialogo en laude de las mujeres*, ed. Angela González Simón, 2d ed. (Madrid: CSIC, 1946), 17.

69. Ibid., 311.

70. Juan Pérez de Moya, *Varia historia de santas e illustres mujeres en todo genero de virtudes* (Madrid: Francisco Sánchez, 1583), prologo, np.

71. Ibid., ffs. 153v–154, 201v–203v.

72. Ibid., ffs. 268, 320.

73. Ibid., f. 231v.

74. Andrade, *Libro de la guía de la virtud*, 3:130–132.

75. Ibid., 133–134, 142–146.

76. Bernardino de Villegas, *La esposa de Cristo instruido con la vida de Santa Lutgarda virgen monja de S. Bernardo* (Madrid: Juan Fernandez de Fuentes, 1635), 555–556.

77. Miguel Batista de Lanuza, *Vida de la venerable madre Jerónima de San Esteban carmelita descalza* (Zaragoza: Domingo de la Puyada, 1653), "al lector," np.

78. Montalvo, *Vida prodigiosa*, "Censura de los RR. PP. Fr. Pascual Ximénez Lector de Theologia y Fr. Juan Cebrian Predicador," np.

79. AHN, Inquisition, "papeles originales tocantes al espiritu de María Antonia Hortola," leg. 532, exp. 1.

80. Francisco de Acosta, Fray. *Vida prodigiosa, y heroicas virtudes de la V.M. María de Jesús* (Madrid: Domingo García y Morrás, 1648), 333.

81. A typical example of the organization of women for devotional practices was the group of neighborhood women formed by Isabel de Briñas to say the rosary in unison. Her confessor Juan de la Puente supervised the group. AHN, Inquisition, September 22, 1639, leg. 102, exp. 5.

82. Espinosa, *Dialogo en laude*, 247–249.

83. Montalvo, *Vida prodigiosa*, dedication, np.

84. Manuela de la Santissima Trinidad, *Fundación del convento de la Purissima Concepción de franciscas descalzas de la ciudad de Salamanca* (Salamanca: María Estevez, 1696), 121–122.

85. Fr. Alonso de Villerino, *Esclarecido solar de las religiosas recoletas de nuestro padre San Augustín*, 2 vols. (Madrid: Bernarda de Villa-Diego, 1690), 2:506–508.

86. Pinto Crespo, *Inquisición y control*, 87.

87. Fr. Lope Paez, *Espejo de virtudes en la vida y muerte de la venerable madre Francisca Inés de la Concepción* (Toledo: Juan Ruiz de Pareda, 1653), "aprobación," np.

88. Batista de Lanuza, *Vida de la venerable madre*, "Remission del Señor Doctor D. Juan Chrisostomo de Exea en 6 de Noviembre de 1653 al Señor D. Diego Antonio Frances de Urrutigati."

89. Poutrin, *Le voile et la plume*, 253.

90. Batista de Lanuza, *Vida de la sierva de Díos*, "Respuesta del ilustrissimo y reverendissimo Señor Inquisidor general a la dedicatoria y lo que de este escrito siente su ilustrissima," July 2, 1659, np.

91. Ibid., "Censura del nunca dionamente alabado venerable padre Juan Eusevio Nieremberg," March 20, 1658, 55–57.

92. Fr. Antonio Daza, *Historia, vida y milagros de la bienaventurada virgen Santa Juana de la Cruz* (Madrid: Luis Sánchez, 1610), September 16, 1610, np.

93. Poutrin, *Le voile et la plume*, 248.

94. Daza, *Historia, vida y milagros*, "Paracer y censura del maestro Fray Don Ignacio de Ibero," September 16, 1610, np.

95. Montalvo, *Vida prodigiosa*, "Aprobación del M.R.P. Fr. Juan de Ascargorta."

96. Ibid., "Censura del M.R.P. Fray Francisco de Silva," December 17, 1713, np.

97. A.G. Dickens, *The Counter-Reformation* (New York: Norton, 1979), 114.

98. Lea, *A History of the Inquisition*, 2:21–23.

99. Galindo, *Parte segundo del directorio de penitentes*, 501–502.

100. Diego Franco de Villalba, *La heroica religiosa Sor Inés de Jesús y Franco* (Zaragoza: Francisco Revilla, 1733), 34.

101. Manuel de San Gerónimo, *Edades y virtudes, empleos y prodigios, de la V.M. Gabriela de San Joseph.* (Jaen: Tómas Copado, 1703), 68.

102. Fr. Fernando de San Antonio Capilla, *Vida singular de la madre María de Christo venerable por esclarecida virgen y por fundadora de los beaterios de La Parra y Almendradejo* (Madrid: Manuel Ruiz de Murga, 1716), 110–111.

103. Moya Salaberria, *Vida prodigiosa*, 196, 200–201.

104. Fr. Antoinio de Lorea, *La venerable madre*, 199–201.

105. Moya Salaberria, *Vida prodigiosa*, 122, 125, 134.

106. AHN. Inquisition, September 2, 1666, leg. 1701, exp. 10.

107. AHN, Inquisition, May 11, 1670, leg. 1701, exp. 10.

108. AHN, Inquisition, October 26, 1635, leg. 115, exp. 2.

109. AHN, Inquisition, October 4, 1636, leg. 115, exp. 2.

110. AHN, Inquisition, January 21, 1638, leg. 115, exp. 2.

111. Pedro de Ribadeneyra, S.J. *Flos Sanctorum, de las vidas de los Santos* (Madrid: Joachin Ibarra, 1761), 185–187.

112. AHN, Inquisition, January 22, 1638, leg. 115, exp. 2.

113. AHN, Inquisition, January 19, 1638, leg 115, exp. 2.

114. AHN, Inquisition, August 18, 1675, leg. 118, exp. 6.

115. AHN, Inquisition, December 9, 1675, leg. 118, exp. 6.

116. AHN, Inquisition, July 11, 1675, leg. 118, exp. 6.

117. AHN, Inquisition, December 2, 1675, leg. 118, exp. 6.

118. AHN, Inquisition, April 14, 1639, leg. 102, exp. 2.

119. AHN, Inquisition, July 13, 1639, leg. 102, exp. 2.

120. Montalvo, *Vida prodigiosa de la extatica virgen*, 386, 401.

Chapter 4

1. Weinstein and Bell, *Saints and Society*, 194–195.

2. Raymond de Roover, *The Rise and Decline of the Medici Bank 1397–1494* (New York: Norton, 1966), 10–12.

3. Weinstein and Bell, *Saints and Society*, 196–199.

4. Henry Kamen, *Spain: 1469–1714, A Society of Conflict* (London: Longman, 1991), 245.

5. Stephen Haliczer, *Inquisition and Society in the Kingdom of Valencia, 1478–1834* (Berkeley: University of California Press, 1990),174–176.

6. Fr. Tomás de Montalvo, *Vida prodigiosa, de la extatica virgin y V.M. sor Beatriz María de Jesús* (Granada: Francisco Dominguez 1719), 2.

7. Fr. Antonio de Lorea, *La venerable madre, Hipolita de Jesús Rocaberti religiosa de la orden de Santo Domingo* (Valencia: Vicente Cabrera, 1679), 3–4.

8. Batista de Lanuza, *Vida de la venerable madre,* "censura del muy R. P. Gerónimo de San Josef," November 28, 1653. np.

9. Fr. Juan de Palma, *Vida de la serenísima Infanta sor Margarita de la Cruz, religiosa descalza de Santa Clara* (Madrid: Imprenta Real, 1636).

10. Montalvo, *Vida prodigiosa,* 1.

11. Ibid., 137.

12. Lope Paez, *Espejo de virtudes*, 10–11.

13. Fr. Juan Bernal, *Compendiosa noticia, de la ejemplar vida y singulares virtudes de la venerable hermana Francisca Badia* (Valencia: Joseph Garcia, 1755), 11.

14. José-Miguel Palop Ramos, *Fluctuaciones de precios y abastecimiento en la Valencia del siglo XVIII* (Valencia: Diputación Provincial, 1977), 131–143.

15. Bernal, *Compendiosa noticia*, 19–25.

16. Fr. Antonio Daza, *Historia, vida y milagros, de la bienaventurada virgen santa Juana de la Cruz* (Madrid: Luis Sanchez, 1610), ffs. 10v-12.

17. Antonio de Lorea, *Las siervas de Dios, sor Catalina de San Lucas y sor Maria de San Andres* (Valencida: Vicento Cabrera, 1671), 168–170.

18. Francisco de Arcos, *La sabia de Coria, vida de la venerable madre Maria de Jesús* (Madrid: Francisco Nieto, 1671), 4.

19. Fr. Rafael María López-Melus, *Beata Inés de Benigánim* (Valencia: Madres Agustinas Descalzas, 1982), 81, 88–90.

20. Teresa of Jesús, *The Complete Works, of Saint Teresa of Jesus*, ed. E.A. Peers, 3 vols. (London and New York: Sheed and Ward, 1982), 1:10–13, 23.

21. Fr. José Ximénez Samaniego, *Prologo Galeato: Vida de Sor María de Ágreda*, Biblioteca de Autores Españoles 109 (Madrid: Atlas, 1958), 272–273; María de Jesús de Ágreda, *Relación breve de la vida y muerte del padre Fr. Francisco Coronel, de su condición y cualidades; y de su madre Sor Catalina de Arana*, Biblioteca de Autores Españoles 109 (Madrid: Atlas, 1958), 209.

22. Lorea, *La venerable madre*, 83, 167.

23. Luis Ignacio Zevallos, *Vida y virtudes, favores del cielo, milagros y prodigious de la V. Madre sor María Ángela Astorch* (Madrid: Jerónimo Rojo, 1733), 51–53.

24. Lázero Iriarte, *Beata María Ángela Astorch: clarisa capuchina (1592–1665), La mística del brevario* (Valencia: Asis Editorial, 1982), 25, 50–51.

25. Fr. Andrés de Maya, Salaberria, *Vida prodigiosa y exercicio admirable de virtudes de la V.M. sor Martina de los Ángeles y Arilla* (Zaragoza: Herederas de Pedro Lanaja y Lamarca, *1678*), 4, 12.

26. Arcos, *La sabia de Coria*, 21–22.

27. Lorea, *La venerable madre*, 192.

28. Batista de Lanuza, *Vida de la sierva de Dios*, "censura del nunca dionamente alavado venerable padre Juan Eusebio Nieremberg," 56.

29. Ibid., 233.

30. Lea, *The Inquisition of Spain*, 4:359–361.

31. Fernando de San Antonio Capilla, *Vida singular de la madre María de Christo*, (Madrid: Manuel Ruiz de Murga, 1716), 240.

32. Ibid., 282–283.

33. Kamen, *Inquisition and Society*, 202.

34. Salaberria, *Vida prodigiosa de admirable exercicio*, 83.

35. Isabel of Jesús, *Tesoro del carmelo escondido*, 255.

36. Batista de Lanuza, *Virtudes de la V. M. Teresa de Jesús Vela*, 25.

37. Joaquín Pérez Villanueva, "Sor María de Agreda y Felipe IV," un epistolerio en su tiempo" in Ricardo Garcia Villoslada, ed. *Historia de la Iglesia en España*, 5 vols. (Madrid: La Editorial Católica, 1979) 4,pt. 1:378–380, 389–390.

38. Teresa of Jesús, *The Complete Works*, 3:121, 142, 151.

39. Fr. Angel Manrique, *La venerable madre Ana de Jesús discipula y compañera de la S. M. Teresa de Jesús* (Brussels: Lucas de Meerbeeck, 1632), 71, 78–79.

40. Teresa of Jesús, *The Complete Works*, 3:79–80, 85.

41. Ibid., 3: 48–49.

42. Fr. Manuel de San Gerónimo, *Edades y virtudes, empleos y prodigios, de le V. M. Gabriela de San Joseph.* (Jaen: Tomás Copado, 1703) f. 151v.

43. Lorea, *La venerable madre*, 189.

44. Arcos, *La sabia de Coria*, 24–33.

45. Ibid., 34–37, 40–45, 47–49, 53.

46. Salaberria, *Vida prodigiosa de admirable exercicio*, 164–165.

47. Lorea, *La venerable madre*, 191.

48. Teresa of Jesús, *The Complete Works*, 3:13.

49. Ibid., 3:71–72.

50. Ibid., 1:231–32, 3:64, 175.

51. Batista de Lanuza, *Vida de la sierva de Dios*, 46–47.

52. Teresa of Jesús, *The Complete Works*, 3:4–6.

53. Batista de Lanuza, *Virtudes de la V. M. Teresa de Jesús Vela*, 218–221.

54. Lorea, *La venerable madre*, 266.

55. San Gerónimo, *Edades y virtudes, empleos y prodigios*, 194.

56. Lope Paez, *Espejo de virtudes*, 36, 47.

57. San Gerónimo, *Edades y virtudes, empleos y prodigios*, 195.

58. Salaberria, *Vida prodigiosa de admirable exercicio*, 114.

59. Iriarte, *Beata María Ángela Astorch*, 152, 182.

60. Richard Kagan, *Students and Society in Early Modern Spain* (Baltimore: Johns Hopkins University Press, 1974), 234.

61. Joël Saugnieux, *Les jansénistes et le renouveau de la prédication dans l'espagne de la seconde moité du XVIIIe siècle* (Lyons: Presses Universitaires de Lyon, 1976), 81–82.

62. Batista de Lanuza, *Vida de la sierva de Dios*, "Aprobación del Señor Doctor D. Manuel de Salinas y Lizana, canonigo de la Iglesia Cathedral de Huesca," 22–23.

63. Galindo, *Parte segundo del directorio de penitentes*, 492–493.

64. Bernal, *Compendioso noticia*, "Censura de la M. R. P. M. Fr. Thomás Lop, del orden de predicadores," September 12, 1755.

65. Batista de Lanuza, *Virtudes de la V. M. Teresa de Jesús Vela*, 222–223.

66. Isaac Vázquez, "Las controversias doctrinales postridentinas hasta finales del siglo XVII," in Ricardo García-Villoslada, ed. *Historia de la Iglesia en España*, 5 vols. (Madrid: La Editorial Católica, 1979) 4:5/4: 438–439.

67. Fr. Bartolomé Valperga, *Vida, muerte y milagros de Sor Caterina Thomasa* (Mallorca: Manuel Rodríguez y Juan Piza, 1627), ffs. 118v–119.

68. Samaniego, *Vida de Sor María de Ágreda*, 346.

Chapter 5

1. AHN, Inquisition, November 21, 1639, leg. 102, exp. 2.

2. AHN, Inquisition, April 6, 1639, "Inventario de los bienes de María Bautista," leg. 102, exp. 2.

3. AHN, Inquisition, November 11, 1639, leg. 102, exp. 2.

4. AHN, Inquisition, March 30, 1639, leg. 102, exp. 2.

5. AHN, Inquisition, May 18, 1639, leg. 102, exp. 2.

6. AHN, Inquisition, January 13, 1670, leg. 1710, exp. 10.

7. AHN, Inquisition, December 12, 1699, leg. 1710, exp. 10.

8. AHN, Inquisition, August 22, 1670, leg. 1710, exp. 10.

9. AHN, Inquisition, February 6, 1670, leg. 1710, exp. 10.

10. AHN, Inquisition, May 11, 1670, leg. 1710, exp. 10.

11. AHN, Inquisition, January 26, 1576, leg. 113, exp. 5.

12. AHN, Inquisition, October 10, 1575, leg. 113, exp. 5.

13. AHN, Inquisition, April 13, 1578, leg. 113, exp. 5.

14. AHN, Inquisition, July 8, 1675, leg. 114, exp. 6.

15. AHN, Inquisition, October 5, 1575, leg. 113, exp. 5.

16. AHN, Inquisition, February 1, 1639, leg. 115, exp. 2.

17. AHN, Inquisition, June 6, 1634, leg. 107, exp. 4.

18. AHN, Inquisition, April 14, 1726, leg. 532#2, exp. 1.

19. AHN, Inquisition, July 18, 1636, leg. 114, exp. 9.

20. AHN, Inquisition, November 22, 1725, leg. 532#2, exp. 1.

21. AHN, Inquisition, June 21, 1708, June 10, 1709, leg. 105, exp. 4.

22. AHN, Inquisition, April 25, 1708, leg. 105, exp. 4.

23. AHN, Inquisition, January 19, 1638, leg. 115, exp. 2.

24. AHN, Inquisition, July 18, 1636, leg. 114, exp. 9.

25. AHN, Inquisition, December 9, 1675, leg. 114, exp. 6.

26. AHN, Inquisition, January 25, 1576, April 6, 1575, leg. 113, exp. 5.

27. AHN, Inquisition, August 11, 1575, leg. 113, exp. 5.

28. AHN, Inquisition, August 12, 1675, leg. 114, exp. 6.

29. AHN, Inquisition, June 28, 1675, leg. 114, exp. 6.

30. AHN, Inquisition, May 13, 1675, leg. 114, exp. 6.

31. AHN, Inquisition, June 9, 1645, leg. 106, exp. 3.
32. AHN, Inquisition, September 18, 1645, leg. 106, exp. 3.
33. AHN, Inquisition, October 1, 1646, leg. 106, exp. 3.
34. AHN, Inquisition, June 18, 1636, leg. 114, exp. 9.
35. AHN, Inquisition, October 4, 1639, leg. 102, exp. 5.
36. AHN, Inquisition, June 6, 1639, leg. 102, exp. 5.
37. AHN, Inquisition, July 10, 1646, leg. 106, exp. 3.
38. AHN, Inquisition, December 11, 1646, leg. 106, exp. 3.
39. AHN, Inquisition, October 11, 1639, leg. 102, exp. 5.
40. AHN, Inquisition, March 26, 1639, leg. 102, exp. 5.
41. AHN, Inquisition, October 18 and 27, 1640; November 14, 1641, leg. 1823, exp. 1.
42. AHN, Inquisition, October 11, 1640; November 11, 1640, leg. 1823, exp. 1.
43. AHN, Inquisition, January 18 and 19, 1638; December 9, 1640, leg. 115, exp. 2.
44. AHN, Inquisition, October 24, 1635, leg. 115, exp. 2.
45. AHN, Inquisition, June 21, 1708; June 10, 1709, leg. 105, exp. 4.
46. AHN, Inquisition, November 16, 1725; July 18, 1723, leg. 532#2, exp. 1.
47. AHN, Inquisition, April 20, 1638, leg. 107, exp. 4.
48. AHN, Inquisition, June 17, 1634, leg. 107, exp. 4.
49. AHN, Inquisition, September 6, 1639, leg. 102, exp. 5.
50. AHN, Inquisition, June 4, 1670, leg. 1707, exp. 10.
51. AHN, Inquisition, October 25, 1639, leg. 102, exp. 5.
52. AHN, Inquisition, May 26, 1639; September 24, 1639, leg. 102, exp. 5.
53. AHN, Inquisition, October 28, 1575, leg. 113, exp. 5.
54. AHN, Inquisition, October 12, 1575, leg. 113, exp. 5.
55. AHN, Inquisition, April 12, 1575, leg. 113, exp. 5.
56. AHN, Inquisition, July 17 and November 4, 1575, leg. 113, exp. 5.
57. AHN, Inquisition, June 25, 1639, leg. 102, exp. 5.
58. AHN, Inquisition, June 3, 1639, leg. 102, exp. 5.
59. AHN, Inquisition, October 30, 1640; November 4, 5, 1641, leg. 1823, exp. 1.
60. AHN, Inquisition, October 29, November 8, 1641, leg. 1823, exp. 1.
61. AHN, October 24, 1640, November 5, 1641, leg. 1823, exp. 1.

Chapter 6

1. Gerónimo Planes, *Tratado del examen de las revelaciones verdaderas y falsas y de los raptos* (Valencia: Viuda de Juan Chrysostomo Garriz, 1634), ffs. 344–347.
2. Ibid., 325v.
3. AHN, Inquisition, August 30, 1648, leg. 104, exp. 5.
4. Planes, *Tratado del examen*, ffs. 269–269v; Eire, *From Madrid to Purgatory*, 494.
5. AHN, Inquisition, September 7, 1634, leg. 104, exp. 5.
6. Lea, *A History of the Inquisition*, 4:2–9.
7. A. G. Dickens, *The Counter-Reformation* (New York: Norton, 1968) 21–22.
8. Lea, *A History of the Inquisition*, 4:8.
9. Ibid., 4:31–33.
10. AHN, Inquisition, June 1, 1645, leg. 1823, exp. 1.
11. AHN, Inquisition, September 23, 1635, leg. 106, exp. 2.
12. Planes, *Tratado del examen*, ffs. 265–266v.

13. AHN, Inquisition, June 13, 1634, leg. 107, fol. 4.

14. Horozco y Covarrubias, *Tratado*, ffs. 26–28.

15. AHN, Inquisition, June 13, 1634, leg. 107, exp. 4.

16. BNM, MS 6744, "Alegaciones y memoriales, informes y apuntamientos en derecho," ffs. 444–444v.

17. AHN, Inquisition, July 11, 1675, leg. 114, exp. 6.

18. Horozco y Covarrubias, *Tratado,* f.43v.

19. BNM, MS 6744, f. 442.

20. Planes, *Tratado del examen,* f. 326.

21. AHN, Inquisition, May 23, 1634, leg. 107, exp. 4.

22. Patrocinio García Barriúso, *La monja de Carrión* (Madrid: Ediciones Monte Casino, 1986), 431.

23. Fr. Pedro de Balbás, *Memorial informativo en defensa de Sor Luisa de la Ascensión monja profesa de Santa Clara de Carrión* (Madrid: Diego Diaz de Carerra, 1643), ffs. 15v–17, 26–27.

24. AHN, Inquisition, June 13, 1634, leg. 107, exp. 4.

25. AHN, Inquisition, August 1, 1645, leg. 1823, exp. 1.

26. AHN, Inquisition, August 21, 1645, leg. 1823, exp. 1.

27. Fr. Luis de Granada, "Sermón contra los escándalos de las caídas públicas," in Imirizaldu, *Monjas y beatas embaucadoras,* 204.

28. AHN, Inquisition, October 4, 1633, leg. 107, exp. 4.

29. AHN, Inquisition, September 11, 1638, leg. 107, exp. 4.

30. AHN, Inquisition, April 16, 1640, leg. 1823, exp. 1.

31. AHN, Inquisition, November 4, 1641, leg. 1823, exp. 1.

32. AHN, Inquisition, November 7, 1641, leg. 1823, exp. 1.

33. AHN, Inquisition, April 10, 1639, leg. 102, exp. 2.

34. AHN, Inquisition, October 6, 1636, leg. 114, exp. 9.

35. AHN, Inquisition, April 2, 1639, leg. 102, exp. 2.

36. AHN, Inquisition, November 25, 1639, leg. 102, exp. 5.

37. Lea, *A History of the Inquisition,* 2:180–185.

38. AHN, Inquisition, December 12, 1642, May 22, 1644, leg. 1823, exp. 1.

39. AHN, Inquisition, November 16, 1634, leg. 107, exp. 4.

40. AHN, Inquisition, November 28, 1645, leg. 106, exp. 2.

41. Lea, *A History of the Inquisition,* 2:321.

42. AHN, Inquisition, February 1, 1639, leg. 115, exp. 2.

43. AHN, Inquisition, December 3, 1575, October 15, 1576, leg. 113, exp. 5.

44. AHN, Inquisition, nd, leg. 107, exp. 3.

45. AHN, Inquisition, June 13, 1634, leg. 107, exp. 4.

46. Bartolomé Valperga, *Vida, muerte y milagros de sor Caterina Thomasa,* (Mallorca: Manuel Rodriquez y Juan Piza, 1627), 65.

47. AHN, Inquisition, May 9, 1642, leg. 1823, exp. 1.

48. AHN, Inquisition, July 13, 1639, leg. 102, exp. 2.

49. For the Illuminists' negative attitudes toward external devotions and their questioning of the value of such things as fasting and physical discipline, see the testimony in the case of Pedro de Alcaraz, AHN, Inquisition, December 29 and 30 and February 17 and 28, 1525, leg. 106, exp. 5.

50. AHN, Inquisition, January 27, 1576, leg. 113, exp. 5.

51. AHN, Inquisition, September 1, 1644, leg. 1823, exp. 1.

52. AHN, Inquisition, March 16, 1638, leg. 107, exp. 4.

53. AHN, Inquisition, August 27, 1640, leg. 102, exp. 5.

54. AHN, Inquisition, April 17, 1638, leg. 107, exp. 4.

55. AHN, Inquisition, April 20, 1638, leg. 107, exp. 4.

56. AHN, Inquisition, April 19, 1638, leg. 107, exp. 4.

57. Elizabeth Rapley, *The Dévotes: Women and the Church in Seventeenth Century France* (Montreal and Kingston: McGill-Queen's University Press, 1990), 44–48.

58. AHN, Inquisition, May 16, 1575, leg. 113, exp. 5.

59. AHN, Inquisition, March 10, 1641, leg. 115, exp. 2.

Chapter 7

1. Greven, *Spare the Child,* 134, 148–168.

2. Fr. Manuel de San Gerónimo, *Edades y virtudes,* f. 8v.

3. Fr. Pedro de San Cicilio, *Dios prodigioso en Teresa de Jesús,* 84, 112.

4. Ibid., 95.

5. Ibid., 78, 137.

6. AHN, Inquisition, February 14, 1636, leg. 107, exp. 4.

7. AHN, Inquisition, September 27, 1675, leg. 114, exp. 6.

8. Fr. Lope Paez, *Espejo de virtudes,* ffs. 4–4v.

9. Fr. Manuel de San Gerónimo, *Edades y virtudes,* 16.

10. Batista de Lanuza, *Virtudes de la V. M. Teresa de Jesús Vela,* 6.

11. Fr. Manuel de San Gerónimo, *Edades y virtudes,* 10.

12. Fr. José Ximénez de Samaniego, *Prologo Galeato,* 276–278.

13. Fr. Pedrode San Cicilio, *Dios prodigioso en Teresa de Jesús,* 199–200.

14. Fr. Antonio de Lorea, *La venerable madre Sor María de la Santissima Trinidad religiosa de la tercera orden de Santo Domingo* (Madrid: Francisco Sanchez, 1671), 6.

15. Mâle, *L'Arte religieux,* 329–331.

16. Jesús, *Tesoro del carmelo escondido,* 5.

17. Franco de Villalba, *La heroica religiosa,* 8.

18. Fr. Antonio Arbiol, *Ejemplar de religiosas en la penitente, virtuosa y maravillosa vida de la venerable Sor Jacinta de Atondo* (Zaragoza: Manuel Roman, 1716), 8.

19. Fr. Andrés de Maya Salaberria, *Vida prodigiosa y exercicio admirable de virtudes de la V.M. sor Martina de los Angeles y Arilla* (Zaragoza: Herederes de Pedro Lanaja y Lamarca, 1678), 3.

20. San Antonio Capilla, *Vida singular de la madre María de Christo,* 17.

21. Fr. José Ximénez de Samaniego, *Prólogo Galeato,* 275–276.

22. Salaberria, *Vida prodigiosa,* 12.

23. AHN, Inquisition, June 9, 1635, leg. 106, exp. 3.

24. Fr. Fernando de San Antonio Capilla, *Vida singular de la madre María de Christo,* 17.

25. Fr. Tomás de Montalvo, *Vida prodigiosa de la extatica virgen y V.M. sor Beatriz Mariá de Jesus.* (Granada: Francisco Dominguez, 1719), 3–4.

26. Fr. Antonio de Lorea, *La venerable madre* Hipolita intro., np.

27. Fr. Antonio Arbiol, *Epitome de la virtuosa y evangelica vida,* 6.

28. Fr. Lope Paez, *Espejo de virtudes,* ffs. 4v-6.

29. Fr. Antonio Arbiol, *La familia regulada con doctrina de la segrada escritura y santos padres de la iglesia católica, para todos los que regularmente componen una casa segular a fin de que cada uno en su estado y en su grado sirva a Dios nuestro señor con toda perfección y salve su alma* (Zaragoza: Herederos de Manuel Roman, 1715), 356–357.

30. Ibid., 477–481.

31. Ibid., 513–514, 518.

32. Fr. Manuel de San Gerònimo, *Edades y virtudes*, 15v.

33. Fr. Bartolomé Valperga, *Vida, muerte y milagros*, 4.

34. Ibid., 15.

35. AHN, Inquisition, May 14, 1725, leg. 532#2, exp. 1.

36. Luis de la Puente, *Vida maravillosa de la venerable virgen Doña Marina de Escobar* (Madrid: Francisco Nieto, 1665), ffs. 9–10.

37. Ibid., f.11v.

38. Ibid., ffs. 16–17.

39. Ibid., ffs. 19v-20, 48v-49.

40. Jesús, *Tesoro de carmelo escondido*, 40.

41. Luis Ignacio Zevallos, *Vida y virtudes, favores del cielo y prodigios sor Maria Ángela Astorch* (Madrid: Jeronimo Rojo, 1733) 6–7.

42. Iriarte, *Beata María Ángela Astorch*, 14.

43. Batista de Lanuza, *Virtudes de la V. M. Teresa de Jesús Vela*, 5.

44. Fr. Bartolomé Valperga, *Vida, muerte y milagros*, f. 5.

45. Ibid., ffs. 7v-8.

46. Ibid., f. 9.

47. Ibid., ffs. 17–18.

48. Lloyd de Mause, "The History of Child Abuse," *Journal of Psychohistory* 25 (1998): 218–219. For a high correlation between physical and sexual abuse and dissociation as measured by the standard Dissociative Experiences Scale, see Jeffrey A. Atlas, Kim Weissman, and Susan Liebowitz, "Adolescent Inpatients' History of Abuse and Dissociative Identity Disorder," *Psychological Reports* 80 (1997): 1086. See also Nicolas P. Spanos, *Multiple Identities and False Memories: A Sociocognitive Perspective* (Washington, D.C.: American Psychological Association, 1996), 265. For an up-to-date discussion of imaginary companions among children with dissociative disorders, see Frank W. Putnam, *Dissociation in Children and Adolescents: A Developmental Perspective* (New York: Guilford Press, 1997), 191–193. Putnam's conclusion that "the most striking difference lay in the vividness of the IC experiences" between normal and multiple personality disorder children is especially suggestive and important for this study. See also Jody Davies and Mary Frawley, *Treating the Adult Survivor of Childhood Sexual Abuse: A Psychoanalytic Perspective* (New York: Basic Books, 1994), 114.

49. Fr. Pedro de San Cecilio, *Dios prodigioso en Teresa de Jesús*, 38, 47.

50. Salaberria, *Vida prodigiosa*, 18. Fear of men is highly correlated to childhood histories of sexual victimization among women victims in the trauma symptom checklist. John Briers, *Therapy for Adults Molested as Children* (New York: Springer, 1989), 183–186. See also Jaima Jasper Jacobson, *Psychiatric Sequelae of Child Abuse* (Springfield, Ill.: Charles C. Thomas, 1986), 179.

51. Ibid., 44.

52. Salaberria, *Vida prodigiosa*, 56.

53. AHN, Inquisition, September 27, 1675, leg. 114, exp. 6.

54. Salaberria, *Vida prodigiosa*, ffs. 3–14.

55. Fr. Antonio Arbiol, *Ejemplar de religiosas*, 3–6.

56. Ibid., 15–16.

57. Ibid., 44–45.

58. The increased severity of dissociative symptoms in patients who suffered mistreatment from family members has been demonstrated by Chu and Dill using

the Dissociative Experiences Scale. They point out that such abuse "would represent a greater level of betrayal of trust and violation of boundaries than abuse by someone outside the family." James A. Chu and Diana L. Dill, "Dissociative Symptoms in Relation to Childhood Physical and Sexual Abuse," *American Journal of Psychiatry* 147 (1990): 886, 891.

59. Fr. Antonio Arbiol, *Ejemplar de religiosas*, 20.

Chapter 8

1. Cerda, *Libro intitulado vida política*, f. 8v.

2. Andrés Ferrer de Valcedebro, *Gobierno general, moral y politico, hallado en las aves más generosas y nobles, sacado de sus naturales virtudes y propiedades* (Barcelona: Tomás Loriente, 1696), 341.

3. Juan Luis Vives, *Libro llamado instrucción de la mujer cristiana* (Madrid: Benito Cano, 1793), 112.

4. Fr. Antonio Arbiol, *Ejemplar de religiosas*, 86–87.

5. Ibid., 90.

6. Ibid., 91.

7. Ibid., 93, 110, 111, 125.

8. Fr. Bartolomé Valperga, *Vida, muerte y milagros*, ffs. 27–27v.

9. Ibid., ffs. 35–36.

10. Fr. Lope Paez, *Espejo de virtudes*, 8, 17.

11. AHN, Inquisition, May 23, 1634, leg. 107, exp. 4.

12. AHN, Inquisition, March 15, 1638, leg. 115, exp. 2.

13. AHN, Inquisition, June 2, 1672, leg. 533, exp. 7; AHN, Inquisition, leg. 1952, (1585) exp. 4b.

14. Cerda, *Libro intitulado vida politica*, ffs. 9v, 11v.

15. Batista de Lanuza, *Virtudes de la V. M. Teresa de Jesús Vela*, 10–12, 21–22, 24.

16. Fr. José Ximénez de Samaniego, *Prólogo Galeato*, 272.

17. Cerda, *Libro intitulado vida politica*, ffs. 12–13.

18. Fr. José Ximénez de Samaniego, *Prólogo Galeato*, 274–275.

19. Ibid., 276.

20. Ibid., 277.

21. Ibid., 285–290.

22. Jesús y Rocaberti, *Libro primero de su admirable vida*, 4–5.

23. Gaspar de Astete, *Tratado del gobierno de la familia y estado de las viudas y doncellas* (Burgos: Felipe Junta, 1603), 192. In Mariló Vigil, *La vida de las mujeres en los siglos XVI y XVII* (Madrid: Siglo Veintiuno, 1986), 79.

24. James A. Brundage, *Law, Sex and Christian Society in Medieval Europe* (Chicago: University of Chicago Press, 1987), 369–370, 514–515.

25. Antonio Domínguez Ortiz, *Sociedad y estado en el siglo XVIII español* (Barcelona: Ariel, 1976), 359–360.

26. AHN, Inquisition, July 3, 1622, leg. 1712, exp. 15.

27. Fr. Francisco de Arcos, *La Sabia de Coria: vida de venerable madre María de Jesús* (Madrid: Francis Nieto, 1671), 9.

28. Fr. Juan de Palma, *Vida de la sereníssima Infanta*, ffs. 43–46.

29. Mariana de Jesús, *Autobiografia*, in *La madre Martina. Aportaciones a la vida de una Madrileña,* ed. Gómez Domínguez (Madrid: Editorial Tirso de Molina, 1965), 241.

30. AHN, Inquisition, December 14, 1622, leg. 1705, exp. 5.

31. Brundage, *Law, Sex and Christian Society*, 581.

32. Galindo, *Excelencias de la castidad*, ffs. 5–5v.

33. Galindo, *Parte segundo*, f. 160.

34. Galindo, *Excelencias de la castidad*, ffs. 8v-9.

35. Ibid., f. 8.

36. AHN, Inquisition, December 9, 1619, leg. 1705, exp. 3.

37. Fr. Antonio de Lorea, *Las siervas de Dios*, 6–9.

38. Mesa, *Vida, favores y mercedes*, 9–10.

39. Ibid., 14.

40. Fr. Manuel de San Gerónimo, *Edades y virtudes*, f. 20.

41. Ibid., ffs. 21–23v.

42. Fr. Antonio Daza, *Historia, vida y milagros*, ffs. 10v-15.

43. Fr. Marcos de San Antonio, *Vida prodigiosa de la venerable madre Sor Clara de Jesús María virgen admirable, religiosa de la vela blanco en el monestario de la merced de la ciudad de Toro* (Madrid: Francisco Xavier García, 1765), 138.

44. Ibid., 148.

45. Fr. Ferdinand San Antonio Capilla, *Vida singular de la madre María de Christo*, 22–23, 32–34.

46. Fr. Francisco de Acosta, *Vida prodigiosa y heroicas virtudes de la V. M. María de Jesús Carmelita descalza de Toledo* (Madrid: Domingo Garcia y Morras, 1648), 25.

47. AHN, Inquisition, May 11 and 14, 1725, leg. 532, exp. 1.

48. Batista de Lanuza, *Vida de la venerable madre*, 5.

49. Fr. Antonio de Lorea, *La venerable madre Hipolita de Jesús Rocaberti*, 148.

50. Ibid., 27.

51. Ibid., 12–13, 46, 102–103.

52. Fr. Juan de Palma, *Vida de la sereníssima Infanta*, ffs. 63–63v, 104v.

53. Fr. Ferdinand San Antonio Capilla, *Vida singular de la madre María de Christo*, 30–32.

54. Mary Elizabeth Perry, *Gender and Disorder in Early Modern Seville* (Princeton, N.J.: Princeton University Press, 1990), 79.

55. Tomás de Montalvo, *Vida prodigiosa de la extatica virgen y V. M. sor Beatria María de Jesús* (Granada: Francisco Domínguez, 1719), 427.

56. Ibid., 424.

57. Arbiol, *Ejemplar de religiosas*, 162.

58. Fr. Juan de Palma, *Vida de la sereníssima Infanta*, ffs. 87v-88.

59. Fr. Ferdinand San Antonio Capilla, *Vida singular de la madre María de Christo*, 40–41.

60. Montalvo, *Vida prodigiosa de la extatica virgen*, 431–432.

61. Teresa of Jesus, *Complete Works of Saint Teresa of Jesus*. 3 vols. Translated and edited by E. A. Peers. 11th ed. (London and New York: Sheed and Ward, 1982), 3:223–224.

62. Ibid., 3:222.

63. Montalvo, *Vida prodigiosa de la extatica virgen,* 431, describes those entering the convent as having come from aristocratic homes where they were brought up "in the greatest luxury" and "loving tenderness." Anyone with even a slight familiarity with the childhood of such women would find it difficult to accept this description as valid for even the majority of those who entered convents, although some girls would certainly be used to more comforts than they would get in religious life.

64. Teresa of Jesus, *Complete Works*, 3:224–225.

65. Montalvo, *Vida prodigiosa de la extatica virgen*, 431.

66. Fr. Juan de Palma, *Vida de la sereníssima Infanta*, f. 76.

67. Fr. Francisco de Acosta, *Vida prodigiosa y heroicas virtudes*, 97, 99, 100–101.

68. Ibid., 96.

69. Fr. Angel Manrique, *La venerable madre Ana de Jesús*, 152–153.

70. Teresa of Jesus, *Complete Works*, 3:224.

71. Fr. Bartolomé Valperga, *Vida, muerte y milagros*, 46.

72. Ibid., 47.

73. Batista de Lanuza, *Virtudes de la V. M. Teresa de Jesús,* 128–129.

74. Fr. Antonio de Lorea, *La venerable madre Hipolita de Jesús Rocaberti*, 8.

75. Fr. Lope Paez, *Espejo de virtudes*, 42–43.

76. Batista de Lanuza, *Vida de la sierva de Dios*, 38.

77. Ibid., 65.

78. Ibid., 40, 45, 51.

79. AHN, Inquisition, December 6 and 7, 1622, leg. 1705, exp. 5.

Chapter 9

1. Fr. Manuel de San Gerónimo, *Edades y virtudes*, f. 84v.

2. Ibid., f. 85.

3. Ibid., f. 163v.

4. Ibid., f. 164.

5. Ibid., f. 165.

6. Fr. Antonio Daza, *Historia, vida y milagros*, f. 52.

7. Marina Warner, *Alone of All Her Sex: The Myth and the Cult of the Virgin Mary* (New York: Vintage, 1983), 262–263.

8. Fr. Antonio Daza, *Historia, vida y milagros*, ffs. 88–89v.

9. AHN, April 3, 1634, leg. 107, exp. 4.

10. Ibid.

11. AHN, Inquisition, February 5, 1634, leg. 107 exp. 4.

12. AHN, Inquisition, September 3, 1675, leg. 114, exp. 6.

13. See the testimony of Quiteria Sánchez, AHN, Inquisition, June 28, 1675, leg. 114, exp. 6.

14. AHN, Inquisition, May 13, 1675, leg. 114, exp. 6.

15. AHN, Inquisition, June 28, 1675, leg. 114, exp. 6.

16. AHN, Inquisition, January 13, 1670, leg. 1707, exp. 10.

17. AHN, Inquisition, December 19, 1669, leg. 1707, exp. 10.

18. AHN, Inquisition, May 28, 1670, leg. 1707, exp. 10.

19. Ibid.

20. AHN, Inquisition, July 4, 1670, leg. 1707, exp. 10.

21. AHN, Inquisition, March 13, 1670, leg. 1707, exp. 10.

22. Ibid.

23. Fr. Antonio Daza, *Historia, vida y milagros*, f. 56v.

24. Ibid., ffs. 58v–60v.

25. Ibid., f. 57.

26. Ibid., f. 58.

27. Ibid., ffs. 62v–63v.

28. AHN, Inquisition, September 17, 1703, leg. 533, exp. 7.

29. Fr. Bartolomé Valperga, *Vida, muerte y milagros*, f. 38v.

30. Pedro de Ribadeneyra, *Flos Sanctorum de las vidas de los santos*; 2 vols. (Madrid: Joachin Ibarra, 1761) 1:186–190.

31. Ibid., ffs. 53–53v.

32. Ibid., ffs. 55v–56.

33. Ibid., f. 54.

34. Ibid., f. 65.

35. Luis Ignacio Zevallos; *Vida y virtudes; favores del cielo y prodigios de la V. M. Madre sor María Ángela Astorch religiosa capuchina, natural de Barcelona.* (Madrid: Jerónimo Rajo, 1733), 102.

36. Iriarte, *Beata María Ángela Astorch*, 66–68.

37. Fr. Pedro de Balbes, *Memorial informativo en defensa de Sor Luisa de la Ascensión*, ffs. 17v, 19.

38. Ibid., ffs. 16v–17.

39. Iriarte, *Beata María Ángela Astorch*, 68–69.

40. Fr. Angel Manrique, *La venerable madre Ana de Jesús*, 154.

41. Fr. Fernando de San Antonio Capilla, *Vida singular*, 119–121.

42. Ibid., 130.

43. Ibid., 131.

44. Fr. Manuel de San Gerónimo, *Edades y virtudes*, f. 187v.

45. Fr. Francisco de Arcos, *La Sabia de Coria*, 134.

46. Tomás de Montalvo, *Vida prodigiosa de la extatica virgen y V. M. sor Beatriz María de Jesús* (Granada: Francisco Dominguez, 1710), 244.

47. Ibid., 387.

48. Ibid., 406.

49. Batista de Lanuza, *Virtudes de la V. M. Teresa de Jesús Vela*, 97.

50. Fr. Bartolomé Valperga, *Vida, muerte y milagros*, 122.

51. Fr. Antonio Arbiol, *Ejemplar de religiosas*, 120, 62.

52. Kendrick, *Mary of Agreda*, 159–164.

53. Fr. Antonio de Lorea, *La venerable madre Sor María de la Santissima Trinidad*, ffs. 153–155, 156v–157.

54. Andrés de Maya Salaberria, *Vida prodigiosa y exercicio admirable de virtudes de la V. M. sor Martina de los Angeles y Arilla* (Zaragoza: Herederos de Pedro Lanaja y Lamarca, 1678), 69.

55. Teresa of Jesus, *Complete Works of Saint Teresa of Jesus*. 3 vols. Translated and edited by E. A Peers. 11th ed. (London and New York: Sheed and Ward, 1982) 2:186, 353–355.

56. Fr. José Ximénez de Samaniego, *Prologo Galeato*, 348.

57. Fr. Antonia Arbiol, *Ejemplar de religiosas*, 149.

58. Isabel de Jesús, *Tesoro del carmelo*, 372.

59. Batista de Lanuza, *Virtudes de la V. M. Teresa de Jesús Vela*, 50, 187.

60. Antonio de Quintanadueñas, *Espejo grande de los trabajos de Jesús crucificado* (Valladolid: Bartolomé Portales, 1656), 54.

61. Brundage, *Law, Sex and Christian Society*, 80.

62. Juan de Avila y Chicona, *Libro espiritual que trata de los malos lenguajes del mundo, carne y demonio y de los remedios contra ellos* (Madrid: Pedro Cosin, 1574), ffs. 17v-18.

63. Ibid., f. 81.

64. Francisco de Posadas, *Cartas del esposo Christo a las religiosas sus esposas* (Toledo: Francisco Martín, 1748), 24–25.

65. Avila y Chicona, *Libro espiritual*, f. 89v.

66. Fr. Angel Manrique, *La venerable madre Ana de Jesús*, 15–16.

67. Teresa of Jesus, *Complete Works*, 1:13–14.

68. Fr. Angel Manrique, *La venerable madre Ana de Jesús*, 22–23.

69. Paez, *Espejo de virtudes*, f. 34.

70. Ibid., 38.

71. AHN, Inquisition, June 28, 1675, leg. 114, exp. 6.

72. Isabel de Jesús, *Tesoro del carmelo*, 223.

73. Fr. Lope Paez, *Espejo de virtudes*, f. 38v.

74. AHN, Inquisition, September 3, 1675, leg. 114, exp. 3.

75. AHN, Inquisition, August 22, 1666, leg. 1707, exp. 10.

76. AHN, Inquisition, September 20, 1666, and December 6, 1669, leg. 1707, exp. 10.

77. AHN, Inquisition, September 17, 1637, leg. 107, exp. 4.

78. Franco de Villalba, *La heroica religiosa*, 70, 95–96, 99, 102.

79. Batista de Lanuza, *Virtudes de la V. M. Teresa de Jesús Vela*, 190.

80. Fr. Fernando de San Antonio Capilla, *Vida singular*, 191.

81. Salaberria, *Vida prodigiosa*, 62.

82. Ibid., 62–63, 67, 70.

83. Ibid., 111.

84. Mâle, *L'Arte religieux*, 326–329.

85. Fr. Juan de Palma, *Vida de la serenissima Infanta*, ffs. 225–225v.

86. Ibid., ffs. 223–224v.

87. AHN, Inquisition, September 17, 1703, leg. 533, exp. 7.

88. AHN, Inquisition, "papeles originales tocantes al espiritu de María Antonia Hortola," leg. 532, exp. 1.

89. Ibid., ffs. 223–223v.

90. Fr. Francisco de Acosta, *Vida prodigiosa y heroicas virtudes*, 325.

91. Mesa, *Vida, favores y mercedes*, 139–142.

92. AHN, Inquisition, May 24 and 25, 1725, leg. 532, exp. 1.

93. For Teresa's famous description of the transverberation of her heart by a beautiful angel, see Teresa of Jesus, *Complete Works*, 1:192–193. For the experience of Martina de los Ángeles y Arilla, see Salaberria, *Vida prodigiosa*, 239.

94. Fr. Francisco de Acosta, *Vida prodigiosa y heroicas virtudes*, 57.

95. Fr. Manuel de San Gerónimo, *Edades y virtudes*, 128–129.

96. Fr. Juan de Palma, *Vida de la sereníssima Infanta*, f. 162v.

97. Luis de La Puente, *Tesoro escondido en las enfermedades y trabajos*, (Madrid: Manuel Fernandez, 1750), 6.

98. Ibid., 17.

99. Ibid., 112–113, 127–128.

100. Ibid., 67–70.

101. Iriarte, *Beata María Ángela Astorch*, 90.

102. AHN, Inquisition, October 20, 1640, leg. 1823, exp. 1.

103. Fr. Juan de Palma, *Vida de la sereníssima Infanta*, f. 166–167v.

104. AHN, Inquisition, July 18, 1671, leg. 533, exp. 4.

105. AHN, Inquisition, October 20, 1671, leg. 533, exp. 4.

106. AHN, Inquisition, October 26, 1671, leg. 533, exp. 4.

107. In his report to the tribunal, Dr. Gerónimo Ramón also declared that she suffered from "destemplanza en la cabeza." AHN, Inquisition, May 15, 1673, leg. 533, exp. 4.

108. Pedro de Galves, who had known Juana for fourteen years, testified that she had wandered the streets of the village, raving and screaming, and had also disrupted church services. AHN, Inquisition, October 6, 1636, leg. 114, exp. 9.

109. AHN, Inquisition, February 20, 1673, leg. 533, exp. 4.

110. Fr. José Ximénez de Samaniego, *Prologo Galeato*, 383, 381.

111. Fr. Juan de Palma, *Vida de la sereníssima Infanta*, f. 257.

112. Philippe Ariès, *L'homme devant la mort* (Paris: Editions du Seuil, 1977), 107–112.

113. Eire, *From Madrid to Purgatory*, 525.

114. Martínez Gil, *Muerte y sociedad*, 36–50.

115. Ibid., 63.

116. Fr. José Ximénez de Samaniego, *Prologo Galeato*, 376–377.

117. Ibid., 380–381.

118. Ibid., 382.

119. Isabel de Jesús, *Tesoro del carmelo*, 423.

120. Ibid., 738, 741–742.

Chapter 10

1. Caroline Walker Bynum, "Women Mystics and Eucharistic Devotion in the Thirteenth Century," *Women's Studies* 2 (1984): 180.

2. Juan Daza y Berrio, *Tesoro de confesores y perla de la conciencia para todos estados* (Madrid: Imprenta Real, 1648), ffs. 2v, 100.

3. Diego Pérez de Valdivia, *Tratado de la frecuente comunión y medios para ella principalmente del modo y orden para buen confesar* (Barcelona: Pedro Malo, 1589), 27.

4. AHN, Inquisition, July 7, 1723, leg. 532, exp. 1.

5. Iriarte, *Beata María Ángela Astorch*, 58, 156–157, 181.

6. Bynum, "Women Mystics," 185.

7. AHN, Inquisition, June 28, 1675, leg. 114, exp. 6.

8. Luis Ignacio Zevallos, *Vida y virtudes favores del cielo y prodigios de la V Madre sor María Ángela Astorch religiosa capuchina natural de Barcelona* (Madrid: Jeronimo Rojo, 1733), 321.

9. AHN, Inquisition, October 27, 1635, leg. 115, exp. 2.

10. Richard Herr, *The Eighteenth Century Revolution in Spain* (Princeton, N.J.: Princeton University Press, 1969), 151–152.

11. Fr. Pedro de San Cicilio, *Dios prodigioso*, 166.

12. Pedro de Ribadeneyra, *Flos Sanctorum de las vidas de los santos*. 2 vols (Madrid: Joachin Ibarra, 1761), 5.

13. Antoniode Quintanadueñas, *Espejo grande de los trabajos de Jesús crucificado* (Valladolid: Bartolome Portoles, 1656), 96–99.

14. AHN, Inquisition, September 27, 1675, leg. 114, exp. 6.

15. Fr. Andrés de Maya Salaberria, *Vida prodigiosa y exercicio admirable de virtudes de la V.M. sor Martina de los Angeles Y Arilla* (Zaragoza: Herederos de Pedro Lanaja y Lamarca, 1678), 50.

16. BNM, MS 387; 872 Mariana de Jesús, *Espejo purissima de la vida, pasión, muerte y resurrección de Christo buen nuestro*, 1617.

17. Isabelle Poutrin, "Les stigmatisées et les clerics: Interprétation et répression d'un signe, Espagne, XVIIe siècle," in *Les signes de Dieu au XVI et XVII siècles*, ed.

Geneviève Demerson and Bernard Dompnier (Clermont Ferrand: Université Blaise-Pascual, 1993), 193.

18. AHN, Inquisition, November 20, 1725, leg. 532, exp. 1.

19. Ibid., 74–75.

20. Ibid., 135.

21. AHN, Inquisition, May 9, 1642, leg. 1823, exp. 1.

22. This testimony came from her cellmate Juana de San Agustín. AHN, Inquisition, November 4, 1641, leg. 1823, exp. 1.

23. AHN, October 29, 1641, leg. 1823, exp. 1.

24. AHN, Inquisition, May 9, 1642, leg. 1823, exp. 1.

25. AHN, Inquisition, September 3, 1644, exp. 1.

26. AHN, Inquisition, December 9, 1669, leg. 1707, exp. 10.

27. AHN, Inquisition, September 16, 1666, leg. 1707, exp. 10.

28. Iriarte, *Beata María Ángela Astorch*, 96.

29. Eire, *From Madrid to Purgatory*, 171.

30. Joseph Boneta, *Gritos del purgatorio y medios para acallarlos* (Zaragoza: Gaspar Martínez, 1699), prologue, ii.

31. Ibid., 2.

32. Ibid., 41.

33. Batista de Lanuza, *Vida de la sierva de Dios*, 119–121.

34. Boneta, *Gritos del purgatorio*, 7, 202.

35. Batista de Lanuza, *Vida de la sierva de Dios*, "consulta con que D. Miguel presento al rey nuestro señor esta historia y lo que su magestad fue servido responderle."

36. Fr. Martín de Roa, *Estado de las almas de purgatorio* (Barcelona: Pedro de la Cavalleria, 1630), dedication, np.

37. AHN, Inquisition, March 15, 1638, leg. 115, exp. 2.

38. Eire, *From Madrid to Purgatory*, 174–175.

39. Fr. Martin de Roa, *Estado de las almas*, ffs. 28, 31v-32.

40. Zevallos, *Vida y virtudes*, 298–299. For a fuller reference, see María Ángela Astorch, *Opúsculos espirituales*, ed. Lazaro Iriarte (Madrid: Hermanos Menores Capuchinos de la Provincia de Navarra-Cantabria-Aragón, 1985), 624–628.

41. Boneta, *Gritos del purgatorio*, 35.

42. Eire, *From Madrid to Purgatory*, 174.

43. Fr. Lope Paez, *Espejo de virtudes*, 57.

44. Fr. Manuel de San Gerónimo, *Edades y virtudes*, f. 72v.

45. Batista de Lanuza, *Vida de la sierva de Dios*, 155.

46. AHN, Inquisition, May 6, 1639, leg. 102, exp. 5.

47. AHN, Inquisition, June 15, 1639, leg. 102, exp. 5.

48. AHN, Inquisition, June 4, 1639, leg. 102, exp. 5.

49. AHN, Inquisition, May 25, 1639, leg. 102, exp. 5.

50. AHN, Inquisition, May 30, 1639, leg. 102, exp. 5.

51. Fr. Francisco de Acosta, *Vida prodigiosa y heroicas virtudes*, 10.

52. Fr. Antonio Arbiol, *Ejemplar de religiosas*, 36.

53. María de Jesús de Agreda, *The City of God*, trans. G. Blatter (Bloomington: Indiana University Press, 1915), 569; quoted in Warner, *Alone of All Her Sex*, 329.

54. AHN, Inquisition, October 5, 1575, leg. 113, exp. 5.

55. Warner, *Alone of All Her Sex*, 308.

56. BNM, MSS 9196, March 24, 1696; AHN, Inquisition, May 11, 1725, leg. 532, exp. 1.

57. Fr. Antonio Arbiol, *Ejemplar de religiosas*, 37.

58. Fr. Rafael María López-Melus, *Beata Inés de Benigánim* (Valencia: Madres Agustinas Descalzas de Benigánim, 1982), 135.

59. AHN, Inquisition, September 28, 1639, leg. 102, exp. 5.

60. AHN, Inquisition, December 9, 1640, leg. 115, exp. 2.

61. Fr. José Ximénez de Samaniego, *Prologo Galeato,* 341.

62. Balbas, *Memorial informativo,* ffs. 11v, 26–27.

63. Francisco Silvela, *Cartas de la venerable madre Sor María de Agreda y del Sr. Rey D. Felipe IV.* 2 vols. (Madrid: Sucesores de Rivadenera, 1885–1886), 179.

64. AHN, Inquisition, September 17, 1703, leg. 533, exp. 7.

65. AHN, Inquisition, November 5, 1641, leg. 1823, exp. 1.

66. Warner, *Alone of All Her Sex,* 313.

67. AHN, Inquisition, November 28, 1634, leg. 107, exp. 4.

68. R. J. W. Evans, *The Making of the Habsburg Monarchy 1550–1700: An Interpretation* (Oxford: Clarendon Press, 1979), 117.

69. Fr. Juan de Palma, *Vida de la sereníssima Infanta,* 241.

70. Lea, *A History of the Inquisition,* 3:359–360.

71. AHN, Inquisition, July 16, 1638, leg. 3692, f. 23.

72. Fr. Luis de la Puente, *Vida maravillosa de la venerable virgen Mariana de Escobar* (Madrid: Francisco Nieto, 1665), 403–406.

73. Eugene Glendlin, *Experiencing and the Creation of Meaning* (Evanston, Ill.: Northwestern University Press, 1997), 276–279.

74. Jesús y Rocaberti, *Libro primero de su admirable vida,* 6, 37, 39.

75. Batista de Lanuza, *Vida de la sierva de Dios,* 173.

76. Ibid., 247.

77. AHN, Inquisition, October 6, 1636, leg. 114, exp. 9.

78. AHN, Inquisition, July 18, 1671, leg. 533, exp. 4. On May 18, 1673, Dolz was judged *falta de juicio* and *illusa passive* by the tribunal.

79. Fr. Antonio Arbiol, *Ejemplar de religiosas,* 459.

80. Ibid., 47–48. In one of her journal entries (p. 459), Jacinta states her fear that the strong desire to sleep that she felt almost all the time could be the work of the devil.

81. Fr. Juan de Palma, *Vida de la sereníssima Infanta,* ffs. 87v-88.

82. Teresa of Jesus, *The Complete Works of Saint Teresa, of Jesus.* 3 vols. Translated and edited by E.A. Peers. 11th ed. (London and New York: Sheed and Ward, 1982), 3:219.

83. Fr. Manuel de San Gerónimo, *Edades y virtudes,* 32.

84. Isabel de Jesús, *Tesoro de carmelo,* 45.

85. Ibid., 279.

86. Harvey Babkoff, "Perceptual Distortions and Hallucinations Reported during the Course of Sleep Deprivation," *Perceptual and Motor Skills* 68 (1989): 787.

87. Michael V. Vitiello, "Sleep in Alzheimer's Disease and Other Dementing Disorders," *Canadian Journal of Psychology* 45 (1991): 230–231.

88. Tomoka Takeuchi, "Laboratory-Documented Hallucination during Sleep-Onset REM Period in a Normal Subject," *Perceptual and Motor Skills* 78 (1994): 980–982.

89. Fr. Antonio Arbiol, *Ejemplar de religiosas,* 87.

90. Zevallos, *Vida y virtudes,* 100–101, 485–488.

91. AHN, Inquisition, September 27, 1711, leg. 105, exp. 4.

92. Fr. Angel Manrique, *La venerable madre,* 192–193, 141–150.

93. Isabel de Jesús, *Tesoro de carmelo,* 420–421.

94. AHN, Inquisition, June 28, 1675, leg. 114, exp. 6.

95. Batista de Lanuza, *Vida de la sierva de Dios*, 236–237.

96. Fr. Antonio de Lorea, *La venerable madre Sor María de la Santissima Trinidad*, 177. In the convent where María worshiped, there were statues of St. Blas and St. Sebastian. Both saints figured among those she saw in visions.

97. Weinstein and Bell, *Saints and Society*, 220–221. It is interesting to note that although María Antonia Hortola had visions that included St. Catherine of Siena, when she became ill in 1724 the saints who acted to cure her were all male. AHN, Inquisition, "papeles originales tocantes al espiritu de María Antonia Hortola," leg. 532, exp. 1 n.d.

98. Ibid., f. 135.

99. Batista de Lanuza, *Virtudes de la V. M. Teresa de Jesús Vela*, 121–122.

100. Peers, *The Complete Works of Saint Teresa of Jesus*, 1: introduction, xliii–xlv.

101. Fr. Juan Bernal, *Compendiosa noticia*, 190–191. See also Eire, *From Madrid to Purgatory*, 472–493, for a discussion of Teresa's apparitions.

102. AHN, Inquisition, July 13, 1639, leg. 102, exp. 2.

103. Zevallos, *Vida y virtudes*, pp. 44–49.

104. Jesús y Rocaberti, *Libro primero de su admirable vida*, 50.

105. David Hugh Farmer, *The Oxford Dictionary of Saints* (Oxford: Oxford University Press, 1997), 105–106.

106. Ibid., 135.

107. Ibid., 235.

108. Peter Brown, *The Cult of the Saints: Its Rise and Function in Latin Christianity* (Chicago: University of Chicago Press, 1981), 8.

109. Ribadeneyra, *Flos Sanctorum*, 1:662.

110. Farmer, *Saints*, 472–473.

111. Dominique de Courcelles, *Les histoires des saints, la prière et la mort en Catalogne* (Paris: Publications de la Sorbonne, 1990), 7.

112. Jean-Marc Depluvrez, "Les retours de saint Eugène et sainte Léocadie a Tolède en 1565 et 1567," in *Les signes de Dieu aux XVI et XVII siècles*, ed. Geneviève Demerson and Bernard Dompnier (Clermont-Ferrand: Université Blaise-Pascal, 1993), 120–130.

113. Isabel de Jesús, *Tesoro de carmelo*, 359.

114. Weinstein and Bell, *Saints and Society*, 82–83.

115. López-Melus, *Beata Inés de Benigánim*, 148–149.

116. Farmer, *Saints*, 328.

117. According to the legend as related by Ribadeneyra, Praxedes spent much of her fortune on assisting the poor, and Cosmas and Damian were physicians who cured the sick without asking for money. Ribadeneyra, *Flos Sanctorum*, 2:382–383; Farmer, *Saints*, 116.

118. Farmer, *Saints*, 91–92.

119. Fr. Antonio Arbiol, *Ejemplar de religiosas*, ffs. 22–23v, 27, 35.

120. Salaberria, *Vida prodigiosa*, 9, 13.

121. AHN, Inquisition, September 17, 1703, leg. 533, exp. 7.

122. Farmer, *Saints*, 218. Ribadeneyra, *Flos Sanctorum*, 1:487, stresses his role in the conversion of the English.

123. Farmer, *Saints*, 92–93.

124. AHN, Inquisition, April 17, 1575, leg. 113, exp. 5.

125. Batista de Lanuza, *Virtudes de la V. M. Teresa de Jesús Vela*, 84.

126. Isabel de Jesús, *Tesoro de carmelo*, 245.

127. Farmer, *Saints*, 27-28.

128. Jean-Michel Sallmann has noted the continued popularity of the saint cult in early modern Naples, based on a high degree of superstition among all classes and widespread belief in the material efficacy of invocation of the saints for a variety of social and environmental problems. Jean-Michel Sallmann, "Il santo e le rappresentazioni della santità. Problemi di metodo," *Quaderno Storici* 41 (1979): 592-593.

Chapter 11

1. Magdalena S. Sánchez, *The Empress the Queen, and the Nun: Women and Power at the Court of Philip III of Spain* (Baltimore: Johns Hopkins University Press, 1998), 148.

2. Fr. Lope Paez, *Espejo de virtudes*, ffs. 58-58v.

3. Sánchez, *The Empress*, 151-153, 177-178.

4. Jean Bérenger, *A History of the Habsburg Empire 1273-1700* (New York: Longman, 1994), 223-224.

5. Fr. Angel Manrique, *La venerable madre*, 120.

6. Carlos Seco Serrano, *Cartas de Sor María de Agreda de Jesús y de Felipe IV*, (Madrid: Biblioteca de Autores Españoles, 1958), 4: 19-20, 22. In her letter of June 14, 1645, Sor María advised the king to provide his garrisons in the castles and towns near Rosas with everything they needed to defend against French attack. Of course, the king had already thought of this, as he informed her in his reply of June 22.

7. Ibid., 19.

8. Ibid., 91.

9. The king's pathetic letter of February 12, 1648, in which he speaks of his "weakness" and lack of merit in the eyes of God, is just one among many. Ibid., 138-139.

10. Iriarte, *Beata María Ángela Astorch*, 140.

11. Rafael María López-Melus, *Beata Inés de Benigánim* (Valencia: Madres Agustinas Descalzas de Benigánim, 1982), 183.

12. AHN, Inquisition, November 11 and 25, 1639, leg. 102, exp. 2.

13. Ibid., f. 155v.

14. Teresa of Jesus. *The Complete Works of Saint Teresa of Jesus*. 3 vols. Ed. E. A. Peers. (London and New York: Sheed and Ward, 1982), 3:79, 178.

15. López-Melus, *Beata Inés de Benigánim*, 192-193.

16. It was Juan Tomás de Rocaberti who paid for the publication of Hipolita de Jesús y Rocaberti's autobiography, which was published in 1679 before he became inquisitor general. The connection with the Holy Office was already present, however, since the book was printed by Francisco Mestre, official printer to the Valencia tribunal.

17. Fr. Lope Paez, *Espejo de virtudes*, 52.

18. AHN, Inquisition, May 28, 1670, leg. 1707, exp. 10.

19. Fr. Manuel de San Gerónimo, *Edades y virtudes*, 90v.

20. AHN, Inquisition, October 11, 1575, leg. 113, exp. 5.

21. Tomás Montalvo, *Vida prodigiosa de la extatica virgen y venerable madre sor Beatriz Madría de Jesús* (Granada: Francisco Dominguez, 1719). 389.

22. AHN, Inquisition, September 10, 1570, leg. 113, exp. 5.

23. Fr. José Ximénez de Samaniego, *Prologo Galeato*, 341.

24. Montalvo, *Vida prodigiosa*, 331.

25. AHN, April 20, 1638, leg. 115, exp. 2.

26. For the increased level of officially sponsored sexual repression, see Haliczer, *Sexuality in the Confessional*, 149–152.

27. Montalvo, *Vida prodigiosa*, 351.

28. Haliczer, *Sexuality in the Confessional*, 16–17, 36–38.

29. Fr. Angel Manrique, *La venerable madre*, 201–202.

30. Fr. Francisco de Acosta, *Vida prodigiosa y heroicas virtudes*, 290.

31. Luis de la Puente, *Vida maravillosa de la V. Virgen Doña Marina de Escobar* (Madrid: Francisco Nieto, 1665), 100–103. Escobar even went about the streets talking to passersby about mental prayer.

32. AHN, Inquisition, September 17, 1703, leg. 533, exp. 7.

33. AHN, Inquisition, January 18 and 19, 1638; February 20, 1640, leg. 115, exp. 2.

34. Ibid., ffs. 57–58, 65.

35. Ibid., f. 60.

36. Mesa, *Vida, favores y mercedes*, 398.

37. Fr. Antonia de Lorea, *Las siervas de Dios*, 219–220.

38. Ibid., 103–104.

39. Fr. Francisco de Arcos, *La Sabia de Coria*, 97–98.

40. Salaberria, *Vida prodigiosa*, 205.

41. AHN, Inquisition, May 28, 1639, leg. 102, exp. 5.

42. Fr. Antonio de Lorea, *Las siervas de Dios*, 221.

43. Fr. Antonio de Lorea, *La venerable madre*, 116.

44. Stuart A. Vyse, *Believing in Magic: The Psychology of Superstition* (New York: Oxford University Press, 1997), 116.

45. Ibid., 114–115, 161–168.

46. Fr. Antonio de Lorea, *La venerable madre*, 113.

47. Vyse, *Believing in Magic*, 112–113.

48. Fr. Antonio de Lorea, *La venerable madre*, 209.

49. Contreras and Henningsen, "Forty-Four Thousand Cases," 8–119.

50. AHN, Inquisition, July 24, 1723, leg. 532, exp. 1.

51. AHN, Inquisition, July 6, 1725, leg. 532, exp. 1.

52. Fr. Antonio de Lorea, *La venerable madre*, 214.

53. Fr. Antonio Arbiol, *Epitome de la virtuosa y evangelica vida,* 36.

54. Fr. Lope Paez, *Espejo de virtudes*, ffs. 17–17v.

55. Gerónimo Planes, *Tratado del examen de las revelaciones verdaderas y falsas y de los raptos* (Valencia: Viuda de Juan Chrysostomo Garriz, 1634), f. 355.

56. Montalvo, *Vida prodigiosa*, 208.

57. Jesús, *Tesoro del carmelo*, f. 225.

58. Andres de Maya Salaberria, *Vida prodigiosa y exercicio admirable de virtudes de la V. M. Sor Martina de los Angeles y Arilla* (Zaragoza: Herederos de Pedro Lanaja y Lamarca, 1678), 174.

59. AHN, Inquisition, October 3, 1575, leg. 113, exp. 5.

60. Salaberria, *Vida prodigiosa*, 166–168.

61. Weinstein and Bell, *Saints and Society*, 160–161.

62. Fr. Antonio de Lorea, *Las siervas de Dios*, 91.

63. Poutrin, *Le voile et la plume*, 297–298.

64. Fr. Antonio de Lorea, *La venerable madre*, 32.

65. Ibid., 34. David Farmer, *The Oxford Dictionary of Saints* (Oxford: Oxford University Press 1997), 493.

66. Fr. Antonio de Lorea, *La venerable madre*, 35

67. Fr. José Ximénez de Samaniego, *Prologo Galeato*, 296–301.

68. Ellen G. Friedman, *Spanish Captives in North Africa in the Early Modern Age* (Madison: University of Wisconsin Press, 1983), 22.

69. Friedman notes that, in general, captives were discouraged from apostatizing. Ibid., 88.

70. AHN, Inquisition, October 25, 1635, leg. 115, exp. 2.

71. Salaberria, *Vida prodigiosa*, 139.

72. Jesús, *Tesoro del carmelo*, 245.

73. Rapley, *The Dévotes*, 28–33. The Bull of Suppression of January 31, 1631, mentions specifically that the women had taken on functions reserved for male clerics.

74. AHN, Inquisition, June 21, 1628, leg. 3691, exp. 1.

75. AHN, Inquisition, January 26, 1576, leg. 113, exp. 5.

76. AHN, Inquisition, January 25, 1576, leg. 113, exp. 5.

77. Ibid.

78. AHN, Inquisition, May 13, 1575, leg. 113, exp. 5.

79. John Elliott, *Imperial Spain, 1469–1716* (New York: New American Library, 1966), 225.

Chapter 12

1. Fr. Lope Paez, *Espejo de virtudes*, 68v.

2. Fr. Antonio Daza, *Historia, vida y milagros*, ffs. 58v–60.

3. AHN, Inquisition, October 29, 1661, leg. 1823, exp. 1.

4. AHN, Inquisition, November 6, 1641, leg. 1823, exp. 1.

5. AHN, Inquisition, October 11, 1640, leg. 1823, exp. 1.

6. AHN, Inquisition, October 25, 1640, leg. 1823, exp. 1.

7. Tomás de Montalvo, *Vida prodigiosa, de la extatica virgen y V.M. sor Beatriz María de Jesús* (Granada: Francisco Dominguez, 1719), 33, 347.

8. AHN, Inquisition, May 28, 1670, leg. 1707, exp. 10.

9. AHN, Inquisition, August 27, 1666, leg. 1707, exp. 10.

10. AHN, Inquisition, July 6, 1639, leg. 102, exp. 5.

11. Fr. Antonio Daza, *Historia, vida y milagros*, ffs. 35v–36v, 38.

12. García Barriúso, *La Monja*, 271.

13. Ibid., 273.

14. AHN, Inquisition, July 3, 1639, leg. 102, exp. 5. The supporter, Beatriz Ponce de Leon, had actually gone to visit Sor Luisa in Carrión.

15. AHN, Inquisition, August 13, 1640, leg. 102, exp. 5.

16. AHN, Inquisition, June 13 and September 6, 1639, leg. 102, exp. 5.

17. Fr. Andres de Maya Salaberria, *Vida prodigiosa y exercicio admirable de virtudes de la V. M. sor Martina de los Ángeles y Arilla* (Zaragoza: Herederos de Pedro Lanaja y Lamarca, 1678), 140, 149.

18. Ibid., 247–248, 255.

19. Ibid., 284.

20. AHN, Inquisition, nd, 1639, leg. 102, exp. 5.

21. AHN, Inquisition, May 25 and June 5, 1639, leg. 102, exp. 5.

22. Mesa, *Vida, favores y mercedes*, 1089.

23. AHN, Inquisition, May 22, 1639, leg. 102, exp. 5.

24. AHN, Inquisition, September 6, 1639, leg. 102, exp. 5.

25. Montalvo, *Vida prodigiosa*, censorship review by Juan de Ascargorta, October 13, 1713, np.

26. Ibid., 125.

27. Ibid., 418.

28. Salaberria, *Vida prodigiosa,* 181, 189–190.

29. Ibid., 249.

30. Ibid., 125.

31. Ibid., ffs. 187v, 193v.

32. Ibid., f. 183.

33. Mesa, *Vida, favores y mercedes*, 619–620.

34. Ibid., 621–622.

35. AHN, Inquisition, November 4, 1636, leg. 3704, exp. 4.

36. Fr. Bartolomé Valperga, *Vida, muerte y milagros*, ffs. 114–116.

37. Imprenta Guasp, *Colección de xilografías mallorquinas de la Imprenta de Guasp fundada en 1579* (Palma de Mallorca: Imprenta de Guasp, 1950), 209–210.

38. Fr. Bartolomé Valperga, *Vida, muerte y milagros*, ffs. 113–113v.

39. Iriarte, *Beata María Ángela Astorch*, 232–233.

40. Fr. Lope Paez, *Espejo de virtudes*, 89.

41. R. Po-chia Hsia, *The World of Catholic Renewal 1540–1770* (Cambridge: Cambridge University Press, 1998), 129. According to Fr. Francisco de Ribera, *La vida de la Madre Teresa de Jesús*, 517, she lost her left arm in 1585 when her body was removed to Avila.

42. Yepes, *Vida, virtudes y milagros*, 4:13–34.

43. Fr. Antonio de Lorea, *La venerable madre sor María de la Santissima Trinidad*, 282–283.

44. Ibid., 280.

45. Fr. Antonio de Arbiol, *Ejemplar de religiosas, en la penitente, virtuosa y maravillosa vida de sor Jacinta de Atondo* (Zaragoza: Manuel Roman, 1716), 234–235.

46. Iriarte, *Beata María Ángela Astorch*, 234–235.

47. Jesús, *Tesoro del carmelo*, 741–742.

48. Elliott, *Imperial Spain*, 349.

49. Fr. Antonio de Lorea, *La venerable madre Hipolita*, 210.

50. Poutrin, *La voile et la plume*, 431.

51. Fr. Manuel de San Gerónimo, *Edades y virtudes*, ffs. 181v–185.

52. Fr. Martín de Roa, *Flos sanctorum*, ffs. 153, 158, 5–15v.

53. Montalvo, *Vida prodigiosa*, 419.

54. Fr. Bartolmé Valperga, *Vida, muerte y milagros*, np.

55. Mesa, *Vida, favores y mercedes*, "Aprobación del reverendissimo padre fray Francisco Guzman Ponce de Leon," np.

56. Weinstein and Bell, *Saints and Society*, 167.

57. Yepes, *Vida, virtudes y milagros*, 2:325.

58. Po-chai Hsia, *The World of Catholic Renewal*, 127–128.

59. Ibid., 134–137.

60. Ibid., 127–128.

61. Fr. Francisco de Ribera, *La vida de la Madre Teresa de Jesús*, 528–560; see also Eire, *From Madrid to Purgatory*, 450–454, for an account of the unearthly fragrance coming from the oil exuded from her corpse.

62. D. P. Walker, *Spiritual and Demonic Magic from Ficino to Campanella* (London: Warburg Institute, 1958), 200.

63. Mesa, *Vida, favores y mercedes*, 368.

64. AHN, Inquisition, July 15, 1639, leg. 102, exp. 5.

65. Thomas Dormandy, *The White Death: A History of Tuberculosis* (New York: New York University Press, 1999), 4.

66. Manrique, *La venerable madre*, 186–187.

67. Fr. Antonio de Lorea, *La venerable madre sor Maria de la Santissima Trinidad*, 289.

68. Fr. Angel Manrique, *La venerable madre*, 273, 294.

69. Mary O'Neil, "Magical Healing, Love Magic and the Inquisition in Late Sixteenth-Century Modena," in *Inquisition and Society in Early Modern Europe*, ed. Stephen Haliczer (London: Croom Helm, 1987), 91.

70. Montalvo, *Vida prodigiosa*, 126.

71. Fr. Antonio de Lorea, *La venerable madre sor María de la Santissima Trinidad*, 111.

72. Weinstein and Bell, *Saints and Society*, 147.

73. Farmer, *Oxford Dictionary of Saints*, 334.

74. Salaberria, *Vida prodigiosa*, 244.

75. Fr. Franciso de Acosta, *Vida prodigiosa*, 306.

76. Ibid.

77. Fr. Angel Manrique, *La venerable madre*, 299–300.

78. Vyse, *Believing in Magic*, 102–109.

79. Salaberria, *Vida prodigiosa*, 173.

80. AHN, Inquisition, December 19, 1666, leg. 1707, exp. 10.

81. Montalvo, *Vida prodigiosa*, 420.

82. Fr. Bartolomé Valperga, *Vida, muerte y milagros*, 129.

83. Franco de Villalba, *La heroica religiosa*, 165, 173–176.

84. Ibid., 185–186.

85. Fr. Antonio Arbiol, *Ejemplar de religiosas*, 564–565.

86. Fr. Manuel de San Gerónimo, *Edades y virtudes*, 190.

87. Poutrin, *Le voile et la plume*, 318.

88. See the discussion of this clause in Yepes, *Vida, virtudes y milagros*, 273–275, 334, 339.

89. Poutrin, *Le voile et la plume*, 287.

90. Francis Lannon, *Privilege, Persecution and Prophecy: The Catholic Church in Spain 1875–1975* (Oxford: Clarendon Press, 1987), 249.

91. Ibid., 246–247.

92. For Jesuit support for the miracle cures of Padre Hoyos S.J. in 1936, see Mary Vincent, *Catholicism in the Second Spanish Republic: Religion and Politics in Salamanca* (Oxford: Clarendon Press, 1996), 76–77. For their success in establishing new sodalities in the 1930s, see ibid., 102–197.

93. José María Javierre, foreword to *Escritos Intimos*, by Sor Angela de la Cruz (Madrid: Biblioteca de Autores Cristianos, 1974), 24–25, 36.

94. Baldomero Jiménez Duque, *La espiritualidad en el siglo XIX español* (Madrid: Fundación Universitaria Española, 1974), 173–177.

95. For an expression of the hostility and fear felt by conservative Catholics toward mass democracy and socialism, see especially M. Arboleya Martínez, *Sermón Perdido* (Madrid: Mundo Latino, 1930), 18–19.

96. José Nakans, *Milagros comentados* (Madrid: Establecimiento Tipográfico, 1913), 272–273.

97. Segismundo Pey Ordeix, *Sor Sicalipsis* (Barcelona: Maucci, 1931), 115.

98. Ibid., 167–175.

99. Ibid., 186–188.

100. Ibid., 199–200.

101. Ibid., 231–232.

102. Kenneth L. Woodward, *Making Saints* (New York: Simon and Schuster, 1990), 171, 162.

103. Kenneth L. Woodward, "Hail Mary," *Newsweek*, 25 August 1997, 50.

104. Woodward, *Making Saints*, 209.

105. Woodward, "Hail Mary," 55; Gustav Niebuhr, "Semi-Comatose Massachusetts Girl Draws Pilgrims Seeking Sign of God," *New York Times*, 30 August 1998, 1, 24.

Bibliography

Archival Sources

Archivo Histórico Nacional, Sección Inquisición, Legajos, 102, 103, 105, 106, 107, 113, 114, 115, 118, 227, 231, 503, 532, 533, 1701, 1705, 1707, 1710, 1821, 1823, 1825, 1827, 4463.

Biblioteca Nacional Madrid: MS 387, 872, 12668, Mariana de Jesús, "Espejo purissima de la vida, pasión, muerte y resurrección de Christo buen nuestro." (1617)

Biblioteca Nacional Madrid: MS 2080 Fray Francisco Monteron, "Historia apologetica donde se cuenta el beneficio singular que ha hecho Dios en estos tiempos del año 1643 al rey D. Felipe IV en haverse enbiado a muchos siervos suyos con un espiritu profetico desde diversas partes de la christianidad."

Biblioteca Nacional Madrid: MS 6732 Papeles varios de D. Francisco Bejar. "Carta sobre haberse puesto en el indice la mistica ciudad de Dios." (1705)

Biblioteca Nacional Madrid: MS 6744 "Alegaciones y memoriales, informes y apuntamientos en derecho."

Biblioteca Nacional Madrid: MS 6035 "Sentencia de la priora María de la Visitación priora que fue del monasterio de la Annunciada de la ciudad de Lisboa." (1588)

Biblioteca Nacional Madrid: MS 9196 "Mariana de Austria, reina de España, Inventario de bienes" (1696)

Biblioteca Nacional Madrid: MS 20711-8.

Biblioteca Nacional Madrid: MS 20711-9.

Primary Sources

Agustín de San Ildefonso, Fray. *Theologia mystica, sciencia y sabaduria de Dios misteriosa, oscura, y levantada para muchos.* Madrid, 1683.

Alonso de Villerino, Fray. *Esclarecido solar de las religiosas recoletas de nuestro padre San Augustín.* 2 vols. Madrid: Bernarda de Villa-Diego, 1690.

Andrés de Maya Salaberria, Fray. *Vida prodigiosa y exercicio admirable de virtudes de la V. M. sor Martina de los Ángeles y Arilla.* Zaragoza: Herederos de Pedro Lanaja y Lamarca, 1678.

Angel Manrique, Fray. *La venerable madre Ana de Jesús discipula y compañera de la S. M. Teresa de Jesús.* Brussels: Lucas de Meerbeeck, 1632.

Antonio Arbiol, Fray. *Desengaños misticos a las almas detenidas o engañadas en el camino de la perfección.* Zaragoza: Manuel Roman, 1706.

————. *Ejemplar de religiosas en la penitente, virtuosa y maravillosa vida de la venerable Sor Jacinta de Atondo.* Zaragoza: Manuel Roman, 1716.

————. *Epitome de la virtuosa y evangelica vida de Fray Ignacio García fundador y guardian del colegio seminario de misionarios apostólicos de la regular observancia de S. Francisco de la villa de Calamocha.* Zaragoza: Pedro Carreras, 1720.

————. *La familia regulada con doctrina de la segrada escritura y santos padres de la iglesia católica, para todos los que regularmente componen una casa segular a fin de que cada uno en su estado y en su grado sirva a Dios nuestro señor con toda perfección y salva su alma.* Zaragoza: Herederos de Manuel Roman, 1715.

Antonio Daza, Fray. *Historia, vida y milagros de la bienaventurada virgen Santa Juana de la Cruz.* Madrid: Luis Sánchez, 1610.

Antonio de Guzman, Fray. *Historia del inocente trinitario el Santo Niño de la Guardia.* Madrid: Diego Martínez Abad, 1720.

Antonio de Lorea, Fray. *Las siervas de Dios Sor Catalina de San Lucas y Sor María de San Andrés.* Valencia: Vicente Cabrera, 1671.

————. *La venerable madre Hipolita de Jesús Rocaberti, religiosa de la orden de Santo Domingo en el monestario de Nuestra Señora de los Angeles de la ciudad de Barcelona.* Valencia: Vicente Carrera, 1679.

————. *La venerable madre Sor María de la Santissima Trinidad religiosa de la tercera orden de Santo Domingo.* Madrid: Francisco Sanchez, 1671.

Antonio Rojo, Fray. *Historia de San Diego de Alcalá.* Madrid: Imprenta Real, 1663.

Avilay Chicona, Juande. *Libro espiritual que trata de los malos lenguajes del mundo, carne y demonio y de los remedios contra ellos.* Madrid: Pedro Cosin, 1574.

Bartolomé Valperga, Fray. *Vida, muerte y milagros de Sor Caterina Thomasa.* Mallorca: Manuel Rodríguez y Juan Piza, 1627.

Batista de Lanuza, Miguel. *Vida de la sierva de Dios Francisca del Santissimo Sacramento.* Pamplona: Joseph Martínez, 1727.

————. *Vida de la venerable madre Jerónima de San Esteban carmelita descalza.* Zaragoza: Domingo de la Puyada, 1653.

————. *Virtudes de la V. M. Teresa de Jesús Vela carmelita descalza.* Madrid: Pedro de Villafranca, 1656.

Boneta, Joseph. *Gritos del purgatorio y medios para acallarlos.* Zaragoza: Gaspar Martínez, 1699.

Calderon, Juan Alonso. *Memorial historico-juridicio-politico que dio a la Magestad Católica del Rey D. Philipe Quarto.* Madrid: Díaz del Carrete, 1651.

Calisbeta, Manuel. *Enseñanzas espirituales para el mayor provecho de las almas, doce doctrinas a favor de la comunión cotidiana.* Madrid: Pablo de Val, 1663.

Cerda, Juan de la. *Libro intitulado vida política de todos los estados de mujeres.* Alcalá de Henares: Juan Gracián, 1599.

Costa Mattos, Vicente. *Discurso contra los judíos.* Translated by Fr. Diego Gavilian Vega. Madrid: Viuda de Melchor Alegre, 1680.

Cyrasco de Figueroa, Bartolomé. *Templo militante, Flos Sanctorum y triunfos de virtudes*. Lisbon: Pedro Crasbeeck, 1613.

Daza y Berrio, Juan. *Tesoro de confesores y perla de la consciencia para todos los estados*. Madrid: Imprenta Real, 1648.

Delmau, Jusepe. *Relaciones de los regozijos y fiestas con que celebró este ciudad de Barcelona la felice beatificación de la Madre Santa Teresa de Jesús*. Barcelona: Sebastián Mathevat, 1614.

Espinosa, Juan de. *Dialogo en laude de las mujeres*. Madrid: CSIC, 1946.

Fernando de San Antonio Capilla, Fray. *Vida singular de la madre María de Christo venerable por esclarecida virgen y por fundadora de los beatarios en las villas de La Parra y Almendradejo*. Madrid: Manuel Ruiz de Murga, 1716.

Ferrer de Valcedebro, Andrés. *Gobierno general, moral y politico, hallado en las aves más generosas y nobles, sacado de sus naturales virtudes y propiedades*. Barcelona: Tomás Loriente, 1696.

Francisco de Acosta, Fray. *Vida prodigosa y heroicas virtudes de la V. M. María de Jesús carmelita descalza de Toledo*. Madrid: Domingo García y Morrás, 1648.

Francisco de Arcos, Fray. *La Sabia de Coria: vida de la venerable madre María de Jesús*. Madrid: Francisco Nieto, 1671.

Francisco de Ribera, Fray. *La vida de la Madre Teresa de Jesús, fundadora de las descalças y desçalcos Carmelitas*. Salamanca: Pedro Lasso, 1590.

Francisco de San Bernardo, Fray. *Vida del prodigioso Job de estos siglos, el venerable padre Fray Tomás de la Virgen*. Madrid: Roque Rico de Miranda, 1678.

Franco de Villalba, Diego. *La heroica religiosa Sor Ines de Jesús y Franco*. Zaragoza: Francisco Revilla, 1733.

Galindo, Pedro. *Excelencias de la castidad y virginidad*. Madrid: Mateo de Espinosa y Arteaga, 1681.

———. *Parte segundo del directorio de penitentes y práctica de una buena y prudente confesíon*. Madrid: Antonio de Zafra, 1680.

Horozco y Covarrubias, Juan de. *Tratado de la verdadera y falsa prophecia*. Segovia: Juan de la Cuesta, 1588.

Jesús, Isabel de. *Tesoro del carmelo escondido en el campo de la iglesia, hallado y descubierto en la muerte y vida que de si dexó escrita por orden de su confesor la venerable madre Isabel de Jesús*. Madrid: Julian de Paredes, 1685.

Jesús y Rocaberti, Hipolita. *Discurso de mi vida*. Edited by Lazaro Iriarte. Madrid: Hermanos Menores Capuchinos de la Provincia de Navarra-Cantabria-Aragón, 1985.

———. *Libro primero de su admirable vida y doctrina, que escribío de su mano por mandado de sus prelados y confesores*. Valencia: Francisco Mestre, 1679.

José Ximénez de Samaniego, Fray. *Prologo Galeato: Vida de Sor María de Ágreda*. Biblioteca de Autores Españoles 109. Edited by Carlos Seco Serrano. Madrid: Atlas, 1958.

Juan Bernal, Fray. *Compendiosa noticia de la ejemplar vida y singulares virtudes de la venerable hermana Francisca Badia*. Valencia: Joseph García, 1755.

Juan de Ellacuriaga, Fray. *Vida de la venerable madre Ana Phelipa de los Angeles, recoleta augustina profesa en el convento de la villa de Medina del Campo*. Madrid: Alonso Balbàs, 1728.

Juan de Palma, Fray. *Vida de la serenísima Infanta Sor Margarita de la Cruz religiosa descalza de Santa Clara*. Madrid: Imprenta Real, 1636.

Juan de Torres, Fray. *Vida y milagros de Santa Isabel Regna de Portugal*. Madrid: Imprenta Real, 1625.

Juan Interian de Ayala, Fray. *Epitome de la admirable vida, virtudes y milagros de Santa María de Cervellón.* Salamanca: Eugenio Antonio García, 1695.

La Puente, Luis de. *Tesoro escondido en las enfermedades y trabajos.* Madrid: Manuel Fernandez, 1750.

Leandro de Granada, Fray. *Vida y revelaciones de Santa Gertrudis la Magna.* Madrid: Melchor Alcarez, 1689.

Llaño, Isabel de. *Historia de la vida, muerte y milagros de la santa Catalina de Sena compuesta en octava rima.* Valladolid: Luis Sánchez, 1604.

Lope Paez, Fray. *Espejo de virtudes en la vida y muerte de la venerable madre Francisca Inés de la Concepción.* Toledo: Juan Ruiz de Pareda, 1653.

Luis de Granada, Fray. *Historia de Sor María de la Visitación.* Barcelona: Juan Flors, 1962.

Luis de Leon, Fray. *La perfecta casada.* Barcelona: Hymsa, 1953.

Manuel de San Gerónimo, Fray. *Edades y virtudes, empleos, y prodigios de la V. M. Gabriela de San Joseph, religiosa carmelita descalza en su convento de la concepción de Ubeda.* Jaen: Tómas Copado, 1703.

Marcos de San Antonio, Fray. *Vida prodigiosa de la venerable madre Sor Clara de Jesús María virgen admirable, religiosa de la vela blanco en el monestario de la merced de la ciudad de Toro.* Madrid: Francisco Xavier García, 1765.

Marcos de Torres, Fray. *Vida y virtudes de V. S. Doña María de Pol.* Madrid: Pablo de Val, 1661.

Martín de Roa, Fray. *Ecija, sus santos, su antigüedad ecclesiastica y segular.* Seville: Manuel de Sanda, 1629.

———. *Estado de las almas de purgatorio.* Barcelona: Pedro de la Cavalleria, 1630.

———. *Flos Sanctorum, fiestas y santos naturales de la ciudad de Córdoba.* Seville: Alonso Rodriguez Gomarra, 1615.

Martyr Rizo, Juan Pablo. *Defensa de la verdad que escrivió D. Francisco de Quevedo Villegas en favor del patronato del apostol único patron de España.* Malaga: Juan Renè, 1628.

Mesa, Luis de. *Vida, favores y mercedes que Christo N. S. hizo a la venerable hermana Mariana de Jesús.* Madrid: Imprenta Real, 1678.

Morovelli de Puebla, Francisco. *Defiende el patronato de Santa Teresa de Jesús, patrona illustrissima de España, y responde a Francisco de Quevedo.* Málaga: Juan Renè, 1628.

Nakans, José. *Chaparrón de milagros.* Madrid: Domingo Blanco, 1912.

———. *Milagros comentados.* Madrid: Establecimiento Tipográfico, 1913.

Nieremberg, Juan Eusebio. *Causa y remedio de los males públicos.* Madrid: María de Quiñones, 1642.

———. *Oculta filosofía de la sympatia y antipatia de las cosas, artificio de la naturaleza y noticia natural del mundo.* Madrid: Imprenta del Reino, 1636.

Pedro de Balbás, Fray. *Memorial informativo en defensa de Sor Luisa de la Ascensión monja profesa de Santa Clara de Carrión.* Madrid: Diego Diaz de Carerra, 1643.

Pedro de Corazón de Jesús, Fray. *Glorias de la beata María Ana de Jesús mercedaria descalza publicados en los solemnes fiestas de su beatificación.* Salamanca: Domingo Cosero, 1783.

Pedro de Riba de Neyra, S. J. *Flos Sanctorum de las vidas de los santos.* 2 vols. Madrid: Joachin Ibarra, 1761.

Pedro de San Cecilio, Fray. *Dios prodigioso en Teresa de Jesús niña que murío a los cinco años un mes y diez y siete días.* Madrid: Dionosio Idalgo, 1669.

Pérez de Moya, Juan. *Varia historia de santas e illustres mujeres en todo genero de virtudes*. Madrid: Francisco Sánchez, 1583

Pérez de Valdivia, Diego. *Tratado de la frecuente comunión y medios para ella principalmente del modo y orden para buen confesar*. Barcelona: Pedro Malo, 1589.

Posadas, Francisco de. *Cartas del esposo Christo a las religiosas sus esposas*. Toledo: Francisco Martín, 1748.

Quintanaduñas, Antonio de. *Espejo grande de los trabajos de jesús crucificado*. Valladolid: Bartolome Portales, 1656.

Santissima Trinidad, Manuela de. *Fundación del convento de la Purissima Concepción de franciscas descalzas de la ciudad de Salamanca*. Salamanca: María Estevez, 1696.

Teresa of Jesus. *The Complete works of Saint Teresa of Jesus*. 3 vols. Translated and edited by E. A. Peers. 11th ed. London and New York: Sheed and Ward, 1982.

Tomás de Montalvo, Fray. *Vida prodigiosa de la extatia, virgen y V. M. sor Beatriz María de Jesús*. Granada: Francisco Domínguez, 1719.

Villegas, Bernardino de. *La esposa de Cristo instruido con la vida de Santa Lutgarda virgen monja de S. Bernardo*. Madrid: Juan Fernández de Fuentes, 1635.

Xarque, Francisco. *Sacra consolatoria del tiempo en las guerras y otras calamidades públicas de la Casa de Austria y Católica monarquia*. Valencia: Garriz, 1642.

Yepes, Diego de. *Vida, virtudes y milagros de la bienaventurada virgen Teresa de Jesús madre y fundadora de la nueva reformación de la orden de los descalços y descalças de Nuestra Señora del Carmen*. Zaragoza: Angelo Tavanno, 1606.

Zevallos, Luis Ignacio. *Vida y virtudes, favores del cielo y prodigios de la V. Madre sor María Ángela Astorch religiosa capuchina, natural de Barcelona*. Madrid: Jerónimo Rojo, 1733.

Secondary Sources

Atlas, Jeffrey, Kim Weissman, and Susan Liebowitz. "Adolescent Inpatients' History of Abuse and Dissociative Identity Disorder." *Psychological Reports* 80 (1997): 1086.

Babkoff, Harvey. "Perceptual Distortions and Hallucinations Reported during the Course of Sleep Deprivation." *Perceptual and Motor Skills* 68 (1989): 787–798.

Bataillon, Marcel. *Erasmo y España*. Mexico, D.F.: Fondo de Cultura Ecónomica, 1950.

Brassloff, Audrey. *Religion and Politics in Spain: The Spanish Church in Transition, 1962–96*. New York: St. Martin's Press, 1998.

Briers, John. *Therapy for Adults Molested as Children*. New York: Springer, 1989.

Brooke, J. H. *Science and Religion: Some Historical Perspectives*. Cambridge: Cambridge University Press, 1991.

Brown, Jonathan, and J. H. Elliott. *A Palace for a King: The Buen Retiro and the Court of Philip IV*. New Haven: Yale University Press, 1980.

Brown, Peter. *The Cult of the Saints: Its Rise and Function in Latin Christianity*. Chicago: University of Chicago Press, 1981.

Brundage, James A. *Law, Sex and Christian Society in Medieval Europe*. Chicago: University of Chicago Press, 1987.

Burke, Peter. "How to Be a Counter-Reformation Saint." In *Religion and Society in Early Modern Europe*, edited by Kaspar von Greyerz, 45–55. London: George Allen and Unwin, 1984.

————. *Popular Culture in Early Modern Europe.* New York: Harper and Row, 1978.

Bynum, Caroline Walker. "Women Mystics and Eucharistic Devotion in the Thirteenth Century." *Women's Studies* 2 (1984): 179–214.

Callahan, William. *Church, Politics and Society in Spain, 1750–1874.* Cambridge: Harvard University Press, 1984.

Cardaillac, Louis. "Vision simplifcatrice des groupes marginaux par le groupe dominant dans l'Espagne des XVI et XVII siècles." In *Les problèmes de l'exclusion en Espagne,* edited by Augustin Redondo, 219–226. Paris: Sorbonne, 1983.

Casey, James. *The Kingdom of Valencia in the Seventeenth Century.* Cambridge: Cambridge University Press, 1979.

Certeau, Michel de. *La fable mystique.* Paris: Gallimard, 1982.

Checa Cremades, Fernando. "La imagen impresa en el Renacimiento y el Manierismo." In *El grabado en España: siglos XV al XVIII,* Fernando Checa Cremades, and Valeriano Bozal, 11–200. *In Summa Artes: Historia General del Arte.* 32 vols. edited by Juan Carrete Parrondo, Madrid: Espasa Calpe, 1987.

Christian, William. *Person and God in a Spanish Valley.* New York: Seminar Press, 1972.

Christianson, Gale. *In the Presence of the Creator: Isaac Newton and His Times.* New York: Free Press, 1984.

Chu, James A., and Diana Dill. "Dissociative Symptoms in Relation to Childhood Physical and Sexual Abuse." *American Journal of Psychiatry* 147 (1990):887–892.

Contreras, Jaime, and Gustav Henningsen. "Forty-Four Thousand Cases of the Spanish Inquisition (1540–1700): Analysis of a Historical Data Bank." In *The Inquisition in Early Modern Europe: Studies on Sources and Methods,* edited by Gustav Henningsen, John Tedeschi, and Charles Amiel, 100–129. DeKalb: Northern Illinois University Press, 1986.

Courcelles, Dominique de. *Les histoires des saints, la prière et la mort en Catalogne.* Paris: Publications de la Sorbonne, 1990.

Cueto Ruiz, Ronald. "La tradición profética en la monarquía católica en los siglos 15, 16 y 17." *Arquivos do Centro Cultural Portugues* 17 (1982): 411–444.

Dansey Smith, Hilary. *Preaching in the Spanish Golden Age.* Oxford: Oxford University Press, 1978.

Davies, Jody, and Mary Frawley. *Treating the Adult Survivor of Childhood Sexual Abuse: A Psychoanalytic Perspective.* New York: Basic Books, 1994.

Defourneaux, Marcelin. *L'Inquisition espagnole et les livres français au XVIII siécle.* Paris: PUF, 1963.

Delehaye, Hippolyte. *The Legends of the Saints.* Translated by Donald Attwater. New York: Fordham University Press, 1962.

Delooz, Pierre. *Sociologie et canonisations.* The Hague: Martinus Nijhoff, 1969.

DeMause, Lloyd. "The History of Child Abuse." *Journal of Psychohistory* 25 (1998): 216–236.

Denzin, Norman, and Yvonna Lincoln, eds., *Collecting and Interpreting Qualitative Materials.* Thousand Oaks, Calif.: Sage, 1998.

Depluvrez, Jean-Marc. "Les retours de saint Eugène et sainte Léocadie a Tolède en 1565 et 1567." In *Les signes de Dieu aux XVI et XVII siècles,* edited by Geneviève Demerson and Bernard Dompnier, 113–132. Clermont-Ferrand: Université Blaise Pascal, 1993.

Domínguez, Gómez. *La madre Martina. Aportaciones a la vida de una Madrileña.* Madrid: Editorial Tirso de Molina, 1965.

Domínguez Ortiz, Antonio, and Bernard Vincent. *Historia de los moriscos, vida y tragedia de una minoría*. Madrid: Revista de Occidente, 1978.

Domínguez Ortiz, Antonio. *Sociedad y estado en el siglo XVIII español*. Barcelona: Ariel, 1976.

Dormandy, Thomas. *The White Death: A History of Tuberculosis*. New York: New York University Press, 1999.

Eire, Carlos M. N. *From Madrid to Purgatory: The Art and Craft of Dying in Sixteenth-Century Spain*. Cambridge: Cambridge University Press, 1995.

Elliott, John. *The Count-Duke of Olivares: The Statesman in an Age of Decline*. New Haven: Yale University Press, 1988.

———. *Imperial Spain 1469–1716*. New York: New American Library, 1966.

Evans, R. J. W. *The Making of the Habsburg Monarchy 1550–1700*: Oxford: Clarendon Press, 1979.

Farmer, David Hugh. *The Oxford Dictionary of Saints*. Oxford: Oxford University Press, 1997.

Finnegan, Mary Jeremy. *The Women of Helfta: Scholars and Mystics*. Athens: University of Georgia Press, 1991.

Friedman, Ellen. *Spanish Captives in North Africa in the Early Modern Period*. Madison: University of Wisconsin Press, 1983.

García Barriúso, Patrocinio. *La monja de Carrión*. Madrid: Ediciones Monte Casino, 1986.

García Cárcel, Ricardo. *Orígenes de la Inquisición Española: el tribunal de Valencia*. Barcelona: Península, 1976.

García Sanz, Angel. *Desarrollo y crisis del Antiguo Régimen en Castilla la Vieja: economía y sociedad en tierras de Segovia 1500–1814*. Madrid: Akal, 1977.

Gendlin, Eugene. *Experiencing and the Creation of Meaning*. Evanston, Ill.: Northwestern University Press, 1997.

Greven, Philip. *Spare the Child*. New York: Knopf, 1991.

Guyer, Paul, ed. *The Cambridge Companion to Kant*. Cambridge: Cambridge University Press, 1992.

Haliczer, Stephen. *Sexuality in the Confessional: A Sacrament Profaned*. New York: Oxford University Press, 1996.

Herr, Richard. *The Eighteenth Century Revolution in Spain*. Princeton, N. J.: Princeton University Press, 1969.

Hill, Christoper. *The Century of Revolution 1603–1714*. New York: Norton, 1966.

Hsia, R. Po-chia. *The World of Catholic Renewal 1540–1770*. Cambridge: Cambridge University Press, 1998.

Huerga, Alvaro. *Historia de los Alumbrados*. 2 vols. Madrid: Fundación Universitaria Española, 1978.

Imirizaldu, Jesús. *Monjas y beatas embaucadoras*. Madrid: Editorial Nacional, 1977.

Imprenta Guasp. *Colección de xilografías mallorquinas de la Imprenta de Guasp fundada en 1579*. Palma de Mallorca: Imprenta de Guasp, 1950.

Iriarte, Lázaro. *Beata María Ángela Astorch: clarrisa capuchina (1592–1665), la mística del brevario*. Valencia: Asis Editorial, 1982.

Javierre, José María. Foreword to *Escritos íntimos*, by Sor Ángela de la Cruz. Madrid: Biblioteca de Autores Cristianos, 1974.

Jiménez Duque, Baldomero. *La espiritualidad en el siglo XIX español*. Madrid: Fundación Universitaria Española, 1974.

José Vicente Benavent y Alabort, Fray. *Breve compendio de la vida de la beata Josefa de Santa Inés de Benigánim y Novena*. Valencia: J. Nacher, 1963.

Kamen, Henry. *Inquisition and Society in Spain in the Sixteenth and Seventeenth Centuries.* Bloomington: Indiana University Press, 1985.

———. *Spain 1469–1714: A Society of Conflict.* London: Longman, 1991.

———. *The War of Succession in Spain 1700–1715.* London: Weidenfeld and Nicolson, 1969.

Kendrick, Thomas, D. *Mary of Agreda: The Life and Legend of a Spanish Nun.* London: Routledge and Kegan Paul, 1967.

Lannon, Frances. *Privilege, Persecution and Prophecy: The Catholic Church in Spain 1875–1975.* Oxford: Clarendon Press, 1987.

Lea, Henry Charles. *A History of the Inquisition of Spain.* 4 vols. New York: Macmillan, 1906–1907.

López Piñero, José María. *Ciencia y técnica en la sociedad española de los siglos XVI y XVII.* Barcelona: Labor, 1979.

Maclean, Ian. *The Renaissance Notion of Women.* Cambridge: Cambridge University Press, 1980.

Mâle, Émile. *L'Arte religieux de la fin du moyen âge en France.* Paris: Armand Colin, 1932.

María de Hornedo, Rafael. "Teatro e iglesia en los siglos XVII y XVII." In *Historia de la Iglesia en España,* edited by Ricardo García Villoslada, 4:311–356. 5 vols. Madrid: La Editorial Católica, 1979.

Martinengo, Alessandreo. "De la intolerencia intelectual: algo más sobre los herejes del Sueños del Infierno." In *Les problèmes de l'exclusion en Espagne,* edited by Augustin Redondo, 219–226. Paris: Sorbonne, 1983.

Martínez, M. Arboleya *Sermón Perdido.* Madrid: Mundo Latino, 1930.

Martínez Gil. Fernando. *Muerte y sociedad en la España de las Austrias.* Madrid: Siglo Veintiuno, 1993.

Mckindrick, Meelvena. *Women and Society in the Spanish Drama of the Golden Age: A Study of the Mujer Varonil.* Cambridge: Cambridge University Press, 1974.

Mecklin, John. *The Passing of the Saint: A Study of a Culture Type.* Chicago: University of Chicago Press, 1941.

Mestre, Antonio. *Ilustración y reforma de la iglesia: pensamiento político-religioso de Don Gregorio Mayans y Siscar (1699–1781).* Valencia: Ayuntamiento de Oliva, 1968.

———. "Religion y cultura en el siglo XVII español." In *Historia de la iglesia en España,* edited by Ricardo García Villoslada, 4:586–739. 5 vols. Madrid: Editora, 1979–1980.

Moreira de Freitas Carvalho, José Adriano. *Gertrudes de Helfta e Espanha.* Porto: Instituto Nacional de Investigação Científica, 1981.

O'Neil, Mary. "Magical Healing, Love Magic and the Inquisition in Late Sixteenth-Century Modena." In *Inquisition and Society in Early Modern Europe,* edited by Stephen Haliczer, 88–114. London: Croom Helm, 1987.

Orensanz, Aurelio. *Religiosidad popular española 1940–1965.* Madrid: Editora Nacional, 1974.

Palma Martínez-Burgos, García. *Ídolos e imágenes: la controversia del arte religioso en el siglo XV español.* Valladolid: Universidad de Valladolid, 1990.

Palop Ramos, José-Miguel. *Fluctuaciones de precios y abastecimiento en la Valencia del siglo XVIII.* Valencia: Diputación Provincial, 1977.

Pérez Villanaeva, Joaquín. *Sor María de Agreda y Felipe IV, un epistolario en su tiempo In Historia de la Iglesia en España,* edited by Ricardo García Villoslada, 5 vols. Madrid: La Editorial Católica, 1979.

Perry, Mary Elizabeth. *Gender and Disorder in Early Modern Seville.* Princeton, N.J.: Princeton University Press, 1990.

Pinto Crespo, Virgilio. *Inquisición y control ideológico en la España del siglo XVI.* Madrid: Taurus, 1983.

Poutrin, Isabelle. *La voile et la plume: autobiographie et sainteté féminine dans l' Espagne moderne.* Madrid: Casa de Velázquez, 1995.

———. "Les stigmatisées et les clerics: Interprétation et répression d'un signe, Espagne, XVII siècle." In *Les signes de Dieu au XVI et XVII siècles,* edited by Geneviève Demerson and Bernard Dompnier, 189–199. Clermont Ferrand: Université Baise-Pascual, 1993.

Praz, Mario. *Studies in Seventeenth-Century Imagery.* Rome: Edizioni di Storia e Leterratura, 1964.

Putnam, Frank W. *Dissociation in Children and Adolescents: A Developmental Perspective.* New York: Guilford Press, 1997

Puyol Buil, Carlos. *Inquisición y política en el reinado de Felipe IV.* Madrid: CSIC, 1993.

Rafael María López-Melus, Fray. *Beata Inés de Benigánim.* Valencia: Madres Agustinas Descalzas de Benigánim, 1982.

Rapley, Elizabeth. *The Dévotes: Women and the Church in Seventeenth-Century France.* Montreal and Kingston: McGill-Queen's University Press, 1990.

Sallmann, Jean-Michel. "Il Santo e le rappresentazioni della santità. Problemi di metodo." *Quaderni storici* 41 (1979): 585–601.

Sánchez, Magdalena S. *The Empress, The Queen and The Nun: Women and Power at the Court of Philip III of Spain.* Baltimore: Johns Hopkins University Press, 1998.

Sauzet, Robert. "La religion populaire Bas-Languedocienne au XVII siècle entre la réforme et la contra-réforme." In *Colloques Internationaux du Centre National de la Recherche Scientifique: Proceedings of a Symposium in Paris, France, October 17–19, 1977,* by the Centre National de la Recherche Scientifique, 103–108.Paris: Éditions du Centre National de la Recherche Scientifique, 1979.

Sicroff, Albert. *Les controverses des statutes de pureté de sang en Espagne du XV au XVII siècle.* Paris: Marciel Didier, 1960.

Simón Díaz, José. "Hagiografías individuales publicadas en español de 1480 á 1700." *Hispania Sacra* 30 (1977): 1–57.

Spanos, Nicolas P. *Multiple Identities and False Memories: A Sociocognative Perspective.* Washington, DC: American Psychological Association, 1996.

Takeuchi, Tomoka. "Laboratory-Documented Hallucination During Sleep-Onset REM Period in a Normal Subject." *Perceptual and Motor Skills* 78 (June 1994): 979–985.

Thomas, Keith. *Religion and the Decline of Magic.* London: Weidenfeld and Nicolson, 1971.

Tous, Jerónimo Juan. *Grabadores Mallorquines.* Palma de Mallorca: Diputación Provincial de Baleares, 1977.

Valentin, Jean-Marie. *Le théâtre des Jésuites dans les pays de langue allemande.* 3 vols. Bern, Frankfurt, Las Vegas: Peter Lang, 1978.

Vauchez, André. *La sainteté en occident aux derniers siècles du moyen age.* Rome: École Française de Rome, 1981.

Vecchi, Alberto. *Il culto delle immagini nelle stampe popolari.* Firenze: Leo S. Olschki Editore, 1968.

Vilar, Jean. *Literatura y economía: La figura satírica del arbitrista en el siglo de oro.* Madrid: Revista de Occidente, 1973.

Vincent, Mary. *Catholicism in the Second Spanish Republic.* Oxford: Clarendon Press, 1996.

Vitiello, Michael V. "Sleep in Alzheimer's Disease and Other Dementing Disorders." *Canadian Journal of Psychology* 45(2) (1991): 221–239.

Vyse, Stuart. *Believing in Magic: The Psychology of Superstition.* New York: Oxford University Press, 1997.

Walker, D. P. *Spiritual and Demonic Magic From Ficino to Campanella.* London: The Warburg Institute, 1958.

Warner, Marina. *Alone of All Her Sex: The Myth and the Cult of the Virgin Mary.* New York: Vintage, 1983.

Weiner, Jack. "La *Numancia* de Cervantes y al alianza entre Dios y Israel." *Neophilogus* 81 (May 1997): 62–70.

Weinstein, Donald. *Saints and Society: The Two Worlds of Western Christendom, 1000–1700.* Chicago: The University of Chicago Press, 1982.

Weisser, Michael. "The Decline of Castile Revisited: The Case of Toledo." *The Journal of European Economic History* 2 (1973): 614–640.

Wiesner, Merry E. *Women and Gender in Early Modern Europe.* Cambridge: Cambridge University Press, 2000.

Winstead, Karen. *Virgin Martyrs: Legends of Sainthood in Late Medieval England.* Ithaca: Cornell University Press, 1997.

Wold, Kenneth. *Christian Martyrs in Muslim Spain.* Cambridge: Cambridge University Press, 1988.

Index

345